Lecture Notes in Computer Science 14128

The series Lecture Notes in Computer Science (LNCS), including its subseries Lecture Notes in Artificial Intelligence (LNAI) and Lecture Notes in Bioinformatics (LNBI), has established itself as a medium for the publication of new developments in computer science and information technology research, teaching, and education.

LNCS enjoys close cooperation with the computer science R & D community, the series counts many renowned academics among its volume editors and paper authors, and collaborates with prestigious societies. Its mission is to serve this international community by providing an invaluable service, mainly focused on the publication of conference and workshop proceedings and postproceedings. LNCS commenced publication in 1973.

Junji Shikata · Hiroki Kuzuno
Editors

Advances in Information and Computer Security

18th International Workshop on Security, IWSEC 2023
Yokohama, Japan, August 29–31, 2023
Proceedings

Springer

Editors
Junji Shikata
Yokohama National University
Yokohama, Japan

Hiroki Kuzuno
Kobe University
Kobe, Japan

ISSN 0302-9743 ISSN 1611-3349 (electronic)
Lecture Notes in Computer Science
ISBN 978-3-031-41325-4 ISBN 978-3-031-41326-1 (eBook)
https://doi.org/10.1007/978-3-031-41326-1

This Springer imprint is published by the registered company Springer Nature Switzerland AG
The registered company address is: Gewerbestrasse 11, 6330 Cham, Switzerland

Preface

The Eighteenth International Workshop on Security (IWSEC 2023) was held as a hybrid event, mainly onsite and online, in Yokohama, Japan, between August 29 and 31, 2023. The workshop was co-organized by the Technical Committee on Information Security in Engineering Sciences Society (ISEC) of the Institute of Electronics, Information and Communication Engineers (IEICE) and the Special Interest Group on Computer Security (CSEC) of the Information Processing Society of Japan (IPSJ).

Following IWSEC's tradition, this year we also had two tracks, Track A: Cryptography and Track B: Cybersecurity, Usable Security, and Privacy, with two separate Program Committees. In total we received 47 submissions, 34 to Track A and 13 to Track B, each of which was then reviewed in a double-blind fashion by three experts in the pertinent fields. After comprehensive review, we accepted 14 papers, eleven in Track A and three in Track B, and included their revised and refined versions in this publication. Among them the Best Paper Award went to "$a\mathcal{P}lon\mathcal{K}$: Aggregated $\mathcal{P}lon\mathcal{K}$ from Multi-Polynomial Commitment Schemes" by Miguel Ambrona, Marc Beunardeau, Anne-Laure Schmitt, and Raphael Toledo; and the Best Student Paper Award went to "A New Security Analysis Against MAYO and QR-UOV Using Rectangular MinRank Attack" by Hiroki Furue and Yasuhiko Ikematsu.

Three keynote talks were presented by Meltem Sonmez Turan, National Institute of Standards and Technology, Gernot Heiser, University of New South Wales, and Kris Shrisha, Irish Council for Civil Liberties.

We extend our heartfelt gratitude to all those who contributed to the remarkable success of IWSEC 2023 following the challenging period of the COVID-19 pandemic. We express our sincere appreciation to the authors who submitted their works to the workshop. We are immensely thankful to the Program Committees and external reviewers for their diligent reviews and insightful discussions, which led to the creation of an outstanding program. Last but not least, we would like to acknowledge the exceptional leadership of the general co-chairs Goichiro Hanaoka and Koji Chida for the workshop, and, we would also like to thank the tremendous efforts of all members of the Organizing Committee, whose great work ensured the success of the event.

August 2023

Junji Shikata
Hiroki Kuzuno

Organization

General Co-chairs

Goichiro Hanaoka	National Institute of Advanced Industrial Science and Technology, Japan
Koji Chida	Gunma University, Japan

Program Committee Co-chairs

Junji Shikata	Yokohama National University, Japan
Hiroki Kuzuno	Kobe University, Japan

Poster Chair

Naoto Yanai	Osaka University, Japan

Publication Chair

Kazuhiko Minematsu	NEC, Japan and Yokohama National University, Japan

Local Organizing Committee

Atsushi Fujioka	Kanagawa University, Japan
Yujie Gu	Kyushu University, Japan
Masaki Hashimoto	Institute of Information Security, Japan
Hyungrok Jo	Yokohama National University, Japan
Shohei Kakei	Nagoya Institute of Technology, Japan
Motohiro Kambashi	Sumitomo Mitsui Banking Corporation, Japan
Ai Kuwagata	National Institute of Advanced Industrial Science and Technology, Japan
Mamoru Mimura	National Defense Academy, Japan
Yasuhiro Murasaki	Japan Broadcasting Corporation, Japan

Takayuki Nagane	National Institute of Advanced Industrial Science and Technology, Japan
Misato Nakabayashi	NTT Social Informatics Laboratories, Japan
Takeshi Nakai	Toyohashi University of Technology, Japan
Shohei Satake	Kumamoto University, Japan
Kazumasa Shinagawa	Ibaraki University, Japan
Kuniyasu Suzaki	Institute of Information Security, Japan
Yuntao Wang	Osaka University, Japan
Yohei Watanabe	University of Electro-Communications, Japan
Sven Wohlgemuth	SECOM Intelligent Systems Laboratory, Japan
Kyosuke Yamashita	Osaka University, Japan

Program Committee

Track A: Cryptography

Yoshinori Aono	National Institute of Information and Communications Technology, Japan
Charles Bouillaguet	Sorbonne Université, France
Chen-Mou Cheng	BTQ AG, Liechtenstein
Sherman S. M. Chow	Chinese University of Hong Kong, China
Bernardo David	IT University of Copenhagen, Denmark
Thomas Espitau	NTT, Japan
Antonio Faonio	EURECOM, France
Hanwen Feng	University of Sydney, Australia
Junqing Gong	East China Normal University, China
Takanori Isobe	University of Hyogo, Japan
Mitsugu Iwamoto	University of Electro-Communications, Japan
Tetsu Iwata	Nagoya University, Japan
Alexander Koch	IRIF, Université de Paris, France
Florian Mendel	Infineon Technologies, Germany
Kirill Morozov	University of North Texas, USA
Akira Otsuka	Institute of Information Security, Japan
Junji Shikata	Yokohama National University, Japan
Daniel Slamanig	Austrian Institute of Technology, Austria
Willy Susilo	University of Wollongong, Australia
Tsuyoshi Takagi	University of Tokyo, Japan
Shota Yamada	National Institute of Advanced Industrial Science and Technology, Japan
Ilsun You	Kookmin University, Republic of Korea
Rui Zhang	Chinese Academy of Sciences, China

Track B: Cybersecurity, Usable Security, and Privacy

Josep Balasch	KU Leuven, Belgium
Gregory Blanc	Télécom SudParis, France
Herve Debar	Télécom SudParis, France
Josep Domingo-Ferrer	Universitat Rovira i Virgili, Catalonia
Koki Hamada	NTT, Japan
Pieter Hartel	Technische Universiteit Delft, The Netherlands
Ayako Hasegawa	NICT, Japan
Hiroki Kuzuno	Kobe University, Japan
Frederic Majorczyk	DGA-MI/CentraleSupélec, France
Weizhi Meng	Technical University of Denmark, Denmark
Alexios Mylonas	University of Hertfordshire, UK
Kotzanikolaou Panayiotis	University of Piraeus, Greece
Masaya Satoh	Okayama Prefecture University, Japan
Toshiki Shibahara	NTT, Japan
Dario Stabili	University of Modena and Reggio Emilia, Italy
Tsubasa Takahashi	LINE Corporation, Japan
Giorgos Vasiliadis	Hellenic Mediterranean University/ICS-FORTH, Greece
Takumi Yamamoto	Mitsubishi Electric Corporation, Japan
Naoto Yanai	Osaka University, Japan
Kuo-Hui Yeh	National Dong Hwa University, Taiwan
Stefano Zanero	Polytechnic University of Milan, Italy

Additional Reviewers

Andrey Kim
Jongkil Kim
Anshu Yadav
Le Trieu Phong
Jakub Klemsa
Kaoru Takemure
Jiafan Wang
Martin Schläffer
Yaacov Belenky
Valerio Cini
Luigi Russo
Keisuke Hara
Abida Haque
Damien Vergnaud
Yuntao Wang
Shuhei Nakamura
Masaya Yasuda
Dooho Choi
Behnam Zahednejad
Seonghan Shin
Kazumasa Shinagawa
Erkan Tairi
Maria Eichlseder

Contents

System and Hardware Security

Power Analysis Pushed too Far: Breaking Android-Based Isolation with Fuel Gauges 3
Vincent Giraud and David Naccache

The Good, the Bad, and the Binary: An LSTM-Based Method for Section Boundary Detection in Firmware Analysis 16
Riccardo Remigio, Alessandro Bertani, Mario Polino, Michele Carminati, and Stefano Zanero

Reliability of Ring Oscillator PUFs with Reduced Helper Data 36
Julien Béguinot, Wei Cheng, Jean-Luc Danger, Sylvain Guilley, Olivier Rioul, and Ville Yli-Mäyry

Symmetric Key Cryptography

Improved Boomerang Attacks on Deoxys-BC 59
Jiahao Zhao, Nana Zhang, Qianqian Yang, Ling Song, and Lei Hu

PMAC*r*x: A Vector-Input MAC for High-Dimensional Vectors with BBB Security 77
Isamu Furuya, Hayato Kasahara, Akiko Inoue, Kazuhiko Minematsu, and Tetsu Iwata

Public Key Cryptography

A New Security Analysis Against MAYO and QR-UOV Using Rectangular MinRank Attack 101
Hiroki Furue and Yasuhiko Ikematsu

Improved Hybrid Attack via Error-Splitting Method for Finding Quinary Short Lattice Vectors 117
Haiming Zhu, Shoichi Kamada, Momonari Kudo, and Tsuyoshi Takagi

Total Break of a Public Key Cryptosystem Based on a Group of Permutation Polynomials 137
Max Cartor, Ryann Cartor, Mark Lewis, and Daniel Smith-Tone

Extractable Witness Encryption for the Homogeneous Linear Equations Problem 152
Bénédikt Tran and Serge Vaudenay

Making Classical (Threshold) Signatures Post-quantum for Single Use on a Public Ledger 173
Laurane Marco, Abdullah Talayhan, and Serge Vaudenay

Zero Knowledge Proofs

aPlonK: Aggregated *PlonK* from Multi-polynomial Commitment Schemes 195
Miguel Ambrona, Marc Beunardeau, Anne-Laure Schmitt, and Raphaël R. Toledo

TENET: Sublogarithmic Proof and Sublinear Verifier Inner Product Argument without a Trusted Setup 214
Hyeonbum Lee and Jae Hong Seo

Card Based Cryptography

Efficient Card-Based Millionaires' Protocols via Non-binary Input Encoding 237
Koji Nuida

Check Alternating Patterns: A Physical Zero-Knowledge Proof for Moon-or-Sun 255
Samuel Hand, Alexander Koch, Pascal Lafourcade, Daiki Miyahara, and Léo Robert

Author Index 273

System and Hardware Security

Power Analysis Pushed too Far: Breaking Android-Based Isolation with Fuel Gauges

Vincent Giraud[1,2(✉)] and David Naccache[1,2]

[1] DIENS, École Normale Supérieure, Université PSL, CNRS, Paris, France
{vincent.giraud,david.naccache}@ens.fr
[2] Ingenico, Suresnes, France

Abstract. Efficient power management is critical for embedded devices, both for extending their lifetime and ensuring safety. However, this can be a challenging task due to the unpredictability of the batteries commonly used in such devices. To address this issue, dedicated Integrated Circuits (ICs) known as "fuel gauges" are often employed outside of the System-on-Chip (SoC). These devices provide various metrics about the available energy source and are highly accurate. However, their precision can also be exploited by malicious actors to compromise platform confidentiality if the Operating System (OS) fails to intervene. Depending on the fuel gauge and OS configuration, several attack scenarios are possible. In this article, we focus on Android and demonstrate how it is possible to bypass application isolation to recover Personal Identification Numbers (PINs) entered in other processes.

Keywords: Fuel gauge · Embedded system · Confidentiality

1 Introduction

Lithium-based batteries have been the go-to choice for embedded devices for several decades. These batteries offer high energy density and low self-discharge, and do not suffer from memory effect. However, predicting and analyzing their behavior can be a challenging task. The voltage at their poles is not directly proportional to the remaining energy level, and their discharge is affected by various factors such as the platform's dynamic consumption, temperature, age, and total capacity. Consequently, managing power on an embedded system is a complex process. Furthermore, end-user expectations have evolved significantly in recent years. Knowing a battery's charge level only up to the nearest quarter is no longer acceptable, as users now expect to have an estimate up to the nearest percentage.

Managing power consumption on embedded devices can be a challenging responsibility, requiring a significant investment of time and expertise. One approach is to implement the necessary operations and modeling at the OS level, or at least execute them on the central processor. However, this approach can impose an additional burden on an already heavily utilized component. Furthermore, obtaining reliable measurements from this environment, such as capturing

J. Shikata and H. Kuzuno (Eds.): IWSEC 2023, LNCS 14128, pp. 3–15, 2023.
https://doi.org/10.1007/978-3-031-41326-1_1

accurate temperature readings, can be complicated. This is because the processor itself can significantly influence the readings, rather than the battery. Additionally, it becomes more difficult to estimate the quality and age of the power source with this implementation. Managing multiple distinct batteries can exacerbate these challenges further.

To facilitate power management in embedded devices, many designers incorporate fuel gauges, which are integrated circuits dedicated to analyzing and monitoring various metrics related to the energy source. These metrics include the voltage of the source, the current drawn from or injected into it, and the temperature, among others. However, an overlooked aspect of these components that is worthy of interest in the field of security is their remarkable accuracy [3]. This accuracy allows fuel gauges to produce precise estimations of the battery's age, charge, and health, which are among their flagship features.

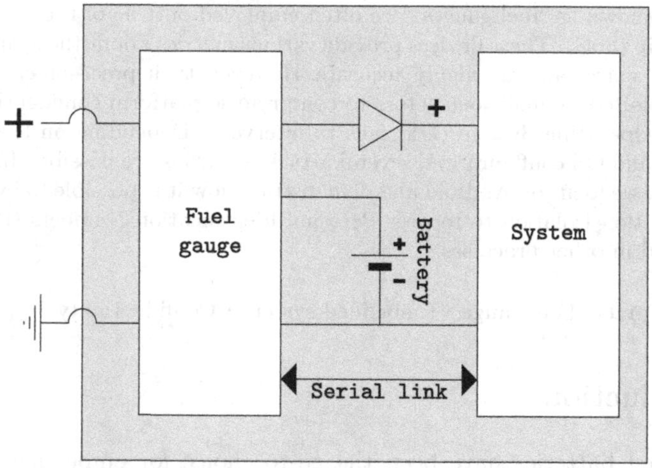

Fig. 1. Diagram representing a typical fuel gauge implementation in an embedded system.

The use of integrated fuel gauges in embedded devices frees device designers and OS developers from the responsibility of managing the power source. Fuel gauges provide more accurate measurements because they are located closer to the battery and handle the necessary calculations and algorithms. The software running on the SoC only needs to request the desired metrics or data, which are communicated through a serial link connecting the fuel gauge and the main system, as illustrated in Fig. 1. This communication channel typically corresponds to an I^2C communication bus, which is managed by a driver residing in the kernel space. This delegation of responsibility is common in smartphones, tablets, and portable video game consoles, particularly in high-end products. However, since fuel gauges can be expensive, it should be noted that less accurate measurements and estimates are often used in devices aimed at more modest price ranges.

Fuel Gauge Presence. Determining whether a phone or tablet is equipped with a fuel gauge before purchase can be a challenging task, as manufacturers do not indicate the presence or absence of this component on their data sheets or documentation. However, after purchasing the device, one can visually inspect its printed circuit to confirm the presence of a fuel gauge. In the case of an Android device, it is possible to determine the presence of a fuel gauge in the system without necessarily having root access by probing the equipment related to power through a terminal.

Listing 1.1. Terminal output when determining the power-related equipments in the Pixel 6 smartphone.

```
$ ls -a /sys/class/power_supply
battery
dc
gcpm
gcpm_pps
main-charger
maxfg
pca9468-mains
tcpm-source-psy-i2c-max77759tcpc
usb
wireless
```

Upon inspection of the resulting list, fuel gauges are often found in Google's Nexus and Pixel lines, particularly in the Pixel 6, as illustrated in Listing 1.1. While the number of listed elements may be substantial, the nomenclature can assist in identifying the IC of interest. In this specific case, the `maxfg` device draws our attention: `max` signifies the Maxim Integrated brand, while `fg` denotes the fuel gauge.

1.1 Software Context in Android

The Android OS is based on a Linux kernel, with a user environment that is radically different from the ones usually found in conventional computer distributions. A decisive choice in the design of Android was to assign each application a different Unix user, thus allowing the system to benefit from the isolation traditionally imposed between processes. The SELinux module is deployed from version 4.3 to reinforce this policy. Outside the kernel space, on top of a minimal layer of libraries and native executables, Zygote acts as a model process for instantiating applications: at each such request, it forks itself, and changes the user associated with the child process to respect the paradigm mentioned. The abstraction layers present on an Android system are illustrated in a simplified way in Fig. 2.

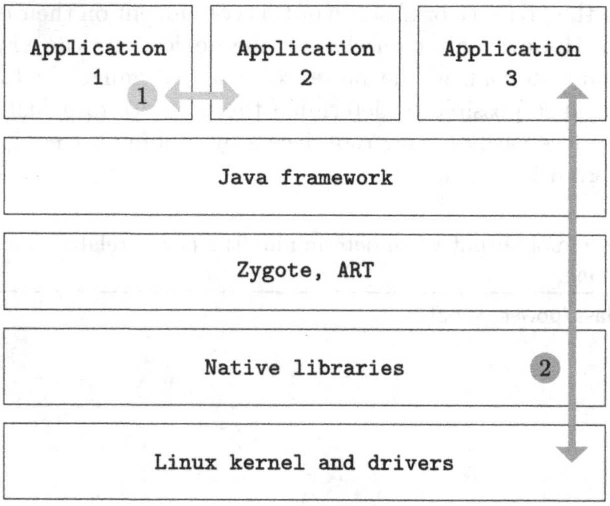

Fig. 2. Simplified view of the abstraction model in Android systems. The first, green arrow represents horizontal accesses. The second, red arrow represents vertical accesses. (Color figure online)

At the application level, interactions between applications in Android are limited, and they are not possible directly. Instead, communications or calls between applications must be negotiated via Binder, the inter-process communication manager specific to Android[1]. This component takes care of calls between services and activities, which is a cardinal aspect of the Android operating system. While horizontal accesses, which refer to interactions between applications, are dictated by explicit rules, this is less the case for vertical interactions, where an application requires hardware resources provided by the platform. In the case of smartphones and tablets, these resources may include components such as a light meter, an accelerometer, a gyroscope, a microphone, and one or more cameras. Access to these features is regulated according to the Android version and the platform manufacturer, and it depends on the nature of the resource and the type of interaction desired. From an application's perspective, these permissions are often discovered at runtime. Access to energy monitoring is regulated

[1] Binder is not documented, but it can be found in Android's common kernel tree's drivers: https://android.googlesource.com/kernel/common/+/refs/heads/android12-5.10/drivers/android/binder.c.

according to the same logic. The possibility of a risk resting on it has prompted us to explore this area further.

1.2 Key Issues and Contribution

Due to their possible presence in an essential brick of embedded systems, it is advisable to perform a risk analysis concerning fuel gauges. The state of the art of security assessment around these integrated circuits is non-existent. Although fuel gauges do not have control over the supply of electricity, unlike Power Management Integrated Circuits (PMICs) (although they may be included in a PMIC), there is reason to consider privacy risks, especially on platforms such as phones and tablets, which can contain a substantial amount of personal information. This is because fuel gauges can expose particularly precise measurements [3]. To mitigate these risks, it is essential to understand the possible attack scenarios and the potential impact of an attack. One approach is to perform a threat modeling exercise to identify potential attackers and their motivations, as well as the potential vulnerabilities of the system. This can help inform the selection of appropriate security controls, such as encryption and access controls, to protect the system against unauthorized access or disclosure.

Contribution. In this article, we focus on embedded systems featuring the Android OS. We summarize the evolution of the access policy to hardware power sensors and outline the consequences of an unsuitable policy. By demonstrating that information about a PIN code can be recovered while it is being typed, we show that concrete and actual risks exist. We also address the question of what measures can be put in place to confront this security hazard. In Sect. 2, we describe the security policy in Android regarding hardware sensors and the risks it can create. In Sect. 3, we explain how we managed to exploit these risks. In Sect. 4, we discuss the implications of our findings. Finally, in Sect. 5, we provide closing remarks on the importance of addressing these security risks in embedded systems.

2 Risk Analysis

2.1 Interactions Between Systems and Their Fuel Gauge

The `BatteryManager` system service has existed since the early days of Android. At the beginning, it only allowed to know the status of the battery regarding its health (`GOOD`, `OVERHEAT`, `DEAD`, `OVER_VOLTAGE`...) or its use (`CHARGING`, `DISCHARGING`, `FULL`...), as well as, if applicable, the charging source (`USB` or `AC`). It has been expanded over time, until in version 5.0 (called *Lollipop*), constants were added to form queries that can be redirected to a fuel gauge[2]. These

[2] See: https://android.googlesource.com/platform/frameworks/base/+/refs/heads/lollipop-release/core/java/android/os/BatteryManager.java.

include `CURRENT_NOW` to obtain the instantaneous current entering or leaving the battery in microamps, `CAPACITY` for the remaining capacity in percentage, and `ENERGY_COUNTER` for the remaining energy in nanowatt-hours.

Technically, any application running on an Android system can access the `BatteryManager` service and request any of the available attributes during its execution. The information in question is retrieved by probing the lower abstraction layers and, possibly, by consulting the fuel gauge. As a first step, we investigated whether any controls were in place in any of the layers of the system. We found that the SELinux configuration did not enforce any restrictions, although it could have. Other layers that are prone to this type of moderation include the Android framework in Java or the ART virtual machine, but no such measures were found here either. As expected, the native executables and libraries on the system did not block these requests either. After checking on version 12 and earlier, we can confirm that Android does not block these requests, regardless of the client application or the requested attribute.

This can already be a problem for the end-user, since he can't object to the sharing of power data. When an application puts in place the technical means to retrieve it, even if for legitimate purposes such as energy saving, one can then question the real use that is made of it. The company Uber, which was the target of such suspicions in 2016, had to publicly deny this kind of exploitation[3].

Incidentally, we should also note that some web browsers allow the Javascript code delivered by some sites to consult the status of the battery and its charge, via an interface of the same name, `BatteryManager`. The Javascript engine then transmits the request following the same procedure as any other application.

Another aspect that requires special attention is the ability to capture these measurements at any time, including when other applications are in use, or when the phone is in sleep mode. Since Android 9 (known as *Pie*), there is a `FOREGROUND_SERVICE` permission[4], required by the activity manager when an application requests to run a task normally in the background. Here too, this one is granted without any request from the user. However, to obtain it, you must have a notification in the list dedicated to this purpose in the system's graphical interface. There are now many applications that require a permanent notification, so as not to be sacrificed by the battery saver, or to be able to receive communications directly without going through the Google services. This could be a case of spoofing, where an application that is supposed to be for chatting or playing a video game is actually probing the fuel gauge in the background.

The next consideration is how often the fuel gauge can be checked. From Android 12 onwards, the `HIGH_SAMPLING_RATE_SENSORS` permission has appeared in the Java framework[5]. This permission is intended to limit scans 200 Hz. However, since it is a normal permission, it can be requested without

[3] See: https://www.forbes.com/sites/amitchowdhry/2016/05/25/uber-low-battery/.

[4] See: https://android.googlesource.com/platform/frameworks/base/+/refs/heads/pie-release/services/core/java/com/android/server/am/ActiveServices.java.

[5] See: https://android.googlesource.com/platform/frameworks/base/+/refs/heads/android12-release/core/java/android/hardware/SystemSensorManager.java.

visual warning to the user. Moreover, it does not concern fuel gauges anyway, as shown in the extract in Listing 1.2. In versions prior to 12, this measure does not exist.

Listing 1.2. Extract of Android's system sensor manager since version 12.

```
/**
 * Checks if a sensor should be capped according to
 * HIGH_SAMPLING_RATE_SENSORS permission.
 *
 * This needs to be kept in sync with the list defined on the native side
 * in frameworks/native/services/sensorservice/SensorService.cpp
 */
private boolean isSensorInCappedSet(int sensorType) {
    return (sensorType == Sensor.TYPE_ACCELEROMETER
            || sensorType == Sensor.TYPE_ACCELEROMETER_UNCALIBRATED
            || sensorType == Sensor.TYPE_GYROSCOPE
            || sensorType == Sensor.TYPE_GYROSCOPE_UNCALIBRATED
            || sensorType == Sensor.TYPE_MAGNETIC_FIELD
            || sensorType == Sensor.TYPE_MAGNETIC_FIELD_UNCALIBRATED);
}
```

In practice, we see that while Android does indeed transmit measurement requests as quickly as it can, many consecutive readings return the same value. The explanation lies in the design of the fuel gauges themselves: for each metric, they contain a physical register that is updated with a certain frequency. If nothing (except the limitations of the serial link) prevents you from scanning as fast as you want, the data read will be limited by this frequency, which varies with the model of integrated circuit. On the market, one can find refreshments around 4 10 Hz, which disqualifies, among others, attacks aiming at the execution of cryptographic code: the attack presented in [8] requires, for example, measurements at the microsecond scale. These frequencies nevertheless leave malicious exploitations on human speed uses within reach. It should also be noted that even if the `HIGH_SAMPLING_RATE_SENSORS` permission mentioned above were applied to fuel gauges, it would still be useless due to this inherent limitation of the hardware.

2.2 State of the Art and Its Applicability to Fuel Gauges

The most judicious category of attack in this context is the side channel attacks. They rely on exploiting information from the operation of a system, rather than a design, specification or protocol flaws. A founding example is the recovery of secrets for Diffie-Hellman, RSA or DSS based on execution times [8]. For personal identification codes, an attack based on electromagnetic emissions during sequence verification is presented in [9]. On the targeted platforms, fuel gauges offer the potential to exploit a major side channel, real-time current consumption, without requiring any additional equipment.

PIN entry on phones has already been targeted in several ways. In [4] and [11], it is spied on Android 2, via motion or rotation sensors, and requires training data. This technique will be pushed in [2], where the authors merge readings on several different sensors of various natures, still requiring training, presumably on Android 5 or 6. [6] explains a spying technique applicable when the phone is charging through its USB port: specific sensing hardware, plugged into the line, intercepts the current and infers the position of touches using a convolutional neural network, also trained but only by the attacker.

By exploiting fuel gauges, we aim at proposing a PIN code attack that does not require training or scanning of a wide variety of onboard sensors.

2.3 Identified Risks

Regarding the state of the art and fuel gauges applications, three risks are identified:

- The first one is a privacy risk. An attacker can log to the second events such as the use or not of the phone, the activation or deactivation of wireless connectivity, the reception or transmission of communication, etc.
- A second one due to the creation of a hidden communication channel on the platform: the real-time consumption tracking. We have seen that it would be accessible in reading mode by all applications. We must also consider that all the actors have a *de facto* inalienable right to write on it, since each one can, by its execution, cause a lesser or additional consumption. Thus, for example, an application `A`, having access to sensitive data but not to the network, could transmit them, by means of certain signal modulation techniques, to an application `B`, having access to the network but not to the sensitive contents.
- A third one, particularly aimed at implementations of secure and sensitive solutions: on many fuel gauges, the refresh rate, although low, is of the same order of magnitude as human interactions. One can then fear the harvesting of information during the entry of a secret data.

In the following, we will focus on the latter, in order to retrieve a PIN, intended for another process.

3 Sensitive Data Recovery Through Fuel Gauges

3.1 Testing Tools

To demonstrate this attack, we focused on exploiting Android versions between 9 and 12. Targeting earlier versions should not pose any obstacle except for the lack of standard fuel gauge support before version 5 (*Lollipop*). Our testing was conducted on devices in Google's Nexus and Pixel lines, both with and without a USB cable connected to the platform. When the fuel gauge is not connected to a power source, it returns negative values for the instantaneous current consumption as energy is being drained from the battery. However, when a charging cable is connected, the charging current is stable enough not to question the attack, and positive values are obtained if the system consumes less energy than it absorbs via the cable. In our testing, we were able to prototype the attack successfully. To facilitate our temporal attack, we developed a simple target application, as shown in Fig. 3, which prompts the user to enter a PIN code using a virtual numeric keypad. The entry must be confirmed using a validation key located in a known location on the screen, thus creating a time lapse between each press that can be exploited by the attacker. Additionally, the keypad is not perfectly square, with varying distances between certain keys, which can also slightly work in favor of the attacker. It is worth noting that most phones come with a factory configuration that includes a vibration feedback when a key is pressed, which requires substantial energy to activate, representing an aggravating factor in this situation. Overall, our prototype attack demonstrates the vulnerability of Android devices to temporal attacks, which can be exploited by an attacker with the knowledge and resources to do so.

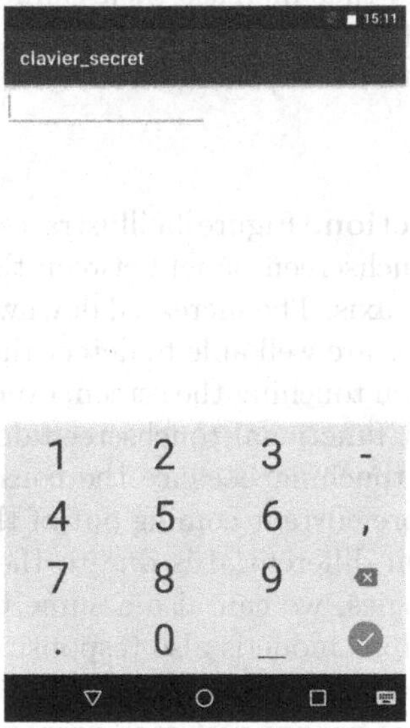

Fig. 3. Screenshot of the target application.

We also developed an Android application dedicated to the attack. The application includes an Android service that can scan the fuel gauge without interfering with the user interface and can do so even when the phone is in standby mode or the user switches to another app. As energy readings accumulate, they are stored in memory and can be accessed later to avoid lowering the signal-to-noise ratio that could occur with real-time extraction via a wired or wireless Android Debug Bridge (ADB) link. For the purposes of this demonstration, we will display a graph directly showing the data collected from the fuel gauge.

The X-axis represents the number of measurements collected, and the Y-axis indicates the instantaneous current consumption. It's important to note that we only rely on the instantaneous current consumption metric for this attack. Other metrics such as voltage, temperature, or remaining charge are either not precise enough or not representative of the instantaneous activity on the platform.

3.2 Exploitation

When setting up a timing-based attack, there are two main aspects to consider: capturing the data and detecting significant events, and analyzing the data to reduce the secret's space. The first aspect can be based on various metrics or physical phenomena, including the one we introduced in this article. The second aspect relies on methods that should be applicable regardless of the technique used to capture the data. These methods are aimed at analyzing the data to reduce the space of possible secrets that could have generated the captured timing data. By applying these methods, an attacker can gain insights into the possible values of the secret and thus increase their chances of successfully cracking it. Overall, timing-based attacks are a powerful tool in an attacker's arsenal, and it is essential to consider both the capture and analysis of the data to successfully execute such an attack.

Temporal Position Detection. Figure 4a illustrates a sequence where we have our finger resting on the touchscreen panel between the 12,500 and 22,500 measurements, counted on the x-axis. The increased downward variance in this region indicates that the fuel gauges are well able to detect the delta in power consumption of a phone or tablet when touching the screen, even without vibration. Using a device with a cracked but functional touchscreen does not change this result. The curve decreases when touching because the consumption increases during these moments (there is more current coming out of the battery). While we can guess that this consumption differential is due to the physical phenomenon at play on capacitive technologies, we can also assume that a software processing necessary to manage this input mode is also responsible. On the Fig. 4b, we can see a typical sequence corresponding to a 4-digit code entry, with validation. The fact that the vibration is triggered at each press makes the reading obvious: the peaks corresponding to each entry are clearly visible to the naked eye. In this case, it is not necessary to deploy signal analysis techniques to conduct the attack. However, the low update rate of the fuel gauges makes us lack precision to conduct a temporal attack. The capture in Fig. 4c illustrates the same dataset as in the middle one, but where we have magnified the first two peaks. The three curves concentrated at the bottom of the screen correspond to the gyroscopic readings, which are also withdrawn. These can allow us to refine the temporal contact points: under an energy peak, we can retain the points where the derivatives of the three axes of rotation reach zero at the same instant after a variation.

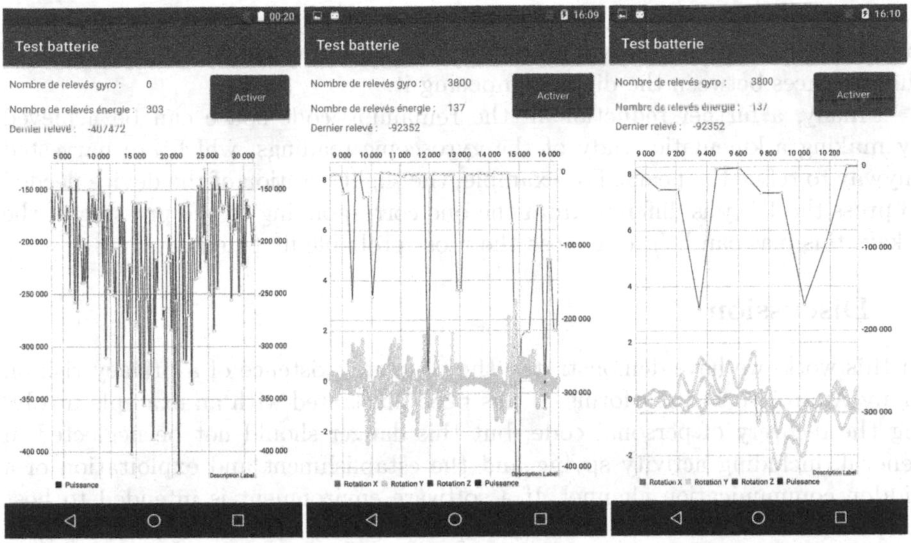

(a) (b) (c)

Fig. 4. Screenshots of the application used for the attack.

Temporal Attack. Once the delays between the inputs have been precisely identified, we can carry out a temporal attack on the code.

On our side, we have developed a recursive and deterministic algorithm, which, depending from the time lapses provided, unrolls the tree of the possible codes starting from the end, as illustrated in Listing 1.3 with values obtained from captures such as the one in Fig. 4b. It works in reverse order, since we know the user is required to confirm the PIN by pressing the validation key. This way, by observing the delays, we can infer on the most likely digits introduced right before, and so on. Thus, in the tree of most possible codes, the validation key, represented with the number 10, is the root, and the first digit of each possible PIN are the end of the branches. This method is conceptually close to the one presented in [5].

Listing 1.3. Example output from the developed deterministic algorithm. The 10-key represents the validation one, pressed at the end of the sequence. The proposed sequences are in reverse.

```
(arbre '(1.74 2 2.01 2.52) (cons '(10) '()) 0)
=> ((((((10 6 8 2 3) (10 6 8 2 1))) (((10 6 2 8 9) (10 6 2 8 7))))))
```

The state of the art shows that temporal analysis can provide convincing results by exploiting several possible techniques, often applied to beep tones emitted by physical pin pads. In [7], the possible PIN codes are extracted with the help of Hidden Markov Models (HMMs). However in [10], the use of machine learning techniques was highlighted. In all cases, quantifying the rate of success is not easy, since it depends a lot on the PIN itself, mostly on the variability in the distances between the digits composing it.

Finally, a further reduction in the remaining code space can be achieved by making a kinematic study of the gyroscopic readings, which are harvested anyway to refine the peaks. For example, the slight rotation of the device needed to press the 1 key is different from the one corresponding to the pressing of the 0 key: this bias can help to choose the most probable first digit.

4 Discussion

In this work, we have demonstrated the concrete existence of a privacy risk on many Android-based platforms. It has been illustrated with an example involving the recovery of personal code, but this danger should not be neglected in general, including activity spying and the establishment and exploitation of a hidden communication channel. If a software environment is intended to host executable content from various third-party actors, then the system designer should pay particular attention to the integration of a fuel gauge. Delegation of responsibility for energy management may indeed bring additional security considerations. Similarly, while this article has focused on the case of Android due to its widespread presence today, the risk presented is not specific to this OS. There are several devices on the market that embed a fuel gauge in different environments. One example is the Nintendo Switch, which is based on a FreeBSD kernel and has such an integrated circuit as part of its battery management. This danger can easily be taken into account when one controls the platform and its OS, since in this case it is sufficient to act on the security policy governing access to such components. This approach has been applied in [1] to regulate access to sensors in general, by means of modifications to the native system libraries, and to the applications before their installation. However, mitigation is much more complex when one is an actor with access only to the application layer, such as a third-party developer. Securing such a sensitive process is then a new task, where one can no longer rely on inter-application isolation. Moreover, thwarting auxiliary channels attacks is particularly complex when working with intermediate code generated from Java or Kotlin sources, as it is mostly the case on Android. This work is currently under study.

5 Conclusion

In this article, we have seen that some autonomous devices embed a fuel gauge and that this, due to its capabilities, can imply privacy risks. We have shown that their inclusion in the Android system is vulnerable to this, by setting up one of the possible exploits, namely secret spying. Since this danger contradicts the guarantee of isolation normally provided by the environment, it has serious consequences on the production of sensitive applications. It is therefore necessary for third-party developers to adopt measures and precautions. These solutions are currently being studied.

Acknowledgments. The authors would like to thank Guillaume Bouffard, for his creative contributions and support throughout this work.

References

1. Bai, X., Yin, J., Wang, Y.-P.: Sensor Guardian: prevent privacy inference on Android sensors. EURASIP J. Inf. Secur. **2017**(1), 1–17 (2017). https://doi.org/10.1186/s13635-017-0061-8
2. Berend, D., Jungk, B., Bhasin, S.: There goes your PIN: exploiting smartphone sensor fusion under single and cross user setting (2017). https://eprint.iacr.org/2017/1169
3. Bokhari, M.A., Xia, Y., Zhou, B., Alexander, B., Wagner, M.: Validation of internal meters of mobile android devices (2017). https://doi.org/10.48550/arXiv.1701.07095. https://arxiv.org/abs/1701.07095
4. Cai, L., Chen, H.: TouchLogger: inferring keystrokes on touch screen from smartphone motion (2011)
5. Cardaioli, M., Conti, M., Balagani, K., Gasti, P.: Your PIN sounds good! on the feasibility of PIN inference through audio leakage (2019). https://doi.org/10.48550/arXiv.1905.08742. Number: arXiv:1905.08742
6. Cronin, P., Gao, X., Yang, C., Wang, H.: Charger-surfing: exploiting a power line side-channel for smartphone information leakage (2021)
7. Foo Kune, D., Kim, Y.: Timing attacks on PIN input devices. In: Proceedings of the 17th ACM Conference on Computer and Communications Security. Association for Computing Machinery (2010). https://doi.org/10.1145/1866307.1866395
8. Kocher, P.C.: Timing attacks on implementations of Diffie-Hellman, RSA, DSS, and other systems. In: Koblitz, N. (ed.) CRYPTO 1996. LNCS, vol. 1109, pp. 104–113. Springer, Heidelberg (1996). https://doi.org/10.1007/3-540-68697-5_9
9. Le Bouder, H., Barry, T., Couroussé, D., Lanet, J.L., Lashermes, R.: A template attack against VERIFY PIN algorithms. In: SECRYPT 2016 (2016). https://hal.inria.fr/hal-01383143
10. Panda, S., Liu, Y., Hancke, G.P., Qureshi, U.M.: Behavioral acoustic emanations: attack and verification of PIN entry using keypress sounds (2020)
11. Xu, Z., Bai, K., Zhu, S.: TapLogger: inferring user inputs on smartphone touchscreens using on-board motion sensors. In: Proceedings of the Fifth ACM Conference on Security and Privacy in Wireless and Mobile Networks. WISEC 2012 (2012). https://doi.org/10.1145/2185448.2185465

The Good, the Bad, and the Binary: An LSTM-Based Method for Section Boundary Detection in Firmware Analysis

Riccardo Remigio, Alessandro Bertani(✉), Mario Polino, Michele Carminati, and Stefano Zanero

Politecnico di Milano, Milan, Italy
riccardo.remigio@mail.polimi.it,
{alessandro.bertani,mario.polino,michele.carminati,
stefano.zanero}@polimi.it

Abstract. Static analysis tools need information about the ISA and the boundaries of the code and data sections of the binary they analyze. This information is often not readily available in embedded systems firmware, often provided only in a non-standard format or as a raw memory dump. This paper proposes a novel methodology for ISA identification and code and data separation, that extends and improves the state of the art. We identify the main shortcoming of state-of-the-art approaches and add a capability to classify packed binaries' architecture employing an entropy-based method. Then, we implement an LSTM-based model with heuristics to recognize the section boundaries inside a binary, showing that it outperforms state-of-the-art methods. Finally, we evaluate our approach on a dataset of binaries extracted from real-world firmware.

Keywords: Binary Analysis · Reverse Engineering · Machine Learning · Embedded Systems

1 Introduction

Unlike general computing systems, which rely on an underlying operating system, embedded devices implement a custom software called *firmware*, which runs only on a specific device and is often proprietary. Furthermore, embedded systems have heterogeneous hardware. Consequently, despite progress in dynamic analysis and emulation, third-party security auditors must still rely on static binary analysis and reverse engineering to discover vulnerabilities and reconstruct the behavior of a program [1]. Many tools implement static analysis techniques, ranging from disassemblers and decompilers to complex analysis frameworks [2,3] that combine static analysis with other techniques, primarily symbolic execution [4,5], fuzzing [6,7], or both [8]. The reverse engineering of a binary through static analysis is challenging and requires disassembling

J. Shikata and H. Kuzuno (Eds.): IWSEC 2023, LNCS 14128, pp. 16–35, 2023.
https://doi.org/10.1007/978-3-031-41326-1_2

the executable file's machine instructions. Unfortunately, perfect disassembly is undecidable [9]: modern disassemblers often fall short on real-world files, such as firmware. Additionally, static analysis tools need information about the binary's Instruction Set Architecture (ISA) and the boundaries of the code and data sections. Without this prior knowledge, the disassembler does not know how to interpret the sequences of bytes and even the analysis's starting point.

In this paper, we tackle the problem of separating instructions from data in a binary program (code discovery problem) to support the static analysis without metadata – i.e., information about the ISA and the layout of a binary file (code and data sections). For ISA identification, we improve upon a state-of-the-art technique, *ELISA* [10], a methodology based on supervised machine learning that identifies the architecture and separates code from data in raw binary files when no metadata is available. We identify the main shortcoming of *ELISA* and add a capability to classify packed binaries' architecture employing an entropy-based method. We implement an LSTM-based model with heuristics to recognize the section boundaries inside a binary for code and data separation. We evaluate our approach on a dataset of binaries extracted from real-world firmware, showing that it outperforms *ELISA*'s CRF-based method, improving the performance up to 74.03%. Additionally, we present our results through novel metrics that are more suitable in the domain under analysis and better catch the context peculiarities concerning the traditional metrics of accuracy, precision, and recall. In this paper, we make the following contributions:

- We extend and improve upon *ELISA* [10] to classify packed binaries' architecture employing an entropy-based method.
- We present a novel approach to better recognize the boundaries of the code and data sections inside the binary, having only the ISA as prior information. In our approach, we leverage an LSTM-based model with heuristics.
- We propose domain-specific metrics that better express the performance in the context under analysis.

2 Background and Related Work

Architecture classification, *code from data separation*, and *function boundaries identification* are well-known problems in static binary analysis. Commercial disassembly tools need to perform, at least implicitly, these three tasks, especially when analyzing header-less files. Even if they are not directly related to our work, we take inspiration from these works to develop our model and heuristics.

Architecture Classification. In this context, signature matching, statistical, and machine learning techniques have been proposed, usually leveraging differences in the distribution of byte frequency among different file types [11–14].

Clemens et al. [15] address the ISA identification problem as a machine learning classification problem, using features extracted from the byte frequency distribution of the files and comparing 10 different machine learning models (i.e., on the same dataset). The dataset is formed by the binaries of 20 different architectures taken by the Debian Linux distribution and some samples from Arduino and CUDA compiled code. The main limitation is that the features are extracted only from the executable sections of the binaries. In our case, this is not possible since, in our scenario, we cannot extract such information from the binaries. Moreover, the models were trained and tested without a phase of hyperparameter tuning. Without tuning the hyperparameters, the results obtained from the models can be less reliable. This phase could increase the performance of some models and change the decision to choose one model over another. A completely different approach leverages static signatures: the Angr static analysis framework [4] includes a tool (Boyscout) to identify the CPU architecture of an executable by matching the file to a set of signatures containing the byte patterns of function prologues and epilogues of known architectures, and picking the architecture with most matches; as a drawback, the signatures require maintenance, and their quality and completeness are critical for the quality of the classification; also, this method may fail on heavily optimized or obfuscated code lacking of function prologues and epilogues. Lyda et al. [16] address the problem of classifying an executable as native, compressed, or encrypted, measuring the entropy of the binary file under analysis and comparing its value with confidence intervals computed on a dataset of packed binaries. Unfortunately, the paper does not clearly define the classification step procedure. `Cpu_rec` [17] is a plugin for the popular `binwalk` [18] tool that uses a statistical approach, based on Markov chains with similarity measures by cross-entropy computation, to detect the CPU architecture or a binary file, or of part of a binary file, among a corpus of 72 architectures. The authors of *ISADetect* [19] implement Clemens and *ELISA* approaches and validate the results on a wider dataset. They also provide an open-source dataset and toolset, which achieves lower scores than *ELISA* on the architecture identification task.

Code and Section Identification. Andriesse et al. [20] analyze the performance of state-of-the-art x86 and x86-64 disassemblers, evaluating the accuracy of detecting instruction boundaries: for this task, linear sweep disassemblers have an accuracy of 99.92%, with a false positive rate of 0.56% for the most challenging dataset, outperforming recursive traversal ones (accuracy between 99% and 96%, depending on the optimization level of the binaries). Despite this, simple obfuscation techniques such as inserting junk bytes in the instruction stream are enough to make linear disassemblers misclassify 26%-30% of the instructions [21]. Kruegel et al. [22] address the code discovery problem in obfuscated binaries and propose a hybrid approach that combines control-flow-based and statistical techniques to deal with such obfuscation techniques. Wartell et al. [9] segment x86 machine code into valid instructions and data based on a Predication by Partial Matching model (PPM), aided by heuristics, that overcomes the performance of a state-of-the-art commercial recursive traversal disassembler, IDA Pro, when evaluated with a small dataset of Windows binaries. The model evaluation is done by manually comparing the model output with the disassembly from IDA Pro because precise ground truth for the binaries in the training set is not available. This limitation does not allow testing the method on many binaries. This approach supports a single architecture (x86) and relies on architecture-specific heuristics: supporting a new ISA requires implementing the new heuristics. Chen et al. [23] address the code discovery problem in the context of static binary translation, specifically targeted ARM binaries; they only consider the difference between 32-bit ARM instructions and 16-bit Thumb instructions that can be mixed in the same executable. Karampatziakis et al. [24] present the code discovery problem in x86 binaries as a supervised learning problem over a graph, using structural SVMs to classify bytes as code or data.

Function Identification. Rosenblum et al. [25] address the problem of Function Entry Point identification in stripped binaries, using linear-chain Conditional Random Fields [26] for structured classification in sequences, the same model proposed in ELISA to tackle the problem of code discovery. ByteWeight [27] uses statistical techniques to tackle the function identification problem (i.e., function prologue and epilogue) inside the code sections of a binary by exploiting a weighted prefix tree and the construction of a Control Flow Graph (CFG). The authors test their approach on a dataset comprising 2048 binaries for Linux and Windows, compiled for x86 and x86-64 architectures, with GCC and ICC compilers and 4 optimization levels. ByteWeight gives better results concerning all the compared techniques, disassemblers, and analysis tools (i.e., Dyninst, BAP, and IDA Pro). Shin et al. [28] use supervised machine learning techniques to recognize boundaries of functions inside a binary. They implement different recurrent neural network models: RNN, GRU, LSTM, and bidirectional RNN. They test each model on the same dataset of ByteWeight [27], showing that the proposed approach outperforms state-of-the-art techniques.

ELISA. *ELISA* [10] is a framework based on supervised machine learning that aims to perform code discovery in header-less binary executable files and is intended as a practical aid to aid static analysis and reverse engineering tasks. Code discovery aims to separate the bytes containing executable instructions from the ones containing data, given an arbitrary sequence of bytes containing machine instructions and data and without the support of any metadata, such as headers of debug symbols. As we use supervised machine learning models, *ELISA* is signature-less: its set of supported architectures can be extended by extending the training set without developing architecture-specific heuristics. To accomplish this goal, *ELISA* follows a two-step approach. First of all, if the ISA of the binary executable file to be analyzed is unknown, *ELISA* detects it using an algorithm based on logistic regression (*architecture classifier*). Then, using the detected ISA, it identifies the boundaries of the code sections and performs fine-grained identification of data inside the code sections (*section identification*). Both code section identification and fine-grained data identification are performed using an algorithm based on supervised machine learning and, specifically, on Conditional Random Fields (CRFs). To this extent, a model is trained for each supported architecture. The original design of *ELISA* sports good performance on the architecture identification task provided the dataset comprises binaries where the code section is prevalent concerning the data section or where part of the code section is neither compressed nor encrypted

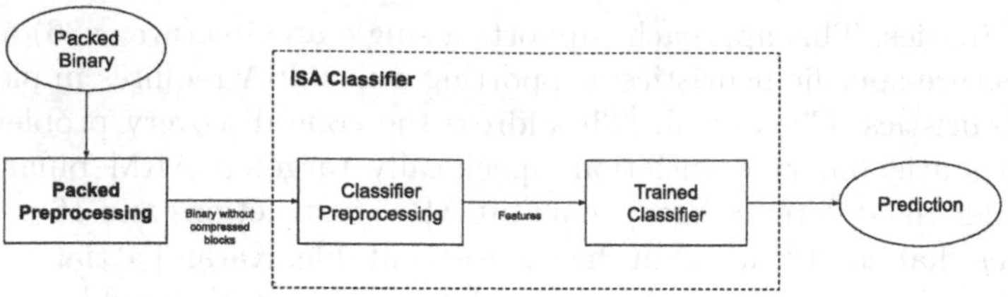

Fig. 1. High-level scheme of the extended ISA classification module

(i.e., packed binaries). A second limitation of the original design is precision in predicting the *beginning* of the code section, which is detected without errors in only 12% of the binaries part of the evaluation dataset, making the tool difficult to use in practice. In this paper, we propose an extension to the ISA identification step of *ELISA*. We also compare the performances of our novel methodology for code and data separation with those of *ELISA*.

3 Approach

3.1 Architecture Classifier

We implement the architecture classifier for the packed binaries by extending *ELISA*'s implementation of the classifier [10]. We decide to use the architecture classifier of *ELISA* because it is a simple machine learning model based on a Logistic Regression that performs well with respect to the state of the art, with an F-Score of 99% over different architectures. Moreover, extending the training set with new binaries makes it easy to extend the model to new architectures. Figure 1 shows how our preprocessing phase interacts with the *ELISA* classifier. The *Packed Preprocessing* block represents the preprocessing phase we implemented.

One of the main shortcomings in the original implementation of *ELISA* is that it cannot classify the architecture of binaries where the code section is packed or otherwise encrypted. To achieve this goal, we implement an approach working with a training set of unpacked binaries and rooted into extracting from a packed binary the executable portion composed of raw instructions (e.g., the loader of the packed binary). Using a model that works with a training set of unpacked binaries allows using the same model and training set for classifying both packed and unpacked binary executables.

Because of the structure of a packed binary, an architecture classifier for uncompressed binaries could predict a wrong ISA. In this case, the architecture classifier would extract the Byte-Frequency Distribution (BFD) from the whole binary, including the compressed sections. The compression algorithm alters the bytes inside the binary, which are no more correlated with its architecture. This can lead to an altered BFD of the binary that would fool the classifier. Our objective is to delete the compressed sections and extract the BFD from uncompressed bytes, excluding the noise of the compressed parts. We integrate a preprocessing phase with an architecture classifier for non-packed binaries.

We use an approach based on **entropy** computation to recognize the compressed parts of the binary. Since the entropy is based on the frequency of the bytes inside the binary, the compression algorithm also alters the entropy value. Usually, data compression increases the entropy value of the data, which can be considered a measure of how much information the data contains [29]. Since we are applying lossless data compression (we want to reconstruct the original data perfectly), the information in compressed and uncompressed data is the same. After the compression, we represent the same information in fewer data or bytes. Another way to interpret entropy is through the redundancy of the information. If the data have high redundancy, they have low entropy. The objective of a compression algorithm is to remove the redundancy inside the data, so we want to represent the same information but with the least possible amount of data [30]. Thus, the predictability of a bit decreases, and the probability of the bit assuming the value 0 or 1 goes towards 0.5, which represents random data. The more the compression algorithm can remove redundancy, the higher the entropy value is. Thus, by computing the entropy value, we can classify a sequence of bytes as compressed or uncompressed.

Preprocessing for the Architecture Classifier. To implement our preprocessing phase, we use an approach similar to the one discussed in the work of Lyda et al. [16]. We divide the binary into blocks of fixed length, and for each block, we compute the entropy. We consider a block as a sequence of bytes of fixed size. We choose to set the block size to 256 bytes. The entropy of a block x is given by $H(x) = -\sum_{i=1}^{n} p(i) \log_2 p(i)$, where, in our case, $p(i)$ represents the frequency of the byte i inside the block x and n is the number of values that a byte can assume, so 256. In this case, the entropy is a real value between 0 and 8, representing the lowest and the highest possible entropy, respectively. After computing the entropy of each block of the binary, we delete a block if its entropy value is over a certain threshold, which means that we consider the block compressed. Following empirical analysis, we set this threshold to 6.3: further details are explained in Appendix A. Then, we collect all the bytes of the uncompressed blocks and use them in the preprocessing phase of the architecture classifier. In this way, the classifier extracts the features only from bytes relevant to the architecture's recognition, and it should not be fooled by an altered BFD given by the compression algorithm. Our approach is used before the preprocessing phase of the architecture classifier and only during the prediction task, so it would also work on a pre-trained model used to classify unpacked binaries. For the same reason, this approach can be used on every model that uses features based on the distribution of the bytes.

3.2 Section Identification

During section identification, we classify each byte of the binary as belonging to a section of code or data using a Bidirectional LSTM, which is a supervised learning model. To the best of our knowledge, the only work that tries to solve the same problem is *ELISA*, in which the authors use a linear chain CRF model. This model can consider not only the context of a feature, that in this case is a sequence of bytes but also the correlation between the model outputs associated with adjacent bytes. LSTM is among the most used models in the state of the art and a valid alternative to the Linear Chain CRF [31]. In work done by Shin et al. [31], the authors use an LSTM model to recognize the boundaries of the functions inside a binary. They take a sequence of bytes and try to classify each byte as the beginning of a function, the end of a function, or code. This scenario can be compared to our problem since we try to classify each byte of a sequence as code or data. This work shows that the LSTM gives results that overcome the state of the art. For these reasons, we decide to implement a Bidirectional LSTM that allows us to consider the context before and after a certain byte. The section identification process can be divided into 4 steps: Preprocessing, Training, Prediction, and Postprocessing.

Training Set Preprocessing. In our scenario, we are dealing with binaries of which we do not have any information besides their ISA. During the preprocessing phase, we extract the features used to train the model that, in our case, are the bytes of the binary. Our choice is also common in other works like ELISA [10] and the work of Shin et al. [31]. We decide to use the one-hot-encoding representation of the bytes to treat the bytes as categorical features. This way, we are considering each possible value of a byte as a different category and not as an integer that could lead the model to learn an order relation between the bytes that does not exist. Thus, the byte is represented by a vector of 256 elements, which are the values that a byte can take, in which the i-th element is set to 1 if the value of the byte is i. Since our model works on sequences of samples (bytes) that are fixed, we have to split the binary into sequences of fixed length. The preprocessing phase differs a little during the training and prediction tasks. During the training phase, we randomly choose a binary from the dataset, read the binary as a stream of bytes and randomly take a point in the binary. From the chosen point on, we take a number of bytes equal to the length of the sequence. If the chosen point is near the end of the binary could happen that the sequence goes over the end of the binary. After the last available byte of the binary, to complete the sequence, we add a padding formed by vectors of 256 elements in which each element has a value equal to 0. This way, we have our first sequence of samples to pass to the model. To extract more sequences to create the complete feature matrix, we repeat this procedure until we have extracted a number of bytes equal to the total size in bytes of the training set. This way, we obtain a set of sequences that are randomly selected. This is done to prevent the network from training first on long sequences of samples of a class and then on long sequences of the other class since this could lead to a wrong tuning of the parameters. In the training phase, in addition to the features, we extract the ground truth from the information contained inside the section header of the binaries, in which are stored which sections are executable and the exact boundaries of each section, more precisely, the beginning of a section and its size. With this information, we create a vector of the size of the binary in which the i-th position is equal to 1 if the i-th byte of the binary belongs to a section of code, 0 otherwise. For example, if we have a binary of 10 bytes and the bytes from index 3 to 7 are in an executable section, the vector of the ground truth would be: $y = (0, 0, 0, 1, 1, 1, 1, 1, 0, 0)$. During the prediction phase, we split the binary into fixed-length sequences of bytes, where the model structure gives the sequence length. If the length of the binary in bytes is not divisible by the length of the sequence, we add padding to the last part of the binary. As for training, before the prediction, we transform each byte in the one-hot-encoding representation of their values.

Training. During the training phase, we use the sequences of samples extracted during the preprocessing phase to update all the model parameters. We use a Cross-Entropy loss function to do this because it is the most common choice when we have a binary classification problem. It is defined as $Loss = -(y_i \log(\hat{y_i}) + (1 - y_i)\log(1 - \hat{y_i}))$, where y_i is the actual label of the sample i and $\hat{y_i}$ is the prediction for the sample i that, in our case, is the output of the sigmoid of the output layer. We use the Adam optimization method [32], which optimizes the learning phase adapting the learning rate individually for each network parameter. We divide the training dataset into mini-batches. The computation of the gradient of the loss function for each sample can cause a large variance in the gradients since each sample can differ significantly from the other. So we use small batches of samples that allow averaging the gradients and decreasing the variance. In addition, this also increases the performance since the weights are updated only once for all the samples of the batch. All the training phase, considered as the training of the network over all the sequences extracted from the training set, is done a fixed number of times called epochs.

Prediction. For the prediction phase, we execute the preprocessing phase described before on the binary we want to analyze. After preprocessing, we obtain a vector with a size equal to the number of bytes in the binary where each item with index i in the vector has value 1 if the i-th byte of the binary belongs to a section of code, 0 if it belongs to a section of data. The output vector has the same structure as the ground truth vector extracted during preprocessing.

Postprocessing. For the postprocessing phase, we apply 3 different techniques to improve the results of the model further. These 3 approaches are used in the same order as they are described. The first technique used for the postprocessing phase is the one developed by the authors of ELISA [10]. Since our model outputs a vector equal in structure to the output vector of ELISA, we can use their postprocessing phase as it is. We decide to reuse this technique since it is based on a simple approach that increases the model's performance and is entirely independent of the model used. As described by the authors of ELISA, this phase is needed because code sections may contain small pieces of data. This phase is based on an iterative algorithm that removes the smallest chunk of data or code by merging it with the surrounding section. This algorithm inverts the labels of the bytes of a chunk c if the total number of chunks is greater than the minimum number of section set and if the length of c is less than the longest chunk times a multiplicative factor. The minimum number of sections and the multiplicative factor called *Cutoff* are parameters set manually. The second technique is based on the model developed by the authors of Byteweight [33], which is used to recognize the prologue of the functions inside a binary. To employ this approach, we analyze the position of the functions inside the binaries. To extract this information, we used two datasets, the one used to train the Byteweight model and a dataset formed by binaries extracted from the firmware of embedded devices. We implement the approach used in the Byteweight paper to recognize the function prologue through the weighted prefix tree. We use the same dataset used in Byteweight to update the tree weights. We take the *Coreutils*, *Binutils*, and *Findutils* sources and compile them for different architectures. We compile the binaries with debug symbols to extract the ground truth and with 4 different compiler optimization levels.

We use the Byteweight prefix tree to improve the performance of our model as follows. We predict the sections of a binary with our model, so we have the output vector of the classifier. We find the functions prologue inside the binary and perform this check for each predicted code section. If the beginning of the section coincides with a function prologue, we consider the prediction correct. Otherwise, we search for a function prologue around the beginning of the section, given a determined offset value. If we find it, we update the beginning of the section to match the position of the function prologue. This approach works because, usually, the error offset between the predicted start of a section and its actual start is lower than 6 bytes. The last technique is the one based on the frequency of the instructions. First, we create a dictionary of instructions. Each instruction is associated with a value that represents an estimated probability of the appearance of that instruction. To compute these probabilities, we use the same dataset used to generate the Byteweight tree. For each architecture, we disassemble all the binaries. For each found instruction, we compute the frequency f_i of instruction i as $f_i = Occ_i/N$ where Occ_i is the number of occurrences of instruction i in all the disassembled instructions of the dataset, and N is the total number of disassembled instructions in the dataset. After we obtain the instruction statistics, we can apply this postprocessing phase to the prediction of the LSTM model. We disassemble each predicted code section starting from the bytes around the start of the section. We take 4 bytes as the window in which we search for instructions. This allows us to minimize wrong modifications of the prediction, i.e., when the model has correctly predicted the beginning of the section, and we change the prediction because we find an instruction with a higher frequency. If the prediction is correct, the disassembly run on the bytes around the considered position should lead to an instruction that is less used (low-frequency value) or to a not existing instruction. Then, we take the instruction with the highest frequency and modify the start of the section to coincide with the beginning of the chosen instruction.

We use more than one dataset to!TEX root = ../paper.tex

Table 1. Composition of the five datasets: eight (BW), Debian (DEB), Debian Packed (DEBP), Firmware (FW), Firmware Packed (FWP).

Architecture	BW	DEB	DEBP	FW	FWP
amd64	588	385	277	971	75
arm32	572	-	-	275	75
arm64	572	382	-	496	19
armel	531	385	237	1000	762
armhf	-	385	192	-	-
i386	440	385	249	422	181
mips	572	384	255	795	398
mips64	572	-	-	482	-
mipsel	572	384	257	983	567
powerpc	572	-	-	934	282
ppc64el	-	380	278	-	-

4 Experimental Evaluation

In this section, we describe the datasets used, the metrics that we implemented and we show the results of our model. We also comment on the results we obtain and compare them with the current state of the art. Through these results, we want to demonstrate that our approach obtains better performance with the respect to the state-of-the-art approaches.

4.1 Dataset Composition

To evaluate and train the different models that we use in this paper. For simplicity, we give each dataset a label. ① **Byteweight**: this dataset is built from the same sources as the one used in the Byteweight paper to update the weights of the prefix tree. We download the source code of *Coreutils*, *Findutils*, and *Binutils* utilities of Linux. Then we use the GNU toolchain to compile the source code with 4 optimization levels and debug symbols for 9 different architectures. ② **Debian**: this is the dataset used by De Nicolao et al. [10]. It comprises the binaries taken by the Debian package repository and compiled for 8 different architectures. ③ **Debian packed**: this dataset is built by running the UPX compression tool on every binary of the Debian dataset. ④ **Firmware**: this dataset comprises binaries extracted from the firmware of embedded devices, which is based on Linux: the extracted binaries are ELF files. The firmware is taken by a collection built during the work of Mkhatvari [34], which contains the firmware of embedded devices downloaded from the vendor sites through web scraping. The authors of the paper used the Firmadyne [35] web scraper to download the firmware images from the site of known vendors: Linksys, Tp-Link, Netgear, Tenda, D-link, Ubiquiti Networks, and Asus. ⑤ **Firmware packed**: this dataset is built by running the UPX compression tool on every binary of the Firmware dataset.

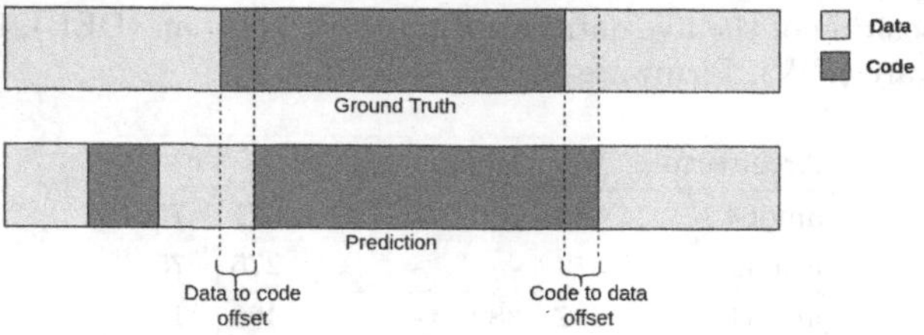

Fig. 2. Section identification metrics

The Debian packed and Firmware packed datasets contain fewer binaries with respect to the Debian and Firmware datasets because the UPX tool was not able to pack some binaries. Some architectures are not supported by UPX, and some types of binaries can not be packed, like relocatable kernel modules. The composition of the five datasets is shown in Table 1.

4.2 Metrics

We use several metrics to evaluate the architecture classification and section identification models. Accuracy, Precision, Recall, and F-Score are traditionally used to evaluate machine learning classifiers. These metrics evaluate a model through the number of samples correctly or wrongly predicted, and they are expressed in terms of True Positive (TP), True Negative (TN), False Positive (FP), and False Negative (FN). In the section identification evaluation, the positive class is the one that represents the code, and the negative class represents the data. Since there are more classes in the architecture classification, these metrics are defined for each class. We use the macro average of each metric computed between the classes to give a general result. This way, we give the same importance to each class.

We also implement three metrics that we use to evaluate the performances of our model on the section identification task: ① **Data to Code offset** (DC) measures the number of bytes between the beginning of a real section of code and the beginning of the corresponding predicted section of code; ② **Code to Data offset** (CD) measures the number of bytes between the beginning of a real section of data and the beginning of the corresponding predicted section of data; ③ **Wrong Sections** (WS) is the difference between the number of sections in the binary and the number of sections in the prediction. If we have contiguous sections of code (data), we consider them a single section because we cannot distinguish different sections of the same type.

Since it can happen that the number of sections of the prediction is not correct, we cannot compute the offsets matching each section by their position. To correctly compute the offsets, we calculate them between the overlapping sections. As shown in Fig. 2, the offset is computed only for the second code section, which overlaps with the one in the ground truth, and not for the first code section considered wrongly predicted. This approach could lead to a wrong evaluation when two predicted sections overlap with a single section of the ground truth.

Table 2. Results of *ELISA* and our architecture classifier on the Debian Packed dataset. In the Table we report precision (P), recall(R), and F1-Score (F1).

Class	ELISA			Our approach			Samples
	P	R	F1	P	R	F1	
amd64	1.000	0.018	0.035	0.829	0.776	0.830	277
armel	0.000	0.000	0.000	0.585	0.726	0.648	237
armhf	0.124	1.000	0.221	0.159	0.073	0.100	192
i386	1.000	0.076	0.142	0.830	0.763	0.795	249
mips	1.000	0.455	0.625	0.740	0.949	0.832	255
mipsel	1.000	0.027	0.053	0.903	0.942	0.922	257
ppc64el	1.000	0.194	0.325	0.869	0.932	0.899	278
Total	0.732	0.253	0.200	0.711	0.737	0.718	1745

However, this situation is rare since the section offsets of our model are usually small, as we will show in the results.

We decide to use these metrics because the classic accuracy, precision, and recall metrics are insufficient to evaluate our approach. They consider each classified byte with the same weight, while we want to give more importance to the bytes on the boundaries. More precisely, we want to know if our classifier can correctly predict each section's beginning and end, as our objective is to perform static analysis on a binary that does not have metadata: one necessary information is the exact boundaries of each section.

4.3 Architecture Classification

To evaluate the architecture classification of packed binaries, we test our model on the Debian and Firmware datasets. We want to show the difference between the base classifier of *ELISA* and our extended version, demonstrating the improvement of performance given by our approach when dealing with packed binaries. For each model, we used unpacked binaries' datasets as a training set and all the packed binaries as a test set. The UPX tool compresses and adds a portion of code at the end of the binary with the decompression routine. This way, the BFD of the binaries is completely altered.

We show the results of our tests in Table 2 and Table 3. As expected, *ELISA*'s classifier does not perform well with packed binaries. For some architectures we have an high precision given by a low level of false positives, but, as we can see from the recall score, we have also an high number of false negatives. As we can see from the recall value of the armhf architecture (when using the Debian dataset), the classifier tends to classify most of the binaries with that class. We can see a similar behaviour with the same model trained on the Firmware dataset. In fact, there are some binaries that are correctly classified but the general trend of the values is highly variable between the classes.

We can see that the results of our approach are better, with an average F-Score of 71.8% on the Debian dataset and 89.0% on the Firmware dataset. In the first case, the values are homogeneous between the architectures other than the armel and armhf architectures. This behaviour is given by the fact that the

Table 3. Results of *ELISA* and our architecture classifier on the Firmware Packed dataset. In the Table we report precision (P), recall(R), and F1-Score (F1).

Class	ELISA			Our approach			Samples
	P	R	F1	P	R	F1	
amd64	1.000	0.520	0.684	0.881	0.787	0.831	75
arm32	0.000	0.000	0.000	0.951	0.773	0.853	75
arm64	1.000	0.158	0.273	1.000	0.789	0.882	19
armel	0.730	0.298	0.423	0.814	0.987	0.892	762
i386	1.000	0.387	0.558	1.000	0.751	0.858	181
mips	0.227	0.997	0.370	0.935	0.942	0.939	398
mipsel	0.695	0.229	0.345	0.974	0.850	0.980	567
powerpc	0.000	0.000	0.000	1.000	0.922	0.959	282
Total	0.582	0.324	0.332	0.944	0.850	0.890	2359

Table 4. Results of *ELISA* and our Bidirectional LSTM with/without heuristics on the section identification task on the Firmware dataset. Higher is better for CD and DC, lower is better for WS.

Architecture	ELISA			ELISA + H			Bi-LSTM			Bi-LSTM + H		
	CD	DC	WS	CD	DC	WS	CD	DC	WS	CD	DC	WS
amd64	85.0%	61.1%	10.7%	85.0%	63.9%	10.7%	85.8%	90.6%	6.3%	85.8%	91.0%	6.3%
arm32	60.7%	88.4%	18.1%	60.7%	94.8%	18.1%	58.7%	96.1%	14.8%	58.7%	96.1%	14.8%
arm64	18.9%	40.4%	48.9%	18.9%	45.5%	48.9%	35.4%	77.9%	39.1%	35.4%	77.9%	39.1%
armel	54.6%	90.3%	25.3%	54.6%	92.5%	25.3%	68.3%	86.5%	25.2%	68.3%	93.8%	25.2%
i386	78.2%	62.9%	41.4%	78.2%	63.3%	41.4%	88.1%	85.1%	38.7%	88.1%	90.4%	38.7%
mips	50.8%	**16.0%**	53.6%	50.8%	**72.2%**	53.6%	66.5%	63.9%	52.3%	66.5%	**74.2%**	52.3%
mips64	38.3%	**10.6%**	38.6%	38.3%	**81.6%**	38.6%	80.5%	74.6%	36.6%	80.5%	**84.6%**	36.6%
mipsel	66.1%	**8.4%**	59.9%	66.1%	**40.5%**	59.9%	66.5%	29.2%	59.9%	66.5%	**47.9%**	59.9%
powerpc	76.5%	53.4%	50.7%	76.5%	60.1%	50.7%	77.0%	57.9%	49.4%	77.0%	64.9%	49.4%

armel and armhf architectures share almost the same instructions and the same endianness. Differently from the scenario in which we are dealing with unpacked binaries, in this case we do not have enough bytes to distinguish a binary between these two architectures. By repeating the same experiment removing the armhf architecture from the dataset, we obtained better results: the average F1-score goes up to 91%. In the case of the Firmware dataset, the recall of the amd64, arm32 and arm64 binaries is a little under the average, but this could be because of the low number of tested samples.

4.4 Section Identification

To test the Bidirectional LSTM, we use a training set composed by 120 binaries for each architecture, and a test set composed by the rest of the binaries. We first tested *ELISA* and our model on the Firmware dataset: the results show that our model performs better, but the average F1-score improvement is 0.007. Using classic metrics, we had small room for improvement, since *ELISA* already had scores around 0.99. To have a better evaluation of the model and extract

Table 5. Bidirectional LSTM improvements with respect to *ELISA*.

Architecture	amd64	arm32	arm64	armel	i386	mips	mips64	mipsel	powerpc
CD	+0.8%	−1.9%	+16.5%	+13.8%	+9.9%	+15.7%	+42.2%	+0.5%	+0.5%
DC	+29.9%	+7.7%	+38.0%	+3.4%	+27.5%	+58.2%	+74.0%	+39.5%	+11.4%
WS	−4.3%	−3.2%	−9.8%	−0.1%	−2.7%	−1.3%	−2.0%	0%	−1.4%

Table 6. Binaries with predicted section boundary offset less or equal to 6 bytes.

Architecture	amd64	arm32	arm64	armel	i386	mips	mips64	mipsel	powerpc
CD	97.5%	92.3%	59.0%	84.9%	97.7%	87.8%	80.2%	85.6%	95.2%
DC	96.4%	98.1%	94.7%	96.5%	99.7%	82.2%	94.4%	73.2%	73.3%

relevant information we have to check the results given through our new metrics: *Code to Data, Data to Code, Wrong Sections*, already covered in Sect. 4.2. For *Data to Code*, we consider the number of binaries in which the model predicts the beginning of all code sections with a data-to-code offset equal to zero. For *Code to Data*, we consider the number of binaries in which the model predicts the beginning of all data sections with a code-to-data offset equal to zero. For *Wrong Sections*, we consider the number of binaries where the real sections number and the predicted one differ. All these metrics are reported as percentages over the total number of binaries for each architecture.

In Table 4, we report the results of the test for both *ELISA* and our model, both evaluated without applying the heuristics described in Sect. 3.2 first, and applying the heuristics then. In this Table, we can see how our model performs better than *ELISA* in the Mips and Mips64 architectures. In these two architectures, we have an average improvement of 66% in recognizing the beginning of the code sections. From these results, we can see that the heuristics that we implemented give our model an improvement for some architectures.

We test the heuristics also on *ELISA*: we can see that the greatest improvement is given on Mips, Mips64, and Mipsel with an average increase of 53% between these three architectures on the data-to-code metric. In Table 5, we show the improvement of our model with respect to *ELISA*: we present the percentage improvements between *ELISA* and the bidirectional LSTM with heuristics applied. The only architecture in which we have results that are slightly worse than the *ELISA* one is arm32, in which our model has a code to data decrease of 2%. A graphic visualization of the comparison between Elisa and the bidirectional LSTM model with the heuristics applied is in Figs. 3a and 3b. In these two graphs, we show the number of binaries in which the models correctly predict the code-to-data transition and the data-to-code transition. Finally, in Table 6 we report the number of binaries in which the offset between each predicted section boundary and the corresponding section boundary of the ground truth is less or equal to 6 bytes. In these results, we can see that 88% of the binaries, on average, have an error between the predicted section boundary and real section boundary of fewer than 6 bytes. This is also the reason why we implemented

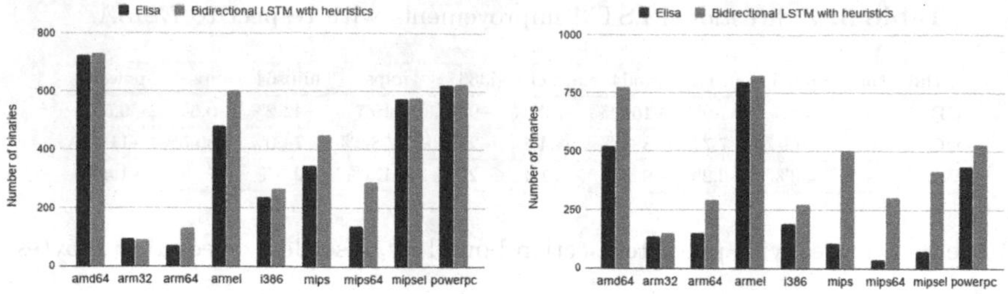

(a) Code to Data (b) Data to Code

Fig. 3. Number of binaries with offsets equal to 0.

the heuristics that work in a little range around the section boundary. For all the considered architectures preprocessing took between 3 and 108 min, training took between 5 and 19 min and testing took between 3 an 105 min.

5 Conclusion

We implement our approach for the architecture classifier extending an existent work, *ELISA*. We add a preprocessing phase that allows us to extract the features only from the relevant bytes that belong to uncompressed blocks. For section identification, we implement a novel approach based on a Bidirectional LSTM model that uses one-hot-encoding of bytes as features. To further improve the results of this classifier we added three postprocessing phases. In Sect. 4, we show the improvements given by our approach with respect to the base classifier of *ELISA*. We tested both approaches on the Debian dataset and on the Firmware dataset. For the section identification, we show that, with both "traditional" and new metrics, our model performs better. With our metrics, we can see a greater improvement.

Limitations and Future Work. As we stated in the introduction the approaches described in this paper can be used to analyze binaries that do not have any metadata associated, as our approach is able to recognize even the architecture of packed binary. This information can enable the analysis of the file. However, an attacker could easily alter the binary to avoid its analysis by putting some constant data inside the blocks of the binary. In this way, they alter the BFD of the binary and decrease the entropy of the blocks. In this situation, our approach would not extract the compressed blocks and the classifier would extract an altered BFD that leads to a wrong prediction.

In some architectures, our model still has pretty low results. Possible future works could be the implementation of heuristics that are able to delete the sections that are wrongly predicted by the model and the exploration of new models. As we have seen, in this scenario, the models used for sequential predictions seem to perform well. Researchers can try other models used in the field of Natural

Language Processing (NLP). Another approach could be to use more complex structures combining different models together.

A Hyperparameter Tuning

In this appendix, we describe how we found the optimal values for some of the hyperparameters used in our approach.

A.1 Architecture Classifier

In our approach, we have to set two parameters to extract the uncompressed blocks from the binary. The first one is the size of the blocks on which we compute the entropy. We tried different values of the block size (128, 256, 512, 1024, 2048, 3072) and we found that the best value is 256. From 256 to 1024 the performances of the model remain the same, while from 2048 on we see that the performances of the classifier tend to decrease. We chose to use 256 as size as we want to extract compressed blocks in a more fine-grained way. This result is consistent with the value used in Lyda et al. [16]. The second parameter is the entropy threshold used to classify a block as compressed or not. To find the optimal value of this parameter we check the entropy of blocks inside the binaries. First, we compute the maximum entropy between the blocks of code inside a binary. Then we compute the mean between the maximum entropy of each binary for each architecture. In Table 7 we report the results of the mean maximum entropy for the different architectures. We can see that the entropy value is almost homogeneous between the architectures. In this way, we have an estimate of the value of the entropy of the blocks that we want to extract. Starting from a value of 6 as the entropy threshold, we test higher values and we find that the optimal value is 6.3. This value is also consistent with the confidence interval computed in Lyda et al. [16].

Table 7. Mean maximum code entropy of unpacked binaries

Architecture	amd64	arm32	arm64	armel	i386	mips	mipsel	powerpc
Mean Entropy	5.89	5.68	5.81	5.74	5.86	5.41	5.28	5.93

A.2 Section Identification

Bidirectional LSTM Hyperparameters. The first two hyperparameters are the dimension of the input and the dimension of the output vector of the LSTM cell. To tune these hyperparameters we perform a grid search between different values. As a starting point, we take the values used by Shin et al. for their model [28]. We define a vector of values for the input dimension [500, 1000,

Table 8. Hyperparamters values for LSTM model

Architecture	amd64	arm32	arm64	armel	i386	mips	mips64	mipsel	powerpc
Input dimension	25	70	75	100	25	50	50	50	50
LSTM output dimension	24	24	24	24	32	32	32	16	32

2000] and for the dimension of the LSTM output [8, 16, 24, 32, 40]. The number of different models created through these values is the Cartesian product of the dimension of the two vectors since we want to check all the permutations. The model is evaluated on a validation set formed by 120 binaries taken from the Firmware dataset and with the new metrics. Since we use custom metrics, we are not able to use existent libraries to decide which hyperparameter value is better than another. The solution is to evaluate each model on the dataset and check the results by hand. The results show that for high dimensions of the input, the performances seem to decrease. So, we train and test the model again with different values of the input dimension that are [25, 50, 75, 100]. With these values, we see a great improvement in the performance of the model. Each model seems to have different best values for these hyperparameters, however, these values are included in a limited range that could be easily explored. The Table 8 shows the values of the hyperparameters used. We do not perform a grid search for the batch size: we take the same value used in the paper of Shin et al. The batch size can modify the time that the model takes to converge to an optimal solution, but should not have a great impact on the performance of the model with respect to the previous hyperparameters. The number of epochs for which the model has to train is set to 5. To decide this value we run a training phase on the model and we see that after 5 epochs the value of the loss function is low and it remains pretty constant on the successive epochs.

Postprocessing Parameters. For the postprocessing phase, we have to tune the parameters of the *ELISA* and Byteweight approach. The postprocessing phase of *ELISA* takes two parameters as input: the minimum number of sections that the prediction vector must have, and the maximum size of the chunk that can be eliminated, represented as the percentage of the size of the biggest chunk. These two parameters were already optimized by the authors of *ELISA*, so we decide to use the same values: 4 as the minimum number of sections and 0.1 for the chunk size. The postprocessing phase that we implemented takes two parameters as input. These two values define the range around the beginning of a section in which we search for a function prologue. To define this range we use two values that represent the positive offset and the negative offset from the section boundary. To find the optimal value for the positive offset, we used the Byteweight dataset to make an estimate of the positions of the functions prologue. We discovered that in some binaries, if the section does not begin with a function, the first encountered function is at an offset of 4 bytes. In order to avoid wrong modification of the start of a code section, we set the positive offset parameter to 3. For the negative offset parameter, we manually tested some values but, over a certain value, the results do not seem to change: only for large values of the offset (e.g., 500 bytes), the performance seems to decrease. We do not expect to find functions in a data section, but the Byteweight model can wrongly predict a function prologue. After some tests, we decide to set this parameter to 40 in order to prevent the Byteweight model from predicting a function in the data section.

References

1. Cova, M., Felmetsger, V., Banks, G., Vigna, G.: Static detection of vulnerabilities in x86 executables. In: Proceedings 22nd Annual Computer Security Applications Conference, ACSAC, pp. 269–278. IEEE (2006)
2. Song, D., et al.: BitBlaze: a new approach to computer security via binary analysis. In: Sekar, R., Pujari, A.K. (eds.) ICISS 2008. LNCS, vol. 5352, pp. 1–25. Springer, Heidelberg (2008). https://doi.org/10.1007/978-3-540-89862-7_1
3. Brumley, D., Jager, I., Avgerinos, T., Schwartz, E.J.: BAP: a binary analysis platform. In: Gopalakrishnan, G., Qadeer, S. (eds.) CAV 2011. LNCS, vol. 6806, pp. 463–469. Springer, Heidelberg (2011). https://doi.org/10.1007/978-3-642-22110-1_37
4. Shoshitaishvili, Y., et al.: SoK: (state of) the art of war: offensive techniques in binary analysis. In: Proceedings of 2016 IEEE Symposium on Security and Privacy, SP, pp. 138–157 (2016)
5. Shoshitaishvili, Y., Wang, R., Hauser, C., Kruegel, C., Vigna, G.: Firmalice-automatic detection of authentication bypass vulnerabilities in binary firmware. In: Proceedings of 2015 Network and Distributed System Security Symposium, NDSS (2015)
6. Haller, I., Slowinska, A., Neugschwandtner, M., Bos, H.: Dowsing for overflows: a guided fuzzer to find buffer boundary violations. In: Proceedings 22nd USENIX Security Symposium, USENIX Security 2013, pp. 49–64 (2013)
7. Corina, J., et al.: Difuze: interface aware fuzzing for kernel drivers. In: Proceedings of the 2017 ACM SIGSAC Conference on Computer and Communications Security, CCS 2017, pp. 2123–2138 (2017)
8. Stephens, N., et al.: Driller: augmenting fuzzing through selective symbolic execution. In: Proceedings of 2016 Network and Distributed System Security Symposium, NDSS, vol. 16, pp. 1–16 (2016)
9. Wartell, R., Zhou, Y., Hamlen, K.W., Kantarcioglu, M., Thuraisingham, B.: Differentiating code from data in x86 binaries. In: Gunopulos, D., Hofmann, T., Malerba, D., Vazirgiannis, M. (eds.) ECML PKDD 2011. LNCS (LNAI), vol. 6913, pp. 522–536. Springer, Heidelberg (2011). https://doi.org/10.1007/978-3-642-23808-6_34
10. De Nicolao, P., Pogliani, M., Polino, M., Carminati, M., Quarta, D., Zanero, S.: ELISA: ELiciting ISA of raw binaries for fine-grained code and data separation. In: Giuffrida, C., Bardin, S., Blanc, G. (eds.) DIMVA 2018. LNCS, vol. 10885, pp. 351–371. Springer, Cham (2018). https://doi.org/10.1007/978-3-319-93411-2_16
11. McDaniel, M., Heydari, M.H.: Content based file type detection algorithms. In: Proceedings of 36th Annual Hawaii International Conference on System Sciences (2003)
12. Li, W.-J., Wang, K., Stolfo, S.J., Herzog, B.: Fileprints: identifying file types by n-gram analysis. In: Proceedings of the 6th Annual IEEE SMC Information Assurance Workshop, IAW 2005, pp. 64–71. IEEE (2005)

13. Sportiello, L., Zanero, S.: Context-based file block classification. In: Peterson, G., Shenoi, S. (eds.) DigitalForensics 2012. IAICT, vol. 383, pp. 67–82. Springer, Heidelberg (2012). https://doi.org/10.1007/978-3-642-33962-2_5
14. Penrose, P., Macfarlane, R., Buchanan, W.J.: Approaches to the classification of high entropy file fragments. Digit. Investig. **10**(4), 372–384 (2013)
15. Clemens, J.: Automatic classification of object code using machine learning. Digit. Invest. **14**, S156–S162 (2015)
16. Lyda, R., Hamrock, J.: Using entropy analysis to find encrypted and packed malware. IEEE Secur. Priv. **5**, 40–45 (2007)
17. Granboulan, L.: cpu_rec: recognize CPU instructions in an arbitrary binary file (2017). https://github.com/airbus-seclab/cpu_rec
18. ReFirmLabs: Binwalk
19. Kairajärvi, S., Costin, A., Hämäläinen, T.: Isadetect: usable automated detection of CPU architecture and endianness for executable binary files and object code. In: Proceedings of the Tenth ACM Conference on Data and Application Security and Privacy, CODASPY 2020, pp. 376–380. Association for Computing Machinery, New York (2020)
20. Andriesse, D., Chen, X., Van Der Veen, V., Slowinska, A., Bos, H.: An in-depth analysis of disassembly on full-scale x86/x64 binaries. In: Proceedings of 25th USENIX Security Symposium, USENIX Security 2016, pp. 583–600 (2016)
21. Linn, C., Debray, S.: Obfuscation of executable code to improve resistance to static disassembly. In: Proceedings of 10th ACM Conference on Computer and Communications Security, CCS 2003, pp. 290–299. ACM (2003)
22. Kruegel, C., Robertson, W., Valeur, F., Vigna, G.: Static disassembly of obfuscated binaries. In: Proceedings of 13th USENIX Security Symposium (2004)
23. Chen, J.-Y., Shen, B.-Y., Ou, Q.-H., Yang, W., Hsu, W.-C.: Effective code discovery for ARM/Thumb mixed ISA binaries in a static binary translator. In: Proceedings of 2013 International Conference on Compilers, Architectures and Synthesis for Embedded Systems, CASES 2013, pp. 1–10 (2013)
24. Karampatziakis, N.: Static analysis of binary executables using structural SVMs. In: Lafferty, J.D., Williams, C.K.I., Shawe-Taylor, J., Zemel, R.S., Culotta, A. (eds.) Advances in Neural Information Processing Systems, vol. 23, pp. 1063–1071. Curran Associates Inc. (2010)
25. Rosenblum, N., Zhu, X., Miller, B., Hunt, K.: Learning to analyze binary computer code. In: Proceedings of 23th AAAI Conference on Artificial Intelligence, AAAI 2008, pp. 798–804. AAAI Press (2008)
26. Lafferty, J.D., McCallum, A., Pereira, F.C.N.: Conditional random fields: probabilistic models for segmenting and labeling sequence data. In: Proceedings of 18th International Conference on Machine Learning, ICML 2001, pp. 282–289. Morgan Kaufmann Publishers Inc. (2001)
27. Bao, T., Burket, J., Woo, M., Turner, R., Brumley, D.: ByteWeight: learning to recognize functions in binary code. In: Proceedings of 23rd USENIX Security Symposium, pp. 845–860 (2014)
28. Shin, E.C.R., Song, D., Moazzezi, R.: Recognizing functions in binaries with neural networks. In: Proceedings of 24th USENIX Security Symposium, pp. 611–626 (2015)
29. Shannon, C.E.: A mathematical theory of communication. Bell Syst. Tech. J. **27**(3), 379–423 (1948)
30. Huffman, D.A.: A method for the construction of minimum-redundancy codes. Proc. IRE **40**(9), 1098–1101 (1952)

31. Shin, E.C.R., Song, D., Moazzezi, R.: Recognizing functions in binaries with neural networks. In: 24th USENIX Security Symposium (USENIX Security 2015), (Washington, D.C.), pp. 611–626. USENIX Association (2015)
32. Kingma, D.P., Ba, J.: Adam: a method for stochastic optimization (2014)
33. Bao, T., Burket, J., Woo, M., Turner, R., Brumley, D.: BYTEWEIGHT: learning to recognize functions in binary code. In: 23rd USENIX Security Symposium (USENIX Security 2014), (San Diego, CA), pp. 845–860. USENIX Association (2014)
34. Mkhatvari, N.: Towards big scale firmware analysis (2018)
35. Chen, D., Egele, M., Woo, M., Brumley, D.: Towards automated dynamic analysis for linux-based embedded firmware (2016)

Reliability of Ring Oscillator PUFs with Reduced Helper Data

Julien Béguinot[1(✉)], Wei Cheng[1,2], Jean-Luc Danger[1], Sylvain Guilley[1,2], Olivier Rioul[1], and Ville Yli-Mäyry[3]

[1] LTCI, Télécom Paris, Institut Polytechnique de Paris, 19 place Marguerite Perey, 91120 Palaiseau, France
{julien.beguinot,wei.cheng,jean-luc.danger,sylvain.guilley, olivier.rioul}@telecom-paris.fr

[2] Secure-IC S.A.S., 104 Bd du Montparnasse, 75014 Paris, France
{wei.cheng,sylvain.guilley}@secure-ic.com

[3] Secure-IC K.K., 2-15-1 Konan, Minato-ku, Level 28 Shinagawa Intercity Tower A, Tokyo, Japan
ville-oskari.ylimayry@secure-ic.com

Abstract. Enhancing the reliability of natively unstable Physically Unclonable Functions (PUFs) is a major requirement when the PUF is to generate secret identifiers like cryptographic keys. One traditional method is to rely on an addition of a public word: the Helper Data. However, it involves extra complexity and constitutes a vulnerability against attacks manipulating it. In this work, we show that for PUFs based on oscillations, such as Loop-PUFs (LPUF) can simultaneously increase the stability of the PUFs responses and reduce the required amount of helper data to decrease the complexity and increase the security. We proceed in two steps: First, we improve the reliability of the LPUF using dynamically determined repeated measurements and decision process. The number of repetitions per challenge is automatically tuned according to its reliability level and measurement window. Second, we investigate lightweight helper data (less than one byte). Experimental validation of our approach is carried out on 640 LPUFs to characterize the PUF reliability under different temperatures. This provides the assessment of the probability that a given Key Error Rate (KER) is achieved. This, in turn, yields the probability that there is an oscillator with arbitrarily low KER among any given number of oscillators. Performances remain notably stable when subject to increasing temperature.

Keywords: Ring Oscillator PUF · Reliability · Adaptively Controlled PUF · Sequential Probability Ratio Test · Lightweight Helper Data

1 Introduction

When using cryptographic primitives, cryptographic keys are at the basis of encryption, digital signatures, etc., and their security is of utmost importance. Traditionally, physically adding a key to a device and providing key storage is delegated to the fabrication plants, assembly factories, and other third parties.

J. Shikata and H. Kuzuno (Eds.): IWSEC 2023, LNCS 14128, pp. 36–56, 2023.
https://doi.org/10.1007/978-3-031-41326-1_3

Malicious subcontractors may potentially change, record, or alter the keys provided to the device. Furthermore, keys embedded in silicon, or programmed into one-time-programmable memory can be read-back by reverse-engineering after production.

Physically Unclonable Functions (PUFs) have been introduced to avoid these problems. Taking advantage of minute manufacturing variations, the PUF gives a "close to random" *response* output from a *challenge* input. Often, however, the response data of various PUF constructions show some instability: Given a challenge, the PUF output exhibits some dynamic noise, so that the output for a given challenge input is not consistently the same. Such noise is essentially due to transistor-level noise and environmental sources (uncontrollable fluctuations in supply voltage, temperature variations, etc.).

The idea of using additional *helper data* to aid in PUF robustness was first introduced in works by Linnartz et al. [28] and Dodis et al. [12]. However, the use of helper data has various drawbacks: additional cost, PUF output bias conditioned on the helper data, manipulation attacks, etc. These act as motivation for designing PUFs with less helper data.

In this article, we present a method applicable to Ring Oscillator PUFs like Loop-PUFs (LPUFs) that allows to trade an increase in latency during key reconstruction to mitigate the problems induced by helper data. For that we proceed in two steps. First we improve the reliability of the LPUF [6] by adaptively controlling the number of required oscillations (as hinted in [21]). Second, we investigate the performances of lightweight helper data (less than one byte).

1.1 Related Works

Four previous works try to enhance PUF reliability without using helper data:

- Che et al. [5] present a physically unclonable function without helper data based on non-volatile memory. It is nonetheless questionable whether this construct is a PUF, as it keeps its value even when not powered.
- Wang et al. [43] leverage locally enhanced defectivity of *direct self assembly* to generate stable PUFs without helper data. Their construction differs from classical constructions in that it is not parametric but relies on random but permanent connection in the hardware layout.
- Herkle et al. [21] present an eye-opening oscillator for arbiter PUFs, which exploit the dead-zone of the arbiter PUF to decide whether a bit is reliable or not, and automatically request new oscillations accordingly. Monte-Carlo simulation with transient noise and 50 repetitions yields an expected Bit Error Rate (BER) of $9.2\cdot10^{-5}\pm7.7\cdot10^{-4}$. However, this work is not validated experimentally and does not propose a mathematical model (only heuristics).
- Temporal majority voting improves the reliability of a decision without helper data [10]. The PUF is repeated a given (odd) number of times and the key is obtained by majority vote at the bit level. This amounts to using a repetition code over time.

Fueller et al. [14] proposed a construction for computational fuzzy extractor based on the learning with error problem. Based on Fueller construction, Herder et al. [20] construct a computational fuzzy extractor based on the Learning Parity with Noise (LPN) computational hardness. As in our work, these constructions use side information retrieved on the fly as a trapdoor.

1.2 Contributions

This paper has four main contributions.

1. Using a stochastic model, we determine the survival function of the BER of the ring-oscillator based LPUF consolidating results from Schaub et al. [35].
2. By controlling adaptively the number of repetitions of a given oscillator, we then improve the reliability of the LPUF at the cost of higher latency. The reliability of the proposed system can be set by the user. A feedback-based mode of operation monitors each bits independently and decides when it is reliable enough in order to minimize the global Key Error Rate (KER). This formalizes the eye-opening concept used in Herkle et al. [21].
3. We validate our analysis on a hardware implementation on FPGA. We analyze through experiments on 640 different oscillators and different controlled temperatures (using a climate chamber) the results of the design.
4. We evaluate performances of a set of different lightweight helper data on our design, and also present a case where design is used without any helper data.

1.3 Outline

The paper is organized as follows. Section 2 recalls the vanilla LPUF design [6] and introduces our novel adaptive design. Section 3 addresses reliability in the context of LPUF and provides the distribution of the BER. Section 4 specifies the adaptive design threshold function and grounds it theoretically with its relation to sequential analysis. Section 5 integrates our design within a full fledged PUF and real measurements show that it achieves satisfactory reliability with lightweight helper data. Namely, we show how to reach arbitrary high reliability.

1.4 Notations

We use the following notations. Random variables are denoted in upper case and their realizations in lower case. The probability density function (p.d.f.) of a random variable X is denoted by f_X or simply f if not ambiguous. The survival function is denoted $\varPhi_X$ or $\varPhi$. The p.d.f. of the standard normal distribution is denoted by ϕ and its survival function by Q. Vector values are in typeset bold and sets are denoted with calligraphic symbols. The XOR operation is denoted $\oplus$ and operates bit-wisely on vector values.

2 LPUF Model

2.1 Model for a Single LPUF (Vanilla LPUF)

Ring oscillator PUF designs were first suggested by Gassend et al. [15,16]. A number of works followed this design such as [29,30,39,44]. A LPUF [6] is a reconfigurable ring oscillator made up of n delay elements. That is, for a fixed challenge word $c \in \{0,1\}^n$ the ring oscillator outputs a noisy observation of the sum of the configured delays $\sum_{i=1}^{n} d_i^{c_i}$, where $d_i^{c_i}$ denotes the corresponding delay of the i-th element when challenged by a bit $c_i \in \{0,1\}$. Typically, each c_i selects one of two possible paths, and the delay $d_i^{c_i}$ is modeled as Gaussian with unknown mean and fixed variance.

The LPUF operates differentially to eliminate part of the noise due to environmental conditions (temperature, voltage, etc.) and to center the delay measurements. It measures the delay for both challenge codeword c and its complementary $\bar{c}$, and outputs the difference of the two delays. The resulting LPUF output on challenge word c is $\Delta_c = \sum_{i=1}^{n}(d_i^{c_i} - d_i^{\bar{c}_i}) = \sum_{i=1}^{n}(-1)^{c_i}\Delta_i$, where the $\Delta_i = d_i^0 - d_i^1$ are normally distributed with zero mean and fixed variance $\mathcal{N}(\delta = 0, \tau^2)$. Typically, the random bit generated by the PUF is $B_c = \text{sign}(\Delta_c)$.

The dynamic noise can be described as flicker noise (a.k.a. $1/f$-noise or pink noise) which is a low frequency noise arising from the transistor commutation in the ring oscillator. For simplicity it is considered here to be zero-mean additive white Gaussian noise (AWGN) $\mathcal{N}(0, \sigma^2)$.

2.2 System Modeling for LPUF

We consider the following system modeling for the LPUF, that subjects to

1. **Randomness** measured by entropy: $H(\mathbf{S}|\mathbf{W}) \geq E$ (or $H_\infty(\mathbf{S}|\mathbf{W}) \geq E$)
2. **Reliability** subject to two parameters α, β: $\mathbb{P}_{PUF}(\mathbb{P}(\mathbf{S} \neq \hat{\mathbf{S}}|PUF) \geq \alpha) \leq \beta$
3. **Lightweight**: low memory and efficiently computation.

There are four degrees of freedom to optimize these three properties:

Challenge Code. The LPUF is restricted to a given set $\mathcal{C} = \{c_1, \ldots, c_M\}$ of M challenges which forms a binary code of length n and size M. In this work we focus on weak PUF or physically obfuscated key with a small number of challenges. Rioul et al. [34] show how to select optimally the first $M = n$ codewords. At most $M = n$ challenges with independent responses can be selected, and up to equivalence, these challenges are given by the Hadamard code of length n. The entropy can be increased by selecting more challenges, yet the orthogonality cannot be preserved anymore. Solé et al. [36] suggested that selecting the vector that minimizes the deviation from the family of vector is optimal with respect to the entropy. In the sequel we restrict the PUF input to $2^6 = 64$ Hadamard challenges for two reasons: (a) it is easy to construct Hadamard matrices of size 2^i by iterative tensor product, which facilitates hardware implementation; (b) LPUF are prone to modeling attacks (with machine learning techniques) when the challenges are not orthogonal.

Helper Data Algorithms [28]. These include error correcting codes [10], bit selection [10,35] or even zero-leakage helper data [17,18,38]. From a theoretical point of view with the framework of secure sketch, fuzzy extractor [12], robust fuzzy extractor [3,11] and computational fuzzy extractor [14,20] are used.

Quantization Procedures are used for zero-leakage helper data [18,38], Two-Metric helper data [9], modelling resistance [37] or to increase entropy [25]. In this work, for simplicity, we only keep the most significant bit (i.e. the sign) of the output.

Noise Channel. Assuming a binary symmetric channel (BSC), information theoretic limits can be derived for the code-offset construction [19,24]. Maringer et al. [31] suggest an improved model with varying BSC and shows that channel state information increases the capacity of the PUF by more than 25% compared to the case where no such information is available.

The main objective of this paper is to design an adaptive procedure that modifies the noise channel to improve the reliability of the LPUF. For this aim, we add a feedback link to the channel and request retransmissions to achieve a given reliability constraint. As a byproduct we use less helper data. The system modeling of LPUF is depicted in Fig. 1 and the generic procedure is described in Algorithm 1.

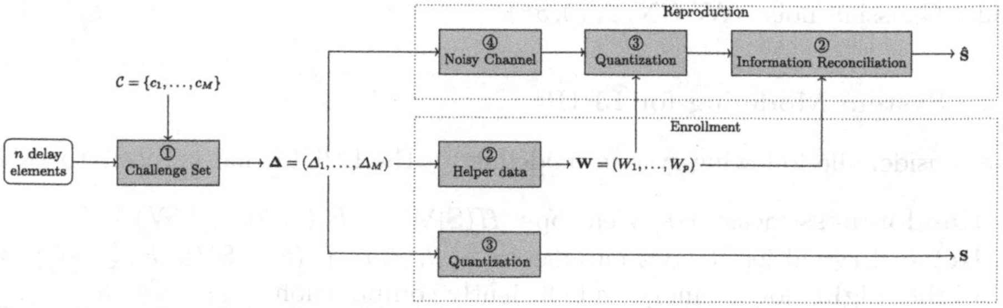

Fig. 1. System modeling of the LPUF

Algorithm 1: Adaptive LPUF

Data: A threshold function $A : \mathbb{N}^* \mapsto \mathbb{R}^+$, a maximal number of repetitions T_{max} and PUF which can be called by a codeword c of a fixed code $\mathcal{C}$.
Result: LPUF key whose reliability is ensured by A.

for $c \in \mathcal{C}$ **do**
  $\Delta_{acc} \leftarrow 0$ `/* Accumulated Measurements */`
  $t \leftarrow 0$ `/* Number of measurements */`
  $ok \leftarrow 0$ `/* Feedback */`
  while *not ok* **do**
    $\Delta_{acc} \leftarrow \Delta_{acc} + PUF(c)$ `/* New measure */`
    $t \leftarrow t + 1$
    $ok \leftarrow (|\Delta_{acc}| \geq A(t)$ or $t \geq T_{max})$ `/* Feedback exit condition */`
  $B_c \leftarrow (\Delta_{acc} \geq 0)$ `/* Final quantization */`
return $(B_c)_{c \in \mathcal{C}}$

2.3 Hardware Description

The proposed vanilla LPUF design FPGA architecture is depicted in Fig. 2. It is implemented in a Basys3 board relying on Artix-7 FPGA. We repeated the

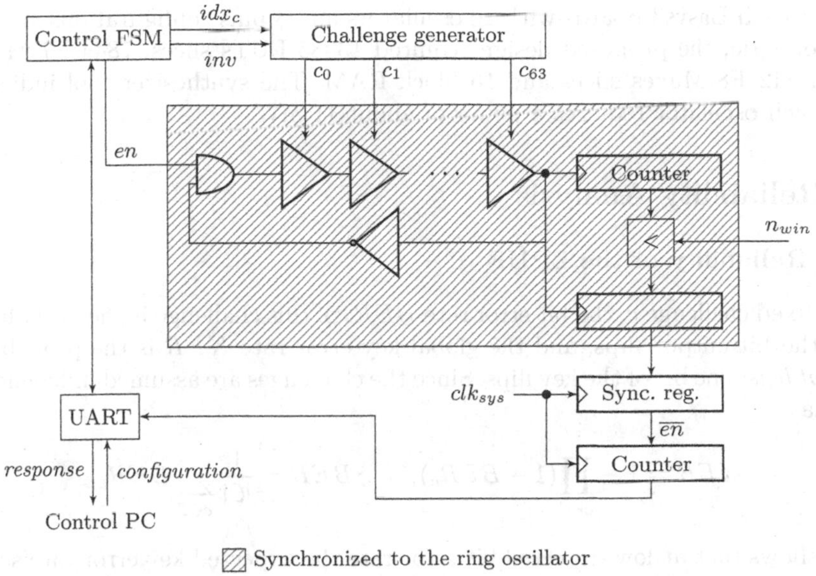

Fig. 2. Overview of the experimental PUF hardware implementation. Elements depicted inside the red area are timed with the ring oscillator as the clock signal. (Color figure online)

test on 5 instances of the same board (see Fig. 8). We expect the results to be consistent with different placement within the same FPGA and with different FPGAs. Namely even if the signal to noise ratio may differ from one instance to another the mechanism should work alike. The PUF interface uses the UART communication with a control PC. The PUF core consists of a single ring oscillator implemented with 64 5-input LUTs as delay elements. As the delay element requires only two inputs (the signal to be delayed and the challenge bit), this leaves three bits, which we call "pins" subsequently, to configure the 8 delay paths inside each look-up table. Hence, a single ring oscillator can have 8 different delay chains by the pins configuration. In Fig. 2, the area shaded in red denotes the parts of the implementation that are synchronized to the ring oscillator. Registers and logic outside of the shaded area are synchronized to the system clock of the FPGA design. The design can be configured with window size n_{win}, which defines the number of LPUF periods the design uses to time the counter (synchronized to the system clock) interval.

During the ring oscillator measurement, first, a challenge is chosen from the possible challenges. Its bits are used to configure the delay elements. Then, the delay loop is activated and the amount of pulses during a given time frame (n_{win}) is counted. Next, the *inv* bit in Fig. 2 is set, and the inverse of the same challenge is used to evaluate the ring oscillator loop count. Finally, the difference of the counts is considered the result of the measurement for the given challenge.

For each Basys3 boards with 16 oscillators and 8 pins configurations and the control logic, the proposed design required 13585 LUTs slices, 7844 F7 Muxes slices, 242 F8 Muxes slices and 16 block RAM. The synthesizer tool indicates that each oscillator requires a power of about 11 mW.

3 Reliability Analysis

3.1 Reliability of the LPUF

For a fixed challenge c, the bit error rate BER_c of this challenge is the probability that the bit output flips, and the global key error rate KER is the probability that *at least* one bit of the key flips. Since the challenges are assumed independent one has

$$KER = 1 - \prod_{c\in\mathcal{C}}(1 - BER_c), \qquad BER = \frac{1}{|\mathcal{C}|}\sum_{c\in\mathcal{C}} BER_c. \tag{1}$$

This shows that at low expected bit error rate the expected key error rate scales linearly with n. Lemma 1 shows that for a fixed average BER, the KER is minimized when all bit error rates are equal:

Lemma 1 (Equal BERs). *One has $KER \geq 1 - (1 - BER)^n$ with equality if and only if all bit error rates BER_c are equal.*

Proof. Arithmetic-geometric mean inequality applied to the $1 - BER_c$. □

Our first take-away is that for a fixed average BER we should target uniform BERs for all the challenges.

The delay difference Δ_c is drawn from $\mathcal{N}(\delta, \tau^2)$. The design sequentially requests new measurements $X_1, X_2, \ldots$ which are i.i.d. $\mathcal{N}(\Delta_c, \sigma^2)$. The goal is to decide optimally the sign of Δ_c. This can be reformulated as a Bayesian statistical hypothesis testing problem: $H_0 : \Delta_c \geq 0$ against $H_1 : \Delta_c < 0$. At step t, $X^t = \sum_{i=1}^t X_i$ is stored and the other measurements $\mathbf{X} = (X_1, \ldots, X_t)$ are discarded without loss of optimality, since X^t is an *sufficient statistic*:

Lemma 2. $X^t = \sum_{i=1}^t X_i = S(\mathbf{X})$ *is an sufficient statistic of the parameter* $\theta = sgn(\Delta_c)$.

Proof. Apply the Fisher-Neyman factorization theorem:

$$f_\theta(\mathbf{X}) = \prod_{i=1}^t e^{-\frac{(\theta|\Delta_c| - X_i)^2}{2\sigma^2}} = \exp\left(-\frac{1}{2\sigma^2}\sum(\Delta_c^2 + X_i^2) - \frac{\theta|\Delta_c|}{\sigma^2}X^t\right) = h(\mathbf{X})g_\theta(S(\mathbf{X})).$$

The second take-away is that for white noise the optimal decision is based only on the sum of the past delays. In particular, for an optimal design it is enough to store this sum. The Bayes decision for the problem is to take the sign of this statistic. We recall the expression for the expected BER and KER when this optimal procedure is used assuming that the delays are not biased ($\delta = 0$):

Lemma 3 (Expected BER [35]). *The BER and expected BER with t repetitions obtained with the same derivations as Schaub et al. are*

$$BER_c(t) = Q(\frac{|\delta_c|}{\sqrt{t}\sigma}) \qquad \mathbb{E}[BER](t) = \frac{1}{\pi}\arctan(\frac{1}{\sqrt{t\gamma}}). \tag{2}$$

where $\gamma = \tau^2\sigma^{-2}$ *denotes the signal-to-noise ratio (SNR).*

From these expressions we can go further in the analysis by deriving the probability density function of the bit error rate and its survival function:

Theorem 1 (BER Distribution). *The BER p.d.f. is*

$$f_{BER}(u) = 2(t\gamma)^{-\frac{1}{2}}\exp\Big(-\frac{Q^{-1}(u)^2}{2}((t\gamma)^{-1}-1)\Big). \tag{3}$$

If the SNR $\gamma = 1$ *the bit error rate is uniformly distributed in* $[0, \frac{1}{2}]$, *else* $f_{BER}(0) = +\infty$ *and* $f_{BER}(\frac{1}{2}) = 2(t\gamma)^{-\frac{1}{2}}$. *The bit error rate survival function is*

$$\Phi_{BER}(u) = 1 - 2Q((t\gamma)^{-\frac{1}{2}}Q^{-1}(u)) \overset{t\gamma\to\infty}{\approx} \sqrt{\frac{2}{\gamma\pi t}}Q^{-1}(u). \tag{4}$$

Proof. The survival function is derived from Lemma 3 and the distribution of Δ_c. The p.d.f. is obtained from the survival function by computing its derivative.

Corollary 1. $\mathbb{P}(BER < \alpha) = \beta$ *for* $\gamma t = Q^{-1}(\alpha)^2 Q^{-1}(\frac{1-\beta}{2})^{-2} \overset{\beta\to 0}{\approx} 8\pi Q^{-1}(\alpha)^2\beta^{-2}$.

Proof. Apply Theorem 1 and Taylor expansion of Q^{-1} about $\frac{1}{2}$.

The expression of Theorem 1 lead to our third take away:

- First, it shows that the bit error rate distribution does not vanish in $\frac{1}{2}$ and is bounded away from 0 by a factor $2(t\gamma)^{-\frac{1}{2}}$. This "large tail" is detrimental to the PUF. Even with large SNR we cannot get rid of very bad bit error rate. Increasing the SNR and number of repetitions t is not enough to get rid of all errors. That is increasing n_{win} is not enough to remove all errors.
- Second, the expression of the survival function enables us to compute the probability β that the bit error rate of a challenge exceed a targeted bit error rate α as shown in Theorem 1. This scales to a n bit key since the probability β_n that the worst bit error rate of the key exceed α is $\beta_n = 1-(1-\beta)^n \approx n\beta$.

3.2 Comparison with Temporal Majority Voting

Temporal majority voting is a technique introduced to make a decision more reliably [10]. It repeats measurements t times and decide the bit by majority voting. If there are t repetitions and a bit error rate of BER, then the new corrected error is given by the survival function of the binomial distribution of parameter n and parameter BER evaluated in $\frac{n-1}{2}$ [10]. This technique is relevant when no information about the reliability is available. It is yet sub-optimal for the LPUF for which a side information on the reliability of the bit is available. Indeed, for temporal majority voting we have $BER(t) = \sum_{t=\frac{n-1}{2}}^{n} \binom{n}{t} BER(1)^t (1-BER(1))^{n-t}$, and with our method (Bayes decision), using the equation of Lemma 3, we have the exponentially better evaluation: $BER(t) = Q(\sqrt{t}Q^{-1}(BER(1)))$.

Our fourth take away is that while temporal majority voting makes sense for PUF constructions without a "confidence information" about the PUF outputs for oscillation based PUF it is preferable to use the optimal strategy based on the sign of the sum of the accumulated difference.

4 Sequential Probability Ratio Test (SPRT)

We now refine the previous approach where the PUF estimates the reliability of the bits on the fly. This requests repetitions for each bit until a certain reliability is achieved. Instead of fixing the number of repetitions in advance, the number of repetitions is chosen adaptively to minimize the required number of sample for a fixed targeted probability of error. The number of repetitions is *not* constant, but found as a (S_t)-*stopping time* denoted T which depends only on (S_t). The requested quality of service imposes some constraints on T. In particular, the number of repetitions should be bounded and not too long on average: $\mathbb{P}(T \leq T_{max}) = 1$ and $\mathbb{E}[T] \leq T_{avg}$.

4.1 Sequential Analysis

We recall that the posterior distribution of Δ_c given X^t is normally distributed:

Lemma 4 (Ex 3.7 [13]**).** *The delay Δ_c given the observation $X^t = x$ is normally distributed with mean $\delta_{t,x}$ and variance τ_{tx}^2 given by $\delta_{t,x} = \frac{x\tau^2+\sigma^2\delta}{\tau^2 t+\sigma^2}$ and $\tau_{t,x}^2 = \frac{\sigma^2\tau^2}{t\tau^2+\sigma^2}$. Interestingly, the posterior variance does not depend on the observations but only on the prior distribution and the number t of repetitions.*

Proof. By factorization under canonical form: Using Bayes' formula,

$$\log f_{\Delta|X^t=x}(u) \propto \frac{(u-\delta)^2}{\tau^2} + \frac{(ut-x)^2}{t\sigma^2} = u^2 \underbrace{\left(\tau^{-2} + t\sigma^{-2}\right)}_{\tau_{t,x}^{-2}} - 2u \underbrace{\left(\delta\tau^{-2} - x\sigma^{-2}\right)}_{\tau_{t,x}^{-2}\delta_{t,x}} + cst.$$

This expression can be simplified by making a change of variable as suggested in [2]. Let $t_0 = \gamma^{-1}$ and $T = t + t_0$. The normalised process $S_t = \frac{X^t + t_0\delta}{\sigma\sqrt{T}}$ is also a sufficient statistic; the posterior distribution of Δ_c given $S_t = s$ is now given by $\delta_{t,s} = \frac{\sigma s}{\sqrt{T}}$ and $\tau_{t,s} = \frac{\sigma}{\sqrt{T}}$. From this expression we can compute the posterior probability of H_0 and H_1 as given in Theorem 2.

Theorem 2. *One has $\mathbb{P}(H_0|S_t = s) = 1 - \mathbb{P}(H_1|S_t = s) = Q(-s) = 1 - Q(s)$, and In particular the Bayes decision at step t is to decide the sign of Δ_c to be the sign of S_t and the posterior probability of error is $\mathbb{P}_e(s) = Q(|s|)$, which corresponds to a Neyman-Pearson test of H_0 against H_1.*

Proof. Immediate from Lemma 4.

We recall that Neyman-Pearson test is the most powerful test[1] at level α to test simple hypothesis. By Karlin-Rubin theorem [27], it is also universally most powerful test for composite hypothesis whose likelihood is non decreasing.

The expression of Theorem 2 can help to correct error more efficiently using this information for soft decoding [10]. It was already observed that for ring oscillator a confidence information could be re-derived [20]. This is one advantage of the LPUF over SRAM-PUF for which deriving a probability of error seems harder as it would require multiple power up.

4.2 Wald's Sequential Probability Ratio Test and Constant Boundary

A first approach is to force the probability of error to reach a given level α before taking a decision as suggested in Sect. 3 with Lemma 1. Using Theorem 2 this is equivalent to set $\alpha \geq Q(|S_T|)$ i.e. $|X^T| \geq \sigma Q^{-1}(\alpha)\sqrt{T}$.

Proposition 1 (Square Root Boundary). *If $A(t) = \sigma Q^{-1}(\alpha)\sqrt{\gamma^{-1} + t}$ in Algorithm 1 then the BER of the LPUF is at most α.*

This is equivalent to set the likelihood ratio of the two hypothesis to a given level. We recognize Wald's sequential probability ratio test (SPRT) [41]. Wald's SPRT has been proven to be optimal for testing simple hypothesis [42]. If a sequential test achieves the same probability of detection and false alarm it requires at least as many measurements as Wald's test. Though, contrary to Neyman-Pearson test, the optimality result does not extend to composite hypothesis testing. This indicates that the procedure can be improved. For the LPUF, the SPRT is truncated since $T \leq T_{max}$ is imposed. As a consequence, the bit error rate is higher since a proportion β of the challenges is not stabilized with the SPRT as they require more than T_{max} measurement repetitions on average. This proportion is $\beta = 1 - 2Q(\frac{\sigma Q^{-1}(\alpha)}{\sqrt{T_{max}}}) \approx \sqrt{\frac{2\sigma^2 Q^{-1}(\alpha)^2}{\pi T_{max}^2}}$. It is useless to decrease further α if a high proportion of the challenges cannot be stabilized. If we target $\beta \approx \alpha$, we obtain that we should have $T_{max} \approx \sqrt{\frac{2}{\pi}}\frac{\sigma Q^{-1}(\alpha)}{\alpha}$.

The simplest sequential test to implement is the constant boundary. The probability β that the expected measurement time for a challenge exceed T_{max} is $\beta = 1 - 2Q(\frac{a}{\sqrt{\gamma T_{max}}}) \approx \sqrt{\frac{2a^2}{\pi\gamma T_{max}^2}}$.

[1] The power of a statistical test is the probability that it correctly rejects H_0.

4.3 Improving the Boundary

Both Wald SPRT test and the constant boundary are sub-optimal solutions. Some works to test the sign of the mean of a Gaussian process or to test the sign of the drift of a Wiener process already exists [2,4,7,8]. These works explores diverse prior assumptions, and loss functions. The main approach is to consider this problem as a Markov decision problem where the terminal cost function is the probability of error with a constant sampling cost $c > 0$ and to approximate the process as a drifted Wiener process. With the recursive equation provided in [2] we computed an approximation of the optimal solution in the finite horizon case for different sampling cost as shown in Fig. 3. If Wald's test was optimal, then the solution in the s state would be a constant. Results show that this is not the case. If we look at the x state representation, we observe that the optimal boundary increases rapidly to a maximum and then decreases slowly to zero. Moreover, the horizon T_{max} does not affect the shape of the boundary.

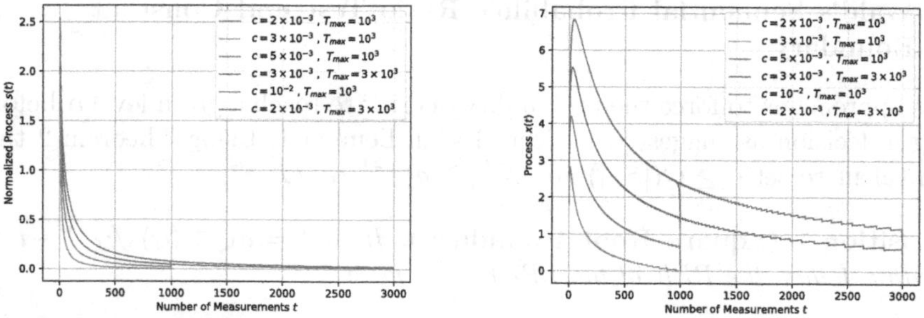

(a) Results in the s state space representation.

(b) Results mapped back into the X^t state space representation.

Fig. 3. Results with dynamic programming for different sampling costs and horizon.

Bather [2] shows that an asymptotic for the optimal boundary is $(8\pi ct)^{-\frac{1}{2}}$ for large values of t. Chernoff [4,7,8] obtains a similar first order term with a terminal cost function proportional to the amplitude of the drift/delay.

5 Combining with Lightweight Helper Data

We repeat the vanilla LPUF measurement 10^3 to verify how the output changes over the time and show the results in Fig. 4. We see that the responses are stable in time and perturbed by noise. We can visualize when errors happen i.e. when the trajectory for a given challenge crosses the line $y = 0$. We consider two different window-sizes $n_{win} = 2^{12}, 2^{19}$ and observe that even by multiplying the window-size by 2^7 the LPUF output is not stabilized even if the results improve. These results have to be compared with the result of the adaptive design for both boundaries. Compared to the classical design where increasing n_{win} "scales" the

LPUF outputs the new design "push away" the delay difference close to zero. On two sub-figures on the right we see that their remain some bits that could not be stabilized by the design. In the first case (square root boundary) there was not enough measurements for the delays. As some errors persists we investigate a set of small helper data.

5.1 Bit Flipping

The posterior probabilities of error can be used as a side information to construct the list of the k most likely key from the PUF outputs. We validate this approach by computing the expected number of guesses necessary to find the correct key. This quantity is known as *guessing entropy* and introduced by Massey for cryptographic purposes [32]. Using the lower bound of Arikan [1] improved by Rioul [33] we obtain when $\gamma \neq 1$, $\frac{1}{\ln(2^{n+1}+1)}\left(1+4\int_0^\infty \phi(\delta)\sqrt{Q(\delta\sqrt{\gamma})Q(-\delta\sqrt{\gamma})}\,\mathrm{d}\delta\right)^n \leq GE \leq \frac{1}{2}\left(1+4\int_0^\infty \phi(\delta)\sqrt{Q(\delta\sqrt{\gamma})Q(-\delta\sqrt{\gamma})}\,\mathrm{d}\delta\right)^n + \frac{1}{2}$. For $\gamma = 3\cdot 10^2$, $5\cdot 10^2$ and 10^3 it follows that 47, 18 and 7 trials are respectively required on average.

5.2 Correction with Few Bits of Parity

We suggest to use few bits of parity to improve the reliability of the LPUF design. The syndrome of the PUF output is stored as a helper data [10,12]. A code offset construction would work as well but it would require to store a whole codeword as helper data. The experiments performed in this section are computed with the 64 challenges of 5 Basys 3 FPGA boards with 16 independent LPUF implementations in parallel using 8 different internal routing configurations. As a reference Van Herrewege et al. [22] use a $[255, 21, t = 55]_2$ BCH code with 234 bits of helper data correcting up to 55 errors for a key of length 255.

Parity Check Code. The parity check code requires a single bit of redundancy. Since its minimal distance is 2, it can detect one error but cannot correct any. However, the parity check code can correct one erasure. We erase the least reliable bit using the reliability information of the LPUF and correct this erasure. This is related to the idea of soft decoding for PUF as suggested by Delvaux et al. [10].

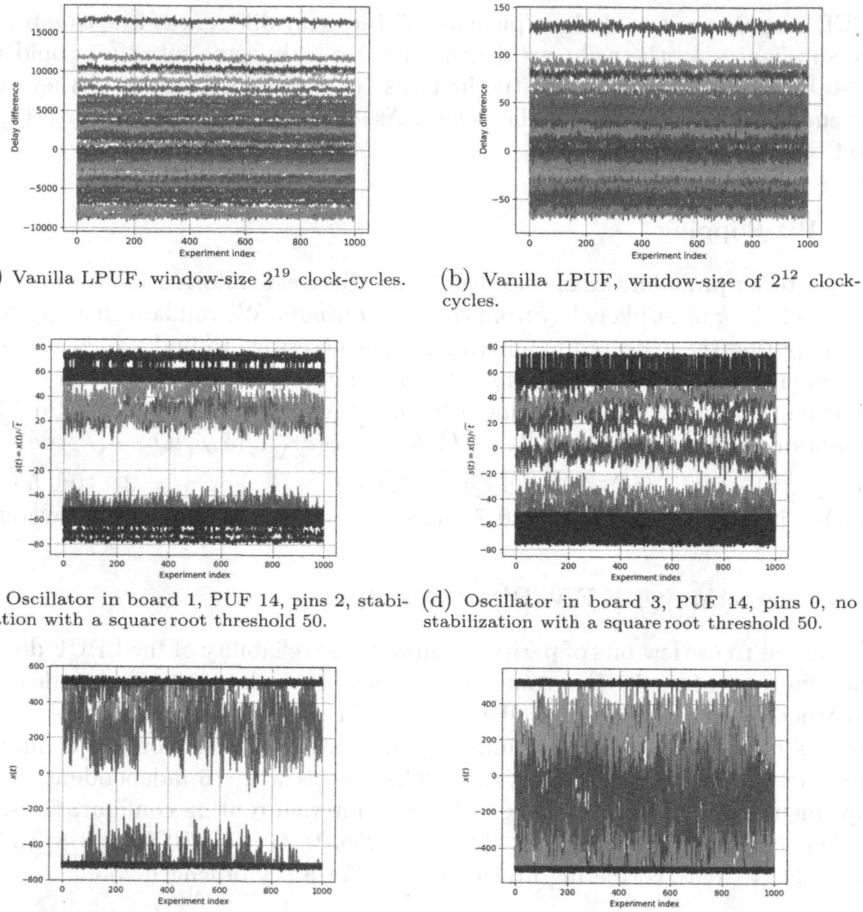

(a) Vanilla LPUF, window-size 2^{19} clock-cycles.

(b) Vanilla LPUF, window-size of 2^{12} clock-cycles.

(c) Oscillator in board 1, PUF 14, pins 2, stabilization with a square root threshold 50.

(d) Oscillator in board 3, PUF 14, pins 0, no stabilization with a square root threshold 50.

(e) Oscillator in board 1, PUF 14, pins 2, stabilization with the constant threshold 500.

(f) Oscillator in board 3, PUF 14, pins 0, no stabilization with the constant threshold 500.

Fig. 4. Example of results of the LPUF design with two types of boundary thresholds.

Parity Check Codes in Parallel (PCP). The n bits output of the LPUF is split into N (where N divides n) blocks of size N/n, and a parity check code in each block is applied. The idea of codes in parallel was first suggested by Delvaux et al. [10]. This scheme requires N bit of parity. We apply the decoding procedure for a parity check code in each of the N blocks. We tried this approach with $N \in \{1, 2, 4, 8, 16\}$ blocks.

Single Error Correction Double Error Detection (SECDED) Code. We can consider a SECDED code [23] which requires 8 bits of helper data. We consider a SECDED code of length 64 punctured from the $[127, 120, 3]_2$ Hamming code and extended with a parity check equation. In particular, the minimum distance of this code is at least 4. For this approach we investigate two different decoders.

The first decoding procedure (SECDED-ALG) is as follows. We compute the syndrome of the reproduced keys and xor it with the helper data. If there is no error we return the key as is. Else there are two cases:

- If the last parity-check bit is a one, there is an odd number of error. If the syndrome correspond to a one error pattern, the bit indicated by the syndrome is flipped. Else, there is a least three errors. A pair of unreliable bits is flipped until a one error pattern is found.
- If the last parity-check bit is even, there is an even number of errors. One unreliable bit is flipped until the syndrome corresponds to a one error pattern.

The second decoding procedure (SECDED-ML) does not exploit the algebraic structure of the code. It enumerates key candidates "by decreasing order of likelihood" until a syndrome without error is found as already suggested in [10]. This second option provides better results but requires a bit more computations. It differs from [10] exhaustive enumeration in that we try key candidates by decreasing likelihood. As the guessing entropy computed in the previous section is small, the computation overhead is limited on average contrarily to a naive exhaustive enumeration.

Hash of the Key? For the SECDED code we suggested an exhaustive search decoder which does not use the algebraic property of the code. The code structure is not compulsory to correct the PUF output. As a proof of concept, we verify that the key can be found if the a hash of the key (SHA256) is stored as helper data. This is not information theoretic secure but computationally secure if the hash function is one way. The underlying idea is to consider cases where successive keys in a list can be tried. For instance, if the key is used to decrypt and AES-GCM, different keys can be tried until success. The main issue here is that this implies a larger computational overhead. In a sense, this is a computational fuzzy extractor scheme. Eventually, the construction based on the LPN problem would be more relevant here. Sieving a list of key candidates with a "tag" was first suggested by Dodis [12], our suggestion differs in that we don't sieve a list obtained by the list decoding of a code but rather sort the key candidates by decreasing likelihood.

Configuring the LPUF in the Most Favorable Pin Configuration. The LPUF design is a re-configurable ring oscillator whose delay elements are implemented by LUT-5. 2 wires are used for the challenge and output which leaves 3 wires for configuring the LPUF (8 configurations). One way to improve the LPUF results is to use the most favorable pin configuration out of m configurations. For an ASIC implementation, we could consider the best oscillator among a list of different oscillators. This selection has two beneficial impacts on the design. It reduces the key error rate, and also reduces the latency of the design.

5.3 Key Error Rate of the Adaptive Design

The performance is estimated with 1000 iterations for the 640 available oscillators with $n_{win} = 2^{10}$ and maximum 300 repetitions. Experimental results are shown in Fig. 5 and 6.

The average KER obtained at 30° is about 0.37 without any helper data, 3.1×10^{-2} with SECDED-ML and 6.4×10^{-3} with a tag (SHA256). If we choose the best pin configuration among the 8 pins configuration the KER reduces to 1.5×10^{-3} with SECDED-ML. The figures can be read as follows: by looking for a given targeted KER on the y-axis we obtain on the x-axis the probability that an oscillator achieves a KER lower than the targeted KER. For instance, for SECDED-ML the probability that the KER is lower than 10^{-3} is little less than 0.8. The ideal case corresponds to a vertical line in $w = 1$ and the worst case corresponds to the horizontal line $y = 1$. It happens that some vertical curves super-impose in the final vertical line (in Fig. 6).

We do not observe significant changes in performances between the square-root boundary and the constant boundary. Hence we advocate to use the simpler constant boundary as introduced by Herkle et al. [21]. It is interesting to observe that despite higher temperature should increase the KER because of larger noise variance the performances are barely affected by the temperature. This shows that the proposed design compensate well larger temperature by dynamically adapting the number of required repetitions to achieve the targeted reliability. Selecting the most reliable oscillators among a list of m oscillators enables to reduce arbitrarily the KER as shown in Fig. 6. Equivalently, discarding bad oscillators greatly improves the performances. At 30° with SECDED-ML the average KER of the 79% best oscillators reduces to 10^3.

Admittedly, removing all helper data while maintaining a very low key error rate seems impossible in general. The proposed design has some limits:

- The impact of repetitions on low frequency noise is limited. Especially its impact on the Pink noise arising from transistor commutations is limited.
- We do not claim that the design prevent errors due to unstable power supply.

The number of measurements at 30° is shown in Fig. 7. The average number of repetitions is approximately 81 (and increases to 83 at 60°). Most of the challenges are stabilized in a first bump. Then we observe a final bump at $T_{max} = 300$ which corresponds to challenges that could not be stabilized and reached the maximum number of repetitions. If we increase T_{max}, the height of this bump (and the KER) would decrease at the cost of a larger latency.

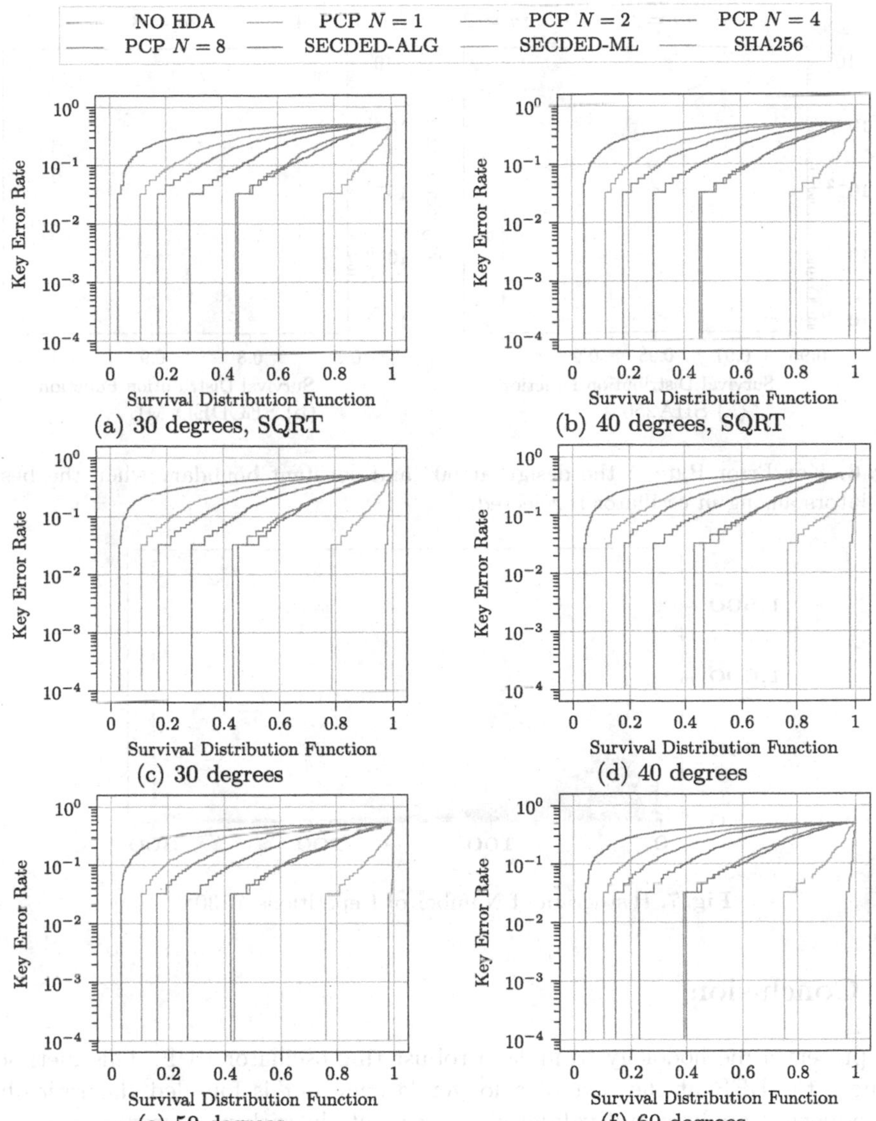

(a) 30 degrees, SQRT
(b) 40 degrees, SQRT
(c) 30 degrees
(d) 40 degrees
(e) 50 degrees
(f) 60 degrees

Fig. 5. KER of the design under different temperatures with light HDAs.

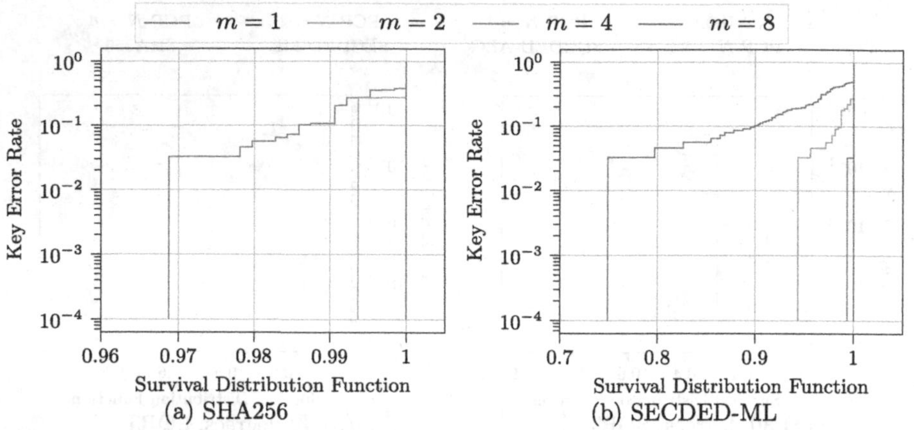

Fig. 6. Key Error Rate of the design at 60° and constant boundary when the best oscillators among m oscillator is selected.

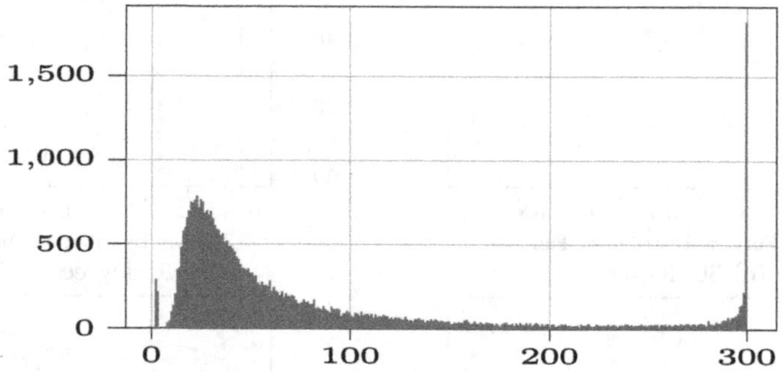

Fig. 7. Histogram of Number of Repetitions at 30°

6 Conclusion

We present a methodology to make a robust ring oscillator PUF. This method reduces the BER at the cost of a longer latency but is founded theoretically on sequential analysis and validated experimentally with measurements on an FPGA board. We investigate a set of lightweight helper data and show that the key error rate can decrease further. In some practical use cases, the LPUF can even be used "without any helper data" provided that a signature or a valid hash with the enrolled secret is available.

There remain multiple aspects to investigate for future works. For example, the impact of correlated noise on the errors and the optimal boundary. The energy consumption could also be studied as in the one hand repeated measurements lead to more energy consumption, but on the other hand we limit post-processing. Depending on the device constraints there should exists an optimal trade-off to exhibit. Potential side-channel attacks are also left as perspectives.

In particular, it should be confirmed that the fact that this design is not constant time is not a problem in this case (timing attack). Further, it would be interesting to know whether the repeated measurements facilitates power or electromagnetic side-channel attacks. As the response is not stored in a flip-flop until the decision is made the effect on side channel attack at the output should be benign. Though, one may identify if a challenge is stable through its corresponding measurement time. Still an efficient countermeasure against side-channel has already been proposed and discussed in [40].

The python code used for the analysis is available at [26].

A Experimental Setup

Fig. 8. Initial experimental setup with 6 boards at room temperature.

References

1. Arikan, E.: An inequality on guessing and its application to sequential decoding. IEEE Trans. Inf. Theory **42**(1), 99–105 (1996)
2. Bather, J.: Bayes procedures for deciding the sign of a normal mean (1962)
3. Becker, G.T.: Robust fuzzy extractors and helper data manipulation attacks revisited: theory versus practice. IEEE Trans. Dependable Secure Comput. **16**, 783–795 (2019)

4. Breakwell, J., Chernoff, H.: Sequential tests for the mean of a normal distribution. II. (large t) (1964)
5. Che, W., Plusquellic, J., Bhunia, S.: A non-volatile memory based physically unclonable function without helper data. In: 2014 IEEE/ACM International Conference on Computer-Aided Design (ICCAD), pp. 148–153. IEEE (2014)
6. Cherif, Z., Danger, J.L., Guilley, S., Bossuet, L.: An easy-to-design PUF based on a single oscillator: the loop PUF. In: 15th Euromicro Conference on Digital System Design, DSD 2012, Çeşme, Izmir, Turkey, 5–8 September 2012, pp. 156–162. IEEE Computer Society (2012). https://doi.org/10.1109/DSD.2012.22
7. Chernoff, H.: Sequential tests for the mean of a normal distribution (1961)
8. Chernoff, H.: Sequential tests for the mean of a normal distribution. III. (small t) (1965)
9. Danger, J.L., Guilley, S., Schaub, A.: Two-metric helper data for highly robust and secure delay PUFs. In: IEEE 8th International Workshop on Advances in Sensors and Interfaces, IWASI 2019, Otranto, Italy, 13–14 June 2019, pp. 184–188. IEEE (2019). https://doi.org/10.1109/IWASI.2019.8791249
10. Delvaux, J., Gu, D., Schellekens, D., Verbauwhede, I.: Helper data algorithms for PUF-based key generation: overview and analysis. IEEE Trans. Comput. Aided Des. Integr. Circuits Syst. **34**(6), 889–902 (2015). https://doi.org/10.1109/TCAD.2014.2370531
11. Dodis, Y., Ostrovsky, R., Reyzin, L., Smith, A.: Fuzzy extractors: how to generate strong keys from biometrics and other noisy data. SIAM J. Comput. **38**(1), 97–139 (2008)
12. Dodis, Y., Reyzin, L., Smith, A.: Fuzzy extractors: how to generate strong keys from biometrics and other noisy data. In: Cachin, C., Camenisch, J.L. (eds.) EUROCRYPT 2004. LNCS, vol. 3027, pp. 523–540. Springer, Heidelberg (2004). https://doi.org/10.1007/978-3-540-24676-3_31
13. Ekström, E., Vaicenavicius, J.: Bayesian sequential testing of the drift of a brownian motion (2015). https://doi.org/10.48550/ARXIV.1509.00675. https://arxiv.org/abs/1509.00675
14. Fuller, B., Meng, X., Reyzin, L.: Computational fuzzy extractors. Cryptology ePrint Archive, Paper 2013/416 (2013). https://eprint.iacr.org/2013/416
15. Gassend, B., Clarke, D., van Dijk, M., Devadas, S.: Controlled physical random functions. In: 18th Annual Computer Security Applications Conference, Proceedings, pp. 149–160 (2002). https://doi.org/10.1109/CSAC.2002.1176287
16. Gassend, B., Clarke, D., van Dijk, M., Devadas, S.: Silicon physical random functions. In: Proceedings of the 9th ACM Conference on Computer and Communications Security, CCS 2002, pp. 148–160. Association for Computing Machinery, New York (2002). https://doi.org/10.1145/586110.586132
17. de Groot, J., Škorić, B., de Vreede, N., Linnartz, J.P.: Information leakage of continuous-source zero secrecy leakage helper data schemes. IACR Cryptology ePrint Archive 2012, 566 (2012). http://eprint.iacr.org/2012/566
18. de Groot, J., Škorić, B., de Vreede, N., Linnartz, J.-P.: Quantization in zero leakage helper data schemes. EURASIP J. Adv. Signal Process. **2016**, 54 (2016). https://doi.org/10.1186/s13634-016-0353-z
19. Günü, O., Schaefer, R.F.: Low-complexity and reliable transforms for physical unclonable functions. In: ICASSP 2020–2020 IEEE International Conference on Acoustics, Speech and Signal Processing (ICASSP), pp. 2807–2811 (2020). https://doi.org/10.1109/ICASSP40776.2020.9053107

20. Herder, C., Ren, L., van Dijk, M., Yu, M.D., Devadas, S.: Trapdoor computational fuzzy extractors and stateless cryptographically-secure physical unclonable functions. IEEE Trans. Dependable Secure Comput. **14**(1), 65–82 (2017). https://doi.org/10.1109/TDSC.2016.2536609
21. Herkle, A., Becker, J., Ortmanns, M.: An Arbiter PUF employing eye-opening oscillation for improved noise suppression. In: 2018 IEEE International Symposium on Circuits and Systems (ISCAS), pp. 1–5 (2018). https://doi.org/10.1109/ISCAS.2018.8351361
22. Van Herrewege, A., et al.: Reverse fuzzy extractors: enabling lightweight mutual authentication for PUF-enabled RFIDs. In: Keromytis, A.D. (ed.) FC 2012. LNCS, vol. 7397, pp. 374–389. Springer, Heidelberg (2012). https://doi.org/10.1007/978-3-642-32946-3_27
23. Hsiao, M.Y.: A class of optimal minimum odd-weight-column SEC-DED codes. IBM J. Res. Dev. **14**(4), 395–401 (1970)
24. Ignatenko, T., Willems, F.M.J.: Information leakage in fuzzy commitment schemes. IEEE Trans. Inf. Forensics Secur. **5**, 337–348 (2010)
25. Immler, V., Hiller, M., Liu, Q., Lenz, A., Wachter-Zeh, A.: Variable-length bit mapping and error-correcting codes for higher-order alphabet PUFs. In: Ali, S.S., Danger, J.-L., Eisenbarth, T. (eds.) SPACE 2017. LNCS, vol. 10662, pp. 190–209. Springer, Cham (2017). https://doi.org/10.1007/978-3-319-71501-8_11
26. Julien, B.: https://github.com/JulienBeg/Reliability-Ring-Oscillator-PUF
27. Karlin, S., Rubin, H.: Distributions possessing a monotone likelihood ratio. J. Am. Stat. Assoc. **51**(276), 637–643 (1956)
28. Linnartz, J.-P., Tuyls, P.: New shielding functions to enhance privacy and prevent misuse of biometric templates. In: Kittler, J., Nixon, M.S. (eds.) AVBPA 2003. LNCS, vol. 2688, pp. 393–402. Springer, Heidelberg (2003). https://doi.org/10.1007/3-540-44887-X_47
29. Maiti, A., Schaumont, P.: Improving the quality of a physical unclonable function using configurable ring oscillators. In: 2009 International Conference on Field Programmable Logic and Applications, pp. 703–707 (2009). https://doi.org/10.1109/FPL.2009.5272361
30. Maiti, A., Schaumont, P.: Improved ring oscillator PUF: an FPGA-friendly secure primitive. J. Cryptol. **24**(2), 375–397 (2010). https://doi.org/10.1007/s00145-010-9088-4
31. Maringer, G., et al.: Analysis of communication channels related to physical unclonable functions. arXiv preprint arXiv:2112.02198 (2021)
32. Massey, J.L.: Guessing and entropy. In: Proceedings of 1994 IEEE International Symposium on Information Theory, p. 204. IEEE (1994)
33. Rioul, O.: Variations on a theme by massey. IEEE Trans. Inf. Theory **68**(5), 2813–2828 (2022)
34. Rioul, O., Solé, P., Guilley, S., Danger, J.L.: On the entropy of physically unclonable functions. In: IEEE International Symposium on Information Theory, ISIT (2016)
35. Schaub, A., Danger, J.L., Guilley, S., Rioul, O.: An improved analysis of reliability and entropy for delay PUFs. In: 21st Euromicro Conference on Digital System Design (2018)
36. Solé, P., Cheng, W., Guilley, S., Rioul, O.: Bent sequences over hadamard codes for physically unclonable functions. In: 2021 IEEE International Symposium on Information Theory (ISIT), pp. 801–806 (2021). https://doi.org/10.1109/ISIT45174.2021.9517752

37. Stangherlin, K., Wu, Z., Patel, H., Sachdev, M.: Enhancing Strong PUF Security with Non-monotonic Response Quantization (2022). https://doi.org/10.48550/ARXIV.2206.03440. https://arxiv.org/abs/2206.03440
38. Stanko, T., Nur Andini, F., Skoric, B.: Optimized quantization in zero leakage helper data systems. Trans. Info. For. Sec. **12**(8), 1957–1966 (2017). https://doi.org/10.1109/TIFS.2017.2697840
39. Suh, G.E., Devadas, S.: Physical unclonable functions for device authentication and secret key generation. In: 2007 44th ACM/IEEE Design Automation Conference, pp. 9–14 (2007)
40. Tebelmann, L., Danger, J.-L., Pehl, M.: Self-secured PUF: protecting the loop PUF by masking. In: Bertoni, G.M., Regazzoni, F. (eds.) COSADE 2020. LNCS, vol. 12244, pp. 293–314. Springer, Cham (2021). https://doi.org/10.1007/978-3-030-68773-1_14
41. Wald, A., Wald, A.: The sequential probability ratio test for testing a simple hypothesis H0 against a single alternative H1. Seq. Anal. **37**, 70 (1947)
42. Wald, A., Wolfowitz, J.: Optimum character of the sequential probability ratio test. Ann. Math. Stat. 326–339 (1948)
43. Wang, W.C., Yona, Y., Diggavi, S., Gupta, P.: LEDPUF: stability-guaranteed physical unclonable functions through locally enhanced defectivity. In: 2016 IEEE International Symposium on Hardware Oriented Security and Trust (HOST), pp. 25–30. IEEE (2016)
44. Yin, C.E.D., Qu, G.: LISA: maximizing RO PUF's secret extraction. In: 2010 IEEE International Symposium on Hardware-Oriented Security and Trust (HOST), pp. 100–105 (2010). https://doi.org/10.1109/HST.2010.5513105

Symmetric Key Cryptography

Improved Boomerang Attacks on Deoxys-BC

Jiahao Zhao[1,2], Nana Zhang[1,2], Qianqian Yang[1,2(✉)], Ling Song[3,4], and Lei Hu[1,2]

[1] State Key Laboratory of Information Security, Institute of Information Engineering, Chinese Academy of Sciences, Beijing, China
{zhaojiahao,zhangnana,yangqianqian,hulei}@iie.ac.cn

[2] School of Cyber Security, University of Chinese Academy of Sciences, Beijing, China

[3] College of Cyber Security, Jinan University, Guangzhou, China

[4] National Joint Engineering Research Center of Network Security Detection and Protection Technology, Jinan University, Guangzhou, China

Abstract. In this paper, we present two techniques to improve the previous attack against the tweakable block cipher Deoxys-BC. First, we apply the idea of "key bridging" to Deoxys-BC and get a better attack on the 9-round Deoxys-BC-256 whose time complexity is decreased from 2^{168} to 2^{147} and memory complexity is decreased from 2^{129} to 2^{100}. Second, we adjust the distinguisher to utilize the additional sieve to filter the data better. Then we apply this method to the 14-round attack on Deoxys-BC-384 and reduce the time complexity from $2^{278.8}$ to $2^{260.4}$ and the memory complexity from 2^{129} to $2^{125.4}$.

Keywords: Block ciphers · Boomerang attacks · Deoxys-BC · Key-bridging · Additional filters

1 Introduction

The block cipher, as one part of the symmetric cipher, is one of the most critical parts of cryptography. Since the first widely used block cipher DES [S+99] was proposed, the development in the field of the block cipher has been very rapid. More and more advanced and complex technology has been applied to many kinds of block ciphers in both directions of the design and the analysis.

As a well-studied and secure block cipher, AES [DR02] has attracted much attention since its publication. Many scholars and institutes have done a variety of cryptanalysis, such as differential cryptanalysis [BS91], boomerang cryptanalysis [Wag01], Demirci-Selçuk meet-in-the-middle attack [DS08] and so on. Regarding the single-key setting, the best-ever known attack is the Demirci-Selçuk meet-in-the-middle attack. More specifically, the most successful key recovery attack against AES-128/192/256 is the 7/9/9-round DS-MITM attack in the single-key setting, due to Derbez *et al.* [DFJ13] and an improvement by Li *et al.* [LJW15]. Correspondingly, the boomerang attack is the best attack that

J. Shikata and H. Kuzuno (Eds.): IWSEC 2023, LNCS 14128, pp. 59–76, 2023.
https://doi.org/10.1007/978-3-031-41326-1_4

covers the most rounds under the related-key setting. To the best of our knowledge, Biryukov *et al.* gave the results of a 12-round (the full version) amplified boomerang attack on AES-192 and a 14-round (also the full version) boomerang attack on AES-256 under the related-key setting respectively [BK09, BKN09].

Due to the good properties of the round function of AES, some designers use it as an important part of their new ciphers. The examples are Kiasu [JNP14a, JNP14b], Deoxys [JNPS16, JNPS21], TNT-AES [BGGS20], TweAES [CDJ+20] and TIAOXIN [Nik14]. In this paper, we focus on the tweakable block cipher (TBC) Deoxys-BC underlying the authenticated encryption scheme Deoxys. Deoxys is one of the six candidates in the final portfolio of the CAESAR competition.[1] Furthermore, Deoxys-BC has been standardized by ISO/IEC.[2]

Up to now, the development history of the attacks on Deoxys-BC can be organized as follows: In [JNPS16], the designers of Deoxys-BC gave the results of the upper bounds of the possibilities of the best round-reduced related-tweakey differential characteristics in different rounds. They also described the security against linear cryptanalysis, meet-in-the-middle attacks, and other attacks. Recently in [JNPS21], they improved their previous results.

Besides, Cid *et al.* [CHP+17] applied the rectangle attack to the variants of Deoxys-BC, and they gave the results of 9/10 and 12/13-round attacks against Deoxys-BC-256 and Deoxys-BC-384 respectively. For Deoxys-BC-256, the best time complexity of their attack is 2^{118} and 2^{204} in 9 and 10 rounds; for Deoxys-BC-384, the best time complexity is 2^{127} and 2^{270} in 12 and 13 rounds. In 2018, the same authors used the boomerang connectivity tool to improve the 10-round distinguisher against Deoxys-BC-384 used in [CHP+17] and obtained better results [CHP+18] by increasing the probability of the distinguisher. In [ZDJ19], Zhao *et al.* modified the MILP model used in the search for boomerang distinguisher and utilized the BDT technique to get the 10 and 11-round related-key boomerang and rectangle attacks against Deoxys-BC-256 and the 12, 13 and 14-round attacks against Deoxys-BC-384. The authors also gave some other results of 13 and 14-round key recovery rectangle attacks against Deoxys-BC-384 in [ZDJM19] by improving their technique. Dong *et al.* [DQSW22] proposed a new key guessing strategy for linear key-schedule algorithm to decrease the time complexity of 14-round rectangle attack on Deoxys-BC-384 from $2^{282.7}$ to about 2^{260}. At EUROCRYPT 2023, Bariant *et al.* [BL23] present a framework of boomerang attacks using the idea of truncated differentials, and they gave their results using a new evaluation model. Song *et al.* [SZY+23] put forward a unified and generic framework for key recovery rectangle attacks and gave an 11-round related-key rectangle attack with the time complexity of $2^{222.49}$ and an 11-round related-key boomerang attack with the time complexity of $2^{218.65}$ against Deoxys-BC-256.

Additionally, other kinds of attacks have been studied by different researchers. Mehrdad *et al.* [MS+18] gave the results of 8/9-round impossible differential attacks against Deoxys-BC-256 in the single-key and related-key settings.

[1] For more details, we recommend the readers refer to the homepage of the CAESAR competition. http://competitions.cr.yp.to/caesar.html.

[2] The readers can go to https://www.iso.org/obp/ui/#iso:std:iso-iec:18033:-7:ed-1:v1:en to find more information about this standard.

In [ZDW19], the authors presented a 10-round impossible differential attack against Deoxys-BC-256 using a newly found 6-round related-tweakey impossible distinguisher. Besides, Hadipour *et al.* [HSE23] utilized a CP-based method to find several zero-correlation (ZC)-based integral distinguishers for Deoxys-BC-256 and Deoxys-BC-384.

Table 1. Results of boomerang attacks against variants of Deoxys-BC

Model	Round	Data	Time	Mem	Ref
RTK1	8	2^{82}	2^{82}	2^{81}	[BL23]
RTK1	9	2^{129}	2^{168}	2^{129}	[BL23]
RTK1	9	2^{129}	2^{147}	2^{100}	Sect. 3.2
RTK2	8	2^{27}	2^{27}	2^{27}	[BL23]
RTK2	9	2^{55}	2^{55}	2^{55}	[BL23]
RTK2	10	2^{90}	2^{90}	2^{89}	[BL23]
RTK2	11	2^{129}	2^{218}	2^{129}	[BL23]
RTK3	10	$2^{19.4}$	$2^{19.4}$	2^{18}	[BL23]
RTK3	11	$2^{32.7}$	$2^{32.7}$	$2^{32.7}$	[BL23]
RTK3	12	$2^{67.4}$	$2^{67.4}$	2^{65}	[BL23]
RTK3	13	$2^{126.4}$	$2^{169.7}$	$2^{126.4}$	[BL23]
RTK3	14	2^{129}	$2^{278.8}$	2^{129}	[BL23]
RTK3	14	2^{129}	$2^{260.4}$	$2^{125.4}$	Sect. 4.2

Our Contributions. Considering all the attacks described above, the most widely studied and effective attack against this cipher is the boomerang and rectangle attack. Based on this fact, we try to improve the previous boomerang attack to achieve the best attack. The results of our attacks are shown in Table 1.

In this paper, we utilize two tricks to improve the previous boomerang attack in [BL23]. First, we exploit the relation among round keys based on the tweakey schedule algorithm to decrease the number of the subtweakey bits that need to be guessed. Then we use this technique for the 9-round attack on Deoxys-BC-256. Second, we try to adjust the part of the distinguisher in [BL23] to achieve a better filtering effect. Next, we apply it to the 14-round attack on Deoxys-BC-384.

Different from the attack against Deoxys-BC-256, which uses the assumption that the size of the key is required to be a certain value, the attack against Deoxys-BC-384 is more general because it does not use any extra conditions. Consequently, we think the technique of this attack can be freely extended to other attacks.

Organization. In Sect. 2, we give some preliminaries and notations about our attacks. The "key bridging" technique and its application to the 9-round attack on Deoxys-BC-256 are discussed in Sect. 3. Section 4 describes the adjustment of the previous distinguisher and the improved 14-round attack on Deoxys-BC-384. Finally, we make a summary in Sect. 5.

2 Preliminaries

2.1 Specification of Deoxys-BC

Deoxys-BC was first introduced by Jérémy *et al.* on CAESAR competition [JNPS16]. Deoxys-BC is an `AES`-like tweakable block cipher. It has two variants: Deoxys-BC-256 and Deoxys-BC-384. The size of the internal state is 128 bits (viewed as a 4×4 matrix of bytes). The round function of Deoxys-BC consists of the following four operations: `AddRoundTweakey`, `SubBytes`, `ShiftRows`, `MixBytes`. These four operations are described in detail as follows:

`AddRoundTweakey` The 128-bit round subtweakey is XORed to the internal state.
`SubBytes` The 8-bit `AES` S-box is applied to each of the 16 bytes of the internal state.
`ShiftRows` The 4-byte i-th row is rotated left by $\rho[i]$ positions, where $\rho = (0, 1, 2, 3)$.
`MixBytes` The internal state is multiplied by the 4×4 constant MDS matrix of `AES`.

After the last round, there is another final `AddRoundTweakey` operation to be done to generate the ciphertext.

The input of Deoxys-BC consists of three parts: a plaintext P (or a ciphertext C), a key K, and a *tweak* T. In Deoxys-BC-256, the sum of the lengths of K and T is 256 bits, while in Deoxys-BC-384, the sum of the lengths of K and T is 384 bits. The number r of rounds for Deoxys-BC-256 and Deoxys-BC-384 is 14 and 16.

The round subtweakeys used in the `AddRoundTweakey` operation are generated by the tweakey schedule algorithm. The designers of Deoxys-BC denote the concatenation of the key K and the *tweak* T as KT, i.e., $KT = K||T$. Then, they divide the tweakey state into words of 128 bits. More precisely, in Deoxys-BC-256, the size of KT is 256 bits with the first (most significant) 128 bits of KT being denoted W_1, while the second W_2. For Deoxys-BC-384, the size of KT is 384 bits, with the first (most significant) 128 bits of KT being denoted W_1, the second W_2 and the third W_3. Finally, STK_i is the representation of the subtweakey (a 128-bit word) that is added to the state at round i of the cipher during the `AddRoundTweakey` operation. For Deoxys-BC-256, a subtweakey is defined as:

$$STK_i = TK_i^1 \oplus TK_i^2 \oplus RC_i,$$

yet for the case of Deoxys-BC-384 it is defined as:

$$STK_i = TK_i^1 \oplus TK_i^2 \oplus TK_i^3 \oplus RC_i.$$

The 128-bit words TK_i^1, TK_i^2, TK_i^3 are produced by a tweakey schedule algorithm, initialized with $TK_0^1 = W_1$ and $TK_0^2 = W_2$ for Deoxys-BC-256 and with $TK_0^1 = W_1, TK_0^2 = W_2$ and $TK_0^3 = W_3$ for Deoxys-BC-384. The tweakey schedule algorithm is defined as

$$TK_{i+1}^1 = h(TK_i^1),$$

$$TK_{i+1}^2 = h(LFSR_2(TK_i^2)),$$

$$TK_{i+1}^3 = h(LFSR_3(TK_i^3)),$$

where the byte permutation h is defined as:

$$\begin{pmatrix} 0 & 1 & 2 & 3 & 4 & 5 & 6 & 7 & 8 & 9 & 10 & 11 & 12 & 13 & 14 & 15 \\ 1 & 6 & 11 & 12 & 5 & 10 & 15 & 0 & 9 & 14 & 3 & 4 & 13 & 2 & 7 & 8 \end{pmatrix},$$

and where the authors number the 16 bytes of a 128-bit tweakey word by the usual ordering:

$$\begin{pmatrix} 0 & 4 & 8 & 12 \\ 1 & 5 & 9 & 13 \\ 2 & 6 & 10 & 14 \\ 3 & 7 & 11 & 15 \end{pmatrix}.$$

The $LFSR_2$ and $LFSR_3$ functions are simply the application of an LFSR to each of the 16 bytes of a 128-bit tweakey TK_i^j. The details of these two functions are not important in this work, so we omit the detailed descriptions here.

2.2 The Boomerang Attack

The boomerang attack was first proposed by Wagner [Wag01], which combines two relatively short differentials to obtain a longer and relatively high-probability distinguisher. In the boomerang attack, we divide the cipher E into two parts, i.e., $E = E_1 \circ E_0$. Suppose we can find a differential $\alpha \rightarrow \beta$ with probability p for E_0 and another differential $\gamma \rightarrow \delta$ with probability q for E_1 as we can see in Fig. 1, then for the cipher E, given a plaintext x, we can find that the following formula holds:

$$Pr[E^{-1}(E(x) \oplus \delta) \oplus E^{-1}(E(x \oplus \alpha) \oplus \delta) = \alpha] = p^2q^2.$$

Due to the formula above, one can easily understand that the boomerang attack requires a certain amount of adaptively chosen plaintexts and ciphertexts. However, the premise of this attack is that the two parts of the cipher E are independent of each other. It has been found that this assumption is not accurate enough in some attacks [Mur11] during more and more research. Later, Dunkelman *et al.* suggested the sandwich attack [DKS10] which divides the cipher E into three parts: E_0, E_m, E_1 and estimates the probability by p^2q^2r. The probability r is the probability of the middle part E_m. In 2018, Cid *et al.* introduced a tool named boomerang connectivity table (BCT) [CHP+18], which was used to calculate the probability r correctly when E_m is an S-Box layer.

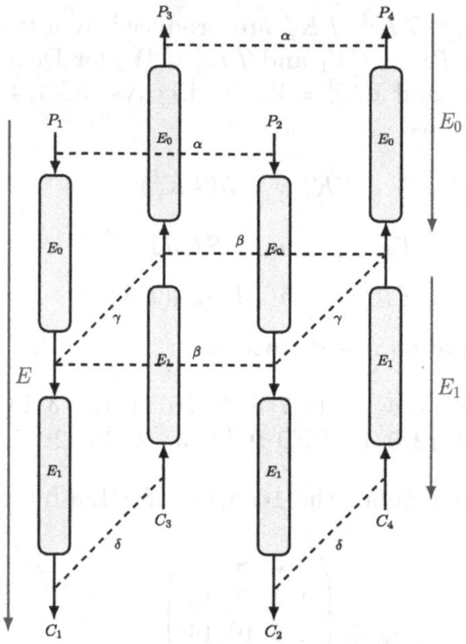

Fig. 1. The boomerang attack

2.3 Notations and Overview of the Boomerang Key Recovery Attack

Song *et al.* presented a unified and generic key recovery algorithm for the rectangle attack at ASIACRYPT 2022 [SZY+23]. The authors use multiple methods to get the best possible result. In this paper, we use the same notations as in their article.

As shown in Fig. 2, given a boomerang distinguisher over E_d, we can propagate the input difference α of E_0 to α' via E_b^{-1} and propagate the output difference δ of E_1 to δ' via E_f^{-1}, where E_d, E_0, E_b^{-1}, E_1, E_f^{-1} represent several round functions or the inverse of round function.

We denote V_b as the space spanned by all possible α' where $r_b = \log_2 |V_b|$, k_b as the subset of subkey bits which are employed in E_b and affect the propagation $\alpha' \to \alpha$. Notations of the other side are similar. The idea of propagating the definite difference to a set of possible differences was first formalized by Biham *et al.* in 2002 [BDK02]. And they called it the structure technique. In our work, we also use this method.

Let $m_b = |k_b|$ and $m_f = |k_f|$ be the number of bits in k_b and k_f, respectively. We can guess some bits of k_b and k_f to verify the differential propagations partially. In the following, we will denote the guessed bytes of k_b and k_f as k_b' and k_f'. By doing this, we may get more balanced and better results.

Now let us introduce the framework used in our paper to mount the related-key boomerang key recovery attack.

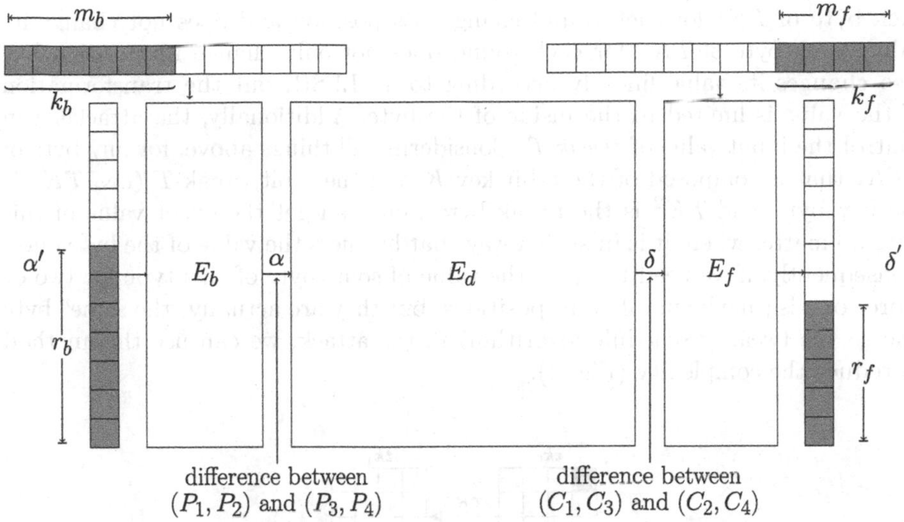

Fig. 2. Outline of boomerang key recovery attack from [SZY+23]

1. First, we determine the number of structures we need according to the parameters of the attack and initialize the data in the structures.
2. Next, we guess some parts of the involved key bits of k_b and k_f and set counters for their remaining unknown bits.
3. For every value of our guess, we do partial encryptions and decryptions to the structures and get the intermediate value. We denote the intermediate value of a quartet by four sets S_1, S_2, S_3, and S_4.
4. Construct pairs according to the direction of the attack.
5. Construct and sieve quartets.
6. Extract key information using the remaining quartets.
7. Determine the remaining unknown key bits by an exhaustive search.

3 Relation Among Round Keys Based on the Tweakey Schedule Algorithm

In this section, we introduce a trick called "key bridging" to improve the boomerang key recovery attack against Deoxys-BC.

3.1 Apply the Key-Bridging Technique to Deoxys-BC

Let us revisit the tweakey schedule algorithm. We can easily observe that for Deoxys-BC-256 if we guess the one-byte value of a round subtweakey, i.e., $STK_i[j]$ (it means the j-th byte in the i-th round subtweakey state STK_i), we can get some equations for the corresponding bits of $TK_i^1[j]$ and $TK_i^2[j]$ ($RC_i[j]$ is constant so we omit it here). According to the tweakey schedule algorithm, each byte of TK^1 for each round changes its position and does not change its value; each byte of TK^2 for each round does not only change its position but also changes its value linearly according to an LFSR, but the transformation of the value is limited to the inside of the byte. Additionally, the attacker can control the input value of *tweak* T. Considering all things above, for any byte of STK_i that is composed of the 8-bit key K and the 8-bit tweak T (i.e., TK^1 is the key byte, and TK^2 is the tweak byte), one can get the exact value of this byte no matter where it is in such a way that he guess the value of the byte once. Consequently, if we need to guess the value of some byte of this type for two or more rounds (maybe in different positions, but they are actually "the same" byte due to the tweakey schedule algorithm) in the attack, we can use this method to reduce the complexity (Fig. 3).

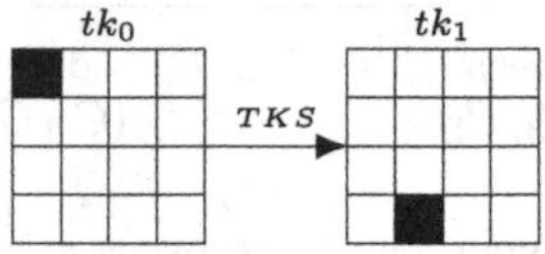

Fig. 3. An example of key-bridging technique applied to Deoxys-BC-256

For example, suppose that we guess the byte 0 of the tweakey state tk_0, according to the tweakey schedule algorithm, $TK_0^1[0]$ will be transformed to $TK_1^1[7]$, and the order of the bits in this byte will not change. However, the condition of $TK_0^2[0]$ will be a little different from $TK_0^1[0]$. Though it will be shifted to the same position, the order and the value of the bits will change depending on the $LFSR_2$. If this byte consists of the 8-bit key and the 8-bit tweak, the attackers can fix the value of the tweak, and then they can determine the value of the key. Consequently, if $STK_1[7]$ should be guessed, the attackers need not guess the value again and can calculate it easily.

Now let us consider the more complex version: Deoxys-BC-384. The situation is similar to Deoxys-BC-256, but there exist some tiny differences in Deoxys-BC-384. First of all, the value of a byte of a round subtweakey consists of three parts: TK_i^1, TK_i^2, and TK_i^3. What's more, these three parts are composed of the key K and the tweak T in a cascade way. So there may be two types of byte values obtained from K and T XORed in STK_i: one byte of K and two bytes of T, or two bytes of K and one byte of T (of course, there may also occur the situation that a byte of TK_i^j consists of some bits of K and some bits of T simultaneously, but it is slightly complex and not significant so that we only consider this problem from the perspective of the byte level).

The first situation is almost the same as the situation in Deoxys-BC-256. The only distinction is that the attacker can only fix one byte of T for Deoxys-BC-256; however, for Deoxys-BC-384, he can fix two bytes of T because the tweak can be longer. The second situation is more interesting because if we guess the one-byte value of STK_i, it seems that we can not get the value of two bytes of K. Nevertheless, we can get eight equations between $TK_i^1[j]$, $TK_i^2[j]$ and $TK_i^3[j]$. Suppose the value of $TK_i^3[j]$ is known, we still have two variables for the one-bit value of $STK_i[j][k]$. Therefore we can get the values of two variables by guessing this byte again, i.e., guessing the value of this byte (perhaps in a different position) in another round. Because of this, one can reduce the complexity if he needs to guess the "same" byte that appears in three or more rounds during the attack.

Next, we will apply this trick to Deoxys-BC-256 to improve its previous attack complexity.

3.2 9-Round Attack on Deoxys-BC-256

Both two distinguishers used in our work are based on the distinguishers proposed by Bariant *et al.* in [BL23] (Fig. 4).

The first attack is a 9-round attack on Deoxys-BC-256. The diagram of the attack is shown below. This 9-round attack is obtained by extending a 7-round distinguisher forward and backward one round, respectively. The length of the key K is 152 bits in this attack, i.e., $TK_0^2[3:15]$ is the tweak T. The parameters of this attack are $P_d = 2^{-96}$, $r_b = 96$, $r_f = 32$, $m_b = 120$, $m_f = 32$. The attack starts from the plaintext side. The process is as follows :

1. Let s be the expected number of right quartets, so the number of structures $y = s \times 2^{-r_b}/P_d = 4$ if $s = 4$. Each structure contains 2^{96} plaintexts. We represent a structure and its corresponding structure with S and $\overline{S}$, respectively. The form of each S and $\overline{S}$ is :

$$S = \{P | P[0:1, 3:6, 9:12, 14:15] \in \{0,1\}^{96}, \\ P[2, 7:8, 13] = constant\},$$

$$\overline{S} = \{\overline{P} | \overline{P}[0:1, 3:6, 9:12, 14:15] \in \{0,1\}^{96}, \\ \overline{P}[2] \oplus P[2] = 9a, \\ \overline{P}[7:8, 13] = P[7:8, 13]\}.$$

Encrypt each plaintext in S and $\overline{S}$ with K_1 and K_2 respectively. K_1 and K_2 are the keys that satisfy the difference of the round subtweakey required in the E_0 stage. The time complexity of this step is 2^{99}, and the memory complexity is 2^{99}.

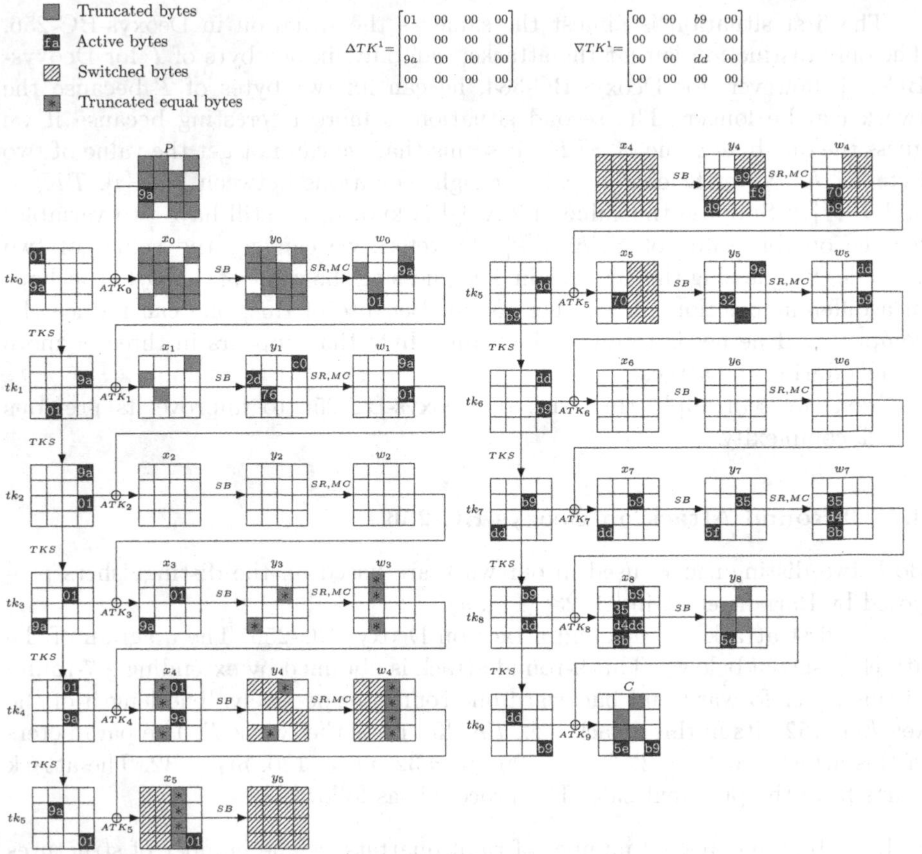

Fig. 4. 9-round attack on Deoxys-BC proposed in [BL23]

2. Next we choose to guess $tk_9[5:6,8,10]$ and $tk_0[4,14]$. Due to the tweakey schedule algorithm, we can get the value of $tk_0[3,9:10,15]$ and $tk_1[6]$ according to the guess. For each guess, we follow the steps below :
   (a) Initialize a list of key counters for $tk_0[0:1,5:6,11:12]$ and $tk_1[1,12]$. The memory complexity is 2^{64}.
   (b) For each data in S and $\overline{S}$, do partial encryptions and decryptions under the guessed bytes. Let $P^* = Enc_{k'_b}(P)$, $\overline{P}^* = Enc_{k'_b}(\overline{P})$ ($P \in S$ and $\overline{P} \in \overline{S}$), $C^* = Dec_{k'_f}(C)$ and $\overline{C}^* = Dec_{k'_f}(\overline{C})$. Taking the pair (P, C) as an example, the partially encrypted bytes of P^* in this attack correspond to the bytes of $w_0[4:5,7]$ and $y_1[6]$, and the partially decrypted bytes of C^* corresponds to the bytes of $x_8[5:6,8,10]$. The rest pairs of the quartet are processed in the same way. After that, XOR the output difference δ of the

distinguisher to C^* and $\overline{C}^*$ to get the corresponding C'^* and $\overline{C}'^*$. For C'^* and $\overline{C}'^*$, we use the guessed bits to encrypt them to get C' and $\overline{C}'$. Then we utilize K_3 and K_4 to decrypt them to get the corresponding P' and $\overline{P}'$. Finally we do partial encryptions under k_b' and let $P'^* = Enc_{k_b'}(P')$, $\overline{P}'^* = Enc_{k_b'}(\overline{P}')$. Construct four sets S_1, S_2, S_3 and S_4 to store the data processed by four keys K_1, K_2, K_3 and K_4, i.e.

$$S_1 = \{(P^*, C^*) | C^* = Dec_{k_1}(C), P^* = Enc_{k_1}(P), (P, C) \in S\},$$

$$S_2 = \{(\overline{P}^*, \overline{C}^*) | \overline{C}^* = Dec_{k_2}(\overline{C}), \overline{P}^* = Enc_{k_2}(\overline{P}), (\overline{P}, \overline{C}) \in \overline{S}\},$$

$$S_3 = \{(P'^*, C'^*) | C'^* = C^* \oplus \delta, C' = Enc_{k_3}(C'^*),$$
$$P' = Dec_{K_3}(C'), P'^* = Enc_{k_3}(P'), (P^*, C^*) \in S_1\},$$

$$S_4 = \{(\overline{P}'^*, \overline{C}'^*) | \overline{C}'^* = \overline{C}^* \oplus \delta, \overline{C}' = Enc_{k_4}(\overline{C}'^*),$$
$$\overline{P}' = Dec_{K_4}(\overline{C}'), \overline{P}'^* = Enc_{k_4}(\overline{P}'), (\overline{P}^*, \overline{C}^*) \in S_2\}.$$

k_i means the guessed parts in the corresponding key K_i. The time complexity of this step is $2^{48} \times 2^{99} = 2^{147}$, and the memory complexity is $2^2 \times 2^{98} = 2^{100}$.

(c) Construct two sets $S_{1,3}$ and $S_{2,4}$,

$$S_{1,3} = \{(P^*, C^*, P'^*, C'^*) | C'^* = C^* \oplus \delta, (P^*, C^*) \in S_1, (P'^*, C'^*) \in S_3\},$$

$$S_{2,4} = \{(\overline{P}^*, \overline{C}^*, \overline{P}'^*, \overline{C}'^*) | \overline{C}'^* = \overline{C}^* \oplus \delta, (\overline{P}^*, \overline{C}^*) \in S_2, (\overline{P}'^*, \overline{C}'^*) \in S_4\}.$$

The size of each set is 2^{98}. The time complexity of this step is $2^{48} \times 2^{99} = 2^{147}$, the memory complexity is 2^{99}.

(d) Insert $S_{1,3}$ into a hash table by

$$(P^*[4:5, 7:11], P^*[6] \oplus 76)$$

and

$$(P'^*[4:5, 7:11], P'^*[6] \oplus 76).$$

Due to the number of structures being 4, the size of the hash table is at most $2^{2+32} \times 2^{64} = 2^{98}$. What's more, because we can get the value of $tk_0[10, 15]$, we can get linear relation among the bytes of $P^*[0:3]$ and $P'^*[0:3]$ respectively, and it makes us have another 2-byte condition to filter quartets better. Consequently, the expected number of quartets is $2^{98 \times 2 - 98 - 16} = 2^{82}$ under every guess. The time complexity of this step is $2^{48+98} = 2^{146}$, the memory complexity is 2^{98}.

(e) Extract key information using the remaining quartets.

(f) Determine the remaining unknown key bits by an exhaustive search.

The time complexity of the whole attack is 2^{147}, the memory complexity is 2^{100}, the data complexity is $2 \times 2^{128} = 2^{129}$.

4 Adjusting the Distinguisher for Additional Filters

In this section, we discuss the new discovery by reviewing the results of Deoxys-BC made by Bariant *et al.* [BL23] at EUROCRYPT 2023.

4.1 More Sieves by Regulating the Distinguisher

The inspiration comes from the distinguisher of Fig. 15 in [BL23]. If we transform the distinguisher into a traditional one, we find that we can make the distinguisher change a little to get a more low-complexity attack. What we can do is change two active but unknown differences in x_1 into two fixed differences whose probabilities are both 2^{-7}. By doing so, the bits of m_b are reduced from 112 to 96. Additionally, we can have more filters. The details of the sieve are shown below.

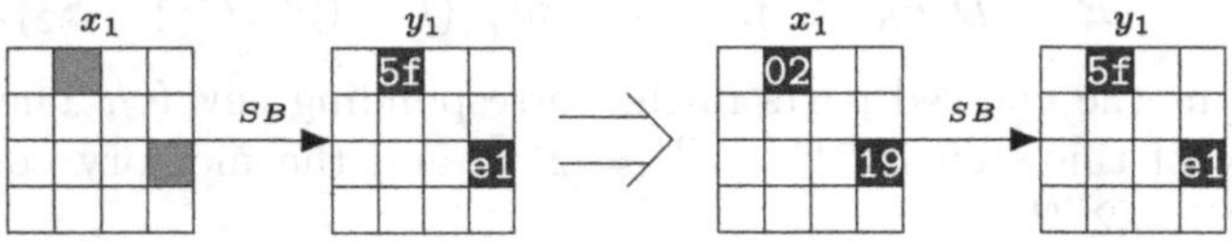

Fig. 5. An example of additional filters

Let us consider a more specific situation, i.e., two fixed differences in x_1 are 02 and 19, as shown in Fig. 5 respectively, for example. In our attack, we guess all 12 bytes of k_b. We can calculate all values of the second column and the fourth column in w_0 of P_1 when constructing the quartet. Because we have determined the fixed differences, we can find all possible transformations by looking up the DDT. We can deduce all possible values of two bytes in tk_1 of K_1, i.e., byte 4 and byte 14, according to the DDT. Because of the dependency among four keys that are used to encrypt the quartet, we can also deduce the two bytes in tk_1 of K_3. Then we can check the rationality of whether the quartets conform to the distinguisher. The filtering effect strongly depends on the entries of the DDT we choose. Given that the entry of the DDT of the S-box of AES is at most 4 except for the entry of $(0, 0)$, we can, of course, choose the entry which is 4, but it will lead to a more complex situation. Considering this, we finally make a tradeoff. However, the principle is completely the same. So we omit the details of choosing the value of 4 here.

4.2 14-Round Attack on Deoxys-BC-384

This 14-round attack is obtained from the attack shown below (Fig. 6). We exploit the framework of the attack and apply our new technique to improve the attack. There are no additional restrictions on the key and tweak lengths as long as this attack is more effective than the exhaustive search attack with the

$$\Delta TK^1=\begin{bmatrix}00&00&a9&00\\00&00&00&00\\00&00&8c&00\\3c&00&00&00\end{bmatrix}\quad \nabla TK^1=\begin{bmatrix}00&00&00&00\\00&53&00&00\\00&7b&00&00\\00&28&00&00\end{bmatrix}$$

$$\Delta TK^2=\begin{bmatrix}00&00&53&00\\00&00&00&00\\00&00&4f&00\\82&00&00&00\end{bmatrix}\quad \nabla TK^2=\begin{bmatrix}00&00&00&00\\00&34&00&00\\00&c8&00&00\\00&fc&00&00\end{bmatrix}$$

$$\Delta TK^3=\begin{bmatrix}00&00&8f&00\\00&00&00&00\\00&00&b9&00\\44&00&00&00\end{bmatrix}\quad \nabla TK^3=\begin{bmatrix}00&00&00&00\\00&d4&00&00\\00&32&00&00\\00&e6&00&00\end{bmatrix}$$

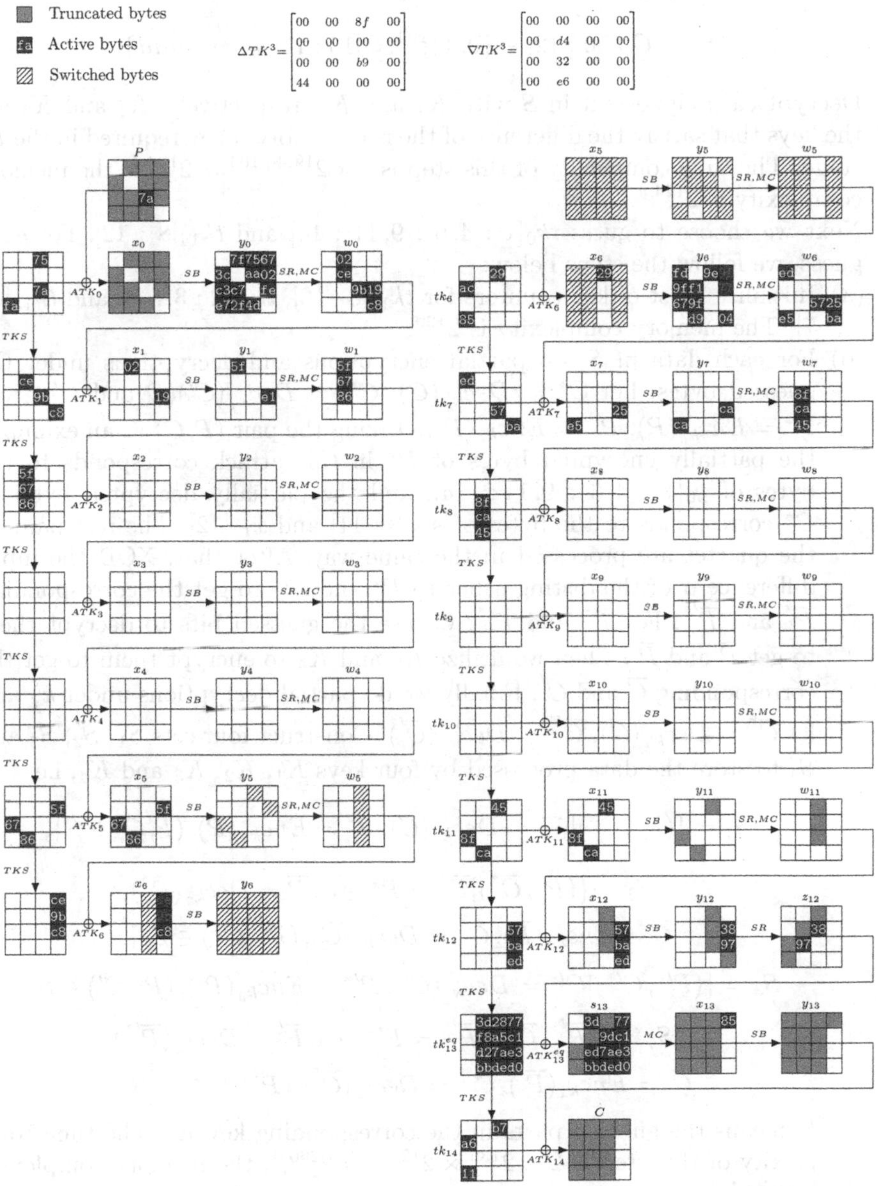

Fig. 6. Improved 14-round attack on Deoxys-BC-384

same sizes of K and T. The parameters of this attack are $P_d = 2^{-121.4}$, $r_b = 96$, $r_f = 104$, $m_b = 96$, $m_f = 104 + 32 + 24 = 160$. The attack starts from the ciphertext side. The process is as follows:

1. Let s be the expected number of right quartets, so the number of structures $y = s \times 2^{-r_f}/P_d = 2^{2+121.4-104} = 2^{19.4}$ if $s = 4$. Each structure contains 2^{104} ciphertexts. We represent a structure with S. The form of each S is :

$$S = \{C|C[0:12] \in \{0,1\}^{104}, C[13:15] = constant\}.$$

   Decrypt each ciphertext in S with K_1 and K_3, respectively. K_1 and K_3 are the keys that satisfy the difference of the round subtweakey required in the E_1 stage. The time complexity of this step is $2 \times 2^{19.4+104} = 2^{124.4}$, the memory complexity is $2^{124.4}$.
2. Next we choose to guess $tk_0[1:4, 6:9, 11:14]$ and $tk_{14}[8:12]$. For each guess, we follow the steps below:
   (a) Initialize a list of key counters for $tk_{12}[8:10]$, $tk_{13}[2:3, 5, 8]$ and $tk_{14}[0:7]$. The memory complexity is 2^{120}.
   (b) For each data in S, do partial encryptions and decryptions under the guessed bytes. Let $C^* = Dec_{k'_f}(C)$, $C'^* = Dec_{k'_f}(C')(C$ and $C' \in S)$, $P^* = Enc_{k'_b}(P)$, $P'^* = Enc_{k'_b}(P')$. Taking the pair (P, C) as an example, the partially encrypted bytes of P^* in this attack corresponds to the bytes of $y_0[1:4, 6:9, 11:14]$, and the partially decrypted bytes of C^* corresponds to the bytes of $s_{13}[8:11]$ and $x_{13}[12]$. The rest pairs of the quartet are processed in the same way. After that, XOR the input difference α of the distinguisher to P^* and P'^* to get the corresponding $\overline{P}^*$ and $\overline{P}'^*$. For $\overline{P}^*$ and $\overline{P}'^*$, we use the guessed bits to decrypt them to get $\overline{P}$ and $\overline{P}'$. Then we utilize K_2 and K_4 to encrypt them to get the corresponding $\overline{C}$ and $\overline{C}'$. Finally we do partial decryptions under k'_f and let $\overline{C}^* = Dec_{k'_f}(\overline{C})$, $\overline{C}'^* = Dec_{k'_f}(\overline{C}')$. Construct four sets S_1, S_2, S_3 and S_4 to store the data processed by four keys K_1, K_2, K_3 and K_4, i.e.

$$S_1 = \{(P^*, C^*)|C^* = Dec_{k_1}(C), P^* = Enc_{k_1}(P), (P, C) \in S\},$$

$$S_2 = \{(\overline{P}^*, \overline{C}^*)|\overline{P}^* = P^* \oplus \alpha, \overline{P} = Dec_{k_2}(\overline{P}^*),$$
$$\overline{C} = Enc_{k_2}(\overline{P}), \overline{C}^* = Dec_{k_2}(\overline{C}), (P^*, C^*) \in S_1\},$$

$$S_3 = \{(P'^*, C'^*)|C'^* = Dec_{k_3}(C'), P'^* = Enc_{k_3}(P'), (P', C') \in S\},$$

$$S_4 = \{(\overline{P}'^*, \overline{C}'^*)|\overline{P}'^* = P'^* \oplus \alpha, \overline{P}' = Dec_{k_4}(\overline{P}'^*),$$
$$\overline{C}' = Enc_{k_4}(\overline{P}'), \overline{C}'^* = Dec_{k_4}(\overline{C}'), (P'^*, C'^*) \in S_3\}.$$

   k_i means the guessed parts in the corresponding key K_i. The time complexity of this step is $2 \times 2^{136} \times 2^{123.4} = 2^{260.4}$, the memory complexity is $2^{125.4}$.

(c) Construct two sets $S_{1,2}$ and $S_{3,4}$,

$$S_{1,2} = \{(P^*, C^*, \overline{P}^*, \overline{C}^*) | \overline{P}^* = P^* \oplus \alpha,\\ (P^*, C^*) \in S_1, (\overline{P}^*, \overline{C}^*) \in S_2\},$$

$$S_{3,4} = \{(P'^*, C'^*, \overline{P}'^*, \overline{C}'^*) | \overline{P}'^* = P'^* \oplus \alpha,\\ (P'^*, C'^*) \in S_3, (\overline{P}'^*, \overline{C}'^*) \in S_4\}.$$

We can use the hash table to help us construct the sets like we do while obtaining the quartets. When constructing the two sets, we can utilize our technique to filter the pairs. Where it can be applied is the 38 cell of y_{12} and z_{12}. We can determine the value of the third column of s_{13}, and then we will deduce a 6-bit condition(the possibility of $57 \rightarrow 38$ is 2^{-6}). Due to the sieve, the number of pairs that can satisfy the distinguisher is $2^{123.4-6} = 2^{117.4}$. The time complexity of this step is $2^{136} \times 2 \times 2^{123.4} = 2^{260.4}$, the memory complexity is $2 \times 2^{123.4} = 2^{124.4}$.

(d) Insert $S_{1,2}$ into a hash table by

$$(C^*[9] \oplus 9d, C^*[10] \oplus 7a, C^*[11] \oplus de,\\ C^*[12] \oplus 77, C^*[13:15]),$$

$$(\overline{C}^*[9] \oplus 9d, \overline{C}^*[10] \oplus 7a, \overline{C}^*[11] \oplus de,\\ \overline{C}^*[12] \oplus 77, \overline{C}^*[13:15])$$

and the possible value of $tk_1[4, 14]$ that is generated by K_3. It should be noted that the additional sieves for quartets are only valid for one side because of the dependency among the four keys. The number of quartets that can pass the filter is $2^{117.4 \times 2 - 19.4 - 32 - 24 - 32 - 14} = 2^{113.4}$. The time complexity of this step is $2^{136} \times 2^{117.4} = 2^{253.4}$, the memory complexity is $2^{117.4} \times 2^2 = 2^{119.4}$.

(e) Extract key information using the remaining quartets.

(f) Determine the remaining unknown key bits by an exhaustive search.

The time complexity of the whole attack is $2^{260.4}$, the memory complexity is $2^{125.4}$, the data complexity is $2 \times 2^{128} = 2^{129}$.

Remark. It may be noticed that the method we utilize in this attack can even be generalized to the distinguishers of other block ciphers. So we think this technique is able to improve some existing attacks if the distinguisher can be coordinated appropriately.

5 Summary

Two approaches are raised to improve the previous boomerang attacks on Deoxys-BC. First, we find the inherent connection among subtweakeys in different rounds and take advantage of this connection to lower the time and memory complexity of the 9-round attack against Deoxys-BC-256 proposed in [BL23]. Second, we show the effect of the extra filters after adjusting the distinguisher and demonstrate the ability of the sieve using an example of a 14-round attack against Deoxys-BC-384.

Acknowledgements. We would like to thank anonymous reviewers for their helpful comments and suggestions. This paper is supported by the National Key Research and Development Program (No. 2018YFA0704704, No.2022YFB2701900, No.2022YFB2703003) and the National Natural Science Foundation of China (Grants 62202460, 62022036, 62132008, 62172410).

References

BDK02. Biham, E., Dunkelman, O., Keller, N.: New results on boomerang and rectangle attacks. In: Daemen, J., Rijmen, V. (eds.) FSE 2002. LNCS, vol. 2365, pp. 1–16. Springer, Heidelberg (2002). https://doi.org/10.1007/3-540-45661-9_1

BGGS20. Bao, Z., Guo, C., Guo, J., Song, L.: TNT: how to tweak a block cipher. In: Canteaut, A., Ishai, Y. (eds.) EUROCRYPT 2020. LNCS, vol. 12106, pp. 641–673. Springer, Cham (2020). https://doi.org/10.1007/978-3-030-45724-2_22

BK09. Biryukov, A., Khovratovich, D.: Related-key cryptanalysis of the full AES-192 and AES-256. In: Matsui, M. (ed.) ASIACRYPT 2009. LNCS, vol. 5912, pp. 1–18. Springer, Heidelberg (2009). https://doi.org/10.1007/978-3-642-10366-7_1

BKN09. Biryukov, A., Khovratovich, D., Nikolić, I.: Distinguisher and related-key attack on the full AES-256. In: Halevi, S. (ed.) CRYPTO 2009. LNCS, vol. 5677, pp. 231–249. Springer, Heidelberg (2009). https://doi.org/10.1007/978-3-642-03356-8_14

BL23. Bariant, A., Leurent, G.: Truncated boomerang attacks and application to AES-based ciphers. In: Hazay, C., Stam, M. (eds.) Advances in Cryptology - EUROCRYPT 2023. EUROCRYPT 2023. LNCS, vol. 14007, pages 3–35. Springer, Cham (2023). https://doi.org/10.1007/978-3-031-30634-1_1

BS91. Biham, E., Shamir, A.: Differential cryptanalysis of DES-like cryptosystems. J. Cryptology **4**(1), 3–72 (1991). https://doi.org/10.1007/BF00630563

CDJ+20. Chakraborti, A., Datta, N., Jha, A., Mancillas-López, C., Nandi, M., Sasaki, Y.: ESTATE: a lightweight and low energy authenticated encryption mode. IACR Trans. Symmetric Cryptology **350–389**, 2020 (2020)

CHP+17. Cid, C., Huang, T., Peyrin, T., Sasaki, Y., Song, L: A security analysis of Deoxys and its internal tweakable block ciphers. IACR Trans. Symmetric Cryptol. **2017**(3), 73–107 (2017)

CHP+18. Cid, C., Huang, T., Peyrin, T., Sasaki, Yu., Song, L.: Boomerang connectivity table: a new cryptanalysis tool. In: Nielsen, J.B., Rijmen, V. (eds.) EUROCRYPT 2018. LNCS, vol. 10821, pp. 683–714. Springer, Cham (2018). https://doi.org/10.1007/978-3-319-78375-8_22

DFJ13. Derbez, P., Fouque, P.-A., Jean, J.: Improved key recovery attacks on reduced-round , in the single-key setting. In: Johansson, T., Nguyen, P.Q. (eds.) EUROCRYPT 2013. LNCS, vol. 7881, pp. 371–387. Springer, Heidelberg (2013). https://doi.org/10.1007/978-3-642-38348-9_23

DKS10. Dunkelman, O., Keller, N., Shamir, A.: A practical-time related-key attack on the KASUMI cryptosystem used in GSM and 3G telephony. In: Rabin, T. (ed.) CRYPTO 2010. LNCS, vol. 6223, pp. 393–410. Springer, Heidelberg (2010). https://doi.org/10.1007/978-3-642-14623-7_21

DQSW22. Dong, X., Qin, L., Sun, S., Wang, X.: Key guessing strategies for linear key-schedule algorithms in rectangle attacks. In: Dunkelman, O., Dziembowski, S. (eds.) Advances in Cryptology - EUROCRYPT 2022. EUROCRYPT 2022, Part III, LNCS, vol. 13277, pp. 3–33. Springer, Cham (2022). https://doi.org/10.1007/978-3-031-07082-2_1

DR02. Daemen, J., Rijmen, V.: The design of Rijndael, vol. 2. Springer, Berlin (2002). https://doi.org/10.1007/978-3-662-60769-5

DS08. Demirci, H., Selçuk, A.A.: A meet-in-the-middle attack on 8-round AES. In: Nyberg, K. (ed.) FSE 2008. LNCS, vol. 5086, pp. 116–126. Springer, Heidelberg (2008). https://doi.org/10.1007/978-3-540-71039-4_7

HSE23. Hadipour, H., Sadeghi, S., Eichlseder, M.: Finding the impossible: automated search for full impossible-differential, zero-correlation, and integral attacks. In: Hazay, C., Stam, M. (eds.) Advances in Cryptology - EUROCRYPT 2023. EUROCRYPT 2023, Part IV, LNCS, vol. 14007, pp. 128–157. Springer, Cham (2023). https://doi.org/10.1007/978-3-031-30634-1_5

JNP14a. Jean, J., Nikolic, I., Peyrin, T.: KIASU v1. Submitted to the CAESAR competition (2014)

JNP14b. Jean, J., Nikolić, I., Peyrin, T.: Tweaks and keys for block ciphers: the TWEAKEY framework. In: Sarkar, P., Iwata, T. (eds.) ASIACRYPT 2014. LNCS, vol. 8874, pp. 274–288. Springer, Heidelberg (2014). https://doi.org/10.1007/978-3-662-45608-8_15

JNPS16. Jean, J., Nikolic, I., Peyrin, T., Seurin, Y.: Deoxys v1. 41. Submitted CAESAR **124** (2016)

JNPS21. Jean, J., Nikolić, I., Peyrin, T., Seurin, Y.: The deoxys aead family. J. Cryptology **34**(3), 31 (2021)

LJW15. Li, L., Jia, K., Wang, X.: Improved single-key attacks on 9-round AES-192/256. In: Cid, C., Rechberger, C. (eds.) FSE 2014. LNCS, vol. 8540, pp. 127–146. Springer, Heidelberg (2015). https://doi.org/10.1007/978-3-662-46706-0_7

MS+18. Moazami, F., Soleimany, H., et al. Impossible differential cryptanalysis on Deoxys-BC-256. Cryptology ePrint Archive (2018)

Mur11. Murphy, S.: The return of the cryptographic boomerang. IEEE Trans. Inf. Theor. **57**(4), 2517–2521 (2011)

Nik14. Nikolic, I.: Tiaoxin-346. Submission to the CAESAR competition (2014)

S+99. Data Encryption Standard et al. Data encryption standard. Federal Information Processing Standards Publication, vol. 112 (1999)

SZY+23. Song, L., et al.: Optimizing rectangle attacks: a unified and generic framework for key recovery. In: Agrawal, S., Lin, D. (eds.) Advances in Cryptology - ASIACRYPT 2022. ASIACRYPT 2022, Part I, LNCS, vol. 13791, pp. 410–440. Springer, Cham (2022). https://doi.org/10.1007/978-3-031-22963-3_14

Wag01. Wagner, D.: The boomerang attack. In: Knudsen, L. (ed.) FSE 1999. LNCS, vol. 1636, pp. 156–170. Springer, Heidelberg (1999). https://doi.org/10.1007/3-540-48519-8_12

ZDJ19. Zhao, B., Dong, X., Jia, K.: New related-tweakey boomerang and rectangle attacks on Deoxys-BC including BDT effect. IACR Trans. Symmetric Cryptol. **2019**(3), 121–151 (2019)

ZDJM19. Zhao, B., Dong, X., Jia, K., Meier, W.: Improved related-Tweakey rectangle attacks on reduced-round Deoxys-BC-384 and Deoxys-I-256-128. In: Hao, F., Ruj, S., Sen Gupta, S. (eds.) INDOCRYPT 2019. LNCS, vol. 11898, pp. 139–159. Springer, Cham (2019). https://doi.org/10.1007/978-3-030-35423-7_7

ZDW19. Zong, R., Dong, X., Wang, X.: Related-tweakey impossible differential attack on reduced-round Deoxys-BC-256. Sci. China Inf. Sci. **62**(3), 1–12 (2019). https://doi.org/10.1007/s11432-017-9382-2

PMACrx: A Vector-Input MAC for High-Dimensional Vectors with BBB Security

Isamu Furuya[1(✉)], Hayato Kasahara[2], Akiko Inoue[1], Kazuhiko Minematsu[1], and Tetsu Iwata[2]

[1] NEC, Kawasaki, Japan
isamu-furuya@nec.com
[2] Nagoya University, Nagoya, Japan

Abstract. At Eurocrypt 2006, Rogaway and Shrimpton presented the idea of vector-input MAC that accepts a vector consisting of variable-length bitstrings. They proposed S2V as a concrete instantiation of the vector-input MAC and S2V is more efficient than the classical method, encoding a vector into a single bitstring and then applying a conventional MAC such as CMAC. However, S2V severely limits the maximum number of elements in a vector. Moreover, the security is up to the birthday bound with respect to the block length of the underlying block cipher (i.e., $n/2$-bit security for n-bit block). To overcome these drawbacks, we use tweakable block ciphers (TBCs) and present a new vector-input MAC, called PMACrx, taking PMAC2x by List and Nandi (CT-RSA 2017) as the baseline scheme. Our proposal allows a significantly larger number of elements than S2V and enjoys the beyond-the-birthday-bound (BBB) security. PMACrx is more efficient than the encode-then-PMAC2x method with respect to the number of primitive calls, as in the case of S2V (where the comparison is made with CMAC).

Keywords: MAC · Vector · S2V · Tweakable block cipher

1 Introduction

A message authentication code (MAC) is a symmetric-key cryptographic function for ensuring the authenticity of a message. Conventional MACs such as CMAC [12] and PMAC [6,24] are defined over bitstrings, i.e., $\{0,1\}^*$. However, in many practical situations, data that we want to authenticate have specific formats or structures. One classical method to authenticate such data is to encode the target datum into a single bitstring and to apply a conventional MAC. For example, consider a vector B of bitstrings, such as $B = (11001, 01, 1011, 1, 000101101)$. One simple method to convert B into a single bitstring is (i) to prefix a bitstring $0^{|B_i|-1}1$ to each element B_i, where $|B_i|$ denotes the length of B_i, and (ii) to concatenate all the results[1]. In this way,

[1] This is a simple application of Elias gamma coding [9].

J. Shikata and H. Kuzuno (Eds.): IWSEC 2023, LNCS 14128, pp. 77–97, 2023.
https://doi.org/10.1007/978-3-031-41326-1_5

B is converted to 000011100101010001101111000000001000101101. We call the above method the encode-then-MAC method. While this always works in principle, there is a potential efficiency loss because of the encoding process. This problem was first studied by Rogaway and Shrimpton at Eurocrypt 2006 (RS06) [25]. They considered vectors, namely lists of variable-length bitstrings, and proposed a *vector-input MAC*, called S2V, the first MAC dedicated to vector structured data. In this paper, we call a MAC a vector-input MAC if it takes vector format data as input and processes more efficiently than the encode-then-MAC method using the baseline MAC. S2V consists of an arbitrary bitstring-input MAC such that $F_K : \{0,1\}^* \rightarrow \{0,1\}^n$, and is more efficient than the encode-then-MAC method using F_K. RS06 presented a concrete instantiation of S2V, where F_K is implemented by CMAC. Furthermore, they designed a seminal misuse-resistant authenticated encryption called SIV using this CMAC-based vector-input MAC. From now on, we refer to the above CMAC-based instantiation as S2V.

While S2V shows a clear efficiency advantage over the encode-then-MAC method, it has two practical drawbacks. First, it accepts at most $n-1$ elements (the number of bitstrings in a vector), where n is the block length. Second, assuming the underlying block cipher is a pseudo-random permutation, RS06 proved that S2V is secure, but the security bound is $O(\sigma^2/2^n)$ for total σ input blocks. This implies that S2V has $n/2$-bit security, also called up-to-the-birthday-bound (upBB) security. UpBB security could be a practical issue if n is not large enough, as in legacy ciphers (e.g., TDES) or modern lightweight block ciphers, such as PRESENT [7] or GIFT [3], whose block lengths are relatively small, 64 bits or even smaller, due to implementation efficiency. Even in the case of $n = 128$ (e.g., AES), it might be insufficient in the future, as suggested by the public comments responding to NIST's review on FIPS 197 that specifies AES [1]. We also remark that while generic SIV constructions of RS06 have attracted significant interest, the idea of the vector-input MAC has received much less attention despite its potential usefulness. A follow-up work by Minematsu [18] also suffers the same drawback as S2V. Hirose, Kuwakado and Yoshida [11] proposed another vector-input MAC that allows a large number of elements; however, the security is still up to the birthday bound and the keyed function to process each vector element is serial.

Our Contributions. In this paper, we propose a new vector-input MAC that overcomes the aforementioned drawbacks of S2V: the number of maximum elements and the upBB security. Instead of conventional block ciphers, we use tweakable block ciphers (TBCs) [15], which generally enables us to achieve stronger security efficiently and achieve beyond-the-birthday-bound (BBB) security. TBC is known to be a powerful primitive and often enables the security level of what is difficult to achieve (or possible but inefficiently) with conventional block ciphers. A famous example is OCB and its TBC-based idealization (ΘCB3) [14], where the former is up to birthday bound secure ($n/2$-bit) while the latter has n-bit security. Our work is to show this phenomenon in the constructions of vector-input MAC. Taking the PMAC2x by List and Nandi [16,17] as the baseline TBC-based MAC, we present PMACrx, a vector-input MAC that accepts a much larger number of elements than S2V and enjoys n-bit (BBB) security. Note that the original PMAC2x has a flaw [20], and we adopt the fixed version [16].

The core idea of PMAC*rx* is the use of multiplications by multiple field constants in the two n-bit chaining values to represent the end of the element; PMAC2x uses a single constant for one chaining value and the other value is just an XOR of all TBC outputs (See Fig. 3). This technique allows PMAC*rx* to reduce the number of TBC calls over the encode-then-MAC method using PMAC2x while preserving n-bit security. Thus, PMAC*rx* satisfies the above definition of the vector-input MAC, i.e., it is more efficient than the baseline bitstring-input MAC. The number of acceptable elements of PMAC*rx* (represented as a parameter $r_{\max}$ in this paper) depends on the maximum number of blocks in each element (a parameter $m_{\max}$) and $r_{\max}$ is in the range of 2^{10} to 2^{24} if the block length of TBC is $n = 128$. This is much larger than the number of acceptable elements of S2V: 127. Each element can also be very large; $m_{\max} = 2^{100}$ or more, thus there is no practical utility loss compared to S2V.

Proving the security of PMAC*rx* requires analysis of collision probabilities on chaining values. This analysis is the most involved part of our security proof since we have to consider a pair of distinct vectors rather than bitstrings; the former requires significantly more cases in how they differ. This previous work considered only the cases where j is in a small range (at most 2^{10}). This parameter j corresponds to $r_{\max}$ in PMAC*rx*, and thus we study an extended analysis. We conduct a computer-based search to show a set of acceptable lists for $(m_{\max}, r_{\max})$, which could be used for other applications.

2 Preliminaries

2.1 Basic Notations

Let $[i]$ be $\{1, 2, \cdots, i\}$ and $[i..j]$ denote $\{i, i+1, \ldots, j\}$ for integers $i < j$. For a set S, an element $a = a_1, a_2, \cdots, a_n$ ($a_i \in S$) of S^* is called a *sequence*, where $|a| = n$ denotes its *length*. For clarity, we sometimes write the sequence as $(a_1, a_2, \cdots, a_n)$ with parentheses. Conversely, we omit the symbols if it seems clear and represent as in $a_1 a_2 \cdots a_n$. A sequence obtained by arbitrarily deleting elements from a is called a *subsequence* of a. For example, $a_1 a_3 a_4$ is a subsequence of $a_1 a_2 a_3 a_4 a_5$.

A sequence of bits $\{0,1\}^*$ is called a *bitstring*. A bitstring of length 0 is called an *empty bitstring*. Let $B_1 \parallel \cdots \parallel B_m \xleftarrow{n} B$ mean that a bitstring B is partitioned by every n bits into m bitstrings $B_1, \cdots, B_m$. In this paper, a *vector* means a sequence of bitstrings, namely, $B = (B_1, B_2, \cdots, B_n)$ is a vector, where each B_i is a bitstring and called an *element* or *dimension* of B. Even if an element B_i is empty, we regard it as a single element. For example, let ε be an empty bitstring, then we understand that (B_1, B_2, ε) and (B_1, B_2) are distinct vectors.

In this paper, we assume that arithmetic operations are defined over $\mathrm{GF}(2^n)$ and we use $x^{128} + x^7 + x^2 + x + 1$ as the primitive polynomial for $n = 128$, which is commonly used in other designs. We write polynomials x and $x+1$ over $\mathrm{GF}(2^n)$ as 2 and 3, respectively, following [24].

2.2 (Tweakable) Block Cipher

Let $\mathcal{K}$ be a key space and let B and B' be bitstrings such that $B, B' \in \{0,1\}^n$. Then, a keyed permutation E over $\{0,1\}^n$ with an arbitrarily key $K \in \mathcal{K}$ such that $E(K, B) = B'$ is called a *block cipher*, where n denotes its *block length*.

A *tweakable block cipher (TBC)* [15] is an extension of a block cipher that accepts an additional value called a *tweak*. Namely, let $\mathcal{T}$ be a tweak space, then TBC is a keyed permutation $\tilde{E}$ over $\{0,1\}^n$ with arbitrarily key $K \in \mathcal{K}$ and tweak $T \in \mathcal{T}$ such that $\tilde{E}(K, T, B) = B'$. Hereinafter, we use the symbol n as the block length of TBC (or block cipher) used in the target structure. Moreover, let $\tilde{E}_K^T$ mean a TBC $\tilde{E}$ using a key K and a tweak T. That is, we write $\tilde{E}(K, T, B) = B'$ as $\tilde{E}_K^T(B) = B'$.

2.3 MAC

A *MAC (message authentication code)* is a symmetric-key cryptographic function ensuring data authenticity. MAC functions can be implemented as modes of block cipher (or TBC) operations. A MAC is a keyed function F_K such that $F_K(X) = Y$, where K is a key, X is a bitstring of variable length, and Y is a bitstring of fixed length. Specifically, the input bitstring is called a *message*, and the output bitstring is called a *tag*.

The practical operation of message authentication is as follows. For the target message X, we generate a tag Y such that $F_K(X) = Y$ with a MAC F in advance. We store the message and tag, but the original X and Y may have been modified while we store them. Let the possibly modified message and tag be X' and Y', respectively. Then, we generate a tag $\hat{Y}$ such that $F_K(X') = \hat{Y}$ and compare $\hat{Y}$ with Y'. If $Y' = \hat{Y}$, then $(X, Y) = (X', Y')$ holds with high confidence, implying that the original message is authenticated. Otherwise, $(X, Y) \neq (X', Y')$ always holds, implying that the original message or tag has been modified.

2.4 Security Notions and Proof Techniques [5]

An *adversary* is a probabilistic polynomial time algorithm with access to a real or ideal oracle. After a given number of queries, an adversary estimates whether the queried oracle is real or ideal and outputs a bit 0 or 1 that indicates the distinguished value. The correspondence between bits and oracles can be either if it is agreed in advance.

Tweakable Block Cipher. To define the security notion for TBC, we define $\mathcal{T} \times \{0,1\}^n \rightarrow \{0,1\}^n$ as a *tweakable permutation*. This is a permutation on $\{0,1\}^n$ if we determine $T \in \mathcal{T}$. A *TRP (tweakable random permutation)*, denoted as $\widetilde{\mathsf{P}}$, is a random variable that is uniformly distributed over the set of all tweakable permutations. The security notion of TBC $\tilde{E}$, which is called *TPRP (tweakable pseudo-random permutation)*, is defined as the indistinguishability between $\tilde{E}$ and $\widetilde{\mathsf{P}}$ under chosen plaintext attack and thus defined as follows.

$$\mathbf{Adv}_{\tilde{E}}^{\mathsf{TPRP}}(\mathcal{A}) := |\Pr[\mathcal{A}^{\tilde{E}} \Rightarrow 1] - \Pr[\mathcal{A}^{\widetilde{\mathsf{P}}} \Rightarrow 1]|,$$

MAC Security. UF-CMA (unforgeability under chosen message attack) is the standard security notion for MAC. An upper bound of UF-CMA of a MAC F is evaluated by PRF advantage $\mathbf{Adv}_F^{\mathsf{PRF}}(\mathcal{A})$ defined as follows.

$$\mathbf{Adv}_F^{\mathsf{PRF}}(\mathcal{A}) := |\Pr[\mathcal{A}^{\mathfrak{R}} \Rightarrow 1] - \Pr[\mathcal{A}^{\mathfrak{I}} \Rightarrow 1]|,$$

where $\mathfrak{R}$ is a real oracle that implements F and returns the outputs of F for queries and $\mathfrak{I}$ is an ideal oracle that returns uniformly random values irrespective of queries (assuming $\mathcal{A}$ makes no repeating queries). $\Pr[\mathcal{A}^{\mathfrak{R}} \Rightarrow 1]$ (or $\Pr[\mathcal{A}^{\mathfrak{R}} \Rightarrow 1]$) means the probability that $\mathcal{A}$ with access to $\mathfrak{R}$ (or $\mathfrak{I}$) outputs 1 as the distinguished value. This probability is determined by the randomness of $\mathfrak{R}$ itself and the randomness generated internally by $\mathcal{A}$ as necessary.

H-Coefficient. H-Coefficient [8,22] is known as a common proof technique for modes of operations. We show notations and a lemma of the H-Coefficient technique used in this paper in the following Definition 1 and Lemma 1. For example, we can find the proof of Lemma 1 in [8].

Definition 1 (Transcript and attainable set). *Let $\mathcal{A}$ be an adversary who uses q queries to a real oracle $\mathfrak{R}$ or an ideal oracle $\mathfrak{I}$. Let X_i be the i-th query that $\mathcal{A}$ uses and Y_i be the corresponding output from the oracle. Then, a* transcript *is the sequence of (X_i, Y_i) in the query order, such as $(X_1, Y_1), \ldots, (X_q, Y_q)$.*

Let $\Theta^{\mathfrak{I}}$ be a random variable generated by $\mathcal{A}$ and $\mathfrak{I}$, and S be a set of possible values of a transcript. Then, we say that a subset of S is attainable *and denote it by S^a, if $\mathsf{S}^a = \{\tau \in \mathsf{S} : \Pr[\Theta^{\mathfrak{I}} = \tau] > 0\}$ holds.*

Lemma 1. *Let $\mathcal{A}$ be an adversary who queries a real oracle $\mathfrak{R}$ or an ideal oracle $\mathfrak{I}$, and $\Theta^{\mathfrak{R}}$ and $\Theta^{\mathfrak{I}}$ be random variables of transcripts generated by $\mathcal{A}$ with $\mathfrak{R}$ and $\mathfrak{I}$, respectively. Assume that the attainable set of transcripts is partitionable into two exclusive subsets E_{good} and E_{bad}. Here, if $\frac{\Pr[\Theta^{\mathfrak{R}}=\tau]}{\Pr[\Theta^{\mathfrak{I}}=\tau]} \geq 1 - \epsilon_1$ and $\Pr[\Theta^{\mathfrak{I}} \in E_{\text{bad}}] \leq \epsilon_2$ for $\epsilon_1, \epsilon_2 \in [0, 1]$ and any $\tau \in E_{\text{good}}$, then $\mathbf{Adv}_F^{\mathsf{PRF}}(\mathcal{A}) \leq \epsilon_1 + \epsilon_2$ holds.*

3 Proposed Method

3.1 Baseline Bitstring-Input MAC

We present a vector-input MAC taking the PMAC2x by List and Nandi [16,17] as the baseline TBC-based MAC. PMAC2x is a refinement of Naito's proposals [21]. It is based on TBC and has a beyond-the-birthday-bound; more concretely, it achieves n-bit security with n-bit block TBCs. It is parallelizable and requires one TBC call to process an n-bit input block. As stated in Sect. 1, we adopt the fixed version [16] instead of the original one [20]. We show the structure of PMAC2x in Fig. 3 in Appendix B.

3.2 PMACrx

Our proposal PMACrx accepts a vector $M = (M^1, \cdots, M^r)$ ($M^i \in \{0,1\}^*$), where r is the (variable) number of elements, as input message and outputs a tag of length $2n$ bits. In this paper, we assume that each M^i is preprocessed by injective encoding, and the bit length is aligned to a multiple of n, the block length. For example, each M^i is changed to $M^i 10^{n-q-1}$, where q is a nonnegative integer such that $pn + q = |M^i|$ with a nonnegative integer p.

The procedure of PMACrx is as follows. Firstly, each element M^i is divided into blocks of n bits each. Let $M^i[j]$ be the j-th block and m^i be the number of generated blocks, i.e., $M^i = M^i[1], \cdots, M^i[m^i]$. For each M^i, let $Z^i[j]$ be the output obtained by inputting $M^i[j]$ into TBC $\tilde{E}_K^{0,i,j}$, i.e., $Z^i[j] = \tilde{E}_K^{0,i,j}(M^i[j])$, and Z^i be the sequence of these outputs in ascending order by j, i.e., $Z^i = Z^i[1], \cdots, Z^i[m^i]$. Let $X^i = \bigoplus_{1 \le j \le m^i} Z^i[j]$ and $Y^i = \bigoplus_{1 \le j \le m^i} 2^{m^i - j + 1} Z^i[j]$. Each $Z^i[j]$ is n bits, and then X^i and Y^i are also n bits each. Hereinafter, we denote the function to derive (X^i, Y^i) from M^i as described above by H^i and write it as $H_K^i(M^i) = (X^i, Y^i)$ with a key K. We illustrate the structure of the function H^i in Fig. 1. Let $V = \bigoplus_{1 \le i \le r} X^i$ and $W = \bigoplus_{1 \le i \le r} 3^{r-i+1} Y^i$. Here, X^i and Y^i are n bits each, and then V and W are also n bits each. We denote the function to derive (V, W) from M by G and write it as $G_K(M)$. Let $U = \tilde{E}_K^{1,W,r}(V)$ and $L = \tilde{E}_K^{2,V,r}(W)$. We call the procedure of deriving (U, L) from (V, W) *finalization*[2], and call a TBC composing the procedure a *finalization TBC*.

PMACrx consists of the above $G_K(M)$ and the finalization procedure. Finalization TBCs have n-bit input/output, and then U and L are bitstrings of n bits each. PMACrx finally outputs the pair (U, L) as a MAC tag of $2n$ bits. We illustrate the structures of the function G and the finalization in Fig. 2. We show the entire procedure of PMACrx in Algorithm 1.

3.3 Analysis of Acceptable Parameters for Input Vectors

As stated in the previous Sect. 3.2, PMACrx performs multiplications by 2 and 3 in the calculation of the chaining value W. To prove the security of PMACrx in Sect. 4, we have to determine possible ranges of i and j so that $2^i 3^j$ in GF(2^{128}) are all distinct values. One possible such range was shown in [24], and it is $(i, j) \in [-2^{115}..2^{115}] \times [-2^{10}..2^{10}]$. However, we consider that this range of j is not large enough to demonstrate the practical usefulness of PMACrx adequately. This section analyzes j in a larger range and shows the results.

Let $m_{\max}$ be the maximum block length of each element in the input vector, and $r_{\max}$ be the maximum number of elements in the input vector. For any $(i, j), (i', j') \in [-m_{\max}..m_{\max}] \times [-r_{\max}..r_{\max}]$ and $(i, j) \ne (i', j')$, we require $2^i 3^j \ne 2^{i'} 3^{j'}$ in GF(2^{128}). Let $\alpha = i - i'$, and $\beta = j - j'$, and we calculate

[2] PMAC2x uses a regular function Conv (see, Fig. 3) for the case that the length of the tweak is less than n bits. In our method, the length of the tweak is always n bits, and we leave out the function.

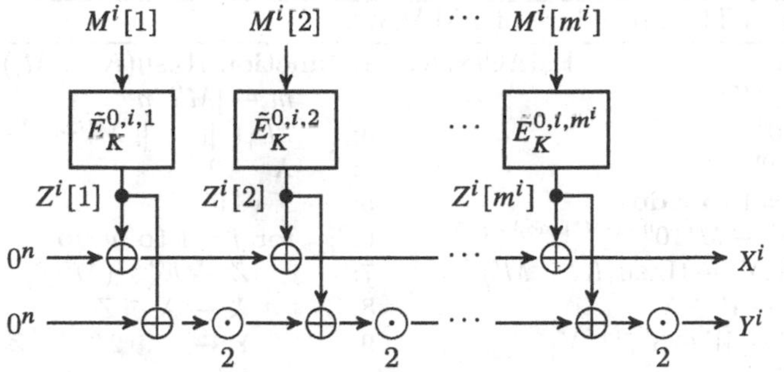

Fig. 1. The structure of the function H^i, where $\odot$ with 2 is a multiplication by 2 in $\mathrm{GF}(2^n)$. This corresponds to HASH in Algorithm 1.

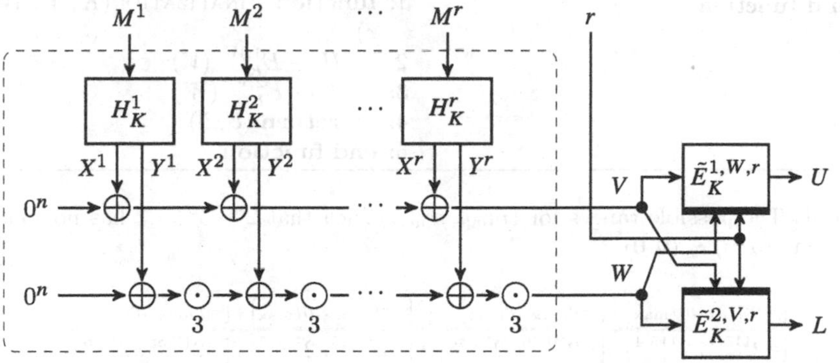

Fig. 2. The structures of the function G and the finalization, where $\odot$ with 3 is a multiplication by 3 in $\mathrm{GF}(2^n)$. The area surrounded by the dashed line corresponds to the function G.

their ranges such that $2^\alpha \cdot 3^\beta = 1$ has no solution other than $(\alpha, \beta) = (0, 0)$ in the same way as [24]. We present the results in Table 1. Note that we limit the maximum value of β to 2^{25} at most, namely $r_{\max} \leq 2^{24}$, because of the computational resources since the method of [24] needs an exponential time of the maximum value of β. Our results may be enough for practical applications such as authenticating the sequences of database entries. Still, if one needs a larger $r_{\max}$, we can take a different approach, such as one based on lattice reduction shown in the remark of Sect. 3.5 in [10]. Hereinafter, we assume that $(m_{\max}, r_{\max})$ is selected based on the ranges shown in Table 1.

4 Security of PMACrx

The proof basically follows those of similar designs [17,21]. However, the bad event probability analysis, which is essentially bounding several types of collision probabilities on the chaining values, needs to consider significantly more cases as we deal with vectors instead of bitstrings. Here, we define oracles and show

Algorithm 1. The procedure of PMACrx.

1: **function** PMACrx(K, $(M^1, \cdots, M^r)$)
2:     $V \leftarrow 0^n$
3:     $W \leftarrow 0^n$
4:     **for** $i = 1$ to r **do**
5:         $M' \leftarrow M^i 10^{n-(|M^i| \bmod n)-1}$
6:         $(X, Y) \leftarrow$ Hash(K, i, M')
7:         $V \leftarrow V \oplus X$
8:         $W \leftarrow W \oplus 3^{r-i+1} Y$
9:     **end for**
10:     $(U, L) \leftarrow$ Finalization(K, V, W, r)
11:     **return** (U, L)
12: **end function**

1: **function** Hash(K, i, M')
2:     $m \leftarrow |M'|/n$
3:     $M'[1] \| \cdots \| M'[m] \overset{n}{\leftarrow} M'$
4:     $X \leftarrow 0^n$
5:     $Y \leftarrow 0^n$
6:     **for** $j = 1$ to m **do**
7:         $Z \leftarrow \tilde{E}_K^{0,i,j}(M'[j])$
8:         $X \leftarrow X \oplus Z$
9:         $Y \leftarrow Y \oplus 2^{m-j+1} Z$
10:     **end for**
11:     **return** (X, Y)
12: **end function**

1: **function** Finalization(K, V, W, r)
2:     $U \leftarrow \tilde{E}_K^{1,W,r}(V)$
3:     $L \leftarrow \tilde{E}_K^{2,V,r}(W)$
4:     **return** (U, L)
5: **end function**

Table 1. The possible ranges for $(m_{\max}, r_{\max})$ such that $2^\alpha \cdot 3^\beta = 1$ has no solution other than $(\alpha, \beta) = (0, 0)$.

$[-m_{\max}..m_{\max}]$	$[-r_{\max}..r_{\max}]$	$[-m_{\max}..m_{\max}]$	$[-r_{\max}..r_{\max}]$
$[-2^{115.1}..2^{115.1}]$	$[-2^{10.40}..2^{10.40}]$	$[-2^{107.5}..2^{107.5}]$	$[-2^{17.55}..2^{17.55}]$
$[-2^{114.5}..2^{114.5}]$	$[-2^{11.00}..2^{11.00}]$	$[-2^{107.3}..2^{107.3}]$	$[-2^{18.50}..2^{18.50}]$
$[-2^{113.5}..2^{113.5}]$	$[-2^{11.70}..2^{11.70}]$	$[-2^{105.0}..2^{105.0}]$	$[-2^{20.70}..2^{20.70}]$
$[-2^{113.4}..2^{113.4}]$	$[-2^{12.40}..2^{12.40}]$	$[-2^{104.9}..2^{104.9}]$	$[-2^{20.90}..2^{20.90}]$
$[-2^{108.4}..2^{108.4}]$	$[-2^{17.50}..2^{17.50}]$	$[-2^{100.2}..2^{100.2}]$	$[-2^{24.00}..2^{24.00}]$

the security bound of PMACrx in Theorem 1, which implies PMACrx achieves BBB security. In the subsequent parts, we show some lemmas and then present the proof of the theorem.

The function G in PMACrx consists of a TBC. Here, we consider an idealized version of G using a TRP instead of a TBC and denote it by $\tilde{G}$. Moreover, let us denote a PMACrx implementation consisting of $\tilde{G}$ by $\mathcal{F}$.

Definition 2. (Real and Ideal oracles $\mathcal{R}$ and $\mathcal{I}$). *Suppose adversary $\mathcal{A}$ who uses q queries with no time complexity restriction. Let $\mathcal{R}$ be an oracle that accepts M as an input (query), returns the output of $\mathcal{F}$ denoted by (U, L), and returns $(V_1, W_1), \ldots, (V_q, W_q)$ after q queries made by $\mathcal{A}$, where each (V_i, W_i) is the output of $\tilde{G}$ for the i-th input M_i. Let ρ be an ideal random function that accepts a vector of the same format as the one accepted by $\mathcal{F}$ and returns a bitstring of length $2n$ bits. Then, let $\mathcal{I}$ be an oracle that accepts M as input, returns* *the output of $\rho(M)$ denoted by (U, L), and returns $(V_1, W_1), \ldots, (V_q, W_q)$ after q queries, where each (V_i, W_i) is the output of $\tilde{G}$ for the i-th input M_i.*

Note that the internal (V, W) tuples are only given to the adversary after all queries are made; hence the adversary cannot make further queries. This is a common technique to reduce proof complexity.

Theorem 1. *Let $\mathcal{A}$ be an adversary against $\mathcal{F}$ who uses q queries to either $\mathcal{R}$ or $\mathcal{I}$. Then, $\mathbf{Adv}_{\mathcal{F}}^{\mathsf{PRF}}(\mathcal{A}) \leq \frac{3q^2}{2^{2n}}$ holds.*

This security bound is for the idealized version of PMACrx, where the underlying TBC $\tilde{E}$ is replaced by a TRP. We can derive the security bound when using TBC by adding the term $\mathbf{Adv}_{\tilde{E}}^{\mathsf{TPRP}}(\mathcal{A}')$ to the above bound, where the resource of $\mathcal{A}'$ is determined by that of $\mathcal{A}$.

For simplicity, we assume that adversaries in the following proofs do not repeat the same query. Such an assumption does not affect the results because of the definitions for oracles (Definition 2). We prove Theorem 1 following H-Coefficient technique shown in Sect. 2. We show necessary propositions in the following Lemmas 2 to 5.

By Definition 2, the adversary $\mathcal{A}$ in Theorem 1 obtains $(V_1, W_1), \ldots, (V_q, W_q)$ after using q queries, regardless of whether $\mathcal{A}$ queries $\mathcal{R}$ or $\mathcal{I}$. Hereinafter, we use $\tau = \tau_1\tau_2\cdots\tau_q$, a sequence of $\tau_i = (M_i, V_i, W_i, U_i, L_i)$, as the transcript and let $\Theta^{\mathcal{R}}$ and $\Theta^{\mathcal{I}}$ be random variables of transcripts obtained from $\mathcal{R}$ and $\mathcal{I}$, respectively.

Definition 3 (Bad events). *Let E_{bad1}, E_{bad2}, and E_{bad3} be sets of transcripts such that there exist (i, j) satisfying conditions as follows.*

E_{bad1}: $r_i = r_j$ *and* $V_i = V_j$ *and* $W_i = W_j$,
E_{bad2}: $r_i = r_j$ *and* $V_i \neq V_j$ *and* $W_i = W_j$ *and* $U_i = U_j$,
E_{bad3}: $r_i = r_j$ *and* $V_i = V_j$ *and* $W_i \neq W_j$ *and* $L_i = L_j$,

where r_i is the number of elements in the vector M_i. E_{bad} denotes their union set, namely, $E_{\text{bad}} = E_{\text{bad1}} \cup E_{\text{bad2}} \cup E_{\text{bad3}}$. An element of E_{bad} is called a bad event. *In contrast, an attainable transcript other than a bad event is called a* good event, *where E_{good} denotes the set consisting of all of them.*

Here, E_{bad1} denotes the simultaneous collision in the two chaining values (V and W). E_{bad2} and E_{bad3} denote an impossible input/output tuple for the real oracle. Since the tweak in the finalization takes r, we only need to define these bad events for the vectors of the identical number of elements.

In the following Lemma 2 and 3, we present the collision probabilities on chaining values represented by V and W. The results are required to prove the bad event probability, which we show in Lemma 4.

Lemma 2. *Let $M = (M^1, \cdots, M^r)$ and $\tilde{M} = (\tilde{M}^1, \cdots, \tilde{M}^r)$ be distinct vectors with the same number of elements r, and let $G_K(M) = (V, W)$ and $G_K(\tilde{M}) = (\tilde{V}, \tilde{W})$. Then, $\Pr[(V, W) = (\tilde{V}, \tilde{W})] \leq 2/2^{2n}$ holds.*

Proof. Let m^i and $\tilde{m}^i$ be the number of blocks of each M^i and $\tilde{M}^i$, respectively. Below we show that $\Pr[(V,W) = (\tilde{V}, \tilde{W})] \leq 1/(2^n - 1)^2$ by dividing it into cases. Here, we can assume that n is large enough, namely, $n \geq 2$. Thus,

$$2^{2n} - 4 \cdot 2^n + 2 = (2^n - 2)^2 - 2 \geq 0 \iff 1/(2^n - 1)^2 \leq 2/2^{2n} \tag{1}$$

holds, and the proposition is then shown.

Case 1. There exists only one i such that $M^i \neq \tilde{M}^i$. We further divide this case into the following Case 1.1 and 1.2.

Case 1.1. $\tilde{m}^i = m^i + 1$. In this case, we have

$$\begin{aligned} X^i &= Z^i[1] \oplus \cdots \oplus Z^i[m^i], \quad \tilde{X}^i = \tilde{Z}^i[1] \oplus \cdots \oplus \tilde{Z}^i[m^i] \oplus \tilde{Z}^i[m^i+1], \\ Y^i &= 2^{m^i-1+1} Z^i[1] \oplus \cdots \oplus 2^{m^i-m^i+1} Z^i[m^i], \\ \tilde{Y}^i &= 2^{m^i-1+2} \tilde{Z}^i[1] \oplus \cdots \oplus 2^{m^i-m^i+2} \tilde{Z}^i[m^i] \oplus 2^{m^i-(m^i+1)+2} \tilde{Z}^i[m^i+1]. \end{aligned}$$

Thus, the following holds.

$$V = \tilde{V} \iff X^i \oplus \tilde{X}^i = 0^n \iff \bigoplus_{1 \leq \ell \leq m^i} (Z^i[\ell] \oplus \tilde{Z}^i[\ell]) \oplus \tilde{Z}^i[m^i+1] = 0^n, \tag{2}$$

$$\begin{aligned} W = \tilde{W} &\iff 3^{r-i+1} Y^i \oplus 3^{r-i+1} \tilde{Y}^i = 0^n \\ &\iff \bigoplus_{1 \leq \ell \leq m^i} (2^{m^i-\ell+1} Z^i[\ell] \oplus 2^{m^i-\ell+2} \tilde{Z}^i[\ell]) \oplus 2^1 \tilde{Z}^i[m^i+1] = 0^n. \end{aligned} \tag{3}$$

We can derive $\Pr[(V,W) = (\tilde{V}, \tilde{W})]$ from the probability that (2) and (3) hold. Below we consider the probability by dividing into Case 1.1.1 and 1.1.2. Note that the argument here similarly holds if $m^i = \tilde{m}^i + 1$.

Case 1.1.1. $M^i[\ell] = \tilde{M}^i[\ell]$ for any ℓ such that $1 \leq \ell \leq m^i$. In this case,

$$\begin{aligned} (2) &\iff \tilde{Z}^i[m^i+1] = 0^n, \\ (3) &\iff \bigoplus_{1 \leq \ell \leq m^i} (2^{m^i-\ell+1} \oplus 2^{m^i-\ell+2}) \tilde{Z}^i[\ell] \oplus 2^1 \tilde{Z}^i[m^i+1] = 0^n \end{aligned} \tag{4}$$

hold. If we arbitrarily fix the elements of $\tilde{Z}^i$ except $\tilde{Z}^i[m^i]$ and $\tilde{Z}^i[m^i+1]$,

$$(4) \iff (2^1 \oplus 2^2) \tilde{Z}^i[m^i] \oplus 2^1 \tilde{Z}^i[m^i+1] = \mathtt{Cst}$$

holds, where $\mathtt{Cst}$ is a constant. Thus, $\begin{bmatrix} 0 & 1 \\ 2^2 \oplus 2^1 & 2 \end{bmatrix} \begin{bmatrix} \tilde{Z}^i[m^i] \\ \tilde{Z}^i[m^i+1] \end{bmatrix} = \begin{bmatrix} 0^n \\ \mathtt{Cst} \end{bmatrix}$ holds. Since the coefficient matrix on the left side above is regular, its inverse exists. Hence, we have $\begin{bmatrix} \tilde{Z}^i[m^i] \\ \tilde{Z}^i[m^i+1] \end{bmatrix} = \begin{bmatrix} 0 & 1 \\ 2^2 \oplus 2^1 & 2 \end{bmatrix}^{-1} \begin{bmatrix} 0^n \\ \mathtt{Cst} \end{bmatrix}$. This implies that only one such $(\tilde{Z}^i[m^i], \tilde{Z}^i[m^i+1])$ exists. Since both $\tilde{Z}^i[m^i]$ and $\tilde{Z}^i[m^i+1]$ take 2^n possible values, the probability that (2) and (3) hold is at most $1/(2^n \cdot 2^n)$.

Case 1.1.2. $\boldsymbol{M^i[\ell] \neq \tilde{M}^i[\ell]}$ **for at least one** $\boldsymbol{\ell}$ **such that** $\boldsymbol{1 \leq \ell \leq \tilde{m}^i}$**.** If we arbitrarily fix the elements of $\tilde{Z}^i$ except $\tilde{Z}^i[\ell]$ and $\tilde{Z}^i[m^i+1]$, we have

$$
\begin{aligned}
&(2) \iff \tilde{Z}^i[\ell] \oplus \tilde{Z}^i[m^i+1] = \mathtt{Cst},\\
&(3) \iff 2^{m^i-\ell+1}\tilde{Z}^i[\ell] \oplus 2^1\tilde{Z}^i[m^i+1] = \mathtt{Cst}',
\end{aligned}
$$

where $\mathtt{Cst}$ and $\mathtt{Cst}'$ are constants. Similar to Case 1.1.1, we find that there exists only one $(\tilde{Z}^i[\ell], \tilde{Z}^i[m^i+1])$ such that the above two hold simultaneously. Note that the number of possible values of $\tilde{Z}^i[\ell]$ is $2^n - 1$ since it does not overlap with the fixed $Z^i[\ell]$, while $\tilde{Z}^i[m^i+1]$ takes 2^n possible values. Therefore, the probability that (2) and (3) hold is at most $1/(2^n(2^n-1))$.

Case 1.2. $\boldsymbol{\tilde{m}^i \geq m^i + 2}$**.** In this case,

$$
\begin{aligned}
&X^i = Z^i[1] \oplus \cdots \oplus Z^i[m^i],\ \ \tilde{X}^i = \tilde{Z}^i[1] \oplus \cdots \oplus \tilde{Z}^i[m^i] \oplus \cdots \oplus \tilde{Z}^i[\tilde{m}^i-1] \oplus \tilde{Z}^i[\tilde{m}^i],\\
&Y^i = 2^{m^i-1+1}Z^i[1] \oplus \cdots \oplus 2^{m^i-m^i+1}Z^i[m^i],\\
&\tilde{Y}^i = 2^{\tilde{m}^i-1+1}\tilde{Z}^i[1] \oplus \cdots \oplus 2^{\tilde{m}^i-m^i+1}\tilde{Z}^i[m^i] \oplus \cdots \oplus 2^2\tilde{Z}^i[\tilde{m}^i-1] \oplus 2^1\tilde{Z}^i[\tilde{m}^i].
\end{aligned}
$$

Thus, we have

$$
V = \tilde{V} \iff \bigoplus_{1\leq\ell\leq m^i} (Z^i[\ell] \oplus \tilde{Z}^i[\ell]) \oplus \cdots \oplus \tilde{Z}^i[\tilde{m}^i-1] \oplus \tilde{Z}^i[\tilde{m}^i] = 0^n, \tag{5}
$$

$$
\begin{aligned}
W = \tilde{W} \iff &\bigoplus_{1\leq\ell\leq m^i} (2^{m^i-\ell+1}Z^i[\ell] \oplus 2^{\tilde{m}^i-\ell+1}\tilde{Z}^i[\ell]) \oplus \cdots\\
&\oplus 2^2\tilde{Z}^i[\tilde{m}^i-1] \oplus 2^1\tilde{Z}^i[\tilde{m}^i] = 0^n.
\end{aligned} \tag{6}
$$

If we arbitrarily fix the elements of Z^i and $\tilde{Z}^i$ except $\tilde{Z}^i[\tilde{m}^i-1]$ and $\tilde{Z}^i[\tilde{m}^i]$,

$$
(5) \iff \tilde{Z}^i[\tilde{m}^i-1] \oplus \tilde{Z}^i[\tilde{m}^i] = \mathtt{Cst},\quad (6) \iff 2^2\tilde{Z}^i[\tilde{m}^i-1] \oplus 2^1\tilde{Z}^i[\tilde{m}^i] = \mathtt{Cst}'
$$

hold, where $\mathtt{Cst}$ and $\mathtt{Cst}'$ are constants. Therefore, similarly to Case 1.1.1, the probability that (5) and (6) hold is at most $1/(2^n \cdot 2^n)$. Note that the argument here similarly holds if $m^i \geq \tilde{m}^i + 2$.

Case 1.3. $\tilde{m}^i = m^i$. In this case,

$$
\begin{aligned}
&X^i = Z^i[1] \oplus \cdots \oplus Z^i[m^i],\ \ Y^i = 2^{m^i-1+1}Z^i[1] \oplus \cdots \oplus 2^{m^i-m^i+1}Z^i[m^i],\\
&\tilde{X}^i = \tilde{Z}^i[1] \oplus \cdots \oplus \tilde{Z}^i[m^i],\ \ \tilde{Y}^i = 2^{m^i-1+1}\tilde{Z}^i[1] \oplus \cdots \oplus 2^{m^i-m^i+1}\tilde{Z}^i[m^i].
\end{aligned}
$$

Thus, we have

$$
V = \tilde{V} \iff \bigoplus_{1\leq\ell\leq m^i} (Z^i[\ell] \oplus \tilde{Z}^i[\ell]) = 0^n, \tag{7}
$$

$$
W = \tilde{W} \iff \bigoplus_{1\leq\ell\leq m^i} (2^{m^i-\ell+1}Z^i[\ell] \oplus 2^{m^i-\ell+1}\tilde{Z}^i[\ell]) = 0^n. \tag{8}
$$

Below we consider the probability (7) and (8) hold by dividing into Case 1.3.1 and 1.3.2.

Case 1.3.1. There exists only one different block. Let ℓ be the index of the different block (i.e., $M^i[\ell] \neq \tilde{M}^i[\ell]$). Then, we have

$$(7) \iff Z^i[\ell] \oplus \tilde{Z}^i[\ell] = 0^n,$$

$$(8) \iff 2^{m^i-\ell+1} Z^i[\ell] \oplus 2^{m^i-\ell+1} \tilde{Z}^i[\ell] = 0^n \iff Z^i[\ell] \oplus \tilde{Z}^i[\ell] = 0^n.$$

Therefore, (7) and (8) hold simultaneously only if there exists $(Z^i[\ell], \tilde{Z}^i[\ell])$ such that $Z^i[\ell] = \tilde{Z}^i[\ell]$. However, this contradicts the assumption that $M^i[\ell] \neq \tilde{M}^i[\ell]$. Hence, the probability that (7) and (8) hold is 0.

Case 1.3.2. There exist two or more different blocks. Let ℓ and s ($\ell \leq s$) be the indices of the different blocks (i.e., $M^i[\ell] \neq \tilde{M}^i[\ell]$ and $M^i[s] \neq \tilde{M}^i[s]$). If we arbitrarily fix the elements of Z^i and $\tilde{Z}^i$ except $Z^i[\ell]$, $\tilde{Z}^i[\ell]$, $Z^i[s]$, and $\tilde{Z}^i[s]$, then we have

$$(7) \iff (Z^i[\ell] \oplus \tilde{Z}^i[\ell]) \oplus (Z^i[s] \oplus \tilde{Z}^i[s]) = \texttt{Cst},$$

$$(8) \iff 2^{m^i-\ell+1}(Z^i[\ell] \oplus \tilde{Z}^i[\ell]) \oplus 2^{m^i-s+1}(Z^i[s] \oplus \tilde{Z}^i[s]) = \texttt{Cst}',$$

where $\texttt{Cst}$ and $\texttt{Cst}'$ are constants. Since $m_{\max}$ is appropriately selected, there exists only one $(Z^i[\ell] \oplus \tilde{Z}^i[\ell], Z^i[s] \oplus \tilde{Z}^i[s])$ such that the above two hold simultaneously and the number of possible values of such $(Z^i[\ell], \tilde{Z}^i[\ell], Z^i[s], \tilde{Z}^i[s])$ is $2^n \cdot 1 \cdot 2^n \cdot 1 = 2^{2n}$. Note that $Z^i[\ell] \neq \tilde{Z}^i[\ell]$ and $Z^i[s] \neq \tilde{Z}^i[s]$, by the assumption, then the probability that (7) and (8) hold is at most $2^{2n}/(2^n(2^n-1)2^n(2^n-1)) = 1/(2^n-1)^2$.

Case 2. There exist i and j ($i < j$) such that $M^i \neq \tilde{M}^i$ and $M^j \neq \tilde{M}^j$. If we arbitrarily fix X, $\tilde{X}$, Y, and $\tilde{Y}$ except X^i, $\tilde{X}^i$, Y^i, $\tilde{Y}^i$, X^j, $\tilde{X}^j$, Y^j, and $\tilde{Y}^j$,

$$V = \tilde{V} \iff X^i \oplus X^j \oplus \tilde{X}^i \oplus \tilde{X}^j = \texttt{Cst}, \tag{9}$$

$$W = \tilde{W} \iff 3^{r-i+1}Y^i \oplus 3^{r-j+1}Y^j \oplus 3^{r-i+1}\tilde{Y}^i \oplus 3^{r-j+1}\tilde{Y}^j = \texttt{Cst}' \tag{10}$$

hold, where $\texttt{Cst}$ and $\texttt{Cst}'$ are constants. Below we consider the probability that (9) and (10) hold by dividing into Case 2.1 to Case 2.4.

Case 2.1. $\tilde{m}^i > m^i$ and $\tilde{m}^j > m^j$. If we arbitrarily fix the elements of Z and $\tilde{Z}$ except $\tilde{Z}^i[\tilde{m}^i]$ and $\tilde{Z}^j[\tilde{m}^j]$, we have

$$(9) \iff \tilde{Z}^i[\tilde{m}^i] \oplus \tilde{Z}^j[\tilde{m}^j] = \texttt{Cst},$$

$$(10) \iff 3^{r-i+1}2^1\tilde{Z}^i[\tilde{m}^i] \oplus 3^{r-j+1}2^1\tilde{Z}^j[\tilde{m}^j] = \texttt{Cst}',$$

where $\texttt{Cst}$ and $\texttt{Cst}'$ are constants (that possibly different from the constants in (9) and (10)). Similar to Case 1.3.2, since $r_{\max}$ is appropriately selected, there exists only one $(\tilde{Z}^i[\tilde{m}^i], \tilde{Z}^i[\tilde{m}^j])$ such that the above two hold simultaneously. Since both $\tilde{Z}^i[\tilde{m}^i]$ and $\tilde{Z}^i[\tilde{m}^j]$ take 2^n possible values, the probability that (9) and (10) hold is at most $1/(2^n \cdot 2^n)$.

Case 2.2. $\tilde{m}^i > m^i$ and $\tilde{m}^j < m^j$. If we arbitrarily fix the elements of Z and $\tilde{Z}$ except $Z^j[m^j]$ and $\tilde{Z}^i[\tilde{m}^i]$, we have

$$(9) \iff \tilde{Z}^i[\tilde{m}^i] \oplus Z^j[m^j] = \texttt{Cst},$$

$$(10) \iff 3^{r-i+1}2^1\tilde{Z}^i[\tilde{m}^i] \oplus 3^{r-j+1}2^1 Z^j[m^j] = \texttt{Cst}',$$

where Cst and Cst′ are constants. Similarly to Case 2.1, the probability that (9) and (10) hold is at most $1/(2^n \cdot 2^n)$.

Case 2.3. $\tilde{m}^i > m^i$ **and** $\tilde{m}^j = m^j$. For M^j and $\tilde{M}^j$, let s be the index of the different block (i.e., $M^j[s] \neq \tilde{M}^j[s]$), and assume that we arbitrarily fix the elements of $\tilde{Z}^i[\tilde{m}^i]$ and $\tilde{Z}^j[s]$ except $\tilde{Z}$ and Z. Then, we have

$$\begin{aligned}(9) &\iff \tilde{Z}^i[\tilde{m}^i] \oplus \tilde{Z}^j[s] = \mathtt{Cst},\\ (10) &\iff 3^{r-i+1}2^1\tilde{Z}^i[\tilde{m}^i] \oplus 3^{r-j+1}2^{\tilde{m}^j-s+1}\tilde{Z}^j[s] = \mathtt{Cst}',\end{aligned}$$

where Cst and Cst′ are constants, and thus

$$\begin{bmatrix} 1 & 1 \\ 3^{r-i+1}2^1 & 3^{r-j+1}2^{\tilde{m}^j-s+1}\end{bmatrix}\begin{bmatrix}\tilde{Z}^i[\tilde{m}^i] \\ \tilde{Z}^j[s]\end{bmatrix} = \begin{bmatrix}\mathtt{Cst} \\ \mathtt{Cst}'\end{bmatrix} \tag{11}$$

holds. If the coefficient matrix on the left side is not regular, then $3^{r-j+1}2^{\tilde{m}^j-s+1} \oplus 3^{r-i+1}2^1 = 0 \iff 3^{i-j}2^{\tilde{m}^j-s} = 1$ holds. However, by the assumption, $(m_{\max}, r_{\max})$ is selected based on the ranges shown in Table 1, then there is no $(i, j, \tilde{m}^j, s)$ that satisfies the above. Therefore, the coefficient matrix is regular, and then there exists only one $(\tilde{Z}^i[\tilde{m}^i], \tilde{Z}^j[s])$ such that (11) holds. Note that the number of possible values of $\tilde{Z}^i[s]$ is $2^n - 1$ since it does not overlap with the fixed $Z^i[s]$, while $\tilde{Z}^i[m^i+1]$ takes 2^n possible values. Hence, the probability that (9) and (10) hold is at most $1/(2^n(2^n-1))$.

Case 2.4. $\tilde{m}^i = m^i$ **and** $\tilde{m}^j = m^j$. Let ℓ and s be the indices of the different blocks for M^i and $\tilde{M}^i$, and M^j and $\tilde{M}^j$, respectively, (i.e., $M^i[\ell] \neq \tilde{M}^i[\ell]$, $M^j[s] \neq \tilde{M}^j[s]$), and assume that we arbitrarily fix the elements of Z and $\tilde{Z}$ except $Z^i[\ell]$, $\tilde{Z}^i[\ell]$, $Z^j[s]$, and $\tilde{Z}^j[s]$. Then, we have

$$\begin{aligned}(9) &\iff (Z^i[\ell] \oplus \tilde{Z}^i[\ell]) \oplus (Z^j[s] \oplus \tilde{Z}^j[s]) = \mathtt{Cst},\\ (10) &\iff 3^{r-i+1}2^{m^i-\ell+1}(Z^i[\ell] \oplus \tilde{Z}^i[\ell]) \oplus 3^{r-j+1}2^{m^j-s+1}(Z^j[s] \oplus \tilde{Z}^j[s]) = \mathtt{Cst}',\end{aligned}$$

where Cst and Cst′ are constants. Similarly to Case 2.3, the probability that (9) and (10) hold is at most $1/(2^n-1)^2$. □

Lemma 3. *Let* $M = (M^1, \cdots, M^r)$ *and* $\tilde{M} = (\tilde{M}^1, \cdots, \tilde{M}^r)$ *be distinct vectors with the same number of elements r, and let* $G_K(M) = (V, W)$ *and* $G_K(\tilde{M}) = (\tilde{V}, \tilde{W})$. *Then,* $\Pr[V = \tilde{V}] \leq 1/(2^n - 1)$ *and* $\Pr[W = \tilde{W}] \leq 1/(2^n - 1)$ *hold.*

The proposition can be proved in the same way as Lemma 2 and we relegate the proof to Appendix A.

Lemma 4. $\Pr[\Theta^I \in E_{\mathrm{bad}}] \leq 3q^2/2^{2n}$ *holds.*

Proof. By Definition 3, for the left-hand side,

$$\Pr[\Theta^I \in E_{\mathrm{bad}}] \leq \Pr[\Theta^I \in E_{\mathrm{bad1}}] + \Pr[\Theta^I \in E_{\mathrm{bad2}}] + \Pr[\Theta^I \in E_{\mathrm{bad3}}] \tag{12}$$

holds. Below we show an upper bound of each term on the right-hand side of (12) and prove that their sum is bounded by $3q^2/2^{2n}$.

(i) $\Pr[\Theta^{\mathcal{I}} \in E_{\text{bad1}}]$. In this case, for i and j $(i \neq j)$, the input and the tweak for the finalization TBC are the same (i.e., $V_i = V_j$ and $W_i = W_j$) but the outputs are different (i.e., $U_i \neq U_j$ or $L_i \neq L_j$). Hence, by Lemma 2, the following holds.

$$\Pr[\Theta^{\mathcal{I}} \in E_{\text{bad1}}] \leq \sum_{i,j} \Pr[V_i = V_j \wedge W_i = W_j] \leq \sum_{i,j} 2/2^{2n} \leq q^2/2^{2n} \quad (\text{by } i \leq j \leq q).$$

(ii) $\Pr[\Theta^{\mathcal{I}} \in E_{\text{bad2}}]$. In this case, for i and j $(i \neq j)$, the tweaks for the finalization TBC are the same and the inputs are different (i.e., $W_i = W_j$ and $V_i \neq V_j$), but the outputs are partially the same (i.e., $U_i = U_j$). Hence, by Lemma 3 and (1) in Lemma 2, the following holds.

$$\begin{aligned}\Pr[\Theta^{\mathcal{I}} \in E_{\text{bad2}}] &\leq \sum_{i,j} \Pr[W_i = W_j \wedge U_i = U_j] \leq \sum_{i,j} (1/(2^n - 1) \cdot 1/2^n) \\ &\leq \sum_{i,j} 1/(2^n - 1)^2 \leq \sum_{i,j} 2/2^{2n} \leq q^2/2^{2n} \quad (\text{by } i \leq j \leq q)\end{aligned}$$

(iii) $\Pr[\Theta^{\mathcal{I}} \in E_{\text{bad3}}]$. In this case, for i and j $(i \neq j)$, the tweaks for the finalization TBC are the same and the inputs are different (i.e., $V_i = V_j$ and $W_i \neq W_j$), but the outputs are partially the same (i.e., $L_i = L_j$). Therefore, similarly to (ii), $\Pr[\Theta^{\mathcal{I}} \in E_{\text{bad3}}] \leq q^2/2^{2n}$ holds.

Thus, by the above (i) to (iii), the proposition holds. □

Lemma 5. *For any* $\tau \in E_{\text{good}}$, $\frac{\Pr[\Theta^{\mathcal{R}}=\tau]}{\Pr[\Theta^{\mathcal{I}}=\tau]} \geq 1$ *holds.*

Proof. For each $\tau_i = (M_i, V_i, W_i, U_i, L_i)$ in a transcript $\tau = \tau_1\tau_2\cdots\tau_q$, let $\dot{\tau}_i = (M_i, V_i, W_i)$ and $\ddot{\tau}_i = (U_i, L_i)$, $\dot{\tau}$ and $\ddot{\tau}$ be their sequences in query order, respectively. That is, $\dot{\tau} = \dot{\tau}_1\dot{\tau}_2\cdots\dot{\tau}_q$ and $\ddot{\tau} = \ddot{\tau}_1\ddot{\tau}_2\cdots\ddot{\tau}_q$.

Let $\Theta^{\mathcal{R}}_i$ and $\Theta^{\mathcal{I}}_i$ be random variables of transcripts corresponding to each i-th query for $\mathcal{R}$ and $\mathcal{I}$, respectively. Furthermore, similarly to the above $\dot{\tau}_i$ and $\ddot{\tau}_i$, let us define $\dot{\Theta}^{\mathcal{R}}_i$, $\ddot{\Theta}^{\mathcal{R}}_i$, $\dot{\Theta}^{\mathcal{I}}_i$, and $\ddot{\Theta}^{\mathcal{I}}_i$ for (M_i, V_i, W_i) and (U_i, L_i), and $\dot{\Theta}^{\mathcal{R}}$, $\ddot{\Theta}^{\mathcal{R}}$, $\dot{\Theta}^{\mathcal{I}}$, and $\ddot{\Theta}^{\mathcal{I}}$ be their sequences in query order, respectively. That is, $\dot{\Theta}^{\mathcal{R}} = \dot{\Theta}^{\mathcal{R}}_1\dot{\Theta}^{\mathcal{R}}_2\cdots\dot{\Theta}^{\mathcal{R}}_q$, $\ddot{\Theta}^{\mathcal{R}} = \ddot{\Theta}^{\mathcal{R}}_1\ddot{\Theta}^{\mathcal{R}}_2\cdots\ddot{\Theta}^{\mathcal{R}}_q$, $\dot{\Theta}^{\mathcal{I}} = \dot{\Theta}^{\mathcal{I}}_1\dot{\Theta}^{\mathcal{I}}_2\cdots\dot{\Theta}^{\mathcal{I}}_q$, and $\ddot{\Theta}^{\mathcal{I}} = \ddot{\Theta}^{\mathcal{I}}_1\ddot{\Theta}^{\mathcal{I}}_2\cdots\ddot{\Theta}^{\mathcal{I}}_q$.

By Definition 2, the probability distribution of (M_i, V_i, W_i) is the same for both $\mathcal{R}$ and $\mathcal{I}$, thus $\Pr[\dot{\Theta}^{\mathcal{R}} = \dot{\tau}] = \Pr[\dot{\Theta}^{\mathcal{I}} = \dot{\tau}]$ holds. Hence, for the left-hand side of the proposition, we obtain as follows.

$$\frac{\Pr[\Theta^{\mathcal{R}} = \tau]}{\Pr[\Theta^{\mathcal{I}} = \tau]} = \frac{\Pr[\dot{\Theta}^{\mathcal{R}} = \dot{\tau}]\Pr[\ddot{\Theta}^{\mathcal{R}} = \ddot{\tau} \mid \dot{\Theta}^{\mathcal{R}} = \dot{\tau}]}{\Pr[\dot{\Theta}^{\mathcal{I}} = \dot{\tau}]\Pr[\ddot{\Theta}^{\mathcal{I}} = \ddot{\tau} \mid \dot{\Theta}^{\mathcal{I}} = \dot{\tau}]} = \frac{\Pr[\ddot{\Theta}^{\mathcal{R}} = \ddot{\tau} \mid \dot{\Theta}^{\mathcal{R}} = \dot{\tau}]}{\Pr[\ddot{\Theta}^{\mathcal{I}} = \ddot{\tau} \mid \dot{\Theta}^{\mathcal{I}} = \dot{\tau}]}. \quad (13)$$

Here, for real oracle $\mathcal{R}$,

$$\Pr[\ddot{\Theta}^{\mathcal{R}} = \ddot{\tau} \mid \dot{\Theta}^{\mathcal{R}} = \dot{\tau}] = \prod_{i=1}^{q} \Pr[\ddot{\Theta}^{\mathcal{R}}_i = \ddot{\tau}_i \mid \dot{\Theta}^{\mathcal{R}}_i = \dot{\tau}_i, \ddot{\Theta}^{\mathcal{R}}_1 = \ddot{\tau}_1, \cdots, \ddot{\Theta}^{\mathcal{R}}_{i-1} = \ddot{\tau}_{i-1}] \quad (14)$$

holds. This similarly holds even if the order of elements τ_i is changed.

If the number of elements in M_i is different, then the tweak for finalization TBC always differs. This implies that the probability $\Pr[\ddot{\Theta}_i^{\mathcal{R}} = \ddot{\tau}_i \mid \dot{\Theta}_i^{\mathcal{R}} = \dot{\tau}_i, \ddot{\Theta}_1^{\mathcal{R}} = \ddot{\tau}_1, \cdots, \ddot{\Theta}_{i-1}^{\mathcal{R}} = \ddot{\tau}_{i-1}]$ in (14) is independent of another probability if r_i is different (note that r_i denotes the number of elements in M_i and can be obtained from τ_i). Let $\dot{\tau}^k$ be a subsequence of $\dot{\tau}$ consisting of all $\dot{\tau}_i$ such that $r_i = k$, and let $\ddot{\tau}^k$, $\dot{\Theta}^{\mathcal{R},k}$, and $\ddot{\Theta}^{\mathcal{R},k}$ be similar subsequences for $\ddot{\tau}$, $\dot{\Theta}^{\mathcal{R}}$, and $\ddot{\Theta}^{\mathcal{R}}$, respectively. Then, from (14) we have $\prod_{k \in \mathbf{r}} \Pr[\ddot{\Theta}^{\mathcal{R},k} = \ddot{\tau}^k \mid \dot{\Theta}^{\mathcal{R},k} = \dot{\tau}^k]$, where $\mathbf{r}$ is a subset of $\{r_1, \cdots, r_q\}$ obtained by selecting all elements that differ from each other[3].

The above discussion similarly holds for $\mathcal{I}$. Hence, with (13), we have

$$\prod_{k \in \mathbf{r}} \frac{\Pr[\ddot{\Theta}^{\mathcal{R},k} = \ddot{\tau}^k \mid \dot{\Theta}^{\mathcal{R},k} = \dot{\tau}^k]}{\Pr[\ddot{\Theta}^{\mathcal{I},k} = \ddot{\tau}^k \mid \dot{\Theta}^{\mathcal{I},k} = \dot{\tau}^k]}. \tag{15}$$

Let J^k be a subsequence of the index sequence of τ obtained by deleting all i such that $r_i \neq k$, where q^k denotes the length of J^k. Then,

$$\begin{aligned}\Pr[\ddot{\Theta}^{\mathcal{R},k} = \ddot{\tau}^k \mid \dot{\Theta}^{\mathcal{R},k} = \dot{\tau}^k] &\geq \prod_{j \in J^k} \Pr[E_K^{1,W_j,k}(V_j) = U_j] \Pr[E_K^{2,V_j,k}(W_j) = L_j] \\ &\geq \left(\frac{1}{2^n}\right)^{q^k} \left(\frac{1}{2^n}\right)^{q^k}\end{aligned} \tag{16}$$

holds. Whereas, for the same J^k,

$$\Pr[\ddot{\Theta}^{\mathcal{I},k} = \ddot{\tau}^k \mid \dot{\Theta}^{\mathcal{I},k} = \dot{\tau}^k] = \prod_{j \in J^k} \Pr[\rho(M_j) = U_j L_j] = \left(\frac{1}{2^{2n}}\right)^{q^k} \tag{17}$$

also holds. Recall that ρ is an ideal random function that $\mathcal{I}$ uses (Definition 2). Hence, by (16) and (17), we obtain $\frac{\Pr[\ddot{\Theta}^{\mathcal{R},k} = \ddot{\tau}^k \mid \dot{\Theta}^{\mathcal{R},k} = \dot{\tau}^k]}{\Pr[\ddot{\Theta}^{\mathcal{I},k} = \ddot{\tau}^k \mid \dot{\Theta}^{\mathcal{I},k} = \dot{\tau}^k]} \geq \frac{\left(\frac{1}{2^n}\right)^{q^k} \left(\frac{1}{2^n}\right)^{q^k}}{\left(\frac{1}{2^{2n}}\right)^{q^k}} = 1$.

By this and (15), the proposition holds. □

Proof. (***Proof of Theorem*** 1). By Lemma 4, $\Pr[\Theta_{\mathcal{I}} \in E_{\text{bad}}] \leq \frac{3q^2}{2^{2n}}$ holds, and by Lemma 5, $\frac{\Pr[\Theta^{\mathcal{R}} = \tau]}{\Pr[\Theta^{\mathcal{I}} = \tau]} \geq 1$ holds for any $\tau \in E_{\text{good}}$. By Definition 3, $E_{\text{good}} \cup E_{\text{bad}}$ is an attainable set, and E_{good} and E_{bad} are its exclusive subsets. Therefore, by Lemma 1, $\mathbf{Adv}_{\mathcal{F}}^{\mathsf{PRF}}(\mathcal{A}) \leq \frac{3q^2}{2^{2n}}$ holds. □

5 Extensions

For dedicated TBCs, the tweak length is usually a fixed parameter [2, 4]. Depending on the parameters $(m_{\max}, r_{\max})$, it may be the case that the minimum tweak

[3] We use another notation $\mathbf{r}$ to emphasize that there is no duplicate in k, whereas the notation $\{r_1, \cdots, r_q\}$ also represents the same set as $\mathbf{r}$ in theory since duplicate elements in a set are regarded as the same ones.

length needed for the finalization exceeds that for the message hashing procedure (Hash of Algorithm 1). When this happens, we somehow need to extend the tweak length to run the finalization.

This issue can be overcome by applying XTX [19] or XT [13] (a CPA-secure version of XTX) to the finalization. For example, using a TBC of n-bit tweak, XTX can extend its tweak length to $2n$ bits by four additional TBC calls. The resulting TBC has n-bit security [13,19]; hence adopting XTX preserves the n-bit security of PMACrx. We can find more details about XTX in [19]. Concerning the proposed method, we execute the XOR operation among V, W, and values obtained by inputting r into TBCs. For example, the finalization could be $U = \tilde{E}_K^{1,W \oplus r_1}(V \oplus r_2)$ and $L = \tilde{E}_K^{2,V \oplus r_3}(W \oplus r_4)$, where $r_1 = \tilde{E}_K^{3,1}(r)$, $r_2 = \tilde{E}_K^{3,2}(r)$, $r_3 = \tilde{E}_K^{3,3}(r)$, and $r_4 = \tilde{E}_K^{3,4}(r)$. In this way, the number of TBCs in the finalization increases, but it is 4 regardless of r.

6 Conclusions

We have presented a vector-input MAC based on a TBC called PMACrx. Our scheme enables us to handle a significantly larger number of elements in the input vector and achieves stronger security (BBB security) than the existing known vector-input MAC, S2V. PMACrx is based on PMAC2x, and is more efficient than the method of encoding the input vector to a bitstring and then inputting it to PMAC2x. TBCs are known to be more powerful primitives than conventional block ciphers and are useful for constructing highly secure modes more easily than using block ciphers. In this paper, we have demonstrated it in the construction of a vector-input MAC.

PMACrx is the first TBC-based vector-input MAC, and several topics remain to be explored. For example, it uses an injective encoding to align the length of each element input to a TBC with n-bit block, which is wasted if the element length is already a multiple of n. Removing such (potentially) redundant calls will further improve efficiency while preserving n-bit security. In a broader context, designing authenticated encryption for vectors would be an interesting direction. By combining (a variant of) PMACrx with an appropriate TBC-based encryption scheme (e.g. one from SCT [23] or ZAE [13]), we can construct a deterministic authenticated encryption in the same manner as SIV. Extending the input format to other data structures would also be worth studying.

The proposed PMACrx outputs a tag of length $2n$ bits. This is derived from the structure of PMAC2x, but it is also possible to make it an n bits tag by using the structure based on PMACx [17]. Even in that case, n-bit security should be guaranteed since the knowledge that the adversary can obtain is also reduced.

In this paper, we construct vector-input MAC by using TBCs. If we want a (not tweakable) block cipher-based construction, further work is required. As introduced in Sect. 1, the encode-then MAC method is still one way to treat vector format data, and in such methods, BBB-security can be achieved simply by using BBB-secure MAC. In such schemes, we can achieve the objective of accepting vector input by applying an efficient block cipher-based MAC such as

PMAC_Plus [26] (note that the security of PMAC_Plus is $2n/3$-bit rather than n-bit and a simple comparison with PMACrx is difficult because of the difference in the primitives). Overall, there is little discussion about vector-input MAC at present. Ways to make vector-input MAC simpler and/or more efficient or the efficiency limitation are issues to be addressed in the future.

Acknowledgements. We thank the reviewers for their useful and interesting comments.

A Proof of Lemma 3

Proof. We prove only for $\Pr[V = \tilde{V}] \leq 1/(2^n - 1)$. Although there are some formal differences with respect to the inner coefficients 2 or 3, $\Pr[W = \tilde{W}] \leq 1/(2^n - 1)$ can be proved similarly to $\Pr[V = \tilde{V}] \leq 1/(2^n - 1)$.

Let m^i and $\tilde{m}^i$ be the number of blocks of each M^i and $\tilde{M}^i$, respectively. Below we show that $\Pr[V = \tilde{V}] \leq 1/(2^n - 1)$ by dividing into cases in the same way as the proof of Lemma 2.

Case 1. There exists only one i such that $M^i \neq \tilde{M}^i$.

Case 1.1. $\tilde{m}^i = m^{i+1}$. In this case, $X^i = Z^i[1] \oplus \cdots \oplus Z^i[m^i]$ and $\tilde{X}^i = \tilde{Z}^i[1] \oplus \cdots \oplus \tilde{Z}^i[m^i] \oplus \tilde{Z}^i[m^i + 1]$. Thus, we have

$$V = \tilde{V} \iff X^i \oplus \tilde{X}^i = 0^n \iff \bigoplus_{1 \leq \ell \leq m^i} (Z^i[\ell] \oplus \tilde{Z}^i[\ell]) \oplus \tilde{Z}^i[m^i + 1] = 0^n. \tag{18}$$

Case 1.1.1. $M^i[\ell] = \tilde{M}^i[\ell]$ for any ℓ such that $1 \leq \ell \leq m^i$. In this case, (18) $\iff \tilde{Z}^i[m^i + 1] = 0^n$ holds. Since $\tilde{Z}^i[m^i + 1]$ takes 2^n possible values, the probability that (18) holds is at most $1/2^n$.

Case 1.1.2. $M^i[\ell] \neq \tilde{M}^i[\ell]$ for at least one ℓ such that $1 \leq \ell \leq \tilde{m}^i$. If we arbitrarily fix the elements of Z^i and $\tilde{Z}^i$ except $\tilde{Z}^i[m^i + 1]$, we have (18) $\iff \tilde{Z}^i[m^i + 1] = \mathtt{Cst}$, where $\mathtt{Cst}$ is a constant. Since $\tilde{Z}^i[m^i + 1]$ takes 2^n possible values, the probability that (18) holds is at most $1/2^n$.

Case 1.2. $\tilde{m}^i \geq m^i + 2$. In this case, $X^i = Z^i[1] \oplus \cdots \oplus Z^i[m^i]$ and $\tilde{X}^i = \tilde{Z}^i[1] \oplus \cdots \oplus \tilde{Z}^i[m^i] \oplus \cdots \oplus \tilde{Z}^i[\tilde{m}^i - 1] \oplus \tilde{Z}^i[\tilde{m}^i]$. Thus,

$$V = \tilde{V} \iff \bigoplus_{1 \leq \ell \leq m^i} (Z^i[\ell] \oplus \tilde{Z}^i[\ell]) \oplus \cdots \oplus \tilde{Z}^i[\tilde{m}^i - 1] \oplus \tilde{Z}^i[\tilde{m}^i] = 0^n \tag{19}$$

holds. If we arbitrarily fix the elements of Z^i and $\tilde{Z}^i$ except $\tilde{Z}^i[\tilde{m}^i]$, we have (19) $\iff \tilde{Z}^i[\tilde{m}^i] = \mathtt{Cst}$, where $\mathtt{Cst}$ is a constant. Since $\tilde{Z}^i[\tilde{m}^i]$ takes 2^n possible values, the probability that (19) holds is at most $1/2^n$.

Case 1.3. $\tilde{m}^i = m^i$. In this case, $X^i = Z^i[1] \oplus \cdots \oplus Z^i[m^i]$ and $\tilde{X}^i = \tilde{Z}^i[1] \oplus \cdots \oplus \tilde{Z}^i[m^i]$. Thus,

$$V = \tilde{V} \iff \bigoplus_{1 \le \ell \le m^i} (Z^i[\ell] \oplus \tilde{Z}^i[\ell]) = 0^n. \qquad (20)$$

Case 1.3.1. There exists only one different block. Let ℓ be the index of the different block (i.e., $M^i[\ell] \neq \tilde{M}^i[\ell]$). Then, we have (20) $\iff Z^i[\ell] \oplus \tilde{Z}^i[\ell] = 0^n$. The above holds only if there exists $(Z^i[\ell], \tilde{Z}^i[\ell])$ such that $Z^i[\ell] = \tilde{Z}^i[\ell]$, but this contradicts the assumption that $M^i[\ell] \neq \tilde{M}^i[\ell]$. Therefore, the probability that (20) holds is 0.

Case 1.3.2. There are two or more different blocks. Let ℓ be one of the indices of the different blocks (i.e., $M^i[\ell] \neq \tilde{M}^i[\ell]$), and assume that we arbitrarily fix the elements of Z^i and $\tilde{Z}^i$ except $Z^i[\ell]$ and $\tilde{Z}^i[\ell]$. Then, we have (20) $\iff Z^i[\ell] \oplus \tilde{Z}^i[\ell] = \texttt{Cst}$, where $\texttt{Cst}$ is a constant. There exists only one $(Z^i[\ell], \tilde{Z}^i[\ell])$ that satisfies the above, and such $(Z^i[\ell], \tilde{Z}^i[\ell])$ takes $2^n \cdot 1 = 2^n$ possible values. By the assumption, $Z^i[\ell] \neq \tilde{Z}^i[\ell]$ holds and then $(Z^i[\ell], \tilde{Z}^i[\ell])$ takes $2^n(2^n - 1)$ possible values. Therefore, the probability that (20) holds is at most $2^n/(2^n(2^n - 1)) = 1/(2^n - 1)$.

Case 2. There exist i and j $(i < j)$ such that $M^i \neq \tilde{M}^i$ and $M^j \neq \tilde{M}^j$. If we arbitrarily fix X except X^i and $\tilde{X}^i$, we have

$$V = \tilde{V} \iff X^i \oplus X^j \oplus \tilde{X}^i \oplus \tilde{X}^j = \texttt{Cst}, \qquad (21)$$

where $\texttt{Cst}$ is a constant.

Case 2.1. $\tilde{m}^i > m^i$ and $\tilde{m}^j > m^j$ In this case, $X^i = Z^i[1] \oplus \cdots \oplus Z^i[m^i]$, $\tilde{X}^i = \tilde{Z}^i[1] \oplus \cdots \oplus \tilde{Z}^i[m^i] \oplus \cdots \oplus \tilde{Z}^i[\tilde{m}^i]$, $X^j = Z^j[1] \oplus \cdots \oplus Z^j[m^j]$, and $\tilde{X}^j = \tilde{Z}^j[1] \oplus \cdots \oplus \tilde{Z}^j[m^j] \oplus \cdots \oplus \tilde{Z}^j[\tilde{m}^j]$. If we arbitrarily fix Z and $\tilde{Z}$ except $\tilde{Z}^i[\tilde{m}^i]$ and $\tilde{Z}^j[\tilde{m}^j]$, we have (21) $\iff \tilde{Z}^i[\tilde{m}^i] \oplus \tilde{Z}^j[\tilde{m}^j] = \texttt{Cst}$, where $\texttt{Cst}$ is a constant. There exists only one $(Z^i[\tilde{m}^i], \tilde{Z}^j[\tilde{m}^j])$ that satisfies the above and such $(Z^i[\tilde{m}^i], \tilde{Z}^j[\tilde{m}^j])$ takes $2^n \cdot 1 = 2^n$ possible values, while $(Z^i[\tilde{m}^i], \tilde{Z}^j[\tilde{m}^j])$ takes $2^n \cdot 2^n$ possible values. Therefore, the probability that (21) holds is at most $2^n/(2^n \cdot 2^n) = 1/2^n$.

Case 2.2. $\tilde{m}^i > m^i$ and $\tilde{m}^j < m^j$ If we arbitrarily fix the elements of Z and $\tilde{Z}$ except $\tilde{Z}^i[\tilde{m}^i]$ and $Z^j[m^j]$, we have (21) $\iff \tilde{Z}^i[\tilde{m}^i] \oplus Z^j[m^j] = \texttt{Cst}$, where $\texttt{Cst}$ is a constant. Then, similarly to Case 2.1, the probability that (21) holds is at most $1/2^n$.

Case 2.3. $\tilde{m}^i > m^i$ and $\tilde{m}^j = m^j$ If we arbitrarily fix the elements of Z and $\tilde{Z}$ except $\tilde{Z}^i[\tilde{m}^i]$, we have (21) $\iff \tilde{Z}^i[\tilde{m}^i] = \texttt{Cst}$, where $\texttt{Cst}$ is a constant. Hence, the probability that (21) holds is at most $1/2^n$.

Case 2.4. $\tilde{m}^i = m^i$ and $\tilde{m}^j = m^j$ Let ℓ be one of the indices of the different blocks for M^i and $\tilde{M}^i$ (i.e., $M^i[\ell] \neq \tilde{M}^i[\ell]$), and assume that the elements of Z^i and $\tilde{Z}^i$ except $Z^i[\ell]$ and $\tilde{Z}^i[\ell]$. Then, we have (21) $\iff Z^i[\ell] \oplus \tilde{Z}^i[\ell] = \texttt{Cst}$, where $\texttt{Cst}$ is a constant. Therefore, similarly to Case 1.3.2, the probability that (21) holds is at most $1/(2^n - 1)$. □

B The structure of PMAC2x

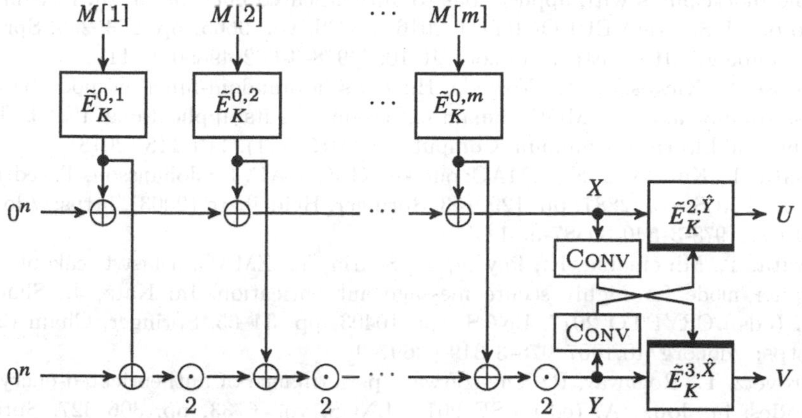

Fig. 3. The structure of PMAC2x [16,17], where $\odot$ with 2 is a multiplication by 2 in $GF(2^n)$), Conv is a regular function $\{0,1\}^n \to \{0,1\}^n$, and $\hat{X}$ and $\hat{Y}$ are the outputs of Conv for X and Y, respectively. Here, a function is called regular iff all outputs are produced by an equal number of inputs.

References

1. https://csrc.nist.gov/csrc/media/Projects/crypto-publication-review-project/documents/initial-comments/sp800-38a-initial-public-comments-2021.pdf
2. Avanzi, R.: The QARMA block cipher family. IACR Trans. Symm. Cryptol. **2017**(1), 4–44 (2017). https://doi.org/10.13154/tosc.v2017.i1.4-44
3. Banik, S., Pandey, S.K., Peyrin, T., Sasaki, Yu., Sim, S.M., Todo, Y.: GIFT: a small present. In: Fischer, W., Homma, N. (eds.) CHES 2017. LNCS, vol. 10529, pp. 321–345. Springer, Cham (2017). https://doi.org/10.1007/978-3-319-66787-4_16
4. Beierle, C., et al.: The SKINNY family of block ciphers and its low-latency variant MANTIS. In: Robshaw, M., Katz, J. (eds.) CRYPTO 2016. LNCS, vol. 9815, pp. 123–153. Springer, Heidelberg (2016). https://doi.org/10.1007/978-3-662-53008-5_5
5. Bellare, M., Desai, A., Jokipii, E., Rogaway, P.: A concrete security treatment of symmetric encryption. In: 38th FOCS, pp. 394–403. IEEE Computer Society Press, October 1997. https://doi.org/10.1109/SFCS.1997.646128
6. Black, J., Rogaway, P.: A block-cipher mode of operation for parallelizable message authentication. In: Knudsen, L.R. (ed.) EUROCRYPT 2002. LNCS, vol. 2332, pp. 384–397. Springer, Heidelberg (2002). https://doi.org/10.1007/3-540-46035-7_25
7. Bogdanov, A., et al.: PRESENT: an ultra-lightweight block cipher. In: Paillier, P., Verbauwhede, I. (eds.) CHES 2007. LNCS, vol. 4727, pp. 450–466. Springer, Heidelberg (2007). https://doi.org/10.1007/978-3-540-74735-2_31
8. Chen, S., Steinberger, J.: Tight security bounds for key-alternating ciphers. In: Nguyen, P.Q., Oswald, E. (eds.) EUROCRYPT 2014. LNCS, vol. 8441, pp. 327–350. Springer, Heidelberg (2014). https://doi.org/10.1007/978-3-642-55220-5_19

9. Elias, P.: Universal codeword sets and representations of the integers. IEEE Trans. Inf. Theory **21**(2), 194–203 (1975). https://doi.org/10.1109/TIT.1975.1055349
10. Granger, R., Jovanovic, P., Mennink, B., Neves, S.: Improved masking for tweakable blockciphers with applications to authenticated encryption. In: Fischlin, M., Coron, J.-S. (eds.) EUROCRYPT 2016. LNCS, vol. 9665, pp. 263–293. Springer, Heidelberg (2016). https://doi.org/10.1007/978-3-662-49890-3_11
11. Hirose, S., Kuwakado, H., Yoshida, H.: A Pseudorandom-function mode based on lesamnta-lw and the MDP domain extension and its applications. IEICE Trans. Fundam. Electron. Commun. Comput. Sci. **101-A**(1), 110–118 (2018)
12. Iwata, T., Kurosawa, K.: OMAC: one-key CBC MAC. In: Johansson, T. (ed.) FSE 2003. LNCS, vol. 2887, pp. 129–153. Springer, Heidelberg (2003). https://doi.org/10.1007/978-3-540-39887-5_11
13. Iwata, T., Minematsu, K., Peyrin, T., Seurin, Y.: ZMAC: a fast tweakable block cipher mode for highly secure message authentication. In: Katz, J., Shacham, H. (eds.) CRYPTO 2017. LNCS, vol. 10403, pp. 34–65. Springer, Cham (2017). https://doi.org/10.1007/978-3-319-63697-9_2
14. Krovetz, T., Rogaway, P.: The software performance of authenticated-encryption modes. In: Joux, A. (ed.) FSE 2011. LNCS, vol. 6733, pp. 306–327. Springer, Heidelberg (2011). https://doi.org/10.1007/978-3-642-21702-9_18
15. Liskov, M., Rivest, R.L., Wagner, D.: Tweakable block ciphers. J. Cryptology **24**(3), 588–613 (2011). https://doi.org/10.1007/s00145-010-9073-y
16. List, E., Nandi, M.: Revisiting full-PRF-secure PMAC and using it for beyond-birthday authenticated encryption. Cryptology ePrint Archive, Report 2016/1174 (2016). https://eprint.iacr.org/2016/1174
17. List, E., Nandi, M.: Revisiting Full-PRF-secure PMAC and using it for beyond-birthday authenticated encryption. In: Handschuh, H. (ed.) CT-RSA 2017. LNCS, vol. 10159, pp. 258–274. Springer, Cham (2017). https://doi.org/10.1007/978-3-319-52153-4_15
18. Minematsu, K.: A short universal hash function from bit rotation, and applications to blockcipher modes. In: Susilo, W., Reyhanitabar, R. (eds.) ProvSec 2013. LNCS, vol. 8209, pp. 221–238. Springer, Heidelberg (2013). https://doi.org/10.1007/978-3-642-41227-1_13
19. Minematsu, K., Iwata, T.: Tweak-length extension for tweakable blockciphers. In: Groth, J. (ed.) IMACC 2015. LNCS, vol. 9496, pp. 77–93. Springer, Cham (2015). https://doi.org/10.1007/978-3-319-27239-9_5
20. Minematsu, K., Iwata, T.: Cryptanalysis of pmacx, pmac2x, and sivx. IACR Trans. Symm. Cryptol. **2017**(2), 162–176 (2017). https://doi.org/10.13154/tosc.v2017.i2.162-176
21. Naito, Y.: Full PRF-secure message authentication code based on tweakable block cipher. In: Au, M.-H., Miyaji, A. (eds.) ProvSec 2015. LNCS, vol. 9451, pp. 167–182. Springer, Cham (2015). https://doi.org/10.1007/978-3-319-26059-4_9
22. Patarin, J.: The "Coefficients H" technique. In: Avanzi, R.M., Keliher, L., Sica, F. (eds.) SAC 2008. LNCS, vol. 5381, pp. 328–345. Springer, Heidelberg (2009). https://doi.org/10.1007/978-3-642-04159-4_21
23. Peyrin, T., Seurin, Y.: Counter-in-tweak: authenticated encryption modes for tweakable block ciphers. In: Robshaw, M., Katz, J. (eds.) CRYPTO 2016. LNCS, vol. 9814, pp. 33–63. Springer, Heidelberg (2016). https://doi.org/10.1007/978-3-662-53018-4_2

24. Rogaway, P.: Efficient instantiations of tweakable blockciphers and refinements to modes OCB and PMAC. In: Lee, P.J. (ed.) ASIACRYPT 2004. LNCS, vol. 3329, pp. 16–31. Springer, Heidelberg (2004). https://doi.org/10.1007/978-3-540-30539-2_2
25. Rogaway, P., Shrimpton, T.: A provable-security treatment of the key-wrap problem. In: Vaudenay, S. (ed.) EUROCRYPT 2006. LNCS, vol. 4004, pp. 373–390. Springer, Heidelberg (2006). https://doi.org/10.1007/11761679_23
26. Yasuda, K.: A new variant of PMAC: beyond the birthday bound. In: Rogaway, P. (ed.) CRYPTO 2011. LNCS, vol. 6841, pp. 596–609. Springer, Heidelberg (2011). https://doi.org/10.1007/978-3-642-22792-9_34

Public Key Cryptography

A New Security Analysis Against MAYO and QR-UOV Using Rectangular MinRank Attack

Hiroki Furue[1(✉)] and Yasuhiko Ikematsu[2(✉)]

[1] Department of Mathematical Informatics, The University of Tokyo, 7-3-1, Hongo, Bunkyo-ku, Tokyo, Japan
furue-hiroki261@g.ecc.u-tokyo.ac.jp

[2] Institute of Mathematics for Industry, Kyushu University, 744, Motooka, Nishi-ku, Fukuoka, Japan
ikematsu@imi.kyushu-u.ac.jp

Abstract. Multivariate public-key cryptography (MPKC) is considered as one of the main candidates for post-quantum cryptography (PQC). In MPKC, the MinRank attacks, which try to solve the MinRank problem obtained from a public key, are important since a lot of multivariate schemes are broken by these attacks. Among them, the rectangular MinRank attack was recently proposed for the Rainbow scheme by Beullens, and it tries to solve a new kind of MinRank problem obtained by transforming the public key of Rainbow. Due to this attack, it is known that the security level of Rainbow was reduced. Rainbow is a multi-layered variant of the UOV scheme, and UOV has a resistance to all MinRank attacks since it does not have a structure of MinRank problem. Recently, there have been proposed two new variants of the UOV scheme having a small public key, MAYO and QR-UOV. In this paper, we show that the rectangular MinRank is applicable to new variants MAYO and QR-UOV. Moreover, we estimate the complexity of the attack.

Keywords: post-quantum cryptography · multivariate public-key cryptography · UOV · QR-UOV · MAYO · MinRank attack

1 Introduction

Multivariate public-key cryptography (MPKC) [8] is considered as one of the main candidates for post-quantum cryptography (PQC) [2]. A lot of multivariate schemes have been proposed so far, and the UOV signature scheme [13], which was proposed by Kipnis et al. in 1999, is considered as a secure multivariate scheme.

Rainbow [9] is an improved signature scheme obtained by layering the structure of UOV, and was proposed by Ding et al. in 2005. Since Rainbow has more complicated structure than UOV, there exist a lot of attacks against Rainbow. In particular, MinRank attacks, which try to solve a MinRank problem obtained by the matrices of the public key, are applicable to Rainbow but not to UOV.

J. Shikata and H. Kuzuno (Eds.): IWSEC 2023, LNCS 14128, pp. 101–116, 2023.
https://doi.org/10.1007/978-3-031-41326-1_6

Since Rainbow was considered to be more efficient than UOV even taking into account various attacks containing MinRank attacks, it was submitted to NIST PQC standardization [15] in 2016, and proceeded to the third round [10] in 2020. However, in 2021, Beullens broke the proposed parameters [10] of Rainbow in the third round by the simple attack [6] that uses a multi-layered structure of Rainbow. As a result, Rainbow is considered to be inefficient compared with UOV, and was not selected as a NIST PQC standardization scheme.

In 2020, Beullens proposed another attack (the rectangular MinRank attack [3]) before the proposal of the simple attack [6]. The 0 tries to solve a different MinRank problem obtained by transforming the matrices of the public key of Rainbow. It is known that the rectangular MinRank attack reduces the security level of the parameters in the third round [10], but not as much as the simple attack.

Recently, there have been proposed two new variants of the UOV scheme having a small public key: MAYO [4] at SAC 2021 and QR-UOV [11] at ASIACRYPT 2021. Since these two schemes do not have the multi-layered structure unlike Rainbow, MinRank attacks were not applied, and the security analysis was done based on basic attacks of UOV: direct attack and UOV attack [14] and so on. Since MAYO and QR-UOV are compact signature schemes compared with UOV, they will attract attention in the additional standardization process for digital signature schemes by NIST [16]. Thus, further security analysis for them are important.

In this paper, we show that the rectangular MinRank is applicable to MAYO and QR-UOV. To do so, we see that the transformation of the public key of MAYO and QR-UOV has a MinRank problem. Moreover, we estimate the complexity of the attack following Beullens' estimation [3] in his rectangular MinRank attack against Rainbow, and we check by some experiments whether our estimation is reasonable. We see that the proposed parameters of MAYO and QR-UOV are secure against the rectangular MinRank attack, while the complexity of the attack is reasonably close to that of the best known attack (See Table 2 and 4). The rectangular MinRank attack against MAYO and QR-UOV is different from the existing attacks since it uses the MinRank problem hidden in MAYO and QR-UOV. Therefore, we consider that it is important to take the attack into consideration when a new parameter of MAYO or QR-UOV is chosen.

Our paper is organized as follows. In Sect. 2, we explain the construction of some multivariate public key cryptosystems. In Sect. 3, we recall the rectangular MinRank attack against Rainbow proposed by Beullens [3]. In Sect. 4 and 5, we describe the rectangular MinRank attack against MAYO [4] and QR-UOV [11], respectively. Finally, we conclude our paper in Sect. 6.

2 Multivariate Signature Schemes

In this section, we explain the constructions of some multivariate public key cryptosystems, UOV [13] and Rainbow [9]. Let $\mathbb{F}_q$ be a finite field with q elements throughout this paper.

2.1 General Construction of MPKC

Let n and m be two positive integers and we denote by $\mathbb{F}_q[x_1, \ldots, x_n]$ the polynomial ring in n variables over $\mathbb{F}_q$. For m quadratic polynomials $f_1, \ldots, f_m \in \mathbb{F}_q[x_1, \ldots, x_n]$, we set the quadratic polynomial map $\mathcal{F} = (f_1, \ldots, f_m)$ as follows:

$$\mathcal{F} : \mathbb{F}_q^n \ni \mathbf{x} \mapsto (f_1(\mathbf{x}), \ldots, f_m(\mathbf{x})) \in \mathbb{F}_q^m.$$

If a solution $\mathbf{x} \in \mathbb{F}_q^n$ to $\mathcal{F}(\mathbf{x}) = \mathbf{y}$ for any $\mathbf{y} \in \mathbb{F}_q^m$ can be computed easily and efficiently, then $\mathcal{F}$ is called an easily-invertible map. A multivariate scheme is constructed using such an easily-invertible map $\mathcal{F}$. Once $\mathcal{F}$ is given, randomly choose two invertible linear maps $\mathcal{T} : \mathbb{F}_q^m \to \mathbb{F}_q^m$ and $\mathcal{S} : \mathbb{F}_q^n \to \mathbb{F}_q^n$, and then compute the composite

$$\mathcal{P} := \mathcal{T} \circ \mathcal{F} \circ \mathcal{S} : \mathbb{F}_q^n \to \mathbb{F}_q^m.$$

The public key is given by $\mathcal{P} = \{p_1, \ldots, p_m\} : \mathbb{F}_q^n \to \mathbb{F}_q^m$. The secret key consists of $\{\mathcal{F}, \mathcal{T}, \mathcal{S}\}$.

The signature generation is performed as follows. For a message $\mathbf{m} \in \mathbb{F}_q^m$, first compute $\mathbf{m}' = \mathcal{T}^{-1}(\mathbf{m})$. Next, find a solution $\mathbf{x} = \mathbf{m}''$ to $\mathcal{F}(\mathbf{x}) = \mathbf{m}'$. Here, since $\mathcal{F}$ is easily-invertible, it can be solved easily. Finally, compute $\mathbf{s} = \mathcal{S}^{-1}(\mathbf{m}'')$ and this $\mathbf{s} \in \mathbb{F}_q^n$ is a signature of the message $\mathbf{m}$.

The verification is done by checking whether $\mathcal{P}(\mathbf{s}) = \mathbf{m}$.

2.2 UOV

We briefly explain the construction of the UOV signature scheme [13].

Let v and o be two integers such that $v > o > 0$ and set $n := v+o$. We use two variable sets $\mathbf{x}_v = (x_1, \ldots, x_v)$, and $\mathbf{x}_o = (x_{v+1}, \ldots, x_n)$, and put $\mathbf{x} = (\mathbf{x}_v, \mathbf{x}_o)$.

The key generation is performed as follows. Randomly choose o quadratic polynomials in $\mathbb{F}_q[x_1, \ldots, x_n]$ in the following form:

$$f_k(\mathbf{x}) = f_k(\mathbf{x}_v, \mathbf{x}_o) = \sum_{i,j=1}^{v} a_{i,j}^{(k)} x_i x_j + \sum_{i=1}^{v} \sum_{j=v+1}^{n} a_{i,j}^{(k)} x_i x_j, \quad (1 \le k \le o).$$

Then, $\mathcal{F} = (f_1, \ldots, f_o) : \mathbb{F}_q^n \to \mathbb{F}_q^m$ is an easily-invertible map as seen below. We randomly choose a linear invertible map $\mathcal{S} : \mathbb{F}_q^n \to \mathbb{F}_q^n$. The public key is given by the composite $\mathcal{P} := \mathcal{F} \circ \mathcal{S} = \{p_1, \ldots, p_o\}$, and the secret key is $\{\mathcal{F}, \mathcal{S}\}$. Note that an invertible linear map $\mathcal{T} : \mathbb{F}_q^o \to \mathbb{F}_q^o$ is not necessary, since it does not change the structure of the UOV scheme.

The signature generation and verification processes are done as explained in 2.1. Here, in the signature generation, the equation $\mathcal{F}(\mathbf{x}) = \mathbf{m}'$ is easily solved as follows. Randomly choose an element $\mathbf{c} = (c_1, \ldots, c_v) \in \mathbb{F}_q^v$, and find a solution $\mathbf{d} \in \mathbb{F}_q^o$ to the following linear equations in $\mathbf{x}_o$:

$$f_1(\mathbf{c}, \mathbf{x}_o) = m_1', \cdots, f_o(\mathbf{c}, \mathbf{x}_o) = m_o',$$

where $\mathbf{m}' = (m_1', \ldots, m_o')$. Here, if there is no solution, we choose another element $\mathbf{c}$. The obtained vector $(\mathbf{c}, \mathbf{d}) \in \mathbb{F}_q^n$ is a solution to $\mathcal{F}(\mathbf{x}) = \mathbf{m}'$.

2.3 Rainbow

The Rainbow scheme [9] was proposed as a multi-layer variant of the UOV scheme. The construction of the Rainbow signature scheme is as follows.

Let v, o_1 and o_2 be positive integers and set $n := v + o_1 + o_2$, $m := o_1 + o_2$. We use three variable sets

$$\mathbf{x}_v = (x_1, \ldots, x_v)$$
$$\mathbf{x}_{o_1} = (x_{v+1}, \ldots, x_{v+o_1})$$
$$\mathbf{x}_{o_2} = (x_{v+o_1+1}, \ldots, x_n)$$

and put $\mathbf{x} = (\mathbf{x}_v, \mathbf{x}_{o_1}, \mathbf{x}_{o_2})$.

The easily-invertible map is generated as follows. Randomly choose m quadratic polynomials in $\mathbb{F}_q[x_1, \ldots, x_n]$ in the following form:

$$f_1(\mathbf{x}) = \sum_{i,j=1}^{v} a_{i,j}^{(1)} x_i x_j + \sum_{i=1}^{v} \sum_{j=v+1}^{v+o_1} a_{i,j}^{(1)} x_i x_j,$$
$$\vdots$$
$$f_{o_1}(\mathbf{x}) = \sum_{i,j=1}^{v} a_{i,j}^{(o_1)} x_i x_j + \sum_{i=1}^{v} \sum_{j=v+1}^{v+o_1} a_{i,j}^{(o_1)} x_i x_j.$$

$$f_{o_1+1}(\mathbf{x}) = \sum_{i,j=1}^{v+o_1} a_{i,j}^{(o_1+1)} x_i x_j + \sum_{i=1}^{v+o_1} \sum_{j=v+o_1+1}^{n} a_{i,j}^{(o_1+1)} x_i x_j,$$
$$\vdots$$
$$f_m(\mathbf{x}) = \sum_{i,j=1}^{v+o_1} a_{i,j}^{(m)} x_i x_j + \sum_{i=1}^{v+o_1} \sum_{j=v+o_1+1}^{n} a_{i,j}^{(m)} x_i x_j.$$

Then, $\mathcal{F} = (f_1, \ldots, f_m) : \mathbb{F}_q^n \to \mathbb{F}_q^m$ is an easily-invertible map of the Rainbow scheme. We randomly choose two linear invertible map $\mathcal{S} : \mathbb{F}_q^n \to \mathbb{F}_q^n$ and $\mathcal{T} : \mathbb{F}_q^m \to \mathbb{F}_q^m$. The public key is given by the composite $\mathcal{P} := \mathcal{T} \circ \mathcal{F} \circ \mathcal{S} = \{p_1, \ldots, p_m\}$, and the secret key is $\{\mathcal{F}, \mathcal{T}, \mathcal{S}\}$.

The signature generation is almost the same as UOV. In UOV, how to solve $\mathcal{F}(\mathbf{x}) = \mathbf{m}'$ is done by substituting a random value $\mathbf{c}$ in $\mathbf{x}_v$ and solving linear equations of $f_1, \ldots, f_o$ in $\mathbf{x}_o$. On the other hand, in Rainbow, it is done by substituting in $\mathbf{x}_v$ and solving linear equations of $f_1, \ldots, f_{o_1}$ in $\mathbf{x}_{o_1}$ and solving linear equations of $f_{o_1+1}, \ldots, f_m$ in $\mathbf{x}_{o_2}$. (See [9] for the detail.)

3 The Rectangular MinRank Attack Against Rainbow

In this section, we explain the rectangular MinRank attack against the Rainbow scheme proposed by Beullens [3]. In Sect. 3.1, we state a lemma regarding matrix representations of the public key and secret key in order to describe the rectangular MinRank attack. In Sect. 3.2, we explain the idea of the rectangular MinRank attack. The description of the rectangular MinRank attack explained here is based on [12].

3.1 Matrix Representation and Deformation

First, we recall the matrix representation of quadratic polynomials. Let $g \in \mathbb{F}_q[x_1, \ldots, x_n]$ be a homogeneous quadratic polynomial. Then there exists a unique symmetric matrix $G \in M_n(\mathbb{F}_q)$ such that

$$\mathbf{x} \cdot G \cdot {}^t\mathbf{y} = g(\mathbf{x}+\mathbf{y}) - g(\mathbf{x}) - g(\mathbf{y}) \quad \mathbf{x}, \mathbf{y} \in \mathbb{F}_q^n.$$

We call G the representation (symmetric) matrix of g.

Let $\mathcal{F} = (f_1, \ldots, f_m)$ be an easily-invertible map of a multivariate scheme and $\mathcal{P} = (p_1, \ldots, p_m)$ a corresponding public key. We set F_i to be the representation matrix of f_i and P_i that of p_i. Recall that the public key $\mathcal{P}$ satisfies $\mathcal{P} = \mathcal{T} \circ \mathcal{F} \circ \mathcal{S}$ for some invertible linear maps $\mathcal{T}$ and $\mathcal{S}$. If we take $S \in M_n(\mathbb{F}_q)$ and $T \in M_m(\mathbb{F}_q)$ as $\mathcal{S}(\mathbf{x}) = \mathbf{x} \cdot S$ and $\mathcal{T}(\mathbf{y}) = \mathbf{y} \cdot T$, then, from an easy computation, we have

$$(P_1, \ldots, P_m) = \left(S \cdot F_1 \cdot {}^tS, \ldots, S \cdot F_m \cdot {}^tS\right) \cdot T \tag{1}$$

By using this relation, some attacks for MPKC have been proposed so far, such as MinRank attacks. However, the rectangular MinRank attack [3] was proposed by using a deformation of the representation matrices $P_1, \ldots, P_m$. We explain such a deformation in the following.

Let $(G_1, \ldots, G_m)$ be a set of n-by-n matrices over $\mathbb{F}_q$, and $\mathbf{g}_i^{(j)}$ denotes the j-th column vector of G_i, namely,

$$G_i = \left(\mathbf{g}_i^{(1)}\ \mathbf{g}_i^{(2)}\ \cdots\ \mathbf{g}_i^{(n)}\right) \in M_n(\mathbb{F}_q).$$

Then, we define the new set $(\tilde{G}_1, \ldots, \tilde{G}_n)$ of n-by-m matrices as follows:

$$\begin{aligned}
\tilde{G}_1 &:= \left(\mathbf{g}_1^{(1)}\ \mathbf{g}_2^{(1)}\ \cdots\ \mathbf{g}_m^{(1)}\right), \\
\tilde{G}_2 &:= \left(\mathbf{g}_1^{(2)}\ \mathbf{g}_2^{(2)}\ \cdots\ \mathbf{g}_m^{(2)}\right), \\
&\ \ \vdots \\
\tilde{G}_n &:= \left(\mathbf{g}_1^{(n)}\ \mathbf{g}_2^{(n)}\ \cdots\ \mathbf{g}_m^{(n)}\right).
\end{aligned}$$

Then, when we apply this deformation to $(P_1, \ldots, P_m)$ and $(F_1, \ldots, F_m)$, the following lemma is easily proven from (1):

Lemma 1. *[12, Lemma 5]*

$$\left(\tilde{P}_1, \ldots, \tilde{P}_n\right) = \left(S \cdot \tilde{F}_1 \cdot T, \ldots, S \cdot \tilde{F}_n \cdot T\right) \cdot {}^tS.$$

3.2 Rectangular MinRank Attack Against Rainbow

We explain the rectangular MinRank attack [3] using Lemma 1. Let $(F_1, \ldots, F_m)$ be the set of representation matrices of the easily-invertible map $\mathcal{F}$ of the Rainbow scheme in Subsect. 2.3. Then, it is shown that $\tilde{F}_i$ has the following form:

$$\tilde{F}_i = \begin{cases} \begin{pmatrix} *_{v\times o_1} & *_{v\times o_2} \\ *_{o_1\times o_1} & *_{o_1\times o_2} \\ 0_{o_2\times o_1} & *_{o_2\times o_2} \end{pmatrix} & (1 \le i \le v), \\ \begin{pmatrix} *_{v\times o_1} & *_{v\times o_2} \\ 0_{o_1\times o_1} & *_{o_1\times o_2} \\ 0_{o_2\times o_1} & *_{o_2\times o_2} \end{pmatrix} & (v+1 \le i \le v+o_1), \\ \begin{pmatrix} 0_{v\times o_1} & *_{v\times o_2} \\ 0_{o_1\times o_1} & *_{o_1\times o_2} \\ 0_{o_2\times o_1} & 0_{o_2\times o_2} \end{pmatrix} & (v+o_1+1 \le i \le n). \end{cases}$$

Let $(P_1, \ldots, P_m)$ be the set of representation matrices of the public key $\mathcal{P}$ of the Rainbow scheme in Subsect. 2.3. Then, by Lemma 1, we have

$$(\tilde{P}_1, \ldots, \tilde{P}_n) = (S\tilde{F}_1T, \ldots, S\tilde{F}_nT) \cdot {}^tS.$$

Since $\tilde{F}_{v+o_1+1}, \ldots, \tilde{F}_n$ are of rank $\le o_2$, there exists a linear combination of $\tilde{P}_1, \ldots, \tilde{P}_n$ whose rank is $\le o_2$. Thus, $(\tilde{P}_1, \ldots, \tilde{P}_n)$ is an instance of MinRank problem with target rank o_2.

Now, we explain the rectangular Min Rank attack against Rainbow. Its purpose is to find a non-zero element of $\mathcal{O}_2 \cdot S^{-1}$ using the above MinRank problem, where

$$\mathcal{O}_2 := \left\{ (\overbrace{0, \ldots, 0}^{v+o_1}, \overbrace{*, \ldots, *}^{o_2}) \in \mathbb{F}_q^n \right\}.$$

By finding such an element, we can recover an equivalent secret key of the Rainbow scheme. We omit the method to recover an equivalent secret key, since the dominant part is to find a non-zero element of $\mathcal{O}_2 \cdot S^{-1}$. See [3] for the detail.

More precisely, the rectangular MinRank attack is explained as follows. Since $\dim \mathcal{O}_2 \cdot S^{-1} = o_2$, there exists a non-zero n-by-1 vector with the following form:

$$\mathbf{a} = (a_1, a_2, \ldots, a_{v+o_1+1}, 0, \ldots, 0) \in \mathcal{O}_2 \cdot S^{-1}.$$

We want to find such an element $\mathbf{a}$ by constructing two problems that $\mathbf{a}$ satisfies. First, from $\mathbf{a} \cdot S \in \mathcal{O}_2$, it is shown that

$$\sum_{i=1}^{v+o_1+1} a_i\tilde{P}_i = (\tilde{P}_1, \ldots, \tilde{P}_n) \cdot {}^t\mathbf{a} = (S\tilde{F}_1T, \ldots, S\tilde{F}_nT) \cdot {}^t(\mathbf{a} \cdot S)$$

is a linear combination of $S\tilde{F}_{v+o_1+1}T, \ldots, S\tilde{F}_nT$. Thus, this linear combination $\sum_{i=1}^{v+o_1+1} a_i\tilde{P}_i$ is of rank $\le o_2$. Namely, the vector $\mathbf{a}$ is a solution to the

MinRank problem for $(\tilde{P}_1, \dots, \tilde{P}_{v+o_1+1})$ with the target rank o_2. Second, since $\mathcal{F} = (f_1, \dots, f_m)$ is zero on $\mathcal{O}_2$, the public key $\mathcal{P} = (p_1, \dots, p_m)$ is zero on $\mathcal{O}_2 \cdot S^{-1}$. Thus we have

$$p_1(\mathbf{a}) = \cdots = p_m(\mathbf{a}) = 0.$$

As a result, the non-zero vector $\mathbf{a} = (a_1, a_2, \dots, a_{v+o_1+1}, 0, \dots, 0)$ we want to find is a common solution of the following problems.

$$\text{(i) Rank}\left(\sum_{i=1}^{v+o_1+1} a_i \tilde{P}_i\right) \leq o_2, \qquad \text{(ii) } p_1(\mathbf{a}) = \cdots = p_m(\mathbf{a}) = 0.$$

The rectangular MinRank attack [3] is the kind of attack that finds a common solution $\mathbf{a}$ of above problems (i) and (ii). These problems are solved using the support minor modeling method [1] and the bilinear XL algorithm [17]. We omit the complexity estimation for solving these problems, since it is similar to that of the rectangular MinRank attacks against MAYO and QR-UOV, which will be explained in Sect. 4 and 5.

Remark 1. If we apply the deformation of the representation matrices of the easily-invertible map $\mathcal{F} = (f_1, \dots, f_o)$ of the original UOV scheme in Subsect. 2.2, then all of $(\tilde{F}_1, \dots, \tilde{F}_n)$ are of full-rank. Thus, the corresponding deformation $(\tilde{P}_1, \dots, \tilde{P}_n)$ of the public key does not have a MinRank problem. Therefore, the rectangular MinRank attack can not be applied for the original UOV scheme.

4 Rectangular MinRank Attack Against MAYO

In this section, we show that the rectangular MinRank attack is applicable to MAYO [4]. Moreover, we give the complexity estimation following Beullens' estimation [3].

4.1 MAYO Signature Scheme

MAYO signature scheme is a variant of the UOV scheme proposed by Beullens [4]. The key generation is almost same as that of UOV, but how to take parameters is slightly different. Let v, o, m be positive integers and set $n := v + o$. Randomly choose m quadratic polynomials $\mathcal{F} = (f_1, \dots, f_m)$ in $\mathbb{F}_q[x_1, \dots, x_n]$ in the following form:

$$f_k(\mathbf{x}) = f_k(\mathbf{x}_v, \mathbf{x}_o) = \sum_{i,j=1}^{v} a_{i,j}^{(k)} x_i x_j + \sum_{i=1}^{v} \sum_{j=v+1}^{n} a_{i,j}^{(k)} x_i x_j, \quad (1 \leq k \leq m). \quad (2)$$

Next, randomly choose an invertible linear map $\mathcal{S} : \mathbb{F}_q^n \to \mathbb{F}_q^n$. Finally, the public key is given by $\mathcal{P} := \mathcal{F} \circ \mathcal{S} : \mathbb{F}_q^n \to \mathbb{F}_q^m$. As seen in (2), the number m of polynomials f_i is not necessarily equal to o. More precisely, the number m would be taken larger than o in MAYO. This is the difference between UOV and MAYO in the key generation. The signature process is achieved by some techniques such as "whipping transformation". Since the attack stated below uses only information of the public key $\mathcal{P}$, we skip the details of signature and verification processes. See Sect. 3 in [4] for the details.

4.2 Rectangular MinRank Attack

In this subsection, we explain that the rectangular MinRank attack can be applied to MAYO [4].

Let $(F_1, \ldots, F_m)$ be the set of representation matrices of the easily-invertible map $\mathcal{F}$ of MAYO. For the proposed parameters of MAYO in [4], we have $m > v > o$. From this relation, it is easily seen that the deformation matrices $\tilde{F}_{v+1}, \ldots, \tilde{F}_n \in M_{n\times m}(\mathbb{F}_q)$ are of rank $\leq v$ since they have the following form:

$$\begin{pmatrix} *_{v\times m} \\ 0_{o\times m} \end{pmatrix}.$$

Thus, as in Rainbow, the rectangular MinRank attack can be applied to MAYO. To estimate the complexity in Subsect. 4.3, we describe the attack in detail.

Let $(P_1, \ldots, P_m)$ be the set of representation matrices of the public key $\mathcal{P}$ of MAYO. Then, by Lemma 1, we have $(\tilde{P}_1, \ldots, \tilde{P}_n) = (S\tilde{F}_1, \ldots, S\tilde{F}_n) \cdot {}^tS$. Since $\tilde{F}_{v+1}, \ldots, \tilde{F}_n$ are of rank $\leq v$, there exists a linear combination of $\tilde{P}_1, \ldots, \tilde{P}_n \in M_{n\times m}(\mathbb{F}_q)$ whose rank is $\leq v$.

The rectangular MinRank attack against MAYO tries to find a non-zero element of $\mathcal{O} \cdot S^{-1}$, where

$$\mathcal{O} := \left\{ (\overbrace{0, \ldots, 0}^{v}, \overbrace{*, \ldots, *}^{o}) \in \mathbb{F}_q^n \right\}.$$

As in the case of Rainbow, the rectangular MinRank attack against MAYO is constructed as follows. Since $\dim \mathcal{O} \cdot S^{-1} = o$, there exists a non-zero n-by-1 vector with the following form:

$$\mathbf{a} = (a_1, a_2, \ldots, a_{v+1}, 0, \ldots, 0) \in \mathcal{O} \cdot S^{-1}.$$

Then, it is shown that

$$\sum_{i=1}^{v+1} a_i \tilde{P}_i = (\tilde{P}_1, \ldots, \tilde{P}_n) \cdot {}^t\mathbf{a} = (S\tilde{F}_1, \ldots, S\tilde{F}_n) \cdot {}^t(\mathbf{a} \cdot S)$$

is a linear combination of $S\tilde{F}_{v+1}, \ldots, S\tilde{F}_n$. Thus, this linear combination is of rank $\leq v$. Namely, the vector $\mathbf{a}$ gives a solution to the MinRank problem for $(\tilde{P}_1, \ldots, \tilde{P}_{v+1})$ with the target rank v. Moreover, for $i = 1, \ldots, m$, we have $p_1(\mathbf{a}) = \cdots = p_m(\mathbf{a}) = 0$, where $\mathcal{P} = (p_1, \ldots, p_m)$ is a public key of MAYO. As a result, the vector $\mathbf{a} = (a_1, a_2, \ldots, a_{v+1}, 0, \ldots, 0)$ we want to find is a common solution of the following problems.

$$\text{(i) Rank}\left(\sum_{i=1}^{v+1} a_i \tilde{P}_i\right) \leq v, \qquad \text{(ii) } p_1(\mathbf{a}) = \cdots = p_m(\mathbf{a}) = 0.$$

4.3 Complexity Analysis

In this subsection, we describe the estimation of the complexity to solve above problems (i) and (ii). This is done along Beullens' estimation [3] for the rectangular MinRank attack against Rainbow.

First, consider problem (i). Fix an integer m' such that $v+1 \leq m' \leq m$. Let $\tilde{P}'_i$ be the $n \times m'$ submatrix constructed from the $(1,1)$-component to the (n, m')-component of $\tilde{P}_i$. Then one considers to apply the support minor modeling method [1] to the MinRank problem $(\tilde{P}'_1, \ldots, \tilde{P}'_{v+1})$ with the target rank v. Let I' be the ideal in $\mathbb{F}_q[\mathbf{a}, \mathbf{c}]$ generated by the bilinear equations obtained from the support minor modeling, where $\mathbf{c}$ is the set of $\binom{m'}{v}$ minor variables. (See [1] and [3] for the detail description.) For $b \in \mathbb{N}_{\geq 1}$, set

$$R'(b) := \sum_{i=1}^{b} (-1)^{i+1} \binom{m'}{v+i} \binom{n+i-1}{i} \binom{v+b-i}{b-i}.$$

Let $I'_{b,1}$ be the subspace of $(b,1)$-degree homogeneous polynomials of I' in $\mathbb{F}_q[\mathbf{a}, \mathbf{c}]$. If the above MinRank problem behaves like a random instance, then $\dim_{\mathbb{F}_q} I'_{b,1}$ is predicted as $R'(b)$ for $1 \leq b \leq v+1$ by the result of Bardet et al. [1].

Next, one considers adding problem (ii) to I'. We assume that $p_1(\mathbf{a}), \ldots, p_m(\mathbf{a})$ behaves like a semi-regular system, where $\mathbf{a} = (a_1, a_2, \ldots, a_{v+1}, 0, \ldots, 0)$. Let I be the ideal generated by I' and $p_1(\mathbf{a}), \ldots, p_m(\mathbf{a})$, namely,

$$I := I' + \langle p_1(\mathbf{a}), \ldots, p_m(\mathbf{a}) \rangle \subset \mathbb{F}_q[\mathbf{a}, \mathbf{c}].$$

We define

$$b_{\min} := \min \left\{ b \in \mathbb{N} \mid \dim_{\mathbb{F}_q} I_{b,1} = \dim_{\mathbb{F}_q} \mathbb{F}_q[\mathbf{a}, \mathbf{c}]_{b,1} - 1 \right\}. \tag{3}$$

By applying to $I_{b_{\min},1}$ the bilinear XL algorithm [17] with Wiedemann algorithm [7,18], we can find a solution $\mathbf{a}$ to problems (i) and (ii) with the following complexity:

$$(2(\log_2 q)^2 + \log_2 q) \cdot 3 \binom{m'}{v}^2 \binom{v+b_{\min}}{b_{\min}}^2 (v+1)^2. \tag{4}$$

Here, $2(\log_2 q)^2 + \log_2 q$ is the factor to convert from the number of multiplications in $\mathbb{F}_q$ to the gate count.

Following the idea of Beullens' estimation [3], in order to guess $b_{\min}$, we define the following two series in t_1 and t_2:

$$G'(t_1, t_2) := \frac{1}{(1-t_1)^{v+1}} + \binom{m'}{v} t_2 + \sum_{b=1}^{v+1} \left(\binom{m'}{v} \binom{v+b}{b} - R'(b) \right) t_1^b t_2$$

$$G(t_1, t_2) := G'(t_1, t_2) \cdot (1 - t_1^2)^m.$$

These series are derived to compute a part of the Hilbert series of $\mathbb{F}_q[\mathbf{a}, \mathbf{c}]/I'$ and $\mathbb{F}_q[\mathbf{a}, \mathbf{c}]/I$. However, due to some non-trivial syzygies, these are not perfectly equal to the Hilbert series of them (See also Remark 2). We consider that $b_{\min}$ is predicted by

$$b_{\min}^{(\text{predict})} := \min\{b \in \mathbb{N} \mid G(t_1, t_2)_{b,1} \le 1\}, \tag{5}$$

where $G(t_1, t_2)_{b,1}$ is the coefficient of $t_1^b t_2$. In Table 1, we experimented whether $b_{\min}$ is equal to $b_{\min}^{(\text{predict})}$ for some parameters. As seen in the table, we have $b_{\min} = b_{\min}^{(\text{predict})}$ for each m' between $v+1$ and m.

Table 1. Experiments for $b_{\min}$ and $b_{\min}^{(\text{predict})}$

(q,v,o,m)	m'	$b_{\min}$	$b_{\min}^{(\text{predict})}$
$(7,5,1,6)$	6	4	4
$(7,8,1,10)$	9	5	5
	10	4	4
$(7,8,2,10)$	9	5	5
	10	4	4
$(16,5,1,6)$	6	4	4
$(16,8,1,10)$	9	5	5
	10	4	4
$(16,8,2,10)$	9	5	5
	10	4	4

From the above experiments, we use $b_{\min}^{(\text{predict})}$ instead of $b_{\min}$, and theoretically estimate the time complexity of the rectangular MinRank attack against MAYO by (4). Table 2 shows the complexity of the attack against the parameters proposed in [5]. Here, m' in Table 2 represents the value between $v+1$ and m such that the complexity of the attack is minimum. The value $b_{\min}^{(\text{predict})}$ is given by (5) for this m'. "RecMin" in the table means the complexity of the rectangular MinRank attack against MAYO given by (4) as $b_{\min} = b_{\min}^{(\text{predict})}$. "Best" means the best complexity among the existing attacks stated in [5].

Table 2. Estimated gate count of the rectangular MinRank attack (RecMin) in Subsect. 4.3 and the best known attack (Best) in [5]

(q,v,o,m)	m'	$b_{\min}^{(\text{predict})}$	RecMin $\log_2(\#\text{gates})$	Best $\log_2(\#\text{gates})$
$(16,58,8,64)$	59	22	159	143
$(16,60,18,64)$	62	21	168	143
$(16,89,10,96)$	90	33	231	207
$(16,121,12,128)$	122	46	310	272

For example, for $(q, v, o, m) = (16, 58, 8, 64)$, the value m' runs between 59 and 64, and $m' = 59$ minimizes the complexity of the rectangular MinRank attack. Also, for $m' = 59$, we have $b_{\text{min}}^{(\text{predict})} = 22$, and then the complexity of the attack is 2^{159} gates.

From Table 2, we see that the rectangular MinRank attack in Subsect. 4.2 does not reduce the security level for the proposed parameters in [5]. However, since the complexity of the rectangular MinRank attack is reasonably close to that of the best known attack, we consider that one can not ignore the influence of the attack in setting a new parameter.

Remark 2. Define

$$R(b) := \binom{m'}{v}\binom{v+b}{b} - G(t_1, t_2)_{b,1}.$$

Following Beullens' estimation [3], it is considered that $R(b)$ predicts the dimension of $I_{b,1}$. Since there had been non-trivial syzygies in the quadratic equations obtained by problems (i) and (ii), $R(b)$ did not equal to the dimension of $I_{b,1}$ in our experiments in Table 1. However, since $R(b) - \dim I_{b,1}$ was very small, the values of b_{min} and $b_{\text{min}}^{(\text{predict})}$ matched. From this, we can expect that those non-trivial syzygies do not affect the values of b_{min} and $b_{\text{min}}^{(\text{predict})}$.

Note that if we take the influence of those syzygies into account, we have $b_{\text{min}} \geq b_{\text{min}}^{(\text{predict})}$. Thus, the estimated complexity of the rectangular MinRank attack by $b_{\text{min}}^{(\text{predict})}$ gives a lower bound of the accurate complexity. Therefore, it does not change the fact that the currently proposed parameters of MAYO is secure against the rectangular MinRank attack.

5 Rectangular MinRank Attack Against QR-UOV

In this section, we show that the rectangular MinRank attack is applicable to QR-UOV [11]. Moreover, we give the complexity estimation following Beullens' estimation [3]. In QR-UOV, we assume that q is not even.

5.1 QR-UOV Signature Scheme

QR-UOV is a variant of the UOV scheme proposed by Furue et al. [11]. It is constructed by using representation of an extension field in a matrix algebra over $\mathbb{F}_q$.

Let V, O, l be positive integers and set

$$v := Vl, o := Ol, N := V + O, n := v + o = Nl.$$

For an irreducible polynomial $f(t) \in \mathbb{F}_q[t]$ with degree l, we define the embedding

$$\phi : \mathbb{F}_{q^l} = \mathbb{F}_q[t]/(f(t)) \to M_l(\mathbb{F}_q)$$

by $(1, t, \ldots, t^{l-1}) \cdot \phi(g) = (g, gt, \ldots, gt^{l-1})$ for $g \in \mathbb{F}_{q^l}$. Then, by Theorem 1 in [11], there exists an invertible symmetric matrix $W \in M_l(\mathbb{F}_q)$ such that $W\phi(g)$ is symmetric for any $g \in \mathbb{F}_{q^l}$. We also define the following extended embedding:

$$\phi : M_N(\mathbb{F}_{q^l}) \ni (a_{ij}) \mapsto (\phi(a_{ij})) \in M_n(\mathbb{F}_q).$$

Then, we have $W^{(N)} \cdot \phi({}^tS) = {}^t\phi(S) \cdot W^{(N)}$ for any $S \in M_N(\mathbb{F}_{q^l})$, where

$$W^{(N)} := \begin{pmatrix} W & & \\ & \ddots & \\ & & W \end{pmatrix} \in M_n(\mathbb{F}_q).$$

QR-UOV is constructed by using these facts and achieved the small public key compared with UOV.

The key generation is done as follows. Randomly choose o symmetric matrices $F_1, \ldots, F_o$ in $M_N(\mathbb{F}_{q^l})$ in the following form:

$$F_i = \begin{pmatrix} *_V & *_{V\times O} \\ *_{O\times V} & 0_O \end{pmatrix}.$$

The easily-invertible map of QR-UOV is given by

$$f_i(\mathbf{x}) := \mathbf{x} \cdot W^{(N)} \cdot \phi(F_i) \cdot {}^t\mathbf{x} \quad (1 \leq i \leq o),$$

where $\mathbf{x} = (x_1, \ldots, x_n)$. Next, randomly choose an invertible matrix $S \in M_N(\mathbb{F}_{q^l})$. The public key $\mathcal{P} = (p_1, \ldots, p_o)$ is given by

$$p_i(\mathbf{x}) := \mathbf{x} \cdot {}^t\phi(S) \cdot W^{(N)} \cdot \phi(F_i) \cdot \phi(S) \cdot {}^t\mathbf{x}, \quad (1 \leq i \leq o). \tag{6}$$

The signature and verification processes are the same of those of UOV scheme.

5.2 Rectangular MinRank Attack

In this subsection, we explain that the rectangular MinRank attack can be applied to QR-UOV [11].

First, since $W^{(N)} \cdot \phi(F_i)$ and ${}^t\phi(S) \cdot W^{(N)} \cdot \phi(F_i) \cdot \phi(S)$ are symmetric, the representation matrix P_i of p_i is equal to $2 \cdot {}^t\phi(S) \cdot W^{(N)} \cdot \phi(F_i) \cdot \phi(S)$. Next, by ${}^t\phi(S) \cdot W^{(N)} = W^{(N)} \cdot \phi({}^tS)$, we have

$$2^{-1} \cdot W^{(N),-1} \cdot P_i = \phi({}^tS \cdot F_i \cdot S).$$

Thus, an attacker can obtain the matrices $\{{}^tS \cdot F_1 \cdot S, \ldots, {}^tS \cdot F_o \cdot S\}$ from the public key $\{p_1, \ldots, p_m\}$. Then we define the following quadratic polynomials over $\mathbb{F}_{q^l}$:

$$\bar{p}_i(\mathbf{y}) := \mathbf{y} \cdot {}^tS \cdot F_i \cdot S \cdot {}^t\mathbf{y},$$

where $\mathbf{y} = (y_1, \ldots, y_N)$. Here, note that $\{\bar{p}_1, \ldots, \bar{p}_o\}$ can be considered as the public key of MAYO with the parameter $v_{MAYO} = V, o_{MAYO} = O$ and

$m_{MAYO} = o$, where v_{MAYO} is the number of vinegar-variables in MAYO and so on. For practical parameters of QR-UOV [11], we have $o > V$. Thus, as in the case of MAYO, we can apply the rectangular MinRank attack to $\bar{p}_1, \dots, \bar{p}_o$. In this case, we want to find a common solution $\mathbf{a}$ of the following problems.

$$\text{(i) Rank}\left(\sum_{i=1}^{V+1} a_i \bar{\bar{P}}_i\right) \le V, \qquad \text{(ii) } \bar{p}_1(\mathbf{a}) = \cdots = \bar{p}_o(\mathbf{a}) = 0.$$

Here $\mathbf{a} = (a_1, \dots, a_{V+1}, 0, \dots, 0)$ is a non-zero element of $\mathbb{F}_{q^l}^N$, and $\bar{\bar{P}}_i \in M_{N\times o}(\mathbb{F}_{q^l})$ are the deformations of representation matrices $\bar{P}_i = 2 \cdot {}^tS \cdot F_i \cdot S$ of $\bar{p}_i$.

5.3 Complexity Analysis

In this subsection, we describe the estimation of the complexity to solve above problems (i) and (ii). This is also done along Beullens' estimation [3] for the rectangular MinRank attack against Rainbow. Note that the characteristic of $\mathbb{F}_q$ is always odd in QR-UOV.

First, consider problem (i). Fix an integer o' such that $V+1 \le o' \le o$. Let $\bar{\bar{P}}'_i$ be the $n \times o'$ matrix obtained by removing the column vectors from $(o'+1)$-th to o-th of $\bar{\bar{P}}_i$. Then one considers to apply the support minor modeling method [1] to the MinRank problem $(\bar{\bar{P}}'_1, \dots, \bar{\bar{P}}'_{V+1})$ with the target rank V. Let I' be the ideal in $\mathbb{F}_{q^l}[\mathbf{a}, \mathbf{c}]$ generated by the bilinear equations obtained from the support minor modeling, where $\mathbf{c}$ is the set of $\binom{o'}{V}$ minor variables. For $b \in \mathbb{N}$, let $I'_{b,1}$ be the subspace of $(b,1)$-degree homogeneous polynomials of I' in $\mathbb{F}_{q^l}[\mathbf{a}, \mathbf{c}]$, and set

$$R'(b) := \sum_{i=1}^{b} (-1)^{i+1} \binom{o'}{V+i} \binom{n+i-1}{i} \binom{V+b-i}{b-i}.$$

Next, one considers adding problem (ii). We assume that $\bar{p}_1(\mathbf{a}), \dots, \bar{p}_o(\mathbf{a})$ behave as a semi-regular system, where $\mathbf{a} = (a_1, a_2, \dots, a_{V+1}, 0, \dots, 0)$. Let I be the ideal generated by I' and $\bar{p}_1(\mathbf{a}), \dots, \bar{p}_o(\mathbf{a})$ in $\mathbb{F}_{q^l}[\mathbf{a}, \mathbf{c}]$. Moreover, set

$$G'(t_1, t_2) := \frac{1}{(1-t_1)^{v+1}} + \binom{o'}{V} t_2 + \sum_{b=1}^{V+1} \left(\binom{o'}{V} \binom{V+b}{b} - R'(b) \right) t_1^b t_2,$$

$$G(t_1, t_2) := G'(t_1, t_2) \cdot (1 - t_1^2)^o.$$

Let $b_{\min} \in \mathbb{N}$ be the minimum of b such that

$$\dim_{\mathbb{F}_{q^l}} I_{b,1} = \dim_{\mathbb{F}_q} \mathbb{F}_{q^l}[\mathbf{a}, \mathbf{c}]_{b,1} - 1.$$

Finally, by applying to $I_{b_{\min},1}$ the bilinear XL algorithm [17] with Wiedemann algorithm [7,18], we can find a solution $\mathbf{a}$ to problem (i) and (ii) with the following complexity:

$$(2(\log_2 q^l)^2 + \log_2 q^l) \cdot 3 \binom{o'}{V}^2 \binom{V+b_{\min}}{b_{\min}}^2 (V+1)^2. \qquad (7)$$

Here, $2(\log_2 q^l)^2 + \log_2 q^l$ is the factor to convert from the number of multiplications in $\mathbb{F}_{q^l}$ to the gate count.

Following the idea of Beullens' estimation, we can state that $b_{\min}$ is predicted by

$$b_{\min}^{(\text{predict})} := \min\{b \mid G(t_1, t_2)_{b,1} \leq 1\}, \tag{8}$$

where $G(t_1, t_2)_{b,1}$ is the coefficient of $t_1^b t_2$. In Table 3, we experimented that $b_{\min}$ is equal to $b_{\min}^{(\text{predict})}$ for some parameters. Here, since $\bar{p}_1, \cdots, \bar{p}_o$ are considered as the public key of MAYO with parameter $v_{MAYO} = V, o_{MAYO} = O$ and $m_{MAYO} = o = Ol$, we experimented for MAYO with such a parameter. As seen in Table 3, we have $b_{\min} = b_{\min}^{(\text{predict})}$.

Table 3. Experiments for $b_{\min}$ and $b_{\min}^{(\text{predict})}$

(q, V, O, l)	o'	$b_{\min}^{(\text{predict})}$	$b_{\min}$
$(7, 5, 2, 3)$	6	4	4
$(7, 6, 3, 3)$	7	3	3
	8	3	3
	9	2	2
$(7, 7, 3, 3)$	8	4	4
	9	3	3
$(7, 8, 3, 3)$	9	5	5

From the above experiments, we use $b_{\min}^{(\text{predict})}$ instead of $b_{\min}$, and theoretically estimate the time complexity of the rectangular MinRank attack against QR-UOV. Table 4 shows the complexity of the attack against the proposed parameters in [11]. Here, o' in Table 4 represents the value between $V + 1$ and o such that the complexity of the attack is minimum. The value $b_{\min}^{(\text{predict})}$ is given by (8) for this o'. "RecMin" means the complexity of the rectangular MinRank attack against QR-UOV given by (7) as $b_{\min} = b_{\min}^{(\text{predict})}$. "Best" means the best complexity among the existing attacks stated in [11].

Table 4. Estimated gate count of the rectangular MinRank attack (RecMin) in Subsect. 4.2 and the best known attack (Best) in [11]

(q, V, O, l)	o'	$b_{\min}^{(\text{predict})}$	RecMin $\log_2(\#\text{gates})$	Best $\log_2(\#\text{gates})$
$(7, 63, 24, 3)$	64	21	162	149
$(7, 97, 37, 3)$	98	30	228	214
$(7, 137, 54, 3)$	138	37	290	279

For example, for $(q, V, O, l) = (7, 63, 24, 3)$, the value o' runs between 64 and 72, and $o' = 64$ minimizes the complexity of the rectangular MinRank attack. Also, for $o' = 64$, we have $b_{\min}^{(\text{predict})} = 21$, and then the complexity of the attack is 2^{162} gates.

From Table 4, we see that the proposed parameters of QR-UOV are secure against the rectangular MinRank attack in Subsect. 5.2. However, the complexity of the rectangular MinRank attack is close to that of the best known attack.

6 Conclusion

MAYO and QR-UOV are multivariate signature schemes obtained by improving the UOV signature scheme. Since they are compact signature schemes compared with UOV, they will attract attention as multivariate signature schemes in the additional standardization process for digital signature schemes by NIST. The security analysis of these two schemes were done based on basic attacks: direct attack and UOV attack and so on. Thus, further security analysis for them are important. In this paper, we showed that the rectangular MinRank attack, which was originally proposed by Beullens against Rainbow, can be applied to MAYO and QR-UOV. Moreover, we estimated the complexity of the attack following Beullens' estimation. We checked that our estimation is reasonable from some experiments in which the indicator $b_{\min}$ was equal to $b_{\min}^{(\text{predict})}$. As a result, we saw that the proposed parameters of MAYO and QR-UOV are secure against the rectangular MinRank attack, while the complexity of the attack is close to that of the best known attack. For example, the parameter $(q, v, o, m) = (16, 58, 8, 64)$ in MAYO has 2^{143} gates security for the existing attacks and 2^{159} gates for the rectangular MinRank attack. Therefore, we consider that it is necessary to analyze the rectangular MinRank attack when a new paramcter of MAYO or QR-UOV is chosen.

Acknowledgements. This work was supported by JST CREST Grant Number JPMJCR2113, Japan, and JSPS KAKENHI Grant Number JP19K20266, JP22KJ0554 and JP22K17889, Japan.

References

1. Bardet, M., et al.: Improvements of algebraic attacks for solving the rank decoding and MinRank problems. In: Moriai, S., Wang, H. (eds.) ASIACRYPT 2020. LNCS, vol. 12491, pp. 507–536. Springer, Cham (2020). https://doi.org/10.1007/978-3-030-64837-4_17
2. Bernstein, D.J., Buchmann, J., Dahmen, E. (eds.) Post-Quantum Cryptography, Springer, Berlin (2009). https://doi.org/10.1007/978-3-540-88702-7
3. Beullens, W.: Improved cryptanalysis of UOV and rainbow. In: Canteaut, A., Standaert, F.-X. (eds.) EUROCRYPT 2021. LNCS, vol. 12696, pp. 348–373. Springer, Cham (2021). https://doi.org/10.1007/978-3-030-77870-5_13

4. Beullens, W.: MAYO: practical post-quantum signatures from oil-and-vinegar maps. In: AlTawy, R., Hülsing, A. (eds.) SAC 2021. LNCS, vol. 13203, pp. 355–376. Springer, Cham (2022). https://doi.org/10.1007/978-3-030-99277-4_17
5. Beullens, W., Campos, F., Celi, S., Hess, B., Kannwischer, M.: The specification of MAYO. https://pqmayo.org/assets/specs/mayo.pdf
6. Beullens, W.: Breaking Rainbow Takes a Weekend on a Laptop. In: Dodis, Y., Shrimpton, T. (eds) Advances in Cryptology - CRYPTO 2022. CRYPTO 2022. LNCS, vol. 13508, pp. 464–479. Springer, Cham (2022). https://doi.org/10.1007/978-3-031-15979-4_16
7. Cheng, C.-M., Chou, T., Niederhagen, R., Yang, B.-Y.: Solving quadratic equations with XL on parallel architectures. In: Prouff, E., Schaumont, P. (eds.) CHES 2012. LNCS, vol. 7428, pp. 356–373. Springer, Heidelberg (2012). https://doi.org/10.1007/978-3-642-33027-8_21
8. Ding, J., Petzoldt, A., Schmidt, D.S.: Multivariate Public Key Cryptosystems. 2nd edn, Springer, New York (2020). https://doi.org/10.1007/978-1-0716-0987-3
9. Ding, J., Schmidt, D.: Rainbow, a new multivariable polynomial signature scheme. In: Ioannidis, J., Keromytis, A., Yung, M. (eds.) ACNS 2005. LNCS, vol. 3531, pp. 164–175. Springer, Heidelberg (2005). https://doi.org/10.1007/11496137_12
10. Ding, J., Chen, M.S., Petzoldt, A., Schmidt, D.S., Yang, B.Y.: 'Rainbow', Technical report, National institute of standards and technology, post-quantum cryptography, https://csrc.nist.gov/Projects/Post-Quantum-Cryptography/Round-3-submissions
11. Furue, H., Ikematsu, Y., Kiyomura, Y., Takagi, T.: A new variant of unbalanced oil and vinegar using quotient ring: QR-UOV. In: Tibouchi, M., Wang, H. (eds.) ASIACRYPT 2021. LNCS, vol. 13093, pp. 187–217. Springer, Cham (2021). https://doi.org/10.1007/978-3-030-92068-5_7
12. Ikematsu, Y., Nakamura, S., Takagi, T.: Recent progress in the security evaluation of multivariate public-key cryptography. IET Inf. Secur. **17**(2), 210–226 (2022)
13. Kipnis, A., Patarin, J., Goubin, L.: Unbalanced oil and vinegar signature schemes. In: Stern, J. (ed.) EUROCRYPT 1999. LNCS, vol. 1592, pp. 206–222. Springer, Heidelberg (1999). https://doi.org/10.1007/3-540-48910-X_15
14. Kipnis, A., Shamir, A.: Cryptanalysis of the oil and vinegar signature scheme. In: Krawczyk, H. (ed.) CRYPTO 1998. LNCS, vol. 1462, pp. 257–266. Springer, Heidelberg (1998). https://doi.org/10.1007/BFb0055733
15. National institute of standards and technology: post-quantum cryptography standardization. https://csrc.nist.gov/projects/post-quantum-cryptography
16. National institute of standards and technology: call for additional digital signature schemes for the post-quantum cryptography standardization process. https://csrc.nist.gov/csrc/media/Projects/pqc-dig-sig/documents/call-for-proposals-dig-sig-sept-2022.pdf
17. Smith-Tone D., Perlner, R.A.: Rainbow band separation is better than we thought, IACR Cryptology ePrint Archive, 2020/702
18. Wiedemann, D.: Solving sparse linear equations over finite fields. IEEE Trans. Inform. Theory **32**(1), 54–62 (1986)

Improved Hybrid Attack via Error-Splitting Method for Finding Quinary Short Lattice Vectors

Haiming Zhu[1], Shoichi Kamada[2(✉)], Momonari Kudo[3], and Tsuyoshi Takagi[1]

[1] Department of Mathematical Informatics, The University of Tokyo, Tokyo, Japan
[2] Institute of Systems and Information Engineering, University of Tsukuba, Tsukuba, Japan
kamada.shoichi.ft@u.tsukuba.ac.jp
[3] Faculty of Information Engineering, Fukuoka Institute of Technology, Fukuoka, Japan

Abstract. Plenty of lattice-based cryptosystems use ternary or quinary sparse short vectors to accelerate the computing procedure. The hybrid attack, proposed by Howgrave-Graham, utilizes the sparsity of the short non-zero vector. Some improved hybrid attack presents a state-of-the-art performance in solving SVPs with ternary short vectors. However, the efficiency of the hybrid attack decreases when the short vector becomes quinary. Although there are several works for the ternary case, few of them focus on the situation that the infinite norm is larger than 1.

In this paper, we propose a new attack for lattice-based schemes using quinary short vectors, called the ESHybrid attack. Our attack is based on the structure of the hybrid attack, with the Meet-LWE algorithm [25] that replaces the traditional meet-in-the-middle structure. To solve the open question that Meet-LWE can not be applied to the hybrid attack, we propose the Error-Splitting (ES) technique. This technique utilizes the structure of quinary vectors and also makes the Meet-LWE procedure faster. We give a complete analysis of the complexity of this algorithm. The evaluation from practical parameter sets ensures that our ESHybrid attack is faster than the ordinary lattice reduction approach and the existing hybrid attack.

Keywords: Shortest Vector Problem · Hybrid Attack · Meet-in-the-Middle · Sparse Vector

1 Introduction

Lattice-based cryptography is one of the most promising directions of post-quantum cryptography. Basically, the evidence of the hardness in lattice-based cryptography is the shortest vector problem (SVP), which is a problem to find

This work was done when all authors belonged to The University of Tokyo, and was supported by JST CREST Grant Number JPMJCR2113, Japan.

J. Shikata and H. Kuzuno (Eds.): IWSEC 2023, LNCS 14128, pp. 117–136, 2023.
https://doi.org/10.1007/978-3-031-41326-1_7

the shortest non-zero vector in a given lattice. Notion of the q-ary lattice covers many of lattice-based cryptosystems. Especially, NTRU and Falcon schemes were candidates of post-quantum lattice-based cryptosystems in the NIST PQC standardization process. At present, Falcon scheme is standardized but NTRU scheme become a finalist.

For the design of lattice-based schemes, most of them consider the characteristics that can reduce the time consumption of these schemes. One common technique uses a short integer vector whose the (Hamming) weight and the infinite norm are specified. In some situation, one sometimes uses a short integer vector of infinity norm 1, which is called ternary. There are plenty of schemes equipped with ternary short vectors (e.g. [9, 18–20, 22, 27]).

Although the ternary setting provides efficiency for the calculation, its security becomes one of the pivotal concerns. The security level of the ternary setting is not well-understood. Some proposed attack presents the risk of sparse short vectors, but this topic is still controversial up to now.

The hybrid attack, proposed by Howgrave-Graham [23], utilizes the sparsity and limited infinite norm of the target cryptosystems. This attack combines the reduction attack and the meet-in-the-middle method, and achieves a better result compared to the previous attacks in some lattices. The hybrid attack is considered to be one of the most efficient attacks on q-ary lattices with the ternary setting. Most lattice-based schemes selected by NIST standardization also evaluate their security under the hybrid attack.

Our method improves the hybrid attack when a cryptosystem transitions from ternary to quinary settings, where quinary cryptosystems require finding short vectors whose infinity norms are at most 2. The larger infinite norm significantly expands the searching space on the meet-in-the-middle part in the hybrid attack with minimal compromise to running efficiency. Although not as widespread as ternary settings, quinary cryptosystems like Giophantus [1] still exist. Therefore, analyzing the security of lattice-based schemes with quinary settings is important. While there are plenty of research analyzing the ternary settings, few of them focus on quinary schemes. In this paper, we estimate the security of q-ary lattices in the quinary settings.

The quinary setting maintains sparsity, so the hybrid attack is still viable. However, it becomes inefficient because the larger searching space makes the meet-in-the-middle attack impractical. To improve the hybrid attack, we can replace the meet-in-the-middle part with other colliding methods. In 2021, May [25] proposed the Meet-LWE attack. However, Meet-LWE can not be applied directly to the hybrid attack because of its smaller candidate set. Our motivation is to investigate this problem.

1.1 Related Works

The hybrid attack on q-ary SVP is first proposed by Howgrave-Graham in [23], utilizing the meet-in-the-middle attack. In the hybrid attack, there are mainly two parts: the lattice reduction part and the guessing part. This hybrid structure is also extended to solve the Learning With Errors (LWE) problem. The direct version of the hybrid attack from the SVP to the LWE is called the hybrid decoding attack or the hybrid primal attack. After that, Albrecht et al. [2] proposed the hybrid dual attack on the decisional LWE, which combines the hybrid attack and the dual attack. Note that in the original hybrid dual attack of the LWE problem, the guessing part uses the exhaustive search method.

Howgrave-Graham [23] analyzes the time complexity of the hybrid attack. Wunderer [28] models the theoretical complexity of the hybrid attack. Espitau et al. [15] and Bi et al. [11] accelerate the guessing phase with matrix multiplication and optimal pruning. Cheon et al. [14] replace exhaustive search with the meet-in-the-middle attack, while Bi et al. [10] replace the meet-in-the-middle part with Meet-LWE attack [25] in the hybrid dual attack on the LWE problem. The Meet-LWE attack on non-ternary attacks is analyzed in [16] with the improved nested collision method, but some application of their method to the hybrid attack on SVP is not mentioned.

1.2 Our Contribution

We propose ESHybrid attack by combining hybrid attack and Meet-LWE with the Error-Splitting (ES) technique. The attack aims to solve SVP of q-ary lattices with designed shortest vector as quinary. The ES technique extracts the error by finding two vectors with smaller norms and meeting rather than checking all possible errors. This reduces the searching time complexity for finding the shortest non-zero vector and improves upon existing attacks.

In the proposal of evaluating the time complexity, we present a detailed analysis of the ESMeet algorithm. The results of the theoretical evaluation are based on some reasonable assumptions. Numerical results are also provided. Experiments are provided in different settings of parameters, with the direct reduction method and the existing hybrid attack as the baseline. The experiment results support our anticipation in the theoretical.

2 Preliminaries

Let $\mathcal{A}_k = \{-k, -k+1 \dots, -1, 0, 1, \dots, k-1, k\}$. For $\boldsymbol{\omega} = (\omega_1, \omega_2, \dots, \omega_k)^T \in \mathbb{Z}^k_{>0}$, a set $\mathcal{A}^n_k(\boldsymbol{\omega})$ is defined as follows.

$$\mathcal{A}^n_k(\boldsymbol{\omega}) := \{(v_1, v_2, \dots, v_n) \in \mathcal{A}^n_k \colon |\{i : v_i = j\}| = \omega_{|j|},\ j \in \mathcal{A}_k \setminus \{0\}\}.$$

In this paper, we utilize the Local Sensitive Hash (LSH) Function [24] to judge the collision between two vectors.

Definition 1. *For $c \in \mathbb{Z}_{>0}$, a function $l_c : \mathbb{R}^n \to 2^{\{0,1\}^n}$ is called the **Odlyzko's Local Sensitive Hash Function** if for a vector $\boldsymbol{x} = (x_1, x_2, \dots, x_n)^T \in \mathbb{R}^n$, each of binary sequences $\boldsymbol{y} = (y_1, y_2, \cdots, y_n)^T \in l_c(\boldsymbol{x})$ satisfies*

$$y_i := \begin{cases} 1 & \text{if } x_i > \lceil c/2 \rceil - 1, \\ 0 & \text{if } x_i < -\lfloor c/2 \rfloor, \\ 0 \text{ or } 1 & \text{otherwise.} \end{cases}$$

*Given $\boldsymbol{x}_1, \boldsymbol{x}_2 \in \mathbb{Z}^n$ and $c \in \mathbb{Z}$, we say that $(l_c(\boldsymbol{x}_1), l_c(\boldsymbol{x}_2))$ is a **matching** if $l_c(\boldsymbol{x}_1) \cap l_c(-\boldsymbol{x}_2) \neq \emptyset$.*

Here, we give the definition of the Shortest Vector Problem (SVP).

Definition 2. *(**Shortest Vector Problem (SVP)**) Given a lattice Λ of dimension n, the shortest non-zero vector problem asks if one finds $\boldsymbol{v}_0 \in \Lambda \backslash \{\boldsymbol{0}\}$ such that $\|\boldsymbol{v}\|_2 \geq \|\boldsymbol{v}_0\|_2$ for all $\boldsymbol{v} \in \Lambda$.*

The hardness of the SVP in q-ary lattices provides the security foundation of lots of cryptosystems. In our attack, we focus on solving SVP in a q-ary lattice, which is defined as follows.

Definition 3. **(q-ary lattice)** *Given a full rank matrix $\boldsymbol{B} \in \mathbb{R}^{n \times n}$, the lattice $\Lambda(\boldsymbol{B})$ is defined as follows:*

$$\Lambda(\boldsymbol{B}) := \{\boldsymbol{B}\boldsymbol{z} : \boldsymbol{z} \in \mathbb{Z}^n\}.$$

*A lattice Λ of dimension n is called a **q-ary lattice** if $\Lambda \subseteq \mathbb{Z}^n$ and $q\mathbb{Z}^n \subseteq \Lambda$.*

Reduction Algorithm. Lattice reduction is one of the most common attacks on the SVP for a general lattice. Given an input lattice basis, a lattice reduction algorithm outputs another basis of the same lattice of a relatively orthogonal shape. The BKZ algorithm, first proposed in [26], is one of the most popular lattice reduction algorithms used to analyze lattice problems. Due to [12], the related RHF can be simulated by the following function for a BKZ-reduced basis:

$$\delta \approx (\beta \cdot (\pi\beta)^{1/\beta}/(2\pi e))^{1/(2(\beta-1))}.$$

The time complexity of the BKZ reduction algorithm is exponentially related to the block size. If the block size increases, then the time consumption of the algorithm grows and the quality of the reduced basis becomes better. The time complexity of the BKZ reduction highly depends on the applied worst-case SVP oracle. Several models [3,4,6,8,13] estimate the time consumption of BKZ reduction with different types of SVP oracle. Albrecht et al. [5] listed these cost models to show their differences. In this paper, BKZ reduction is utilized as a tool and its complexity models are not further investigated. For the convenience of comparing the results, following the settings of [29], we use the enumeration technique as the SVP oracle. The concrete model we used will be explained in Sect. 5.2 in detail. In this paper, the BKZ algorithm is not only a tool but also a baseline in order to estimate the performance of our attack.

3 Existing Attacks with Some Searching Methods

3.1 The Hybrid Attack for q-ary Lattices

The hybrid attack proposed by Howgrave-Graham [23] tries to find a short vector in a lattice of some special form, typically in a q-ary lattice. This attack successfully applies when the infinite norm of the short vector is restricted. Currently, the hybrid attack only works well when the short vector is ternary, but its mechanism does not prevent it from working in the quinary situation. In what follows, we introduce this specific version of the hybrid attack for quinary vectors.

Let $\Lambda(\boldsymbol{B}')$ be a q-ary lattice with the basis $\boldsymbol{B}' \in \mathbb{Z}^{m\times m}$ given by

$$\boldsymbol{B}' = \begin{pmatrix} \boldsymbol{B} & \boldsymbol{C} \\ \boldsymbol{0} & \boldsymbol{I} \end{pmatrix}, \tag{1}$$

where $\boldsymbol{B} \in \mathbb{Z}^{(m-r)\times(m-r)}$; $\boldsymbol{C} \in \mathbb{Z}^{(m-r)\times r}$; $\boldsymbol{I} \in \mathbb{Z}^{r\times r}$ is the unit matrix. Suppose that $\boldsymbol{v} \in \Lambda(\boldsymbol{B}') \cap \mathcal{A}_2^m$ is one shortest vector in $\Lambda(\boldsymbol{B}')$. For every possible candidate in the short vectors, this attack exploits the structure of the lattice basis by dividing the candidate vector into two parts:

$$\boldsymbol{v} = (\boldsymbol{v}_l, \boldsymbol{v}_g)^T = \boldsymbol{B}'(\boldsymbol{x}, \boldsymbol{v}_g)^T = (\boldsymbol{B}\boldsymbol{x} + \boldsymbol{C}\boldsymbol{v}_g, \boldsymbol{v}_g)^T,$$

where $\boldsymbol{v}_l \in \mathcal{A}_2^{m-r}$, $\boldsymbol{v}_g \in \mathcal{A}_2^r$, $\boldsymbol{x} \in \mathbb{Z}^{m-r}$. If the exact $\boldsymbol{v}_g$ is determined, then it holds that

$$\boldsymbol{C}\boldsymbol{v}_g = -\boldsymbol{B}\boldsymbol{x} + \boldsymbol{v}_l. \tag{2}$$

Since $\boldsymbol{v}_l \in \mathcal{A}_2^{m-r}$ is small, this formula can be viewed as finding a lattice vector that is close to the input target vector $\boldsymbol{C}\boldsymbol{v}_g$ on the $(m-r)$-dimensional lattice $\Lambda(\boldsymbol{B})$. The upper part $\boldsymbol{v}_l$ of the secret vector $\boldsymbol{v}$ can be recovered by the nearest plane (NP) algorithm [7], denoted by $\mathrm{NP}_{\boldsymbol{B}}(\boldsymbol{x})$, on lattice $\Lambda(\boldsymbol{B})$ when the valid $\boldsymbol{C}\boldsymbol{v}_g$ is known and $\Lambda(\boldsymbol{B})$ is fully reduced.

Let $\boldsymbol{x} \in \mathbb{Z}^{m-r}$. By the Furst and Kannan's lemma [17], if the basis $\boldsymbol{B}$ is sufficiently reduced, then with high probability, we have $\| \mathrm{NP}_{\boldsymbol{B}}(\boldsymbol{x})\|_\infty \leq 2$ and $\boldsymbol{x} - \mathrm{NP}_{\boldsymbol{B}}(\boldsymbol{x}) \in \Lambda(\boldsymbol{B})$. Therefore, the Eq. (2) with the variable vector $\boldsymbol{v}_l$ could be solved by the nearest plane algorithm, i.e.

$$\boldsymbol{v}_l = \mathrm{NP}_{\boldsymbol{B}}(\boldsymbol{C}\boldsymbol{v}_g). \tag{3}$$

Meet-in-the-Middle Searching Method. Howgrave-Graham [23] presents the Meet-in-the-Middle method which fits the colliding part of the hybrid attack. Suppose that $\mathcal{A}_2^r(\omega_1, \omega_2)$ is a candidate set of $\boldsymbol{v}_g$. Howgrave-Graham's colliding splits a candidate vector into the summation of two candidate sub-vectors $\boldsymbol{v}_g'$ and $\boldsymbol{v}_g''$ in $\mathcal{A}_2^r(\omega_1/2, \omega_2/2)$. This method uses the Odlyzko's Local Sensitive Hash function (Definition 1) on $\mathrm{NP}_{\boldsymbol{B}}(\boldsymbol{C}\boldsymbol{v}_g')$ to judge their collisions. With the Birthday Paradox, the time complexity of colliding is much lower than that of exhaustive searching. To avoid the redundancy of calculating the NP result for each $\boldsymbol{v}_g' + \boldsymbol{v}_g''$ and reduce the time complexity, only candidates $\boldsymbol{v}_g'$ and $\boldsymbol{v}_g''$ satisfying

$$\mathrm{NP}_{\boldsymbol{B}}(\boldsymbol{C}\boldsymbol{v}_g') + \mathrm{NP}_{\boldsymbol{B}}(\boldsymbol{C}\boldsymbol{v}_g'') = \mathrm{NP}_{\boldsymbol{B}}(\boldsymbol{C}(\boldsymbol{v}_g' + \boldsymbol{v}_g'')) \tag{4}$$

are considered. Condition (4) will be called **additively homomorphic condition**. The final check is to check that whether $(\mathrm{NP}_{\boldsymbol{B}}(\boldsymbol{C}(\boldsymbol{v}_g' + \boldsymbol{v}_g'')), \boldsymbol{v}_g' + \boldsymbol{v}_g'')^T$ is a vector in $\Lambda(\boldsymbol{B}')$. The specification of the hybrid attack is stated in Algorithm 1.

Algorithm 1. The existing hybrid attack on SVP on a q-ary Lattice

Input: $m, r \in \mathbb{Z}_{>0}$, $\boldsymbol{B}'$ is of (1);
Output: $\boldsymbol{v} = (\boldsymbol{v}_g, \boldsymbol{v}_l)^T \in \Lambda(\boldsymbol{B}') \cap \mathcal{A}_2^m$;
Implementing BKZ reduction on $\Lambda(\boldsymbol{B})$
Initialize sets $D_{\boldsymbol{d}} = \emptyset$ for every $\boldsymbol{d} \in \{0,1\}^m$;
for $\boldsymbol{v}_g' \in \mathcal{A}_2^r(\omega_1/2, \omega_2/2)$ **do**
  for $\boldsymbol{g} \in l_2(\mathrm{NP}_{\boldsymbol{B}}(\boldsymbol{C}\boldsymbol{v}_g'))$ **do**
    $D_{\boldsymbol{g}} = D_{\boldsymbol{g}} \cup \left\{\boldsymbol{v}_g'\right\}$
    $D_{\overline{\boldsymbol{g}}} = D_{\overline{\boldsymbol{g}}} \cup \left\{\boldsymbol{v}_g'\right\}$
    if there exists $\boldsymbol{v}_g'' \in D_{\boldsymbol{g}} \cup D_{\overline{\boldsymbol{g}}}$ with $\boldsymbol{v}_g'' \neq \boldsymbol{v}_g'$ **then**
      if $\boldsymbol{v}_g'$ and $\boldsymbol{v}_g''$ satisfies $\left(\mathrm{NP}_{\boldsymbol{B}}(\boldsymbol{C}(\boldsymbol{v}_g' + \boldsymbol{v}_g'')), (\boldsymbol{v}_g' + \boldsymbol{v}_g'')\right)^T \in \mathcal{A}_2^m$ **then**
        return $\boldsymbol{v} := \left(\mathrm{NP}_{\boldsymbol{B}}(\boldsymbol{C}(\boldsymbol{v}_g' + \boldsymbol{v}_g'')), (\boldsymbol{v}_g' + \boldsymbol{v}_g'')\right)^T$;
      end if
    end if
  end for
end for
return $\perp$

The current hybrid attack exhibits satisfactory performance when the infinite norm of the desired short vector $\|\boldsymbol{v}\|_\infty$ does not exceed 1. This is because the search space is comparably small. However, the collision complexity increases significantly as the dimensionality of the candidate short vectors grows from the ternary to the quinary case.

3.2 May's Meet-LWE

The Meet-LWE technique, introduced by May [25], presents a novel approach for searching and colliding in lattice analysis. While this method cannot be readily applied to the hybrid attack, it suggests a promising aspect for exploiting the process of finding $\boldsymbol{v}_g$. Among the various versions of the Meet-LWE algorithm, we select the "Rep-0" version as the fundamental framework. The proposed Meet-LWE algorithm can be readily extended to quinary scenarios by straightforwardly enlarging the search spaces of the error vectors and secret vectors.

Let $(\boldsymbol{A}, \boldsymbol{b}) \in \mathbb{Z}_q^{n \times m} \times \mathbb{Z}_q^m$ be a quinary LWE instance satisfying $\boldsymbol{A}\boldsymbol{s} + \boldsymbol{e} = \boldsymbol{b}$ for some $\boldsymbol{s} \in \mathcal{A}_2^n(\omega_1, \omega_2)$ and $\boldsymbol{e} \in \mathcal{A}_2^m$. The Meet-LWE attack finds a pair of quinary vectors $(\boldsymbol{s}_1, \boldsymbol{s}_2)$ satisfying $\boldsymbol{s} = \boldsymbol{s}_1 + \boldsymbol{s}_2$. This pair can be easily obtained by arranging half of the i-entries and $(-i)$-entries of $\boldsymbol{s}$ to $\boldsymbol{s}_1$ and the others to $\boldsymbol{s}_2$ for $i \in \{1, 2\}$. Here, we shall call a pair $(\boldsymbol{s}_1, \boldsymbol{s}_2)$ a **valid representation** of $\boldsymbol{s}$. Let the R be the set of valid representations of $\boldsymbol{s}$. Then the cardinality $|R|$ is given by

$$|R| = \binom{\omega_1}{\omega_1/2}^2 \binom{\omega_2}{\omega_2/2}^2.$$

Define a target dimension t by $t = \arg\max\{t' \in \mathbb{Z}: q^{t'} \leq R\}$. Let $\pi_t : \mathbb{Z}_q^m \to \mathbb{Z}_q^t$ be the projection such that $\pi_t((x_1, x_2, \cdots, x_m)) = (x_1, x_2, \cdots, x_t)$. It can be checked that the projection π_t is an additive homomorphism. Assume that the projection of a valid error vector $\pi_t(\boldsymbol{e}) \in \mathcal{A}_1^r$ is known. We randomly choose $\boldsymbol{b}_1 \xleftarrow{\$} \mathbb{Z}_q^t$ and let $\boldsymbol{b}_2 := \boldsymbol{b} - \boldsymbol{b}_1$. Note that there exist vectors $\boldsymbol{e}_+, \boldsymbol{e}_- \in \{0, 1, 2\}^t$ such that $\pi_t(\boldsymbol{e}) = \boldsymbol{e}_+ - \boldsymbol{e}_-$. Indeed, these vectors $\boldsymbol{e}_+$ and $\boldsymbol{e}_-$ can be found by determining their entries with the following constraints:

$$(\boldsymbol{e}_+)_i = \begin{cases} (\pi_t(\boldsymbol{e}))_i & \text{if } (\pi_t(\boldsymbol{e}))_i > 0, \\ 0 & \text{otherwise,} \end{cases} (\boldsymbol{e}_-)_i = \begin{cases} -(\pi_t(\boldsymbol{e}))_i & \text{if } (\pi_t(\boldsymbol{e}))_i < 0, \\ 0 & \text{otherwise,} \end{cases} \quad (5)$$

where $(\pi_t(\boldsymbol{e}))_i$ is the i-th entry of $\pi_t(\boldsymbol{e})$. It is clear that $\boldsymbol{e}_+$ and $\boldsymbol{e}_-$ represent the positive part and the negative part of the projection $\pi_t(\boldsymbol{e})$ of a valid short error $\boldsymbol{e}$ respectively. $\pi_t(\boldsymbol{e})$, respectively. Since $q^t \approx R$, it is expected that at least one valid representation $(\boldsymbol{s}_1, \boldsymbol{s}_2)$ satisfies $\pi_t(\boldsymbol{A}\boldsymbol{s}_1 + \boldsymbol{e}_+) = \pi_t(\boldsymbol{b})$. At this time, $\boldsymbol{s}_2$ must satisfy $\pi_t(\boldsymbol{A}\boldsymbol{s}_2 - \boldsymbol{e}_-) = \boldsymbol{b}_2$. Therefore, for every possible $\pi_t(\boldsymbol{e}) \in \mathcal{A}_1^t$, namely $\pi_t(\boldsymbol{e}_+), \pi_t(\boldsymbol{e}_-) \in \{0, 1\}^t$, we construct the colliding lists:

$$L_1 = \{\boldsymbol{s}_1 \colon \pi_t(\boldsymbol{A}\boldsymbol{s}_1 + \boldsymbol{e}_+) = \boldsymbol{b}_1\}, L_2 = \{\boldsymbol{s}_2 \colon \pi_t(\boldsymbol{A}\boldsymbol{s}_2 - \boldsymbol{e}_-) = \boldsymbol{b}_2\}.$$

It holds that $\pi_t(\boldsymbol{A}(\boldsymbol{s}_1 + \boldsymbol{s}_2) + \boldsymbol{e}_+ - \boldsymbol{e}_-) = \pi_t(\boldsymbol{b})$ for every $\boldsymbol{s}_1 \in L_1$ and $\boldsymbol{s}_2 \in L_2$. Therefore, only the $n - t$ remaining dimensions need to be collided by meet-in-the-middle methods. These collisions of the remaining dimensions are found by Odlyzko's LSH function with $c = 2$. Since there are 5^t different possible candidates for a vector $\pi_t(\boldsymbol{e})$, the problem of solving the original LWE instance is changed to the problem of solving two smaller LWE-like instances for 5^t times in the average case with the list constructing process. The hash function used in the Meet-LWE algorithm can not find an unbalanced error vector that has no minus entry when the attacker plans to find $\boldsymbol{s}_1$ with colliding techniques, which means that the error vector should be pre-determined for the construction of the lists. As a result, eliminating the guessing component is challenging.

Given that the Meet-LWE algorithm does not systematically iterate all possible vectors in the searching space $\mathcal{A}_2^n(\omega_1/2, \omega_2/2)$, it can achieve a faster collision detection than traditional methods. Nonetheless, this feature limits the applicability of the Meet-LWE algorithm to the hybrid attack, as it requires a valid representation $(\boldsymbol{v}_g', \boldsymbol{v}_g'')$ that satisfies the additively homomorphic condition (4).

4 Error-Splitting Hybrid Attack

In this section, we introduce the Error-Splitting Hybrid (ESHybrid) attack for solving q-ary SVP lattices with a quinary shortest non-zero vector.

Let $\boldsymbol{B}'$ be a basis for a q-ary lattice given in (1). Following the basic thought of the existing hybrid attack, r denotes the colliding dimension. When r is fixed, we assume that the knowledge of weights in the last r of $\boldsymbol{v}$ is given: ω_1, ω_2 are known if $\boldsymbol{v} = (\boldsymbol{v}_l, \boldsymbol{v}_g)^T$ for $\boldsymbol{v}_g \in \mathcal{A}_2^r(\omega_1, \omega_2)$.

Similar to the existing hybrid attack, the ESHybrid attack aims at finding a short vector $\boldsymbol{v} = (\boldsymbol{v}_l, \boldsymbol{v}_g)^T \in \mathcal{A}_2^m$ where $\boldsymbol{v}_l \in \mathcal{A}_2^{m-r}$ and $\boldsymbol{v}_g \in \mathcal{A}_2^r(\omega_1, \omega_2)$. The ESHybrid attack still seeks the collisions in the lower entries of a short non-zero vector and uses the nearest plane algorithm to find the upper part of the valid short vector. However, instead of the ordinary meet-in-the-middle attack, the ESHybrid attack employs the Meet-LWE to reduce the searching time consumption. To overcome the difficulty noted in [25], saying that Meet-LWE can not be applied to the hybrid attack, we apply the so-called Error-Splitting technique in the searching procedure. This technique leverages the special structure of quinary vectors and improves the efficiency of the attack as well.

As described by the core Eq. (3), the process of finding $\boldsymbol{v}_l$ in the ESHybrid attack is somewhat like solving an "altered" LWE instance with the vector $\boldsymbol{b} = \boldsymbol{0}$. Therefore, the Meet-LWE attack can be applied. Let $t < r$ be a colliding target dimension. Generally, the ESHybrid attack constructs lists L_1 and L_2 containing vectors that collide in the first t entries and searches for a valid representation in these two lists.

The hybrid attack selects a target vector $\boldsymbol{t} \in \mathbb{Z}^t$ randomly. The colliding part of the ESHybrid attack chooses candidates $\boldsymbol{v}_g^{'}, \boldsymbol{v}_g^{''} \in \mathcal{A}_2^r(\omega_1/2, \omega_2/2)$ uniformly and searches for a valid short non-zero vector from them. When the target vector $\boldsymbol{t}$ is fixed, we only search for a vector $\boldsymbol{v}_g^{'}$ such that the difference between $\mathrm{NP}_{\boldsymbol{B}}(\boldsymbol{C}\boldsymbol{v}_g^{'})$ and $\boldsymbol{t}$ and the first t entries of $\mathrm{NP}_{\boldsymbol{B}}(\boldsymbol{C}\boldsymbol{v}_g^{'})$ is ternary. Whenever the difference is not ternary, the ESHybrid attack does not accept it even if $(\boldsymbol{v}_g^{'}, \boldsymbol{v}_g^{''})$ a valid representations of $\boldsymbol{v}_g$. For $\boldsymbol{v}_g^{''}$, we seek a similar condition, while the target vector becomes $-\boldsymbol{t}$. From basic arithmetic, the sum of these two ternary sub-vectors can be a quinary sub-vector. Therefore, the goal of the colliding is converted to searching all the vectors $\boldsymbol{v}_g^{'} \in \mathcal{A}_2^r(\omega_1/2, \omega_2/2)$ and construct the list:

$$L_1^{(1)} = \left\{(\boldsymbol{v}_g^{'}, l_2(\boldsymbol{v}_g^{'})) \colon \left\|\pi_t(\mathrm{NP}_{\boldsymbol{B}}(\boldsymbol{C}\boldsymbol{v}_g^{'})) - \boldsymbol{t}\right\|_\infty \leq 1\right\}. \tag{6}$$

Also, finding all the vectors $\boldsymbol{v}_g^{''} \in \mathcal{A}_2^r(\omega_1/2, \omega_2/2)$ and construct the list:

$$L_2^{(1)} = \left\{(\boldsymbol{v}_g^{''}, l_2(\boldsymbol{v}_g^{''})) \colon \left\|\pi_t(\mathrm{NP}_{\boldsymbol{B}}(\boldsymbol{C}\boldsymbol{v}_g^{''})) + \boldsymbol{t}\right\|_\infty \leq 1\right\}, \tag{7}$$

where l_2 is the Odlyzko's LSH with $c = 2$. The procedure of candidates to $L_1^{(1)}$ and $L_2^{(1)}$ is stated as Layer 2.

If the lists in (6) are constructed, then for every $(\boldsymbol{v}_g^{'}, \boldsymbol{v}_g^{''}) \in L_1^{(1)} \times L_2^{(1)}$, it holds from the basic arithmetic that

$$\left\|\pi_t(\mathrm{NP}_{\boldsymbol{B}}(\boldsymbol{C}\boldsymbol{v}_g^{'}) + \mathrm{NP}_{\boldsymbol{B}}(\boldsymbol{C}\boldsymbol{v}_g^{''}))\right\|_\infty \leq 2. \tag{8}$$

Indeed, if the additively homomorphic property (4) is assumed for the nearest plane algorithm on $\boldsymbol{C}\boldsymbol{v}_g^{'}$ and $\boldsymbol{C}\boldsymbol{v}_g^{'}$, then the inequality can be converted into (8). This fact means that all $\boldsymbol{v}_g^{'}$ in $L_1^{(1)}$ and $\boldsymbol{v}_g^{''}$ in $L_2^{(1)}$ matches in the first t entries of the last r entries of $\boldsymbol{B}^{'}$ which is a necessary condition for $\boldsymbol{v}_g^{'}$ and $\boldsymbol{v}_g^{''}$ to be a valid representation. If a valid representation is guaranteed to be in $L_1^{(1)} \times L_2^{(1)}$, then it can be found by colliding all elements from the lists by the assumption on the additively homomorphic property (4). The procedure of finding the valid vector is said to be Layer 1 in the algorithm.

The determination of the target dimension t is a crucial step in the ESHybrid attack. To take the additively homomorphic condition (4) into account, t needs to be chosen relatively small compared to the LWE version. The whole procedure

Algorithm 2. Colliding for the ESHybrid Attack on SVP

Input: $q, m, r, t, \omega_1, \omega_2 \in \mathbb{Z}_{>0}$, where B' is of (1);
Output: A vector $v_g \in \mathcal{A}_2^r(\omega_1, \omega_2)$ such that $(v_l, v_g)^T \in \Lambda(B')$ for some $v_l \in \mathcal{A}_2^{m-r}$;
1: Initialize empty lists L_1,L_2;
2: $R_1^{\mathrm{CR}} = \binom{\omega_1}{\omega_1/2}^2 \binom{\omega_2}{\omega_2/2}^2$;
3: Randomly select $t \in \mathcal{A}_1^r$;
4: Constructing $L_1^{(1)}$ as (6);
5: Constructing $L_2^{(1)}$ as (7);
6: **for** $((v_g', \mathcal{H}_1), (v_g'', \mathcal{H}_2)) \in L_1 \times L_2$ s.t. $(\mathcal{H}_1, \mathcal{H}_2)$ is a matching **do**
7:     **if** $\|\pi_t(\mathrm{NP}_B(C(v_g' + v_g'')))\|_\infty \leq 2$ **then**
8:         **return** $v_g = v_g' + v_g''$;
9:     **end if**
10: **end for**
11: **return** $\perp$

in colliding a valid v_g is shown in Algorithm 2. Layer 2 starts from Line 4 to Line 5; Layer 1 starts from Line 6 to Line 10. Directly combining Algorithm 2 and a lattice reduction on B creates the whole ESHybrid attack.

5 Theoretical Analysis

Theoretical complexity analysis of the ESHybrid Attack on SVP of q-ary lattices is provided in this section. We consider the overestimate and underestimate of the attacker's ability. To represent the complexity, we use the abbreviated symbol to represent the multinomial symbol

$$\binom{n}{n_1, n_2, \ldots, n_k, \cdot} := \binom{n}{n_1, n_2, \ldots, n_k, n - \sum_{i=1}^k n_i}.$$

Overestimate and Underestimate. In our analysis of the heuristic theoretical time complexity, for a given attacking algorithm (such as the ESHybrid attack in this section), we consider two "extreme" situations: overestimate and underestimate of the complexity (of the attack algorithm). The overestimate assumes that the subroutines of the attack in the algorithm achieve their goals in the worst case, while the underestimate assumes that the algorithm runs in the optimal case. Due to the black-box situation of the running environment in the analysis, these inaccuracies are unavoidable. We provide both the overestimate and the underestimate of the complexity analysis in this analysis to give a general perspective of the ESHybrid attack.

5.1 Theoretical Analysis of the Colliding Part

In this section, we present a theoretical analysis of the time complexity of the ESHybrid attack. This attack is divided into two main parts: the reduction part and the colliding part. The reduction procedure of solving lattice problems has been extensively investigated in works like [12], so we mainly focus on the time complexity of the colliding procedure. To address this problem, we compute the expected number of loops required to find a valid representation based on a series of assumptions.

Operation Estimation. Following the fashion of [23,29], during the theoretical analysis, the complexity of NP algorithm C_{NP} acts as the unit and the time consumption of the total algorithm is roughly multiple numbers of C_{NP}. We use the heuristic time complexity calculated by Hirschhorn et al. in [21] to modify the time consumption of one call to the NP algorithm:

Lemma 1. *Let the expected bit operation number of one call to* $\mathrm{NP}_{\boldsymbol{B}}(\boldsymbol{t})$ *be* $C_{\mathrm{NP,over}}$ *if the complexity is overestimated; and be* $C_{\mathrm{NP,under}}$ *if the complexity is underestimated. Then*

$$C_{\mathrm{NP,over}} = (m-r)/2^{1.06},\ \ C_{\mathrm{NP,under}} = (m-r)^2/2^{1.06}.$$

Probability of Admissibility. The task of the colliding algorithm is to produce a pair $(\boldsymbol{v}_g^{'}, \boldsymbol{v}_g^{''})$ satisfying the following condition: (1) $\boldsymbol{v}_g^{'}$ and $\boldsymbol{v}_g^{''}$ are $\boldsymbol{v}_l$-admissible for some $\boldsymbol{v}_l \in \mathcal{A}_1^n$;
(2) $(\mathrm{NP}_{\boldsymbol{B}}(\boldsymbol{C}\boldsymbol{v}_g^{'}), \mathrm{NP}_{\boldsymbol{B}}(\boldsymbol{C}\boldsymbol{v}_g^{''}))$ is a matching; (3) For a given target dimension t and target vector $\boldsymbol{t} \in \mathbb{Z}_q^t$,

$$\|\pi_k(\mathrm{NP}_{\boldsymbol{B}}(\boldsymbol{C}\boldsymbol{v}_g^{'})) - \boldsymbol{t}\|_\infty \leq 1, \|\pi_k(\mathrm{NP}_{\boldsymbol{B}}(\boldsymbol{C}\boldsymbol{v}_g^{''})) + \boldsymbol{t}\|_\infty \leq 1.$$

To ensure that the ESHybrid algorithm can find at least one representation that satisfies the previous necessary conditions, the target dimension t must guarantee that at least one representation, which satisfies the additively homomorphic condition (4), matches the randomly chosen vector in the first t entries.

Howgrave-Graham [23] introduced the concept "admissibility" in order to analyze the hybrid attack which allows us to view the nearest plane algorithm as a required additive homomorphism.

Definition 4. *Given* $\boldsymbol{x}, \boldsymbol{y} \in \mathbb{Z}^n$, $\boldsymbol{x}$ *is said to be* $\boldsymbol{y}$*-admissible (with respect to* $\boldsymbol{B}$*) if it holds that*

$$\mathrm{NP}_{\boldsymbol{B}}(\boldsymbol{x}-\boldsymbol{y}) + \boldsymbol{y} = \mathrm{NP}_{\boldsymbol{B}}(\boldsymbol{x}).$$

[23] states that $\boldsymbol{t}$-admissible vectors preserve the additively homomorphic property (4) by the following lemma.

Lemma 2. *Suppose that $\boldsymbol{x}_1, \boldsymbol{x}_2 \in \mathbb{R}^m$ are two arbitrary vectors. Then the following statements are equivalent:*

(1) $\mathrm{NP}_{\boldsymbol{B}}(\boldsymbol{x}_1 + \boldsymbol{x}_2) = \mathrm{NP}_{\boldsymbol{B}}(\boldsymbol{x}_1) + \mathrm{NP}_{\boldsymbol{B}}(\boldsymbol{x}_2)$.
(2) $\boldsymbol{x}_i$ *is* $(\boldsymbol{x}_1 + \boldsymbol{x}_2)$*-admissible for each* $i \in \{1, 2\}$.

From Lemma 2, if $\boldsymbol{v}_g^{'}$ and $\boldsymbol{v}_g^{''}$ fulfill the condition of $\boldsymbol{v}_l$-admissible for some $\boldsymbol{v}_l \in \mathbb{Z}^{m-r}$, then the key condition (4) makes our hybrid attack applicable. In order to deduce the complexity, we define the concept of probability of admissibility in the colliding procedure.

Definition 5. *Let $\mathcal{P}(\boldsymbol{B})$ be the fundamental region of a lattice $\Lambda(\boldsymbol{B})$. Given $k_1, k_2, t \in \mathbb{Z}_{>0}$ and a lattice $\Lambda(\boldsymbol{B})$ with basis $\boldsymbol{B} \in \mathbb{Z}^{(m-r)\times(m-r)}$, suppose $\boldsymbol{x} \xleftarrow{\$} \mathcal{P}(\boldsymbol{B}^*)$, $\boldsymbol{y} \xleftarrow{\$} \mathcal{A}_2^n((m-r)k_1/m, (m-r)k_2/m)$, $\boldsymbol{z} \xleftarrow{\$} \mathcal{A}_1^n(\tau)$, where $\boldsymbol{y}$ and $\boldsymbol{x}$ are independent; $\boldsymbol{y}$ and $\boldsymbol{z}$ are independent. The probability p_1 is defined by*

$$p_1(\omega_1, \omega_2, \tau, t) := \Pr[\boldsymbol{x} \textit{ is } \boldsymbol{y}\textit{-admissible}].$$

Let $\mathcal{P}^{'}(\boldsymbol{B}^*) := \{\boldsymbol{s} \in \mathbb{R}^t \colon \pi_t(\boldsymbol{u}) = \boldsymbol{s},\ \boldsymbol{u} \in \mathcal{P}(\boldsymbol{B}^*)\}$. Then the probability p_2 is defined by

$$p_2(\omega_1, \omega_2, \tau, t) := \Pr[\pi_t(\boldsymbol{z} + \boldsymbol{y}) \in \mathcal{P}^{'}(\boldsymbol{B}^*)].$$

When all the parameters are clear in the context, we use $p_1 := p_1(\omega_1, \omega_2, \tau, t)$ and $p_2 := p_2(\omega_1, \omega_2, \tau, t)$.

The intuition of this definition is that p_2 models the probability that when $\boldsymbol{v}_g^{'}, \boldsymbol{v}_g^{''} \xleftarrow{\$} \mathcal{A}_2^r(\omega_1/4, \omega_2/4)$, the condition (4) holds. Since it is hard to model this probability without any predetermined conditions, we propose the following assumption.

Assumption 1. *The events of p_1 and p_2 satisfy the following two statement:*

(1) The events of p_1 and p_2 are independent.
(2) The events of p_1 and p_2 have no relationship with the angle between every $\boldsymbol{b}_i^*$ and the every coordinate axis.

Remark 1. We do not know that Assumption 1 holds in practice. So, we leave this as an open problem.

The first statement of Assumption 1 means that the event of admissibility in each layer should be considered independent of that of the other layer. the second statement is based on the randomness of the reduced result of BKZ. Both of the statements simplify the theoretical analysis.

Lemma 3. *Let*

$$p_{y_i}^{(j)} := \begin{cases} (\|\boldsymbol{b}_i\| - j)/\|\boldsymbol{b}_i\| & \text{if } \|\boldsymbol{b}_i\| > j, \\ 0 & \text{otherwise.} \end{cases}$$

If Assumptions 1 is true, then p_1 *and* p_2 *are calculated as*

$$p_1 = \prod_{i=1}^{m-r} \left(\frac{2k_1}{m} p_{y_i}^{(1)} + \frac{2k_2}{m} p_{y_i}^{(2)} + \frac{m - 2k_1 - 2k_2}{m} \right),$$

$$p_2 = \prod_{i=1}^{t} \left(\frac{k_1 + 2k_2}{m} p_{y_i}^{(1)} + \frac{m - 2k_1 - 2k_2}{m} \right).$$

This lemma can be verified by considering each entry of the short vector independently.

Note that p_1 models the probability that a random vector in the list L_1 of Layer 1 in Algorithm 2 is $\boldsymbol{y}$-admissible for some $\boldsymbol{y} \in \mathcal{P}^*(\boldsymbol{B})$ in the last $r-t$ entries. p_2 models the probability that in the first t entries. With these components, We provide the complexities of each parts of Algorithm 2 and then give the theorem that states the total consumption of the ESHybrid attack.

Lemma 4. *The average list construction complexity* $C_{List}^{(2)}$ *of Layer* 2 *in Algorithm 2 is calculated as* $C_{List}^{(2)} := |L^{(2)}| := |\mathcal{A}_2^r(\omega_1/4, \omega_2/4)|$.

Proof. Since lists in Layer 2 contain the whole searching space to find the correct representation, the size of the list in Layer 2 is exactly the cardinality of the searching space. In our setting, we assume that all of the possible candidates in $L^{(2)}$ should be considered and calculated. This means that $C_{\text{List}}^{(2)}$ is just the size of the colliding space $L^{(2)}$:

$$C_{\text{List}}^{(2)} := |L^{(2)}| := |\mathcal{A}_2^r(\omega_1/4, \omega_2/4)|.$$

Notice that in the colliding procedure of Layer 2, the calling of the NP algorithm is integrated into the construction of the list of Layer 1. This fact means that the Layer 2 colliding complexity $C_{\text{Col}}^{(2)}$ can be ignored.

Lemma 5. *The average list construction complexity* $C_{List}^{(1)}$ *of Layer* 1 *in Algorithm 2 is calculated as* $C_{List}^{(1)} := (3/q)^t |\mathcal{A}_2^r(\omega_1/2, \omega_2/2)|$; *the average colliding complexity* $C_{Col}^{(1)}$ *of Layer* 1 *in Algorithm 2 is calculated as* $C_{Col}^{(1)} := (C_{List}^{(1)})^2 / 2^{m-r}$.

Proof. Due to the mechanism of the construction of $L^{(1)}$ and $L^{(2)}$, the possible candidates of must be around the target vector $\boldsymbol{t}$ in the first t entries. Viewing the results $\text{NP}_{\boldsymbol{B}}(\boldsymbol{Cs})$ are randomly distributed in its first t dimension, than $|L^{(1)}| = 3^t |S| / q^t$, where S is the original searching space utilized in the existing hybrid attack. The definition of S indicates that it goes over all vector in $\mathcal{A}_2^r(\omega_1/2, \omega_2/2)$, where $|S| := |\mathcal{A}_2^r(\omega_1/2, \omega_2/2)| = \binom{r}{\omega_1/2, \omega_1/2, \omega_2/2, \omega_2/2, \cdot}$.

The list construction complexity equals to the size. After the list construction, a valid representation can be found by constructing the list with complexity around $C^{(1)}_{\text{Col}} := |L^{(1)}|^2/2^{m-r}$ in average.

With the components mentioned above, the complexity of the colliding period of our algorithm can be calculated as Theorem 2:

Theorem 2. *Let p_1, p_2 be defined in Definition 5. Then under Assumptions 1, the time complexity C_{ESCol} of the colliding part of Algorithm 2 is calculated as*

$$C_{ESCol} := C^{(2)}_{List} + C^{(1)}_{List} + C^{(1)}_{Col},$$

where $C^{(2)}_{List}$, $C^{(1)}_{List}$ and $C^{(1)}_{Col}$ are demonstrated in Lemmas 4 and 5.

Proof. Due to Algorithm 2, the colliding procedure of the ESHybrid attack contains two layers, and the process of Layer 1 starts after the end of Layer 2. Therefore, the complexity C_{ESCol} combines all the stated components by addition.

5.2 Total Theoretical Complexity of the ESHybrid Attack

Reduction Complexity. Following the fashion from [29], the enumeration kernel-based method is considered in the experiment, which is a common cost estimate given by the research of Albrecht [3] based on the experiments of Chen [13]. Generally, the cost corresponding to one call to the SVP oracle will be in the form of

$$C_{\text{Red}}(\beta) = 2^{0.187281\beta\log_2(\beta)-1.0192\beta+16.1},$$

while the parameters are different from each other relating to the models. Then the time complexity of the BKZ reduction in our ESHybrid attack in the overestimate and the underestimate situation is set to be

$$C_{\text{Red,over}}(\beta, r) = (m-r)C_{red}(\beta),\ C_{\text{Red,under}}(\beta, r) = (m-r-\beta+1)C_{red}(\beta),$$

separately, where r is the colliding dimension.

Probability of Success. The previous sections have outlined the complexity analysis based on the assumption that the valid secret vector $\boldsymbol{v} = (\boldsymbol{v}_l, \boldsymbol{v}_g)^T \in \mathcal{A}^n_2(k_1, k_2)$ while $\boldsymbol{v}_g \in \mathcal{A}^r_2(k_1, k_2)$. However, in the evaluation of the complexity for attacking a particular lattice-based cryptosystem, it is crucial for the estimator to ensure that the ideal condition is met. Therefore, when dealing with real-world cryptosystems, the probability of the preset condition occurring must be taken into account. We note that this probability acts as a factor in every collision-based method.

Definition 6. ***(Probability of Choosing)*** *If the shortest non-zero vector $\boldsymbol{v} = (\boldsymbol{v}_l, \boldsymbol{v}_g)^T \in \Lambda(\boldsymbol{B})$ satisfies $\boldsymbol{v} \in \mathcal{A}^m_2(k_1, k_2)$. $\boldsymbol{v}_g \in \mathbb{Z}^r$, then the probability of choosing $p_{\text{ch}}(\omega_1, \omega_2)$ is defined by the probability that $\boldsymbol{v}_g \in \mathcal{A}^r_2(\omega_1, \omega_2)$.*

For each SVP-based cryptosystem, the calculation of the probability of choosing is nearly same. From Definition 6, the probability of choosing is given by

$$p_{\text{ch}}(\omega_1, \omega_2) = \binom{r}{\omega_1, \omega_1, \omega_2, \omega_2, \cdot} \Big/ \binom{m}{k_1, k_1, k_2, k_2, \cdot}.$$

However, for some cryptosystems (e.g. NTRU Prime), there is more than one valid short vector. In this case, the calculating formula of p_{ch} needs to be reconsidered due to specific distributions.

Definition 7. ***(Probability of NP)*** *For some $\boldsymbol{v} \in \mathcal{A}_2^m(k_1, k_2)$ and $\boldsymbol{v}_g \in \mathbb{Z}^r$, let $\boldsymbol{v} = (\boldsymbol{v}_l, \boldsymbol{v}_g)^T \in \Lambda(\boldsymbol{B}) \setminus \{\boldsymbol{0}\}$ be shortest. Then p_{NP} is the probability that $\boldsymbol{v}_l = \text{NP}_{\boldsymbol{B}}(\boldsymbol{C}\boldsymbol{v}_g)$.*

According to Assumption 1, p_{NP} is then modeled by estimating the probability for each coordinate, which is denoted as $p_{\text{NP},i}$ for the i-th coordinate. Let $k_0 := m - 2k_1 - 2k_2$. Then the probability $p_{\text{NP},i}$ $(-b_i \le v_{li} \le b_i)$ can be calculated by

$$p_{\text{NP},i} := \sum_{\epsilon=-2}^{2} \frac{k_\epsilon}{m} \theta_i(\epsilon), \text{where } \theta_i(\epsilon) = \begin{cases} 1 & \text{if } |\epsilon| \le b_i, \\ 0 & \text{otherwise.} \end{cases} \tag{9}$$

Then p_{NP} can be computed by taking a product overall $p_{\text{NP},i}$.

$$p_{\text{NP}} := \prod_{i=1}^{m-r} p_{\text{NP},i} = \prod_{i=1}^{m-r} \sum_{\epsilon=-2}^{2} \frac{k_\epsilon}{m} \theta_i(\epsilon). \tag{10}$$

It is revealed that if the events corresponding to p_{ch} and p_{NP} do not happen, then the total procedure of the attack needs to be restarted. They are combined to be the probability of success:

Definition 8. ***(Probability of Success)*** *The probability of success $p_s(\omega_1, \omega_2)$ is defined by $p_s(\omega_1, \omega_2) := p_{\text{ch}}(\omega_1, \omega_2) \cdot p_{\text{NP}}$.*

The total heuristic complexity of the Error-Splitting attack in the overestimating case would be like

$$C_{\text{total,over}} = (C_{\text{Red,over}}(\beta, r) + C_{\text{NP,over}} \cdot C_{\text{ESCol}}(\beta, r))/p_s(\omega_1, \omega_2).$$

In the underestimating situation,

$$C_{\text{total,under}} = (C_{\text{Red,under}}(\beta, r) + C_{\text{NP,under}} \cdot C_{\text{ESCol}}(\beta, r))/p_s(\omega_1, \omega_2).$$

5.3 Applying Conditions

In order to obtain a heuristic formula for the complexity of the ESHybrid attack, the target dimension t must be determined. In the LWE case, the only requirement for t is that $q^t < |R|$, ensuring that at least one representation hits the target. However, in the hybrid attack, we must consider the probability of admissibility p_1 and p_2 when determining t. Consequently, some suitable choice of t significantly reduces the number of potential candidates.

Heuristic 3. *Let* $\boldsymbol{v} = (\boldsymbol{v}_l, \boldsymbol{v}_g)^T \in \mathcal{A}_2^m$ *be a short vector in some q-ary lattice. For the colliding dimension r and the target dimension t, let* $\boldsymbol{v}_g \in \mathcal{A}_2^r(\omega_1, \omega_2)$ *be fixed. Then ESHybrid attack can be successfully implemented when (1):* $(3/q)^t p_1 |R| > 1$*; (2):* $|S|/(p_1|R|) \leq p_2 |\mathcal{A}_2^r(\omega_1/4, \omega_2/4)|^2/q^t$*; where* p_1*,* p_2 *are calculated as Lemma 3.*

We justify this heuristic. Let S denote the searching space in Layer 1 and R denote the set of the valid representations in Layer 1. The cardinality of these two sets can be calculated by the definition. The intuition of Criterion (1) is clear. It guarantees that at least there exists one valid representation satisfying all the conditions. Criterion (2) is based on the fact that the required number of candidates in Layer 1 is different from the supporting candidates provided by Layer 2. Algorithm 2 can recover the required short vector if Layer 2 can provide enough candidate vectors. Specifically, we define the required list size of Layer 1 by $|L^{(1)}|_1$. Based on the Pigeon Hole Principle, we have $|L^{(1)}|_1 := |S|/(p_1|R|)$. Note that the $(3/q)^t$ factor in Heuristic 3 represents the condition of constructing $L^{(1)}$. The p_1 factor here is used to compensate for the loss from the probability of admissibility. The size of candidates that Layer 2 can provide is defined by $\left|L^{(2)}\right|_1$. It is clear that $|L^{(2)}|_1$ is based on the size of the searching space in Layer 2, which is $|L^{(2)}| := |\mathcal{A}_2^r(\omega_1/4, \omega_2/4)|$. By the complexity of colliding, $|L^{(1)}|_2$ could be calculated as $|L^{(1)}|_2 := p_2 |L^{(2)}|^2/q^t$. Then Criterion (2) is generated by asking $|L^{(1)}|_1 < |L^{(1)}|_2$.

Target Dimension Determination. Due to Algorithm 2, a bigger target dimension t will lead to a smaller colliding complexity. Hence, the attacker with ESHybrid tries to use a larger t. However, the Criterion (2) of Heuristic 3 constrains the maximal value for the target dimension t. There also exists another restriction that asks every list of each layer to hold more than one candidate, indicating another upper bound for t. Therefore, the optimal target dimension t satisfies

$$t_{\text{opt}} := \min(\lfloor \log_q (p_1 p_2 |\mathcal{A}_1^2(\omega_1/4 + \omega_2/2)|^2 |R|/|S|) \rfloor, \lfloor \log_{q/3} |S|/(p_1|R|) \rfloor). \quad (11)$$

To ensure that the ESHybrid algorithm can find the vector, more than one candidate may be provided for list L_1, in practical situation t can be smaller than the shown t_{opt} in (11).

6 Numerical Result

6.1 Estimation of Parameters from Existing Cryptosystems

In this section, we evaluate the numerical results of the ESHybrid attack and compare them with the results from previous attacks. All the parameter sets are selected from existing cryptosystems, and are extended to the quinary situation, where k_i means the number of entries whose absolute value is i in the short vector. In our experiments, the ESHybrid attack is compared with the lattice reduction with 2016 estimation [6] and the existing hybrid attack with the estimation from [29]. In Table 1, we show the security evaluation for several schemes. The meaning of parameters in Table 1 is as follows. $r_{\text{hyb, under}}/r_{\text{hyb, over}}$ is the optimal colliding dimension of the existing hybrid attack with under/over-estimate; $r_{\text{ES, under}}/r_{\text{ES, over}}$ is the optimal colliding dimension of ESHybrid attack with under/over-estimate; $\beta_{\text{hyb, under}}/\beta_{\text{hyb, over}}$ is the optimal reduction block size of the existing hybrid attack with under/over-estimate; $\beta_{\text{ES, under}}/\beta_{\text{ES, over}}$ is the optimal reduction block size of ESHybrid attack with under/over-estimate. The 2016 estimate outperforms the existing hybrid attack. This is because of the larger searching space and the larger infinite norm of the quinary setting. Thus, the existing hybrid attack is not considered suitable for the quinary setting. Due to the experimental results, our ESHybrid attack is highly effective in solving q-ary SVPs with quinary short vectors. However, its performance, as in other methods, depends on the sparsity of the cryptosystem. It remains an open question of improving the efficiency when the short vector is not sparse.

Table 1. Security Evaluation of Each Parameter Sets under Different Attacks

m	802	878	1186	1486	1213	1478	1858
q	2048	2048	2048	2048	18749	9829	12953
k_1	202	220	298	374	300	372	233
k_2	64	72	96	120	104	120	152
Optimal β_{2016}	277	311	453	595	348	484	622
2016 est. in Bits	164/171	191/197	312/319	446/452	221/227	341/349	474/481
$r_{\text{hyb,under}}$	98	120	202	261	114	213	264
$r_{\text{hyb,over}}$	110	125	202	263	121	222	286
$\beta_{\text{hyb,under}}$	269	302	453	568	363	464	587
$\beta_{\text{hyb,over}}$	263	291	449	559	358	459	585
Under/Over Sec. of [29]	203/215	224/249	322/334	422/435	234/248	349/377	445/463
Under/Over Sec. of [29] with p_s	214/227	236/262	335/347	435/450	242/261	364/391	460/477
$r_{\text{ES,under}}$	151	172	268	371	194	292	391
$r_{\text{ES,over}}$	152	176	276	367	180	284	390
$\beta_{\text{ES,under}}$	253	271	394	488	323	420	528
$\beta_{\text{ES,over}}$	259	281	387	500	326	412	517
Under/Over Sec. of ESHybrid	144/153	167/173	259/268	354/362	192/202	277/290	375/381
Under/Over Sec. of ESHybrid with p_s	154/166	175/186	267/282	366/376	193/215	278/303	384/396

6.2 Comparison

In this section, we investigate the influence of parameters on the attacking algorithm and verify the theoretical trade-off discussed. Specially, We estimate the effect of the colliding dimension r and block size β. We provide a detailed analysis of specific parameter sets to illustrate the features of the ESHybrid algorithm.

Changes of the Attacking Complexity with Different Dimension r. Figure 1 show the change of the total complexity of the ESHybrid attack and the existing hybrid attack correspond to different r when other parameters (n, q, k_1, k_2) are fixed to be $(1186, 2048, 202, 64)$.

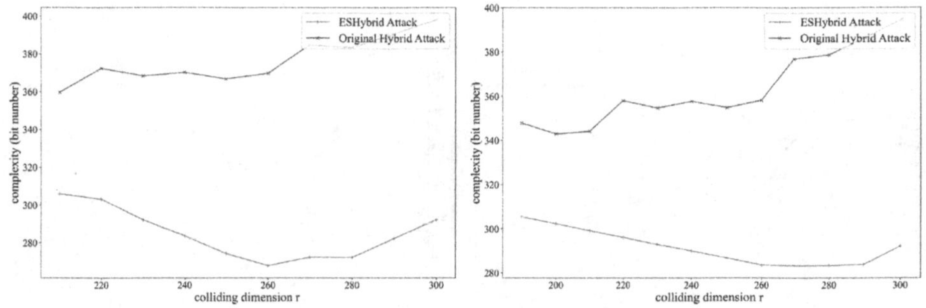

$m = 1186$, $\beta = 200$ $m = 1186$, $\beta = 230$

Fig. 1. Overestimating complexity of ESHybrid and the existing hybrid attack on lattices. The corresponding variable is r.

The colliding dimension r directly determines the searching dimension. Enlarging r exactly means increasing the Layer 2 searching complexity $C_{\text{List}}^{(2)}$. Also, the enlargement of the searching space S increases the Layer 1 searching complexity $C_{\text{List}}^{(1)}$. On the other hand, the increment of r cut down the magnitude of the probability of admissibility p_1 rapidly, disturbing the growth of $C_{\text{List}}^{(1)}$. A larger r also leads to a smaller reduction dimension $m - r$ and cut the complexity of the reduction procedure. Consequently, the optimal r exists by balancing C_{ESCol} and C_{Red} (representing $C_{\text{Red,over}}$ or $C_{\text{Red,under}}$ in different situations).

Note that if the β is sufficiently large, then the influence of r becomes implicit and, in some cases, negligible. This observation is evident from Fig. 1. This is because the reduction complexity C_{Red} plays the main role here. These results also reflect that the theoretical analysis of parameters is not far from a realistic attack.

Changes of the Attacking Complexity with different β. Figure 2 shows the trend of the complexity in the overestimating situation with the parameter set $(n, q, k_1, k_2) = (1478, 9829, 372, 120)$.

Due to the theoretical analysis, a larger block size β leads to a smaller p_1 in calculating the colliding period but increases the reduction complexity exponentially. Similar to the discussion with r, this fact also leads to a trade-off, offering the best choice of β if other parameters are determined. For instance, according to Fig. 2, the optimal point appears in each different parameter set.

Because of the decrease of Layer 1 probability of admissibility p_1, for β smaller than the optimal value, the complexity value becomes smaller with the growth of β. For β bigger than the optimal point, the complexity is mainly dominated by the reduction step, and the complexity grows exponentially. The complexity of ESHybrid and the existing hybrid attack overlaps when the block size becomes larger enough. Note that the optimal value of β for ESHybrid and the existing hybrid attack is different. This is on account of the difference in the colliding complexity between the ESHybrid attack and the existing hybrid attack.

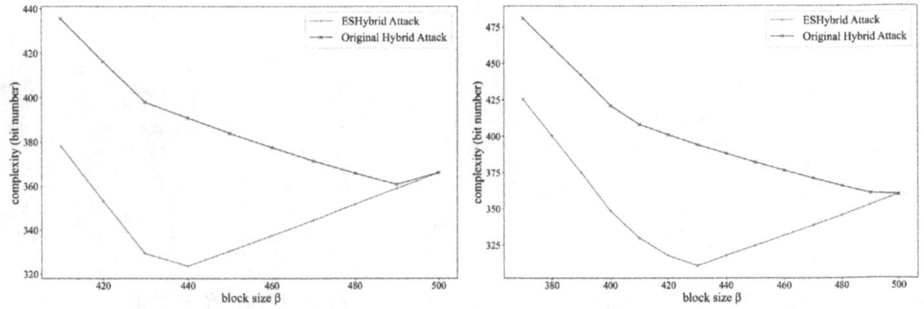

$m = 1478,\ r = 220$ $\qquad$ $m = 1478,\ r = 240$

Fig. 2. Overestimating complexity of ESHybrid Attack (red line) and the Original Hybrid Attack (blue line) on lattices. The corresponding variable is β. (Color figure online)

7 Conclusions

In this paper, we propose the ESHybrid attack, offering a faster solution to q-ary SVPs with quinary short vectors than the previous methods. This attack is based on the Meet-LWE framework, combined with the Error-Splitting technique. This technique enables the Meet-LWE to replace the meet-in-the-middle attack part in the hybrid attack and accelerate the solving of SVPs in the quinary settings. Moreover, We provide a comprehensive theoretical analysis of the time complexity based on several assumptions. This analysis includes the time complexity of the searching, and the embedding of the complexity in the hybrid attack. It also shows how the parameters affect the total complexity of the ESHybrid attack.

One limitation of our work is that it is only effective in the quinary setting. This leads to future work on how to improve the ESHybrid attack and make it suitable for short vectors with a larger infinite norm. Moreover, colliding methods may not perform well when the short vector is not sparse enough. It is interesting to investigate the efficient attacks for non-sparse cases.

References

1. Akiyama, K., Goto, Y., Okumura, S., Takagi, T., Nuida, K., Hanaoka, G.: A public-key encryption scheme based on non-linear indeterminate equations. In: Adams, C., Camenisch, J. (eds.) SAC 2017. LNCS, vol. 10719, pp. 215–234. Springer, Cham (2018). https://doi.org/10.1007/978-3-319-72565-9_11
2. Albrecht, M.R.: On dual lattice attacks against small-secret LWE and parameter choices in hElib and SEAL. In: Coron, J.-S., Nielsen, J.B. (eds.) EUROCRYPT 2017. LNCS, vol. 10211, pp. 103–129. Springer, Cham (2017). https://doi.org/10.1007/978-3-319-56614-6_4
3. Albrecht, M.R., Player, R., Scott, S.: On the concrete hardness of learning with errors. J. Math. Cryptol. **9**(3), 169–203 (2015)
4. Albrecht, M.R., Player, R., Scott, S.: On the concrete hardness of learning with errors. Cryptology ePrint Archive, Paper 2015/046 (2015)
5. Albrecht, M.R., et al.: Estimate all the LWE, NTRU schemes! In: Catalano, D., De Prisco, R. (eds.) SCN 2018. LNCS, vol. 11035, pp. 351–367. Springer, Cham (2018). https://doi.org/10.1007/978-3-319-98113-0_19
6. Alkim, E., Ducas, L., Pöppelmann, T., Schwabe, P.: Post-quantum key exchange - a new hope. In: 25th USENIX Security Symposium, USENIX Security 16, pp. 327–343. USENIX Association (2016)
7. Babai, L.: On Lovász' lattice reduction and the nearest lattice point problem. In: Mehlhorn, K. (ed.) STACS 1985. LNCS, vol. 182, pp. 13–20. Springer, Heidelberg (1985). https://doi.org/10.1007/BFb0023990
8. Becker, A., Ducas, L., Gama, N., Laarhoven, T.: New directions in nearest neighbor searching with applications to lattice sieving. In: SODA 2016, pp. 10–24. SIAM (2016)
9. Bernstein, D.J., Chuengsatiansup, C., Lange, T., van Vredendaal, C.: NTRU prime: reducing attack surface at low cost. In: Adams, C., Camenisch, J. (eds.) SAC 2017. LNCS, vol. 10719, pp. 235–260. Springer, Cham (2018). https://doi.org/10.1007/978-3-319-72565-9_12
10. Bi, L., Lu, X., Luo, J., Wang, K.: Hybrid dual and meet-LWE attack. In: Nguyen, K., Yang, G., Guo, F., Susilo, W. (eds.) Information Security and Privacy. ACISP 2022. LNCS, vol. 13494, pp. 168–188. Springer, Cham (2022). https://doi.org/10.1007/978-3-031-22301-3_9
11. Bi, L., Xianhui, L., Luo, J., Wang, K., Zhang, Z.: Hybrid dual attack on LWE with arbitrary secrets. Cybersecur. **5**(1), 15 (2022)
12. Chen, Y.: Réduction de Réseau et Sécurité Concrète Chiffrement Complètement Homomorphe. PhD thesis, École normale supérieure (2013)
13. Chen, Y., Nguyen, P.Q.: BKZ 2.0: better lattice security estimates. In: Lee, D.H., Wang, X. (eds.) ASIACRYPT 2011. LNCS, vol. 7073, pp. 1–20. Springer, Heidelberg (2011). https://doi.org/10.1007/978-3-642-25385-0_1
14. Cheon, J.H., Hhan, M., Hong, S., Son, Y.: A hybrid of dual and meet-in-the-middle attack on sparse and ternary secret LWE. IEEE Access **7**, 89497–89506 (2019)
15. Espitau, T., Joux, A., Kharchenko, N.: On a dual/Hybrid approach to small secret LWE. In: Bhargavan, K., Oswald, E., Prabhakaran, M. (eds.) INDOCRYPT 2020. LNCS, vol. 12578, pp. 440–462. Springer, Cham (2020). https://doi.org/10.1007/978-3-030-65277-7_20
16. Esser, A., Girme, R., Mukherjee, A., Sarkar, S.: Memory-efficient attacks on small lwe keys. Cryptology ePrint Archive, Paper 2023/243 (2023)

17. Furst, M.L., Kannan, R.: Succinct certificates for almost all subset sum problems. SIAM J. Comput. **18**(3), 550–558 (1989)
18. Gentry, C.: Fully homomorphic encryption using ideal lattices. In: STOC 2009, pp. 169–178. ACM (2009)
19. Halevi, S., Shoup, V.: Design and implementation of helib: a homomorphic encryption library. Cryptology ePrint Archive, Paper 2020/1481 (2020)
20. HEAAB library. https://github.com/snucrypto/HEAAN
21. Hirschhorn, P.S., Hoffstein, J., Howgrave-Graham, N., Whyte, W.: Choosing NTRUEncrypt parameters in light of combined lattice reduction and MITM approaches. In: Abdalla, M., Pointcheval, D., Fouque, P.-A., Vergnaud, D. (eds.) ACNS 2009. LNCS, vol. 5536, pp. 437–455. Springer, Heidelberg (2009). https://doi.org/10.1007/978-3-642-01957-9_27
22. Hoffstein, J., Pipher, J., Silverman, J.H.: NTRU: a ring-based public key cryptosystem. In: Buhler, J.P. (ed.) ANTS 1998. LNCS, vol. 1423, pp. 267–288. Springer, Heidelberg (1998). https://doi.org/10.1007/BFb0054868
23. Howgrave-Graham, N.: A hybrid lattice-reduction and meet-in-the-middle attack against NTRU. In: Menezes, A. (ed.) CRYPTO 2007. LNCS, vol. 4622, pp. 150–169. Springer, Heidelberg (2007). https://doi.org/10.1007/978-3-540-74143-5_9
24. Howgrave-Graham, N., Silverman, J.H., Whyte, W.: A meet-in-the-middle attack on an ntru private key. In: Technical report, vol. 4622 of Technical report, pp. 150–169. NTRU Cryptosystems (2003)
25. May, A.: How to meet ternary LWE keys. In: Malkin, T., Peikert, C. (eds.) CRYPTO 2021. LNCS, vol. 12826, pp. 701–731. Springer, Cham (2021). https://doi.org/10.1007/978-3-030-84245-1_24
26. Schnorr, C.-P.: A hierarchy of polynomial time lattice basis reduction algorithms. Theor. Comput. Sci. **53**, 201–224 (1987)
27. Microsoft SEAL (release 4.1). https://github.com/Microsoft/SEAL. Microsoft Research, Redmond, WA
28. Wunderer, T.: A detailed analysis of the hybrid lattice-reduction and meet-in-the-middle attack. J. Math. Cryptol. **13**(1), 1–26 (2019)
29. Wunderer, T.: On the security of lattice-based cryptography against lattice reduction and hybrid attacks. PhD thesis, Technischen Universität Darmstadt (2018)

Total Break of a Public Key Cryptosystem Based on a Group of Permutation Polynomials

Max Cartor[1], Ryann Cartor[2(✉)], Mark Lewis[1], and Daniel Smith-Tone[1,3]

[1] University of Louisville, Louisville, KY, USA
{maxwell.cartor,mark.lewis.2}@louisville.edu
[2] Clemson University, Clemson, SC, USA
rcartor@clemson.edu
[3] National Institute of Standards and Technology, Gaithersburg, MD, USA
daniel.smith@nist.gov

Abstract. In this paper, we respond to the proposal of the Permutation Polynomial Encryption Scheme, introduced by Singh, Sarma, and Saikia in 2020. We simplify the private key and prove the scheme can be completely broken by a direct attack. Furthermore, we show that the direct attack also completely breaks the ℓIC cryptosystem. Although other attacks on this scheme were known, it was previously incorrectly asserted that Gröbner basis method is not feasible against ℓIC. We also highlight that this attack is effective against any generalization of these schemes that contain specific properties necessary for inversion.

Keywords: Multivariate Cryptography · Permutation Polynomials · Cryptanalysis · Solving Degree · ℓIC

1 Introduction

With advances towards quantum computing, the need for finding quantum-secure cryptosystems is greater than ever. One field of possibly quantum-safe public key cryptography is multivariate cryptography. Multivariate cryptosystems are based on the MQ problem, which is the well known NP-complete problem of solving a system of multivariate quadratic equations over a finite field.

Although several long-lived schemes have recently suffered impactful and damaging cryptanalyses, multivariate schemes remain an interesting and promising field in the study of post quantum cryptography. These schemes often have performance properties that are not easily matched by other potentially quantum-safe schemes. For example, the UOV digital signature scheme, see [5], still has one of the best performance profiles for schemes with offline transmission of the public key.

The first well-known instance of a multivariate crytposystem was C^* [6], introduced in 1988 by Matsumoto and Imai. C^* is an example of a big field scheme, which utilizes computations in both a base field and extension field. The system hides an easily invertible monomial $f = x^{q^\theta+1}$ by composing it with

J. Shikata and H. Kuzuno (Eds.): IWSEC 2023, LNCS 14128, pp. 137–151, 2023.
https://doi.org/10.1007/978-3-031-41326-1_8

two invertible linear transformations. C^* was broken by Patarin in 1995 [8] by finding a linear relationship between the plaintext and the ciphertext variables.

Many new multivariate schemes were introduced after the break of C^*. Patarin attempted to create secure multivariate cryptosystems by introducing Little Dragon and Big Dragon, [9]. In both Dragon cryptosystems, the public key is quadratic in plaintext variables and linear in the ciphertext. This is known as a *mixed type* public key. After Patarin found that the dragon scheme was insecure with one hidden monomial, Singh et al. proposed a Dragon type multivariate cryptosystem using permutation polynomials over finite fields in 2010 [11] and 2011 [12].

In this vein, Singh, Sarma, and Saikia [10] proposed a multivariate public key encryption scheme in 2020 whose structure depends intimately on a group of permutation polynomials. The authors presented an alternative structure of the public keys that differs from the butterfly construction utilized by C^* and many other multivariate cryptosystems. The typical structure of a multivariate cryptosystem is to hide a quadratic function F between two secret invertible linear transformations S and T in the form $P = T \circ F \circ S$. Singh, Sarma, and Saikia, however, proposed an alternative structure of

$$F_1 \circ S_1(y) = T \circ F \circ S(x)$$

where S_1, T, and S are invertible linear or affine transformations. The secret function F is quadratic and invertible in the plaintext variable x. The function $F_1(y)$ is of high degree and invertible in the ciphertext y. Similar to the Dragon cryptosystems, this cryptosystem is of mixed type.

In this paper, we provide a total break of this SSS Permutation Polynomials Scheme presented in [10]. We do this by simplifying the presentation of the public key and deriving affine relations on the input and output of the quadratic map applied to the plaintext variables, leaving us with a system that can be solved using Gröbner basis algorithms at degree 3. We are able to prove this fact explicitly; that is, we prove that the solving degree of the polynomial system generated in our attack is 3 for all possible parameters of the scheme. Therefore, the attack is of polynomial complexity in all cases and the scheme is completely and practically broken.

Surprisingly, we note that there are other schemes in the literature that have a similar sort of structure to the SSS scheme which are susceptible to the same sort of analysis. As an application of our techniques, we generalize our attack model and verify that the method works on other similar schemes, such as ℓIC [3]. Even though ℓIC has long been broken by other means, this fact is quite surprising since our analysis reveals the concerning fact that *even the direct attack* is effective for certain parameter sets. As an example, some of the proposed parameters for 2IC, chosen for encryption applications, are broken with the direct attack at degree 3.

The paper is organized as follows. In the next section, we review two of the schemes that are affected by the generalization of our analysis of the SSS scheme. We first present the SSS Permutation Polynomials encryption scheme of [10] itself. We then introduce the ℓIC scheme of [3] and, in particular, we highlight some parameters proposed for secure encryption in [1]. In Sect. 3.1, we present a great simplification in the form of the private key of the permutation polynomial scheme, allowing for a simpler discussion of its algebraic properties. Then, in Sect. 3.2, we derive relations on the input and output of the quadratic component of the private key and use them to prove that the solving degree of the system of equations derived from the public key by fixing a ciphertext is 3 for all possible parameters. In the subsequent section, we generalize the analysis abstracting away from the specific algebraic structure in the SSS scheme. Even in the generalized setting, we argue that the solving degree of the derived system is low with high probability. The next section contrasts our technique with the analysis of linearization equations, see [9], or higher-order linearization equations, see [2]. In the following section, we present our experimental results in implementing the attack on the SSS scheme and on 2IC. In all cases the constructed quadratic systems were solved explicitly at degree 3 for both schemes, resulting in message recovery. Finally, we conclude with a concerning observation about the apparent long-term lack of careful cryptanalysis by standard techniques of sometimes well-known schemes.

2 Relevant Schemes

The objects of study in this work are multivariate cryptosystems involving a vector-valued function on some commutative algebra over a finite field. The analysis is inspired by the SSS permutation polynomial scheme of [10], but a natural generalization of the idea encompasses schemes such as ℓIC, see [3], and others. In this section, we present the SSS scheme, ℓIC and a natural generalization of these structures that encompasses the two and retains the algebraic properties required for our later cryptanalysis.

2.1 SSS Permutation Scheme

We will denote the elements of $\mathbb{F}_2^m$ which have odd Hamming weight by $O\mathbb{F}_2^m$. The key generation algorithm makes use of the convolution operation which is defined below.

Definition 1 (Convolution). *Given elements $\alpha, \beta \in \mathbb{F}_{q^m}$ with respective $\mathbb{F}_q^m$ representatives $(\alpha_0, \alpha_1, \ldots, \alpha_{m-1})$ and $(\beta_0, \beta_1, \ldots, \beta_{m-1})$, the convolution of α and β is defined as*

$$\alpha * \beta = (\gamma_0, \gamma_1, \ldots, \gamma_{m-1}), \text{ where } \gamma_r = \sum_{i=0}^{m-1} \alpha_i \beta_{(r-i) \mod n}.$$

The key proposed in [10] is generated by the composition and convolution of many affine maps, along with one quadratic map. The encryption function accepts a binary string $(x_0, x_1, \ldots, x_{m-2})$, and then appends an additional bit x_{m-1} to guarantee the weight of the input string has odd parity. This condition on the weight is both necessary and sufficient for the input string to be an invertible element of the ring $\mathbb{F}_2[U]/(U^m - 1)$ (Proposition 2.1 in [10]). The plaintext $\mathbf{x} = (x_0, x_1, \ldots, x_{m-1}) \in O\mathbb{F}_2^m$ is then used to produce a ciphertext $\mathbf{y} = (y_0, y_1, \ldots, y_{2m-1}) \in \mathbb{F}_2^{2m}$ by solving a set of linear equations in y_i. To construct the desired map we first perform the following tasks:

1. Select six random invertible elements from $\mathbb{F}_2[U]/(U^m - 1)$, which is isomorphic to the ring of $m \times m$ circulant matrices. We will denote this ring by C^m.
2. Compose each element chosen from C^m with a random permutation of m bits to form linear maps A_i.
3. Add a random even-weight element of $\mathbb{F}_2^m$ to each A_i to form affine maps T_i.

Now we may form the quadratic central map F using the maps T_i. The authors specify that we will use $F(T_6(\mathbf{x}))$ where $F : O\mathbb{F}_2^m \to \mathbb{F}_2^{2m}$ is defined by

$$F(\mathbf{x}) = \left(T_3\left(T_1(\mathbf{x})^2 * T_2(\mathbf{x})\right), T_4\left(T_1(\mathbf{x}) * T_2(\mathbf{x})\right) + T_5\left(T_1(\mathbf{x})^2 * T_2(\mathbf{x})\right)\right). \quad (1)$$

The expressions on either side of the comma in Eq. 1 each produce m-bit strings, and the output of F is the $2m$-bit string formed by concatenating the pair. To complete the map we now do the following:

1. Select two random invertible elements from $\mathbb{F}_2[U]/(U^{2m} - 1) \cong C^{2m}$.
2. Compose each element chosen from C^{2m} with a random permutation of $2m$ bits to form two linear maps B_1 and B_2.
3. Add a random even-weight element of $\mathbb{F}_2^{2m}$ to each B_i to form affine maps S_1 and S_2.
4. Select random elements $\gamma_1, \gamma_2 \in \mathbb{F}_2^{2m}$ such that γ_1 has even weight and γ_2 has odd weight.

The final map is then expressed by

$$S_2\Big(F\big(T_6(\mathbf{x})\big)\Big) * S_1(\mathbf{y}) + \gamma_1 S_1(\mathbf{y}) + \gamma_2 = 0. \quad (2)$$

The ciphertext is the solution $\mathbf{y} \in \mathbb{F}_2^{2m}$ that satisfies Eq. 2.

2.2 ℓIC

Consider a base field $\mathbb{F}$ of size q and an extension field $\mathbb{E} := GF(q^k)$ where computations in $\mathbb{E}$ are modulo the irreducible polynomial $\pi(t) \in \mathbb{F}[t]$. In the ℓIC framework, n denotes the number of variables over $\mathbb{F}$, m denotes the number of equations over $\mathbb{F}$, ℓ is the length of the cycle, k is the degree of the extension field. In the unmodified scheme, $n = m = \ell k$.

The public key $\mathcal{P} : \mathbb{F}^n \to \mathbb{F}^m$ is defined as

$$\mathcal{P} = T \circ \phi^{-1} \circ P \circ \phi \circ S,$$

where

$$\phi : (x_1, \ldots, x_n) \mapsto \begin{pmatrix} x_1 + x_2 t + \cdots + x_k t^{k-1} \\ x_{k+1} + x_{k+2} t + \cdots + x_{2k} t^{k-1} \\ \vdots \\ x_{(\ell-1)k+1} + x_{(\ell-1)k+2} t + \cdots + x_n t^{k-1} \end{pmatrix}^{\top}$$

and

$$P : \mathbb{E}^\ell \to \mathbb{E}^\ell : (A_1, \ldots, A_\ell) \mapsto (A_1^{q^{\lambda_1}} A_2, \ldots, A_{\ell-1}^{q^{\lambda_{\ell-1}}} A_\ell, A_\ell^{q^{\lambda_\ell}} A_1),$$

where each $\lambda_i \in \{0, \ldots, k-1\}$ and S, T are invertible affine maps.

For encryption, it is recommended in [1] that 2IC is used with central map

$$P : \mathbb{E}^2 \to \mathbb{E}^2 : (A_1, A_2) \mapsto (A_1^q A_2),$$

and the choice of field $\mathbb{F}_2$. The natural and more general choice is to choose the central map

$$P : \mathbb{E}^2 \to \mathbb{E}^2 : (A_1, A_2) \mapsto (A_1^{q^\theta} A_2, A_1 A_2);$$

however, in decryption the additional operation of inverting $(A_1^{q^\theta} A_2)/(A_1 A_2) = A_1^{q^\theta - 1}$ is as costly as inverting a C^* central map. Thus, their choice increases efficiency by eliminating this additional operation.

Encryption and Decryption. Generically, the inversion of ℓIC can be inefficient due to possibly different powers in each coordinate of the central map. For efficiency, the special case of setting all $\lambda_i = 1$ is examined. In this case inversion can be made very simple and efficient. In this case, inversion is accomplished as described in the following Lemma.

Lemma 1 (Inversion, Lemma 1 of [3]). *For a fixed $\ell \geq 2$, let our ℓIC central map $P : (A_1, \ldots, A_\ell) \to (B_1, \ldots, B_\ell)$ be*

$$B_1 := \begin{cases} A_1 A_2 & \text{for } \ell \text{ odd and} \\ A_1^q A_2 & \text{for } \ell \text{ even} \end{cases}, \quad B_i := A_i A_{\mu(i)} \text{ for } 2 \leq i \leq \ell.$$

Then the inverse image of $(B_1 \ldots B_\ell)$, where $B_i \in \mathbf{E}^* := \mathbf{E} \setminus \{0\}$, is given by

$$A_1 := \begin{cases} \sqrt{\dfrac{\prod_{i=0}^{(\ell-1)/2} B_{2i+1}}{\prod_{i=1}^{(\ell-1)/2} B_{2i}}} & \text{for } \ell \text{ odd and} \\ \sqrt[q-1]{\dfrac{\prod_{i=0}^{\ell/2-1} B_{2i+1}}{\prod_{i=1}^{\ell/2} B_{2i}}} & \text{for } \ell \text{ even} \end{cases}, \quad A_i := \frac{B_i}{A_{\mu(i)}}$$

for $2 \leq i \leq \ell$.

2.3 Generalization of SSS and ℓIC

The properties that the SSS scheme and ℓIC rely on for inversion actually can be generalized in such a way to construct a generic scheme with inversion based on relations satisfied by the coordinates of a vector-valued function over an extension ring. We may begin with the defining relation of both schemes.

Let the relation

$$F(\mathbf{y}) = T(G(U(\mathbf{x}))) \tag{3}$$

be satisfied by all plaintext ciphertext pairs $(\mathbf{x}, \mathbf{y})$ of a multivariate cryptosystem, where G is quadratic and both T and U are affine. This structure encompasses the type of cryptosystem presented in [10], where F is a high-degree function of $\mathbf{y}$, as discussed in [10], as well as more traditional schemes in which F above is the identity map and the composition on the right is the public key $\mathcal{P}$. Let us suppose that the central map G has the structure

$$G(\mathbf{x}) = \left(G_1(\mathbf{x}), G_2(\mathbf{x})\right),$$

where $G_1(\mathbf{x}) = B(A(\mathbf{x}), G_2(\mathbf{x}))$, $A(\mathbf{x})$ is an affine function, and B is bilinear.

This property is the essential structure that allows efficient inversion for the SSS permutation polynomial scheme (as will be clear given a greatly simplified description of the private key in Sect. 3.1), but also holds for schemes such as 2IC, see [3] and [1], in which the central map is bivariate over an extension field and has the more obvious and explicit structure

$$G(X_1, X_2) = \left(X_1^{q^\theta} X_2, X_1 X_2\right).$$

In the first case above, the bilinear map is related to multiplication within the ring $\mathcal{R} = \mathbb{F}_2[U]/(U^m - 1)$, whereas in the latter, the bilinear map is multiplication in the extension field.

3 Cryptanalysis of the SSS Permutation Scheme

In this section we present a practical cryptanalysis of the SSS permutation scheme showing that all possible parameters are broken. The proof of the efficacy of the attack depends intimately on the structure of the quadratic component of the secret key acting on the plaintext variables. As a first step, we derive an equivalent, but greatly simplified description of the private key structure.

3.1 Simplifying the Private Key

Given that every T_i and S_i map is affine in Eq. 2, we are able to simplify the expression. First consider the central map. Let

$$\widehat{F}(\mathbf{x}) = \left(\mathbf{x}^2 * \widehat{T}(\mathbf{x}), \mathbf{x} * \widehat{T}(\mathbf{x})\right) \text{ and } \mathbf{M} = \begin{bmatrix} T_3 & T_5 \\ 0 & T_4 \end{bmatrix},$$

where $\widehat{T}$ is affine and $\mathbf{M}$ defines a $2m \times 2m$ block matrix. Observe that

$$\widehat{F}(\mathbf{x})\mathbf{M} = \Big(T_3\big(\mathbf{x}^2 * \widehat{T}(\mathbf{x})\big),\, T_4\big(\mathbf{x} * \widehat{T}(\mathbf{x})\big) + T_5\big(\mathbf{x}^2 * \widehat{T}(\mathbf{x})\big)\Big).$$

Now if we set $T = T_1 \circ T_6$ and $\widehat{T} = T_2 \circ T_1^{-1}$ we have $\widehat{T} \circ T = T_2 \circ T_6$ and it follows that $\widehat{F}\big(T(\mathbf{x})\big)\mathbf{M} = F\big(T_6(\mathbf{x})\big)$ where $F(T_6(\mathbf{x}))$ is our central map. Next we set $S(\mathbf{x}) = S_2(\mathbf{x}\mathbf{M})$ and we have

$$S\Big(\widehat{F}\big(T(\mathbf{x})\big)\Big) = S_2\Big(F\big(T_6(\mathbf{x})\big)\Big). \tag{4}$$

The key features of this simplification are:

(i) T_1 and T_6 have been composed to form a single affine map T.
(ii) The affine maps S_2, T_3, T_4, and T_5 have been absorbed into a single affine map S.
(iii) $\widehat{F}$ has a particularly simple structure which now involves only one affine map $\widehat{T}$ (which accounts for the effects of T_2).

Overall, we can see the familiar butterfly construction of two affine maps composed with a central map, $\widehat{F}$. Furthermore, $\widehat{F}$ now highlights clearly the structure we propose to attack.

3.2 Breaking the Scheme

Consider the matrix representation of multiplication by an element $\mathbf{a} \in C^m$, denoted by $\mathbf{M_a}$. Since we are in characteristic 2, we have

$$\begin{aligned}\widehat{F}(\mathbf{x}) \begin{pmatrix}\mathbf{I}\\ \mathbf{M_x}\end{pmatrix} &= (\mathbf{x}^2 * \widehat{T}(\mathbf{x}),\, \mathbf{x} * \widehat{T}(\mathbf{x})) \begin{pmatrix}\mathbf{I}\\ \mathbf{M_x}\end{pmatrix}\\ &= \mathbf{x}^2 * \widehat{T}(\mathbf{x}) + \mathbf{x}^2 * \widehat{T}(\mathbf{x}) = 0.\end{aligned} \tag{5}$$

Noting Lemma 3.1 from [10], we observe that $\mathbf{x}^2$ is in fact a linear map on the plaintext and consider

$$\widehat{F}(\mathbf{x}) \begin{pmatrix}\mathbf{M_x^{\delta}}\\ \mathbf{M_x^{\delta+1}}\end{pmatrix} = \mathbf{x}^{2+\delta} * \widehat{T}(\mathbf{x}) + \mathbf{x}^{2+\delta} * \widehat{T}(\mathbf{x}) = 0 \tag{6}$$

where $\delta \in \{0, 1\}$. That is, we have two linear maps that each produce m equations. Now let $\mathbf{z} = S_1(\mathbf{y})$ for some fixed ciphertext $\mathbf{y}$. Using our simplification for the central map from Eq. 4 and evaluating at $\mathbf{y}$, Eq. 2 becomes

$$S\Big(\widehat{F}\big(T(\mathbf{x})\big)\Big) * \mathbf{z} + \gamma_1\mathbf{z} + \gamma_2 = 0. \tag{7}$$

Notice that $\gamma_1\mathbf{z} + \gamma_2$ is constant for fixed $\mathbf{y}$ and that the effect of the convolution by $\mathbf{z}$ can be absorbed into S. If we let $\gamma_\mathbf{z} = \gamma_1\mathbf{z} + \gamma_2$ and $S_\mathbf{z}(\mathbf{x}) = S(\mathbf{x}) * \mathbf{z} + \gamma_\mathbf{z}$, then from Eq. 7 we obtain

$$S_\mathbf{z}\Big(\widehat{F}\big(T(\mathbf{x})\big)\Big) = 0. \tag{8}$$

Theorem 1. *The solving degree d_s of the system given by Eq.* (8) *is* 3.

Proof. The critical observation here is that the relation shown in Eq. 6 filters through the affine maps T and $S_{\mathbf{z}}$. We can write $S_{\mathbf{z}}(\mathbf{x}) = L_{\mathbf{z}}(\mathbf{x}) + \xi_{\mathbf{z}}$ where $L_{\mathbf{z}}$ is linear and $\xi_{\mathbf{z}}$ is constant. Hence, there is a linear transformation $L_{\mathbf{z}}^{-1}$ that we can apply to Eq. (8) and then multiply on the right by $\left(\mathbf{M}_{T(\mathbf{x})}^{\delta} \;\; \mathbf{M}_{T(\mathbf{x})}^{\delta+1}\right)^{\mathsf{T}}$ to produce

$$
\begin{aligned}
\mathbf{0} = L_{\mathbf{z}}^{-1}(\mathbf{0}) \begin{pmatrix} \mathbf{M}_{T(\mathbf{x})}^{\delta} \\ \mathbf{M}_{T(\mathbf{x})}^{\delta+1} \end{pmatrix} &= L_{\mathbf{z}}^{-1}\Big(S_{\mathbf{z}}\big(\widehat{F}(T(\mathbf{x}))\big)\Big) \begin{pmatrix} \mathbf{M}_{T(\mathbf{x})}^{\delta} \\ \mathbf{M}_{T(\mathbf{x})}^{\delta+1} \end{pmatrix} \\
&= \widehat{F}(T(\mathbf{x})) \begin{pmatrix} \mathbf{M}_{T(\mathbf{x})}^{\delta} \\ \mathbf{M}_{T(\mathbf{x})}^{\delta+1} \end{pmatrix} + L_{\mathbf{z}}^{-1}(\xi_{\mathbf{z}}) \begin{pmatrix} \mathbf{M}_{T(\mathbf{x})}^{\delta} \\ \mathbf{M}_{T(\mathbf{x})}^{\delta+1} \end{pmatrix} \qquad (9) \\
&= L_{\mathbf{z}}^{-1}(\xi_{\mathbf{z}}) \begin{pmatrix} \mathbf{M}_{T(\mathbf{x})}^{\delta} \\ \mathbf{M}_{T(\mathbf{x})}^{\delta+1} \end{pmatrix}.
\end{aligned}
$$

Since this last quantity is affine in $\mathbf{x}$, we obtain $2m$ linear equations (m for $\delta = 0$ and m for $\delta = 1$) in the m plaintext variables. We argue that this linear system is of full rank, and thus the system is solved at degree 3.

To see this, first observe that

$$\widehat{F}(\mathbf{x}) = (\mathbf{x}^2 * \widehat{T}(\mathbf{x}), \mathbf{x} * \widehat{T}(\mathbf{x}))$$

and recall that $\widehat{T}$ sends odd weight vectors to odd weight vectors. Since T also sends odd weight vectors to odd weight vectors, we have from Eq. (8) that

$$(\mathbf{v}_1 \; \mathbf{v}_2) = L_{\mathbf{z}}^{-1}(\xi_{\mathbf{z}}) = \widehat{F}(T(\mathbf{x}))$$

has the property that both coordinates, $\mathbf{v}_1$ and $\mathbf{v}_2$, are odd-weight vectors. Thus $\mathbf{v}_1$ and $\mathbf{v}_2$ correspond to invertible elements in $\mathbb{F}_2[U]/(U^m - 1)$.

Finally, due to the commutativity of multiplication in $\mathbb{F}_2[U]/(U^m - 1)$, we observe that, even restricting to the case of $\delta = 0$, we obtain

$$
\begin{aligned}
0 = L_{\mathbf{z}}^{-1}(\xi_{\mathbf{z}}) \begin{pmatrix} I_n \\ \mathbf{M}_{T(\mathbf{x})} \end{pmatrix} &= (\mathbf{v}_1 \; \mathbf{v}_2) \begin{pmatrix} I_n \\ \mathbf{M}_{T(\mathbf{x})} \end{pmatrix} \\
&= (\mathbf{1} \; T(\mathbf{x})) \begin{pmatrix} \mathbf{M}_{\mathbf{v}_1} \\ \mathbf{M}_{\mathbf{v}_2} \end{pmatrix}.
\end{aligned}
$$

Multiplying on the right by $\mathbf{M}_{\mathbf{v}_2}^{-1}$, since $\mathbf{v}_2$ is invertible, we obtain

$$(\mathbf{1} \; T(\mathbf{x})) \begin{pmatrix} \mathbf{M}_{\mathbf{v}_1}\mathbf{M}_{\mathbf{v}_2}^{-1} \\ I_n \end{pmatrix} = \mathbf{w} + T(\mathbf{x}),$$

where $\mathbf{w} = \mathbf{v}_1\mathbf{v}_2^{-1} \in \mathbb{F}_2[U]/(U^m - 1)$. Since T is an invertible affine map and $\mathbf{w}$ is a constant, the linear system is of rank m and therefore uniquely solvable. Thus the degree of regularity of the system is 3 with probability 1 for all possible parameters of the scheme. □

The complexity of solving a nonhomogeneous system of equations in m variables at degree d_{reg} with F4 is

$$\mathcal{O}\left(\binom{m+d_{reg}-1}{d_{reg}}^{\omega}\right),$$

where ω is the linear algebra constant. If we use Strassen's algorithm for the linear algebra, we may take $\omega = 2.8$.

In particular, since $d_{reg} = 3$ for all parameters, we have that the complexity of direct message recovery via F4 is

$$\mathcal{O}\left(\binom{m+2}{3}^{\omega}\right) = \mathcal{O}\left(m^{3\omega}\right).$$

Thus, since m is linear in the security parameter, our cryptanalysis is of polynomial complexity in the security parameter.

4 A Generalization of the Analysis: Cryptanalysis of ℓIC

We may generalize the analysis of the direct attack from the previous section to apply to more generic multivariate cryptosystems. Surprisingly, we find that the same analysis implies a low solving degree for the algebraic attack of some older multivariate cryptosystems.

4.1 Attack on General Scheme

Consider the set up described in Sect. 2.3. If we write $T(\mathbf{x}) = \mathbf{x}\mathbf{T} + \delta_T$, we can expand Eq. 3 for a fixed ciphertext $\mathbf{y}$ as

$$F(\mathbf{y}) = \left[B(A(U(\mathbf{x})), G_2(U(\mathbf{x}))),\, G_2(U(\mathbf{x}))\right]\mathbf{T} + \delta_T,$$

and multiplying on the right by $\mathbf{T}^{-1}$ and setting $\delta_T\mathbf{T}^{-1} - F(\mathbf{y})\mathbf{T}^{-1} = (\delta_1, \delta_2)$ we obtain

$$\left[B(A(U(\mathbf{x})), G_2(U(\mathbf{x}))) + \delta_1,\, G_2(U(\mathbf{x})) + \delta_2\right] = 0.$$

The key observation is that since $G_2(\mathbf{x}\mathbf{U} + \delta_U) + \delta_2$ is in the span of the equations $F(\mathbf{y}) = T(G(U(\mathbf{x})))$, we have that $(B(A(\mathbf{x}\mathbf{U}+\delta_U), G_2(\mathbf{x}\mathbf{U}+\delta_U)+\delta_2))$ must be in the span of the equations generated at degree 3 by F4 or XL. Indeed, $(B(A(\mathbf{x}\mathbf{U} + \delta_U), G_2(\mathbf{x}\mathbf{U} + \delta_U) + \delta_2))$ consists coordinate-wise of merely linear combinations of linear forms in the coordinates of $\mathbf{x}$ multiplied by coordinates of $G_2(\mathbf{x}\mathbf{U} + \delta_U) + \delta_2$. By the bilinearity of B, we have that this quantity equals $G_1(U(\mathbf{x})) + B(A(U(\mathbf{x})), \delta_2)$, and given that $G_1(U(\mathbf{x})) + \delta_1$ is in the span of the equations at degree 2, the affine expression $B(A(U(\mathbf{x})), \delta_2) + \delta_1$ is in the span of the equations at degree 3. Thus, the degree of regularity of the system is 3 with extremely high probability (depending on B and A).

We note that this analysis generalizes to many other "big field" or "big ring" cryptosystems in many ways. For example, the linear map A may be replaced with a quadratic or higher degree map or there may be additional "coordinates" over the extension ring. To illustrate this fact, we elucidate the technique when applied to two illuminating examples, 2IC and 3IC.

4.2 Direct Cryptanalysis of 2IC

For our first test case, consider plain 2IC. If we denote by (U_1, U_2) the inputs of the central map G satisfying $(U_1, U_2) = \phi(U(\mathbf{x}))$, we see that the public map can be represented

$$\mathcal{P}(\mathbf{x}) = L_T(\phi^{-1}(U_1^{q^\theta} U_2, U_1 U_2)) + \delta_T,$$

where $T(\mathbf{v}) = L_T(\mathbf{v}) + \delta_T$. Then, multiplying $L_T^{-1}\mathcal{P}$ on the right by

$$\begin{bmatrix} M_{U_1} \\ M_{U_1^{q^\theta}} \end{bmatrix},$$

where M_V is the matrix representation of multiplication by $V \in \mathbb{E}$, we obtain

$$\begin{aligned} L_T^{-1}\mathcal{P}(\mathbf{x}) \begin{bmatrix} M_{U_1} \\ M_{U_1^{q^\theta}} \end{bmatrix} &= \phi^{-1}(U_1^{q^\theta} U_2, U_1 U_2) \begin{bmatrix} M_{U_1} \\ M_{U_1^{q^\theta}} \end{bmatrix} + L_T^{-1}(\delta_T) \begin{bmatrix} M_{U_1} \\ M_{U_1^{q^\theta}} \end{bmatrix} \\ &= L_T^{-1}(\delta_T) \begin{bmatrix} M_{U_1} \\ M_{U_1^{q^\theta}} \end{bmatrix}, \end{aligned}$$

since $U_1^{q^\theta} U_2 * U_1 + U_1 U_2 * U_1^{q^\theta} = 0$. Notice that the final quantity is affine in $\mathbf{x}$ and is recovered at degree 3 in a Gröbner basis calculation.

While the parameters proposed for encryption in [1] seem to suggest exactly this scheme with the choice of $q = 2$ and $\theta = 1$ for efficiency, it is noted in [3] that the direct attack is more efficient for these parameters due to the simple algebraic structure. Since [1] was published two years after [3] and the discussion on the characteristics of 2IC under Gröbner basis is fairly terse, it is not clear if there was a miscommunication or otherwise some reason for recommending 2IC for encryption.

It is interesting to note that in [3] the authors recommend adding a few modifiers to the 2IC construction, including adding a low support rank summand to the central map, embedding in a larger field and adding additional random equations. None of these modifications, however, completely remove the deficiency of 2IC with respect to the direct attack. A projection orthogonal to the support of the internal perturbation results in a scheme with the same linear relations provided above simply by considering linear combinations of the public key avoiding the random polynomials. Also, the much more recent result in [7] shows that the embedding modifier does not, in general, increase the degree of regularity of a polynomial system. Thus, the security of the modified 2IC against direct attacks is still suspect, though mostly moot due to the cryptanalysis in [4] which completely breaks the scheme.

4.3 Direct Cryptanalysis of 3IC

The attack on 3IC is similar, but works at a higher degree. For simplicity of exposition, we simply show the analysis applied to the central map. The translation of the property of the central map into the full attack is identical to that of 2IC in the previous section.

First, recall that the central map of 3IC can be written

$$G(X_1, X_2, X_3) = (X_1^{q^{\lambda_1}} X_2, X_2^{q^{\lambda_2}} X_3, X_1 X_3^{q^{\lambda_3}}).$$

In analogy to the previous sections, note that multiplying on the right by matrices to produce the least common multiple of coordinates of this map results in the elimination of terms. For example, consider

$$G \begin{bmatrix} \mathbf{M}_{X_1 X_3^{q^{\lambda_3}}} \\ \mathbf{0} \\ -\mathbf{M}_{X_1^{q^{\lambda_1}} X_2} \end{bmatrix} = (X_1^{q^{\lambda_1}} X_2, X_2^{q^{\lambda_2}} X_3, X_1 X_3^{q^{\lambda_3}}) \begin{bmatrix} \mathbf{M}_{X_1 X_3^{q^{\lambda_3}}} \\ \mathbf{0} \\ -\mathbf{M}_{X_1^{q^{\lambda_1}} X_2} \end{bmatrix}$$
$$= X_1^{q^{\lambda_1}+1} X_2 X_3^{q^{\lambda_3}} - X_1^{q^{\lambda_1}+1} X_2 X_3^{q^{\lambda_3}} = \mathbf{0}.$$

Since the input and output of G are affinely related to the equations and variables in the public key, and due to the fact that the matrix above consists of quadratic forms in $\mathbf{x}$, we observe that the above equation implies the recovery of a large family of quadratic relations at degree 4 in the direct attack.

We should finally note that although 2IC was recommended for encryption, 3IC and more generally ℓIC was recommended for digital signatures with the change that several equations of the system are not published. This change is the so-called minus modifier and has a much greater impact, as noted in [7], on the first fall degree and solving degree of polynomial systems. Thus, although we expect the solving degree of 3IC to be low, we cannot justify the same conclusion for 3IC-, which was what was actually recommended for applications in digital signatures.

5 Security Estimates

Here we implement the generic attack (using Magma) against the 2IC scheme for parameters proposed in [1], and against the SSS encryption scheme. As previously suggested, the solving degree of the system is consistently 3 across the different parameters. The data for the attack against SSS and 2IC is summarized in Table 1.

Table 1. The complexity of the direct attack against the SSS permutation polynomial scheme and 2IC minus. The timings reported are for the calculation of the Gröbner basis of the public key fixed at a particular constant ciphertext value.

Scheme	(vars, eqns)	Total Degree of PK	Solving Degree	Time (ms)
SSS	(64, 128)	3	3	66
SSS	(128,256)	3	3	2505
2IC	(60, 60)	2	3	8
2IC	(120,120)	2	3	49

6 Comparison with HOLEs Attacks

In [9], Patarin developed an attack on the Matsumoto-Imai, or C^*, scheme of [6]. His attack, as well as ours, related to relations among the inputs and outputs of the quadratic component of the private key. Specifically, Patarin noted that given the map $v = f(u) = u^{q^\theta+1}$ over the finite field $\mathbb{F}_q$, the relationship $uv^{q^\theta} = u^{q^{2\theta}}v$ holds for all input output pairs. Expressing this relation over the plaintext $\mathbf{x}$ and ciphertext $\mathbf{y}$ variables, which are linearly related to u and v, respectively, results in a bilinear relation between all possible plaintext/ciphertext pairs. An attack is accomplished by setting the unknown coefficients of these linearization equations as variables and deriving equations among them by generating many plaintext/ciphertext pairs, solving for the bilinear relation. Once recovered, the bilinear relation itself provides another decryption algorithm consisting of simply plugging in the ciphertext variables and solving linearly for the plaintext variables.

Later, in [2], a generalization of the linearization technique was presented. In that work, it is shown that while the ciphertext $\mathbf{y}$ may be a quadratic function of the plaintext $\mathbf{x}$, it is still possible that there may be relations that are of higher, but still small, degree in $\mathbf{y}$ and still *linear* in $\mathbf{x}$, resulting in a higher-order linearization equations, or HOLEs, attack. Such an attack proceeds by setting the unknown coefficients of this higher-order linearization equation as variables and, again, solving for them by generating many plaintext/ciphertext pairs. Since the resulting equations are linear in the plaintext variables, the same procedure as above allows for efficient message recovery.

While the analysis of our attack does rely on a relation on the input and output of a hidden quadratic map as do the linearization equations and HOLEs attacks, there is an important difference. In linearization equation or HOLEs attacks, pairs of plaintext $\mathbf{x}$ and ciphertext $\mathbf{y}$ are generated and used to derive a relation $H(\mathbf{x}, \mathbf{y}) = 0$ which is then used to complete the attack. In the case of the attack on the SSS scheme, the key relation derives from the fact that adding the first coordinate of the central map $\widehat{F}$ to $T(\mathbf{x})$ times the second coordinate produces 0. Still, when applying this operation to the public key, even though the quadratic component of the private key is eliminated, the resulting quantity from Eq. (8) is linear in $\mathbf{x}$ but of high degree in $\mathbf{y}$.

The reason for this property is that the map $L_{\mathbf{z}}^{-1}$ is the composition of linear maps including a *division* by $\mathbf{y}$. Since inversion in $O\mathbb{F}_2^{2m}$ is a high-degree map, we have that the resulting relation is of very high degree in $\mathbf{y}$. Instead, the attack proceeds by setting $\mathbf{y}$ to a fixed ciphertext, and noting that the elimination of $\widehat{F}$ produces sufficiently many degree falls to generate a full rank linear system in $\mathbf{x}$ with probability 1. Thus, the attack never produces any HOLEs relations.

7 Conclusion

The new SSS multivariate encryption scheme presented in [10] is another in a long line of attempts to create efficient and secure multivariate cryptosystems based on the algebraic structure of some interesting construction. There is a long history in multivariate cryptography of clever schemes that end up not only failing to achieve their security claims, but being practically broken.

We demonstrate in this work that the same deficiency ails the SSS encryption scheme based on groups of permutation polynomials. We present an analysis of the SSS scheme that proves that the simple direct attack completely breaks all parameters of the scheme and that the solving degree is always 3. This result shows that the most generic of all attacks on multivariate schemes is effective in this case.

We extend our analysis to apply to a much larger family of potential multivariate cryptosystems, a family including some old and reasonably well-known cryptosystems including ℓIC. In particular, we show that in the case of 2IC, the only version of ℓIC recommended for encryption, that our analysis leads to a complete break of the scheme by way of the direct attack. In the case of ℓIC for $\ell > 2$, we show that the analysis still exhibits degree falls earlier than one would expect generically and that the solving degree of these schemes is likely quite low, though we acknowledge that these schemes were recommended in conjunction with the minus modifier, which makes the direct attack more difficult.

Finally, we show that this analysis, while certainly related to the linearization equations and HOLEs attacks is fundamentally different. In particular, the implied relation in the case of the SSS scheme, while linear in the plaintext variables, is of very high degree in the ciphertext variables, and so not efficiently recoverable, as discussed in [10].

Results such as the one this article provides should incite some concern from the reader on the state of the science in multivariate cryptography. It is, of course, reasonable to study new algebraic structures to make new proposals for potentially secure primitives. Indeed, it should not be extremely surprising for a new idea depending on a new structure to be broken, and this fact does not detract from the value in the attempt and the progress to be made in adapting tools for use in new circumstances.

In this case, however, the most generic tool possible for cryptanalysis of a multivariate scheme, that is, the direct attack, completely breaks all parameters of the scheme. Our experiments support our mathematical proof that the ideal is resolved at degree 3 in every case. Indeed, the parameter sets recommended for the SSS scheme, that is, setting $m = 128$, are still solved by MAGMA's F4 in about 1.5 seconds and show that the solving degree is 3. This result is the antithesis of the claim in [10] that the "Gröbner basis method is not feasible," and could be checked in just a few minutes with an implementation of the scheme.

The situation with ℓIC is similarly confusing. While [3] indicates that there are anomalies in the Gröbner basis calculations for 2IC, the remedies recommended do not protect the scheme from direct cryptanalysis, at least with the composition of a projection that effectively removes the internal perturbation. In fairness, the analysis of Gröbner basis techniques on projected schemes is a more recent object of study than the publication of ℓIC; however, this fact does not explain why a later report on the scheme seems to recommend parameters that both are exploitable and were previously reported as exploitable via the direct attack in [1].

As scientists, we should be cautious and skeptical of new results and try to verify that standard techniques are not directly applicable. The occurrence of new schemes being broken by old code is one that is perhaps less common today than it was in the early days of multivariate cryptography, but there is still room for improvement.

References

1. Bernstein, D., Buchmann, J., Dahmen, E.: Post-Quantum Cryptography. Springer, Heidelberg (2009). https://doi.org/10.1007/978-3-540-88702-7
2. Ding, J., Hu, L., Nie, X., Li, J., Wagner, J.: High order linearization equation (HOLE) attack on multivariate public key cryptosystems. In: Okamoto, T., Wang, X. (eds.) PKC 2007. LNCS, vol. 4450, pp. 233–248. Springer, Heidelberg (2007). https://doi.org/10.1007/978-3-540-71677-8_16
3. Ding, J., Wolf, C., Yang, B.-Y.: ℓ-invertible cycles for $\mathcal{M}$ultivariate $\mathcal{Q}$uadratic ($\mathcal{MQ}$) public key cryptography. In: Okamoto, T., Wang, X. (eds.) PKC 2007. LNCS, vol. 4450, pp. 266–281. Springer, Heidelberg (2007). https://doi.org/10.1007/978-3-540-71677-8_18
4. Fouque, P.-A., Macario-Rat, G., Perret, L., Stern, J.: Total break of the ℓ-IC signature scheme. In: Cramer, R. (ed.) PKC 2008. LNCS, vol. 4939, pp. 1–17. Springer, Heidelberg (2008). https://doi.org/10.1007/978-3-540-78440-1_1
5. Kipnis, A., Patarin, J., Goubin, L.: Unbalanced oil and vinegar signature schemes. In: Stern, J. (ed.) EUROCRYPT 1999. LNCS, vol. 1592, pp. 206–222. Springer, Heidelberg (1999). https://doi.org/10.1007/3-540-48910-X_15
6. Matsumoto, T., Imai, H.: Public quadratic polynomial-tuples for efficient signature-verification and message-encryption. In: Barstow, D., et al. (eds.) EUROCRYPT 1988. LNCS, vol. 330, pp. 419–453. Springer, Heidelberg (1988). https://doi.org/10.1007/3-540-45961-8_39
7. Øygarden, M., Felke, P., Raddum, H., Cid, C.: Cryptanalysis of the multivariate encryption scheme EFLASH. In: Jarecki, S. (ed.) CT-RSA 2020. LNCS, vol. 12006, pp. 85–105. Springer, Cham (2020). https://doi.org/10.1007/978-3-030-40186-3_5
8. Patarin, J.: Cryptanalysis of the Matsumoto and Imai public key scheme of Eurocrypt'88. In: Coppersmith, D. (ed.) CRYPTO 1995. LNCS, vol. 963, pp. 248–261. Springer, Heidelberg (1995). https://doi.org/10.1007/3-540-44750-4_20

9. Patarin, J.: Asymmetric cryptography with a hidden monomial. In: Koblitz, N. (ed.) CRYPTO 1996. LNCS, vol. 1109, pp. 45–60. Springer, Heidelberg (1996). https://doi.org/10.1007/3-540-68697-5_4
10. Singh, R., Sarma, B., Saikia, A.: A public key cryptosystem using a group of permutation polynomials. Tatra Mountains **77**, 139–162 (2020). https://doi.org/10.2478/tmmp-2020-0013. https://doi.org/10.1006/jsco.1996.0125
11. Singh, R.P., Saikia, A., Sarma, B.K.: Little dragon two: an efficient multivariate public key cryptosystem. CoRR abs/1005.5028 (2010). http://arxiv.org/abs/1005.5028
12. Singh, R.P., Saikia, A., Sarma, B.K.: Poly-dragon: an efficient multivariate public key cryptosystem. J. Math. Cryptol. **4**(4), 349–364 (2011). https://doi.org/10.1515/jmc.2011.002

Extractable Witness Encryption for the Homogeneous Linear Equations Problem

Bénédikt Tran(✉) and Serge Vaudenay

LASEC, Ecole Polytechnique Fédérale de Lausanne, 1015 Lausanne, Switzerland
{benedikt.tran,serge.vaudenay}@epfl.ch

Abstract. Witness encryption is a cryptographic primitive which encrypts a message under an instance of an NP language and decrypts the ciphertext using a witness associated with that instance. In the current state of the art, most of the witness encryption constructions are based on multilinear maps. Following the construction of Choi and Vaudenay based on RSA-related problems, we suggest a novel witness key encapsulation mechanism based on the hardness of solving homogeneous linear Diophantine equations (HLE problem). Our arithmetic-based construction aims to solve an issue raised by these authors where the security might be compromised if the adversary is able to find small solutions to a homogeneous linear Diophantine equation, while avoiding the inefficiency of multilinear maps. The security of our scheme is based on a hidden group order and a knowledge assumption.

Keywords: Witness Encryption · Homogeneous Linear Equations problem · Extractable One-Wayness

1 Introduction

Witness encryption (WE) constructions are introduced by Garg et al. [13] in 2013 and can be summarized as follows: the user encrypts a message under an NP problem instance to produce a ciphertext and any party knowing a witness is guaranteed to recover the plaintext. Witness encryption is a powerful primitive that can be used to incorporate temporal constraints (e.g., time-released encryption) or offer IND-CPA security when the encryption key does *not* belong to the NP language. In the latter case, decryption is unfortunately not possible and thus it might not necessarily be practical. In the current state of the art, witness encryption relies on multilinear maps (Garg's construction uses "approximate" multilinear maps for the Exact Cover NP-complete problem) or obfuscation, yet hardly relies on arithmetic constructions. This work introduces an arithmetic construction to alleviate the primitive construction complexity and focuses on a

B. Tran—Supported by the Swiss National Science Foundation (SNSF) through the project grant № 192364 on Post-Quantum Cryptography.

J. Shikata and H. Kuzuno (Eds.): IWSEC 2023, LNCS 14128, pp. 152–172, 2023.
https://doi.org/10.1007/978-3-031-41326-1_9

stronger notion, namely *extractable witness encryption* (EWE) where the ability to decrypt is informally equivalent to knowing a witness.

In practice, EWE-schemes solve the time-released problem discussed by Timothy May [22] in 1993 and Rivest, Shamir and Wagner [26] in 1996. In contrast to May's trusted agent, the Rivest–Shamir–Wagner construction relies on RSA-based time-lock puzzles, introduced by Merkle [23] in 1978, and on time-consuming computations. Thus, the release time depends on the receiver computational power. In 2018, Liu et al. [21] proposed an alternative by relying on blockchains based on proof-of-works and extractable witness encryption. Since a new block is appended to the blockchain after some time dt, the blockchain can be regarded as an internal clock.

Choi and Vaudenay [7, §4], later improved in [6], constructed a *witness key encapsulation mechanism* (WKEM) based on RSA-like constructions to remove the inefficiency arising from multilinear maps, and proved the security in a generic model under classical assumptions such as the RSA order assumption and the generalized knowledge-of-exponent assumption. They also introduced yet another variant of the *extractable security* notion proposed for instance in [8,11,13].

Their construction considers instances $(\boldsymbol{x}_1, \ldots, \boldsymbol{x}_t, \boldsymbol{s})$ from the NP-complete language Multi-SS, where $\boldsymbol{x}_1, \ldots, \boldsymbol{x}_t$ and $\boldsymbol{s}$ are d-dimensional vectors of nonnegative integers and a witness is a tuple $(a_1, \ldots, a_t)$ of *polynomially bounded* nonnegative integers such that $\sum_{i=1}^{t} a_i \boldsymbol{x}_i = \boldsymbol{s}$. In the one-dimensional case where instances are tuples $(x_1, \ldots, x_t, s)$ of nonnegative integers, the encapsulation generates a tuple (n, ℓ, g, k) of integers, where k is invertible modulo ℓ and the multiplicative order of g modulo n is ℓ. Then, the encapsulated key is $h = g^{k^s} \bmod n$ and the corresponding ciphertext is $(n, g, y_1, \ldots, y_t)$, where $y_i = k^{x_i} \bmod \ell$. Conversely, given a ciphertext $(n, g, y_1, \ldots, y_t)$ and a witness $(a_1, \ldots, a_t)$ for $(x_1, \ldots, x_t, s)$, the decryption recovers the encapsulated key as $h = g^{\prod_{i=1}^{t} y_i^{a_i}} \bmod n$.

Here, $\prod_{i=1}^{t} y_i^{a_i}$ is computed over the integers and this operation is inefficient if some a_i is not sufficiently small. Unfortunately, the security of the scheme collapses if an adversary finds a small solution $(b_1, \ldots, b_t)$ to the homogeneous linear equation (HLE) $\sum_{i=1}^{t} b_i x_i = 0$ since such relation gives rise to a multiple of ℓ that can be used to recover the encapsulated key [7, §4.3]. To mitigate this scenario, Choi and Vaudenay only considered Multi-SS $\cap$ coHLE instances and reformulated the *extractable indistinguishability* (IND-EWE) security notion [6], where they require the extractor to be as effective as a successful adversary. Since this characterization is stronger than the one by Chvojka et al. in [8], Choi and Vaudenay focused on a novel and weaker notion than IND-EWE, namely *extractable one-wayness* (OW-EWE), and provided a generic transformation *à la* Fujisaki-Okamoto turning an OW-EWE scheme into an IND-EWE one.

Our Contributions. We generalize the exact correctness of WKEM to *approximate correctness* and suggest a WKEM for the homogeneous linear equations (HLE) problem. Assuming the NP-completeness of HLE, this results in an efficient WKEM for all NP languages.

Instead of considering Multi-SS instances, we consider HLE instances and turn the "knowledge of a small relation" (which caused the issue in [6]) into the "ability to decrypt". More precisely, given a HLE instance $(\boldsymbol{a}_1, \ldots, \boldsymbol{a}_n)$ of

d-dimensional integral vectors, the encapsulation samples a random prime number p and a primitive root g modulo p. The encapsulated key is $K = p$ and the ciphertext $\mathsf{ct} = (\boldsymbol{x}, \boldsymbol{y})$ is a pair of n-dimensional integral vectors, where $\boldsymbol{x} = (x_1, \ldots, x_n)$ is a random integral linear combination of the rows of the $d \times n$ matrix $[\boldsymbol{a}_1 \cdots \boldsymbol{a}_n]$ and $\boldsymbol{y} \equiv (g^{x_1}, \ldots, g^{x_n}) \pmod p$. Conversely, given a ciphertext $(\boldsymbol{x}, \boldsymbol{y})$ and a tuple $(w_1, \ldots, w_n)$ of integers satisfying $\sum_{i=1}^{n} w_i \boldsymbol{a}_i = \boldsymbol{0}$, let $\delta = \prod_{i:w_i>0} y_i^{w_i} - \prod_{i:w_i<0} y_i^{-w_i} \equiv 0 \pmod p$. Then, $p = \gcd(\delta, \sigma_1, \ldots, \sigma_T)$ where $\sigma_1, \ldots, \sigma_T$ are other multiples of p constructed from δ and $\boldsymbol{x}$ in polynomial-time. To the best of our knowledge, δ must be computed during the decapsulation, thereby requiring the w_i's to be small for keeping polynomial-time complexity. This is similar to the KEA assumption: if an adversary $\mathcal{A}(g, g^s, q)$ outputs (C, Y) such that $C^s \equiv Y \pmod q$, then an extractor finds x such that $g^x \equiv C \pmod q$.

Related Work. In 2019, Chvojka, Jager and Kakvi [8] suggested a generic *witness encryption through obfuscation* primitive. Essentially, the ciphertext is an obfuscated program releasing the plaintext if and only if a relation $\mathcal{R}(x, w)$ holds. Such schemes may arise from *indistinguishability obfuscation* (iO), formalized in 2001 by Barak et al. [2]. The authors proved under reasonably weak assumptions that iO does *not* exist for arbitrary circuits, although it may exist for a restricted class of algorithms. In 2013, Garg et al. [12] suggested iO candidates based on multilinear maps while Lin and Tessaro [19] proposed a construction only requiring trilinear maps. More recently, Jain, Lin and Sahai [15] suggested iO candidates based on the symmetric external Diffie-Hellmann (used in elliptic-curve cryptography), learning with errors and learning plus noise assumptions.

Witness encryption schemes based on obfuscation can also be turned into *offline witness encryption* (OWE) schemes. The OWE primitive introduced by Abusalah, Fuchsbauer and Pietrzak [1] in 2016 requires the encryption to be performed via public-key cryptography and the decryption via obfuscation. This type of construction is motivated by the needs to reduce the encryption complexity at the cost of an external setup algorithm (such as a trusted third-party) and optional additional steps in the decryption, thereby addressing scenarios where the encryptor and the decryptor have different computational power, e.g., in the Bellare and Hoang Asymmetric Password-Based Encryption protocol [3].

The *hash proof system* (HPS) primitive for an NP relation $\mathcal{R}$ introduced by Cramer and Shoup [9] in 2002 is a variant of a non-interactive zero-knowledge proof system. A HPS is characterized by a keypair $(\mathsf{pk}, \mathsf{sk})$ and a pair of hash functions $H_{\mathsf{pk},\cdot}(\cdot)$ and $H_{\mathsf{sk}}(\cdot)$ hashing an NP instance x with the public key and a witness ω for $\mathcal{R}$ or with the secret key respectively, such that $H_{\mathsf{pk},\omega}(x)$ and $H_{\mathsf{sk}}(x)$ match with high probability whenever $\mathcal{R}(x, \omega)$ holds. Thus, the secret key can be considered as a "universal" substitute for a witness. While the HPS original purpose is to turn an IND-CPA public-key encryption (PKE) scheme into an IND-CCA2 PKE in the standard model, the primitive induces an extractable WKEM as follows: the encapsulation of x samples a random keypair $(\mathsf{pk}, \mathsf{sk})$ and outputs an encapsulated key $K = H_{\mathsf{sk}}(x)$ and a ciphertext $\mathsf{ct} = \mathsf{pk}$. Conversely, given a witness ω for x, the decapsulation recovers $K = H_{\mathsf{ct},\omega}(x)$. Since a HPS does not exist for all NP languages, this motivates the construction of an efficient WKEM for an NP-complete problem.

Structure of the Paper. Section 2 introduces the basic notations and presents the NP languages that we will focus on. In Sect. 2.2, we present the Witness Key Encapsulation Mechanism (WKEM) primitive and the associated security notion, extending the definitions from [6] to handle approximate correctness. The construction of our WKEM scheme is presented in Sect. 3, along with the correctness analysis, the hardness assumptions and the complexity analysis. We eventually discuss parameters selection and conclude our report in the last section. Technical details for the correctness proof are given in Appendix A.

2 Preliminaries

We write $P \doteq Q$ to mean that the symbol P is *defined as* the symbol Q. By convention, $\log(x)$ is the binary logarithm of $x > 0$. The set of (nonzero) *positive integers* is denoted by $\mathbb{N}$, the set of *nonnegative integers* by $\mathbb{Z}_{\geq 0}$ and the integral range $\{a, \ldots, b\}$ for $a, b \in \mathbb{Z}$ $(a \leq b)$ by $[\![a, b]\!]$. We denote by $\mathbf{Z}_\ell = \mathbb{Z}/\ell\mathbb{Z}$ the image of the modulo ℓ reduction $\pi_\ell \colon \mathbb{Z} \twoheadrightarrow \mathbb{Z}/\ell\mathbb{Z}$ defined by $x \mapsto x \bmod \ell \in [\![0, \ell - 1]\!]$. The algebra $\mathbb{M}_{m\times n}(\mathbb{Z})$ of $m \times n$ matrices defined over $\mathbb{Z}$ is identified with $\mathbb{Z}^{m\times n}$ and the *transpose* of a matrix $\mathbf{M}$ is denoted by $\mathbf{M}^\top$. The components of a (column) vector $\boldsymbol{v}$ and a matrix $\mathbf{M}$ are denoted by v_i and M_{ij} respectively. For $\boldsymbol{u}, \boldsymbol{v} \in \mathbb{Z}^n$, we write $\langle \boldsymbol{u}, \boldsymbol{v}\rangle = \boldsymbol{u}^\top \boldsymbol{v}$ and $\|\boldsymbol{v}\|_\infty \doteq \max_{1\leq i\leq n} |v_i|$. For $\mathbf{M} \in \mathbb{Z}^{m\times n}$, we define the *integral kernel* to be $\ker(\mathbf{M}) \doteq \{\boldsymbol{v} \in \mathbb{Z}^n : \mathbf{M}\boldsymbol{v} = \mathbf{0}\}$. For $L \in \mathbb{N}$, we define *the bounded kernel* to be $\ker_L(\mathbf{M}) \doteq \ker(\mathbf{M}) \cap [\![-L, L]\!]^n$.

Asymptotic Analysis. A function $f \colon \mathbb{N} \longrightarrow \mathbb{R}$ is said to be *polynomially bounded*, denoted by $\mathsf{poly}(\lambda)$, if there exist $c \in \mathbb{N}$ and $\lambda_0 \in \mathbb{N}$ such that for all $\lambda \geq \lambda_0$, we have $|f(\lambda)| < \lambda^c$. Similarly, f is said to be *negligible*, denoted by $\mathsf{negl}(\lambda)$, if for all $c \in \mathbb{N}$, there exists $\lambda_0 \in \mathbb{N}$ such that for all $\lambda \geq \lambda_0$ we have $|f(\lambda)| < \lambda^{-c}$.

Probability. The *truth function*, denoted by $\mathbb{1}_S$, outputs 1 if a statement S holds and 0 otherwise. The *complement* of an event E is denoted by $\neg E$. The *probability* of an event E is denoted by $\Pr[E]$. Given an algorithm $\mathcal{A}(\rho)$ parametrized by a set of parameters ρ and a source of randomness $\mathcal{S}$, the *deterministic* output of $\mathcal{A}$ with respect to random coins ξ chosen from $\mathcal{S}$ is denoted by $\mathcal{A}(\rho; \xi)$.

Definition 1 (NP language). *An* NP *language is a triplet* $(\mathscr{L}, p, \mathcal{R})$ *consisting of a language* $\mathscr{L} \subseteq \{0,1\}^*$, *a polynomial* $p \colon \mathbb{Z}_{\geq 0} \longrightarrow \mathbb{Z}_{\geq 0}$ *and a deterministic polynomial-time computable predicate* $\mathcal{R}$ *such that*

$$\mathscr{L} = \left\{\alpha \in \{0,1\}^* : \exists \omega \in \{0,1\}^{p(|\alpha|)} \text{ such that } \mathcal{R}(\alpha, \omega) = 1\right\},$$

where $|\alpha|$ *is the length of* α. *A word* $\omega \in \{0,1\}^{p(|\alpha|)}$ *for which* $\mathcal{R}(\alpha, \omega)$ *holds is called a* witness *(or* certificate*) for the instance* α *(with respect to* $\mathscr{L}$ *and* $\mathcal{R}$*).*

Definition 2 (Karp reduction). *A language* $\mathscr{L}_1$ *is said to be* Karp-reducible *to a language* $\mathscr{L}_2$, *denoted by* $\mathscr{L}_1 \leq_p \mathscr{L}_2$, *if there exists a deterministic and polynomial-time Turing machine* $\mathscr{E} \colon \{0,1\}^* \longrightarrow \{0,1\}^*$ *such that an arbitrary word* $\alpha \in \{0,1\}^*$ *belongs to* $\mathscr{L}_1$ *if and only if* $\mathscr{E}(\alpha)$ *belongs to* $\mathscr{L}_2$.

Definition 3 (NP-hard, NP-complete). *A language $\mathscr{L}$ is said to be* NP-*hard if $\mathscr{L}' \leq_p \mathscr{L}$ for all $\mathscr{L}' \in$* NP. *An* NP-*complete language is an* NP-*hard language that also belongs to* NP.

2.1 Subset Sum and Zero-Sum Problems

We extend the unary notation from $\mathbb{Z}_{\geq 0}$ to $\mathbb{Z}$ by mapping 0 to the empty word and $n > 0$ and $n < 0$ to 1^{2n-1} and 1^{-2n} respectively and abusively write 1^{w_i} for $w_i \in \mathbb{Z}$. On the following figure, we present the NP languages for *subset sum* problems such as Multi-SS as described in [7, §4.4] and [6, §2] and *zero-sum* problems that we are interested in (BHLE [10] and HLE).

Subset Sum (SS)	Multi-Subset Sum (Multi-SS)
$\alpha = (a_1, \dots, a_n, s) \in \mathbb{Z}_{\geq 0}^n \times \mathbb{Z}_{\geq 0}$.	$\alpha = (\boldsymbol{a}_1, \dots, \boldsymbol{a}_n, \boldsymbol{s}) \in (\mathbb{Z}_{\geq 0}^d)^n \times \mathbb{Z}_{\geq 0}^d$.
$\omega = (w_1, \dots, w_n) \in \{0, 1\}^n$.	$\omega = (1^{w_1}, \dots, 1^{w_n}) \in \mathbb{Z}_{\geq 0}^n$.
$\mathcal{R}(\alpha, \omega) : w_1 a_1 + \cdots + w_n a_n = s$.	$\mathcal{R}(\alpha, \omega) : w_1 \boldsymbol{a}_1 + \cdots + w_n \boldsymbol{a}_n = \boldsymbol{s}$.

Bounded Homogeneous Linear Equation (BHLE)	Homogeneous Linear Equation (HLE)
$\alpha = (a_1, \dots, a_n, K) \in \mathbb{Z}^n \times \mathbb{N}$.	$\alpha = (\boldsymbol{a}_1, \dots, \boldsymbol{a}_n) \in (\mathbb{Z}^d)^n$.
$\omega = (w_1, \dots, w_n) \in [\![-K, K]\!]^n \setminus \{0\}$.	$\omega = (1^{w_1}, \dots, 1^{w_n}) \in \mathbb{Z}^n \setminus \{\boldsymbol{0}\}$.
$\mathcal{R}(\alpha, \omega) : w_1 a_1 + \cdots + w_n a_n = 0$.	$\mathcal{R}(\alpha, \omega) : w_1 \boldsymbol{a}_1 + \cdots + w_n \boldsymbol{a}_n = \boldsymbol{0}$.

By transitivity, a sufficient condition for an NP language $\mathscr{L}$ to be NP-complete is to satisfy $\mathscr{L}' \leq_p \mathscr{L}$ for some NP-complete language $\mathscr{L}'$ such as 3-SAT. Karp and van Emde-Boas proved the NP-completeness of the SS and BHLE languages in [17] and [10] respectively. Choi and Vaudenay provided a novel proof of the NP-completeness of Multi-SS in [7, Thm. 12] by reducing 3-SAT to Multi-SS.

While it is not known whether HLE is NP-complete, the latter is closely related to the *Short Integer Solution* (SIS) problem which, in the current state of the art, is assumed to be hard. Formally, the $\mathsf{SIS}_{d,n,q,K}$ problem is formulated as follows: given a uniform random matrix $\mathbf{A} \in \mathbf{Z}_q^{d \times n}$, find a nonzero vector $\boldsymbol{z} \in \mathbb{Z}^n$ such that $\mathbf{A}\boldsymbol{z} \equiv \mathbf{0} \pmod q$ and $\|\boldsymbol{z}\|_2 \leq K$, where $\|\boldsymbol{z}\|_2$ denotes the Euclidean norm. In the language of lattices, the problem is equivalent to find a nonzero short vector in the dual lattice $\{\boldsymbol{z} \in \mathbb{Z}^n : \mathbf{A}\boldsymbol{z} \equiv \mathbf{0} \pmod q\}$. Interestingly, HLE is the modulus-free version of SIS with a polynomially bounded L_p-norm for any $p \geq 1$.

The hardness of SIS depends on the underlying parameters, e.g., a large n does not necessarily mean a harder problem as one may simply ignore some columns in $\mathbf{A}$ and force the corresponding coefficients in $\boldsymbol{z}$ to be 0. On the other hand, a large d means more equations to satisfy. Hardness results on worst-case lattice reductions or on SIS can be found in [14, Thm. 9.2] and [24] respectively.

Lattice problems are generally solved by lattice basis reductions techniques such as the Lenstra-Lenstra-Lovász (LLL) [18] algorithm or the Block Korkine-Zolotarev (BKZ) [5,27,28] algorithm. These algorithms may solve BHLE or HLE, yet in exponential time, and thus it is relevant to assume that HLE is hard.

2.2 Witness Key Encapsulation Mechanism

In [7, §4], later reformulated in [6], the authors extended the primitives of witness encryption introduced by Garg et al. [13] and constructed a *key encapsulation mechanism* (KEM) instead of a cryptosystem. The security notions are *extractable one-wayness* (OW-EWE) and *extractable indistinguishability* (IND-EWE). For practical considerations, we extend the correctness property in [6] for the construction proposed in Sect. 3 to be correct up to a negligible error.

Definition 4 (witness key encapsulation mechanism (extends [6])). *A* witness key encapsulation mechanism $\mathrm{WKEM}_{\mathcal{R}}(\mathcal{K}_\lambda, \mathsf{Enc}, \mathsf{Dec})$ *for a predicate* $\mathcal{R}$ *consists of a key domain* $\mathcal{K}_\lambda$ *defined by a security parameter* $\lambda \in \mathbb{N}$ *and two efficient algorithms:*

- $\mathsf{Enc}(1^\lambda, \alpha) \overset{\$}{\rightarrow} (K, \mathsf{ct})$*: a probabilistic polynomial-time algorithm which, given as inputs a security parameter* $\lambda \in \mathbb{N}$ *in unary notation and a word* $\alpha \in \{0,1\}^*$*, outputs a key* $K \in \mathcal{K}_\lambda$ *and a ciphertext* ct.
- $\mathsf{Dec}(\omega, \mathsf{ct}) \overset{\$}{\rightarrow} K/\bot$*: a probabilistic polynomial-time algorithm which, given as inputs a word* $\omega \in \{0,1\}^*$ *and a ciphertext* ct*, outputs a key* $K \in \mathcal{K}_\lambda$ *or a failure symbol* $\bot$ *if a decryption failure occurred.*

The correctness *property is defined as follows: the scheme is* $\varepsilon(\lambda)$-correct *if for any security parameter* $\lambda \in \mathbb{N}$*, any word* $\alpha \in \{0,1\}^*$ *and any witness* ω *for* α *with respect to the predicate* $\mathcal{R}$*, the following holds:*

$$\Pr_{\xi,\xi'}\left[\mathsf{Dec}(\omega, \mathsf{ct}\,; \xi') = K \mid (K, \mathsf{ct}) \leftarrow \mathsf{Enc}(1^\lambda, \alpha\,; \xi)\right] = 1 - \varepsilon(\lambda), \tag{2.1}$$

where the probability is taken over all the choices of random coins ξ *and* ξ'.

Our definition of correctness allows for probabilistic decryption to capture the notion of a failure. Those failures usually occur in code-based key encapsulation mechanisms where decoding is not guaranteed to succeed. We recall the OW-EWE security notion from [6].

Definition 5 (extractable one-way [6]). *A witness key encapsulation mechanism* $\mathrm{WKEM}_{\mathcal{R}}(\mathcal{K}_\lambda, \mathsf{Enc}, \mathsf{Dec})$ *for a predicate* $\mathcal{R}$ *is said to be* extractable one-way *if for any probabilistic and polynomial-time adversary* $\mathcal{A}$*, there exists a probabilistic and polynomial-time extractor* $\mathcal{E}$ *such that for all* $\alpha \in \{0,1\}^*$*, we have*

$$\Pr\left[\mathcal{R}(\alpha, \mathcal{E}(1^\lambda, \alpha)) = 1\right] \geq \min\left(\tfrac{1}{2}, \mathsf{Adv}^{\text{OW-EWE}}_{\mathcal{A},\text{WKEM}}(1^\lambda, \alpha)\right) - \mathsf{negl}(\lambda),$$

where $\mathsf{Adv}^{\text{OW-EWE}}_{\mathcal{A},\text{WKEM}}(1^\lambda, \alpha) \doteq \Pr[\text{OW-EWE}_{\mathcal{A}}(1^\lambda, \alpha) \rightarrow 1]$ *denotes the advantage of the adversary* $\mathcal{A}$ *in the* OW-EWE *game defined as follows:*

$\underline{\text{OW-EWE}_{\mathcal{A}}(1^\lambda, \alpha)}$

1: $\mathsf{Enc}(1^\lambda, \alpha) \overset{\$}{\rightarrow} (K, \mathsf{ct})$
2: $\mathcal{A}(1^\lambda, \alpha, \mathsf{ct}) \rightarrow K'$
3: **return** $\mathbb{1}_{K'=K}$

Similar to the Fujisaki-Okamoto transform which turns an IND-CPA-secure PKC into an IND-CCA-secure KEM in the random oracle model (ROM), [6] provides a simple transformation turning an OW-EWE-secure WKEM into an IND-EWE one in the ROM [6, Thm. 6] by applying a KDF on the encapsulated key. As such, we may simply focus on OW-EWE instead. The construction and the security definitions in [6] were slightly different from [7, §4] but do not differ by essence. Other extractable security definitions, especially for indistinguishability, are found in the works of Chvojka et al. [8], Garg et al. [13] or Faonio et al. [11].

Remark 1. The $\frac{1}{2}$ in the OW-EWE security definition is motivated as follows. When there is no witness, the adversary wins with negligible probability, but if the advantage of the adversary is close to 1, removing $\frac{1}{2}$ implies that the extractor should be as good or better than the adversary. As mentioned by [6], the existence of such extractor may be unnecessarily hard to prove. Morally speaking, OW-EWE-security only cares that the extractor performs substantially well, namely better than $\frac{1}{2}$, or as good as the adversary. Additionally, [6] focused on "substantially good" extractors to amplify the probability of success of the extractor in the proof of the *à la* Fujisaki-Okamoto transform.

3 Hidden Modulus WKEM

Recall that the HLE predicate $\mathcal{R}\colon (\mathbb{Z}^d)^n \times \mathbb{Z}^n \longrightarrow \{0,1\}$ is defined by

$$\mathcal{R}(\alpha, \boldsymbol{\omega})\colon w_1\boldsymbol{a}_1 + \cdots + w_n\boldsymbol{a}_n = \mathbf{0},$$

where $\alpha = (\boldsymbol{a}_1, \ldots, \boldsymbol{a}_n)$ and $\boldsymbol{\omega} = (w_1, \ldots, w_n)$. For convenience, HLE instances can be regarded as tuples $(\boldsymbol{a}_1, \ldots, \boldsymbol{a}_n) \in (\mathbb{Z}^d)^n$ or matrices $[\boldsymbol{a}_1 \cdots \boldsymbol{a}_n] \in \mathbb{Z}^{d\times n}$. As mentioned in the introduction, the WKEM arithmetic construction by Choi and Vaudenay [6] considers Multi-SS instances $(\boldsymbol{a}'_1, \ldots, \boldsymbol{a}'_n, \boldsymbol{s}) \in (\mathbb{Z}^d_{\geq 0})^n \times \mathbb{Z}^d_{\geq 0}$ but the security of their scheme collapses when an adversary finds $\boldsymbol{\omega}' = (w'_1, \ldots, w'_n) \in \mathbb{Z}^n$ with polynomially bounded coefficients such that $w'_1\boldsymbol{a}'_1 + \cdots + w'_n\boldsymbol{a}'_n = \mathbf{0}$, namely witnesses corresponding to the HLE instance $(\boldsymbol{a}'_1, \ldots, \boldsymbol{a}'_n) \in (\mathbb{Z}^d_{\geq 0})^n \subset (\mathbb{Z}^d)^n$.

Our idea is to turn this "attack" into a security "requirement" so that the ability to decrypt is equivalent to the knowledge of a HLE witness. Given a HLE instance $\mathbf{A} = [\boldsymbol{a}_1 \cdots \boldsymbol{a}_n] \in \mathbb{Z}^{d\times n}$, the encapsulation algorithm (Algorithm 1) generates a random λ-bit number p and a primitive root g modulo p. The encapsulated key is defined to be $K = p$ and the corresponding ciphertext to be a pair of *integral vectors* $\mathsf{ct} = (\boldsymbol{x}, \boldsymbol{y}) \in \mathbb{Z}^n \times \mathbb{Z}^n$, where $\boldsymbol{x} = (x_1, \ldots, x_n)$ is a random nonzero integral linear combination of the rows of $\mathbf{A}$ and $\boldsymbol{y} \equiv (g^{x_1}, \ldots, g^{x_n}) \pmod p$. Conversely, given a witness candidate $\boldsymbol{\omega} \in \ker(\mathbf{A})$ and a ciphertext $\mathsf{ct} = (\boldsymbol{x}, \boldsymbol{y})$, the decapsulation algorithm (Algorithm 2) recovers p by taking the greatest common divisor of multiples of p. The decapsulation is additionally parametrized by public parameters discussed in Sect. 3.4. The purpose of $\boldsymbol{x}$ is to reveal some information on $\mathbf{A}$ without the needs of storing it inside the ciphertext (if $\boldsymbol{x}$ were to be replaced by $\mathbf{A}$ in ct, then the size of the ciphertext likely becomes impractical).

Algorithm 1: $\mathsf{Enc}(1^\lambda, \mathbf{A})$

Input: A security parameter $\lambda \in \mathbb{N}$ and a HLE instance $\mathbf{A} \in \mathbb{Z}^{d \times n}$.
Output: An encapsulated key K and a ciphertext $\mathsf{ct} = (\boldsymbol{x}, \boldsymbol{y}) \in \mathbb{Z}^n \times \mathbb{Z}^n$.

Sample distinct λ-bit prime numbers p, q and a primitive root g modulo p.
$\phi \leftarrow p - 1$
repeat
 $\boldsymbol{\mu} \leftarrow\$ \mathbf{Z}_\phi^d$ ▷ $\boldsymbol{\mu} = (\mu_1, \ldots, \mu_d)$
 $\boldsymbol{x} \leftarrow \mathbf{A}^\top \boldsymbol{\mu} \bmod \phi$ ▷ $\boldsymbol{x} = (x_1, \ldots, x_n)$
until $\boldsymbol{x} \neq \mathbf{0}$
$\boldsymbol{\kappa} \leftarrow\$ \mathbf{Z}_q^n$ ▷ $\boldsymbol{\kappa} = (k_1, \ldots, k_n)$
for $i = 1, \ldots, n$ **do**
 $y_i \leftarrow (g^{x_i} \bmod p) + k_i p$
$K \leftarrow p$
$\mathsf{ct} \leftarrow (\boldsymbol{x}, \boldsymbol{y})$
return (K, ct)

Algorithm 2: $\mathsf{Dec}(\boldsymbol{\omega}, \mathsf{ct})$

Parameters: Public parameters $B \ll 2^\lambda$, $T = \mathsf{poly}(\lambda)$ and $L \in \mathbb{N}$.
Input: An element $\boldsymbol{\omega} \in \ker(\mathbf{A})$ and a ciphertext $\mathsf{ct} = (\boldsymbol{x}, \boldsymbol{y}) \in \mathbb{Z}^n \times \mathbb{Z}^n$.
Output: A decapsulated key K' or a failure symbol $\perp$.

[a] $\delta \leftarrow \prod_{i: w_i > 0} y_i^{w_i} - \prod_{i: w_i < 0} y_i^{-w_i}$
if $\delta = 0$ **then**
 return $\perp$
[b] $\delta \leftarrow \max\{d \in \mathbb{N} \colon \delta \equiv 0 \pmod{d} \text{ and } \gcd(y_i, d) = 1 \text{ for all } 1 \leq i \leq n\}$
[c] Discard the ℓ-primary parts of δ for $2 \leq \ell \leq B$.
for $j = 1, \ldots, T$ **do**
 [d] $\boldsymbol{\beta} \leftarrow\$ \ker_L(\boldsymbol{x}^\top) \setminus \{\mathbf{0}\}$ ▷ $\langle \boldsymbol{x}, \boldsymbol{\beta} \rangle = 0, \|\boldsymbol{\beta}\|_\infty \leq L$
 $\boldsymbol{\beta} \rightarrow (b_1, \ldots, b_n)$
 $\sigma_j \leftarrow \prod_{i=1}^n y_i^{b_i} - 1 \bmod \delta$
$K' \leftarrow \gcd(\delta, \sigma_1, \ldots, \sigma_T)$
if K' *is not prime* **then**
 return $\perp$
return K'

[a] This step takes polynomial-time *if and only if* $\boldsymbol{\omega}$ has a small L_1-norm.
[b] This step guarantees $y_i^{b_i} \bmod \delta$ to be well-defined for an *arbitrary* choice of $b_i \in \mathbb{Z}$.
[c] The ℓ-primary part of δ is the largest prime power ℓ^k dividing δ for some $k \geq 1$.
[d] The question on how to *efficiently* sample $\boldsymbol{\beta}$ is discussed in Sect. 3.3.

Intuition Behind the Correctness. We will prove later that δ (line 1 of Algorithm 2) is a nonzero multiple of p. We stress that δ cannot be computed efficiently if the witness coefficients are not polynomially bounded since y_i are integers and not class residues. For now, assume that $\gcd(y_i, \delta) = 1$, up to replacing δ by its largest divisor that fulfils that condition (line 4). If $\boldsymbol{\beta} = (b_1, \ldots, b_n) \in \ker(\boldsymbol{x}^\top) \subset \mathbb{Z}^n$, then $y_i^{b_i} \bmod \delta$ is a well-defined integer (even if $b_i < 0$) and

$$\sigma = \left(\prod_{i=1}^{n} y_i^{b_i} - 1 \bmod \delta\right) \equiv g^{\langle \boldsymbol{x}, \boldsymbol{\beta} \rangle} - 1 \equiv 0 \pmod{p}. \tag{3.1}$$

Since $b_i \in \mathbb{Z}$, it is crucial that the modular exponentiations are well-defined, whence the coprimality condition. By computing $\sigma_1, \ldots, \sigma_T$ according to (3.1) for different choices of $\boldsymbol{\beta} \in \ker_L(\boldsymbol{x}^\top)$ (line 9), we hope that $K' = \gcd(\delta, \sigma_1, \ldots, \sigma_T)$ is p. Intuitively, the larger T, the smaller the probability for K' to be composite. Small smooth factors are avoided by discarding the ℓ-primary parts of δ for every prime $\ell \leq B \ll 2^\lambda$ (line 5). This step is efficient since only polynomial factors are eliminated and may also be performed on K' instead of δ. It is however recommended to do it on δ since this shortens the modulus involved in (3.1) without affecting the divisibility by p. Finally, observe that K' can be lazily computed by defining $K'_0 = \delta$ and $K'_{j+1} = \gcd(K'_j, \sigma_j)$ and substituting δ in (3.1) for K'_j at each iteration (the modulus being used is obtained after line 5 and remains a multiple of p of size $\Omega(p)$). In summary, the proposed decryption algorithm recovers p with high probability.

Correctness Under Heuristic Assumptions. The correctness is essentially characterized by the condition $\gcd(\sigma_1, \ldots, \sigma_T) = p$, i.e., $\gcd(\sigma_1/p, \ldots, \sigma_T/p) = 1$. By Nymann's theorem [25], the probability that $3 \leq T \leq N$ (with $T = \mathsf{poly}(\lambda)$) positive integers chosen uniformly at random from $[\![1, N]\!]$ are coprime is $\frac{1}{\zeta(T)} + O(1/N)$, where $\zeta(s) = \sum_{k=1}^{\infty} \frac{1}{k^s}$ is the Riemann zeta function. In our case, neither $\{\sigma_1, \ldots, \sigma_T\}$ are "uniformly distributed" in $p\mathbb{Z}$ (natural density being the correct notion) nor $\{\sigma_1/p, \ldots, \sigma_T/p\}$ are uniformly distributed modulo δ/p. However, since δ is deprived of small factors, σ_i/p is *almost* uniform modulo δ/p. Thus, we may heuristically claim $\varepsilon(\lambda)$-correctness for $\varepsilon(\lambda) = 1 - \frac{1}{\zeta(\mathsf{poly}(\lambda))} = \mathsf{negl}(\lambda)$.

Roadmap. Section 3.1 focuses on the *formal* correctness of the scheme but the technical claims are proved in Appendix A. Section 3.2 discusses the hardness assumption for our scheme to be OW-EWE-secure and Sect. 3.3 analyses the scheme complexity. In particular, this explains how to sample (p, g) and q in Algorithm 1, compute δ (lines 1 to 5 of Algorithm 2), or sample $\boldsymbol{\beta} \in \ker_L(\boldsymbol{x}^\top)$. We eventually prove that the decapsulation complexity is polynomial *if and only if* $\boldsymbol{\omega}$ has a small coefficients.

3.1 Correctness Proof

Since our construction is probabilistic even during decapsulation, perfect correctness cannot be achieved in the sense of Definition 4. For the rest of the document, we assume that p and q are distinct λ-bit primes, $\mathbf{A} \in \mathbb{Z}^{d \times n}$ is a HLE instance and $\boldsymbol{\omega} \in \mathbb{Z}^n$ is a witness for $\mathbf{A}$. From now on, we use the following notations:

- For a prime number ℓ, we fix a primitive root g_ℓ modulo ℓ and denote the *discrete logarithm in base* g_ℓ by $\mathrm{dlog}_\ell \colon \mathbf{Z}_\ell^\times \longrightarrow \mathbf{Z}_{\varphi(\ell)}$, where φ denotes the Euler totient function. This application naturally extends to $(\mathbf{Z}_\ell^\times)^n$ via componentwise evaluation. We will abusively write $\mathrm{dlog}_\ell(z)$ instead of $\mathrm{dlog}_\ell(z \bmod \ell)$ for $z \in \mathbb{Z}$ such that $\gcd(z, \ell) = 1$.
- With the convention $0^0 = 1$, we define $\boldsymbol{\Delta} \colon \mathbb{Z}^n \times \mathbb{Z}^n \longrightarrow \mathbb{Z}$ by

$$\boldsymbol{\Delta}(\boldsymbol{z}, \boldsymbol{e}) \doteq \prod_{i:e_i>0} z_i^{e_i} - \prod_{i:e_i<0} z_i^{-e_i} = \prod_{i=1}^{n} z_i^{\max(0,e_i)} - \prod_{i=1}^{n} z_i^{\max(0,-e_i)}. \quad (3.2)$$

  We stress that $\boldsymbol{\Delta}(\boldsymbol{z}, \boldsymbol{e})$ is a well-defined integer since $\max(0, \pm e_i) \geq 0$.
- Given $\delta \geq 2$ and $\boldsymbol{z} = (z_1, \ldots, z_n) \in \mathbb{Z}^n$ with $z_i \neq 0$, denote by $\mathcal{M}_\delta(\boldsymbol{z})$ the largest divisor of δ for which $\gcd(z_i, \mathcal{M}_\delta(\boldsymbol{z})) = 1$ for all $i = 1, \ldots, n$. Stated otherwise, $\mathcal{M}_\delta(\boldsymbol{z})$ is the largest divisor ℓ of δ for which $z_1, \ldots, z_n \in \mathbf{Z}_\ell^\times$.

To prove that our scheme is a correct WKEM (Theorem 1), we focus on the following claims:

- The integer $\delta = \boldsymbol{\Delta}(\boldsymbol{y}, \boldsymbol{\omega})$ on line 1 of Algorithm 2 and the integers $\sigma_1, \ldots, \sigma_T$ computed on line 9 are multiples of p (Lemma 1). Additionally, δ is divisible by q with probability at most $\frac{n^2}{4q^2} + \frac{1}{q-1}$ (Lemma 2 and Proposition 1).
- If $T = \mathsf{poly}(\lambda)$ and if $n = o(q)$ and $n = \Omega(\lambda)$, then δ is a multiple of p with high probability (Corollary 1) and $p = \gcd(\delta, \sigma_1, \ldots, \sigma_T)$ holds with high probability (Theorem 1). In particular, the decapsulation algorithm succeeds.

Lemma 1. *Let p and q be distinct λ-bit prime numbers and let g be a primitive root modulo p. Let $\mathcal{Y} \colon \mathbb{Z}^n \times \mathbf{Z}_q^n \longrightarrow \mathbb{Z}^n$ be the application defined by*

$$((x_1, \ldots, x_n), (k_1, \ldots, k_n)) \overset{\mathcal{Y}}{\longmapsto} (g^{x_1} \bmod p + k_1 p, \ldots,, g^{x_n} \bmod p + k_n p). \quad (3.3)$$

Let $(\boldsymbol{x}, \boldsymbol{\kappa}) \in \mathbb{Z}^n \times \mathbf{Z}_q^n$ and $\boldsymbol{y} = (y_1, \ldots, y_n) = \mathcal{Y}(\boldsymbol{x}, \boldsymbol{\kappa})$. If $\boldsymbol{\beta} = (b_1, \ldots, b_n) \in \mathbb{Z}^n$ satisfies $\langle \boldsymbol{x}, \boldsymbol{\beta} \rangle \equiv 0 \pmod{\varphi(p)}$, then

$$\boldsymbol{\Delta}(\boldsymbol{y}, \boldsymbol{\beta}) = \prod_{i:b_i>0} y_i^{b_i} - \prod_{i:b_i<0} y_i^{-b_i} = \prod_{i=1}^{n} y_i^{\max(0,b_i)} - \prod_{i=1}^{n} y_i^{\max(0,-b_i)}$$

is a multiple of p. In particular, if M is a multiple of p for which $\gcd(y_i, M) = 1$ *for all* $i = 1, \dots, n$, *then* $\prod_{i=1}^n y_i^{b_i} - 1 \bmod M$ *is a multiple of p as well.*

Proof. Clearly, $\boldsymbol{\Delta}(\boldsymbol{y}, \boldsymbol{\beta}) \equiv \left(1 - g^{-\langle \boldsymbol{x}, \boldsymbol{\beta}\rangle}\right) \prod_{i=1}^n g^{\max(0,b_i)} \equiv 0 \pmod p$. If $M \in p\mathbb{Z}$ satisfies $\gcd(y_i, M) = 1$ for all $i = 1, \dots, n$, then

$$\left[\prod_{i=1}^n y_i^{b_i} \bmod M\right] \bmod p = \prod_{i=1}^n y_i^{b_i} \bmod p \equiv g^{\langle \boldsymbol{x}, \boldsymbol{\beta}\rangle} \equiv 1 \pmod p.$$

□

In order to prove that δ is a nonzero multiple of p, we simply prove that δ is a multiple of q with negligible probability. For that, we need the following lemma.

Lemma 2. *Let* $\boldsymbol{x} \in \mathbb{Z}^n$ *and let* $\mathcal{K}$ *be uniformly distributed in* $\mathbf{Z}_q^n$. *Consider the random vector* $\mathcal{Y}(\boldsymbol{x}) = \mathcal{Y}(\boldsymbol{x}, \mathcal{K})$ *in* $\mathbb{Z}^n$. *Then,* $\mathcal{Y}(\boldsymbol{x}) \bmod q$ *is uniformly distributed in* $\mathbf{Z}_q^n$. *Additionally, if p and q are distinct prime numbers, then*

$$\Pr_{\boldsymbol{\kappa} \sim \mathcal{K}}\left[\bigcap_{i=1}^n \{\gcd(y_i, q) = 1\} \mid (y_1, \dots, y_n) \leftarrow \mathcal{Y}(\boldsymbol{x}, \boldsymbol{\kappa}) \bmod q\right] = \left(1 - \frac{1}{q}\right)^n.$$

Proof. Since $\mathcal{Y}(\boldsymbol{x}, \mathcal{K})$ solely depends on $\mathcal{K}$, it follows that $\mathcal{Y}(\boldsymbol{x}, \mathcal{K}) \bmod q$ is uniformly distributed in $\mathbf{Z}_q^n$. The second assertion is a consequence of the independence of the components of $\mathcal{Y}(\boldsymbol{x}, \mathcal{K})$ and the fact that $p \neq q$. □

Proposition 1. *Let* $\boldsymbol{x} \in \mathbb{Z}^n$ *and let* $\boldsymbol{\beta} \in \mathbb{Z}^n \setminus \{\boldsymbol{0}\}$ *such that* $\langle \boldsymbol{x}, \boldsymbol{\beta}\rangle = 0$. *Then,*

$$\Pr_{\boldsymbol{y} \sim \mathcal{Y}(\boldsymbol{x})}\left[\boldsymbol{\Delta}(\boldsymbol{y}, \boldsymbol{\beta}) \equiv 0 \pmod q\right] \leq \frac{n^2}{4q^2} + \frac{1}{\varphi(q)}.$$

Proof. Let $\boldsymbol{\beta} = (b_1, \dots, b_n) \in \ker(\boldsymbol{x}^\top) \setminus \{\boldsymbol{0}\}$ and $\boldsymbol{y} = (y_1, \dots, y_n) \sim \mathcal{Y}(\boldsymbol{x}) \in \mathbb{Z}^n$. Let E_+ (resp. E_-) be the event "there exists y_i such that $b_i > 0$ (resp. $b_i < 0$) and y_i is a multiple of q". By Lemma 2, the events E_+ and E_- are independent. Let n_+ and n_- denote the number of nonzero positive and negative components in $\boldsymbol{\beta}$ respectively. Then, $\Pr_{\boldsymbol{y}}[E_\pm] = 1 - \left(1 - \frac{1}{q}\right)^{n_\pm} \leq \frac{n_\pm}{q}$. Observe that if the event $E = E_+ \cap E_-$ holds, then $\boldsymbol{\Delta}(\boldsymbol{y}, \boldsymbol{\beta}) \bmod q = 0$. In particular,

$$\Pr_{\boldsymbol{y}}[E \cap \{\boldsymbol{\Delta}(\boldsymbol{y}, \boldsymbol{\beta}) \bmod q = 0\}] \leq \frac{n_+ n_-}{q^2} \leq \frac{n_+ + n_-}{2q}\sqrt{\frac{n_+ n_-}{q^2}} \leq \frac{n^2}{4q^2},$$

where the second inequality arises from the fact that the function $t \mapsto \sqrt{t(t_0 - t)}$ realizes its maximum over $[0, t_0]$ at $t = \frac{t_0}{2}$. Let S be the support of $\mathcal{Y}(\boldsymbol{x}) \bmod q$. By definition, $\neg E \cap \{\boldsymbol{\Delta}(\boldsymbol{y}, \boldsymbol{\beta}) \bmod q = 0\}$ holds if and only if $(\boldsymbol{y} \bmod q) \in S \cap (\mathbf{Z}_q^\times)^n$ and $\langle \mathrm{dlog}_g(\boldsymbol{y}), \boldsymbol{\beta}\rangle \equiv 0 \pmod{\varphi(q)}$. By assumption, q is prime. It follows that if $\overline{\boldsymbol{y}}$ is uniformly distributed in $S \cap (\mathbf{Z}_q^\times)^n$, then $\langle \mathrm{dlog}_g(\overline{\boldsymbol{y}}), \boldsymbol{\beta}\rangle \bmod \varphi(q)$ is uniformly distributed in $\mathbf{Z}_{\varphi(q)}$. Therefore,

$$\Pr_{\boldsymbol{y}}[\neg E \cap \{\boldsymbol{\Delta}(\boldsymbol{y}, \boldsymbol{\beta}) \bmod q = 0\}] \leq \Pr_{\overline{\boldsymbol{y}}}[\langle \mathrm{dlog}_q(\overline{\boldsymbol{y}}), \boldsymbol{\beta}\rangle \bmod \varphi(q) = 0] = \frac{1}{\varphi(q)}.$$

The desired result then follows from the law of total probability. □

Corollary 1. *Let* $\mathbf{A} \in \mathbb{Z}^{d\times n}$ *and let* $\boldsymbol{\omega} \in \ker(\mathbf{A})$. *Let* $\boldsymbol{\mu} \in \mathbf{Z}^d_{\varphi(p)}$ *and* $\mathcal{K} \in \mathbf{Z}^n_q$ *be uniformly distributed,* $\boldsymbol{x} = \mathbf{A}^\top\boldsymbol{\mu} \bmod \varphi(p)$ *and* $\boldsymbol{y} = \mathcal{Y}(\boldsymbol{x}, \mathcal{K})$ *be random variables in* $\mathbb{Z}^n$. *Then,* $\Pr[\boldsymbol{\Delta}(\boldsymbol{y}, \boldsymbol{\omega}) \in p\mathbb{Z} \setminus \{0\}] \geq 1 - \left(\frac{n^2}{4q^2} + \frac{1}{\varphi(q)}\right)$.

Proof. Since $\langle \boldsymbol{x}, \boldsymbol{\omega}\rangle \equiv 0 \pmod{\varphi(p)}$, Lemma 1 implies that $\delta = \boldsymbol{\Delta}(\boldsymbol{y}, \boldsymbol{\omega}) \in p\mathbb{Z}$. Now, since $\langle \mathbf{A}^\top \boldsymbol{\mu}, \boldsymbol{\omega}\rangle = \langle \boldsymbol{\mu}, \mathbf{A}\boldsymbol{\omega}\rangle = 0$, we have $\langle \boldsymbol{x}, \boldsymbol{\omega}\rangle = 0$ in $\mathbb{Z}$. By Proposition 1, this implies $\Pr[\delta \in q\mathbb{Z}] \leq \frac{n^2}{4q^2} + \frac{1}{\varphi(q)}$. Since p and q are distinct primes,

$$\Pr[\delta = 0] \leq \Pr[\delta = 0 \mid \delta \in p\mathbb{Z}] \leq \Pr[\delta \in q\mathbb{Z} \mid \delta \in p\mathbb{Z}] \leq \Pr[\delta \in q\mathbb{Z}].$$

Therefore, $\Pr[\delta \in p\mathbb{Z} \setminus \{0\}] = \Pr[\delta \neq 0] \geq 1 - \Pr[\delta \in q\mathbb{Z}]$. □

Given $\boldsymbol{z} \in \mathbb{Z}^n$, recall that $\mathcal{M}_\delta(\boldsymbol{z})$ is the largest divisor d of $\delta \in \mathbb{Z}$ for which $\gcd(z_i, d) = 1$. We formalize (3.1) by the function $\sigma_\delta(\boldsymbol{z}, -) \colon \mathbb{Z}^n \longrightarrow \mathbb{Z}$ defined by

$$\boldsymbol{e} = (e_1, \ldots, e_n) \mapsto \sigma_\delta(\boldsymbol{z}, \boldsymbol{e}) \doteq \prod_{i=1}^{n} z_i^{e_i} - 1 \bmod \mathcal{M}_\delta(\boldsymbol{z}). \tag{3.4}$$

Let $\mathsf{ct} = (\boldsymbol{x}, \boldsymbol{y})$ be a ciphertext produced by Algorithm 1 and p be the encapsulated key. Let $\boldsymbol{\beta} \in \ker(\boldsymbol{x}^\top)$ and $\sigma = \sigma_\delta(\boldsymbol{y}, \boldsymbol{\beta}) \in \mathbb{Z}$ be as on line 9 of Algorithm 2. By Corollary 1, we have $\delta \in p\mathbb{Z}$. Thus, $M = \mathcal{M}_\delta(\boldsymbol{y}) \in p\mathbb{Z}$ and $\sigma \in p\mathbb{Z}$ for by Lemma 1. It remains to estimate the probability for M and σ to share a prime factor ℓ other than p as $\boldsymbol{\beta}$ is uniformly distributed in $\ker_L(\boldsymbol{x}^\top) \setminus \{\mathbf{0}\}$ for $L \in \mathbb{N}$. Assume that there exists an event F such that $\Pr[F] = \mathsf{negl}(\lambda)$ and $\Pr[\sigma \in \ell\mathbb{Z} | \neg F] = \mathsf{negl}(\lambda)$. By the law of total probability, this would imply

$$\Pr[\sigma \in \ell\mathbb{Z}] = \Pr[\sigma \in \ell\mathbb{Z}|F] \Pr[F] + \Pr[\sigma \in \ell\mathbb{Z}|\neg F] \Pr[\neg F] = \mathsf{negl}(\lambda).$$

In particular, $K' = \gcd(\delta, \sigma_1, \ldots, \sigma_T) = p$ with high probability (Theorem 1). To show the existence of the event F (later defined as the family of events of the form (3.5)), we need the following results (the proofs are given in Appendix A due to their technical nature).

Claim 1. *Let p and q be distinct prime numbers and let g be a primitive root modulo p. Recall the definition of $\mathcal{Y}\colon \mathbb{Z}^n \times \mathbf{Z}_q^n \longrightarrow \mathbb{Z}^n$ from Lemma 1, namely*

$$((x_1, \ldots, x_n), (k_1, \ldots, k_n)) \overset{\mathcal{Y}}{\longmapsto} (g^{x_1} \bmod p + k_1 p, \ldots, g^{x_n} \bmod p + k_n p).$$

Fix $\boldsymbol{x} \in \mathbb{Z}^n$ and let $\mathcal{K}$ be uniformly distributed in $\mathbf{Z}_q^n$. Let ℓ be a prime number distinct from p and $\mathcal{Y}_\ell(\boldsymbol{x}) \doteq \mathcal{Y}(\boldsymbol{x}, \mathcal{K}) \bmod \ell$. Let r be a prime factor of $\varphi(\ell)$ and

$$\vartheta_{\ell,r}(\boldsymbol{x}) \doteq \Pr_{\boldsymbol{y} \sim \mathcal{Y}_\ell(\boldsymbol{x})} [\exists \varepsilon \in \mathbf{Z}_r^\times : \operatorname{dlog}_\ell(\boldsymbol{y}) \equiv \varepsilon \boldsymbol{x} \pmod r],$$

where the probability is taken over the outcomes for which $dlog_\ell(-)$ is well-defined. Then $\vartheta_{\ell,r}(\boldsymbol{x}) \leq \frac{1}{r^{n-1}}$ if $\ell \geq q$ and $\vartheta_{\ell,r}(\boldsymbol{x}) \leq \frac{1}{r^{n-1}}\left(1 + \frac{r}{q}\right)^n$ if $\ell < q$. In particular,

$$\Pr_{\boldsymbol{y} \sim \mathcal{Y}_\ell(\boldsymbol{x})}\Big[\bigcup_{r \mid \varphi(\ell)} \{\forall \varepsilon \in \mathbf{Z}_r^\times : \operatorname{dlog}_\ell(\boldsymbol{y}) \not\equiv \varepsilon \boldsymbol{x} \pmod r\}\Big] \geq 1 - \frac{1}{2^{n-1}}\left(1 + \frac{2}{q}\right)^n,$$

where the probability is taken over the outcomes for which $dlog_\ell(-)$ is well-defined.

Proof. See Appendix A. □

Claim 2. *Let $\mathsf{ct} = (\boldsymbol{x}, \boldsymbol{y}) \in \mathbb{Z}^n \times \mathbb{Z}^n$ be a ciphertext produced by Algorithm 1 corresponding to a HLE instance $\mathbf{A} \in \mathbb{Z}^{d \times n}$ and a hidden prime p and consider a nonzero vector $\boldsymbol{\omega} \in \ker(\mathbf{A})$. Let $\delta = \boldsymbol{\Delta}(\boldsymbol{y}, \boldsymbol{\omega})$. For every prime factor ℓ of $\mathcal{M}_\delta(\boldsymbol{y})$ distinct from p and every prime factor r of $\varphi(\ell)$, denote by $F_{\ell,r}(\boldsymbol{x}, \boldsymbol{y})$ the event*

$$F_{\ell,r}(\boldsymbol{x}, \boldsymbol{y}) \doteq \big\{\exists \varepsilon \in \mathbf{Z}_r^\times : \operatorname{dlog}_\ell(\boldsymbol{y}) \equiv \varepsilon \boldsymbol{x} \pmod r\big\}. \tag{3.5}$$

Assume that there exists a prime factor ℓ of $\mathcal{M}_\delta(\boldsymbol{y})$ distinct from p and a prime factor r of $\varphi(\ell)$ such that the event $F_{\ell,r}(\boldsymbol{x}, \boldsymbol{y})$ fails[5]*. If $L \geq 2\varphi(\ell)$ is an integer and $\mathcal{U}$ is the uniform distribution over $\ker_L(\boldsymbol{x}^\top) \setminus \{\mathbf{0}\}$, then*

$$\Pr_{\boldsymbol{\beta} \sim \mathcal{U}} [\sigma_\delta(\boldsymbol{y}, \boldsymbol{\beta}) \equiv 0 \pmod \ell \mid \neg F_{\ell,r}(\boldsymbol{x}, \boldsymbol{y})] \leq \left(\frac{3}{4}\right)^n.$$

Proof. See Appendix A. □

Theorem 1 (correctness). *Let λ be a security parameter. Let $n, d \geq 1$ be integers such that $n = o(2^\lambda)$ and $n = \Omega(\lambda)$ and let $\mathbf{A} \in \mathbb{Z}^{d \times n}$ and $\boldsymbol{\omega} \in \ker(\mathbf{A}) \setminus \{\mathbf{0}\}$. If L is sufficiently large, then*

$$\Pr_\xi\big[\mathsf{Dec}(\boldsymbol{\omega}, (\boldsymbol{x}, \boldsymbol{y})) = p \,|\, (p, (\boldsymbol{x}, \boldsymbol{y})) \leftarrow \mathsf{Enc}(1^\lambda, \mathbf{A}; \xi)\big] \geq 1 - \mathsf{negl}(\lambda),$$

---

[5] By Claim 1, this happens with probability at least $1 - \frac{1}{2^{n-1}}\left(1 + \frac{2}{q}\right)^n$.

where $\boldsymbol{y} \sim \mathcal{Y}(\boldsymbol{x}, \boldsymbol{\kappa})$ and the probability is taken over $\xi = (\xi_\mu, \xi_\kappa, \xi_L)$. The random coins ξ_μ and ξ_κ are associated with the uniform distribution of $\boldsymbol{\mu} \in \mathbf{Z}^d_{\varphi(p)}$ and the uniform distribution of $\boldsymbol{\kappa} \in \mathbf{Z}^n_q$ in the encapsulation (Algorithm 1). The random coins ξ_L are associated with the uniform distribution over $\ker_L(\boldsymbol{x}^\top) \setminus \{\mathbf{0}\}$ used for sampling the exponent vectors $\boldsymbol{\beta}_1, \ldots, \boldsymbol{\beta}_T$ during the decapsulation (Algorithm 2).

Proof. If $\boldsymbol{\mu}$ is uniformly distributed in $\mathbf{Z}^d_{\varphi(p)}$, so is $\boldsymbol{x} = \mathbf{A}^\top \boldsymbol{\mu} \bmod \varphi(p)$ in $\mathbf{Z}^n_{\varphi(p)}$. In particular, $\Pr_{\xi_\mu}[\boldsymbol{x} = \mathbf{0}] = O(p^{-n}) = \mathsf{negl}(\lambda)$. Let $\boldsymbol{\Delta}\colon \mathbb{Z}^n \times \mathbb{Z}^n \longrightarrow \mathbb{Z}$ be given by (3.2). Let $\mathcal{K}$ be uniformly distributed in $\mathbf{Z}^n_q$ and $\mathcal{Y}\colon \mathbb{Z}^n \times \mathbf{Z}^n_q \longrightarrow \mathbb{Z}^n$ be given by (3.3). Let $\boldsymbol{y} = (y_1, \ldots, y_n) \sim \mathcal{Y}(\boldsymbol{x}, \mathcal{K})$. Without loss of generality, $\delta = \boldsymbol{\Delta}(\boldsymbol{y}, \boldsymbol{\omega})$ is deprived of its ℓ-primary parts for every prime $\ell \leq B \lll 2^\lambda$ and $\gcd(y_i, \delta) = 1$ for all $1 \leq i \leq n$. In practice, such δ is obtained after executing lines 4 and 5 of Algorithm 2. Since $n = o(2^\lambda) = o(q)$, Proposition 1 implies that

$$\Pr_{\kappa \sim \mathcal{K}}[\delta \equiv 0 \pmod{q}] \leq \frac{n^2}{4q^2} + \frac{1}{q-1} = O(1/q) = \mathsf{negl}(\lambda).$$

In particular, we conclude that $\Pr[\delta \in p\mathbb{Z} \setminus \{0\}] \geq 1 - \mathsf{negl}(\lambda)$ for by Corollary 1.

Let $\sigma_\delta(\boldsymbol{y}, -)\colon \mathbb{Z}^n \longrightarrow \mathbb{Z}$ be given by (3.4) and let $\boldsymbol{\beta}_1, \ldots, \boldsymbol{\beta}_T$ be uniformly distributed in $\ker_L(\boldsymbol{x}^\top) \setminus \{\mathbf{0}\}$. Although δ and $\sigma_j = \sigma_\delta(\boldsymbol{y}, \boldsymbol{\beta}_j)$ have different distributions, $\delta' = \gcd(\sigma_1, \ldots, \sigma_T)$ satisfies $\gcd(\delta, \delta') \neq p$ if there exists a "parasite" prime factor $\ell \neq p$ dividing δ and δ'. Assume that the event $F_{\ell,r}(\boldsymbol{x}, \boldsymbol{y})$ defined by (3.5) fails for some prime factor r of $\varphi(\ell)$. By Claim 1, this happens with probability $\vartheta \geq 1 - \frac{1}{2^{n-1}}\left(1 + \frac{2}{q}\right)^n$. Since $n = \Omega(\lambda)$ and $n = o(q)$ by assumption, it follows that $\vartheta = 1 - \mathsf{negl}(\lambda)$. Thus, the prime ℓ divides δ' with probability at most $(\frac{3}{4})^{nT}$ for by Claim 2. By choosing $T = \mathsf{poly}(\lambda)$, it is clear that the parasite factor ℓ of $\gcd(\delta, \delta')$ is eliminated after a polynomial number of iterations. By iteratively defining $K'_0 \doteq \delta$ and $K'_{j+1} \doteq \gcd(K'_j, \sigma_j)$, the length of K_j reduces until eventually reaching $\log p = \lambda$. □

3.2 Hardness Assumption

The purpose of our construction is to define the *ability to decrypt* as equivalent to the *knowledge of a witness.* Although it is possible to decrypt given sufficient time by choosing $\delta = \boldsymbol{\Delta}(\boldsymbol{y}, \boldsymbol{\omega})$ for some nonzero $\boldsymbol{\omega} \in \ker(\mathbf{A})$ instead of a true witness for $\mathbf{A}$, this process is inefficient due to the exponentiations in the decapsulation and the result may not be relevant at that time. To achieve OW-EWE-security, we need the following hardness assumption:

Assumption 1 (KER assumption). Let $\mathbf{A} \in \mathbb{Z}^{d \times n}$ be a HLE instance and let $(p, (\boldsymbol{x}, \boldsymbol{y})) \sim \mathsf{Enc}(1^\lambda, \mathbf{A})$. If a polynomial-time adversary $\mathcal{A}(\mathbf{A}, \boldsymbol{x}, \boldsymbol{y})$ outputs $s = \pm p$, then there exists exists a polynomial-time extractor $\mathcal{E}(\mathbf{A}, \boldsymbol{x}, \boldsymbol{y})$ which, given the same view, outputs a HLE witness $(1^{w_1}, \ldots, 1^{w_n})$ for $\mathbf{A}$.

Assuming that HLE is hard and that the KER assumption holds, it is clear that our WKEM construction is OW-EWE-secure. To support the hardness of the KER assumption, note that an adversary breaking the KER assumption is likely to break the following problem:

Problem 1 (Hidden Order Problem). Let $\mathbb{G}$ be a finite abelian group of order $m \geq 1$ and let $g \in \mathbb{G}^\times$ be an element of maximal multiplicative order. Given $\boldsymbol{x} = (x_1, \ldots, x_n)$ uniformly distributed in $[\![0, \varphi(m) - 1]\!]^n$ and a random class representative $\boldsymbol{y} = (y_1, \ldots, y_n)$ lifted to $\mathbb{Z}^n$ of $(g^{x_1}, \ldots, g^{x_n}) \bmod \mathbb{G}$ such that $\|\boldsymbol{y}\|_\infty = \Omega(m)$ and $\|\boldsymbol{y}\|_\infty = O(m^2)$, find the order of $\mathbb{G}$.

We argue that the above problem is hard in our settings. By construction, the ciphertext $\mathsf{ct} = (\boldsymbol{x}, \boldsymbol{y})$ is a pair of random integral vectors whose components have no real arithmetic structure, or at least do not leak information on the hidden modulus p (its size is already known). Note that $\boldsymbol{x} = \mathbf{A}^\top \boldsymbol{\mu} \bmod \varphi(p)$ with uniform $\boldsymbol{\mu}$ is uniformly distributed in $\mathbf{Z}^n_{\varphi(p)}$ and satisfies $\|\boldsymbol{x}\|_\infty = O(2^\lambda)$. On the other hand, $\boldsymbol{y}$ consists of random class representatives modulo p such that $\|\boldsymbol{y}\|_\infty = \Omega(2^\lambda)$ and $\|\boldsymbol{y}\|_\infty = O(2^{2\lambda})$, hence looking "almost uniform" in $[\![2^\lambda, 2^{2\lambda}]\!]^n$. In order to break OW-EWE-security, an adversary must *efficiently* recover p with some *a priori* arbitrary $\boldsymbol{\omega} \in \ker(\mathbf{A})$. To the best of our knowledge, this requires the adversary to compute relations modulo p via exponentiations in $\mathbb{Z}$ using $\boldsymbol{y}$ and $\boldsymbol{\omega}$. This inherently restricts *a posteriori* the adversary to small w_i's (otherwise the exponentiations in $\mathbb{Z}$ cannot be evaluated in polynomial-time), i.e., HLE witnesses. In particular, assuming the hardness of HLE, solving the Hidden Order Problem must be at least as hard as breaking the KER assumption.

3.3 Complexity Analysis

We assume that computing the multiplication and division operations or the greatest common divisor of λ-bit numbers take time $O(\lambda^2)$. We also assume that random sampling and basic arithmetic operations have a negligible cost. By [29, Thm. 4.2], computing $a \bmod b$ takes time $O(\log |b| \log |\frac{a}{b}|)$. For primality testing, the Miller-Rabin (MR) test with ρ iterations takes time $\tau_{MR}(\rho, \lambda) = O(\rho\lambda^3)$ on λ-bit inputs and fails with probability at most $4^{-\rho}$. Recall that the p-adic valuation of $n \geq 1$ is computed in $O\big((\log \frac{\log n}{\log p})^\varepsilon\big)$ divisions for some $1 \leq \varepsilon \leq 2$.

Lemma 3. *If $4^{-\rho} \leq \frac{1}{2(\lambda+1)}$, then sampling distinct λ-bit prime numbers p and q and a primitive root g modulo p takes time $O(\lambda^3 \cdot \tau_{MR}(\rho, \lambda)) = O(\rho\lambda^6)$.*

Proof. By [29, §9.6, §11.1], generating a λ-bit prime number together with a primitive root takes time $O(\lambda^3 \cdot \tau_{MR}(\rho, \lambda)) + O(\lambda^4) = O(\lambda^3 \cdot \tau_{MR}(\rho, \lambda))$. □

Theorem 2. *If the number of iterations ρ in the Miller-Rabin primality test satisfies $4^{-\rho} \leq \frac{1}{2(\lambda+1)}$, then the expected time complexity of the encapsulation algorithm (Algorithm 1) for $\mathbf{A} = (A_{ij})_{ij} \in \mathbb{Z}^{d \times n}$ is*

$$O\Big(\lambda^3 \cdot \tau_{MR}(\rho,\lambda) + nd\lambda \log \tfrac{\|\mathbf{A}\|}{2^\lambda} + nd\lambda^2 + n\lambda^3\Big),$$

where $\|\mathbf{A}\| = \max_{i,j} |A_{ij}|$.

Proof. By Lemma 3, generating (p, g) and q take time $O(\lambda^3 \cdot \tau_{MR}(\rho, \lambda))$. Computing $\boldsymbol{x} = \mathbf{A}^\top \boldsymbol{\mu} \bmod \varphi(p)$ in Algorithm 1 for $\boldsymbol{\mu} \in \mathbf{Z}^d_{\varphi(p)}$ requires dn reductions modulo $\varphi(p)$ and a matrix-vector multiplication modulo $\varphi(p)$. These operations take time $O\Big(nd\lambda \log \frac{\|\mathbf{A}\|}{2^\lambda}\Big)$ and $O(nd\lambda^2)$ respectively. Since $\boldsymbol{x} = \mathbf{0}$ happens with negligible probability, $\boldsymbol{x}$ is computed in time $O\Big(nd\lambda \log \frac{\|\mathbf{A}\|}{2^\lambda}\Big) + O(nd\lambda^2)$. Similarly, computing $\boldsymbol{y} = \mathcal{Y}(\boldsymbol{x}, \boldsymbol{\kappa})$ for $\boldsymbol{\kappa} \in \mathbf{Z}^n_q$ is dominated by n modular exponentiations, each of which taking time $O(\lambda^2 \log|x_i|) = O(\lambda^3)$. □

Theorem 3. *If* $L = \Omega(n2^{2\lambda})$, *the expected time complexity of the decapsulation algorithm (Algorithm 2) for* $\mathbf{A} \in \mathbb{Z}^{d\times n}$ *and* $\boldsymbol{\omega} \in \ker(\mathbf{A}) \subseteq \mathbb{Z}^n$ *is*

$$O\Big(\eta^2 + n^2\lambda^2 + \tfrac{\eta^3}{\log \eta} + \tfrac{B}{\log B}\eta^2(\log \eta)^\varepsilon + (n\lambda)^{1+o(1)} + n\lambda\eta + T(n + \log L)\eta^2\Big),$$

where $\eta = \lambda|\boldsymbol{\omega}|_1 = \lambda \sum_{i=1}^n |w_i|$ *and* $\varepsilon \in [1, 2]$ *is a real constant.*

Proof. By construction, $\delta = 2^{O(\lambda|\boldsymbol{\omega}|_1)}$ and $\|\boldsymbol{y}\|_\infty = O(2^{2\lambda})$. By [29, Ex. 3.26], computing $\prod_{i=1}^n y_i^{|w_i|}$ takes time $O(\lambda^2|\boldsymbol{\omega}|_2^2 + \lambda^2|\boldsymbol{\omega}|_1^2) = O(\lambda^2|\boldsymbol{\omega}|_1^2)$. Since subtraction has negligible cost, computing δ (line 1) takes time $O(\lambda^2|\boldsymbol{\omega}|_1^2)$. Let $c_1 = \delta$ and $c_{k+1} = \frac{c_k}{\gcd(c_k, \operatorname{lcm}(y_1,\ldots,y_n))}$. Computing the least common multiple once takes time $O((\log \prod_{i=1}^n |y_i|)^2) = O(n^2\lambda^2)$. Since an integer s has $O\Big(\frac{\log s}{\log\log s}\Big)$ distinct prime factors, $c_k \longrightarrow \mathcal{M}_\delta(\boldsymbol{y})$ in $O\Big(\lambda^2|\omega|_1^2 \frac{\lambda|\omega|_1}{\log \lambda|\omega|_1}\Big)$ steps, thereby giving the complexity of line 4. Since finding the ℓ-adic valuation of $\mathcal{M}_\delta(\boldsymbol{y})$ requires $O((\log \frac{\log|\delta|}{\log \ell})^\varepsilon)$ divisions, each of which taking time $O(\lambda^2|\boldsymbol{\omega}|_1^2)$, discarding the B-smooth factors (line 5) takes time $O\Big(\frac{B}{\log B}\lambda^2|\boldsymbol{\omega}|_1^2(\log \lambda|\boldsymbol{\omega}|_1)^\varepsilon\Big)$.

An integral basis of $\ker(\boldsymbol{x}^\top)$ is obtained in time $O((n\lambda)^{1+o(1)})$ [16] by computing the Hermite decomposition of $\ker(\boldsymbol{x}^\top)$ [31, §6]. For $L = \Omega(n2^{2\lambda})$, taking random small linear combinations of the basis vectors gives an efficient sampling algorithm in $\ker_L(\boldsymbol{x}^\top)$ for line 7. Finally, when arriving at this point of the algorithm, $\gcd(y_i, \delta) = 1$ for all $1 \le i \le n$. Since $\delta = \Omega(2^\lambda)$, computing $(y_1, \ldots, y_n) \bmod \delta$ takes time $O(n\lambda^2|\boldsymbol{\omega}|_1)$. Given $(b_1, \ldots, b_n) \in \ker_L(\boldsymbol{x}^\top)$, computing $y_i^{b_i} \bmod \delta$ takes time $O(\log L \cdot \lambda^2|\boldsymbol{\omega}|_1^2)$ for by [29, §3.4]. As such, $\sigma = \prod_{i=1}^n y_i^{b_i} - 1 \bmod \delta$ is computed in time $O(\log L \cdot \lambda^2|\boldsymbol{\omega}|_1^2) + O(n \cdot \lambda^2|\boldsymbol{\omega}|_1^2)$. □

3.4 Practical Considerations

Estimating the hardness of lattice-based problems is generally achieved by considering the complexity of lattice basis reduction techniques such as BKZ. Linder and Peikert [20] estimated the number of BKZ operations to find a reduced basis achieving Hermite factor γ to be $2^{\frac{1.8}{\log \gamma} - O(1)}$.

Let $\mathbf{A} = \begin{bmatrix} \boldsymbol{a}_1 \cdots \boldsymbol{a}_n \end{bmatrix} \in \mathbb{Z}^{d \times n}$ be a HLE instance and let $\boldsymbol{\omega} \in \mathbb{Z}^n$ be a witness. The larger n is, the better the decapsulation algorithm performs, but this does not necessarily mean better security. Indeed, for $m \gg 1$ and $\boldsymbol{a}'_1, \ldots, \boldsymbol{a}'_m \in \mathbb{Z}^d$, we have $\begin{bmatrix} \boldsymbol{a}_1 \cdots \boldsymbol{a}_n \ \boldsymbol{a}'_1 \cdots \boldsymbol{a}'_m \end{bmatrix} \in \mathsf{HLE}$ since $(w_1, \ldots, w_n, 0, \ldots, 0)$ is a valid witness. Thus, selecting a large n is unlikely to affect the security in the way we expect.

On the other hand, the larger d is, the more equations are to be satisfied. Note that $n = \mathsf{poly}(\lambda)$ and $d = \mathsf{poly}(\lambda)$ are still required to keep the algorithms correct and efficient. If $d < n$, the Bombieri–Vaaler–Siegel lemma [4,30] guarantees the existence of a nonzero $\boldsymbol{z} \in \ker(\mathbf{A})$ satisfying $1 \leq \|\boldsymbol{z}\|_\infty^{n-d} \leq c^{-1}\sqrt{|\det(\mathbf{A}\mathbf{A}^\top)|}$, where c is the greatest common divisor of the determinants of the $d \times d$ minors of $\mathbf{A}$. In particular, this gives an estimate on the size of a solution that an adversary may find.

Choosing the Decapsulation Public Parameters. The parameter $B \ll 2^\lambda$ is used to discard polynomially bounded primes to speed-up the computations and avoid having small factor, hence left to the discretion of the decryptor. The number of iterations T must satisfy $\left(\frac{3}{4}\right)^{nT} = o(1)$ to ensure a negligible failure probability for by Theorem 1. Finally, choosing $L \approx n\delta^2 = O(n2^{2\lambda|\boldsymbol{\omega}|_1}) = \Omega(\mathcal{M}_\delta(\boldsymbol{y}))$ for the upper-bound on the coefficients of elements in $\ker(\boldsymbol{x}^\top)$ allows to efficiently sample in $\ker_L(\boldsymbol{x}^\top)$. This also ensures the correctness of the scheme and the polynomial complexity of the decapsulation according to Theorem 3 if $|\boldsymbol{\omega}|_1 = \mathsf{poly}(\lambda)$.

4 Conclusion and Future Work

In this paper, we suggested an arithmetic construction for a witness encryption scheme proposed as a witness key encapsulation mechanism and similar to what was proposed by Choi and Vaudenay [6]. Our arithmetic construction removes the inefficiency of multilinear maps and achieves correctness with negligible failure probability. Now, the applications highly depend on whether the HLE problem is NP-complete or not, although the cryptographic community believes in the former. Future research should focus on other arithmetic constructions possibly based on the NP-complete problems such as BHLE or related to lattices or linear codes. An important challenge is to study the selection of parameters to ensure a given security as well as the instantiation of HLE instances.

A Correctness Proof

In this section, we prove the unproved assertions of Sect. 3.1. To that end, we need some results involving abstract algebra.

Lemma 4. *Let $L \geq m$ be positive integers. Let $\mathcal{U}$ be the uniform distribution over $\mathbf{Z}_L$ and $\mathcal{Z} = \mathcal{U} \bmod m$. For all $z \in \mathbf{Z}_m$, we have*

$$\Pr[\mathcal{Z} = z] \leq \frac{1}{L}\left(1 + \frac{L}{m}\right) = \frac{1}{m}\left(1 + \frac{m}{L}\right) \leq \frac{2}{m}.$$

Proof. Let $z \in \mathbf{Z}_m$ and $s = |\{a \in \mathbf{Z}_L \mid a \bmod m = z\}|$. Then, $\Pr[\mathcal{Z} = z] = s/L$. Since $\lfloor L/m \rfloor \leq s \leq \lceil L/m \rceil \leq 1 + L/m$, this completes the proof. □

Lemma 5. *Let $L \geq m$ be positive integers and $G \trianglelefteq \mathbb{Z}^n$ be a group. Let $\mathcal{U}$ be the uniform distribution over $G_L \doteq G \cap [\![-L, L]\!]^n$ and let $\mathcal{Z} \doteq \mathcal{U} \bmod m$ be its projection in $G_L \bmod m$. For all $\boldsymbol{z} \in G_L \bmod m$, we have*

$$\Pr[\mathcal{Z} = \boldsymbol{z}] \leq \frac{1}{|G_L|}\left(1 + \frac{L}{m}\right)^n \leq \frac{1}{|G \bmod m|}\left(1 + \frac{1}{\lfloor L/m \rfloor}\right)^n.$$

Proof. Let $\boldsymbol{z} \in G_L \bmod m$ and $s(\boldsymbol{z}) = |\{\boldsymbol{a} \in G_L \colon \boldsymbol{a} \bmod m = \boldsymbol{z}\}|$. A similar argument as in the proof of Lemma 4 establishes $s(\boldsymbol{z}) \leq \lceil L/m \rceil^n \leq (1 + L/m)^n$. On the other hand, since $G \bmod m \subset G_L$, it follows that $s(\boldsymbol{z}) \geq \lfloor L/m \rfloor^n$. In particular, $|G_L| \geq |G \bmod m| \lfloor L/m \rfloor^n$. Therefore,

$$\Pr[\mathcal{Z} = \boldsymbol{z}] \leq \frac{s(\boldsymbol{z})}{|G_L|} \leq \frac{1}{|G \bmod m|}\left(\frac{\lceil L/m \rceil}{\lfloor L/m \rfloor}\right)^n = \frac{1}{|G \bmod m|}\left(1 + \frac{1}{\lfloor L/m \rfloor}\right)^n.$$

□

Proof of Claim 1, page 13. Since $\mathrm{dlog}_\ell \colon \mathbf{Z}_\ell^\times \longrightarrow \mathbf{Z}_{\varphi(\ell)}$ is bijective, $\mathcal{Y}_\ell(\boldsymbol{x})$ and $\mathrm{dlog}_\ell(\mathcal{Y}_\ell(\boldsymbol{x}))$ have the same probability distributions. Thus, $\mathrm{dlog}_\ell(\mathcal{Y}_\ell(\boldsymbol{x})) \bmod r$ solely depends on the distribution of $\mathcal{K} \bmod r$. Let $\varepsilon_0 \in \mathbf{Z}_r^\times$ be *fixed* and assume that $\ell \geq q$. Then, the probability that a given component of $\mathrm{dlog}_\ell(\mathcal{Y}_\ell(\boldsymbol{x})) \bmod r$ is equal to $\varepsilon_0 \in \mathbf{Z}_r^\times \subset \mathbf{Z}_r$ is at most $1/r$. Since these components are identically and independently distributed, it follows that

$$\Pr_{\boldsymbol{y} \sim \mathcal{Y}_\ell(\boldsymbol{x})}[\mathrm{dlog}_\ell(\boldsymbol{y}) \equiv \varepsilon_0 \boldsymbol{x} \pmod r \mid \ell \geq q] \leq \frac{1}{r^n}.$$

On the other hand, assume that $\ell < q$. By Lemma 4 applied to $q \geq r$, we get

$$\Pr_{\boldsymbol{y} \sim \mathcal{Y}_\ell(\boldsymbol{x})}[\mathrm{dlog}_\ell(\boldsymbol{y}) \equiv \varepsilon_0 \boldsymbol{x} \pmod r \mid \ell < q] \leq \frac{1}{q^n}\left(1 + \frac{q}{r}\right)^n = \frac{1}{r^n}\left(1 + \frac{r}{q}\right)^n.$$

Summing these probabilities as ε_0 ranges over $\mathbf{Z}_r^\times$ establishes the desired bounds and the remaining inequality is a consequence of the Fréchet inequality. □

Lemma 6. *Let* $\mathsf{ct} = (\boldsymbol{x}, \boldsymbol{y}) \in \mathbb{Z}^n \times \mathbb{Z}^n$ *be a ciphertext produced by Algorithm 1 corresponding to a* HLE *instance* $\mathbf{A} \in \mathbb{Z}^{d\times n}$ *and a hidden prime* p *and consider a nonzero vector* $\boldsymbol{\omega} \in \ker(\mathbf{A})$. *Let* $\delta = \boldsymbol{\Delta}(\boldsymbol{y}, \boldsymbol{\omega})$ *and assume that there exist a prime factor* ℓ *of* $\mathcal{M}_\delta(\boldsymbol{y})$ *and a prime factor* r *of* $\varphi(\ell)$ *such that the event* $F_{\ell,r}(\boldsymbol{x}, \boldsymbol{y})$ *defined by* (3.5) *does not hold. If* $\bar{\mathcal{U}}$ *denotes the uniform distribution over* $H \doteq \ker(\boldsymbol{x}^\top) \bmod \varphi(\ell)$, *then*

$$\Pr_{\bar{\boldsymbol{\beta}}\sim\bar{\mathcal{U}}}\left[\sigma_\delta(\boldsymbol{y}, \bar{\boldsymbol{\beta}}) \equiv 0 \pmod{\ell}\right] \le \frac{1}{r^n} \le \frac{1}{2^n}. \qquad (^\dagger)$$

Stated otherwise, at most $\frac{|H|}{2^n}$ *elements from* H *give rise to a multiple of* ℓ *under the mapping* $\sigma_\delta(\boldsymbol{y}, -)\colon \mathbb{Z}^n \longrightarrow \mathbb{Z}$ *defined by* (3.4).

Proof. Let $\phi = \varphi(\ell)$. Since ℓ is a prime factor of $\mathcal{M}_\delta(\boldsymbol{y})$ and y_i is invertible modulo $\mathcal{M}_\delta(\boldsymbol{y})$, the latter is invertible modulo ℓ and $\operatorname{dlog}_\ell(\boldsymbol{y})$ is well-defined. In particular, $\sigma_\delta(\boldsymbol{y}, \bar{\boldsymbol{\beta}}) = \prod_{i=1}^n y_i^{\bar{b}_i} - 1 \bmod \mathcal{M}_\delta(\boldsymbol{y}) \equiv 0 \pmod{\ell}$ if and only if $\langle \operatorname{dlog}_\ell(\boldsymbol{y}), \bar{\boldsymbol{\beta}}\rangle \equiv 0 \pmod{\phi}$. Without loss of generality, $H = \ker(\boldsymbol{x}^\top) \bmod \phi$ and $H \cap \ker(\operatorname{dlog}_\ell(\boldsymbol{y})) = \{\boldsymbol{h} \in H \colon \langle \operatorname{dlog}_\ell(\boldsymbol{y}), \boldsymbol{h}\rangle \equiv 0 \pmod{\phi}\} \trianglelefteq H$ are nonempty subgroups of $\mathbf{Z}_\phi^n$. If $\boldsymbol{z}$ uniformly distributed in $\mathbf{Z}_\phi^n$, then

$$\begin{aligned}\bar{\vartheta} \doteq \Pr_{\bar{\boldsymbol{\beta}}\sim\bar{\mathcal{U}}}\left[\langle \operatorname{dlog}_\ell(\boldsymbol{y}), \bar{\boldsymbol{\beta}}\rangle \equiv 0 \pmod{\phi}\right] &= \Pr_{\boldsymbol{z}}[\boldsymbol{z} \in H \cap \ker(\operatorname{dlog}_\ell(\boldsymbol{y})) | \boldsymbol{z} \in H] \\ &\le \frac{\Pr_{\boldsymbol{z}}[\boldsymbol{z} \in H \cap \ker(\operatorname{dlog}_\ell(\boldsymbol{y}))]}{\Pr_{\boldsymbol{z}}[\boldsymbol{z} \in H]}.\end{aligned}$$

Fix an isomorphism $\mathbf{Z}_\phi^n \cong \bigoplus_{k=1}^s \mathbf{Z}_{m_k}^n$ where each $m_k = r_k^{e_k}$ is a prime power and denote by $\rho_k \colon \mathbf{Z}_\phi^n \twoheadrightarrow \mathbf{Z}_{r_k^{e_k}}^n$ the canonical projection onto the r_k-primary component. By definition, there exist integers $0 \le e_k' \le e_k'' \le e_k$ such that

$$\frac{\Pr_{\boldsymbol{z}}[\boldsymbol{z} \in H \cap \ker(\operatorname{dlog}_\ell(\boldsymbol{y}))]}{\Pr_{\boldsymbol{z}}[\boldsymbol{z} \in H]} = \prod_{k=1}^s \frac{|\rho_k(H \cap \ker(\operatorname{dlog}_\ell(\boldsymbol{y})))|}{|\rho_k(H)|} = \prod_{k=1}^s r_k^{n(e_k'-e_k'')}.$$

By assumption, there exists k such that $\operatorname{dlog}_\ell(\boldsymbol{y}) \equiv (\varepsilon x_1, \ldots, \varepsilon x_n) \pmod{r_k}$ has no solution for ε in $\mathbf{Z}_{r_k}^\times$. In particular, the inclusion $\rho_k(H \cap \ker(\operatorname{dlog}_\ell(\boldsymbol{y}))) \triangleleft \rho_k(H)$ is strict, namely $e_k' < e_k''$. Therefore, $\bar{\vartheta} \le \frac{1}{r_k^n} \le \frac{1}{2^n}$. □

Proof of Claim 2, page 13. Let $\phi = \varphi(\ell)$ and $H = \ker(\boldsymbol{x}^\top) \bmod \phi$. Let $\boldsymbol{\beta}$ be uniformly distributed in $\ker_L(\boldsymbol{x}^\top)$. Lemma 5 applied to $G = \ker(\boldsymbol{x}^\top) \subset \mathbb{Z}^n$ implies that $\max_{\boldsymbol{\beta}} \Pr_{\boldsymbol{\beta}}[\boldsymbol{\beta} \bmod \phi] \le \frac{1}{|H|}\left(1 + \frac{1}{\lfloor L/\phi \rfloor}\right)^n \le \frac{1}{|H|}\left(\frac{3}{2}\right)^n$. By Lemma 6, at most $\frac{|H|}{2^n}$ elements in H give rise to a multiple of ℓ via $\boldsymbol{\beta} \mapsto \sigma_\delta(\boldsymbol{y}, \boldsymbol{\beta})$. Therefore,

$$\Pr_{\boldsymbol{\beta}}[\sigma_\delta(\boldsymbol{y}, \boldsymbol{\beta}) \equiv 0 \pmod{\ell}] \le \frac{|H|}{2^n} \cdot \max_{\boldsymbol{\beta}} \Pr_{\boldsymbol{\beta}}[\boldsymbol{\beta} \bmod \phi] \le \left(\frac{3}{4}\right)^n. \qquad (^{\dagger\dagger})$$

□

† For clarity, we omit in Pr[...] the "conditioned to $\neg F_\ell(\boldsymbol{x}, \boldsymbol{y})$" part.

†† ibid.

References

1. Abusalah, H., Fuchsbauer, G., Pietrzak, K.: Offline witness encryption. In: Manulis, M., Sadeghi, A.-R., Schneider, S. (eds.) ACNS 2016. LNCS, vol. 9696, pp. 285–303. Springer, Cham (2016). https://doi.org/10.1007/978-3-319-39555-5_16
2. Barak, B., et al.: On the (im)possibility of obfuscating programs. In: Kilian, J. (ed.) CRYPTO 2001. LNCS, vol. 2139, pp. 1–18. Springer, Heidelberg (2001). https://doi.org/10.1007/3-540-44647-8_1
3. Bellare, M., Hoang, V.T.: Adaptive witness encryption and asymmetric password-based cryptography. In: Katz, J. (ed.) PKC 2015. LNCS, vol. 9020, pp. 308–331. Springer, Heidelberg (2015). https://doi.org/10.1007/978-3-662-46447-2_14
4. Bombieri, E., Vaaler, J.: On Siegel's lemma. Inventiones Mathematicae **73**, 11–32 (1983)
5. Chen, Y., Nguyen, P.Q.: BKZ 2.0: better lattice security estimates. In: Lee, D.H., Wang, X. (eds.) ASIACRYPT 2011. LNCS, vol. 7073, pp. 1–20. Springer, Heidelberg (2011). https://doi.org/10.1007/978-3-642-25385-0_1
6. Choi, G., Vaudenay, S.: Towards witness encryption without multilinear maps. In: Park, J.H., Seo, S. (eds.) ICISC 2021. LNCS, vol. 13218, pp. 28–47. Springer, Cham (2021). https://doi.org/10.1007/978-3-031-08896-4_2
7. Choi, G.: Time in cryptography (2020). https://infoscience.epfl.ch/record/279784
8. Chvojka, P., Jager, T., Kakvi, S.A.: Offline witness encryption with semi-adaptive security. In: Conti, M., Zhou, J., Casalicchio, E., Spognardi, A. (eds.) ACNS 2020. LNCS, vol. 12146, pp. 231–250. Springer, Cham (2020). https://doi.org/10.1007/978-3-030-57808-4_12
9. Cramer, R., Shoup, V.: Universal hash proofs and a paradigm for adaptive chosen ciphertext secure public-key encryption. In: Knudsen, L.R. (ed.) EUROCRYPT 2002. LNCS, vol. 2332, pp. 45–64. Springer, Heidelberg (2002). https://doi.org/10.1007/3-540-46035-7_4
10. van Emde-Boas, P.: Another NP-complete partition problem and the complexity of computing short vectors in a lattice (1981). https://staff.fnwi.uva.nl/p.vanemdeboas/vectors/abstract.html. Accessed 13 Feb 2022
11. Faonio, A., Nielsen, J.B., Venturi, D.: Predictable arguments of knowledge. In: Fehr, S. (ed.) PKC 2017. LNCS, vol. 10174, pp. 121–150. Springer, Heidelberg (2017). https://doi.org/10.1007/978-3-662-54365-8_6
12. Garg, S., Gentry, C., Halevi, S., Raykova, M., Sahai, A., Waters, B.: Candidate indistinguishability obfuscation and functional encryption for all circuits. SIAM J. Comput. **45**(3), 882–929 (2016)
13. Garg, S., Gentry, C., Sahai, A., Waters, B.: Witness encryption and its applications. In: Proceedings of the Forty-Fifth Annual ACM Symposium on Theory of Computing, pp. 467–476 (2013)
14. Gentry, C., Peikert, C., Vaikuntanathan, V.: Trapdoors for hard lattices and new cryptographic constructions. In: Dwork, C. (ed.) Proceedings of the 40th Annual ACM Symposium on Theory of Computing, pp. 197–206. ACM (2008)
15. Jain, A., Lin, H., Sahai, A.: Indistinguishability Obfuscation from Well-Founded Assumptions. Cryptology ePrint Archive, Report 2020/1003 (2020)
16. Kaltofen, E.L., Storjohann, A.: Complexity of computational problems in exact linear algebra. In: Engquist, B. (ed.) Encyclopedia of Applied and Computational Mathematics, pp. 227–233. Springer, Heidelberg (2015)
17. Karp, R.M.: Reducibility among combinatorial problems. In: Miller, R.E., Thatcher, J.W., Bohlinger, J.D. (eds.) Complexity of Computer Computations, pp. 85–103. Springer, Boston (1972). https://doi.org/10.1007/978-1-4684-2001-2_9

18. Lenstra, A.K., Lenstra, H.W., Lovasz, L.: Factoring polynomials with rational coefficients. Math. Ann. **261**, 515–534 (1982)
19. Lin, H., Tessaro, S.: Indistinguishability obfuscation from trilinear maps and block-wise local PRGs. In: Katz, J., Shacham, H. (eds.) CRYPTO 2017. LNCS, vol. 10401, pp. 630–660. Springer, Cham (2017). https://doi.org/10.1007/978-3-319-63688-7_21
20. Lindner, R., Peikert, C.: Better key sizes (and attacks) for LWE-based encryption. In: Kiayias, A. (ed.) CT-RSA 2011. LNCS, vol. 6558, pp. 319–339. Springer, Heidelberg (2011). https://doi.org/10.1007/978-3-642-19074-2_21
21. Liu, J., Jager, T., Kakvi, S.A., Warinschi, B.: How to build time-lock encryption. Des. Codes Crypt. **86**(11), 2549–2586 (2018). https://doi.org/10.1007/s10623-018-0461-x
22. May, T.C.: Time-release crypto (1993). https://cypherpunks.venona.com/date/1993/02/msg00129.html. Accessed 16 Feb 2022
23. Merkle, R.C.: Secure communications over insecure channels. Commun. ACM **21**(4), 294–299 (1978)
24. Micciancio, D., Peikert, C.: Hardness of SIS and LWE with small parameters. In: Canetti, R., Garay, J.A. (eds.) CRYPTO 2013. LNCS, vol. 8042, pp. 21–39. Springer, Heidelberg (2013). https://doi.org/10.1007/978-3-642-40041-4_2
25. Nymann, J.: On the probability that k positive integers are relatively prime. J. Number Theory **4**(5), 469–473 (1972)
26. Rivest, R.L., Shamir, A., Wagner, D.A.: Time-lock puzzles and timed-release Crypto (1996)
27. Schnorr, C.: A hierarchy of polynomial time lattice basis reduction algorithms. Theor. Comput. Sci. **53**, 201–224 (1987)
28. Schnorr, C., Euchner, M.: Lattice basis reduction: improved practical algorithms and solving subset sum problems. Math. Program. **66**, 181–199 (1994)
29. Shoup, V.: A computational introduction to number theory and algebra (2009). https://shoup.net/ntb/ntb-v2.pdf. Accessed 13 Feb 2022
30. Siegel, C.L.: Über einige Anwendungen Diophantischer Approximationen. Abh. Preuss. Akad. Wiss. Phys. Math. Kl **1**, 41–69 (1929). reprinted as pp. 209–266 of Gesammelte Abhandlungen I. Springer, Berlin (1966)
31. Storjohann, A.: Algorithms for matrix canonical forms. Ph.D. thesis, ETH Zurich, Zürich (2000). https://doi.org/10.3929/ethz-a-004141007. Diss., Technische Wissenschaften ETH Zürich, Nr. 13922, 2001

Making Classical (Threshold) Signatures Post-quantum for Single Use on a Public Ledger

Laurane Marco(✉), Abdullah Talayhan, and Serge Vaudenay

EPFL, Lausanne, Switzerland
{laurane.marco,abdullah.talayhan,serge.vaudenay}@epfl.ch

Abstract. The Bitcoin architecture heavily relies on the ECDSA signature scheme which is broken by quantum adversaries as the secret key can be computed from the public key in quantum polynomial time. To mitigate this attack, bitcoins can be paid to the hash of a public key (P2PKH). However, the first payment reveals the public key so all bitcoins attached to it must be spent at the same time (i.e. the remaining amount must be transferred to a new wallet). Some problems remain with this approach: the owners are vulnerable against *rushing adversaries* between the time the signature is made public and the time it is committed to the blockchain. Additionally, there is no equivalent mechanism for threshold signatures. Finally, no formal analysis of P2PKH has been done. In this paper, we formalize the security notion of a *digital signature with a hidden public key* and we propose and prove the security of a generic transformation that converts a classical signature to a post-quantum one that can be used only once. We compare it with P2PKH. Namely, our proposal relies on pre-image resistance instead of collision resistance as for P2PKH, so allows for shorter hashes. Additionally, we propose the notion of a *delay signature* to address the problem of the rushing adversary when used with a public ledger and discuss the advantages and disadvantages of our approach. We further extend our results to threshold signatures.

1 Introduction

The recent progress made on the development of quantum computers poses a threat to public key cryptography schemes that are based on the discrete logarithm and factorization problems. Hence, it has become essential to find post-quantum alternatives to classical public key primitives. In this work, we focus on digital signatures, which are heavily used in cryptocurrencies. Despite a standardization effort made by the NIST, current post-quantum signatures are not yet mature enough, and struggle to compare with their classical counterparts, as shown by the new call for post-quantum signature proposals [11].

An alternative way to achieve post-quantum security of digital signatures, by using a simpler mechanism, is to hide the public key and release it along with the signature for verification. This however restricts key pairs to one-time use only, since in a quantum setting any key pair is trivially broken after its

J. Shikata and H. Kuzuno (Eds.): IWSEC 2023, LNCS 14128, pp. 173–192, 2023.
https://doi.org/10.1007/978-3-031-41326-1_10

release. Bitcoin P2PKH (Pay To Public Key Hash) transactions [6] currently use a similar technique. More precisely, an account address consists of the hash of a public key and as long as a user does not spend the funds available on their account, only their address is revealed. The actual public key is released only when a transaction is made from this account. If a signer fears a quantum attack, they should collect all their unspent assets linked to the public key and make a new transaction to redistribute them to a new address (public key hash). The key pair is indeed broken after the transaction, but the wallet (related to the public key) does not contain any bitcoins left to be stolen.

However, the P2PKH construction has not been formalized nor proven secure, and it is open to attacks by a rushing quantum adversary between the release of the signature and the time the transaction is published to the ledger. Indeed, at this time any adversary who verifies the transaction is able to recover the secret key from the public one, and forge a new signature. If that signature is published on the ledger before the previous one, the attack is successful, and funds can be stolen. Furthermore, to the best of our knowledge, there is no threshold variant of this construction, and the rushing problem becomes worse in the threshold setting. Indeed, any signing participant which outputs the signature can proceed with such an attack, since the public key can be recovered from the signature. Additionally, without guaranteed output delivery, it might be the case that the honest signers do not even learn the original signature by the end of the protocol, while the adversary can forge a new one, since they get access to the common public key.

Our goal is to find a pragmatic solution to these problems that is efficient and secure against quantum adversaries whilst still being compatible with classical algorithms that are already in production. We stress that post-quantum signatures are the obvious solutions, but they are not fully standardized yet, are less efficient and rely on less studied assumptions. We thus propose our construction as a solution for a transitional phase, whilst waiting for efficient, standardized post-quantum signatures. In this work, we propose a generic transform that takes any classically secure signature scheme and turns it into a signature scheme with classical (with unlimited usage) and quantum (limited to one signature) security under minimal assumptions by hiding the public key (Sect. 2). We also formalize the existing construction used in Bitcoin P2PKH, analyze its security and compare it with our approach. Furthermore, we provide a framework for a delayed signature verification that protects the public key against rushing adversaries until the corresponding signature is published on a public ledger (Sect. 3). Finally, since threshold signatures are being used frequently in cryptocurrencies we extend the transform to the threshold setting (Sect. 4). Our extension of the generic transform to the threshold setting does not require a multi-party hash function evaluation (contrary to the post-quantum candidates), at the cost of an increase in the public key and signature size which is linear in the number of participants.

1.1 Related Work

In this section, we discuss current classical signatures and post-quantum signature proposals, and their potential for constructing threshold signatures. We also introduce hash-based signatures as they share similar ideas to our construction.

Cozzo and Smart [5] estimate the performance of threshold versions of the NIST round 3 candidate schemes using generic MPC techniques. The most promising candidates are the multivariate schemes (Rainbow and LUOV), now broken [2,7], as they only require linear secret sharing (LSSS). The other round 3 and 4 candidates (lattice-based, hash-based) are less friendly to generic MPC techniques, and require a tailored approach to be thresholdized. On the other hand, classical signatures, such as Schnorr and ECDSA signatures, already have practical and efficient threshold versions.

Hash-based signatures were introduced by Lamport. They are one-time signatures that rely on hash-functions, and signing requires to reveal the secret key. Since the unforgeability only relies on the security of the underlying one-way function it makes them a good candidate for post-quantum security. In fact, SPHINCS+ [1] has been selected for standardization by NIST and is an instance of hash-based signature. The idea of post-quantum signatures designed for blockchain has already been explored in [4,9]. They construct a post-quantum signature scheme from an optimised hash-based signature scheme with the objective of using it for blockchain applications. However, one common problem about constructing threshold variants of the hash based schemes is the need for multiple hash function evaluations over the secret shares. This problem motivated our approach that does not require a multi-party hash function evaluation. Finally the concept of hiding a public key to guarantee post-quantum security for blockchain transactions was introduced in [3], but it is not formalised nor proven secure, and no extension to the threshold case is considered.

1.2 Overview of the Construction

We now give an overview of our transformation and the methodology for releasing and verifying the signatures in order to give a complete picture of our contribution. We can simply explain our construction by putting together Fig. 2, Fig. 8, and Fig. 10 as follows:

A key pair $(\mathsf{sk}, \mathsf{pk})$, e.g. for ECDSA, is transformed to

- $\mathsf{sk}' = (\mathsf{sk}, \rho, t_1, t_2)$
- $\mathsf{pk}' = (H(\rho), \mathsf{pk} + \rho, H(t_1), H(t_2))$

where ρ, t_1 and t_2 are sampled randomly. Intuitively, the public key is encrypted with a one-time pad key ρ, committed by $H(\rho)$. Two secret tokens t_1 and t_2 are also committed in pk'. Hence, the original public key pk is hidden using a committed secret key.

To sign a message msg, we compute a signature, e.g. ECDSA, on message msg with sk and obtain σ. Then we set:

- $\sigma_1 = H(\sigma, \rho, \mathsf{msg}, \mathsf{open})$
- $\sigma_2 = (\sigma, \rho, \mathsf{open})$

where open is a randomly sampled opening value. In order to publish the signature, the signer posts $(t_1, \sigma_1, \mathsf{msg})$ on the public ledger as a commitment for the actual signature σ (Stage 1). Once the signer observes that this commitment has been safely posted on the ledger, the signer posts t_2 on the ledger and further (t_1, σ_1) pairs are invalid afterwards (Stage 2). Finally, the signer posts σ_2 after confirming that t_2 is safely posted (Stage 3). This prevents forgeries by rushing adversaries. The signature (σ_1, σ_2) is verified for msg with public key $\mathsf{pk}' = (H(\rho), \mathsf{pk} + \rho, H(t_1), H(t_2))$ if the following conditions are satisfied:

1. σ_1 appears in the ledger between a preimage of $H(t_1)$ and a preimage of $H(t_2)$.
2. $(\sigma, \rho, \mathsf{open})$ parsed from σ_2 allows to verify $\sigma_1 = H(\sigma, \rho, \mathsf{msg}, \mathsf{open})$.
3. ρ is a preimage of $H(\rho)$.
4. After recovering pk using ρ, the original signature σ verifies the message msg.

Here, condition 1. checks that the order of commitments correctly appeared on the ledger. Condition 2. checks that the commitments are consistent with each other. Condition 3. verifies that the opening of the key commitment is correct and condition 4. checks if the original signature is actually a valid signature. The key idea is that a commitment on a signature must appear on the ledger between the publication of two tokens and the second token allows to safely publish pk.

For our extension to threshold signatures, the transformation is similar, except that the one-time pad key ρ and the public key pk are secretly shared. More concretely, we assume that each participant with a key pair $(\mathsf{pk}_i, \mathsf{sk}_i)$ will publish $\mathsf{pk}_i + \rho_i$ and keep ρ_i secret. The threshold signature will be augmented with the release of the ρ_i which will be used to uncover pk_i.

We summarize the overhead induced by P2PKH and our transformations in Fig. 1. Note that the compact version refers to the full version [10], Appendix G.

2 Hiding a Public Key

In this section, we give a generic transform that takes any classical signature scheme and hides the public key by adding a uniform masking value in order to obtain a post-quantum secure signature scheme with the single use of a public/private key pair. We then compare this transform with the Bitcoin P2PKH construction where the public key is hidden by using a hash function.

	Key Generation	Signing	Verification	Signature Size	Assumption
P2PKH (Fig. 6)	1H	-	1H	$\lvert G_{\mathsf{el}}\rvert$	CR
HiddenPK (Fig. 2)	$1\mathsf{H} + 1\mathsf{G}_{\mathsf{add}}$	-	$1\mathsf{H} + 1\mathsf{G}_{\mathsf{add}}$	$\lvert G_{\mathsf{el}}\rvert$	2PreIm
DelayL (Fig. 10)	$3\mathsf{H} + 1\mathsf{G}_{\mathsf{add}}$	1H	$2\mathsf{LU} + 4\mathsf{H} + 1\mathsf{G}_{\mathsf{add}}$	$\lvert G_{\mathsf{el}}\rvert + \lvert\mathsf{H}\rvert + \lambda$	RO
Thresh-HiddenPK (Fig. 11)	$n\mathsf{H} + n\mathsf{G}_{\mathsf{add}}$	-	$\lvert S\rvert\mathsf{H} + \lvert S\rvert\mathsf{G}_{\mathsf{add}} + \mathcal{O}(\mathsf{Rec})$	$\lvert S\rvert \cdot \lvert G_{\mathsf{el}}\rvert$	2PreIm
Compact Thresh-HiddenPK ([10], Fig. 23)	$\mathcal{O}(\mathsf{Shr}) + 1\mathsf{H}$	$\mathcal{O}(\mathsf{Rec})$	$1\mathsf{H} + 1\mathsf{G}_{\mathsf{add}}$	$\lvert G_{\mathsf{el}}\rvert$	2PreIm

Fig. 1. Complexity summary of the added overhead of the transformations - H denotes a hash function evaluation, $\mathsf{G}_{\mathsf{add}}$ a group operation, LU a table lookup of tokens, $\mathcal{O}(\mathsf{Shr})$ and $\mathcal{O}(\mathsf{Rec})$ the complexity of secret sharing and reconstruction, $\lvert G_{\mathsf{el}}\rvert$ the size of a group element, n is the number of parties involved in a threshold setting and S is the set of signers. CR stands for collision resistance, 2PreIm for 2nd pre-image resistance and RO for random oracle. λ is the security parameter.

2.1 A Generic Transform

We present a transform that takes any signature scheme and allows one to sign while only disclosing the public key at signing time.

More precisely, it takes as input $\Sigma = (\mathsf{KeyGen}_\Sigma, \mathsf{Sign}_\Sigma, \mathsf{Verify}_\Sigma)$ with security parameter λ, and a hash function H. We assume that the public key domain $\mathcal{D}$ has a finite group structure with law $+$. The transform is illustrated in Fig. 2.

HiddenPK-KeyGen(λ)	HiddenPK-Sign($\tilde{\mathsf{sk}}$, msg)	HiddenPK-Verify($\tilde{\sigma}$, $\tilde{\mathsf{pk}}$, msg)
$(\mathsf{sk}, \mathsf{pk}) \leftarrow\!\!\$\ \mathsf{KeyGen}_\Sigma(\lambda)$	$(\mathsf{sk}, \rho) \leftarrow \tilde{\mathsf{sk}}$	$(\sigma, \rho) \leftarrow \tilde{\sigma}$
$\rho \leftarrow\!\!\$\ \mathcal{D}$	$\sigma \leftarrow \mathsf{Sign}_\Sigma(\mathsf{sk}, \mathsf{msg})$	$(\tilde{\mathsf{pk}}_1, \tilde{\mathsf{pk}}_2) \leftarrow \tilde{\mathsf{pk}}$
$\tilde{\mathsf{sk}} \leftarrow (\mathsf{sk}, \rho)$	$\tilde{\sigma} \leftarrow (\sigma, \rho)$	**if** $H(\rho) = \tilde{\mathsf{pk}}_1$
$\tilde{\mathsf{pk}} \leftarrow (H(\rho), \mathsf{pk} + \rho)$	**return** $\tilde{\sigma}$	$\quad \mathsf{pk} = \tilde{\mathsf{pk}}_2 - \rho$
return $(\tilde{\mathsf{sk}}, \tilde{\mathsf{pk}})$		$\quad$ **return** $\mathsf{Verify}_\Sigma(\sigma, \mathsf{pk}, \mathsf{msg})$
		return 0

Fig. 2. HiddenPK(Σ, λ, H) generic transform.

We now define and prove the security of our transform in both the classical and the quantum setting.

Theorem 1 (Classical security of $\mathsf{HiddenPK}$**).** *The* $\mathsf{HiddenPK}(\Sigma, \lambda, H)$ *transform is secure against existential forgery under chosen-message attack if the underlying signature scheme* Σ *is and if* H *is 2nd pre-image resistant.*

Proof. Consider an EUF-CMA adversary $\mathcal{A}'$ for $\mathsf{HiddenPK}(\Sigma, \lambda, H)$.

Let $\mathsf{2PreIm} = \{\text{Given } \rho \text{ from } \mathsf{sk}, \rho^* \text{ from } \sigma^* : \rho \neq \rho^*, H(\rho^*) = H(\rho)\}$. Since EUF-CMA$(\mathcal{A}') \to 1$ implies that $H(\rho) = H(\rho^*)$, we have:

$$\begin{aligned}\Pr[\text{EUF-CMA}(\mathcal{A}') \to 1] &= \Pr[\text{EUF-CMA}(\mathcal{A}') \to 1 \wedge \mathsf{2PreIm}] \\ &\quad + \Pr[\text{EUF-CMA}(\mathcal{A}') \to 1 \wedge \overline{\mathsf{2PreIm}}] \\ &\leq \Pr[\mathsf{2PreIm}] \\ &\quad + \Pr[\text{EUF-CMA}(\mathcal{A}') \to 1 \wedge \rho = \rho^*]\end{aligned}$$

Intuitively, the first term corresponds to the 2nd pre-image resistance of H and the second to the EUF-CMA security of Σ. We want to show that they are both negligible.

Let us consider an adversary $\mathcal{C}$ for 2nd pre-image resistance (Fig. 3).

We have $\mathsf{negl}(\lambda) = \Pr[\mathcal{C} \text{ wins}] \geq \Pr[\mathsf{2PreIm}]$ because of 2nd pre-image resistance.

Now let us consider an EUF-CMA adversary $\mathcal{A}$ for Σ (Fig. 3).

We have that the view of $\mathcal{A}'$ called as a subroutine of EUF-CMA$(\mathcal{A})$ is the same as the view of $\mathcal{A}'$ in EUF-CMA$(\mathcal{A}')$.

If we assume that $\mathcal{A}'$ succeeds and $\overline{\mathsf{2PreIm}}$ then $\mathcal{A}$ succeeds. Indeed, if we have $\overline{\mathsf{2PreIm}}$ and a success for $\mathcal{A}'$, it implies that $\rho = \rho^*$ and $\mathsf{HiddenPK\text{-}Verify}(m^*, \tilde{\sigma}^*, \tilde{\mathsf{pk}}) = 1$. Hence (m^*, σ^*) is a valid forgery for $\mathcal{A}$.

Therefore we have $\Pr[\text{EUF-CMA}(\mathcal{A}) \to 1] \geq \Pr[\text{EUF-CMA}(\mathcal{A}') \to 1 \wedge \overline{\mathsf{2PreIm}}]$ and the first term is negligible by assumption. □

We now define a similar security notion for a quantum adversary and prove the security of HiddenPK. We want to formalize the fact that a quantum adversary should not be able to recover the private key (otherwise it can trivially forge signatures), and that the key pairs are being used only once for each signature. Contrarily to one-time signatures which remain secure after the signature is released, the same notion does not apply to the case where the key pair is broken by a quantum adversary. So, we rather call it a *zero-time signature*, and we consider key-only security, since each key-pair is discarded after a signature is issued.

Definition 1 (QEUF-KOA security). *A digital signature scheme* (KeyGen, Sign, Verify) *with associated security parameter* λ *is quantum secure against existential forgery under key-only attack if for any* ***quantum*** *polynomial time adversary* $\mathcal{A}$*, the advantage of* $\mathcal{A}$ *in the* QEUF-KOA *game is negligible, i.e.*

$$\mathrm{Adv}_{\mathcal{A}}^{\mathsf{QEUF\text{-}KOA}} = \Pr[\mathsf{QEUF\text{-}KOA}(\mathcal{A}) \to 1] \leq \mathsf{negl}(\lambda)$$

where the QEUF-KOA *game is defined in Fig. 4.*

$\mathcal{C}(\rho)$

- $(\mathsf{sk}, \mathsf{pk}) \leftarrow\!\!\$\ \mathsf{KeyGen}_\Sigma(\lambda)$
- $\tilde{\mathsf{sk}} \leftarrow (\mathsf{sk}, \rho)$
- $\tilde{\mathsf{pk}} \leftarrow (H(\rho), \mathsf{pk} + \rho)$
- $\mathcal{A}'(\tilde{\mathsf{pk}})$
  - **if** query m_i :
    - $\mathcal{C}$ computes $\sigma_i = \mathsf{Sign}(\mathsf{sk}, m_i)$
    - $\mathcal{C}$ returns $\sigma_i' = (\sigma_i, \rho)$ to $\mathcal{A}'$
  - **return** $(m, \tilde{\sigma})$
- $\tilde{\sigma} \rightarrow (\sigma^*, \rho^*)$
- **return** ρ^*

$\mathcal{A}^{\mathsf{OSign}}(\mathsf{pk})$

- $\rho \leftarrow\!\!\$\ G$
- $\tilde{\mathsf{pk}} \leftarrow (H(\rho), \mathsf{pk} + \rho)$
- $\mathcal{A}'(\tilde{\mathsf{pk}})$
  - **if** query m_i :
    - $\sigma_i \leftarrow \mathsf{OSign}_\mathcal{A}(m_i)$
    - $\mathcal{A}$ returns (σ_i, ρ) to $\mathcal{A}'$
  - **return** $(m^*, \tilde{\sigma}^*)$
- $\tilde{\sigma}^* \rightarrow (\sigma^*, \rho^*)$
- **return** (m^*, σ^*)

Fig. 3. Adversary $\mathcal{C}$ calling $\mathcal{A}'$ for 2nd pre-image resistance (left) and adversary $\mathcal{A}$ calling $\mathcal{A}'$ for EUF-CMA($\mathcal{A}$) (right) (Theorem 1).

QEUF-KOA($\mathcal{A}$)

- $\mathsf{KeyGen} \rightarrow (\mathsf{sk}, \mathsf{pk})$
- $\mathcal{A}(\mathsf{pk}) \rightarrow (m^*, \sigma^*)$
- **return** $\mathsf{Verify}(\sigma^*, \mathsf{pk}, m^*)$

Fig. 4. The QEUF-KOA game for zero-time quantum security.

Theorem 2 (Quantum security of HiddenPK). *Consider a digital signature scheme Σ with security parameter λ, if the hash function H is quantum one-way over $\mathcal{D}$ and the statistical distance between the distribution of* pk *in the public key domain $(\mathcal{D}, +)$ and the uniform distribution in $\mathcal{D}$ is negligible, then* HiddenPK(Σ, λ, H) *is zero-time quantum unforgeable (QEUF-KOA).*

Note that this result requires no security assumption related to the underlying signature scheme Σ. It is true even though the underlying scheme is broken by quantum (or classical) adversaries. It is still true for a trivial scheme Σ for which Verify_Σ always returns true. The only security assumption is about the quantum one-wayness of H. The proof consists in saying that breaking HiddenPK implies breaking H.

Proof. In the QEUF-KOA game, the signing key sk is unused. We define $D(\mathsf{pk})$ by the execution of the game after the first step. $D(\mathsf{pk})$ can be seen as a distinguisher between the distribution of pk and the uniform distribution. The advantage is negligible, by assumption on the statistical distance. We can now define $\mathcal{B}$ as on Fig. 5 playing the QOW game. Since ρ and pk are independent, $(H(\rho), \mathsf{pk}+\rho)$ and

$(H(\rho), x)$ have the same distribution when pk is uniform. Hence, QOW returns 1 with the same probability as D. □

$\mathsf{QOW}(\mathcal{B})$	$\mathcal{B}(y)$
$\rho \leftarrow\$ \mathcal{D}$	$x \leftarrow\$ \mathcal{D}$
$y = H(\rho)$	$\tilde{\mathsf{pk}} \leftarrow (y, x)$
$\mathcal{B}(y) \rightarrow \rho^*$	$\mathcal{A}(\tilde{\mathsf{pk}}) \rightarrow (m^*, \tilde{\sigma}^*)$
return $\mathbb{1}_{H(\rho)=H(\rho^*)}$	$(\sigma^*, \rho^*) \leftarrow \tilde{\sigma}^*$
	return ρ^*

Fig. 5. QOW game for adversary $\mathcal{B}$ (Theorem 2).

Note that the HiddenPK transform is generic, and can be further optimized to fit specific signature schemes to obtain shorter signatures. For example, one can tailor it to ECDSA, and have a variant that does not store the masking value in the signature, by making use of the fact that we can recover public keys from the signature directly. We refer to the full version [10], Appendix E.

2.2 Bitcoin P2PKH

The HiddenPK transform differs from the approach taken in Bitcoin P2PKH of hiding the public key behind a hash. We give a generalized version of P2PKH as the HashedPK transform in Fig. 6, applicable to any signature scheme Σ, and analyze its security.

Note that this transform requires a stronger assumption than our HiddenPK transform, namely collision resistance.

HashedPK-KeyGen(λ)	HashedPK-Sign($\tilde{\mathsf{sk}}$, msg)	HashedPK-Verify($\tilde{\sigma}$, $\mathsf{pk}_{\mathcal{H}}$, msg)
$(\mathsf{pk}, \mathsf{sk}) \leftarrow\$ \mathsf{KeyGen}_\Sigma(\lambda)$	$(\mathsf{sk}, \mathsf{pk}) \leftarrow \tilde{\mathsf{sk}}$	$(\sigma, \mathsf{pk}) \leftarrow \tilde{\sigma}$
$\mathsf{pk}_{\mathcal{H}} \leftarrow H(\mathsf{pk})$	$\sigma \leftarrow \mathsf{Sign}_\Sigma(\mathsf{sk}, \mathsf{msg})$	**if** $\mathsf{pk}_{\mathcal{H}} = H(\mathsf{pk})$:
$\tilde{\mathsf{sk}} \leftarrow (\mathsf{sk}, \mathsf{pk})$	$\tilde{\sigma} \leftarrow (\sigma, \mathsf{pk})$	**return** $\mathsf{Verify}_\Sigma(\sigma, \mathsf{pk}, \mathsf{msg})$
return $(\tilde{\mathsf{sk}}, \mathsf{pk}_{\mathcal{H}})$	**return** $\tilde{\sigma}$	**return** 0

Fig. 6. HashedPK(Σ, λ, H) a generic transform from the Bitcoin P2PKH construction.

However, EUF-CMA security can be proven for the HashedPK construction with the additional assumption of collision resistance on H (hence a larger hash length and the need for a hash key). QEUF-KOA security can be proven as in Theorem 2.

Theorem 3 (Classical security of $\mathsf{HashedPK}$**).** *If Σ is EUF-CMA and if H is collision resistant (with a common random* hk*) then* $\mathsf{HashedPK}(\Sigma, \lambda, H)$ *is EUF-CMA.*

Proof. The proof follows similarly to that of Theorem 1, by considering an adversary against collision resistance, instead of second pre-image resistance.

Theorem 4 (Quantum security of $\mathsf{HashedPK}$**).** *Consider a digital signature scheme Σ with associated parameters λ, if the hash function H is quantum one-way over $\mathcal{D}$ and the statistical distance between the distribution of* pk *in the public key domain $(\mathcal{D}, +)$ and the uniform distribution in $\mathcal{D}$ is negligible,* $\mathsf{HashedPK}(\Sigma, \mathsf{pk}, H)$ *is* $\mathsf{QEUF\text{-}KOA}$.

Proof. The proof is similar to that of Theorem 2. □

3 Delayed Signatures

One issue that needs to be addressed is front-running. In our case, if at the end of the protocol a rushing quantum adversary has access to the signature before it is published, the adversary can recover the public key and derive the secret key to produce arbitrarily many new signatures before the original one is registered. We therefore need a mechanism to prevent this behaviour.

We assume that signatures are published in an append-only ledger where everyone can reliably check the contents of the ledger consistently and everyone can append to the ledger with some publication delay.

We propose the idea of a two-stage transaction in which the first stage would consist of announcing a commitment for the signature to be verified, and the second one would release the actual signature for verification. This two stage commit and reveal approach was introduced by Fawkescoin [3]. The high level idea is to commit to the signature $\tilde{\sigma}$ using a commitment scheme with opening value open that returns a commitment value com. Namely, we write $\mathsf{Commit}(\tilde{\sigma}, \mathsf{open}) \rightarrow \mathsf{com}$.

Formally, we consider a signature that is composed of two components, namely σ_1, σ_2. The first component (σ_1) is appended to the ledger as a separate transaction to commit to the signature. The submission of the second transaction follows after the first component being issued to the ledger. We now define the following delayed signature scheme and the corresponding security notion. Note that we switch the naming to *one-time* signatures because only the signatures that are committed are considered valid and hence, a signature released without a valid commitment does not represent a forgery.

Definition 2 (One-Time Delayed Signature). *A One-Time Delayed Signature consists of three algorithms* (Delay-KeyGen, Delay-Sign, Delay-Verify) *such that:*

- $(\mathsf{sk}', \mathsf{pk}') \leftarrow \mathsf{Delay\text{-}KeyGen}(\lambda)$*: A* PPT *algorithm that takes as input a security parameter* λ *and outputs a secret key* sk' *and the corresponding public key* pk'.
- $(\sigma_1, \sigma_2) \leftarrow \mathsf{Delay\text{-}Sign}(\mathsf{sk}', \mathsf{msg})$*: A* PPT *algorithm that takes as input a secret key* sk' *and the message to be signed* msg*. Outputs a two component signature* (σ_1, σ_2) *where* σ_1 *acts as a commitment for the* σ_2 *to be verified after the delay.*
- $0/1 \leftarrow \mathsf{Delay\text{-}Verify}(\mathsf{pk}', (\sigma_1, \sigma_2), \mathsf{msg})$*: A deterministic polynomial time algorithm that takes as input a public key* pk'*, a two component signature* (σ_1, σ_2) *and the message* msg *to be verified. Outputs* 1 *if* (σ_1, σ_2) *is a valid signature tuple for* msg*,* 0 *otherwise.*

Definition 3 (One-Time Delayed Signature Unforgeability). *A One-Time Delay signature scheme is* unforgeable *if for any quantum polynomial time adversary* $\mathcal{A}$ *the advantage of winning the* OTDU *game (Fig. 7) is negligible in* λ*, that is:*

$$\mathsf{Adv}_{\mathcal{A}}^{\mathsf{OTDU}} = \Pr[\mathsf{OTDU}(\mathcal{A}) \rightarrow 1] \leq \mathsf{negl}(\lambda)$$

```
OTDU(A)
  (sk', pk') <-$ Delay-KeyGen(λ)
  msg <- ⊥
  queried <- false
  A^OSig(pk') -> st, L
  A(st, σ2) -> s1, s2, m
  if Delay-Verify(pk', s1, s2, m) ≠ 1
    return 0
  return 1_{s1 ∈ L ∧ m ≠ msg}
```

```
OSig(m)
  if queried
    return ⊥
  queried <- true
  msg <- m
  (σ1, σ2) <- Delay-Sign(sk', m)
  return σ1
```

Fig. 7. OTDU security game.

Intuitively, OTDU game consists of supplying the adversary with the public key pk', then the adversary outputs a list of σ_1 candidates in the list L. During this process, it is possible to query the OSig oracle once, to obtain a valid σ_1 for msg. This behaviour corresponds to the adversary observing a signer posting pk', σ_1 to the ledger. In the second execution of the adversary, it is given σ_2 and it outputs a two component signature s_1, s_2 and the forged message m. This corresponds to the adversary seeing the release of the actual signature within σ_2. The adversary wins if the forged signature verifies successfully, the first component s_1 has been generated in the first execution and the forged message m is not equal to msg.

3.1 Constructing a One-Time Delayed Signature from a HiddenPK Signature

We construct a *One-Time Delayed Signature* from a HiddenPK signature by committing to the signature (σ_1) and releasing the second part of the signature along with the opening (σ_2). The signature is only correctly verified after the signer releasing σ_2 and its opening along with the signature. More concretely, given a HiddenPK signature scheme Σ_{HPK}, a QOW hash function H and a commitment scheme Commit, we construct a delayed signature in Fig. 8.

```
Delay-KeyGen(λ)
  (s̃k, p̃k) ←$ KeyGen_{Σ_HPK}(λ)
  return (s̃k, p̃k)

Delay-Sign(s̃k, msg)
  σ̃ ← Sign_{Σ_HPK}(s̃k, msg)
  open ←$ {0,1}^λ
  com ← Commit(σ̃||msg, open)
  σ1 ← com
  σ2 ← (σ̃, open)
  return (σ1, σ2)

Delay-Verify(p̃k, (σ1, σ2), msg)
  com ← σ1
  (σ̃, open) ← σ2
  if Commit(σ̃||msg, open) ≠ com
    return 0
  return HiddenPK-Verify(σ̃, p̃k, msg)
```

Fig. 8. Delayed signature construction from a HiddenPK signature.

Theorem 5. (QEUF-KOA → OTDU) *For a given* QEUF-KOA *secure* HiddenPK *signature scheme* Σ_{HPK}*, and a random oracle* Commit *with output length* λ*, the resulting delayed signature scheme* DelayHiddenPK *(Fig. 8) is unforgeable.*

Proof. We set G0 to be the OTDU game. Given an adversary $\mathcal{A}$ that wins G0 we reduce G0 to QEUF-KOA as follows:

- G1: We put an additional constraint to G0 that Commit does not have any collisions. Since Commit is a random oracle, the probability of having a collision is negligible. Hence, we have:

$$|\mathsf{Adv}_{\mathcal{A}}^{\mathsf{G1}} - \mathsf{Adv}_{\mathcal{A}}^{\mathsf{G0}}| \leq \mathsf{negl}(\lambda)$$

- G2: We put another additional constraint that the s_1 that is output by $\mathcal{A}$ was returned from a Commit query that is queried before the final Delay-Verify (line 5 of OTDU). Note that this implies that the output s_2, m was queried to the random oracle in the first phase of $\mathcal{A}$. If the constraint is not satisfied, it implies that the adversary has successfully predicted a fresh random oracle query which is negligible in λ. That is:

$$|\mathsf{Adv}_{\mathcal{A}}^{\mathsf{G2}} - \mathsf{Adv}_{\mathcal{A}}^{\mathsf{G1}}| \leq \mathsf{negl}(\lambda)$$

– G3: In order to simulate the second phase of $\mathcal{A}$ we intercept all random oracle queries s_2, parse the values $(\tilde{\sigma}, m, \mathsf{open})$ and their corresponding oracle replies s_1, check if $\mathsf{HiddenPK\text{-}Verify}(\tilde{\sigma}, \tilde{\mathsf{pk}}, \mathsf{m}) = 1$ and we output the correct s_1, s_2, m triplet. Since $|L|$ is polynomial, we can exhaust L for all s_1 values and find the correct triplet with probability 1. Hence, this game is at least as good as G2 in terms of advantage, that is:

$$\mathsf{Adv}_{\mathcal{A}}^{\mathsf{G3}} \geq \mathsf{Adv}_{\mathcal{A}}^{\mathsf{G2}}$$

– G4: We add the constraint that the query $(\tilde{\sigma}, m, \mathsf{open})$ from OSig was not queried by $\mathcal{A}$. Otherwise, it would imply that the adversary correctly guessed a correct opening open for a forged $\tilde{\sigma}$. Hence, the difference between G4 and G3 is negligible:

$$|\mathsf{Adv}_{\mathcal{A}}^{\mathsf{G4}} - \mathsf{Adv}_{\mathcal{A}}^{\mathsf{G3}}| \leq \mathsf{negl}(\lambda)$$

– G5: Since Osig only returns the fresh commitment output σ_1 which is a random oracle output, we simulate Osig oracle by randomly sampling a σ_1 from the output domain of the random oracle. Hence, the advantage remains the same:

$$\mathsf{Adv}_{\mathcal{A}}^{\mathsf{G5}} = \mathsf{Adv}_{\mathcal{A}}^{\mathsf{G4}}$$

The QEUF-KOA adversary $\mathcal{A}'$ runs the adversary $\mathcal{A}$ playing G5. This produces a valid forgery $(\tilde{\sigma}, m)$ on the public key $\tilde{\mathsf{pk}}$. However, since $\mathsf{Adv}_{\mathcal{A},\Sigma_{\mathsf{HPK}}}^{\mathsf{QEUF\text{-}KOA}}$ is negligible, by combining the results for G5, G4, G3, G2 and G1 we have:

$$\mathsf{Adv}_{\mathcal{A}}^{\mathsf{G0}} \leq \mathsf{negl}(\lambda)$$
$$\mathsf{Adv}_{\mathcal{A}}^{\mathsf{OTDU}} \leq \mathsf{negl}(\lambda)$$

□

However, *this model is not strong enough to be practically used.* When using the OTDU notion, we can still face two practical problems: a *Denial of Service* (DoS) attack consisting of flooding the ledger with rogue σ_1 commits, and a rushing adversary who would break the signature after seeing (σ_1, σ_2), and rushing to post a rogue (σ_1', σ_2') before σ_2 is published. We now introduce an enriched security model that captures both of these problems and introduce a three-stage signature process. The first problem is solved by defining an artificial relation between pk' and σ_1 so that pk' values cannot be paired up with arbitrary σ_1 values. The second problem is solved by adding extra mechanisms for explicitly controlling the opening and the closing of the list L on the ledger. We formalize the new approach as follows.

Definition 4 (One-Time Signatures with Delayed Ledger). *A One-Time Signature with Delayed Ledger consists of an append-only ledger L and the following algorithms:*

- $(\mathsf{sk}', \mathsf{pk}') \leftarrow \mathsf{DelayL\text{-}KeyGen}(\lambda)$: *A* PPT *algorithm that takes as input a security parameter and outputs a secret key* sk' *and the corresponding public key* pk'.
- $\mathsf{tok}_1 \leftarrow \mathsf{Open}(\mathsf{sk}')$: *Takes as input the secret key* sk', *outputs the first token associated with the opening of the ledger* L.
- $\mathsf{tok}_2 \leftarrow \mathsf{Close}(\mathsf{sk}')$: *Takes as input the secret key* sk', *outputs the second token associated with the closing of the ledger* L.
- $0/1 \leftarrow \mathsf{VerifyOpen}(\mathsf{pk}', \mathsf{tok}_1)$: *Takes as input the public key* pk' *and an opening token* tok_1, *outputs 1 if the opening value is consistent with the public key.*
- $0/1 \leftarrow \mathsf{VerifyClose}(\mathsf{pk}', \mathsf{tok}_2)$: *Takes as input the public key* pk' *and a closing token* tok_2, *outputs 1 if the opening value is consistent with the public key.*
- $(\sigma_1, \sigma_2) \leftarrow \mathsf{DelayL\text{-}Sign}(\mathsf{sk}', \mathsf{msg})$: *A* PPT *algorithm that takes as input a secret key* sk' *and the message to be signed* msg. *Outputs a two component signature* (σ_1, σ_2) *where* σ_1 *acts as a commitment for the* σ_2 *to be verified after a delay.*
- $0/1 \leftarrow \mathsf{DelayL\text{-}Verify}(\mathsf{pk}', (\sigma_1, \sigma_2), \mathsf{msg})$: *A deterministic polynomial time algorithm that takes as input a public key* pk', *a two component signature* (σ_1, σ_2) *and the message* msg *to be verified. Outputs* 1 *if* (σ_1, σ_2) *is a valid signature tuple for* msg, 0 *otherwise.*

Definition 5 (One-Time Signature Unforgeability with Delayed Ledger). *A One-Time Signature with Delayed Ledger scheme is unforgeable if for any quantum polynomial time adversary* $\mathcal{A}$ *the advantage of winning the* OTDU-L *game (Fig. 9) is negligible in* λ, *that is:*

$$\mathsf{Adv}_{\mathcal{A}}^{\mathsf{OTDU\text{-}L}} = \Pr[\mathsf{OTDU\text{-}L}(\mathcal{A}) \to 1] \leq \mathsf{negl}(\lambda)$$

Intuitively, when a signer wants to sign a message, it opens the ledger L, it posts the signature commitment σ_1. It checks that σ_1 is well posted. It closes the ledger L and only releases σ_2 after checking that the ledger L is closed. Using the OTDU-L notion: The adversary can post arbitrary commitments to L as long as it is open. The adversary has to call OwishOpen in order to call Oopen. That is, it has to observe the correct opening token. Moreover, the adversary has to call OwishClose in order to call Oclose. That is, the commitment of the signer should appear in the list L and σ_2 can only be observed after the closure of L.

3.2 Constructing a One-Time Signature with Delayed Ledger

We can modify the delayed signature construction in Fig. 8 by integrating two one-time tokens t_1 (for opening) and t_2 (for closing) to the secret key and their corresponding hashes to the public key. More concretely, we realize the construction as in Fig. 10.

Theorem 6. (OTDU $\rightarrow$ OTDU-L) *For a given* OTDU *signature scheme* (Delay-KeyGen, Delay-Sign, Delay-Verify), *the resulting signature scheme with delayed ledger* OTDU-L *(Fig. 10) is unforgeable.*

Proof. We need to show that

$$\mathsf{Adv}_{\mathcal{A}}^{\mathsf{OTDU\text{-}L}} = \Pr[\mathsf{OTDU\text{-}L}(\mathcal{A}) \to 1] \leq \mathsf{negl}(\lambda)$$

OTDU-L($\mathcal{A}$)

1 : $(\mathsf{sk}', \mathsf{pk}') \leftarrow\!\!\$ \ \mathsf{Delay\text{-}KeyGen}(\lambda)$
2 : opened, openwish $\leftarrow$ false, false
3 : closed, closewish $\leftarrow$ false, false
4 : queried $\leftarrow$ false
5 : $L \leftarrow$ empty list
6 : msg $\leftarrow \perp$
7 : $\mathcal{A}^{O*}(\mathsf{pk}') \rightarrow s_1, s_2, m$
8 : **reward if** $(s_1 \in L) \wedge \mathsf{Delay\text{-}Verify}(\mathsf{pk}', s_1, s_2, m) \wedge m \neq$ msg

OSig(m)

1 : **if** queried $\vee \neg$openwish $\vee$ closewish
2 :   **return** $\perp$
3 : queried $\leftarrow$ true
4 : msg $\leftarrow m$
5 : $(\sigma_1, \sigma_2) \leftarrow \mathsf{Delay\text{-}Sign}(\mathsf{sk}', m)$
6 : **return** σ_1

Opost(s)

1 : **if** opened $\wedge \neg$closed
2 : $L \leftarrow L \| s$
3 : **return** $\perp$

Oopen(t)

1 : **if** VerifyTokOpen(pk', t)
2 :   opened $\leftarrow$ true
3 :   **reward if** $\neg$openwish
4 : **return** $\perp$

OwishOpen()

1 : openwish $\leftarrow$ true
2 : **return** Open(sk')

Oclose(t)

1 : **if** $\neg$VerifyTokClose(pk', t)
2 :   **return** $\perp$
3 : closed $\leftarrow$ true
4 : **reward if** $\neg$closewish
5 : // returned after closure
6 : **return** σ_2

OwishClose()

1 : **if** $\neg$queried $\vee \sigma_1 \notin L$
2 :   **return** $\perp$
3 : closewish $\leftarrow$ true
4 : **return** Close(sk')

Fig. 9. OTDU-L security game for the signature scheme with delayed ledger.

DelayL-KeyGen(λ)

1 : $(\tilde{\mathsf{sk}}, \tilde{\mathsf{pk}}) \leftarrow\!\!\$ \ \mathsf{Delay\text{-}KeyGen}(\lambda)$
2 : $t_1 \leftarrow\!\!\$ \ \{0,1\}^{\lambda}, t_2 \leftarrow\!\!\$ \ \{0,1\}^{\lambda}$
3 : $\mathsf{sk}' \leftarrow (\tilde{\mathsf{sk}}, t_1, t_2)$
4 : $\mathsf{pk}' \leftarrow (\tilde{\mathsf{pk}}, H(t_1), H(t_2))$
5 : **return** $(\mathsf{sk}', \mathsf{pk}')$

DelayL-Sign(sk', msg)

1 : $(\tilde{\mathsf{sk}}, t_1, t_2) \leftarrow \mathsf{sk}'$
2 : $(\sigma_1, \sigma_2) \leftarrow \mathsf{Delay\text{-}Sign}(\tilde{\mathsf{sk}}, \text{msg})$
3 : **return** (σ_1, σ_2)

Open(sk')

1 : $(\tilde{\mathsf{sk}}, t_1, t_2) \leftarrow \mathsf{sk}'$
2 : **return** t_1

DelayL-Verify($\mathsf{pk}', (\sigma_1, \sigma_2), \text{msg}$)

1 : $(\tilde{\mathsf{pk}}, H(t_1), H(t_2)) \leftarrow \mathsf{pk}'$
2 : **return** Delay-Verify($\mathsf{pk}', (\sigma_1, \sigma_2), \text{msg}$)

VerifyOpen(pk', t)

1 : $(\tilde{\mathsf{pk}}, H(t_1), H(t_2)) \leftarrow \mathsf{pk}'$
2 : **return** $\mathbb{1}_{H(t)=H(t_1)}$

VerifyClose(pk', t)

1 : $(\tilde{\mathsf{pk}}, H(t_1), H(t_2)) \leftarrow \mathsf{pk}'$
2 : **return** $\mathbb{1}_{H(t)=H(t_2)}$

Close(sk')

1 : $(\tilde{\mathsf{sk}}, t_1, t_2) \leftarrow \mathsf{sk}'$
2 : **return** t_2

Fig. 10. Delayed signature (with ledger) construction

We set $\mathsf{G0}$ to be the $\mathsf{OTDU\text{-}L}$ game. Given an adversary $\mathcal{A}$ that wins $\mathsf{G0}$, we reduce $\mathsf{G0}$ to OTDU as follows:

- $\mathsf{G1}$: We replace Oopen by an oracle who does not reward if $\mathsf{openwish}$ is false. The difference between $\mathsf{OTDU\text{-}L}$ and $\mathsf{G1}$ can express as an adversary who break QOW on $H(t_1)$, that is:

$$|\mathsf{Adv}_{\mathcal{A}}^{\mathsf{G1}} - \mathsf{Adv}_{\mathcal{A}}^{\mathsf{G0}}| \leq \mathsf{negl}(\lambda)$$

- $\mathsf{G2}$: We replace Oclose by an oracle which first checks if $\mathsf{closewish}$ is true and returns nothing if $\mathsf{closewish}$ is false. The difference between $\mathsf{G1}$ and $\mathsf{G2}$ can express as an adversary who breaks QOW on $H(t_2)$. Note that Oclose does not have a reward statement anymore.

$$|\mathsf{Adv}_{\mathcal{A}}^{\mathsf{G2}} - \mathsf{Adv}_{\mathcal{A}}^{\mathsf{G1}}| \leq \mathsf{negl}(\lambda)$$

The OTDU adversary $\mathcal{A}'$ simulates $\mathcal{A}$ playing $\mathsf{G2}$ and the oracles that are not present in the OTDU game. That is, it selects (t_1, t_2), simulates Oopen, $\mathsf{OwishOpen}$, Oclose, $\mathsf{OwishClose}$ by using the sampled (t_1, t_2) values. It also simulates Opost by maintaining a list L. Furthermore, $\mathcal{A}'$ stops when it makes the Oclose query which closes L to return the list L and a state st to resume the simulation of $\mathcal{A}$ (Line 3 of the OTDU in Fig. 7). When it resumes, σ_2 is obtained and provided to $\mathcal{A}$ for the rest of the simulation. Note that no calls to the oracle OSig has been made throughout the simulation. Hence, given an adversary $\mathcal{A}$ that wins the $\mathsf{OTDU\text{-}L}$ game, we can construct an adversary $\mathcal{A}'$ that wins OTDU. Since $\mathsf{Adv}_{\mathcal{A}}^{\mathsf{ODTU}}$ is negligible in λ, we have:

$$\mathsf{Adv}_{\mathcal{A}}^{\mathsf{OTDU\text{-}L}} \leq \mathsf{negl}(\lambda)$$

□

Note that it is possible to extend the *One-Time Signature with Delayed Ledger* construction and the corresponding $\mathsf{OTDU\text{-}L}$ notion to *n-time* signatures in a natural way. As long as the underlying signature scheme has $\mathsf{QEUF\text{-}KOA}$ security, it is possible to publish n signature commitments to the ledger under the same public key and wait for the ledger closure before releasing the signatures.

Lifting the Proofs to QROM: Since the challenger only makes a constant number of queries to the random oracle in OTDU and $\mathsf{OTDU\text{-}L}$ both Theorem 5 and Theorem 6 still holds in the QROM model. This is due to the *Lifting Theorem for Search-Type Games* (Theorem 4.2 from [12]). Note that the advantage of the adversary against ROM is divided by $(2q+1)^{2k}$ where q is the number of queries the adversary makes (polynomially bounded in our case) and k is the number of queries the challenger makes to the oracle ($k = 2$ in our case).

Discussion on Practical Instantiations: The construction based on the OTDU-L notion cannot be directly implemented in Bitcoin Mainly due to the fact that after a single *close* transaction (to close the original *open* transaction), no further *open* transactions can be made. However, this behaviour is not currently possible unless the miners manually check for this condition, which would result in a hard fork. Nevertheless, it is possible to practically instantiate this for any ledger that implements this closure mechanism.

Note that our approach of two-stage signatures targets the issue of avoiding publication of wrong stage-1 transactions for a given address. However this does not address the scenario in which a user floods the ledger with correct stage-1 commitments without ever paying the transaction during stage-2, but including stage-1 transactions does consume network resources. Moreover, there is no incentive for miners to even include the stage-1 transactions with commitments. This problem is well-known and has been studied since [3]. We further reflect on this problem by considering the following scenarios:

- **Honest stage-1 transactions with malicious opens**: In this scenario, the goal of the rushing adversary is to add many open transactions to increase the total transaction fee paid by the original signer of the transaction.
  In stage-1, the token t_1 is released and rushing adversaries can create rogue transactions with the same token t_1. This can only be done until the second token t_2 is released (i.e. stage-2). We stress that t_2 is released after t_1 is well posted (i.e. the block confirmation period has passed for the block containing t_1). For instance, Bitcoin requires 6 block confirmations which -assuming the block producing time is 10 min- would translate to an hour.
  If we assume that each miner includes only one transaction per block per t_1, this would multiply the transaction fee by the number of blocks in the block confirmation period.
- **Dishonest stage-1 transactions**: In this scenario, the goal of the adversary (not necessarily rushing) is to create as many stage-1 transactions as possible and never proceed with the stage-2 transaction to cause congestion over the network. In this setting, the miners would not get paid for the transactions that have been already included if stage-2 never occurs. The malicious signer would further lose assets.

Looking at these two scenarios, we see a relation between the denial of service surface of the system and the miner's motivation for including stage-1 transactions. If we motivate the miners to include stage-1 transactions, there is a better opportunity for the adversary to congest the network by dishonest stage-1 transactions, but also the opportunity for the miner to extract more fees from honest stage-1 transactions.

4 Extension to Threshold Signatures

In this section, we extend the construction of Sect. 2 to the case of multi-party signing, and more precisely to threshold signatures. In particular, this means that we present a threshold signature scheme with hidden public key.

Consider a threshold signature scheme Σ with associated parameters λ, we assume that $\mathsf{TSKeyGen}$ has a specific form i.e. it consists of an algorithm $((\mathsf{sk}_i, \mathsf{pk}_i)_{i\in[n]}) \leftarrow \mathsf{TSKeyGen}^1(\lambda)$, which is followed by a final computation $\mathsf{pk} \leftarrow \mathsf{Rec}((\mathsf{pk}_i)_{i\in S})$, where Rec is the linear reconstruction function from the associated linear secret sharing scheme in $\mathcal{D}$. We argue that this assumption is reasonable as it matches all the existing protocols. Hence, we abuse it by calling the transform as a generic one.

Additionally, for simplicity we assume a *trusted setup* during $\mathsf{TSKeyGen}$ in the form of an honest dealer running $\mathsf{TSKeyGen}$. Given such a threshold signature scheme Σ with associated parameters λ, a (t, n) secret sharing scheme $(\mathsf{Shr}_t^n, \mathsf{Rec})$, and a hash function H, the generic threshold with hidden public key transform $\mathsf{ThreshHiddenPK}$ is describe in Fig. 11. Note that this transform makes the public key and the signature grow linear in size and makes the resulting signature transparent (i.e. it is possible to distinguish whether a signature is the result of a threshold signing process). However, the amount of computational overhead is minimal since the key generation is almost non-interactive. It is possible to construct a non-transparent transformation with constant key size by considering a more computationally demanding key generation process.

$\mathsf{ThreshHiddenPK\text{-}KeyGen}(\lambda)$

$(\mathsf{sk}_i, \mathsf{pk}_i)_{i\in[n]} \leftarrow\!\!\$\ \mathsf{TSKeyGen}^1_{\Sigma}(\lambda)$
for $i = 1, ..., n$:
  $\rho_i \leftarrow\!\!\$\ \mathcal{D}$
  $\tilde{\mathsf{sk}}_i \leftarrow (\mathsf{sk}_i, \rho_i)$
$\tilde{\mathsf{pk}}_1 \leftarrow (H(\rho_i))_{i\in[n]}$
$\tilde{\mathsf{pk}}_2 = (\mathsf{pk}_i + \rho_i)_{i\in[n]}$
$\tilde{\mathsf{pk}} \leftarrow (\tilde{\mathsf{pk}}_1, \tilde{\mathsf{pk}}_2)$
return $((\tilde{\mathsf{sk}}_i)_{i\in[n]}, \tilde{\mathsf{pk}})$

$\mathsf{ThreshHiddenPK\text{-}Sign}((\tilde{\mathsf{sk}}_i)_{i\in S}, \mathsf{msg})$

Each P_i does :
$(\mathsf{sk}_i, \rho_i) \leftarrow (\tilde{\mathsf{sk}}_i)$
$\sigma \leftarrow \mathsf{TSSign}_{\Sigma}((\mathsf{sk}_i)_{\in S}, \mathsf{msg})$
$\tilde{\sigma} \leftarrow (\sigma, S, (\rho_i)_{i\in S})$
return $\tilde{\sigma}$

$\mathsf{ThreshHiddenPK\text{-}Verify}(\tilde{\sigma}, \tilde{\mathsf{pk}}, \mathsf{msg})$

$(\sigma, S, (\rho_i)_{i\in S}) \leftarrow \tilde{\sigma}$
$(\tilde{\mathsf{pk}}_1, \tilde{\mathsf{pk}}_2) \leftarrow \tilde{\mathsf{pk}}$
for each $i \in S$:
  if $H(\rho_i) \neq (\tilde{\mathsf{pk}}_1)_i$:
    return 0
for each $i \in S$:
  $\mathsf{pk}_i \leftarrow (\tilde{\mathsf{pk}}_2)_i - \rho_i$
$\mathsf{pk} \leftarrow \mathsf{Rec}((\mathsf{pk}_i)_{i\in S})$
return $\mathsf{Verify}_{\Sigma}(\sigma, \mathsf{pk}, \mathsf{msg})$

Fig. 11. $\mathsf{ThreshHiddenPK}(\Sigma, \lambda, H)$ transform.

Theorem 7 (Classical security of $\mathsf{ThreshHiddenPK}$). *The* $\mathsf{ThreshHiddenPK}$ (Σ, λ, H) *transform is existentially unforgeable under chosen-message attack*

(TEUF-CMA) if the underlying threshold signature scheme Σ is and if H is 2nd pre-image resistant.

Proof. The proof technique can be extended from the single signer setting in a straightforward manner.

We now define and analyze the quantum security of our protocol. We extend our definitions from the single signer setting to the threshold one, and define zero-time threshold signatures as threshold signatures that are quantum secure against existential forgeries under key-only attack.

Definition 6 (TQEUF-KOA security). *A (t, n)-threshold-signature scheme consisting of three algorithms* $(\mathsf{TSKeyGen}, \mathsf{TSSign}, \mathsf{Verify})$ *is quantum existentially unforgeable under key-only attack (TQEUF-KOA) if for any quantum adversary $\mathcal{A}$, and for any set of corrupted players* Corr *chosen by $\mathcal{A}$ such that* $|\mathsf{Corr}| \leq t$, *the advantage of $\mathcal{A}$ in the* TQEUF-KOA *game is negligible i.e.*

$$\mathrm{Adv}_{\mathcal{A}}^{\mathsf{TQEUF\text{-}KOA}} = \Pr[\mathsf{TQEUF\text{-}KOA}(\mathcal{A}) \rightarrow 1] \leq \mathsf{negl}(\lambda)$$

where the TQEUF-KOA *game is defined in Fig. 12.*

$\mathsf{TQEUF\text{-}KOA}(\mathcal{A}, \mathsf{Corr})$	
1 :	$\mathsf{TSKeyGen}(\lambda) \rightarrow ((\mathsf{sk}_i)_{i\in[n]}, \mathsf{pk})$
2 :	$\mathcal{A}(\mathsf{pk}, (\mathsf{sk}_i)_{i\in\mathsf{Corr}}) \rightarrow (\sigma^*, m^*)$
3 :	**return** $\mathsf{Verify}(\sigma^*, \mathsf{pk}, m^*) = 1$

Fig. 12. The TQEUF-KOA game for zero-time quantum security of threshold signatures.

Theorem 8 (Quantum security of ThreshHiddenPK). *The* $\mathsf{ThreshHiddenPK}(\Sigma, \lambda, H)$ *transform is quantum existentially unforgeable under key-only attack if H is quantum one-way and given ρ_i, r_i for $i \in [n]$ uniform and independent then $(H(\rho_i), \mathsf{pk}_i + \rho_i)_{i\in[n]}$ is indistinguishable from $(H(\rho_i), r_i)_{i\in[n]}$.*

Proof. Consider an adversary $\mathcal{A}$ for the TQEUF-KOA game applied to $\mathsf{ThreshHiddenPK}(\Sigma, \lambda, H)$. We construct an adversary $\mathcal{B}$ such that if $\mathcal{A}$ wins TQEUF-KOA then $\mathcal{B}$ breaks the one-wayness of $\mathcal{A}$. Given a quantum one-way challenge y, $\mathcal{B}$ generates key pairs for ThreshHiddenPK and samples a special index j out of the uncorrupted values, for which the hash is set to y. Then they call $\mathcal{A}$ on the public key and the corrupted secrets. Then $\mathcal{B}$ can extract the preimage ρ_j^* of y from the message-signature pair returned by $\mathcal{A}$. If $\mathcal{A}$ wins the TQEUF-KOA game then ρ_j^* will be a valid pre-image for the QOW game.

Using the assumption on the distribution of pk_i and H, the view of $\mathcal{A}$ called as a subroutine of $\mathcal{B}$ is indistinguishable from the view of $\mathcal{A}$ in the TQEUF-KOA game. This implies that if $\mathcal{A}$ wins TQEUF-KOA then $\mathcal{B}$ wins QOW. Hence we have

$$\Pr[\mathsf{TQEUF\text{-}KOA}(\mathcal{A}) \to 1] \leq \Pr[\mathsf{QOW} \to 1] = \mathsf{negl}(\lambda)$$

by assumption on the quantum one-wayness of H. □

Note that the assumption on the pk_i and H can be proven assuming that the vector of pk_is has high min-entropy (denoted H_∞) and that given $K = (k_1, ...k_n)$ and $X = (x_1, ..., x_n)$, the function $h_K(X) = (H(k_i - x_i))_{i\in[n]}$ is a universal hash function.

Let ℓ be the output length of H. We write $\mathsf{PK} = (\mathsf{pk}_i)_{i\in[n]}$, $\mathsf{PK} + \rho = (\mathsf{pk}_i + \rho_i)_{i\in[n]}$ as random vectors and U for a uniform random vector. We consider the function $h_K(\mathsf{PK}) = (H(k_i - \mathsf{pk}_i))_{i\in[n]}$ with $k_i = \rho_i + \mathsf{pk}_i$ of output length $n \cdot \ell$. We have that PK and $\mathsf{PK} + \rho$ are independent, and are independent from uniform U. Furthermore, $\mathsf{PK} + \rho$ is uniformly distributed since ρ_i is uniform for all $i \in [n]$. Since we assume that the min-entropy of PK is high, and h is a universal hash function, we can apply the Leftover Hash Lemma [8] and we get that the distribution of $(h_{\mathsf{PK}+\rho}(\mathsf{PK}), \mathsf{PK} + \rho)$ and that of $(U, \mathsf{PK} + \rho)$ are $\epsilon/2$-indistinguishable, with $\epsilon = \sqrt{2^{n\cdot\ell - \mathsf{H}_\infty(\mathsf{pk})}}$. Since $h_{\mathsf{PK}+\rho}(\mathsf{PK}) = (H(\rho_i))_{i\in[n]}$, we get the desired result. Note that typically, $\mathsf{H}_\infty(\mathsf{pk}_i)$ is close to $t \cdot \log_2(|G|)$ for a group G as the pk_i are t-wise independent and close to uniform in G. This implies that $\ell \leq \frac{t}{n} \cdot \log_2(|G|)$.

Acknowledgements. We thank Loïs Huguenin-Dumittan for discussions about lifting the proofs of Theorem 5 and Theorem 6 to the QROM setting.

References

1. Bernstein, D.J., Hülsing, A., Kölbl, S., Niederhagen, R., Rijneveld, J., Schwabe, P.: The SPHINCS+ signature framework. In: Proceedings of the 2019 ACM SIGSAC Conference on Computer and Communications Security, CCS 2019, pp. 2129–2146. Association for Computing Machinery, New York (2019). https://doi.org/10.1145/3319535.3363229
2. Beullens, W.: Breaking rainbow takes a weekend on a laptop. In: Dodis, Y., Shrimpton, T. (eds.) CRYPTO 2022. LNCS, vol. 13508, pp. 464–479. Springer, Cham (2022). https://doi.org/10.1007/978-3-031-15979-4_16
3. Bonneau, J., Miller, A.: Fawkescoin: a cryptocurrency without public-key cryptography. In: Christianson, B., Malcolm, J., Matyáš, V., Švenda, P., Stajano, F., Anderson, J. (eds.) Security Protocols 2014. LNCS, vol. 8809, pp. 350–358. Springer, Cham (2014). https://doi.org/10.1007/978-3-319-12400-1_35
4. Chalkias, K., Brown, J., Hearn, M., Lillehagen, T., Nitto, I., Schroeter, T.: Blockchained post-quantum signatures. In: 2018 IEEE International Conference on Internet of Things (iThings) and IEEE Green Computing and Communications (GreenCom) and IEEE Cyber, Physical and Social Computing (CPSCom) and IEEE Smart Data (SmartData), pp. 1196–1203 (2018). https://doi.org/10.1109/Cybermatics_2018.2018.00213

5. Cozzo, D., Smart, N.P.: Sharing the LUOV: threshold post-quantum signatures. In: Albrecht, M. (ed.) IMACC 2019. LNCS, vol. 11929, pp. 128–153. Springer, Cham (2019). https://doi.org/10.1007/978-3-030-35199-1_7
6. Developper, B.: Developper guides - transactions. Bitcoin Developper. https://developer.bitcoin.org/devguide/transactions.html
7. Ding, J., Deaton, J., Vishakha, Yang, B.Y.: The Nested subset differential attack. In: Canteaut, A., Standaert, F.X. (eds.) EUROCRYPT 2021. LNCS, vol. 12696, pp. 329–347. Springer, Cham (2021). https://doi.org/10.1007/978-3-030-77870-5_12
8. Impagliazzo, R., Levin, L.A., Luby, M.: Pseudo-random generation from one-way functions. In: Proceedings of the Twenty-First Annual ACM Symposium on Theory of Computing, STOC 1989, pp. 12–24. Association for Computing Machinery, New York (1989). https://doi.org/10.1145/73007.73009
9. van der Linde, W.: Post-quantum blockchain using one-time signature chains (2018)
10. Marco, L., Talayhan, A., Vaudenay, S.: Making classical (threshold) signatures post-quantum for single use on a public ledger. Cryptology ePrint Archive, Paper 2023/420 (2023). https://eprint.iacr.org/2023/420
11. NIST: Request for Additional Digital Signature Schemes for the Post-Quantum Cryptography Standardization Process. https://www.nist.gov/news-events/news/2022/09/request-additional-digital-signature-schemes-post-quantum-cryptography
12. Yamakawa, T., Zhandry, M.: Classical vs quantum random oracles. In: Canteaut, A., Standaert, F.-X. (eds.) EUROCRYPT 2021. LNCS, vol. 12697, pp. 568–597. Springer, Cham (2021). https://doi.org/10.1007/978-3-030-77886-6_20

Zero Knowledge Proofs

aPlonK: Aggregated *PlonK* from Multi-polynomial Commitment Schemes

Miguel Ambrona(✉), Marc Beunardeau, Anne-Laure Schmitt, and Raphaël R. Toledo

Nomadic Labs, Paris, France
{miguel.ambrona,marc.beunardeau,anne-laure.schmitt, raphael.toledo}@nomadic-labs.com

Abstract. *PlonK* is a prominent universal and updatable zk-SNARK for general circuit satisfiability. We present *aPlonK*, a variant of *PlonK* that reduces the proof size and verification time when multiple statements are proven in a batch. Both the aggregated proof size and the verification complexity of *aPlonK* are logarithmic in the number of aggregated statements. Our main building block, inspired by the techniques developed in SnarkPack (Gailly, Maller, Nitulescu, FC 2022), is a multi-polynomial commitment scheme, a new primitive that generalizes polynomial commitment schemes. Our techniques also include a mechanism for involving committed data into *PlonK* statements very efficiently, which can be of independent interest.

We implement an open-source industrial-grade library for zero-knowledge *PlonK* proofs with support for *aPlonK*. Our experimental results show that our techniques are suitable for real-world applications (such as blockchain rollups), achieving significant performance improvements in proof size and verification time.

1 Introduction

In 1985 [GMR85], Goldwasser et al. introduced the notion of zero-knowledge proofs. They allow a *prover* to convince a *verifier* of the validity of a certain statement without leaking any other information, e.g. why the statement is true.

Existing generic protocols that implement zero-knowledge argument systems [BFM88,DMP90,FLS90] for any NP relation have long been perceived as mainly theoretical results. Recently, the research community has witnessed significant improvements on the design of efficient general-purpose zero-knowledge proof systems offering various degrees of practicality [Gro16,BCG+17,BBB+18, MBKM19,LMR19]. Such improvements have been driven by the development of blockchain systems that make use of zero-knowledge arguments to achieve privacy and scalability [BCG+14,DFKP13]. In these systems, communication complexity is one of the most important factors, which has led to an increasing interest and remarkable progress in so-called *succinct non-interactive arguments of knowledge*

J. Shikata and H. Kuzuno (Eds.): IWSEC 2023, LNCS 14128, pp. 195–213, 2023.
https://doi.org/10.1007/978-3-031-41326-1_11

(SNARKs) [GGPR13, BCG+13, PHGR13, Gro16], a class of non-interactive arguments of knowledge with sublinear, if not constant, communication and verification complexity. This, however, comes at the cost of a significantly slower prover. $\mathcal{P}lon\mathcal{K}$ is a universal and updatable zero-knowledge SNARK. Given its significant improvements with respect to its predecessor Sonic [MBKM19], especially on prover efficiency, $\mathcal{P}lon\mathcal{K}$ has become very popular and has been adopted by several state-of-the-art blockchain projects such as Zcash [HBHW], Mina [BMRS20], the Dusk Network [MKF21] or Anoma [GYB21].

We present $a\mathcal{P}lon\mathcal{K}$, a new affluent of the $\mathcal{P}lon\mathcal{K}$ family which focuses on reducing the proof size and verification time when multiple statements are proven in a batch. The aggregated proof size and the verification complexity of $a\mathcal{P}lon\mathcal{K}$ are logarithmic in the number of aggregated statements, making it an appealing building block for blockchain applications, where having low verification complexity is paramount.

1.1 Blockchain Applications of SNARKs

Blockchain developers were among the first to deploy large-scale real-life applications of general purpose zero-knowledge proof systems, starting different lines of research in this area. We can cite Virgo [ZXZS20] and its successors, used for Overeality [Ove22]; STARK [BBHR19], used by Starkware [Sta21]; Halo [BGH19a], used by Zcash [HBHW]; or $\mathcal{P}lon\mathcal{K}$ [GWC19], created by Aztec [Wil18].

In this paper we focus on scalability, which is an inherent issue in blockchain systems. The blockchain throughput cannot be simply increased with additional computing power, since every node should be able to validate state transitions. SNARKs can be of help here when they are used to certify expensive computations (e.g., the validity of multiple transactions), since the SNARK verification can become cheaper than the direct validation of the statement being proven. This idea has been explored in so-called validity rollups. (Note that in this context, zero-knowledge is not necessarily relevant.)

A validity rollup is an alternative chain that runs in parallel to the main chain, but stores a small amount of data on the main chain, e.g., a commitment to the rollup state. Transactions can be sent to a rollup *operator*, who knows the complete rollup state and can update it accordingly. Periodically, the rollup operator will communicate to the main chain a commitment to the most updated version of the rollup state together with a proof that ensures its validity (ergo the name).[1] The blockchain nodes only need to check this single proof (instead of validating all the operations performed between rollup states).[2] The blockchain (layer 1) becomes more scalable at the cost of having to produce such proof, which is generated by an independent operator (in layer 2). The transactions are revealed to the operator but can remain private w.r.t. the blockchain. Unlike in layer 1, the operator can use of extra computing power and parallelization to speedup the process of creating proofs, thus reducing the rollup latency.

[1] A proof that the new committed state has been achieved by applying legitimate operations to the previous committed state.

[2] Remarkably, the blockchain nodes do not even need access to the rollup operations that were involved.

Despite such promising properties and even if the rollup operator can use large computing power, producing proofs is a major bottleneck. A possible idea to reduce the proving cost (and thus the latency) is to split the statement into smaller ones. For example, instead of proving the validity of 10,000 rollup transactions with one proof, one could produce 100 proofs of 100 transactions each. Dealing with smaller proofs reduces the prover cost, whose complexity is linearithmic in the circuit size. Unfortunately, this would require that the blockchain nodes receive and verify 100 proofs instead of 1.

Our techniques in this work are particularly suitable for the above scenario. They allow the prover to combine the batched proofs, producing an aggregated proof that can be efficiently verified by the blockchain nodes. We could alternatively use incrementally verifiable computation (IVC) [Val08]. We discuss the differences between these two approaches in Sect. 1.3.

1.2 Our Contributions

We pursue the study of *PlonK* and establish several general techniques that reduce the proof size and verification time when multiple statements are proven in a batch.

aPlonK . Our main contribution is a multi-statement proving system coined *aggregated PlonK*, or *aPlonK* for short, which allows one to combine k proofs into a single aggregated proof of $\mathcal{O}(\log k)$ group elements that can be verified in $\mathcal{O}(\log k)$ time. The aggregated proofs must be created coordinately, but their computation is highly parallelizable. *aPlonK* is the result of extending the techniques of Gailly, Maller and Nitulescu (SnarkPack) [GMN20], designed over Groth16 [Gro16], to the framework of *PlonK*. This work and SnarkPack both use the generalized inner-product argument [BCC+16] presented in [BMV19].

Multi-polynomial Commitments. We introduce the notion of multi-polynomial commitment schemes, a generalization of polynomial commitment schemes designed to commit to several polynomials at the same time, while achieving sublinear commitment and proof sizes and sublinear verification complexity in the number of committed polynomials.

We then present a generic construction of a multi-polynomial commitment scheme from any homomorphic polynomial commitment scheme whose commitment space is one of the source groups of a set of bilinear groups. Our construction is inspired by the techniques of SnarkPack for building an inner-product argument with logarithmic verification time by combining a modified version of the inner-product argument [BCC+16, BBB+18, BGH19b, BCL+21, DRZ20] with a KZG-like [KZG10] commitment scheme whose commitment space is the target group of a set of bilinear groups.

Our new notion of multi-polynomial commitments captures the essence of SnarkPack, hardcoded in their *ad hoc* construction for aggregating Groth16 [Gro16] proofs. We consider this an important contribution as it provides clarity, intuition and continues the modularity of *PlonK*-based systems.

Improvements over SnarkPack. While the verification of SnarkPack is presented as sublinear[3], their verifier needs to perform a linear number of scalar operations for dealing with public inputs. (This is inherent for verifiable computations.) We observe that for many applications (e.g. a validity rollup) most public inputs can be hidden from the verifier as long as some relation on them is ensured (e.g., they form a chain). Our system can exploit this fact, to achieve actual sublinear verification time, when the use case allows for it.

Furthermore, we double the efficiency of the main subroutine of SnarkPack by observing that their *pair group commitments* [GMN20, Section 3.2] do not need to be binding in order to achieve the desired security properties, if the underlying polynomial commitment scheme is *inner-product binding* and *inner-product extractable* (see Sect. 3). Note that [BMM+21, Section 5.3] proposed an alternative solution to achieve a binding committing function without doubling the commitment size. They use a different SRS without odd powers in one of the source groups. This requires a dedicated trusted setup, something which SnarkPack and this work want to avoid in order to reuse the SRS from existing ceremonies.

Commitments in $\mathcal{P}lon\mathcal{K}$ Relations. En route, we present a mechanism that allows a $\mathcal{P}lon\mathcal{K}$ statement to refer to the data inside a public commitment. Such link does not require a high number of constraints to model the commitment opening, as it is performed *outside of the $\mathcal{P}lon\mathcal{K}$ circuit.* This building block, necessary to instantiate $a\mathcal{P}lon\mathcal{K}$ efficiently, can be of independent interest, as it can be used for building hybrid proving systems or for proving statements modeled with non-deterministic circuits.

Implementation and Evaluation. We implement a general library for (zero-knowledge) $\mathcal{P}lon\mathcal{K}$ proofs with support for $a\mathcal{P}lon\mathcal{K}$. Our library is implemented over the BLS12-381 elliptic curve [Bow17] and uses bindings to the *blst* library [Sup21]. Our experiments show that the techniques described in this work are suitable for real-world applications, providing significant performance improvements in proof size and verification time, while introducing a light overhead on prover complexity. Our code will be publicly available as open-source.

1.3 Related Work

In this section, we compare our techniques with other approaches for combining zero-knowledge proofs and present the main advantages of $a\mathcal{P}lon\mathcal{K}$.

IVC and Recursion. Incrementally verifiable computation (IVC) [Val08], conceived by Valiant, is a framework that provides proof composability: with IVC one can conjunctively combine two proofs of size k into a proof of size k as well. This is a powerful technique that can be used to implement recursion. In the context of SNARKS, recursion allows one to prove statements like the following (parametrized by a state):

[3]It is in terms of elliptic curve operations.

"I know a previous state from which the current state can be reached and I also have a proof of this very statement for such previous state."

This can be achieved by expressing a SNARK verifier in a SNARK circuit. One real-world application is the Mina blockchain [BMRS20], which provides its users with a constant-size proof of validity of its most updated state. In particular, the proof ensures that one transition of the blockchain has been performed correctly and that there exists another proof for the preceding state. This allows the blockchain state to be constant in size.

However, the strength of recursive SNARKs comes with high costs. Expressing a SNARK verifier in a SNARK circuit is very expensive. The current known techniques are (i) using cycles of pairing friendly elliptic curves [CCW19] which require very large group elements, (ii) or implementing non-native operations such as modular arithmetic over a modulus (e.g. the SNARK's base field order) that does not coincide with the SNARK's scalar field order. This typically leads to a decrease in performance of several orders of magnitude.

This performance issue has led to new lines of research exploring alternative techniques for achieving weaker versions of IVC. We can cite, Halo [BGH19a], and its successor Halo2 (using *PlonK* instead of Sonic [MBKM19]), Fractal [COS19], Bünz et al. work [BCMS20], or Nova [KST21], a novel construction based on folding schemes. These works explore the idea of performing a weaker version of recursion by moving some expensive parts of the SNARK verification outside of the circuit. Such steps are accumulated and carried out for future verification. These techniques achieve IVC by using a cycle of (not necessarily pairing-friendly) elliptic curves, leading to better performance.

Proof Aggregation Without Recursion. Proof aggregation can be achieved more efficiently without recursion and still be suitable for many applications such as validity rollups.

Aztec. The company Aztec [Wil18], creator of *PlonK*, achieves a form of proof aggregation which can be seen as a weak version of IVC. Thanks to this simplification, they do not require cycles of elliptic curves. However, they still need to model elliptic curves in a SNARK circuit by simulating non-native field operations. The expensive pairing checks are accumulated as in Halo, by using standard batching techniques.

SnarkPack. Gailly, Maller and Nitulescu [GMN20] provide a framework for aggregating Groth16 proofs. As we explained in Sect. 1.2, their techniques (based on [BMM+21]) are the starting point of this paper and combine a homomorphic pair group commitment scheme with an inner-product argument to achieve logarithmic-size proofs and logarithmic verification complexity (in the number of aggregated proofs).

Our work achieves very efficient proof aggregation without cycles of elliptic curves and without simulating non-native operations. This is an improvement over Halo and Aztec, which brings us at the level of SnarkPack. However, unlike

SnarkPack, $a\mathcal{P}lon\mathcal{K}$ is defined over a universal SNARK. An immediate consequence is that we can aggregate different circuits. Furthermore, we can perform proof aggregation that connects the proven statements in an arbitrary fashion.

2 Preliminaries

2.1 Notation

For a finite set S, we write $a \leftarrow S$ to denote that a is uniformly sampled from S. We denote the security parameter by $\lambda \in \mathbb{N}$. Given two functions $f, g : \mathbb{N} \to [0,1]$, we write $f \approx g$ if the difference $|f(\lambda) - g(\lambda)|$ is asymptotically smaller than the inverse of any polynomial. A function f is said to be *negligible* if $f \approx 0$, whereas it is said to be *overwhelming* when $f \approx 1$. For integers m, n, such that $m \leq n$, we denote by $[m, n]$ the range $\{m, m+1, \dots, n\}$. We denote by $[n]$ the range $[1, n]$. Given $d \in \mathbb{N}$ and a ring R, we denote by $R^{<d}[X]$ the set of univariate polynomials over X with coefficients in R and degree strictly smaller than d. For $n \in \mathbb{N}$, we denote by $\boldsymbol{v} \in R^n$ a vector length n over R, and for every $i \in [n]$, we denote by v_i its i-th component. Furthermore, for any $k \leq n$, $\boldsymbol{v}[:k]$ denotes the vector formed by the first k components of $\boldsymbol{v}$.

We consider a bilinear group generator $\mathcal{G}$ that on input 1^λ, produces a set of bilinear groups $(\mathbb{G}_1, \mathbb{G}_2, \mathbb{G}_t)$ of order p (a λ-bits prime), equipped with a non-degenerate bilinear pairing $e : \mathbb{G}_1 \times \mathbb{G}_2 \to \mathbb{G}_t$, satisfying $e(a\,G, b\,H) = ab \cdot e(G, H)$ for all $G \in \mathbb{G}_1$, $H \in \mathbb{G}_2$ and $a, b \in \mathbb{Z}_p$. We use additive notation for all three groups.[4] Unless specified otherwise, we implicitly assume that all algorithms share the same common set of bilinear groups, sampled from the appropriate security parameter. For $n \in \mathbb{N}$, such that $n \mid p-1$, let $\mathcal{H}_n$ be the subgroup generated by $\omega_n \in \mathbb{Z}_p$, a designated primitive n-th root of unity over $\mathbb{Z}_p$, and let $Z_{\mathcal{H}_n}(X) := X^n - 1$, which vanishes over $\mathcal{H}_n$. For every $i \in [n]$, let $\mathsf{L}_{i,n}$ be the Lagrange polynomial such that $\mathsf{L}_{i,n}(\omega_n^i) = 1$ and $\mathsf{L}_{i,n}(h) = 0$ for all $h \in \mathcal{H}_n \setminus \{\omega_n^i\}$. Throughout the paper, such n will denote the number of constraints in the constraint system of interest.

For the sake of space, we refer the full version for a formal definition of SNARKs, polynomial commitment schemes and a detailed description of the $\mathcal{P}lon\mathcal{K}$ proving system.

2.2 Constraint Systems

A constraint system is a list of polynomial equations over $\mathbb{Z}_p[X_1, \dots, X_m]$, of restricted form. For simplicity in our exposition, in this work we consider polynomials of the form

$$\mathsf{q_L} X_i + \mathsf{q_R} X_j + \mathsf{q_O} X_k + \mathsf{q_M} X_i X_j + \mathsf{q_C} \ ,$$

[4] It is more common to express $\mathbb{G}_t$ in multiplicative notation, since its group operation is typically implemented through a polynomial multiplication.

for certain scalar coefficients $\mathsf{q_L}, \mathsf{q_R}, \mathsf{q_O}, \mathsf{q_M}, \mathsf{q_C} \in \mathbb{Z}_p$. This corresponds to the classical identity considered in the original *PlonK* paper [GWC19]. All our results extend to other versions of *PlonK*, that involve additional custom identities such as [GW19, PFM+22] and even to implementations that use a different number of wires per gate (instead of 3).

Definition 1 (Constraint System). *A constraint system on m variables is a list of tuples $(a, b, c, \mathsf{q_L}, \mathsf{q_R}, \mathsf{q_O}, \mathsf{q_M}, \mathsf{q_C})$ with $a, b, c \in [m]$, $\mathsf{q_L}, \mathsf{q_R}, \mathsf{q_O}, \mathsf{q_M}, \mathsf{q_C} \in \mathbb{Z}_p$. We say a vector $\boldsymbol{x} \in \mathbb{Z}_p^m$ satisfies constraint system $\mathcal{C} = \{(a_i, b_i, c_i, \mathsf{q}_{\mathsf{L}_i}, \mathsf{q}_{\mathsf{R}_i}, \mathsf{q}_{\mathsf{O}_i}, \mathsf{q}_{\mathsf{M}_i}, \mathsf{q}_{\mathsf{C}_i})\}_{i \in [n]}$ if for every $i \in [n]$:*

$$\mathsf{q}_{\mathsf{L}_i} x_{a_i} + \mathsf{q}_{\mathsf{R}_i} x_{b_i} + \mathsf{q}_{\mathsf{O}_i} x_{c_i} + \mathsf{q}_{\mathsf{M}_i} x_{a_i} x_{b_i} + \mathsf{q}_{\mathsf{C}_i} = 0 \ .$$

The *PlonK* proving system is a zk-SNARK for the following relation, defined over so-called *public inputs* $\boldsymbol{x} \in \mathbb{Z}_p^\ell$ and *witness* $\boldsymbol{w} \in \mathbb{Z}_p^{m-\ell}$:

$$\mathrm{PoK}\left\{ \boldsymbol{w} \in \mathbb{Z}_p^{m-\ell} : (\boldsymbol{x}, \boldsymbol{w}) \in \mathbb{Z}_p^m \text{ satisfies } \mathcal{C} \right\} \ . \tag{1}$$

The statement being proved is parametrized by both $\mathcal{C}$ and $\boldsymbol{x}$.

3 Multi-polynomial Commitment Schemes

We introduce the notion of *multi-polynomial commitment schemes*, a generalization of polynomial commitment schemes designed to commit to several polynomials at the same time. We require the commitment size be sublinear in the number of committed polynomials. Furthermore, we require that verification can be performed from a succinct (standard) commitment to the polynomial evaluations. That way, the verifier does not need to obtain the actual evaluations, which allows its running time to be sublinear in the number of polynomials involved.

Definition 2 (Multi-polynomial commitment). *A multi-polynomial commitment scheme over a ring R consists of five polynomial-time algorithms:*

- $\mathsf{Setup}(1^\lambda, d, K) \to (\mathsf{ck}, \mathsf{vk})$, *on input the security parameter λ, a degree bound $d \in \mathbb{N}$, and a vector length bound $K \in \mathbb{N}$, outputs commitment and verification keys $(\mathsf{ck}, \mathsf{vk})$.*[5]
- $\mathsf{Commit\text{-}Polys}(\mathsf{ck}, \boldsymbol{f}) \to \mathsf{com}_{\boldsymbol{f}}$, *given a commitment key ck and a vector of k polynomials $\boldsymbol{f} \in R^{<d}[X]^k$, with $k \leq K$, outputs a commitment $\mathsf{com}_{\boldsymbol{f}}$. We require that the size of $\mathsf{com}_{\boldsymbol{f}}$ be sublinear in k.*
- $\mathsf{Commit\text{-}Evals}(\boldsymbol{v}) \to \mathsf{com}_{\boldsymbol{v}}$, *given a vector $\boldsymbol{v} \in R^k$, with $k \leq K$, outputs a commitment $\mathsf{com}_{\boldsymbol{v}}$. We require that the size of $\mathsf{com}_{\boldsymbol{v}}$ be sublinear in k.*
- $\mathsf{Open}(\mathsf{ck}, \mathsf{com}_{\boldsymbol{f}}, z, \boldsymbol{f}) \to \pi$, *given a commitment key, a commitment $\mathsf{com}_{\boldsymbol{f}}$, an evaluation point $z \in R$ and a vector of k polynomials in $R^{<d}[X]$ (that were committed in $\mathsf{com}_{\boldsymbol{f}}$) with $k \leq K$, outputs a proof π.*

[5]We assume that both keys implicitly contain d and K; and that ck implicitly contains vk.

$\underline{\mathsf{Setup}(1^\lambda, d, K)}$:

$(\mathsf{ck}_\Psi, \mathsf{vk}_\Psi) \leftarrow \Psi.\mathsf{Setup}(1^\lambda, d)$

$\tau \leftarrow \mathbb{Z}_p$; $\mathsf{ck}_\tau := [1, \tau, \tau^2, ..., \tau^{K-1}]_2$

return $(\mathsf{ck} := (\mathsf{ck}_\Psi, \mathsf{ck}_\tau), \mathsf{vk} := (\mathsf{vk}_\Psi, [\tau]_1))$

$\underline{\mathsf{Commit\text{-}Polys}(\mathsf{ck} := (\mathsf{ck}_\Psi, \mathsf{ck}_\tau), \boldsymbol{f})}$:

$\mu_i \leftarrow \Psi.\mathsf{Commit}(\mathsf{ck}_\Psi, f_i)\ \forall i \in [k]$ $(k := |\boldsymbol{f}| \leq K)$

return $\mathsf{com}_{\boldsymbol{f}} := (k, \sum_{i=1}^{k} e(\mu_i, \mathsf{ck}_{\tau i}))$

$\underline{\mathsf{Commit\text{-}Evals}(\boldsymbol{v})}$: Any function that is (sublinearly) *shrinking*, *binding* and admits a succinct proof for relation:

$$\mathrm{PoK}\{\boldsymbol{v} : \mathsf{Commit\text{-}Evals}(\boldsymbol{v}) = \mathsf{com}_{\boldsymbol{v}} \wedge \textstyle\sum_{i=1}^{k} r^{i-1} v_i = \hat{v}\} \quad . \quad (2)$$

$\underline{\mathsf{Open}(\mathsf{ck} := (\mathsf{ck}_\Psi, \mathsf{ck}_\tau), \mathsf{com}_{\boldsymbol{f}} := (k, G), z, \boldsymbol{f})}$:

$\boldsymbol{v} = \boldsymbol{f}(z)$; $\mathsf{com}_{\boldsymbol{v}} := \mathsf{Commit\text{-}Evals}(\boldsymbol{v})$; $k = |\boldsymbol{f}|$; $\kappa := \lceil \log_2(k) \rceil$

$\mu_i \leftarrow \Psi.\mathsf{Commit}(\mathsf{ck}_\Psi, f_i)\ \forall i \in [k]$ ▷ Not necessary if μ_i were stored on Commit-Polys

$r := \mathsf{Hash}(\mathsf{com}_{\boldsymbol{f}}, z, \mathsf{com}_{\boldsymbol{v}})$; $\boldsymbol{r} := (1, r, \ldots, r^{k-1})$; $\hat{f} := \langle \boldsymbol{f}, \boldsymbol{r} \rangle$; $\hat{\mu} := \langle \boldsymbol{\mu}, \boldsymbol{r} \rangle$; $\hat{v} := \langle \boldsymbol{v}, \boldsymbol{r} \rangle$

$\pi_\Psi \leftarrow \Psi.\mathsf{Open}(\mathsf{ck}_\Psi, \hat{\mu}, z, \hat{f}, \hat{v})$ and produce a proof π_v of relation (2) w.r.t $\mathsf{com}_{\boldsymbol{v}}$, $\hat{v}$ and r

$\pi_{\mathsf{IPA}} \leftarrow \mathsf{IPA.Prove}(k, \mathsf{ck}_\tau, (G, r, \hat{\mu}), \boldsymbol{\mu})$ (let $\{u_j\}_{j=1}^{\kappa}$ be the sampled random challenges)

$g(X) := \prod_{j=1}^{\kappa}(u_j^{-1} + u_j X^{2^{\kappa-j}})$; $\rho := \mathsf{Hash}(\pi_{\mathsf{IPA}})$; $v_\rho := g(\rho)$; $h(X) := (g(X) - v_\rho)/(X - \rho)$; $\pi_\tau := [h(\tau)]_2$

return $(\hat{\mu}, \hat{v}, \pi_\Psi, \pi_v, \pi_{\mathsf{IPA}}, \pi_\tau)$

$\underline{\mathsf{Check}(\mathsf{vk} := (\mathsf{vk}_\Psi, [\tau]_1), \mathsf{com}_{\boldsymbol{f}} := (k, G), z, \mathsf{com}_{\boldsymbol{v}}, \pi := (\hat{\mu}, \hat{v}, \pi_\Psi, \pi_v, \pi_{\mathsf{IPA}}, \pi_\tau))}$:

$b_\Psi \leftarrow \Psi.\mathsf{Check}(\mathsf{vk}_\Psi, \hat{\mu}, z, \hat{v}, \pi_\Psi)$ and $r := \mathsf{Hash}(\mathsf{com}_{\boldsymbol{f}}, z, \mathsf{com}_{\boldsymbol{v}})$

let b_v be the result of verifying that π_v is a valid proof of relation (2) w.r.t $\mathsf{com}_{\boldsymbol{v}}$, $\hat{v}$ and r

$b_{\mathsf{IPA}} \leftarrow \mathsf{IPA.Verify}'(k, [\tau]_1, (G, r, \hat{\mu}), \pi_{\mathsf{IPA}})$

$\rho := \mathsf{Hash}(\pi_{\mathsf{IPA}})$; $v_\rho := \prod_{j=1}^{\kappa}(u_j^{-1} + u_j\, \rho^{2^{\kappa-j}})$ ▷ u_j are the challenges computed during IPA.Verify′

$b_\tau := e([\tau]_1 - [\rho]_1, \pi_\tau) \stackrel{?}{=} e([1]_1, G_0 - [v_\rho]_2)$ ▷ $G_0 \in \mathbb{G}_2$ is the last element of π_{IPA}

return $b_\Psi \wedge b_v \wedge b_{\mathsf{IPA}} \wedge b_\tau$

Fig. 1. Multi-polynomial commitment scheme based on an inner-product binding and inner-product extractable polynomial commitment scheme Ψ (over $\mathbb{G}_1$) and inner-product argument IPA.

- $\mathsf{Check}(\mathsf{vk}, \mathsf{com}_{\boldsymbol{f}}, z, \mathsf{com}_{\boldsymbol{v}}, \pi) \to 1/0$, *given a verification key* vk, *a commitment to polynomials* $\mathsf{com}_{\boldsymbol{f}}$, *an evaluation point* z, *a commitment to evaluations* $\mathsf{com}_{\boldsymbol{v}}$, *and a proof* π, *outputs a bit. We require that the verification complexity be sublinear in* K.

Completeness. A multi-polynomial commitment scheme is *complete* if $\forall \lambda, d, K$, all $(\mathsf{ck}, \mathsf{vk}) \leftarrow \mathsf{Setup}(1^\lambda, d, K)$, any $k \leq K$, any vector $\boldsymbol{f} \in R^{<d}[X]^k$, and any $z \in R$, it holds:

$$\mathsf{Check}(\mathsf{vk}, \mathsf{com}_{\boldsymbol{f}}, z, \mathsf{com}_{\boldsymbol{v}}, \mathsf{Open}(\mathsf{ck}, \mathsf{com}_{\boldsymbol{f}}, z, \boldsymbol{f})) = 1 ,$$

where commitment $\mathsf{com}_{\boldsymbol{f}}$ is defined as $\mathsf{Commit\text{-}Polys}(\mathsf{ck}, \boldsymbol{f})$ and $\mathsf{com}_{\boldsymbol{v}} := \mathsf{Commit\text{-}Evals}(\boldsymbol{f}(z))$.

Binding property. A multi-polynomial commitment scheme is *binding* if for every polynomial $d, K \in \mathbb{N}$ and every PPT adversary $\mathcal{A}$, the following probabilities are negligible in λ:

$$\Pr\left[\begin{array}{r} (\mathsf{ck}, \mathsf{vk}) \leftarrow \mathsf{Setup}(1^\lambda, d, K); \\ (\boldsymbol{v}, \boldsymbol{v}') \leftarrow \mathcal{A}(\mathsf{ck}) \end{array} : \begin{array}{c} \boldsymbol{f} \neq \boldsymbol{f}' \\ \wedge\, \boldsymbol{f} \in R^{<d}[X]^k, \boldsymbol{f}' \in R^{<d}[X]^{k'}, k, k' \leq K \\ \mathsf{Commit\text{-}Polys}(\mathsf{ck}, \boldsymbol{f}) = \mathsf{Commit\text{-}Polys}(\mathsf{ck}, \boldsymbol{f}') \end{array}\right],$$

$$\Pr\left[\begin{array}{r} (\mathsf{ck}, \mathsf{vk}) \leftarrow \mathsf{Setup}(1^\lambda, d, K); \\ (\boldsymbol{v}, \boldsymbol{v}') \leftarrow \mathcal{A}(\mathsf{ck}) \end{array} : \begin{array}{c} \boldsymbol{v} \neq \boldsymbol{v}' \wedge \boldsymbol{v} \in R^k, \boldsymbol{v}' \in R^{k'}, k, k' \leq K \\ \mathsf{Commit\text{-}Evals}(\boldsymbol{v}) = \mathsf{Commit\text{-}Evals}(\boldsymbol{v}') \end{array}\right].$$

Knowledge soundness. A multi-polynomial commitment scheme is *knowledge sound* if for every $d, K \in \mathbb{N}$ and every PPT adversary $\mathcal{A}$, there exists an (expected polynomial time) extractor $\mathcal{E}$ such that the following probability is negligible in λ:

$$\Pr\left[\begin{array}{r} (\mathsf{ck}, \mathsf{vk}) \leftarrow \mathsf{Setup}(1^\lambda, d, K) \\ (\mathsf{com}_{\boldsymbol{f}}, z, \mathsf{com}_{\boldsymbol{v}}, \pi) \leftarrow \mathcal{A}(\mathsf{ck}) \\ \boldsymbol{f} \leftarrow \mathcal{E}(\mathsf{ck}) \end{array} : \begin{array}{c} \mathsf{Check}(\mathsf{vk}, \mathsf{com}_{\boldsymbol{f}}, z, \mathsf{com}_{\boldsymbol{v}}, \pi) = 1 \\ \wedge \left(\begin{array}{l} \mathsf{com}_{\boldsymbol{f}} \neq \mathsf{Commit\text{-}Polys}(\mathsf{ck}, \boldsymbol{f}) \\ \vee\, \mathsf{com}_{\boldsymbol{v}} \neq \mathsf{Commit\text{-}Evals}(\boldsymbol{f}(z)) \end{array}\right) \end{array}\right].$$

3.1 A Multi-polynomial Commitment Scheme from KZG and IPA

We present a generic construction of multi-polynomial commitments from:

i) a polynomial commitment scheme which is homomorphic over $\mathbb{G}_1$, inner-product binding and inner-product extractable (as defined below);
ii) a sublinear-verifier argument system for the following relation, parametrized by $\boldsymbol{G} \in \mathbb{G}_2^k$, $C \in \mathbb{G}_t$, $P \in \mathbb{G}_1$ and $r \in \mathbb{Z}_p$, where $\boldsymbol{r} = (1, r, \ldots, r^{k-1})$:

$$\mathrm{PoK}\{\, \boldsymbol{\mu} \in \mathbb{G}_1^k : \langle \boldsymbol{\mu}, \boldsymbol{G} \rangle = C \wedge \langle \boldsymbol{r}, \boldsymbol{\mu} \rangle = P \,\} , \qquad (3)$$

The scheme is depicted in Fig. 1.

The first building block can be instantiated with the celebrated KZG commitment scheme [KZG10] (described in the full version). For the second building block, we propose a modified version of the inner-product argument [BCC+16,BBB+18], inspired by [GMN20] (see full version).

Homomorphic property. A polynomial commitment scheme over group $\mathbb{G}$ of prime order p is *homomorphic* if $\forall\lambda, d \in \mathbb{N}$, $(\mathsf{ck}, \mathsf{vk}) \leftarrow \mathsf{Setup}(1^\lambda, d)$ and all $f, g \in \mathbb{Z}_p^{<d}[X]$, it holds:

$$\mathsf{Commit}(\mathsf{ck}, f) +_{\mathbb{G}} \mathsf{Commit}(\mathsf{ck}, g) = \mathsf{Commit}(\mathsf{ck}, f + g) \ ,$$

Inner-product binding property. A homomorphic polynomial commitment scheme (over $\mathbb{G}_1$) is *inner-product binding* if for all polynomial $d, K \in \mathbb{N}$ and every PPT (stateful) algorithm $\mathcal{A}$, the following probability is negligible in λ:

$$\Pr\left[\begin{array}{c}(\mathsf{ck}, \mathsf{vk}) \leftarrow \mathsf{Setup}(1^\lambda, d)\\ \tau \leftarrow \mathbb{Z}_p\\ \boldsymbol{f}, \boldsymbol{f}' \leftarrow \mathcal{A}(\mathsf{ck}, [\boldsymbol{\tau}]_1, [\boldsymbol{\tau}]_2)\end{array} : \begin{array}{c}\boldsymbol{f} \neq \boldsymbol{f}', \boldsymbol{f}, \boldsymbol{f}' \in \mathbb{Z}_p^{<d}[X]^k, \text{ with } k \leq K\\ \langle \mathsf{Commit}(\mathsf{ck}, \boldsymbol{f}), \boldsymbol{\tau}[:k]\rangle = \langle \mathsf{Commit}(\mathsf{ck}, \boldsymbol{f}'), \boldsymbol{\tau}[:k]\rangle\end{array}\right],$$

where $\mathsf{Commit}(\mathsf{ck}, \boldsymbol{f})$ is a shorthand for $(\mathsf{Commit}(\mathsf{ck}, f_1), \ldots, \mathsf{Commit}(\mathsf{ck}, f_k))$ and $\boldsymbol{\tau} := (1, \tau, \ldots, \tau^{K-1})$.

Proposition 1. *The* KZG *polynomial commitment scheme is inner-product binding.*

We refer to the full version for a proof.

Inner-product extractability. A homomorphic polynomial commitment scheme (over $\mathbb{G}_1$) is *inner-product extractable* if for every polynomial $d, K \in \mathbb{N}$ and every PPT (stateful) algorithm $\mathcal{A}$, there exists an (expected polynomial time) extractor $\mathcal{E}$ such that the following probability is negligible in λ:

$$\Pr\left[\begin{array}{c}(\mathsf{ck}, \mathsf{vk}) \leftarrow \mathsf{Setup}(1^\lambda, d)\\ \tau, r \leftarrow \mathbb{Z}_p\\ G, z, \boldsymbol{v} \leftarrow \mathcal{A}(\mathsf{ck}, [\boldsymbol{\tau}]_1, [\boldsymbol{\tau}]_2)\\ (\boldsymbol{\mu}, \pi) \leftarrow \mathcal{A}(r)\\ \boldsymbol{f} \leftarrow \mathcal{E}(\mathsf{ck}, [\boldsymbol{\tau}]_1, [\boldsymbol{\tau}]_2, r)\end{array} : \begin{array}{c}G \in \mathbb{G}_t, z \in \mathbb{Z}_p, \boldsymbol{v} \in \mathbb{Z}_p^k, \boldsymbol{\mu} \in \mathbb{G}_1^k, \text{ with } k \leq K\\ \langle \boldsymbol{\mu}, \boldsymbol{\tau}[:k]\rangle = G\\ \mathsf{Check}(\mathsf{vk}, \langle \boldsymbol{\mu}, \boldsymbol{r}\rangle, z, \langle \boldsymbol{v}, \boldsymbol{r}\rangle, \pi) = 1\\ (\boldsymbol{f}(z) \neq \boldsymbol{v} \vee \langle \mathsf{Commit}(\mathsf{ck}, \boldsymbol{f}), \boldsymbol{\tau}[:k]\rangle \neq G)\end{array}\right],$$

where $\mathsf{Commit}(\mathsf{ck}, \boldsymbol{f})$ is a shorthand for $(\mathsf{Commit}(\mathsf{ck}, f_1), \ldots, \mathsf{Commit}(\mathsf{ck}, f_k))$, $\boldsymbol{\tau} := (1, \tau, \ldots, \tau^{K-1})$ and $\boldsymbol{r} := (1, r, \ldots, r^{k-1})$.

Proposition 2. *The* KZG *polynomial commitment scheme is inner-product extractable in the algebraic group model.*

We refer to the full version for a proof.

Theorem 1. *If* $\mathsf{Hash} : \{0,1\}^* \to \mathbb{Z}_p$ *is a random oracle, and polynomial commitment scheme* Ψ *is complete, binding, knowledge sound, homomorphic, inner-product binding and inner-product extractable, then the scheme from Fig. 1 is a complete, binding and knowledge sound multi-polynomial commitment scheme in the algebraic group model.*

We refer to the full version for a proof.

Remark 1. Our scheme from Fig. 1 could also be instantiated with a homomorphic commitment scheme Ψ that is neither inner-product binding nor inner-product extractable. In that case, the multi-polynomial commitment scheme would need to be modified by adding a second $\mathbb{G}_t$ element $\sum_{i=1}^{k} e(\mu_i, [\tilde{\tau}^i]_2)$ to com_f for a new $\tilde{\tau}$ independent of τ.[6] This modification would make the committing function binding, which would allow us to prove security without relying on the inner-product binding and inner-product extractability properties of Ψ. Note that proofs of opening would need to include an extra element $\pi_{\tilde{\tau}}$, computed as $[h(\tilde{\tau})]_2$, analogously to π_τ in step 6 of the Open algorithm, which would be verified with a second pairing equation in step 5 of the Check algorithm. Furthermore, the IPA protocol would need to be adapted, as described in the full version.

4 *PlonK* Proof Aggregation from Multi-polynomial Commitments

We study the problem of designing a multi-statement proving system, that can handle several *PlonK* proofs more efficiently than the simple parallel execution on every statement of the traditional *PlonK* system. For the sake of simplicity in our exposition, we assume that all statements are parametrized by the same *PlonK* constraint system (although each statement has its own public inputs). However, most of our techniques apply to the case with different systems.

4.1 *aPlonK*

A simple but effective first optimization is to share the random challenges sampled with Fiat-Shamir across all proofs. This can be beneficial for several reasons. For example, having a common evaluation point ξ for all proofs means that all polynomial commitments are opened at the same point, which can typically lead to significant optimizations by the underlying polynomial commitment scheme. Sharing such random challenges across proofs does not harm security as long as the challenges are computed from the partial transcripts of all proofs. In that case, from an extractor for the aggregated proving system one could build an extractor for any of the individual statements by fixing all other statements. On the other hand, this trick, which is the basis of many of our optimizations, requires that the provers of every different statement run coordinately or at least synchronize at every point where random challenges are sampled. This limitation prevents us from strictly achieving IVC [Val08], but does not limit the distribution of the prover computation. Our system is perfectly applicable to creating a validity rollup (see Sect. 1.1).

Another rather simple optimization is to have a common polynomial T for all proofs, computed from a linear combination of all the identities. In the rest

[6] Such $\tilde{\tau}$ could be the same secret used during the setup of Ψ, if Ψ is such that its structured reference string is formed by the powers of a secret scalar over $\mathbb{G}_1$ and $\mathbb{G}_2$ (such as KZG).

of this section, we describe our more sophisticated optimization techniques. The resulting proving system, that we call *aPlonK*, is described in Fig. 2.

Theorem 2. *If multi-polynomial commitment scheme* Ψ *is complete, binding and knowledge sound, and* $\mathsf{Hash} : \{0,1\}^* \to \mathbb{Z}_p$ *is a random oracle, the protocol described in Fig. 2 constitutes a* SNARK *for relation:*

$$\mathrm{PoK}\left\{ \{\boldsymbol{w}_i \in \mathbb{Z}_p^{m-\ell}\}_{i\in[k]} : (\boldsymbol{x}_i, \boldsymbol{w}_i) \in \mathbb{Z}_p^m \text{ satisfies } \mathcal{C}\ \forall i \in [k] \right\} .$$

We refer to the full version for a proof.

Using a Multi-polynomial Commitment. Replacing the polynomial commitment scheme used by *PlonK* by a multi-polynomial commitment scheme can lead to major improvements in proof size and verification time. It allows us to commit to all wire polynomials together in one single multi-polynomial commitment with sublinear size in the number of aggregated proofs k. With our multi-polynomial commitment scheme from Fig. 1, the commitment size would be constant (1 $\mathbb{G}_\mathsf{t}$ element) instead of linear in k, and the commitment verification complexity would be $\mathcal{O}(\log k)$ instead of $\mathcal{O}(k)$. This technique achieves sublinear complexity (in k) on commitment verification operations. However, the verifier still needs to check all the identities, which involves a $\mathcal{O}(k)$ number of scalar operations. For that, the verifier needs to receive all the evaluations of the committed polynomials (whose validity can be asserted through the already verified evaluation commitment) and use them to verify the identities. Our next technique addresses this issue.

Meta-verification. The verification of identities only involves scalar operations over $\mathbb{Z}_p$, but this is the native field of *PlonK* circuits. This opens the possibility of, instead of verifying the identities, verifying a *PlonK* proof that the identities are correct. Such proof would need to ensure that:

- the prover knows evaluations satisfying all the identities,
- such evaluations coincide with the evaluations verified during the multi-polynomial commitment check.

We formally describe the meta-verification equation in Fig. 3. It is parametrized by the number of constraints n, and the number of aggregated proofs k. The public inputs to the meta-verification circuit are $(\alpha, \beta, \gamma, \delta, \xi, \nu_\mathsf{w}, \nu_\mathsf{z}, \nu_{\bar{\mathsf{z}}}, \nu_\mathsf{t}, \nu_\mathsf{pp}, \{\boldsymbol{x}_j\}_{j\in[k]})$, where $\alpha, \beta, \gamma, \delta, \xi$ are Fiat-Shamir sampled scalars; $\nu_\mathsf{w}, \nu_\mathsf{z}, \nu_\mathsf{t}, \nu_\mathsf{pp}$ are evaluation commitments of (respectively) the wire polynomials, Z polynomial, T polynomial and setup polynomials at ξ; $\nu_{\bar{\mathsf{z}}}$ is (a commitment to) the evaluation of polynomial Z at $\omega\xi$; and for every $j \in [k]$, $\boldsymbol{x}_j$ is the vector of public inputs to the j-th statement. The secret inputs to the meta-verification relation are the actual polynomial evaluations at ξ and $\omega\xi$ of the committed polynomials.

By just verifying a single *PlonK* proof, the verifier can assert the correctness of all identities without performing a $\mathcal{O}(k)$ number of scalar operations. On the other hand, we make three observations that deserve attention:

$\underline{a\mathcal{P}lon\mathcal{K}.\mathsf{Setup}(1^\lambda, \mathcal{C} := \{a_i, b_i, c_i, \mathsf{q_L}_i, \mathsf{q_R}_i, \mathsf{q_O}_i, \mathsf{q_M}_i, \mathsf{q_C}_i\}_{i\in[n]}, k):}$

1: $\mathsf{q_L}(X) := \sum_{i=1}^{n} \mathsf{q_L}_i \mathsf{L}_{i,n}(X)$; define $\mathsf{q_R}, \mathsf{q_O}, \mathsf{q_M}, \mathsf{q_C}$ analogously

2: $\sigma : [3n] \to [3n]$ be $\mathcal{C}_\sigma$; $\mathsf{pp.polys} := (\mathsf{q_L}, \mathsf{q_R}, \mathsf{q_O}, \mathsf{q_M}, \mathsf{q_C}, \mathsf{S}_{\sigma 1}, \mathsf{S}_{\sigma 2}, \mathsf{S}_{\sigma 3})$

3: $(\mathsf{ck}, \mathsf{vk}) \leftarrow \Psi.\mathsf{Setup}(1^\lambda, n, k)$; $\mu_{\mathsf{pp}} \leftarrow \Psi.\mathsf{Commit\text{-}Polys}(\mathsf{ck}, \mathsf{pp.polys})$

4: **return** $\mathsf{pp} := (n, \sigma, \mathsf{ck}, \mathsf{vk}, \mu_{\mathsf{pp}}, \mathsf{pp.polys})$

$\underline{a\mathcal{P}lon\mathcal{K}.\mathsf{Prove}(\mathsf{pp} := (n, \sigma, \mathsf{ck}, \_, \mu_{\mathsf{pp}}, \mathsf{pp.polys}), \{\boldsymbol{x}_j\}_{j\in[k]}, \{\boldsymbol{w}_j\}_{j\in[k]}):}$

1: $\widetilde{\boldsymbol{w}}_j := (\boldsymbol{x}_j, \boldsymbol{w}_j)$ for all $j \in [k]$

2: compute $\text{Wire}_j := \sum_{i=1}^{n} \widetilde{w}_{j,\text{wire}_i} \mathsf{L}_{i,n}(X)$ for wires A, B and C for all $j \in [k]$

3: $\mathbf{W} := (\mathsf{A}_1, \mathsf{B}_1, \mathsf{C}_1, \ldots, \mathsf{A}_k, \mathsf{B}_k, \mathsf{C}_k)$; $\mu_{\mathsf{w}} := \Psi.\mathsf{Commit\text{-}Polys}(\mathsf{ck}, \mathbf{W})$

4: $\beta \leftarrow \mathsf{Hash}(\mu_{\mathsf{w}})$; $\gamma \leftarrow \mathsf{Hash}(\beta)$; $\delta \leftarrow \mathsf{Hash}(\gamma)$

5: $\widehat{\mathsf{A}}(X) := \sum_{j=1}^{k} \delta^j \mathsf{A}_j(X)$; $\widehat{\mathsf{B}}(X) := \sum_{j=1}^{k} \delta^j \mathsf{B}_j(X)$; $\widehat{\mathsf{C}}(X) := \sum_{j=1}^{k} \delta^j \mathsf{C}_j(X)$

6: compute $\mathsf{Z}(X)$, satisfying $\textit{perm-ids}^{\sigma}_{\beta,\gamma}(\widehat{\mathsf{A}}, \widehat{\mathsf{B}}, \widehat{\mathsf{C}}, \mathsf{Z})$ on $\mathcal{H}_n$ ▷ See full version

7: $\mu_{\mathsf{z}} \leftarrow \Psi.\mathsf{Commit\text{-}Polys}(\mathsf{ck}, \mathsf{Z})$ and $\alpha \leftarrow \mathsf{Hash}(\delta, \mu_{\mathsf{z}})$

8: $F_j(X) := (\mathsf{q_L}\mathsf{A}_j + \mathsf{q_R}\mathsf{B}_j + \mathsf{q_O}\mathsf{C}_j + \mathsf{q_M}\mathsf{A}_j\mathsf{B}_j + \mathsf{q_C} + \mathsf{PI}_{\boldsymbol{x}_j})(X)$ for all $j \in [k]$

9: $\textit{ids}(X) := \bigcup_{j\in[k]} F_j(X) \cup \textit{perm-ids}^{\sigma}_{\beta,\gamma}(\widehat{\mathsf{A}}, \widehat{\mathsf{B}}, \widehat{\mathsf{C}}, \mathsf{Z})$; $\mathsf{T}(X) := \frac{\left(\sum_{i\in[|\textit{ids}|]} \alpha^i \textit{ids}_i(X)\right)}{Z_{\mathcal{H}_n}(X)}$

10: $\mu_{\mathsf{t}} \leftarrow \Psi.\mathsf{Commit\text{-}Polys}(\mathsf{ck}, \mathsf{T})$ and $\xi \leftarrow \mathsf{Hash}(\alpha, \mu_{\mathsf{t}})$

11: let $\mathsf{ev}(, , \boldsymbol{f}, x) := (\Psi.\mathsf{Open}(\mathsf{ck}, , , x, \boldsymbol{f}), \Psi.\mathsf{Commit\text{-}Evals}(\mathsf{ck}, \boldsymbol{f}(x)))$; compute $(\pi_{\mathsf{pp}}, \nu_{\mathsf{pp}}) \leftarrow \mathsf{ev}(\mu_{\mathsf{pp}}, \mathsf{pp.polys}, \xi)$, $(\pi_{\mathsf{w}}, \nu_{\mathsf{w}}) \leftarrow \mathsf{ev}(\mu_{\mathsf{w}}, \mathbf{W}, \xi)$, $(\pi_{\mathsf{z}}, \nu_{\mathsf{z}}) \leftarrow \mathsf{ev}(\mu_{\mathsf{z}}, \mathsf{Z}, \xi)$, $(\overline{\pi}_{\mathsf{z}}, \nu_{\overline{\mathsf{z}}}) \leftarrow \mathsf{ev}(\mu_{\mathsf{z}}, \mathsf{Z}, \omega\xi)$, and $(\pi_{\mathsf{t}}, \nu_{\mathsf{t}}) \leftarrow \mathsf{ev}(\mu_{\mathsf{t}}, \mathsf{T}, \xi)$

12: compute the proof of knowledge π_{meta} ▷ See Section 4.1
$\quad \text{PoK}\left\{\boldsymbol{w}_{\mathsf{meta}} : \mathcal{R}_{n,k}(((\alpha, \beta, \gamma, \delta), \xi, \nu_{\mathsf{w}}, \nu_{\mathsf{z}}, \nu_{\overline{\mathsf{z}}}, \nu_{\mathsf{t}}, \nu_{\mathsf{pp}}, \{\boldsymbol{x}_j\}_{j\in[k]}), \boldsymbol{w}_{\mathsf{meta}}) = 1\right\}$

13: **return** $\pi := (\mu_{\mathsf{w}}, \mu_{\mathsf{z}}, \mu_{\mathsf{t}}, \nu_{\mathsf{w}}, \nu_{\mathsf{z}}, \nu_{\overline{\mathsf{z}}}, \nu_{\mathsf{t}}, \nu_{\mathsf{pp}}, \pi_{\mathsf{w}}, \pi_{\mathsf{z}}, \overline{\pi}_{\mathsf{z}}, \pi_{\mathsf{t}}, \pi_{\mathsf{pp}}, \pi_{\mathsf{meta}})$

$\underline{a\mathcal{P}lon\mathcal{K}.\mathsf{Verify}(\mathsf{pp} := (n, \_, \_, \mathsf{vk}, \mu_{\mathsf{pp}}, \_), \{\boldsymbol{x}_j\}_{j\in[k]}, \pi):}$

1: let $(\mu_{\mathsf{w}}, \mu_{\mathsf{z}}, \mu_{\mathsf{t}}, \nu_{\mathsf{w}}, \nu_{\mathsf{z}}, \nu_{\overline{\mathsf{z}}}, \nu_{\mathsf{t}}, \nu_{\mathsf{pp}}, \pi_{\mathsf{w}}, \pi_{\mathsf{z}}, \overline{\pi}_{\mathsf{z}}, \pi_{\mathsf{t}}, \pi_{\mathsf{pp}}, \pi_{\mathsf{meta}}) := \pi$

2: $\beta \leftarrow \mathsf{Hash}(\mu_{\mathsf{w}})$; $\gamma \leftarrow \mathsf{Hash}(\beta)$; $\delta \leftarrow \mathsf{Hash}(\gamma)$; $\alpha \leftarrow \mathsf{Hash}(\delta, \mu_{\mathsf{z}})$; $\xi \leftarrow \mathsf{Hash}(\alpha, \mu_{\mathsf{t}})$

3: $\mathsf{v}(, , \boldsymbol{v}, x, \pi) := \Psi.\mathsf{Check}(\mathsf{vk}, , , x, \boldsymbol{v}, \pi)$

4: $b_\mu := \mathsf{v}(\mu_{\mathsf{w}}, \nu_{\mathsf{w}}, \xi, \pi_{\mathsf{w}}) \wedge \mathsf{v}(\mu_{\mathsf{z}}, \nu_{\mathsf{z}}, \xi, \pi_{\mathsf{z}}) \wedge \mathsf{v}(\mu_{\mathsf{z}}, \overline{\nu_{\mathsf{z}}}, \omega\xi, \overline{\pi}_{\mathsf{z}}) \wedge \mathsf{v}(\mu_{\mathsf{t}}, \nu_{\mathsf{t}}, \xi, \pi_{\mathsf{t}}) \wedge \mathsf{v}(\mu_{\mathsf{pp}}, \nu_{\mathsf{pp}}, \xi, \pi_{\mathsf{pp}})$

5: $b_{\mathsf{meta}} \leftarrow \mathsf{Verify}_{\text{PoK}}(\pi_{\mathsf{meta}}, \mathcal{R}_{n,k}(((\alpha, \beta, \gamma, \delta), \xi, (\nu_{\mathsf{w}}, \nu_{\mathsf{z}}, \nu_{\overline{\mathsf{z}}}, \nu_{\mathsf{t}}, \nu_{\mathsf{pp}}), \{\boldsymbol{x}_j\}_{j\in[k]}), \cdot)$

6: **return** $b_\mu \wedge b_{\mathsf{meta}}$

Fig. 2. *aPlonK* proof system, based on multi-polynomial commitment scheme Ψ.

$$\underline{\mathcal{R}_{n,k}((\text{randomness}, \xi, \nu_{\mathsf{w}}, \text{evals}, \{\mathbb{x}_j\}_{j\in[k]}), (\{\mathsf{a}_j, \mathsf{b}_j, \mathsf{c}_j\}_{j\in[k]}, (\text{polys}, e_{\mathsf{pp}})))} :=$$

$$\begin{aligned}
&\text{let } (\alpha, \beta, \gamma, \delta) := \text{randomness}; \ (\nu_{\mathsf{w}}, \nu_{\mathsf{z}}, \nu_{\overline{\mathsf{z}}}, \nu_{\mathsf{t}}, \nu_{\mathsf{pp}}) := \text{evals}\\
&\text{let } (\mathsf{z}, \overline{\mathsf{z}}, \mathsf{t}) := \text{polys}; \ (\mathsf{e}_{\mathsf{q_L}}, \mathsf{e}_{\mathsf{q_R}}, \mathsf{e}_{\mathsf{q_O}}, \mathsf{e}_{\mathsf{q_M}}, \mathsf{e}_{\mathsf{q_C}}, \mathsf{e}_{\mathsf{s_1}}, \mathsf{e}_{\mathsf{s_2}}, \mathsf{e}_{\mathsf{s_3}}) := e_{\mathsf{pp}}\\
&\mathsf{id}_j := \mathsf{e}_{\mathsf{q_L}}\mathsf{a}_j + \mathsf{e}_{\mathsf{q_R}}\mathsf{b}_j + \mathsf{e}_{\mathsf{q_O}}\mathsf{c}_j + \mathsf{e}_{\mathsf{q_M}}\mathsf{a}_j\mathsf{b}_j + \mathsf{e}_{\mathsf{q_C}} + \mathsf{PI}_{\mathbb{x}_j}(\xi) \ \forall j \in [k]\\
&\hat{\mathsf{a}} := \textstyle\sum_{j=1}^{k} \delta^j \mathsf{a}_j; \quad \hat{\mathsf{b}} := \sum_{j=1}^{k} \delta^j \mathsf{b}_j; \quad \hat{\mathsf{c}} := \sum_{j=1}^{k} \delta^j \mathsf{c}_j\\
&\mathsf{perm\text{-}id}_1 := (\hat{\mathsf{a}} + \beta\xi + \gamma)(\hat{\mathsf{b}} + \beta\eta\xi + \gamma)(\hat{\mathsf{c}} + \beta\eta'\xi + \gamma)\mathsf{z}\\
&\qquad\qquad - (\hat{a} + \beta\mathsf{e}_{\mathsf{s_1}} + \gamma)(\hat{b} + \beta\mathsf{e}_{\mathsf{s_2}} + \gamma)(\hat{c} + \beta\mathsf{e}_{\mathsf{s_3}} + \gamma)\overline{\mathsf{z}}\\
&\mathsf{perm\text{-}id}_2 := (\mathsf{z} - 1)\mathsf{L}_{1,n}(\xi)\\
&b_{\mathsf{ids}} := \left(Z_{\mathcal{H}_n}(\xi) \cdot \mathsf{t} = (\textstyle\sum_{j=1}^{k} \alpha^{j-1}\mathsf{id}_j) + \alpha^k \mathsf{perm\text{-}id}_1 + \alpha^{k+1}\mathsf{perm\text{-}id}_2\right)\\
&\text{return } b_{\mathsf{ids}} \wedge \nu_{\mathsf{w}} = \mathsf{Commit\text{-}Evals}((\mathsf{a}_1, \mathsf{b}_1, \mathsf{c}_1, \ldots, \mathsf{a}_k, \mathsf{b}_k, \mathsf{c}_k))\\
&\qquad\qquad \wedge \nu_{\mathsf{z}} = \mathsf{Commit\text{-}Evals}(\mathsf{z}) \wedge \nu_{\overline{\mathsf{z}}} = \mathsf{Commit\text{-}Evals}(\overline{\mathsf{z}})\\
&\qquad\qquad \wedge \nu_{\mathsf{t}} = \mathsf{Commit\text{-}Evals}(\mathsf{t}) \wedge \nu_{\mathsf{pp}} = \mathsf{Commit\text{-}Evals}(\mathsf{e}_{\mathsf{pp}}) \ .
\end{aligned}$$

Fig. 3. Meta-verification relation for aggregating k proofs of n-constraints circuits. η_2 and η_3 are non-quadratic residues over $\mathbb{Z}_p$

a) The Commit-Evals algorithm needs to be modeled in a $\mathcal{P}lon\mathcal{K}$ circuit. There is flexibility for the choice of such algorithm, but modeling any commitment scheme that is binding will require a significant number of constraints.
b) The verifier complexity is $\mathcal{O}(k)$ on scalar operations, given the public inputs $\{\mathbb{x}_j\}_{j\in[k]}$ to the meta-verification circuit.
c) This technique imposes a bound on k, the number of aggregated proofs, since the meta-verification circuit size is linear in k and there is an inherent upper-bound on the size of $\mathcal{P}lon\mathcal{K}$ circuits.

These issues are addressed in the full version of the paper.

5 Implementation and Evaluation

We have implemented the algorithms described in this work and evaluated their performance in a series of benchmarks presented in Sect. 5.1. Our source code is written in OCaml with bindings to C implementations of the heaviest cryptographic functions. We use the BLS12-381 elliptic curve [Bow17] for pairings through bindings to the *blst* library [Sup21]. Our implementation will be publicly available as open-source.

We compare $\mathcal{P}lon\mathcal{K}$ and $a\mathcal{P}lon\mathcal{K}$ for aggregating a batch of k different proofs of a constraint system of n constraints. In the case of $\mathcal{P}lon\mathcal{K}$, we use KZG and implement a naïve aggregation, but which uses the batch verification optimizations applicable to KZG [GWC19]. In the case of $a\mathcal{P}lon\mathcal{K}$, we implement the scheme described in Fig. 2 instantiated with a multi-polynomial commitment scheme constructed from KZG and the IPA argument. Our experimental results from Sect. 5.1 show that the performance and proof size improvements of *aPlonK* are significant even against the optimized version of *PlonK* that we compare it with, which in turn is a lot more performant than the naïve parallel execution of standard *PlonK*.

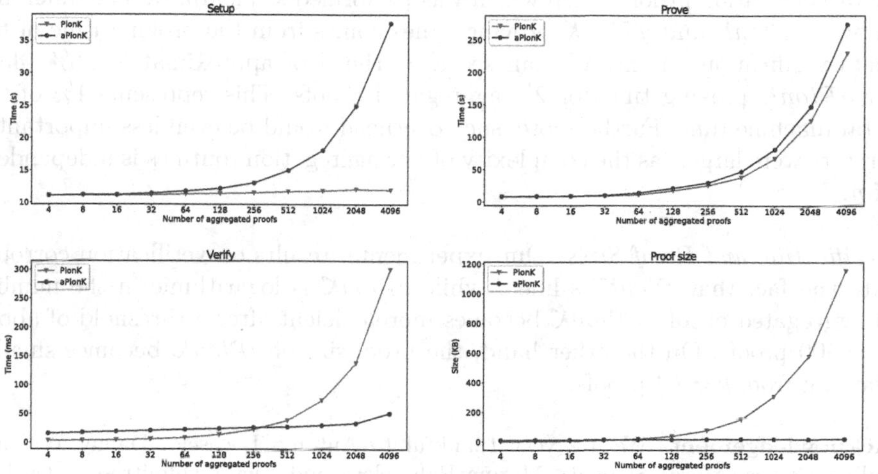

Fig. 4. Times and proof sizes for different number of aggregated proofs of a circuit of 2^{16} constraints.

5.1 Experimental Results

Our experimental results from Fig. 4 include a comparison of the setup, proving and verification times, as well as proof sizes of *PlonK* and *aPlonK*, for different aggregation sizes. All experiments were performed on a 2.9GHz Intel Xeon Platinum 8375C vCPU with 1 TB of RAM and 128 processors.

We use a circuit of $n = 2^{16}$ constraints. Our circuit performs a binary tree computation on the inputs (placed on the leaves, two of them being public), alternating addition and multiplication layers. This guarantees that all selectors $\mathsf{q}_\mathsf{L}, \mathsf{q}_\mathsf{R}, \mathsf{q}_\mathsf{O}, \mathsf{q}_\mathsf{M}, \mathsf{q}_\mathsf{C}$ are dense. Nevertheless, note that the complexity of all algorithms is independent of the actual architecture of the circuit and their performance only depends on the number of constraints n. We choose a rollup-like schedule of public inputs, joined in a chain as described in the previous section.

Setup. The setup of *PlonK* is constant since the circuit of interest always has $n = 2^{16}$ constraints. However, in *aPlonK*, it is linear in k. This is because the size of the meta-verification circuit grows linearly with the number of aggregated proofs. Fortunately, the impact of *aPlonK*'s setup is in the order of seconds for aggregating thousands or proofs. Furthermore, note that the setup performance is not critical, as it is precomputed only once.

Proving. All experiments have used parallelization over all the 128 available cores. When $k \leq 128$ a core is assigned for each proof. After that threshold we can expect a linear growth since each core will need to produce more than one proof. One CPU was also in charge of orchestrating the distribution and computing the meta-verification proof, a step which was performed sequentially. The difference between $\mathcal{P}lon\mathcal{K}$ and $a\mathcal{P}lon\mathcal{K}$ proving times comes from the proving time of the meta-verification circuit. We can see a overhead of approximately 20% (45 s) for $a\mathcal{P}lon\mathcal{K}$ proving time for 2^{12} aggregated proofs. This represents 1% of the total machine time. Furthermore, such overhead would be even less important if circuits were larger, as the complexity of our aggregation routines is independent of n.

Verification and Proof Sizes. Our experimental results on verification corroborate the fact that $\mathcal{P}lon\mathcal{K}$ is linear while $a\mathcal{P}lon\mathcal{K}$ is logarithmic in the number of aggregated proofs. $a\mathcal{P}lon\mathcal{K}$ becomes more efficient after a threshold of about $k = 300$ proofs. On the other hand, the proof size of $a\mathcal{P}lon\mathcal{K}$ becomes smaller starting from $k = 64$ proofs.

Acknowledgement. We are very thankful to Antonio Locascio, Danny Willems, Julien Coolen, Marco Stronati, Marina Polubelova and Victor Dumitrescu, developers and co-authors of our implementation [Nom22], for very fruitful discussions and all their help and feedback. We would also like to thank Mary Maller, for her feedback and clarifications about SnarkPack in the early stages of this project.

References

[BBB+18] Bünz, B., Bootle, J., Boneh, D., Poelstra, A., Wuille, P., Maxwell, G.: Bulletproofs: short proofs for confidential transactions and more. In: 2018 IEEE Symposium on Security and Privacy, pp. 315–334. IEEE Computer Society Press (2018)

[BBHR19] Ben-Sasson, E., Bentov, I., Horesh, Y., Riabzev, M.: Scalable zero knowledge with no trusted setup. In: Boldyreva, A., Micciancio, D. (eds.) CRYPTO 2019, Part III. LNCS, vol. 11694, pp. 701–732. Springer, Cham (2019). https://doi.org/10.1007/978-3-030-26954-8_23

[BCC+16] Bootle, J., Cerulli, A., Chaidos, P., Groth, J., Petit, C.: Efficient zero-knowledge arguments for arithmetic circuits in the discrete log setting. In: Fischlin, M., Coron, J.-S. (eds.) EUROCRYPT 2016, Part II. LNCS, vol. 9666, pp. 327–357. Springer, Heidelberg (2016). https://doi.org/10.1007/978-3-662-49896-5_12

[BCG+13] Ben-Sasson, E., Chiesa, A., Genkin, D., Tromer, E., Virza, M.: SNARKs for C: verifying program executions succinctly and in zero knowledge. In: Canetti, R., Garay, J.A. (eds.) CRYPTO 2013, Part II. LNCS, vol. 8043, pp. 90–108. Springer, Heidelberg (2013). https://doi.org/10.1007/978-3-642-40084-1_6

[BCG+14] Ben-Sasson, E., et al.: Zerocash: decentralized anonymous payments from bitcoin. In: 2014 IEEE Symposium on Security and Privacy, pp. 459–474. IEEE Computer Society Press (2014)

[BCG+17] Bootle, J., Cerulli, A., Ghadafi, E., Groth, J., Hajiabadi, M., Jakobsen, S.K.: Linear-time zero-knowledge proofs for arithmetic circuit satisfiability. In: Takagi, T., Peyrin, T. (eds.) ASIACRYPT 2017, Part III. LNCS, vol. 10626, pp. 336–365. Springer, Cham (2017). https://doi.org/10.1007/978-3-319-70700-6_12

[BCL+21] Bünz, B., Chiesa, A., Lin, W., Mishra, P., Spooner, N.: Proof-carrying data without succinct arguments. In: Malkin, T., Peikert, C. (eds.) CRYPTO 2021, Part I. LNCS, vol. 12825, pp. 681–710. Springer, Cham (2021). https://doi.org/10.1007/978-3-030-84242-0_24

[BCMS20] Bünz, B., Chiesa, A., Mishra, P., Spooner, N.: Proof-carrying data from accumulation schemes. Cryptology ePrint Archive, Report 2020/499 (2020). https://eprint.iacr.org/2020/499

[BFM88] Blum, M., Feldman, P., Micali, S.: Non-interactive zero-knowledge and its applications (extended abstract). In: 20th ACM STOC, pp. 103–112. ACM Press (1988)

[BGH19a] Bowe, S., Grigg, J., Hopwood, D.: Halo: recursive proof composition without a trusted setup. IACR Cryptology ePrint Archive, p. 1021 (2019)

[BGH19b] Bowe, S., Grigg, J., Hopwood, D.: Halo: recursive proof composition without a trusted setup. Cryptology ePrint Archive, Report 2019/1021 (2019). https://eprint.iacr.org/2019/1021

[BMM+21] Bünz, B., Maller, M., Mishra, P., Tyagi, N., Vesely, P.: Proofs for inner pairing products and applications. In: Tibouchi, M., Wang, H. (eds.) ASIACRYPT 2021, Part III. LNCS, vol. 13092, pp. 65–97. Springer, Cham (2021). https://doi.org/10.1007/978-3-030-92078-4_3

[BMRS20] Bonneau, J., Meckler, I., Rao, V., Shapiro, E.: Mina: decentralized cryptocurrency at scale (2020). Whitepaper. https://docs.minaprotocol.com/static/pdf/technicalWhitepaper.pdf

[BMV19] Bünz, B., Maller, M., Vesely, P.: Efficient proofs for pairing-based languages. Cryptology ePrint Archive, Report 2019/1177 (2019). https://eprint.iacr.org/2019/1177

[Bow17] Bowe, S.: BLS12-381: new zk-SNARK elliptic curve construction (2017). ECC Posts. https://electriccoin.co/blog/new-snark-curve/

[CCW19] Chiesa, A., Chua, L., Weidner, M.: On cycles of pairing-friendly elliptic curves. SIAM J. Appl. Algebra Geom. **3**(2), 175–192 (2019)

[COS19] Chiesa, A., Ojha, D., Spooner, N.: Fractal: post-quantum and transparent recursive proofs from holography. Cryptology ePrint Archive, Report 2019/1076 (2019). https://eprint.iacr.org/2019/1076

[DFKP13] Danezis, G., Fournet, C., Kohlweiss, M., Parno, B.: Pinocchio coin: building zerocoin from a succinct pairing-based proof system. In: Proceedings of the First ACM Workshop on Language Support for Privacy-Enhancing Technologies, PETShop 2013, pp. 27–30. Association for Computing Machinery, New York (2013)

[DMP90] De Santis, A., Micali, S., Persiano, G.: Non-interactive zero-knowledge with preprocessing. In: Goldwasser, S. (ed.) CRYPTO 1988. LNCS, vol. 403, pp. 269–282. Springer, New York (1990). https://doi.org/10.1007/0-387-34799-2_21

[DRZ20] Daza, V., Ràfols, C., Zacharakis, A.: Updateable inner product argument with logarithmic verifier and applications. In: Kiayias, A., Kohlweiss, M., Wallden, P., Zikas, V. (eds.) PKC 2020, Part I. LNCS, vol. 12110, pp. 527–557. Springer, Cham (2020). https://doi.org/10.1007/978-3-030-45374-9_18

[FLS90] Feige, U., Lapidot, D., Shamir, A.: Multiple non-interactive zero knowledge proofs based on a single random string (extended abstract). In: 31st FOCS, pp. 308–317. IEEE Computer Society Press (1990)

[GGPR13] Gennaro, R., Gentry, C., Parno, B., Raykova, M.: Quadratic span programs and succinct NIZKs without PCPs. In: Johansson, T., Nguyen, P.Q. (eds.) EUROCRYPT 2013. LNCS, vol. 7881, pp. 626–645. Springer, Heidelberg (2013). https://doi.org/10.1007/978-3-642-38348-9_37

[GMN20] Gailly, N., Maller, M., Nitulescu, A.: Snarkpack: practical snark aggregation. In: Eyal, I., Garay, J. (eds.) FC 2022. LNCS, vol. 13411, pp. 203–229. Springer, Heidelberg (2020). https://doi.org/10.1007/978-3-031-18283-9_10

[GMR85] Goldwasser, S., Micali, S., Rackoff, C.: The knowledge complexity of interactive proof-systems (extended abstract). In: 17th ACM STOC, pp. 291–304. ACM Press (1985)

[Gro16] Groth, J.: On the size of pairing-based non-interactive arguments. In: Fischlin, M., Coron, J.-S. (eds.) EUROCRYPT 2016, Part II. LNCS, vol. 9666, pp. 305–326. Springer, Heidelberg (2016). https://doi.org/10.1007/978-3-662-49896-5_11

[GW19] Gabizon, A., Williamson, Z.J.: The turbo-plonk program syntax for specifying snark programs (2019). https://docs.zkproof.org/pages/standards/accepted-workshop3/proposal-turbo_plonk.pdf

[GWC19] Gabizon, A., Williamson, Z.J., Ciobotaru, O.: PLONK: permutations over lagrange-bases for oecumenical noninteractive arguments of knowledge. Cryptology ePrint Archive, Report 2019/953 (2019). https://eprint.iacr.org/2019/953

[GYB21] Goes, C., Yin, A.S., Brink, A.: Anoma: undefining money: a protocol for private, asset-agnostic digital cash and n-party bartering (2021). https://anoma.network/papers/whitepaper.pdf

[HBHW] Hopwood, D., Bowe, S., Hornby, T., Wilcox, N.: Zcash protocol specifiation. https://zips.z.cash/protocol/protocol.pdf

[KST21] Kothapalli, A., Setty, S., Tzialla, I.: Nova: recursive zero-knowledge arguments from folding schemes. Cryptology ePrint Archive, Report 2021/370 (2021). https://eprint.iacr.org/2021/370

[KZG10] Kate, A., Zaverucha, G.M., Goldberg, I.: Constant-size commitments to polynomials and their applications. In: Abe, M. (ed.) ASIACRYPT 2010. LNCS, vol. 6477, pp. 177–194. Springer, Heidelberg (2010). https://doi.org/10.1007/978-3-642-17373-8_11

[LMR19] Lai, R.W.F., Malavolta, G., Ronge, V.: Succinct arguments for bilinear group arithmetic: practical structure-preserving cryptography. In: Cavallaro, L., Kinder, J., Wang, X.F., Katz, J. (eds.) ACM CCS 2019, pp. 2057–2074. ACM Press (2019)

[MBKM19] Maller, M., Bowe, S., Kohlweiss, M., Meiklejohn, S.: Sonic: zero-knowledge SNARKs from linear-size universal and updatable structured reference strings. In: Cavallaro, L., Kinder, J., Wang, X.F., Katz, J. (eds.) ACM CCS 2019, pp. 2111–2128. ACM Press (2019)

[MKF21] Maharramov, T., Khovratovich, D., Francioni, E.: The dusk network whitepaper (2021). Whitepaper. https://dusk.network/uploads/The_Dusk_Network_Whitepaper_v3_0_0.pdf

[Nom22] Nomadic Labs' Cryptography Team. aPlonK, a library for zero-knowledge proofs and validity rollups (2022). https://gitlab.com/nomadic-labs/privacy-team/

[Ove22] Overeality Labs. Infrastructure for web3 interoperability (2022). https://overeality.io/home

[PFM+22] Pearson, L., Fitzgerald, J., Masip, H., Bellés-Muñoz, M., Muñoz-Tapia, J.L.: Plonkup: reconciling plonk with plookup. Cryptology ePrint Archive, Report 2022/086 (2022). https://ia.cr/2022/086

[PHGR13] Parno, B., Howell, J., Gentry, C., Raykova, M.: Pinocchio: nearly practical verifiable computation. In: 2013 IEEE Symposium on Security and Privacy, pp. 238–252. IEEE Computer Society Press (2013)

[Sta21] StarkWare. ethstark documentation. Cryptology ePrint Archive, Paper 2021/582 (2021). https://eprint.iacr.org/2021/582

[Sup21] Supranational. BLST, a BLS12-381 signature library focused on performance and security (2021). https://github.com/supranational/blst/tree/757aa00a90c03779f70d0ddab6bc84b40861bb4b

[Val08] Valiant, P.: Incrementally verifiable computation or proofs of knowledge imply time/space efficiency. In: Canetti, R. (ed.) TCC 2008. LNCS, vol. 4948, pp. 1–18. Springer, Heidelberg (2008). https://doi.org/10.1007/978-3-540-78524-8_1

[Wil18] Williamson, Z.J.: Aztec network (white paper) (2018). Whitepaper. https://github.com/AztecProtocol/AZTEC/blob/master/AZTEC.pdf

[ZXZS20] Zhang, J., Xie, T., Zhang, Y., Song, D.: Transparent polynomial delegation and its applications to zero knowledge proof. In: 2020 IEEE Symposium on Security and Privacy, SP 2020, San Francisco, CA, USA, 18–21 May 2020, pp. 859–876. IEEE (2020)

TENET: Sublogarithmic Proof and Sublinear Verifier Inner Product Argument without a Trusted Setup

Hyeonbum Lee and Jae Hong Seo(✉)

Department of Mathematics and Research Institute for Natural Sciences, Hanyang University, Seoul 04763, Republic of Korea
{leehb3706,jaehongseo}@hanyang.ac.kr

Abstract. We propose a new inner product argument (IPA), called TENET, which features sublogarithmic proof size and sublinear verifier without a trusted setup. IPA is a core primitive for various advanced proof systems including range proofs, circuit satisfiability, and polynomial commitment, particularly where a trusted setup is hard to apply. At ASIACRYPT 2022, Kim, Lee, and Seo showed that pairings can be utilized to exceed the complexity barrier of the previous discrete logarithm-based IPA without a trusted setup. More precisely, they proposed two pairing-based IPAs, one with sublogarithmic proof size and the other one with sublinear verifier cost, but they left achieving both complexities simultaneously as an open problem. We investigate the obstacles for this open problem and then provide our solution TENET, which achieves both sublogarithmic proof size and sublinear verifier. We prove the soundness of TENET under the discrete logarithm assumption and double pairing assumption.

Keywords: Inner product argument · Transparent setup · Zero knowledge proof

1 Introduction

An argument system is a protocol between two parties, the prover and the verifier, such that the prover can convince the verifier that a statement is true [16]. One of the most useful argument systems is an inner product argument (IPA), an argument for the inner product relation of two committed vectors. Bootle, Cerulli, Chaidos, Groth, and Petit [5] proposed the first IPA with logarithmic proof size under the discrete logarithm assumption, which is a multi-round extension of constant-round discrete logarithm based sublinear argument systems [17,24,25] for linear algebraic relations including inner product. Subsequently, Bünz, Bootle, Boneh, Poelstra, Wuille, and Maxwell [8] and Chung, Han, Ju, Kim, and Seo [12] further improved communication costs and showed IPA's efficacy by applying to prove range and arithmetic circuit relations.

J. Shikata and H. Kuzuno (Eds.): IWSEC 2023, LNCS 14128, pp. 214–234, 2023.
https://doi.org/10.1007/978-3-031-41326-1_12

Kim, Lee, and Seo [20] proposed two pairing-based IPAs without a trusted setup, Protocol2 and Protocol3. Protocol2 and Protocol3 provide sublogarithmic proof size and sublinear verifier costs, respectively. However, they do not achieve both complexity simultaneously and leave it as an open problem.

We focus on generalization of pairing-based IPA without a trusted setup. More concretely, we aim to combine two arguments, Protocol2 and Protocol3, to achieve sublogarithmic proof size and sublinear verifier simultaneously.

1.1 Our Results

Generalization of IPA Without a Trusted Setup. We propose generalization of pairing-based IPA without a trusted setup. Specifically, we focus on a combination of two ideas of pairing-based IPAs, Protocol2 and Protocol3. One of the core ideas of Protocol2 is *commit-and-prove* for relation of group elements, which are messages of the prover. In this phase, pairing-based group commitment scheme [1] is used to commit prover's messages. Meanwhile, the prover's message in Protocol3 belongs to the target group. To combine two schemes, the prover should make commitments of his messages that are not put to pairing-based group commitment schemes.
Structure of Prover's Message: The prover's message consists of multiple target groups of the form $v = \prod_{i,j} e(g[i], H[j])^{a[i,j]}$, where $\boldsymbol{H}$ is public. From the bilinear structure, the message construction can be viewed as $v = \prod_i e(\boldsymbol{g}^{\boldsymbol{a}[j]}, H[j])$. Owing to this structure, we substitute the prover's message v with the source group elements $\boldsymbol{g}^{\boldsymbol{a}[j]}$. After substitution, we apply pairing-based group commitments to $\boldsymbol{g}^{\boldsymbol{a}[j]}$ for a *commit-and-prove* approach.
Optimization Technique for Sublogarithmic Size IPA. We introduce optimization techniques for sublogarithmic size IPAs, specifically Protocol2 and our new IPA called TENET. These optimizations significantly impact the size of the common reference string (CRS), proof size, and verifier cost.

In these optimizations, the prover generates several group vectors denoted as $\boldsymbol{v} \in \mathbb{G}_1^{2d(2d-1)}$, where d is a dividing factor used for reduction. The prover then sends commitments to each group vector along with a knowledge proof for them. The proof size and verifier cost depend on the size of the group vectors, which is originally $O(d^2)$. However, we propose using compressed vectors with a length of $O(d)$, which are sufficient to ensure soundness. This optimization reduces the required size and verifier cost from quadratic to linear in terms of d.
TENET: Sublogarithmic Proof Size and Sublinear Verifier IPA Under DL and DPair. After the generalization and optimization, we analyze the arguments and then find appropriate parameters to achieve both sublogarithm proof size and sublinear verifier cost. Certainly, we prove security of TENET with perfect completeness and computational witness extended emulation under discrete logarithm (DL) and double pairing (DPair) assumption. From our IPA TENET, one can construct sublogarithm proof size and sublinear verifiable polynomial commitment schemes, which can be used on polynomial IOP systems [9] such as Sonic [23], Plonk [15], and Marlin [11] to get efficiency without a trusted setup.

Table 1. Comparison Table of Inner Product Arguments from Discrete Logarithms

	Comm.	$\mathcal{P}$'s cost	$\mathcal{V}$'s cost	Assumption	Trusted Setup
Bootle et al. [5]	$O(\log N)$	$O(N)$	$O(N)$	DL	No
Bünz et al. [8]	$O(\log N)$	$O(N)$	$O(N)$	DL	No
Chung et al. [12]	$O(\log N)$	$O(N)$	$O(N)$	DL	No
Daza et al. [13]	$O(\log N)$	$O(N)$	$O(\log N)$	DL, DPair	Yes
Zhou et al. [27]	$O(\log N)$	$O(N)$	$O(\log N)$	DL, DPair	Yes
Protocol2 [20]	$O(\sqrt{\log N})$	$O(N2^{\sqrt{\log N}})$	$O(N)$	DL, DPair	No
Protocol3 [20]	$O(\log N)$	$O(N)$	$O(\sqrt{N})$	DL	No
Protocol4 [20]	$O(\log N)$	$O(N)$	$O(\sqrt{N}\log N)$	DL	No
TENET(Ours)	$O(\sqrt{\log N})$	$O(N2^{\sqrt{\log N}})$	$O(N/2^{\sqrt{\log N}})$	DL, DPair	No

N: length of witness vectors, DL: discrete logarithm assumption, DPair: double pairing assumption

1.2 Related Work

Inner Product Argument. Inner product arguments are used as building blocks for range proof and zero knowledge proof, which can be used in numerous applications such as verifiable computation, confidential transactions, and decentralized identification.

There are many variants of IPAs [3,9,10,12,13,20,27], which are based on inner product reduction. In [12], the zero knowledge weighted IPA was proposed and used to construct a variant of [8], with a shorter proof size. In [13,27], the structured common reference string and bilinear maps are used to achieve both logarithmic communication and verification. In [20], three IPAs without a trusted setup are proposed: Protocol2 with sublogarithmic proof size, Protocol3 with sublinear verifier, and Protocol4 with sublinear verifier. The difference between Protocol3 and Protocol4 is reliance on pairing-based elliptic curves. We provide a comparison among various IPAs in Table 1.

Zero Knowledge Argument and Polynomial Commitment Schemes. Bootle et al. [5] first proposed the logarithmic size ZK argument for circuit satisfiability without a trusted setup. To construct the ZK argument, they applied their IPA, which provides a logarithm proof size. The core idea to achieve logarithm size is to construct an efficient reduction protocol that can run recursively. This idea is widely used to construct ZK arguments without a trusted setup [6,8,9,22,26].

Kate, Zaverucha, and Goldberg [19] first introduced the polynomial commitment scheme (PCS), which allows the prover to claim the polynomial evaluation at a point without opening the polynomial itself. In addition, they constructed a constant size PCS, called KZG PCS. KZG PCS is the core building block of ZK arguments with a constant proof size [11,15,18,23]. However, the arguments require a trusted setup.

Bünz, Fisch, and Szepieniec [9] proposed PCS without a trusted setup, called DARK, and they introduced the paradigm of construction ZK argument, combining a polynomial interactive oracle proof system [4] and PCS. From their paradigm, they constructed logarithmic proof size and verifiable ZK argument without a trusted setup by replacing KZG PCS with DARK. In their paradigm, the complexity and cryptographic properties of ZK arguments are inherited from those of PCS.

IPA can be converted to a PCS scheme because polynomial evaluations are a kind of inner product relation; thus, some recent works [2,10,22] have focused on efficient IPA to construct efficient PCS and ZK arguments.

2 Preliminary

2.1 Definitions

We first define notations used in the paper. Some notations are inspired by [20]. $[m]$ denotes a set of integers from 1 to m, $\{1, \cdots, m\}$. Specifically, we define two index sets I_d and J_d. I_d is the set of continuous odd integers from $-2d+1$ to $2d-1$, $I_d = \{\pm 1, \pm 3, \cdots, \pm(2d-1)\}$. And J_d is the set of continuous even integers excluding 0 from $-4d+2$ to $4d-2$, $J_d = \{\pm 2, \pm 4, \cdots, \pm(4d-2)\}$. Note that J_d consists of all possible differences between two distinct elements of I_d. We define $\mathcal{G}$ as an asymmetric bilinear group generator. $\mathcal{G}$ takes the security parameter λ and outputs $(p, g, G, \mathbb{G}_1, \mathbb{G}_2, \mathbb{G}_t, e)$, where $\mathbb{G}_1, \mathbb{G}_2$, and $\mathbb{G}_t$ are distinct groups of prime order p of length λ, g and G are generators of $\mathbb{G}_1$ and $\mathbb{G}_2$, respectively; and $e : \mathbb{G}_1 \times \mathbb{G}_2 \to \mathbb{G}_t$ is a non-degenerate bilinear map. We use bold font to represent vectors in $\mathbb{Z}_p^m$ or $\mathbb{G}^m$. For a vector $\boldsymbol{a} \in \mathbb{Z}_p^m$, we use subscript index $i \in I_d$ to denote $2d$-separation of $\boldsymbol{a}$. Starting from 1 for the first upper subvector subscript, following the order: $\{1, -1, 3, -3, \ldots, 2d-1, -2d+1\}$, small absolute value is in front of a large one, and positive is in front of negative, for lower subvector subscript. We denote $\boldsymbol{a}_1 \parallel \boldsymbol{a}_{-1}$ for sticking two vectors $\boldsymbol{a}_1$ and $\boldsymbol{a}_{-1}$, and the notation $\parallel$ can be used when sticking several vectors sequentially. To represent the i-th element of the vector $\boldsymbol{a}$, we use a_i(non-bold style letter with subscript i); that is $\boldsymbol{a} = (a_1, a_2, \ldots, a_m)$. Now, we define notation for some vector operations.

Component-Wise Multiplication: For $\boldsymbol{g}, \boldsymbol{h} \in \mathbb{G}^m$, we denote $\boldsymbol{g} \circ \boldsymbol{h} = (g_1 h_1, \ldots, g_m h_m)$. In general, we denote $\bigcirc_{i \in [I]} \boldsymbol{g}_i = (\prod_{i \in [I]} g_{i,1}, \cdots, \prod_{i \in [I]} g_{i,m})$ for several vectors $\boldsymbol{g}_i = (g_{i,1}, \cdots, g_{i,m}) \in \mathbb{G}^m$ for $i \in I$.
Inner Product: For $\boldsymbol{a}, \boldsymbol{b} \in \mathbb{Z}_p^m$, we denote $\langle \boldsymbol{a}, \boldsymbol{b} \rangle = \sum_{i \in [m]} a_i b_i$.
Multi-Exponentiation: For $\boldsymbol{x} \in \mathbb{Z}_p^m$ and $\boldsymbol{g} \in \mathbb{G}^m$, we denote $\boldsymbol{g}^{\boldsymbol{x}} = \prod_{i \in [m]} g_i^{x_i}$.
Inner Pairing Product: For $\boldsymbol{g} \in \mathbb{G}_1^m$ and $\boldsymbol{H} \in \mathbb{G}_2^m$, we denote $\boldsymbol{E}(\boldsymbol{g}, \boldsymbol{H}) = \prod_{i \in [m]} e(g_i, H_i)$.

Parallel Multi-exponentiations. We denote two types of parallel multi-exponentiation. One is parallel multi-exponentiation of common base elements, and the other is parallel multi-exponentiation to common vectors.

1. Parallel multi-exponentiation of common base elements: Let $\mathbf{a} \in \mathbb{Z}_p^{m\times n}$ be a matrix and $\boldsymbol{g} \in \mathbb{G}^m$ be group elements. We denote $\overrightarrow{\boldsymbol{g}^{\boldsymbol{a}}} := (\boldsymbol{g}^{\boldsymbol{a}_1}, \ldots, \boldsymbol{g}^{\boldsymbol{a}_n})$, where $\boldsymbol{a}_i$ is the i-th column vector of matrix $\boldsymbol{a}$.
2. Parallel multi-exponentiation to common vectors: Let $\mathbf{a} \in \mathbb{Z}_p^n$ be a vector and $\boldsymbol{g} \in \mathbb{G}^{m\times n}$ be a group matrix. We denote $\widehat{\boldsymbol{g}^{\boldsymbol{a}}} := (\boldsymbol{g}_1^{\boldsymbol{a}}, \ldots, \boldsymbol{g}_m^{\boldsymbol{a}})$, where $\boldsymbol{g}_i$ is the i-th row group vector of group matrix $\boldsymbol{g}$.

Outer-Pairing Product. We define an outer pairing product, which is a way of generating a target group matrix from source group vectors. For $\boldsymbol{g} \in \mathbb{G}_1^m$ and $\boldsymbol{H} \in \mathbb{G}_2^n$, we denote

$$\boldsymbol{g} \otimes \boldsymbol{H} = \begin{bmatrix} e(g_1, H_1) & \cdots & e(g_1, H_n) \\ \vdots & \ddots & \vdots \\ e(g_m, H_n) & \cdots & e(g_m, H_n) \end{bmatrix} \in \mathbb{G}_t^{m\times n}$$

Argument System for Relation $\mathcal{R}$. A set $\mathcal{R}$ is a polynomial-time verifiable relation consisting of common reference string (CRS), statement, and witness, denoted by σ, x, and w respectively. From the relation, we define language $\mathcal{L}_\sigma = \{ x \mid \exists\, w \text{ such that } (\sigma, x, w) \in \mathcal{R} \}$. We call the statement x true if the statement belongs to the language $\mathcal{L}_\sigma$, and we call w a witness of the statement x under the relation $\mathcal{R}$ if (σ, x, w) belongs to $\mathcal{R}$. For simplicity, we sometimes omit CRS σ and simply write $(x, w) \in \mathcal{R}$.

An interactive argument system for relation $\mathcal{R}$ consists of three probabilistic polynomial-time algorithms (PPTs), key generation algorithms, prover algorithms, verifier algorithms $(\mathcal{K}, \mathcal{P}, \mathcal{V})$. The $\mathcal{K}$ algorithm takes the security parameter λ and outputs CRS, which is the input of $\mathcal{P}$ and $\mathcal{V}$. $\mathcal{P}$ and $\mathcal{V}$ generate transcript interactively, denoted by $tr \leftarrow \langle \mathcal{P}(\sigma, x, w), \mathcal{V}(\sigma, x)\rangle$. At the end of the transcript, $\mathcal{V}$ outputs a bit, 0 or 1, which means reject or accept, respectively. The purpose of $\mathcal{P}$ is to obtain acceptance from $\mathcal{V}$, and the purpose of $\mathcal{V}$ is to check the statement x belongs to $\mathcal{L}_\sigma$.

Argument of Knowledge. An argument of knowledge (AoK) is a special case of an argument system. Informally, the purpose of $\mathcal{V}$ is to check the knowledge of the witness w of statement x, $(x, w) \in \mathcal{R}$, which guarantees $x \in \mathcal{L}_\sigma$. AoK should satisfy the properties of completeness and witness extractability.

Definition 1 (Perfect Completeness). *Let $(\mathcal{K}, \mathcal{P}, \mathcal{V})$ be an argument system and $\mathcal{R}$ be a polynomial-time verifiable relation. We say that the argument system $(\mathcal{K}, \mathcal{P}, \mathcal{V})$ for the relation $\mathcal{R}$ has* ***perfect completeness*** *if, the following probability equation holds for all $\sigma \leftarrow \mathcal{K}(1^\lambda)$:*

$$\Pr_{(\sigma,x,w)\in\mathcal{R}} \left[\langle \mathcal{P}(\sigma, x, w), \mathcal{V}(\sigma, x)\rangle = 1 \right] = 1.$$

Definition 2 (Computational Witness Extended Emulation). *Let $(\mathcal{K}, \mathcal{P}, \mathcal{V})$ be an argument system and $\mathcal{R}$ be a polynomial-time verifiable relation. We say that the argument $(\mathcal{P}, \mathcal{V})$ has* ***witness-extended emulation*** *if,* *for every deterministic polynomial prover $\mathcal{P}^*$, which may not follow $\mathcal{P}$, there exists a polynomial time emulator $\mathcal{E}$ for which the following inequality holds:*

$$\Pr\left[(\sigma, x, w) \in \mathcal{R} \;\middle|\; \begin{array}{l} \sigma \leftarrow \mathcal{K}(1^\lambda); \\ (tr, w) \leftarrow \mathcal{E}^{\langle \mathcal{P}^*(\sigma,x,s), \mathcal{V}(\sigma,x)\rangle}(\sigma, x) \\ tr \text{ is accepting} \end{array}\right] > 1 - negl(\lambda),$$

where $negl(\lambda)$ is a negligible function in λ. Emulator $\mathcal{E}$ can access the oracle $\langle \mathcal{P}^*(\sigma, x, s), \mathcal{V}(\sigma, x)\rangle$, which outputs the transcript between $\mathcal{P}^*$ and $\mathcal{V}$. $\mathcal{E}$ permits to rewind $\mathcal{P}^*$ at a specific round and rerun $\mathcal{V}$ using fresh randomness. s can be considered as the state of $\mathcal{P}^*$, which includes randomness.

Definition 3. *We say that the argument system $(\mathcal{K}, \mathcal{P}, \mathcal{V})$ is an* argument of knowledge *for relation $\mathcal{R}$ if the argument has (perfect) completeness and (computational) witness-extended emulation.*

Trusted Setup. In some arguments, the CRS generator algorithm takes a trapdoor that should not be revealed to anyone, including the prover and verifier. In this case, CRS generation should be run by a trusted third party. The setting requiring trusted party is called a trusted setup.

Non-interactive Argument in the Random Oracle Model. We call an interactive argument a public coin if $\mathcal{V}$ outputs without decision bits constituting a uniformly random message without dependency of $\mathcal{P}$'s messages. Fiat and Shamir [14] proposed a method to transform any public coin interactive argument into a non-interactive one using the random oracle model. The approach involves replacing $\mathcal{V}$'s random messages with random oracle outputs, where the inputs are derived from previous messages at that point.

Assumptions. Let $\mathcal{G}$ be a group generator. $\mathcal{G}$ takes security parameters λ and then outputs $\mathbb{G}$, describing a group of order p.

Definition 4 Discrete Logarithm Relation Assumption [7]**).** *We say that $\mathbb{G}$ satisfies the discrete logarithm relation (DLR) assumption*[1] *if, for all non-uniform polynomial-time adversaries $\mathcal{A}$, the following inequality holds:*

$$\Pr[\boldsymbol{a} \neq \boldsymbol{0} \wedge \boldsymbol{g}^{\boldsymbol{a}} = 1_{\mathbb{G}} | (p, g, \mathbb{G}) \leftarrow \mathcal{G}(1^\lambda); \boldsymbol{g} \xleftarrow{\$} \mathbb{G}^n; \boldsymbol{a} \leftarrow \mathcal{A}(\boldsymbol{g}, p, g, \mathbb{G})] < negl(\lambda)$$

where $negl(\lambda)$ is a negligible function in λ.

Definition 5 (q-Pairing Assumption [1]**).** *We say that the asymmetric bilinear group generator $\mathcal{G}_b$ satisfies the q-pairing assumption if, for all non-uniform polynomial-time adversaries $\mathcal{A}$, the following inequality holds.*

$$\Pr\left[\boldsymbol{E}(\boldsymbol{g}, \boldsymbol{H}) = 1_{\mathbb{G}_t} \wedge \boldsymbol{g} \neq 1_{\mathbb{G}_1} \;\middle|\; \begin{array}{c} (p, g, H, \mathbb{G}_1, \mathbb{G}_2, \mathbb{G}_t, e) \leftarrow \mathcal{G}(1^\lambda); \\ \boldsymbol{H} \xleftarrow{\$} \mathbb{G}_2^q; \\ \boldsymbol{g} \leftarrow \mathcal{A}(\boldsymbol{H}, (p, g, H, \mathbb{G}_1, \mathbb{G}_2, \mathbb{G}_t, e)) \end{array}\right] < negl(\lambda)$$

[1] To the best of our knowledge, [7] is the oldest reference introducing DLR. Although the DLR is widely used due to the equivalence to the DL, we could not find the original reference that firstly proved the equivalence. Instead, we provide a recent reference [20] for the proof of the equivalence between the DLR and the DL.

The discrete logarithm relation (DLR) assumption is equivalent to the DL assumption. Similarly, the q-pairing assumption is equivalent to the 2-pairing assumption, DPair assumption.

2.2 Inner Product Argument

An IPA is an argument of knowledge for the inner product relation between two vectors [5], which can be written as $\mathcal{R}_{\mathsf{IPA}}$:

$$\mathcal{R}_{\mathsf{IPA}} = \{(\boldsymbol{g}, \boldsymbol{h} \in \mathbb{G}^N, A, B \in \mathbb{G}, c \in \mathbb{Z}_p; \boldsymbol{a}, \boldsymbol{b} \in \mathbb{Z}_p^N) : A = \boldsymbol{g}^{\boldsymbol{a}} \wedge B = \boldsymbol{h}^{\boldsymbol{b}} \wedge c = \langle \boldsymbol{a}, \boldsymbol{b} \rangle\}$$

Bünz et al. [8] proposed an improved IPA by relation reduction. To achieve low communication cost, they provided a reduction technique from relation $\mathcal{R}_{\mathsf{IPA}}$ to the following relation $\mathcal{R}_{\mathsf{BPIP}}$ using Pedersen commitment of the inner product value c:

$$\mathcal{R}_{\mathsf{BPIP}} = \{(\boldsymbol{g}, \boldsymbol{h} \in \mathbb{G}^N, u, P \in \mathbb{G}; \boldsymbol{a}, \boldsymbol{b} \in \mathbb{Z}_p^N) : P = \boldsymbol{g}^{\boldsymbol{a}} \boldsymbol{h}^{\boldsymbol{b}} u^{\langle \boldsymbol{a}, \boldsymbol{b} \rangle}\}$$

After the reduction, they constructed an argument of knowledge for $\mathcal{R}_{\mathsf{BPIP}}$ using recursive reduction. The improved IPA, denoted by $\mathsf{BP}_{\mathsf{IP}}$, provides the $O(\log N)$ proof size and $O(N)$ prover and verifier cost.

Lai, Malavolta, and Ronge [21] proposed an inner pairing product argument, and Bünz, Maller, Mishra, and Vesely [10] optimized it. We denote the inner pairing product argument as IPP, which is an argument for the below relation $\mathcal{R}_{\mathsf{IPP}}$. The core structure of IPP is similar to that of $\mathsf{BP}_{\mathsf{IP}}$, and its complexity is $O(\log N)$ size with the $O(N)$ prover and verifier cost.

$$\mathcal{R}_{\mathsf{IPP}} = \{(\boldsymbol{h} \in \mathbb{G}_2^N, P \in \mathbb{G}_t; \mathbf{g} \in \mathbb{G}_1^N) : P = \boldsymbol{E}(\boldsymbol{g}, \boldsymbol{h})\}$$

Kim, Lee, and Seo [20] proposed two pairing-based IPAs: sublogarithmic proof size $\mathsf{Protocol2}$ and sublinear verifier $\mathsf{Protocol3}$. Before describing our protocols, we briefly explain two schemes: $\mathsf{Protocol2}$ and $\mathsf{Protocol3}$.

Protocol2: Sublogarithm Communication IPA. Protocol2 is an AoK for the relation $\mathcal{R}_{\mathsf{BPIP}}$. The construction of Protocol2 consists of three steps: *round reducing, commit-and-prove, aggregating technique*. First, they construct refined reduction, which induces decreasing total rounds. However, there is no benefit in terms of communication costs because refined reduction results in high communication costs per round. To reduce communication cost, they apply the *commit-and-prove* approach, which commits the prover's message per round and then proves the knowledge of the prover's message. This approach reduces total communication cost, but logarithmic complexity remains. To further reduce communication cost, they apply the *aggregating technique*, which delays the proof for each round until the last time the prover generates proof for the previous claims. To achieve sublogarithm communication, they proposed augmented aggregating multi-exponentiation argument, aAggMEA.

Protocol3: Sublinear Verifier IPA. Protocol3 is an inner product argument with a sublinear verifier for the below relation $\mathcal{R}_{\mathsf{PT3}}$. The reduction process is equivalent to $\mathsf{BP_{IP}}$, but one difference is the common reference string. The CRS of Protocol3 is $\boldsymbol{g}, \boldsymbol{h}$, and $\boldsymbol{H}$, whose length is the square root of the witness length. The CRS structure makes the verifier avoid linear computation.

$$\mathcal{R}_{\mathsf{PT3}} = \left\{ \begin{array}{c} (\boldsymbol{g}, \boldsymbol{h} \in \mathbb{G}_1^m, \boldsymbol{H} \in \mathbb{G}_2^n, u, P \in \mathbb{G}_t; \boldsymbol{a}, \boldsymbol{b} \in \mathbb{Z}_p^{m\times n}) : \\ P = (\boldsymbol{g} \otimes \boldsymbol{H})^{\boldsymbol{a}} \cdot (\boldsymbol{h} \otimes \boldsymbol{H})^{\boldsymbol{b}} \cdot u^{\langle \boldsymbol{a}, \boldsymbol{b} \rangle} \end{array} \right\}$$

RRPT3($\boldsymbol{g}, \boldsymbol{h} \in \mathbb{G}_1^m, \boldsymbol{H} \in \mathbb{G}_2^n, u, P \in \mathbb{G}_t; \boldsymbol{a}, \boldsymbol{b} \in \mathbb{Z}_p^{m\times n}$)

If $m = 1$

$\boxed{\mathcal{P} \,\&\, \mathcal{V}}$: Run $\mathsf{BP_{IP}}(g \otimes \boldsymbol{H}, h \otimes \boldsymbol{H}, u, P; \boldsymbol{a}, \boldsymbol{b})$

Else ($m > 1$): Let $m' = \frac{m}{2d}$. Parse $\boldsymbol{a}, \boldsymbol{b}, \boldsymbol{g}$, and $\boldsymbol{h}$ to

$$\boldsymbol{a} = [\boldsymbol{a}_1 \parallel \boldsymbol{a}_{-1} \parallel \cdots \parallel \boldsymbol{a}_{2d-1} \parallel \boldsymbol{a}_{-2d+1}], \quad \boldsymbol{g} = \boldsymbol{g}_1 \parallel \boldsymbol{g}_{-1} \parallel \cdots \parallel \boldsymbol{g}_{2d-1} \parallel \boldsymbol{g}_{-2d+1},$$
$$\boldsymbol{b} = [\boldsymbol{b}_1 \parallel \boldsymbol{b}_{-1} \parallel \cdots \parallel \boldsymbol{b}_{2d-1} \parallel \boldsymbol{b}_{-2d+1}], \quad \boldsymbol{h} = \boldsymbol{h}_1 \parallel \boldsymbol{h}_{-1} \parallel \cdots \parallel \boldsymbol{h}_{2d-1} \parallel \boldsymbol{h}_{-2d+1}$$

$\boxed{\mathcal{P}}$: Calculate $v[i, j]$ for all distinct $i, j \in I_n$, such that

$$v[i, j] = (\boldsymbol{g}_i \otimes \boldsymbol{H})^{\boldsymbol{a}_j} \cdot (\boldsymbol{h}_j \otimes \boldsymbol{H})^{\boldsymbol{b}_i} \cdot u^{\langle \boldsymbol{a}_j, \boldsymbol{b}_i \rangle} \in \mathbb{G}_t$$

and concatenate $v[i, j]$ to $\boldsymbol{v} \in \mathbb{G}_t^{2d(2d-1)}$ in lexicographic order

$\boxed{\mathcal{P} \rightarrow \mathcal{V}}$: $\boldsymbol{v}$

$\boxed{\mathcal{V} \rightarrow \mathcal{P}}$: $x \xleftarrow{\$} \mathbb{Z}_p^*$

$\boxed{\mathcal{P} \,\&\, \mathcal{V}}$: Set $\boldsymbol{x} = (x^{j-i}) \in \mathbb{Z}_p^{2d(2d-1)}$ in lexicographic order. Then, computes

$$\boldsymbol{g}' = \bigcirc_{i \in I_d} \boldsymbol{g}_i^{x^{-i}}, \quad \boldsymbol{h}' = \bigcirc_{i \in I_d} \boldsymbol{h}_i^{x^i}, \quad P' = P \cdot \boldsymbol{v}^{\boldsymbol{x}}$$

$\boxed{\mathcal{P}}$: Compute

$$\boldsymbol{a}' = \sum_{i \in I_n} \boldsymbol{a}_i x^i \in \mathbb{Z}_p^{m' \times n}, \quad \boldsymbol{b}' = \sum_{i \in I_n} \boldsymbol{b}_i x^{-i} \in \mathbb{Z}_p^{m' \times n}$$

$\boxed{\mathcal{P} \,\&\, \mathcal{V}}$: Run RRPT3($\boldsymbol{g}', \boldsymbol{h}', \boldsymbol{H}, u, P'; \boldsymbol{a}', \boldsymbol{b}'$).

Fig. 1. RRPT3: Round Reduced Protocol3

3 Main Results

3.1 Motivation and Reducing Round

This paper mainly aims to construct a pairing-based inner product argument that provides a sublogarithmic proof size and sublinear verifier cost simultaneously. To construct it, we focus on combining two protocols: Protocol2 and Protocol3. Our approach is to apply the idea of Protocol2 on Protocol3 for the relation $\mathcal{R}_{\mathsf{PT3}}$. Rather than half reduction, it is $2d$ times smaller per round.

The following protocol RRPT3 in Fig. 1 is a round reduced version of Protocol3, applying a *round-reducing* technique.

The next step is *commit-and-prove*. To reduce communication cost per round, we substitute sending whole commitment $\boldsymbol{v}$ with sending commitment to $\boldsymbol{v}$ with proof for $\boldsymbol{v}$. In the case of Protocol2, $2d(2d-1)$ group elements are committed by the pairing-based commitment scheme by Abe et. al. [1] because they belong to the source group $\mathbb{G}_1$. Meanwhile, it is difficult to apply pairing-based group commitments directly on RRPT3 because group elements $\boldsymbol{v}$ belong to the target group $\mathbb{G}_t$. To the best of our knowledge, there are no homomorphic commitment schemes for target group elements of bilinear groups.

Key Idea: Decompose Commitment of $\boldsymbol{a}$ and $\boldsymbol{b}$. To detour the obstacle, we observe the bilinear structure of the following product:

$$(\boldsymbol{g} \otimes \boldsymbol{H})^{\boldsymbol{a}} \cdot (\boldsymbol{h} \otimes \boldsymbol{H})^{\boldsymbol{b}} = \boldsymbol{E}(\overrightarrow{\boldsymbol{g}^{\boldsymbol{a}}} \circ \overrightarrow{\boldsymbol{h}^{\boldsymbol{b}}}, \boldsymbol{H})$$

From the bilinear property, we can change operation order, outer product, and multi-exponentiation to parallel multi-exponentiation and inner pairing product. Let us focus on the term $\overrightarrow{\boldsymbol{g}^{\boldsymbol{a}}} \circ \overrightarrow{\boldsymbol{h}^{\boldsymbol{b}}}$. By DL assumption on $\mathbb{G}_1$, $\overrightarrow{\boldsymbol{g}^{\boldsymbol{a}}} \circ \overrightarrow{\boldsymbol{h}^{\boldsymbol{b}}} \in \mathbb{G}_1^n$ can be a valid binding commitment of $\boldsymbol{a}$ and $\boldsymbol{b}$. In addition, we can apply pairing-based group commitment for $\overrightarrow{\boldsymbol{g}^{\boldsymbol{a}}} \circ \overrightarrow{\boldsymbol{h}^{\boldsymbol{b}}}$.

Inner Product Term. In the above change, we only substitute commitment of witness vectors $\boldsymbol{a}, \boldsymbol{b}$, not their inner product $\langle \boldsymbol{a}, \boldsymbol{b} \rangle$. In Protocol3, the inner product part $\langle \boldsymbol{a}, \boldsymbol{b} \rangle$ is committed using single exponentiation on the base $u \in \mathbb{G}_t$. To apply pairing-based group commitments to the exponentiation $u^{\langle \boldsymbol{a}, \boldsymbol{b} \rangle}$, we use $\mathbb{G}_1$ base for commitment, not $\mathbb{G}_t$. Then, we add additional CRS $U \in \mathbb{G}_2$ to combine vector commitment and inner product terms to one target group element $P \in \mathbb{G}_t$

Now, we describe VRPT3, a variant of RRPT3, as shown in Fig. 2. VRPT3 is an argument of knowledge for the following relation:

$$\mathcal{R}_{\mathsf{VRPT3}} = \left\{ \begin{matrix} (\boldsymbol{g}, \boldsymbol{h} \in \mathbb{G}_1^m, \boldsymbol{H} \in \mathbb{G}_2^n, u \in \mathbb{G}_1, U \in \mathbb{G}_2, P \in \mathbb{G}_t; \boldsymbol{a}, \boldsymbol{b} \in \mathbb{Z}_p^{m \times n}) : \\ P = \boldsymbol{E}(\overrightarrow{\boldsymbol{g}^{\boldsymbol{a}}} \circ \overrightarrow{\boldsymbol{h}^{\boldsymbol{b}}}, \boldsymbol{H}) \cdot e(u, U)^{\langle \boldsymbol{a}, \boldsymbol{b} \rangle} \end{matrix} \right\}$$

Theorem 1. VRPT3 *provides perfect completeness and witness extended emulator under the discrete logarithm assumption.*

The main idea of the proof is similar to that of generalized-BP [20]. For more details, please refer to Appendix A.

3.2 Commit-and-Prove Approach

In this section, we apply the *commit-and-prove* approach to VRPT3. Instead of sending $\boldsymbol{v}, \boldsymbol{w}$, the prover sends commitments $V = \boldsymbol{E}(\boldsymbol{v}, \boldsymbol{F})$ and $W = \boldsymbol{E}(\boldsymbol{w}, \boldsymbol{K})$,

VRPT3($\boldsymbol{g}, \boldsymbol{h} \in \mathbb{G}_1^m, \boldsymbol{H} \in \mathbb{G}_2^n, u \in \mathbb{G}_1, U \in \mathbb{G}_2, P \in \mathbb{G}_t; \boldsymbol{a}, \boldsymbol{b} \in \mathbb{Z}_p^{m\times n}$)

If $m = 1$

$\boxed{\mathcal{P} \,\&\, \mathcal{V}}$: Run $\mathsf{BP_{IP}}(g \otimes \boldsymbol{H}, h \otimes \boldsymbol{H}, u, P; \boldsymbol{a}, \boldsymbol{b})$

Else ($m > 1$): Let $m' = \frac{m}{2d}$. Parse $\boldsymbol{a}, \boldsymbol{b}, \boldsymbol{g}$, and $\boldsymbol{h}$ to

$$\boldsymbol{a} = [\boldsymbol{a}_1 \parallel \boldsymbol{a}_{-1} \parallel \cdots \parallel \boldsymbol{a}_{2d-1} \parallel \boldsymbol{a}_{-2d+1}], \quad \boldsymbol{g} = \boldsymbol{g}_1 \parallel \boldsymbol{g}_{-1} \parallel \cdots \parallel \boldsymbol{g}_{2d-1} \parallel \boldsymbol{g}_{-2d+1},$$
$$\boldsymbol{b} = [\boldsymbol{b}_1 \parallel \boldsymbol{b}_{-1} \parallel \cdots \parallel \boldsymbol{b}_{2d-1} \parallel \boldsymbol{b}_{-2d+1}], \quad \boldsymbol{h} = \boldsymbol{h}_1 \parallel \boldsymbol{h}_{-1} \parallel \cdots \parallel \boldsymbol{h}_{2d-1} \parallel \boldsymbol{h}_{-2d+1}$$

$\boxed{\mathcal{P}}$: Compute $\boldsymbol{v}[i,j]$ and $w[i,j]$ for all distinct $i, j \in I_d$ such that

$$\boldsymbol{v}[i,j] = \overrightarrow{\boldsymbol{g}_i^{\boldsymbol{a}_j}} \circ \overrightarrow{\boldsymbol{h}_j^{\boldsymbol{b}_i}} \in \mathbb{G}_1^n, w[i,j] = u^{\langle \boldsymbol{a}_j, \boldsymbol{b}_i \rangle} \in \mathbb{G}_1$$

and concatenate $\boldsymbol{v}[i,j]$ and $w[i,j]$ to $\boldsymbol{v} \in \mathbb{G}_1^{n\times 2d(2d-1)}$ and $\boldsymbol{w} \in \mathbb{G}_1^{2d(2d-1)}$ in lexicographic order, respectively.

$\boxed{\mathcal{P} \to \mathcal{V}}$: $\boldsymbol{v}, \boldsymbol{w}$

$\boxed{\mathcal{V} \to \mathcal{P}}$: $x \xleftarrow{\$} \mathbb{Z}_p^*$

$\boxed{\mathcal{P} \,\&\, \mathcal{V}}$: Set $\boldsymbol{x} = (x^{j-i}) \in \mathbb{Z}_p^{2d(2d-1)}$ in lexicographic order. Then, compute

$$\nu = \boldsymbol{E}(\widehat{\boldsymbol{v}^{\boldsymbol{x}}}, \boldsymbol{H}) \in \mathbb{G}_t, \quad \mu = \boldsymbol{w}^{\boldsymbol{x}} \in \mathbb{G}_1, \quad P' = P \cdot \nu \cdot e(\mu, U) \in \mathbb{G}_t$$

$$\boldsymbol{g}' = \bigcirc_{i \in I_d} \boldsymbol{g}_i^{x^{-i}} \in \mathbb{G}_1^{m'}, \quad \boldsymbol{h}' = \bigcirc_{i \in I_d} \boldsymbol{h}_i^{x^i} \in \mathbb{G}_1^{m'}$$

$\boxed{\mathcal{P}}$: Compute

$$\boldsymbol{a}' = \sum_{i \in I_n} \boldsymbol{a}_i x^i \in \mathbb{Z}_p^{m'\times n}, \quad \boldsymbol{b}' = \sum_{i \in I_n} \boldsymbol{b}_i x^{-i} \in \mathbb{Z}_p^{m'\times n}$$

$\boxed{\mathcal{P} \,\&\, \mathcal{V}}$: Run VRPT3($\boldsymbol{g}', \boldsymbol{h}', \boldsymbol{H}, u, P'; \boldsymbol{a}', \boldsymbol{b}'$).

Fig. 2. VRPT3: Variant Round Reduced Protocol3

where $\boldsymbol{F} \in \mathbb{G}_2^{n\times 2n(2n-1)}$ and $\boldsymbol{K} \in \mathbb{G}_2^{2n(2n-1)}$ are additional CRS for commitments. After receiving commitments V and W, the verifier sends a random challenge to the Prover. Unlike VRPT3, the verifier cannot update instance P' because the verifier does not know $\boldsymbol{v}$ and $\boldsymbol{w}$. Thus, the prover sends $\nu = \boldsymbol{E}(\widehat{\boldsymbol{v}^{\boldsymbol{x}}}, \boldsymbol{H})$ and $\mu = \boldsymbol{w}^{\boldsymbol{x}}$ to the verifier to update P', and then they run additional argument for knowledge $\boldsymbol{v}$ and $\boldsymbol{w}$. The argument should guarantee knowledge for $\boldsymbol{v}$ and $\boldsymbol{w}$ such that $\nu = \boldsymbol{E}(\widehat{\boldsymbol{v}^{\boldsymbol{x}}}, \boldsymbol{H})$ and $\mu = \boldsymbol{w}^{\boldsymbol{x}}$.

Parallel Multi-Exponentiation Argument. Let us focus on the argument of knowledge for $\boldsymbol{v}$. In the argument system, the prover's claim is the knowledge of $\boldsymbol{v}$, which satisfies $V = \boldsymbol{E}(\boldsymbol{v}, \boldsymbol{F})$ and $\nu = \boldsymbol{E}(\widehat{\boldsymbol{v}^{\boldsymbol{x}}}, \boldsymbol{H})$. We can construct an argument system using the half-reduction idea of $\mathsf{BP_{IP}}$. We denote the argument for $\boldsymbol{v}$ as parallel multi-exponentiation argument (PMEA). PMEA is an argument system for the following relation:

$$\mathcal{R}_{\mathsf{PMEA}} = \left\{ \begin{matrix} (\boldsymbol{F} \in \mathbb{G}_2^{n\times c}, \boldsymbol{x} \in \mathbb{Z}_p^c, \boldsymbol{H} \in \mathbb{G}_2^n, V, \nu \in \mathbb{G}_t; \boldsymbol{v} \in \mathbb{G}_1^{n\times c}) : \\ V = \boldsymbol{E}(\boldsymbol{v}, \boldsymbol{F}) \wedge \nu = \boldsymbol{E}(\widehat{\boldsymbol{v}^{\boldsymbol{x}}}, \boldsymbol{H}) \end{matrix} \right\}$$

Argument of Knowledge for $\boldsymbol{w}$. Certainly, the prover claims knowledge of $\boldsymbol{w}$, which satisfies multi-exponentiation relation $\mu = \boldsymbol{w}^{\boldsymbol{x}}$. We can apply the MEA protocol [20] for knowledge of $\boldsymbol{w}$. Therefore, we do not explain the details of the argument for $\boldsymbol{w}$.

Using two protocols PMEA and MEA, we can construct a reduced communication protocol. However, for a similar reason as constructing Protocol2, we should apply an *Aggregation* technique to achieve sublogarithmic communication cost. The aggregation of multi MEA, called aAggMEA, was already proposed by Kim, Lee, and Seo [20]. Inspired by the idea of aAggMEA, we construct aggregated arguments for PMEA.

Aggregation PMEA**.** In this section, we focus on aggregating PMEA protocols to apply our main protocol. One of the aggregating techniques is random linear combination. However, naïve random combination does not guarantee unuseness of $\boldsymbol{F}_s$ to construct V_ℓ for all $s \neq \ell$. To detour it, we use idea of aAggMEA, which are used in Protocol2. Similarly, we add redundant witness $\boldsymbol{v}_{\ell,r}$ and construct an argument for the following relation.

$$\mathcal{R}_{\mathsf{APMEA}} = \left\{ \begin{matrix} (\boldsymbol{F}_\ell \in \mathbb{G}_2^{n\times c}, \boldsymbol{x}_\ell \in \mathbb{Z}_p^c, \boldsymbol{H} \in \mathbb{G}_2^n, V_\ell, \nu_\ell \in \mathbb{G}_t; \boldsymbol{v}_{\ell,r} \in \mathbb{G}_1^{n\times c}, \ell, r \in [R]) : \\ \wedge_{\ell\in[R]} \left(V_\ell = \prod_{s\in[R]} \boldsymbol{E}(\boldsymbol{v}_{\ell,s}, \boldsymbol{F}_s) \wedge \nu = \boldsymbol{E}(\widehat{\boldsymbol{v}_{\ell,\ell}^{\boldsymbol{x}_\ell}}, \boldsymbol{H}) \right) \\ \wedge \left(\wedge_{\ell,r\in[R]\wedge \ell\neq r} \widehat{\boldsymbol{v}_{\ell,r}^{\boldsymbol{x}_r}} = \boldsymbol{1} \right) \end{matrix} \right\}$$

We construct a protocol APEMA for the relation $\mathcal{R}_{\mathsf{APMEA}}$. We describe details in Fig. 3. APEMA consists of two steps, the aggregation and the recursive reduction. Using the verifier challenges, the protocol lets R distinct commitments V_ℓ and evaluation ν_ℓ aggregate to one group element P. After the aggregating step, the prover and verifier run ProdPMEA for the following relation:

$$\mathcal{R}_{\mathsf{ProdPMEA}} = \left\{ \begin{matrix} (\boldsymbol{F}_\ell \in \mathbb{G}_2^{n\times c}, \boldsymbol{x}_\ell \in \mathbb{Z}_p^c, \boldsymbol{H} \in \mathbb{G}_2^n, P \in \mathbb{G}_t; \boldsymbol{v}_\ell \in \mathbb{G}_1^{n\times c}, \ell \in [R]) : \\ P = \prod_{s\in[R]} \boldsymbol{E}(\boldsymbol{v}_s, \boldsymbol{F}_s) \cdot \boldsymbol{E}(\widehat{\boldsymbol{v}_s^{\boldsymbol{x}_s}}, \boldsymbol{H}) \end{matrix} \right\}$$

Theorem 2. *Let* ProdPMEA *provide perfect completeness and witness extended emulator. Then, the* APMEA *protocol provides perfect completeness and witness extended emulator under the double pairing assumption.*

Theorem 3. *The* ProdPMEA *protocol provides perfect completeness and witness extended emulator under the double pairing assumption.*

Proof Sketch. We sketch the proof for witness extended emulation (WEE) of APMEA. In a similar way to ProdMEA [20], we can construct WEE of ProdPMEA. One difference is that the WEE of ProdPMEA runs the WEE of IPP as a subroutine. Once getting WEE of ProdPMEA, one can construct a WEE of APMEA, which uses the WEE of ProdPMEA as a subroutine. From $2R$ distinct extracted witnesses from the WEE of ProdPMEA, one can extract witness $\boldsymbol{v}_{\ell,r}$.

$\boxed{\mathsf{APMEA}(\boldsymbol{F}_\ell \in \mathbb{G}_2^{n\times c}, \boldsymbol{x}_\ell \in \mathbb{Z}_p^c, \boldsymbol{H} \in \mathbb{G}_2^n, V_\ell, \nu_\ell \in \mathbb{G}_t; \boldsymbol{v}_{\ell,r} \in \mathbb{G}_1^{n\times c}, \ell, r \in [R])}$

$\boxed{\mathcal{V}\to\mathcal{P}}$: $\alpha \xleftarrow{\$} \mathbb{Z}_p^*$

$\boxed{\mathcal{P}\ \&\ \mathcal{V}}$: **Compute** $\boldsymbol{F}'_\ell \in \mathbb{G}_2^{n\times c}, \boldsymbol{x}'_\ell \in \mathbb{Z}_p^c, \boldsymbol{H}' \in \mathbb{G}_2^n, P \in \mathbb{G}_t$ **such that**

$$\boldsymbol{F}'_\ell = \boldsymbol{F}_\ell^{\alpha^{\ell-1}}, \quad \boldsymbol{x}'_\ell = \alpha^{\ell-1}\boldsymbol{x}_\ell, \quad \boldsymbol{H}' = \boldsymbol{H}^{\alpha^R}, \quad P = \prod_{\ell\in[R]} V_\ell^{\alpha^{\ell-1}} \nu_\ell^{\alpha^{R+\ell-1}}$$

$\boxed{\mathcal{P}}$: Compute $\boldsymbol{v}'_\ell = \bigcirc_{s\in[R]} \boldsymbol{v}_{s,\ell}^{\alpha^{s-\ell}}$

$\boxed{\mathcal{P}\ \&\ \mathcal{V}}$: Run $\mathsf{ProdPMEA}(\boldsymbol{F}'_\ell, \boldsymbol{x}'_\ell, \boldsymbol{H}', P; \boldsymbol{v}'_\ell)$

$\boxed{\mathsf{ProdPMEA}(\boldsymbol{F}_\ell \in \mathbb{G}_2^{n\times c}, \boldsymbol{x}_\ell \in \mathbb{Z}_p^c, \boldsymbol{H} \in \mathbb{G}_2^n, P \in \mathbb{G}_t; \boldsymbol{v}_\ell \in \mathbb{G}_1^{n\times c}, \ell \in [R])}$

If $c = 1$

$\boxed{\mathcal{P}\ \&\ \mathcal{V}}$: Set $\boldsymbol{F}'_\ell = \boldsymbol{F}_\ell \circ \boldsymbol{H}_\ell^{x_\ell} \in \mathbb{G}_2^n$, $\forall \ell \in [R]$ and then concatenate ℓ vectors $\boldsymbol{F}'_\ell$ into $\boldsymbol{F}' \in \mathbb{G}_2^{nR}$.

$\boxed{\mathcal{P}}$: Concatenate all of $\boldsymbol{v}_\ell \in \mathbb{Z}_p^n$ into $\boldsymbol{v} \in \mathbb{G}_1^{nR}$

$\boxed{\mathcal{P}\ \&\ \mathcal{V}}$: Run $\mathsf{IPP}(\boldsymbol{F}', P; \boldsymbol{v})$

Else $(c > 1)$: Let $c' = \frac{c}{2}$ and parse $\boldsymbol{F}_\ell$, $\boldsymbol{x}_\ell$, $\boldsymbol{v}_\ell$

$$\boldsymbol{F}_\ell = [\boldsymbol{F}_{\ell,1} \parallel \boldsymbol{F}_{\ell,-1}], \quad \boldsymbol{x}_\ell = \boldsymbol{x}_{\ell,1} \parallel \boldsymbol{x}_{\ell,-1}, \quad \boldsymbol{v}_\ell = [\boldsymbol{v}_{\ell,1} \parallel \boldsymbol{v}_{\ell,-1}]$$

$\boxed{\mathcal{P}}$: Calculate $L, R \in \mathbb{G}_t$ such that

$$L = \prod_{\ell\in[R]} \boldsymbol{E}(\boldsymbol{v}_{\ell,1}, \boldsymbol{F}_{\ell,-1})\boldsymbol{E}(\widehat{\boldsymbol{v}_{\ell,1}{}^{\boldsymbol{x}_{\ell,-1}}}, \boldsymbol{H}), \; R = \prod_{\ell\in[R]} \boldsymbol{E}(\boldsymbol{v}_{\ell,-1}, \boldsymbol{F}_{\ell,1})\boldsymbol{E}(\widehat{\boldsymbol{v}_{\ell,-1}{}^{\boldsymbol{x}_{\ell,1}}}, \boldsymbol{H})$$

$\boxed{\mathcal{P}\to\mathcal{V}}$: L, R

$\boxed{\mathcal{V}\to\mathcal{P}}$: $\alpha \xleftarrow{\$} \mathbb{Z}_p^*$

$\boxed{\mathcal{P}\ \&\ \mathcal{V}}$: Compute $\boldsymbol{F}'_\ell \in \mathbb{G}_2^{n\times c'}, \boldsymbol{x}'_\ell \in \mathbb{Z}_p^{c'}, P' \in \mathbb{G}_t$ such that

$$\boldsymbol{F}'_\ell = \boldsymbol{F}_{\ell,1}^{\alpha^{-1}} \circ \boldsymbol{F}_{\ell,-1}^{\alpha}, \; \boldsymbol{x}'_\ell = \alpha^{-1}\boldsymbol{x}_{\ell,1} + \alpha\boldsymbol{x}_{\ell,-1}, \; P' = L^{\alpha^2} P R^{\alpha^{-2}}$$

$\boxed{\mathcal{P}}$: Compute $\boldsymbol{v}'_\ell = \boldsymbol{v}_{\ell,1}^{\alpha} \circ \boldsymbol{v}_{\ell,-1}^{\alpha^{-1}} \in \mathbb{G}_1^{n\times c'}$

$\boxed{\mathcal{P}\ \&\ \mathcal{V}}$: $\mathcal{P}$ and $\mathcal{V}$ run $\mathsf{ProdPMEA}(\boldsymbol{F}'_\ell, \boldsymbol{x}'_\ell, \boldsymbol{H}, P'; \boldsymbol{v}'_\ell)$

Fig. 3. APMEA: Augmented Aggregating Parallel Multi-Exponentiation Argument

3.3 Main Protocols

In this section, we explain our main protocol TENET, sublogarithm communication, and sublinear verifier without a trusted setup. TENET consists of four phases: row reduction, column reduction, APMEA, and aAggMEA.

The purpose of row reduction is to reduce witness size from $m \times n$ to $\frac{m}{2d} \times n$ per round. For each round, the prover sends commitments V and W to the verifier. After receiving the verifier's challenges, the prover sends evaluation ν and μ to the verifier. Then, the prover and verifier run the protocol recursively without checking the proof for knowledge $\boldsymbol{v}$ and $\boldsymbol{w}$. Rather than checking per round, the prover and verifier store statements $\boldsymbol{v}, \boldsymbol{w}, \nu, \mu$ per round. Then, the prover and verifier run column reduction, which is identical to $\mathsf{BP_{IP}}$ on base $\mathbb{G}_t$. If the $\mathsf{BP_{IP}}$ verifier outputs 1, the prover and verifier run APMEA and aAggMEA using stored statements from row reduction. We describe TENET in Fig. 4, which is applied using the following optimization technique.

$\boxed{\mathsf{TENET}(\boldsymbol{g}, \boldsymbol{h}, \boldsymbol{H}, \boldsymbol{F}_\ell, \boldsymbol{K}_\ell, u, U, P, st_I; \boldsymbol{a}, \boldsymbol{b}, st_W \text{ for } \ell \in [R])}$

If $m = 1$:

$\boxed{\mathcal{P} \,\&\, \mathcal{V}}$: Run $\mathsf{BP_{IP}}(g \otimes \boldsymbol{H}, h \otimes \boldsymbol{H}, e(u, U), P; \boldsymbol{a}, \boldsymbol{b})$

If $st_P = \perp$:

$\boxed{\mathcal{V}}$ *Accept* the protocol.

Else : Let $(V_\ell, \nu_\ell, W_\ell, \mu_\ell, \boldsymbol{x}_\ell; \boldsymbol{v}_{\ell,r}, \boldsymbol{w}_{\ell,r})$ be the ℓ-th row in (st_I, st_W)

$\boxed{\mathcal{P}}$: Set $\boldsymbol{v}_{\ell,\ell} = \boldsymbol{v}_\ell$, $\boldsymbol{w}_{\ell,\ell} = \boldsymbol{w}_\ell$ for all $\ell \in [R]$ and $\boldsymbol{v}_{\ell,r} = \boldsymbol{1}_{\mathbb{G}_1}$, $\boldsymbol{w}_{\ell,r} = \boldsymbol{1}_{\mathbb{G}_1}$ for all distinct $\ell, r \in [R]$

$\boxed{\mathcal{P} \,\&\, \mathcal{V}}$: Run $\mathsf{APMEA}(\boldsymbol{F}_\ell, \boldsymbol{x}_\ell, \boldsymbol{H}, \boldsymbol{K}, V_\ell, \nu_\ell; \boldsymbol{v}_{\ell,r})$, $\mathsf{aAggMEA}(\boldsymbol{K}_\ell, \boldsymbol{x}_\ell, W_\ell, \mu_\ell; \boldsymbol{w}_{\ell,r})$

Else ($m > 1$): Let $m' = \frac{m}{2d}$. Parse $\boldsymbol{a}, \boldsymbol{b}, \boldsymbol{g}$, and $\boldsymbol{h}$ to

$$\boldsymbol{a} = [\boldsymbol{a}_1 \parallel \boldsymbol{a}_{-1} \parallel \cdots \parallel \boldsymbol{a}_{2d-1} \parallel \boldsymbol{a}_{-2d+1}], \quad \boldsymbol{g} = \boldsymbol{g}_1 \parallel \boldsymbol{g}_{-1} \parallel \cdots \parallel \boldsymbol{g}_{2d-1} \parallel \boldsymbol{g}_{-2d+1},$$
$$\boldsymbol{b} = [\boldsymbol{b}_1 \parallel \boldsymbol{b}_{-1} \parallel \cdots \parallel \boldsymbol{b}_{2d-1} \parallel \boldsymbol{b}_{-2d+1}], \quad \boldsymbol{h} = \boldsymbol{h}_1 \parallel \boldsymbol{h}_{-1} \parallel \cdots \parallel \boldsymbol{h}_{2d-1} \parallel \boldsymbol{h}_{-2d+1}$$

$\boxed{\mathcal{P}}$: Compute $\boldsymbol{v}[s] = \bigcirc_{s=i-j} (\overrightarrow{\boldsymbol{g}_i{}^{\boldsymbol{a}_j}} \circ \overrightarrow{\boldsymbol{h}_j{}^{\boldsymbol{b}_i}}) \in \mathbb{G}_1^n, w[s] = \prod_{s=i-j} u^{\langle \boldsymbol{a}_j, \boldsymbol{b}_i \rangle} \in \mathbb{G}_1 \ \forall s \in J_d$, and then concatenate $\boldsymbol{v}[s]$ and $w[s]$ to $\boldsymbol{v} \in \mathbb{G}_1^{n \times 4d-2}$ and $\boldsymbol{w} \in \mathbb{G}_1^{4d-2}$ in ascending order. And then compute $V = \boldsymbol{E}(\boldsymbol{v}, \boldsymbol{F}_\ell)$ and $W = \boldsymbol{E}(\boldsymbol{w}, \boldsymbol{K}_\ell)$

$\boxed{\mathcal{P} \rightarrow \mathcal{V}}$: V, W

$\boxed{\mathcal{V} \rightarrow \mathcal{P}}$: $x \xleftarrow{\$} \mathbb{Z}_p^*$

$\boxed{\mathcal{P}}$: Set $\boldsymbol{x} = (x^s)_{s \in J_d} \in \mathbb{Z}_p^{4d-2}$ in ascending order. Then, compute ν, μ

$$\nu = \boldsymbol{E}(\widehat{\boldsymbol{v}^{\boldsymbol{x}}}, \boldsymbol{H}) \in \mathbb{G}_t, \quad \mu = \boldsymbol{w}^{\boldsymbol{x}} \in \mathbb{G}_1$$

$\boxed{\mathcal{P} \rightarrow \mathcal{V}}$: ν, μ

$\boxed{\mathcal{P} \,\&\, \mathcal{V}}$: Compute $\boldsymbol{g}', \boldsymbol{h}', P'$

$$\boldsymbol{g}' = \circ_{i \in I_d} \boldsymbol{g}_i^{x^{-i}} \in \mathbb{G}_1^{m'}, \ \boldsymbol{h}' = \circ_{i \in I_d} \boldsymbol{h}_i^{x^i} \in \mathbb{G}_1^{m'}, P' = P \cdot \nu \cdot e(\mu, U) \in \mathbb{G}_t$$

Then, update st_I by adding a tuple $(V, \nu, W, \mu, \boldsymbol{x})$ to the bottom.

$\boxed{\mathcal{P}}$: Compute $\boldsymbol{a}' = \sum_{i \in I_n} \boldsymbol{a}_i x^i \in \mathbb{Z}_p^{m' \times n}, \quad \boldsymbol{b}' = \sum_{i \in I_n} \boldsymbol{b}_i x^{-i} \in \mathbb{Z}_p^{m' \times n}$

Then, update st_W by adding a tuple $(\boldsymbol{v}, \boldsymbol{w})$ to the bottom.

$\boxed{\mathcal{P} \,\&\, \mathcal{V}}$: Run $\mathsf{TENET}(\boldsymbol{g}', \boldsymbol{h}', \boldsymbol{H}, \boldsymbol{F}_\ell, \boldsymbol{K}_\ell, u, U, P, st_V; \boldsymbol{a}', \boldsymbol{b}', st_P \text{ for } \ell \in [R-1])$

Fig. 4. TENET: Sublogarithm Proof and Sublinear Verifier IPA

Optimization: Compress Columns of $\boldsymbol{v}$ and $\boldsymbol{w}$. In this section, we present an optimization technique for APMEA and aAggMEA. Certainly, this idea can be applied to Protocol2, which contains aAggMEA as a subprotocol. Let us focus on the prover's message of VRPT3 in Fig. 2. For each round, the prover sends $\boldsymbol{v}$ and $\boldsymbol{w}$, which are commitments to parsed matrices and inner products with $2d(2d-1)$ columns. When computing multi-exponentiation to $\boldsymbol{x}$, each of the columns $\boldsymbol{v}[i,j]$ and $w[i,j]$ meet an exponent x^{j-i}. In this case, some columns meet the same exponent x^{j-i}. More concretely, we can rewrite multi-exponentiation of $4d-2$ group elements by the following equations:

$$\bigcirc_{i,j\in I_d \wedge i\neq j} \boldsymbol{v}[i,j]^{x^{i-j}} = \bigcirc_{s\in J_d} \Big(\bigcirc_{s=i-j} \boldsymbol{v}[i,j] \Big)^{x^s}, \quad \prod_{i,j\in I_d \wedge i\neq j} w[i,j]^{x^{i-j}} = \prod_{s\in J_d} \Big(\prod_{s=i-j} w[i,j] \Big)^{x^s}$$

This implies that only $4d-2$ different terms are sufficient to update P'. Then, is $4d-2$ terms sufficient to guarantee knowledge of witness $\boldsymbol{a}$ and $\boldsymbol{b}$? Let D_s be a set of tuples such that $D_s = \{i,j \in I_d | s = i-j\}$. Then, any tuples in D_s cannot have a common entry with each other. Since the tuple is related to base group elements, $\boldsymbol{v}[i,j] = \boldsymbol{g}_i^{\overrightarrow{a_j}} \circ \boldsymbol{h}_j^{\overrightarrow{b_i}}$ have distinct bases from each other on tuple set D_s. Under the DLR assumption, witness vectors $\boldsymbol{a}_j$ and $\boldsymbol{b}_i$ are extractable from products of $\boldsymbol{v}[i,j]$. For more details on witness extraction, please refer to Appendix A.

Let us define the column-reduced vector $\bar{\boldsymbol{v}} \in \mathbb{G}_1^{n\times 4d-2}$ and $\bar{\boldsymbol{w}} \in \mathbb{G}_1^{4d-2}$ as $\bar{\boldsymbol{v}} = \big(\bigcirc_{(i,j)\in D_s} \boldsymbol{v}[i,j] \big)_{s\in J_d}$ and $\bar{\boldsymbol{w}} = \big(\prod_{(i,j)\in D_s} w[i,j] \big)_{s\in J_d}$. Then, we can adjust the prover's action in VRPT3 by generating $\bar{\boldsymbol{v}}$ and $\bar{\boldsymbol{w}}$ and sending them to the verifier. After applying the *commit-and-prove* approach, the prover's action is changed to sending commitment to $\bar{\boldsymbol{v}}$ and $\bar{\boldsymbol{w}}$ and their proofs, rather than to $\boldsymbol{v}$ and $\boldsymbol{w}$. Since the witness size is reduced from $O(d^2)$(resp. $\boldsymbol{v}, \boldsymbol{w}$) to $O(d)$(resp. $\bar{\boldsymbol{v}}, \bar{\boldsymbol{w}}$), the required CRS size $\boldsymbol{F}$ and $\boldsymbol{K}$ decrease to $O(d)$, and proof size and verifier cost for APMEA and aAggMEA can be decreased.

Uniform Reference Strings. The required common reference strings for TENET are $\boldsymbol{g}, \boldsymbol{h} \in \mathbb{G}_1^m$, $\boldsymbol{H} \in \mathbb{G}_2^n$, $\boldsymbol{F}_\ell \in \mathbb{G}_2^{n\times 4d-2}$, $\boldsymbol{K}_\ell \in \mathbb{G}_2^{4d-2}$, and $(u,U) \in \mathbb{G}_1 \times \mathbb{G}_2$, which are all chosen randomly from a uniform distribution, not depending on a trusted party. The total size of common reference strings is $(2m+1)|\mathbb{G}_1| + (R(4d-2)(n+1)+1)|\mathbb{G}_2|$.

Theorem 4. TENET *provides perfect completeness and witness extended emulator under the discrete logarithm and double pairing assumptions if* APMEA *and* aAggMEA *provide perfect completeness and witness extended emulator.*

Proof Sketch. The proof idea of TENET is similar to that of Protocol2. The witness extended emulator of APMEA and that of aAggMEA extract prover's messages $\boldsymbol{v}$ and $\boldsymbol{w}$ for all rounds. Using them, we can construct a witness extended emulator for TENET following the witness extended emulator of VRPT3.

Efficiency. We explain the cost of TENET, communication cost, verifier computational cost and prover computational cost. We analyze TENET in four parts: row reduction, column reduction, APMEA, and aAggMEA. We describe the efficiency of them in Table 2.

- **Row Reduction.**
  - Communication: For each row reduction, the prover sends 3 $\mathbb{G}_t$ elements and 1 $\mathbb{G}_1$ element. Since the total round of row reduction is $R = \log_{2d} m$, total communication is $O(R)$.
  - Prover's Complexity: To compute $\boldsymbol{v}$ and $\boldsymbol{w}$ per round, the prover computes $\frac{m}{2d} \cdot n \cdot 2d(2d-1)$ $\mathbb{G}_1$-exp with $n \cdot (4d-2)$ pairing and $2d(2d-1)$ $\mathbb{G}_1$-exp with $4d-2$ pairing. After receiving a challenge, the prover constructs ν and μ, whose costs are $n \cdot (4d-2)$ $\mathbb{G}_1$-exp with n pairing and $4d-2$ $\mathbb{G}_1$-exp, respectively. Then, the prover computes $2m$ $\mathbb{G}_1$-exp and mn field operations with constant pairing for updating instance and witness steps. Since the size of m is shrinking by $1/2d$ times per round, the overwhelming term of prover complexity is $O(mnd + nd^2R)$.
  - Verifier's Complexity: The verifier updates instances $\boldsymbol{g}, \boldsymbol{h}$, and P, whose computation costs are $2m$ $\mathbb{G}_1$-exp in total. Similarly prover complexity, the overwhelming term of verifier complexity is $O(m)$.
- **Column Reduction.**
  The column-reduction phase is only running $\mathsf{BP}_{\mathsf{IP}}$ on $\mathbb{G}_t$. However, the CRS update step can be changed to updating $\boldsymbol{H} \in \mathbb{G}_2^n$, rather than $g \otimes \boldsymbol{H} \in \mathbb{G}_t^n$. Therefore, total communication is $O(\log n)$ $\mathbb{G}_t$-exp, and the prover and verifier computation is $O(n)$ $\mathbb{G}_2$-exp.
- **APMEA.**
  - Communication: In the aggregating phase, the verifier sends one challenge to the prover, but sending a challenge can be substituted by using random oracle by the Fiat-Shamir transform [14]. In the recursive reduction phase, the prover sends two $\mathbb{G}_t$ elements per round, so that the total communication cost is $O(\log(ndR)$.
  - Prover's Complexity: In the aggregating phase, the prover computes $n(4d-2)R$ $\mathbb{G}_1$-exp for updating witness $\boldsymbol{v}_\ell$ [2] , $n(4d-2)R$ $\mathbb{G}_2$-exp and n $\mathbb{G}_2$-exp for updating $\boldsymbol{F}_\ell$ and $\boldsymbol{H}$, and R $\mathbb{G}_t$-exp for updating P. In the recursive reduction phase, the prover complexity is linear to witness length $n(4d-2)$. Then, the total prover complexity is $O(ndR)$, which is a overwhelming term.
  - Verifier's Complexity: Since the verifier computes $n(4d-2)R$ $\mathbb{G}_2$-exp for updating $\boldsymbol{F}_\ell$ too, the verifier's complexity is also $O(ndR)$
- **aAggMEA.**
  The complexity of aAggMEA is $O(R + \log d)$, $O(dR)$, and $O(dR)$ for communication prover and verifier cost, respectively [20].

[2] The complexity for computing $\boldsymbol{v}'_\ell$ is $O(ndR^2)$. However, in TENET, the prover sets $\boldsymbol{v}_{s,\ell} = \mathbf{1}$ for all distinct s, ℓ. For this reason, the exponentiation of the redundant terms can be omitted.

Table 2. Complexity Table of TENET

	Communication	$\mathcal{P}$'s computation	$\mathcal{V}$'s computation
Row Reduction	$O(R)\lvert\mathbb{G}_t\rvert$	$O(mnd + nd^2R)E_1$	$O(m)E_1$
Column Reduction	$O(\log n)\lvert\mathbb{G}_2\rvert$	$O(n)E_2$	$O(n)E_2$
APMEA	$O(\log ndR)\lvert\mathbb{G}_t\rvert$	$O(nd^2R)E_1$	$O(ndR)E_2$
aAggMEA	$O(R + \log d)\lvert\mathbb{G}_t\rvert$	$O(d^2R)E_2$	$O(dR)E_2$
Total(TENET)	$O(R + \log nd)$	$O(mnd + nd^2R)$	$O(m + ndR)$

$|\mathbb{G}_i|$: size of group elements in $\mathbb{G}_i$, E_i: group exponentiation on $\mathbb{G}_i$

Parameter Setting. When choosing appropriate parameters on TENET, we can achieve sublogarithm communication and sublinear verifier.

- *Parameter Setting.*: Let $N = mn$ be a length of witness vectors. Set the column size and row size as $n = 2^{\sqrt{\log N}}$ and $m = \frac{N}{n}$, respectively. Then, define dividing factor as $2d = 2^{\sqrt{\log m}}$. Then, the round number of row reduction $R = \log_{2d} m = \sqrt{\log m}$. Let us put all factors from the above results.
- *Communication.*: The communication cost is $O(R + \log nd) = O(\sqrt{\log N})$
- *Prover's Complexity.*: The prover's complexity is $O(N \cdot 2^{\sqrt{\log m}})$. Since m is smaller than N, we have rough bound $O(N \cdot 2^{\sqrt{\log N}})$.
- *Verifier's Complexity.*: For simplicity, we focus on rough bound using substitution $\sqrt{\log m}$ with $\sqrt{\log N}$. Then, the verifier's complexity is $O\left(\frac{N}{2^{\sqrt{\log N}}} + \sqrt{\log N} \cdot 4^{\sqrt{\log N}}\right)$; the term d is substituted with $2^{\sqrt{\log N}}$. The left-term $\frac{N}{2^{\sqrt{\log N}}}$ is larger scale than the right-term $\sqrt{\log N} \cdot 4^{\sqrt{\log N}}$. Hence, we can conclude that the verifier complexity is $O\left(\frac{N}{2^{\sqrt{\log N}}}\right)$, which is smaller than $O\left(\frac{N}{\log N}\right)$.

Acknowledgement. This work was supported in part by the Institute of Information and Communications Technology Planning and Evaluation (IITP) grant funded by the Korea Government (MSIT) (A Study on Cryptographic Primitives for SNARK, under Grant 20210007270012002.)

A Appendix

A.1 Proof of Theorem 1

Proof. (*completeness*) If $m = 1$, completeness holds by perfect completeness of $\mathsf{BP}_{\mathsf{IP}}$. Consider the case $m > 1$.

$$
\begin{aligned}
P' &= P \cdot \nu \cdot e(\mu, U) = P \cdot \boldsymbol{E}(\widehat{\boldsymbol{v}^{\boldsymbol{x}}}, \boldsymbol{H}) \cdot e(\boldsymbol{w}^{\boldsymbol{x}}, U) \\
&= \boldsymbol{E}(\overrightarrow{\boldsymbol{g}^{\boldsymbol{a}} \circ \boldsymbol{h}^{\boldsymbol{b}}}, \boldsymbol{H}) \cdot e(u, U)^{\langle \boldsymbol{a}, \boldsymbol{b} \rangle} \cdot \boldsymbol{E}(\widehat{\boldsymbol{v}^{\boldsymbol{x}}}, \boldsymbol{H}) \cdot e(\boldsymbol{w}^{\boldsymbol{x}}, U) \\
&= \boldsymbol{E}(\overrightarrow{\boldsymbol{g}^{\boldsymbol{a}} \circ \boldsymbol{h}^{\boldsymbol{b}}} \circ \widehat{\boldsymbol{v}^{\boldsymbol{x}}}, \boldsymbol{H}) \cdot e(u^{\langle \boldsymbol{a}, \boldsymbol{b} \rangle} \cdot \boldsymbol{w}^{\boldsymbol{x}}, U)
\end{aligned}
$$

Now, we claim that $\overrightarrow{g^{a}} \circ \overrightarrow{h^{b}} \circ \widehat{v^{x}} = \overrightarrow{g'^{a'}} \circ \overrightarrow{h'^{b'}}$ and $u^{\langle a,b\rangle} \cdot w^{x} = u^{\langle a',b'\rangle}$. From the prover's computation, we achieve the following equations:

$$\begin{aligned}
\overrightarrow{g^{a}} \circ \overrightarrow{h^{b}} \circ \widehat{v^{x}} &= \left(\circ_{i \in I_d} \overrightarrow{g_i^{a_i} \circ h_i^{b_i}} \right) \circ \left(\circ_{i,j \in I_d \wedge i \neq j} (\overrightarrow{g_i^{a_j} \circ h_j^{b_i}})^{x^{j-i}} \right) \\
&= \circ_{i,j \in I_d} (\overrightarrow{g_i^{a_j} \circ h_j^{b_i}})^{x^{j-i}} \\
&= \overrightarrow{\left(\circ_{i \in I_d} g_i^{x^{-i}} \right)^{(\sum_{j \in I_d} x^{j} a_j)}} \circ \overrightarrow{\left(\circ_{j \in I_d} h_j^{x^{j}} \right)^{(\sum_{i \in I_d} x^{-i} b_i)}} \\
&= \overrightarrow{g'^{a'}} \circ \overrightarrow{h'^{b'}}
\end{aligned}$$

$$\begin{aligned}
u^{\langle a,b\rangle} \cdot w^{x} &= \prod_{i \in I_d} u^{\langle a_i, b_i \rangle} \cdot \prod_{i,j \in I_d \wedge i \neq j} u^{\langle a_j x^{j}, b_i x^{-i} \rangle} = \prod_{i,j \in I_d} u^{\langle a_j x^{j}, b_i x^{-i} \rangle} \\
&= u^{\langle \sum_{j \in I_d} a_j x^{j}, \sum_{i \in I_d} b_i x^{-i} \rangle} = u^{\langle a', b' \rangle}
\end{aligned}$$

From the equation $P' = E(\overrightarrow{g'^{a'}} \circ \overrightarrow{h'^{b'}}, H) \cdot e(u, U)^{\langle a', b' \rangle}$, the updated instance-witness pair $(g', h', H, u, U, P'; a', b')$ belongs to the relation $\mathcal{R}$
(*witness extended emulation*) In order to show the computational witness extended emulation, we construct an expected polynomial time extractor whose goal is to extract the witness using a polynomially bounded tree of accepting transcripts. If so, we can apply the general forking lemma [5].

The case $(m = 1)$ is clear because $\mathsf{BP}_{\mathsf{IP}}$ has witness extended emulation [8]. Let us focus on the case $(m > 1)$. We prove that, for each recursive step on input (g, h, H, u, U, P), we can efficiently extract from the prover witness vectors a and b under the DLR assumption, whose instance is the CRS $g \parallel h \parallel u$ on $\mathbb{G}_1$ and $H \parallel u$ on $\mathbb{G}_2$. First, the extractor runs the prover to obtain $v \in \mathbb{G}_1^{n \times 2d(2d-1)}$ and $w \in \mathbb{G}_1^{2d(2d-1)}$. At this point, the extractor rewinds the prover $12d-5$ times and feeds $12d-5$ non-zero challenges x_t such that all x_t^2 are distinct. Then, the extractor obtains $12d-5$ pairs a'_t and b'_t such that for $t \in [12d-5]$,

$$P \cdot \prod_{s \in J_d} (E(v_s, H) e(w_s, U))^{x_t^s} = P'_t = E\left(\bigcirc_{i \in I_d} \overrightarrow{(g_i^{x_t^{-i}})^{a'_t}} \circ \overrightarrow{(h_i^{x_t^{i}})^{b'_t}}, H \right) e\left(u^{\langle a'_t, b'_t \rangle}, U\right) \tag{1}$$

where $\bigcirc_{j-i=s} v[i,j] = v_s \in \mathbb{G}_1^n$, $\bigcirc_{j-i=s} w[i,j] = w_s \in \mathbb{G}_1$.[3]

The left-hand side (LHS) of Eq. (1) has exponentiation of x_t, and its degree takes even integers between $-4n+2$ and $4n-2$. Our $4n+1$ distinct challenges x_t determine P. Then, the extractor can compute v_P, w_P such that $P = E(v_P, H) e(w_P, U)$. By q-pairing assumption whose instance is the CRS

[3] Once v_s and w_s are constructed, the extractor extracts the witness using them. In the extract process, the extractor does not decompose v_s to multi-$v[i,j]$. That is, it does not affect soundness to substitute sending $v \in \mathbb{G}_1^{n \times 2d(2d-1)}$ with $\bar{v} \in \mathbb{G}_1^{4d-2}$ in Sect. 3.3.

$\boldsymbol{H} \parallel U$ on $\mathbb{G}_2$, we can separate the $\boldsymbol{H}$ and U terms. Then, we obtain two equations:

$$\boxed{\boldsymbol{H}\text{ correspondence}} : \boldsymbol{v}_P \circ \big(\bigcirc_{s \in J_d} \boldsymbol{v}_s^{x_t^s} \big) = \bigcirc_{i \in I_d} \overrightarrow{(\boldsymbol{g}_i^{x_t^{-i}})}^{\boldsymbol{a}'_t} \circ \overrightarrow{(\boldsymbol{h}_i^{x_t^i})}^{\boldsymbol{b}'_t} \tag{2}$$

$$\boxed{U\text{ correspondence}} : w_P \cdot \prod_{s \in J_d} w_s^{x_t^s} = u^{\langle \boldsymbol{a}'_t, \boldsymbol{b}'_t \rangle} \tag{3}$$

for all $t \in [12d-5]$.

The extractor knows all the exponents $x_t^{j-i}, x_t^{-i}, x_t^j, \boldsymbol{a}'_t$, and $\boldsymbol{b}'_t$ in Eq. (2) from $4d-2$ distinct challenges. There are $4d-1$ distinct powers of x_t^2 in the LHS in Eq. (2). Thus, by using the inverse matrix of M and elementary linear algebra in the public exponents of the first $4d-1$ equalities in Eq. (2), the extractor can find the exponent matrices $\{\boldsymbol{a}_{P,r}, \boldsymbol{b}_{P,r}\}_{r \in I_d}$ and $\{\boldsymbol{a}_{s,r}, \boldsymbol{b}_{s,r}\}_{r \in I_d}$ for $s \in J_d$ satisfying

$$\boldsymbol{v}_P = \bigcirc_{r \in I_d} \overrightarrow{\boldsymbol{g}_r^{\boldsymbol{a}_{P,r}}} \circ \overrightarrow{\boldsymbol{h}_r^{\boldsymbol{b}_{P,r}}}, \quad \boldsymbol{v}_s = \bigcirc_{r \in I_d} \overrightarrow{\boldsymbol{g}_r^{\boldsymbol{a}_{s,r}}} \circ \overrightarrow{\boldsymbol{h}_r^{\boldsymbol{b}_{s,r}}} \tag{4}$$

We claim that concatenation of submatrices $\boldsymbol{a}_{P,r}, \boldsymbol{b}_{P,r} \in \mathbb{Z}_p^{m' \times n}$ are valid witnesses.

Combine Eq. (4) with Eq. (2):

$$\begin{aligned} \boldsymbol{v}_P \circ \big(\bigcirc_{s \in J_d} \boldsymbol{v}_s^{x_t^s} \big) &= \bigcirc_{r \in I_d} \overrightarrow{\boldsymbol{g}_r^{\boldsymbol{a}_{P,r}}} \circ \overrightarrow{\boldsymbol{h}_r^{\boldsymbol{b}_{P,r}}} \circ \big(\bigcirc_{s \in J_d} \overrightarrow{\boldsymbol{g}_r^{\boldsymbol{a}_{s,r}}} \circ \overrightarrow{\boldsymbol{h}_r^{\boldsymbol{b}_{s,r}}} \big)^{x_t^s} \\ &= \bigcirc_{r \in I_d} \overrightarrow{\boldsymbol{g}_r^{\boldsymbol{a}_{P,r} + \sum_{s \in J_d} \boldsymbol{a}_{s,r} x_t^s}} \circ \overrightarrow{\boldsymbol{h}_r^{\boldsymbol{b}_{P,r} + \sum_{s \in J_d} \boldsymbol{b}_{s,r} x_t^s}} \\ &= \bigcirc_{r \in I_d} \overrightarrow{\boldsymbol{g}_r^{\boldsymbol{a}'_t x_t^{-r}}} \circ \overrightarrow{\boldsymbol{h}_r^{\boldsymbol{b}'_t x_t^r}} \end{aligned} \tag{5}$$

By discrete logarithm relation assumption, we can separate exponents. For all $t \in [12d-5]$ and $r \in I_d$, we obtain

$$\boxed{\boldsymbol{g}_r\text{ exponentiation}} : \boldsymbol{a}_{P,r} + \sum_{s \in J_d} \boldsymbol{a}_{s,r} x_t^s = \boldsymbol{a}'_t x_t^{-r} \tag{6}$$

$$\boxed{\boldsymbol{h}_r\text{ exponentiation}} : \boldsymbol{b}_{P,r} + \sum_{s \in J_d} \boldsymbol{b}_{s,r} x_t^s = \boldsymbol{b}'_t x_t^r \tag{7}$$

Let both Eq. (6) and Eq. (7) be multiplied by x_t^r and x_t^{-r} respectively. Then, both equations have degrees of x_t range between $6d-3$ and $-6d+3$ according to $r \in I_d$ and $s \in J_d$, and it holds for all $t \in [12d-5]$. $12d-5$ distinct challenges $\{x_t\}$ determine polynomials $f, g : \mathbb{Z}_p \to \mathbb{Z}_p^{m \times n}$ satisfying the following equations:

$$\boldsymbol{a}_{P,r} X^r + \sum_{s \in J_d} \boldsymbol{a}_{s,r} X^{s+r} = f(X), \quad \boldsymbol{b}_{P,r} X^{-r} + \sum_{s \in J_d} \boldsymbol{b}_{s,r} X^{s-r} = g(X) \tag{8}$$

for all $r \in I_d$. Notice that the RHSs of Eq. (8) do not depend on the choice of r. Since the possible value of r is between $-2d+1$ and $r = 2d-1$, the polynomials $f(X)$ and $g(X)$ take degrees between $-2d+1$ and $2d-1$. Then, we obtain the following equations:

$$\boldsymbol{a}'_t = \sum_{r \in I_d} \boldsymbol{a}_{P,r} x_t^r, \quad \boldsymbol{b}'_t = \sum_{r \in I_d} \boldsymbol{b}_{P,r} x_t^{-r} \tag{9}$$

In a similar way to obtain exponent vectors $\boldsymbol{a}_{P,r}$ $\boldsymbol{b}_{P,r}$, the extractor can obtain exponents $c_P, c_s \in \mathbb{Z}_p$ such that $w_P = u^{c_P}$ and $w_s = u^{c_s}$. In the RHS in Eq. (2), let us put the results of Eq. (9). Then, we obtain the following equation:

$$u^{c_P} \cdot \prod_{s \in J_d} u^{c_s x_t^s} = u^{\langle \boldsymbol{a}'_t, \boldsymbol{b}'_t \rangle} = \prod_{i,j \in I_d} u^{\sum_{i,j \in I_d} \langle \boldsymbol{a}_{P,j}, \boldsymbol{b}_{P,i} \rangle x_t^{j-i}} \tag{10}$$

The exponents equation $c_P + \sum_{s \in J_d} c_s x_t^s = \sum_{i,j \in I_d} \langle \boldsymbol{a}_{P,j}, \boldsymbol{b}_{P,i} \rangle x_t^{j-i}$ holds by DLR assumption. The $8n-3$ distinct values determine the coefficient of the equation. Therefore, the emulator extracts valid witness $\boldsymbol{a}_P, \boldsymbol{b}_P$, which satisfies $c_P = \sum_{i \in I_d} \langle \boldsymbol{a}_{P,i}, \boldsymbol{b}_{P,i} \rangle = \langle \boldsymbol{a}_P, \boldsymbol{b}_P \rangle$. □

References

1. Abe, M., Fuchsbauer, G., Groth, J., Haralambiev, K., Ohkubo, M.: Structure-preserving signatures and commitments to group elements. J. Cryptol. **29**(2), 363–421 (2016)
2. Arun, A., Ganesh, C., Lokam, S.V., Mopuri, T., Sridhar, S.: Dew: transparent constant-sized zkSNARKs. Cryptology ePrint Archive, Report 2022/419 (2022). https://eprint.iacr.org/2022/419.pdf
3. Attema, T., Cramer, R., Kohl, L.: A compressed σ-protocol theory for lattices. In: Malkin, T., Peikert, C. (eds.) CRYPTO 2021, Part II. LNCS, vol. 12826, pp. 549–579. Springer, Cham (2021). https://doi.org/10.1007/978-3-030-84245-1_19
4. Ben-Sasson, E., Chiesa, A., Spooner, N.: Interactive oracle proofs. In: Hirt, M., Smith, A. (eds.) TCC 2016, Part II. LNCS, vol. 9986, pp. 31–60. Springer, Heidelberg (2016). https://doi.org/10.1007/978-3-662-53644-5_2
5. Bootle, J., Cerulli, A., Chaidos, P., Groth, J., Petit, C.: Efficient zero-knowledge arguments for arithmetic circuits in the discrete log setting. In: Fischlin, M., Coron, J.-S. (eds.) EUROCRYPT 2016. LNCS, vol. 9666, pp. 327–357. Springer, Heidelberg (2016). https://doi.org/10.1007/978-3-662-49896-5_12
6. Bowe, S., Grigg, J., Hopwood, D.: Recursive proof composition without a trusted setup (2019). https://eprint.iacr.org/2019/1021
7. Brands, S.: Untraceable off-line cash in wallet with observers. In: Stinson, D.R. (ed.) CRYPTO 1993. LNCS, vol. 773, pp. 302–318. Springer, Heidelberg (1994). https://doi.org/10.1007/3-540-48329-2_26
8. Bünz, B., Bootle, J., Boneh, D., Poelstra, A., Wuille, P., Maxwell, G.: Bulletproofs: short proofs for confidential transactions and more. In: IEEE Symposium on Security and Privacy 2018, pp. 315–334. IEEE (2018)
9. Bünz, B., Fisch, B., Szepieniec, A.: Transparent SNARKs from DARK compilers. In: Canteaut, A., Ishai, Y. (eds.) EUROCRYPT 2020. LNCS, vol. 12105, pp. 677–706. Springer, Cham (2020). https://doi.org/10.1007/978-3-030-45721-1_24

10. Bünz, B., Maller, M., Mishra, P., Tyagi, N., Vesely, P.: Proofs for inner pairing products and applications. In: Tibouchi, M., Wang, H. (eds.) ASIACRYPT 2021, Part III. LNCS, vol. 13092, pp. 65–97. Springer, Cham (2021). https://doi.org/10.1007/978-3-030-92078-4_3
11. Chiesa, A., Hu, Y., Maller, M., Mishra, P., Vesely, N., Ward, N.: Marlin: preprocessing zkSNARKs with universal and updatable SRS. In: Canteaut, A., Ishai, Y. (eds.) EUROCRYPT 2020. LNCS, vol. 12105, pp. 738–768. Springer, Cham (2020). https://doi.org/10.1007/978-3-030-45721-1_26
12. Chung, H., Han, K., Ju, C., Kim, M., Seo, J.H.: Bulletproofs+: shorter proofs for a privacy-enhanced distributed ledger. IEEE Access **10**, 42067–42082 (2022)
13. Daza, V., Ràfols, C., Zacharakis, A.: Updateable inner product argument with logarithmic verifier and applications. In: Kiayias, A., Kohlweiss, M., Wallden, P., Zikas, V. (eds.) PKC 2020. LNCS, vol. 12110, pp. 527–557. Springer, Cham (2020). https://doi.org/10.1007/978-3-030-45374-9_18
14. Fiat, A., Shamir, A.: How to prove yourself: practical solutions to identification and signature problems. In: Odlyzko, A.M. (ed.) CRYPTO 1986. LNCS, vol. 263, pp. 186–194. Springer, Heidelberg (1987). https://doi.org/10.1007/3-540-47721-7_12
15. Gabizon, A., Williamson, Z.J., Ciobotaru, O.: PLONK: permutations over lagrange-bases for oecumenical noninteractive arguments of knowledge. Cryptology ePrint Archive, Report 2019/953 (2019). https://eprint.iacr.org/2019/953.pdf.
16. Goldwasser, S., Micali, S., Rackoff, C.: The knowledge complexity of interactive proof systems. SIAM J. Comput. **18**, 186–208 (1989)
17. Groth, J.: Linear algebra with sub-linear zero-knowledge arguments. In: Halevi, S. (ed.) CRYPTO 2009. LNCS, vol. 5677, pp. 192–208. Springer, Heidelberg (2009). https://doi.org/10.1007/978-3-642-03356-8_12
18. Groth, J.: On the size of pairing-based non-interactive arguments. In: Fischlin, M., Coron, J.-S. (eds.) EUROCRYPT 2016. LNCS, vol. 9666, pp. 305–326. Springer, Heidelberg (2016). https://doi.org/10.1007/978-3-662-49896-5_11
19. Kate, A., Zaverucha, G.M., Goldberg, I.: Constant-size commitments to polynomials and their applications. In: Abe, M. (ed.) ASIACRYPT 2010. LNCS, vol. 6477, pp. 177–194. Springer, Heidelberg (2010). https://doi.org/10.1007/978-3-642-17373-8_11
20. Kim, S., Lee, H., Seo, J.H.: Efficient zero-knowledge arguments in discrete logarithm setting: sublogarithmic proof or sublinear verifier. In: Agrawal, S., Lin, D. (eds.) ASIACRYPT 2022. LNCS, vol. 13792, pp. 403–433. Springer, Cham (2023). https://doi.org/10.1007/978-3-031-22966-4_14
21. Lai, R.W.F., Malavolta, G., Ronge, V.: Succinct arguments for bilinear group arithmetic: practical structure-preserving cryptography. In: ACM CCS 2019, pp. 2057–2074 (2019)
22. Lee, J.: Dory: efficient, transparent arguments for generalised inner products and polynomial commitments. In: Nissim, K., Waters, B. (eds.) TCC 2021, Part II. LNCS, vol. 13043, pp. 1–34. Springer, Cham (2021). https://doi.org/10.1007/978-3-030-90453-1_1
23. Maller, M., Bowe, S., Kohlweiss, M., Meiklejohn, S.: Sonic: zero-knowledge snarks from linear-size universal and updatable structured reference strings. In: ACM CCS 2019, pp. 2111–2128. Association for Computing Machinery (2019)
24. Seo, J.H.: Round-efficient sub-linear zero-knowledge arguments for linear algebra. In: Catalano, D., Fazio, N., Gennaro, R., Nicolosi, A. (eds.) PKC 2011. LNCS, vol. 6571, pp. 387–402. Springer, Heidelberg (2011). https://doi.org/10.1007/978-3-642-19379-8_24

25. Seo, J.H.: Short round sub-linear zero-knowledge argument for linear algebraic relations. IEICE Trans. Fundam. Electron. Commun. Comput. Sci. **95**(4), 776–789 (2012)
26. Wahby, R.S., Tzialla, I., Shelat, A., Thaler, J., Walfish, M.: Doubly-efficient zkSNARKs without trusted setup. In: IEEE Symposium on Security and Privacy 2018, pp. 926–943. IEEE (2018)
27. Zhou, Z., Zhang, Z., Tao, H., Li, T., Zhao, B.: Efficient inner product arguments and their applications in range proofs. IET Inf. Secur. **17**, 485–504 (2023)

Card Based Cryptography

Efficient Card-Based Millionaires' Protocols via Non-binary Input Encoding

Koji Nuida[1,2(✉)]

[1] Institute of Mathematics for Industry (IMI), Kyushu University, Fukuoka, Japan
nuida@imi.kyushu-u.ac.jp

[2] National Institute of Advanced Industrial Science and Technology (AIST), Tokyo, Japan

Abstract. Comparison of integers, a traditional topic in secure multi-party computation since Yao's pioneering work on "Millionaires' Problem" (FOCS 1982), is also well studied in card-based cryptography. For the problem, Miyahara et al. (Theoretical Computer Science, 2020) proposed a protocol using binary cards (i.e., cards with two kinds of symbols) that is highly efficient in terms of numbers of cards and shuffles, and its extension to number cards (i.e., cards with distinct symbols). In this paper, with a different design strategy which we name "Tug-of-War Technique", we propose new protocols based on binary cards and on number cards. For binary cards, our protocol improves the previous protocol asymptotically (in bit lengths of input integers) in terms of numbers of cards and shuffles when adopting ternary encoding of input integers. For number cards, at the cost of increasing the number of cards, our protocol improves the number of shuffles of the previous protocol even with binary encoding, and more with q-ary encoding where $q > 2$.

Keywords: Card-based protocols · integer comparison · Millionaires' Problem

1 Introduction

Secure multiparty computation (MPC) is a cryptographic technology that enables multiple parties to collaboratively derive a correct output while keeping each party's input secret to the other parties. The notion of MPC was proposed by Yao [12] in 1982, where he discussed the problem of securely comparing two integers, nowadays called "Yao's Millionaires' Problem". Besides such historical importance, comparison of integers has also been an active research topic in the area of MPC from the viewpoints of theoretical interests and ubiquitous practical applications. Moreover, it is also a major topic in card-based cryptography, which is a research area where MPC (as well as zero-knowledge proofs, etc.) is executed by using physical (non-electronic) objects such as a deck of cards [1].

Most of the card-based protocols in the literature are designed assuming a deck of "binary cards" with two kinds of front-side symbols, frequently denoted by ♣ and ♡, and identical back-side symbols. There is also a line of studies for card-based protocols using a deck of "number cards" [8] where all cards have

J. Shikata and H. Kuzuno (Eds.): IWSEC 2023, LNCS 14128, pp. 237–254, 2023.
https://doi.org/10.1007/978-3-031-41326-1_13

distinct front-side symbols, such as the standard playing cards with 52 different symbols (or 53, including a joker). An essential ingredient of card-based protocols is shuffle operations, which permute the sequence of cards according to some probability distribution, untraceably by any party. (We note that there are also card-based protocols using so-called private permutations [7] instead of shuffles, which are out of the scope of the present work.) The efficiency of card-based protocols is mainly evaluated by the numbers of cards and shuffles.

Among the existing card-based protocols based on binary cards in the literature for comparison of two input integers in a range, say $\{0, 1, \dots, m-1\}$, a protocol proposed by Miyahara et al. [3] has the smallest number of cards to the authors' best knowledge and also uses a fairly small number of shuffles. Namely, their protocol uses $4\ell + 2$ cards and $2\ell - 1$ shuffles where $\ell := \lceil \log_2 m \rceil$ denotes the bit length of each input integer. Their basic strategy itself is elementary: they compare the two bits in the binary expressions of two input integers from the most significant to the least significant bits, and adopt the earliest non-tie result. They implemented this strategy by combining known efficient protocols for fundamental gates and also applying some optimizations. In particular, they used the standard encoding of each bit of an input integer into the order of two cards $\boxed{\clubsuit}$ and $\boxed{\heartsuit}$. As their protocol requires just two extra cards in addition to the 4ℓ cards for encoding two ℓ-bit integers, the number of cards cannot be largely reduced when assuming this encoding rule. Consequently, any significant improvement in the number of cards requires a change of encoding rules.

In fact, there is a known encoding technique for a non-binary, say q-ary value in $\{0, 1, \dots, q-1\}$ (with $q > 2$) using the q possible positions of a single card $\boxed{\heartsuit}$ in a sequence of q cards where the other $q-1$ cards are $\boxed{\clubsuit}$. By using $q = 3$, i.e., ternary expressions of integers, the number of cards needed in encoding two input integers can be reduced in comparison to the binary encoding above (due to the effect that the number of digits is decreased). However, the previous protocol in [3] relies on known efficient protocols specific to binary AND and XOR gates, therefore it is not directly extendible to non-binary input encoding. A possible strategy is to apply some efficient protocol tailored to comparison of non-binary (and fairly small) integers, recursively from the most significant to the least significant digits. For example, Nakai et al. [7] proposed a card-based implementation of Yao's original protocol in [12] using private permutations, and its conversion to the shuffle model (i.e., without private permutations) is also described in [3]. However, this protocol has a crucial drawback from the present viewpoint, inherited from Yao's protocol, that it is in nature for only distinguishing two cases $\alpha < \beta$ and $\alpha \geq \beta$, while such a recursive usage as above requires distinguishing three cases $\alpha < \beta$, $\alpha > \beta$, and $\alpha = \beta$. To the authors' best knowledge, an efficient card-based protocol for non-binary inputs that can distinguish these three cases is not known in the literature.

1.1 Our Contributions

In this paper, we introduce a new design strategy for integer comparison protocols, which we name "Tug-of-War Technique", and propose a new card-based protocol based on the technique. Our Tug-of-War subprotocol distinguishes three cases $\alpha_\nu < \beta_\nu$, $\alpha_\nu = \beta_\nu$, and $\alpha_\nu > \beta_\nu$ for q-ary digits α_ν and β_ν of input integers α and β, respectively, therefore it can realize the strategy for recursive comparison mentioned in the previous paragraph. Table 1 shows a comparison of the efficiency of our proposed protocol with the previous protocol in [3], where some cells also include asymptotic values (when $\log_2 m \to \infty$) of the numbers of cards or shuffles. See Sect. 2.4 for definitions of the shuffles appearing in the table. When using binary encoding, our proposed protocol is slightly less efficient compared to [3] in both numbers of cards and shuffles. On the other hand, our proposed protocol with ternary encoding achieves better efficiency than [3]; asymptotically, the number of cards is reduced to approximately 94.6% and the number of shuffles is reduced to 63.1%. (We note that the shuffles used in [3] are random bisection cuts, which are the simplest case of pile-shifting shuffles; while our protocol requires not only random bisection cuts but also more complicated pile-shifting shuffles.) In addition, Table 1 also includes the state-of-the-art protocol by Ono et al. [9] among card-based garbled circuits [11], which uses just a single shuffle but a significantly larger (though still linear in $\log_2 m$) number of cards. See Sect. 3.4 for the details of the comparison of efficiency.

Technical Overview. We explain the central idea of our proposed Tug-of-War Technique for comparison of two input digits α_ν and β_ν, by using the following simple but *insecure* protocol as an example:

1. Arrange cards sequentially (from left to right), where the card ($\boxed{\heartsuit}$, in default) at the middle point O is given in advance and the others are $\boxed{\clubsuit}$'s.
2. Alice shifts the sequence by α_ν to the left.
3. Bob shifts the sequence by β_ν to the right.
4. Alice (respectively, Bob) takes the cards at the left (respectively, right) side, exclusively relative to the point O; a card at the point O remains not taken.

It is easily seen that, if $\alpha_\nu > \beta_\nu$ (respectively, $\alpha_\nu < \beta_\nu$), then Alice (respectively, Bob) takes the card $\boxed{\heartsuit}$ at the end of the protocol; while if $\alpha_\nu = \beta_\nu$, then the card $\boxed{\heartsuit}$ is not taken. (Intuitively, the party who pulls the rope of cards more strongly will get the card $\boxed{\heartsuit}$.) Moreover, when this protocol is repeated recursively from the most significant to the least significant digits, the card $\boxed{\heartsuit}$ is not taken until $\alpha_\nu \neq \beta_\nu$ holds, and once $\alpha_\nu \neq \beta_\nu$ holds, $\boxed{\heartsuit}$ is taken by the party with larger input at the round and $\boxed{\heartsuit}$ does not appear in the subsequent rounds. This realizes correct comparison of input integers. Although the protocol above is insecure (as the position of $\boxed{\heartsuit}$ at the end of a round tells the difference

Table 1. Comparison of (committed-format) protocols for comparing integers $\alpha, \beta \in \{0, 1, \dots, m-1\}$ (with binary output distinguishing $\alpha < \beta$ and $\alpha \geq \beta$): here PSS, CS, and US denote a pile-shifting shuffle, a complete shuffle, and a (complicated) uniform shuffle, respectively; for (*), the bottom row is under an assumption that the cards can be shuffled before generating input commitments and each party is allowed to generate an input commitment by using private permutations (not counted in the table)

Cards	Protocols	# of Cards	# of Shuffles
Binary	Miyahara et al. [3], §6	$4\lceil \log_2 m \rceil + 2$ $\sim 4 \log_2 m$	$(2\lceil \log_2 m \rceil - 1)$ PSS $\sim 2 \log_2 m$
	Ono et al. [9]	$28\lceil \log_2 m \rceil - 16$ $\sim 28 \log_2 m$	1 US
	Ours, Sect. 3 q-ary encoding	$2q\lceil \log_q m \rceil + 2q - 1$ $\sim (2q/\log_2 q) \log_2 m$	$(2\lceil \log_q m \rceil + 2)$ PSS $\sim (2/\log_2 q) \log_2 m$
	Ours, Sect. 3 binary encoding ($q = 2$)	$4\lceil \log_2 m \rceil + 3$ $\sim 4 \log_2 m$	$(2\lceil \log_2 m \rceil + 2)$ PSS $\sim 2 \log_2 m$
	Ours, Sect. 3 ternary encoding ($q = 3$)	$6\lceil \log_3 m \rceil + 5$ $\sim (3.7855\cdots) \log_2 m$	$(2\lceil \log_3 m \rceil + 2)$ PSS $\sim (1.2618\cdots) \log_2 m$
Number	Miyahara et al. [3], §7	$4\lceil \log_2 m \rceil + 4$	$(6\lceil \log_2 m \rceil - 2)$ PSS
	Ours, Sect. 4 q-ary encoding (*)	$(6q - 3)\lceil \log_q m \rceil + 3$	$(3\lceil \log_q m \rceil + 2)$ PSS +1 CS
		$(5q - 3)\lceil \log_q m \rceil + 3$	$(2\lceil \log_q m \rceil + 2)$ PSS +1 CS
	Ours, Sect. 4 binary encoding ($q = 2$) (*)	$9\lceil \log_2 m \rceil + 3$	$(3\lceil \log_2 m \rceil + 2)$ PSS +1 CS
		$7\lceil \log_2 m \rceil + 3$	$(2\lceil \log_2 m \rceil + 2)$ PSS +1 CS

of the input digits), we can convert it into a secure protocol by applying a known technique of computing subtraction of integers (e.g., [10]) and using some post-processing phase to securely determine who has taken the ♡.

Extension to Number Cards. The previous paper [3] also gives a variant of the comparison protocol that uses number cards instead of binary cards. To the authors' best knowledge, it is the protocol with minimal number of cards among such existing protocols using number cards in the literature. In fact, the number of cards is even kept almost unchanged from the case of binary cards. On the other hand, the number of shuffles is increased to almost three times larger than the case of binary cards. This is because the efficient protocols for fundamental gates used originally are tailored to binary cards, and their protocol with number cards has to rely on less efficient building-block protocols.

In contrast, our proposed protocol with binary cards has an advantage that the underlying mechanism, especially that for Tug-of-War subprotocol, is not deeply dependent on the characteristic of binary cards. Our variant of the protocol using number cards is basically obtained by partitioning the number cards in a deck into "♣-cards" and "♡-cards" first and then replacing the originally used binary cards $\boxed{\clubsuit}$ and $\boxed{\heartsuit}$ with random $\clubsuit$-cards and $\heartsuit$-cards, respectively. Here, in fact, we need some additional care about the usage of number cards; e.g., some previously opened cards were reused in later steps for our protocol based on binary cards, but such reuse of cards should be avoided in the case of number cards to achieve the security. Even considering such points, our proposed protocol is still significantly more efficient than [3] in terms of the number of shuffles, while it uses an almost twice larger number of cards than [3]. See Table 1 for more information on the comparison with the previous work, and Sect. 4.3 for the details. We note also that the number of shuffles in our protocol can be decreased further (at the cost of increasing the number of cards) by using q-ary encoding with $q > 2$. It is a future research topic to improve further the trade-off between the number of cards and the number of shuffles.

1.2 Organization of the Paper

In Sect. 2, we summarize basic notations (Sect. 2.1) and our model of card-based protocols (Sect. 2.2), including the encoding rule of input integers (Sect. 2.3) and definitions of shuffles (Sect. 2.4). In Sect. 3, we introduce the Tug-of-War subprotocol (Sect. 3.1), and then describe our main protocol (Sect. 3.2). We also discuss a way of modifying the protocol to deal with ternary and/or non-committed outputs (Sect. 3.3), and explain a comparison with previous work (Sect. 3.4). In Sect. 4, we explain how an integer is encoded using number cards (Sect. 4.1), describe the extension of our proposed protocol based on binary cards to number cards (Sect. 4.2), and explain about the comparison of our protocols with the previous protocol (Sect. 4.3).

2 Preliminaries

2.1 Notations

In the paper, we let $[a..b] := \{a, a+1, \dots, b\} \subseteq \mathbb{Z}$ for two integers a, b. Let S_n denote the symmetric group on n letters. For a condition P, we define $\chi[P] := 1$ if P is satisfied and $\chi[P] := 0$ if P is not satisfied.

Let $\boldsymbol{q} = (q_0, q_1, \dots, q_{\ell-1})$ be a sequence of ℓ integers $q_i \geq 2$. Then we define

$$|\boldsymbol{q}| := q_0 + \cdots + q_{\ell-1}\,,\ \pi(\boldsymbol{q}) := q_0 q_1 \cdots q_{\ell-1}\,,\ \max(\boldsymbol{q}) := \max\{q_0, \dots, q_{\ell-1}\}\ .$$

Now in the same way as ordinary q-ary expressions of integers, for any $a \in [0..\pi(\boldsymbol{q}) - 1]$, there is a unique expression of the form

$$a = \sum_{k=0}^{\ell-1} a_k q_0 q_1 \cdots q_{k-1}\,,\ a_k \in [0..q_k - 1]$$

(where $q_0 q_1 \cdots q_{k-1} := 1$ when $k = 0$). We call it the $\boldsymbol{q}$*-ary expression* of a and write $a = (a_{\ell-1} \cdots a_1 a_0)_{\boldsymbol{q}}$. When the q_k's are a constant value q (as in the case of ordinary q-ary expressions), we also write the sequence $\boldsymbol{q}$ as $q^{\times \ell}$.

2.2 Model of Card-Based Protocols

In the paper, we put the following assumptions on the cards. Each card has a front-side symbol and a back-side symbol. There are two possible states for cards, "face-up" and "face-down", where only the front-side (respectively, back-side) symbol is visible for a face-up (respectively, face-down) card. All cards have identical back-side symbols, denoted by '?', and hence face-down cards are indistinguishable from each other. Face-up cards with identical front-side symbols are also indistinguishable from each other. For the purpose of explanation, we often write a face-down card with invisible front-side symbol s as $\boxed{[s]}$.

In the paper, we deal with the following two kinds of cards.

Binary cards The front-side symbols are ♣ or ♡.

Number cards There are a number, say N, of cards in the deck and each card has a mutually distinct number from 1 to N as the front-side symbol.

The card-based protocols in the paper can be modeled in the following manner (see e.g., [5] for a more formal treatment of card-based protocols). Here we only deal with protocols played by two parties, say Alice and Bob with inputs α and β, respectively, and suppose that the number L of steps in a protocol is constant (possibly depending on a public parameter).

Initial sequence The initial card sequence is the concatenation of three sequences $\mathsf{In}_1(\alpha)$, $\mathsf{In}_2(\beta)$, and Aux, where $\mathsf{In}_1(\alpha)$ and $\mathsf{In}_2(\beta)$ are sequences of face-down cards determined by a certain encoding rule from the input values α and β, respectively, and Aux is a publicly known sequence of face-down cards. Moreover, a list Vis of "visible sequences" is initialized to be empty.

Main loop In ν-th step ($\nu = 1, 2, \ldots, L$), the parties execute one of the following operations on the card sequence according to the current content of Vis, where M denotes the number of cards in the sequence:

Permutation Permute the cards in the sequence according to a publicly known permutation $\sigma \in S_M$.

Turn Switch the states of some (possibly multiple) cards, where we write "open" (respectively, "turn down") to mean changing from "face-down" to "face-up" (respectively, from "face-up" to "face-down").

Shuffle Choose a permutation $\sigma \in S_M$ according to some probability distribution, and permute the card sequence according to σ in a way that σ is kept secret for both parties.

Let vis_ν denote the sequence of visible symbols of the card sequence, called the *visible sequence*, after the operation above. The parties append vis_ν to Vis. For example, if the card sequence after the operation is $\boxed{♣}\boxed{♡}\boxed{?}\boxed{?}\boxed{♡}$, then $\mathsf{vis}_\nu = (♣, ♡, ?, ?, ♡)$. Let $\mathsf{Vis}_{\mathsf{Out}}$ denote the list Vis after the L-th step.

Output (for "non-committed-format" protocols) According to a certain rule from the list $\mathsf{Vis}_{\mathsf{Out}}$, the parties output a value, denoted by Out.

Output (for "committed-format" protocols) According to a certain rule from the list $\mathsf{Vis}_{\mathsf{Out}}$, the parties determine a list of positions, pick up the (face-down) cards at those positions in the card sequence, and output the sequence of those picked cards. Now set Out to be the empty list.

We say that a protocol is *secure* (in the semi-honest model) if for any party with input $\gamma = \alpha$ or $\gamma = \beta$, the conditional probability distribution of $\mathsf{Vis}_{\mathsf{Out}}$ conditioned on a value of (γ, Out) is independent of the other input β or α.

In what follows, a description of a concrete protocol may use some intuitive explanations in order to improve the readability. For example, we allow a protocol to arrange (a part of) the cards in multiple rows rather than a single sequence, or to store cards into (or take cards from) some separate "regions"; such operations can in fact be simulated by some appropriate operations performed on a single sequence of cards as in the model above.

2.3 Encoding of Input Values

We use the following two kinds of encodings of an integer into binary cards.

- We use the term *k-vector commitment* of $a \in [0..k-1]$ and write $\mathsf{vEnc}_k(a)$ to mean a sequence of k face-down binary cards in which the a-th card (counted from the 0-th) from the right has front-side symbol ♡ and the others have front-side symbols ♣. For example, we have $\mathsf{vEnc}_5(3) =$ [♣][♡][♣][♣][♣]. When $k = 2$, it is the same as the standard definition of commitments of bits in card-based cryptography.
- Let $\boldsymbol{q} = (q_0, q_1, \ldots, q_{\ell-1})$ be a sequence of ℓ integers $q_i \geq 2$. For any integer $a \in [0..\pi(\boldsymbol{q}) - 1]$ with $a = (a_{\ell-1} \cdots a_1 a_0)_{\boldsymbol{q}}$ (see Sect. 2.1 for the notations), we use the term *$\boldsymbol{q}$-ary commitment* of a and write $\mathsf{qEnc}_{\boldsymbol{q}}(a)$ to mean the sequence of q_k-vector commitments of each a_k:

$$\mathsf{qEnc}_{\boldsymbol{q}}(a) = (\mathsf{vEnc}_{q_{\ell-1}}(a_{\ell-1}), \ldots, \mathsf{vEnc}_{q_1}(a_1), \mathsf{vEnc}_{q_0}(a_0)) \ .$$

  When $\boldsymbol{q} = 2^{\times \ell}$, it is the same as the standard definition of commitments of integers, which is used in e.g., [3].

2.4 Shuffles Used in the Paper

Complete Shuffle (CS). This is a shuffle that permutes all the target cards uniformly at random.

Pile-Shifting Shuffle (PSS) [2]. Suppose that an array of cards with r rows and c columns is given. A *column*-PSS is a shuffle that cyclically rotates the c columns uniformly at random (where the rows are synchronized). For example, a column-PSS applied to the following 3×3 array of cards

[1]	[2]	[3]
[4]	[5]	[6]
[7]	[8]	[9]

yields one of the following three arrays with probability 1/3 each:

$$\begin{array}{|c|c|c|} \hline [1] & [2] & [3] \\ \hline [4] & [5] & [6] \\ \hline [7] & [8] & [9] \\ \hline \end{array} , \begin{array}{|c|c|c|} \hline [2] & [3] & [1] \\ \hline [5] & [6] & [4] \\ \hline [8] & [9] & [7] \\ \hline \end{array} , \begin{array}{|c|c|c|} \hline [3] & [1] & [2] \\ \hline [6] & [4] & [5] \\ \hline [9] & [7] & [8] \\ \hline \end{array} .$$

We also define a *row*-PSS by switching the roles of rows and columns in a column-PSS. In the example above, a row-PSS yields one of the following three arrays with probability 1/3 each:

$$\begin{array}{|c|c|c|} \hline [1] & [2] & [3] \\ \hline [4] & [5] & [6] \\ \hline [7] & [8] & [9] \\ \hline \end{array} , \begin{array}{|c|c|c|} \hline [4] & [5] & [6] \\ \hline [7] & [8] & [9] \\ \hline [1] & [2] & [3] \\ \hline \end{array} , \begin{array}{|c|c|c|} \hline [7] & [8] & [9] \\ \hline [1] & [2] & [3] \\ \hline [4] & [5] & [6] \\ \hline \end{array} .$$

We note that column-PSSs with $c = 2$ columns and row-PSSs with $r = 2$ rows are equivalent to *random bisection cuts* (RBCs) [6].

3 Our Proposed Protocol with Binary Cards

3.1 Tug-of-War Subprotocol

In this subsection, we introduce a subprotocol as in Protocol 1 used in our proposed protocol, which we name *Tug-of-War subprotocol.* In both of the subprotocol and our main protocol (Sect. 3.2), we use five separate regions named "Main Memory", "♣-Garage", "♡-Garage", "Memory A", and "Memory B". Main Memory is endowed with two-dimensional coordinates and each card is placed at an integer point. For integers $i \geq 1$ and j, we write "Point (i, j)" to mean the j-th column (counted from left to right) of the i-th row (counted from top to bottom) in Main Memory. ♣-Garage and ♡-Garage are for storing face-down cards $\boxed{[\clubsuit]}$ and $\boxed{[\heartsuit]}$, respectively. Memory A and Memory B are for storing face-down cards taken during a protocol by Alice and Bob, respectively.

Figure 1 shows an example of Protocol 1 for $q = 4$, $\alpha = 3$, and $\beta = 1$, i.e., $\mathsf{vEnc}_q(\alpha) = \boxed{[\heartsuit]}\boxed{[\clubsuit]}\boxed{[\clubsuit]}\boxed{[\clubsuit]}$ and $\mathsf{vEnc}_q(\beta) = \boxed{[\clubsuit]}\boxed{[\clubsuit]}\boxed{[\heartsuit]}\boxed{[\clubsuit]}$. Here we suppose that the card originally put at Point $(1, 0)$ is $\boxed{[\heartsuit]}$. In the figure, '$*$' denotes an empty point in Main Memory at which a card will be put. The four numbers in the right side show how the numbers of cards in ♣-Garage, ♡-Garage, Memory A, and Memory B are changed. In the example, at Step 11, one $\boxed{[\heartsuit]}$ and $q-2 = 2$ $\boxed{[\clubsuit]}$'s are taken by Alice and $q - 1 = 3$ $\boxed{[\clubsuit]}$'s are taken by Bob.

Protocol 1 Our Tug-of-War subprotocol using binary cards

Input q-vector commitments $\mathsf{vEnc}_q(\alpha), \mathsf{vEnc}_q(\beta)$ of $\alpha, \beta \in [0..q-1]$
(Main Memory involves only a single face-down card, say C, and it is at Point $(1, 0)$; and $\clubsuit$-Garage must involve at least $2q-2$ cards $\boxed{[\clubsuit]}$)

Output A single face-down card, say C', at Point $(1, 0)$ in Main Memory, and $q-1$ new cards each in Memory A and Memory B, among which at most one card is $\boxed{[\heartsuit]}$ and the others are $\boxed{[\clubsuit]}$, where

- if $C = \boxed{[\heartsuit]}$ and $\alpha > \beta$ (respectively, $\alpha < \beta$), then $\boxed{[\heartsuit]}$ is appended to Memory A (respectively, Memory B);
- if $C = \boxed{[\heartsuit]}$ and $\alpha = \beta$, then $C' = \boxed{[\heartsuit]}$;
- if $C = \boxed{[\clubsuit]}$, then all those cards are $\boxed{[\clubsuit]}$;

and two new cards $\boxed{[\heartsuit]}$ in $\heartsuit$-Garage

1: For each $j \in [1..q-1]$, move a face-down card from $\clubsuit$-Garage to Point $(1, -j)$.
2: Put the cards in $\mathsf{vEnc}_q(\alpha)$ at Points $(2, -(q-1))$ to $(2, 0)$ in reverse order; i.e., the rightmost (the 0-th) card of $\mathsf{vEnc}_q(\alpha)$ comes to Point $(2, -(q-1))$.
3: Apply column-PSS to Main Memory, and open all cards in the second row.
4: For Main Memory, rotate the columns in the two rows synchronously in a way that $\boxed{\heartsuit}$ in the second row comes to the leftmost place (i.e., Point $(2, -(q-1))$).
5: Move $\boxed{\heartsuit}$ and $q-1$ $\boxed{\clubsuit}$'s in the second row to $\heartsuit$-Garage and $\clubsuit$-Garage, respectively, and turn them face-down.
6: For each $j \in [1..q-1]$, move two face-down cards from $\clubsuit$-Garage to Points $(1, j)$ and $(2, -j)$, respectively.
7: Put the cards in $\mathsf{vEnc}_q(\beta)$ at Points $(2, 0)$ to $(2, q-1)$.
8: Apply column-PSS to Main Memory, and open all cards in the second row.
9: For Main Memory, rotate the columns in the two rows synchronously in a way that $\boxed{\heartsuit}$ in the second row comes to the rightmost place (i.e., Point $(2, q-1)$).
10: Move $\boxed{\heartsuit}$ and $2q-2$ $\boxed{\clubsuit}$'s in the second row to $\heartsuit$-Garage and $\clubsuit$-Garage, respectively, and turn them face-down.
11: Move the cards at Points $(1, j)$, $j < 0$ by Alice to Memory A, and move the cards at Points $(1, j)$, $j > 0$ by Bob to Memory B.

Let C be the card originally put at Point $(1, 0)$. In a general case, if the inputs satisfy that $\alpha > \beta$ (respectively, $\alpha < \beta$), then the card C moves $\alpha - \beta$ cells to the left (respectively, $\beta - \alpha$ cells to the right) through Steps 1–10, therefore C is taken by Alice (respectively, Bob) at Step 11. On the other hand, if $\alpha = \beta$, then the card C is still at the middle after Step 10, therefore C remains not taken at Step 11. As for the security, regardless of the input values, the visible sequences (focusing only on the second row) after Steps 3 and 8 are uniformly random sequences of $\heartsuit$ and $q-1$ (respectively, $2q-2$) $\clubsuit$'s, and those after Steps 4 and 9 are public constants specified by the protocol. Hence no information leaks during Protocol 1.

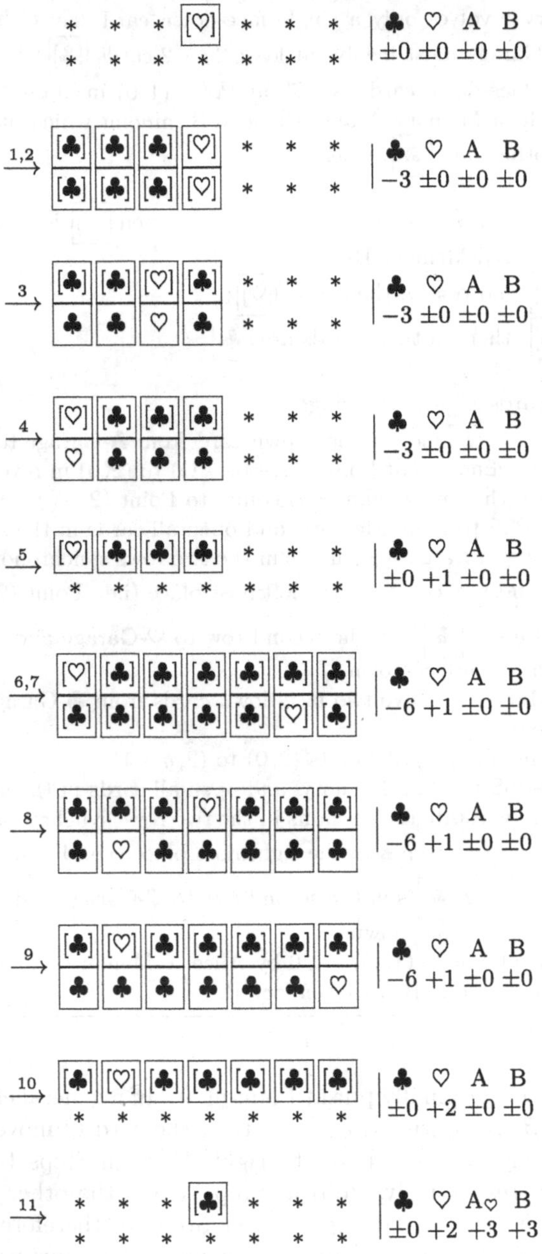

Fig. 1. Example of Protocol 1 for $q = 4$, $\alpha = 3$, $\beta = 1$: the pictures after Step 3 and Step 8 show some possible results of PSS

3.2 The Main Protocol

Based on Tug-of-War subprotocol in Sect. 3.1, we describe our proposed protocol using binary cards in Protocol 2. For $\boldsymbol{q}$-ary commitments $\mathsf{qEnc}_{\boldsymbol{q}}(\alpha)$ and $\mathsf{qEnc}_{\boldsymbol{q}}(\beta)$ of input values $\alpha = (\alpha_{\ell-1} \cdots \alpha_1\alpha_0)_{\boldsymbol{q}}$ and $\beta = (\beta_{\ell-1} \cdots \beta_1\beta_0)_{\boldsymbol{q}}$, respectively, first suppose that $\alpha \neq \beta$ and ν_0 is the largest index with $\alpha_{\nu_0} \neq \beta_{\nu_0}$. Then the card [♡] is not taken by Alice nor by Bob in Tug-of-War subprotocols during the loops with $\nu > \nu_0$, and at the loop with $\nu = \nu_0$, [♡] is taken by Alice (respectively, Bob) if $\alpha_{\nu_0} > \beta_{\nu_0}$ (respectively, $\alpha_{\nu_0} < \beta_{\nu_0}$). On the other hand, if $\alpha = \beta$, then the card [♡] is not taken by Alice nor by Bob during all the loops. As a result, for the 0-th to λ-th columns (where $\lambda := |\boldsymbol{q}| - \ell$) after Step 5, [♡] exists in the first row if $\alpha \geq \beta$ and in the second row if $\alpha < \beta$, while the other cards are [♣]. Now when $\alpha \geq \beta$, the two [♡]'s in Main Memory are at the same (first) row after Step 5, which implies that [♡] comes to Point $(2, -1)$ after Step 8 and therefore the protocol outputs the 2-vector commitment of the bit $0 = \chi[\alpha < \beta]$. On the other hand, when $\alpha < \beta$, the two [♡]'s in Main Memory are at different rows after Step 5, which implies that [♡] comes to Point $(1, -1)$ after Step 8 and therefore the protocol outputs the 2-vector commitment of the bit $1 = \chi[\alpha < \beta]$. Hence Protocol 2 outputs $\mathsf{vEnc}_2(\chi[\alpha < \beta])$ correctly.

Protocol 2 Our proposed protocol using binary cards (committed-format)

Input $\boldsymbol{q}$-ary commitment $\mathsf{qEnc}_{\boldsymbol{q}}(\alpha)$ of $\alpha = (\alpha_{\ell-1} \cdots \alpha_1\alpha_0)_{\boldsymbol{q}}$, and $\boldsymbol{q}$-ary commitment $\mathsf{qEnc}_{\boldsymbol{q}}(\beta)$ of $\beta = (\beta_{\ell-1} \cdots \beta_1\beta_0)_{\boldsymbol{q}}$

Output 2-vector commitment $\mathsf{vEnc}_2(b)$ of the bit $b = \chi[\alpha < \beta]$

1: Put a face-down card [♡] at Point $(1, 0)$; put $2 \cdot \max(\boldsymbol{q}) - 2$ face-down cards [♣] in ♣-Garage; and initialize ♡-Garage, Memory A, and Memory B to be empty.

2: **for** $\nu = \ell - 1, \ldots, 1, 0$ **do**

3: Execute Tug-of-War subprotocol using q_ν-vector commitments $\mathsf{vEnc}_{q_\nu}(\alpha_\nu)$ and $\mathsf{vEnc}_{q_\nu}(\beta_\nu)$ contained in $\mathsf{qEnc}_{\boldsymbol{q}}(\alpha)$ and $\mathsf{qEnc}_{\boldsymbol{q}}(\beta)$, respectively.

4: **end for** `// Each of Memory A and Memory B involves` $\lambda := |\boldsymbol{q}| - \ell$ `cards`

5: Move a card from ♡-Garage to Point $(1, -1)$; put all cards in Memory A at Points $(1, 1), (1, 2), \ldots, (1, \lambda)$; move two cards from ♣-Garage to Points $(2, -1)$ and $(2, 0)$; and put all cards in Memory B at Points $(2, 1), (2, 2), \ldots, (2, \lambda)$.

6: Apply column-PSS to the 0-th to λ-th columns in Main Memory.

7: Apply row-PSS to all cards in Main Memory, and open the cards in the 0-th to λ-th columns in Main Memory.

8: For Main Memory, rotate the rows synchronously in a way that the face-up card [♡] comes to the bottom (i.e., the second row).

9: Output a pair of the face-down cards at Points $(1, -1)$ and $(2, -1)$ in this order.

As for the security, it was shown in Sect. 3.1 that Tug-of-War subprotocol leaks no information. For the remaining steps, as the 0-th to λ-th columns after Step 5 involves precisely one $\boxed{[\heartsuit]}$, the column-PSS in Step 6 has an effect equivalent to the complete shuffle for these columns. Consequently, the visible sequence (focusing only on the 0-th to λ-th columns) after Step 7 is a uniformly random $2 \times (\lambda + 1)$ array of one $\heartsuit$ and $2\lambda + 1$ $\clubsuit$'s regardless of the input values, and the visible sequence after Step 8 is uniquely determined by that after Step 7. Hence Protocol 2 is secure.

As for the efficiency, Protocol 2 uses 2ℓ $\boxed{\heartsuit}$'s and $2|\boldsymbol{q}| - 2\ell$ $\boxed{\clubsuit}$'s for the two $\boldsymbol{q}$-ary commitments; and one $\boxed{\heartsuit}$ and $2 \cdot \max(\boldsymbol{q}) - 2$ $\boxed{\clubsuit}$'s prepared in Step 1 (the cards moved to $\clubsuit$-Garage and $\heartsuit$-Garage during Tug-of-War subprotocols can be reused as the extra $\boxed{\heartsuit}$ and $\boxed{\clubsuit}$'s in Step 5). Therefore the protocol uses $2\ell + 1$ $\boxed{\heartsuit}$'s and $2|\boldsymbol{q}| - 2\ell + 2 \cdot \max(\boldsymbol{q}) - 2$ $\boxed{\clubsuit}$'s, hence $2|\boldsymbol{q}| + 2 \cdot \max(\boldsymbol{q}) - 1$ cards in total. When $\boldsymbol{q} = q^{\times \ell}$, these values are $2\ell + 1$, $2(q-1)\ell + 2q - 2$, and $2q\ell + 2q - 1$. On the other hand, Protocol 2 uses two PSSs per one Tug-of-War subprotocol and two PSSs after the loops, hence $2\ell + 2$ PSSs in total.

3.3 Options for the Protocol

Ternary Output. We can modify Protocol 2 in a way that it will output the 3-vector commitment $\mathsf{vEnc}_3(b)$ of the value b given by $b = 0$ if $\alpha > \beta$, $b = 1$ if $\alpha = \beta$, and $b = 2$ if $\alpha < \beta$. Instead of the array of cards with two rows in Step 5, we let the protocol arrange the face-down cards in a way that the first row is a sequence of $\boxed{[\heartsuit]}$ and the cards in Memory A; the second row is a sequence of $\boxed{[\clubsuit]}$, the card remained (at Point $(1, 0)$) after the loops, and $\lambda - 1$ $\boxed{[\clubsuit]}$'s from $\clubsuit$-Garage; and the third row is a sequence of $\boxed{[\clubsuit]}$ and the cards in Memory B. (The correspondence of the value of b and the three conditions can be made arbitrarily by changing the order of the rows appropriately.) Steps 6–8 are executed similarly, with the only difference that the number of rows is increased by one and the number of columns is decreased by one. Finally, in Step 9, the output is changed to the triplet of the cards at Points $(1, -1)$, $(2, -1)$ and $(3, -1)$ in this order. As for the number of cards, the new Step 5 uses one extra $\boxed{\heartsuit}$ and $\lambda + 1 = |\boldsymbol{q}| - \ell + 1$ extra $\boxed{\clubsuit}$'s, therefore we have to put $\max\{2 \cdot \max(\boldsymbol{q}) - 2, |\boldsymbol{q}| - \ell + 1\}$ $\boxed{\clubsuit}$'s to $\clubsuit$-Garage at Step 1. Hence this option requires $2\ell+1$ $\boxed{\heartsuit}$'s and $2|\boldsymbol{q}| - 2\ell + \max\{2 \cdot \max(\boldsymbol{q}) - 2, |\boldsymbol{q}| - \ell + 1\}$ $\boxed{\clubsuit}$'s, therefore $2|\boldsymbol{q}| + \max\{2 \cdot \max(\boldsymbol{q}) - 1, |\boldsymbol{q}| - \ell + 2\}$ cards in total. When $\boldsymbol{q} = q^{\times \ell}$ and $\ell \geq 2$, these values are $2\ell + 1$, $3q\ell - 3\ell + 1$, and $3q\ell - \ell + 2$. On the other hand, when $\boldsymbol{q} = q^{\times 1}$, these values are 3, $4q - 4$, and $4q - 1$ (note that $q \geq 2$). As for the shuffles, the number of shuffles is not changed by adopting the option.

Non-committed Format. Protocol 2 is easily converted into a non-committed-format protocol by just opening the cards after the column-PSS in Step 6 and tells at which row the [♡] appears (we have $\alpha \geq \beta$ if it is the first row and $\alpha < \beta$ if it is the second row). This option does not require the two cards put at the (-1)-th column (among which the [♣] is a reused card) nor the row-PSS in Step 7. As a result, the number of [♡]'s is decreased by one and the number of [♣]'s is not changed, while the number of PSSs is decreased by one.

This non-committed-format option can be also modified to output a ternary value. In contrast to the committed-format case, here we do not need an extra row. Instead, we just change the procedure in the previous paragraph in a way that the last column-PSS is applied to the 1-th (rather than the 0-th) to λ-th columns; the three possibilities can be distinguished by observing the position of [♡] among the opened cards. This even does not require the card put at Position $(2, 0)$, but as it was a reused card, the number of cards (as well as the number of shuffles) used throughout the protocol is not changed from the previous paragraph.

3.4 Comparison to the Previous Work

To the authors' best knowledge, the existing committed-format protocol in the literature for integer comparison (with binary output) using minimal number of binary cards is the protocol by Miyahara et al. [3, Section 6]. Table 2 shows a comparison of the numbers of cards for our proposed protocol (with binary output in the committed format, i.e., the original Protocol 2) and for the previous one mentioned above. Here m denotes the size of the input domain, i.e., $\alpha, \beta \in [0..m-1]$. For our protocol, we simply use the parameter $\boldsymbol{q} = q^{\times \ell}$ (though the use of $\boldsymbol{q}$ with differing components q_ν may sometimes decrease the number of cards further), where $\ell = \lceil \log_q m \rceil$ to satisfy the requirement $\pi(\boldsymbol{q}) \geq m$. From the table we observe that, our protocol with $q = 2$ requires one more additional card compared to [3] and consequently, the total number of cards for our protocol is also increased by one. On the other hand, when we use $q = 3$, the number of additional cards in our protocol is increased further by two, but now the number of cards for input commitments is asymptotically decreased (note that $6\lceil \log_3 m \rceil \sim (3.7855\cdots) \cdot (\log_2 m)$) due to the effect that the number of digits in the input integers is decreased. As the latter effect is dominant, the total number of cards is also asymptotically decreased.

As for the shuffles, the protocol in [3] has $\lceil \log_2 m \rceil$ loops. Each loop uses the six-card AND protocol in [6] with one RBC, which is equivalent (in our terminology) to row-PSS for two rows, and, except for the first loop, uses the six-card XOR protocol in [6] with one RBC. In total, the protocol in [3] uses $2\lceil \log_2 m \rceil - 1$ PSSs. On the other hand, our protocol (with $\boldsymbol{q} = q^{\times \ell}$) uses $2\lceil \log_q m \rceil + 2$ PSSs. This number is larger than [3] by three when $q = 2$, while it is again asymptotically smaller than [3] when $q = 3$.

Table 2. Comparison of the numbers of binary cards

Protocols	# of Cards		
	Total	For Inputs	Additional
Miyahara et al. [3], §6	$4\lceil \log_2 m \rceil + 2$	$4\lceil \log_2 m \rceil$	2
Ours, Protocol 2 **(any** q**)**	$2q\lceil \log_q m \rceil + 2q - 1$	$2q\lceil \log_q m \rceil$	$2q - 1$
Ours, Protocol 2 ($q = 2$)	$4\lceil \log_2 m \rceil + 3$	$4\lceil \log_2 m \rceil$	3
Ours, Protocol 2 ($q = 3$)	$6\lceil \log_3 m \rceil + 5$	$6\lceil \log_3 m \rceil$	5

We also take into account another line of researches on card-based garbled circuits using only a single shuffle invented by Shinagawa and Nuida [11]. Among its follow-up work, the most efficient (committed-format) protocol known at the present (in the shuffle-based model as in our work, without private permutations) is the one by Ono et al. [9], using $6g + 2n_{\mathsf{In}} + 2n_{\mathsf{Out}}$ cards and a single (uniform, but not necessarily closed) shuffle, where g is the number of gates for a circuit to be computed, n_{In} is the number of input bits, and n_{Out} is the number of output bits. By setting $n_{\mathsf{In}} = 2\lceil \log_2 m \rceil$ and $n_{\mathsf{Out}} = 1$ as in our problem and applying it to the integer comparison circuit used in [3] with $g = 4\lceil \log_2 m \rceil - 3$ gates, it follows that the number of cards used by the protocol of [9] becomes $28\lceil \log_2 m \rceil - 16$, which is still linear in $\lceil \log_2 m \rceil$ but is significantly larger.

4 Our Proposed Protocol with Number Cards

4.1 Encoding of Integers Using Number Cards

Here we extend the definitions of commitments of integers based on binary cards to number cards. We partition the number cards into "♣-cards" and "♡-cards". In our protocol, each ♣-card plays the role of a card [♣], and each ♡-card plays the role of a card [♡]. Now the definitions of k-vector commitments and q-ary commitments are naturally generalized and written in the same notations as the original, by replacing any binary card [♣] with some ♣-card and replacing any binary card [♡] with some ♡-card. For example, when ♣-cards and ♡-cards have front-side symbols in $[1..7]$ and in $\{8, 9\}$, respectively, the two sequences [0][8][3][6] and [4][9][0][1] are examples of 4-vector commitments $\mathsf{vEnc}_4(2)$ of an integer 2.

4.2 Extension of Our Protocol to Number Cards

Our proposed protocol with number cards is obtained basically by replacing the cards [♣] and [♡] in Protocol 2 with ♣-cards and ♡-cards, respectively. Therefore the correctness is inherited from the original protocol.

Regarding the security, the problem in contrast to the case of binary cards is that now the ♣-cards have non-identical front-side symbols. Consequently, the distribution of the ♣-cards opened simultaneously at some step should be independent of the input values. In particular, unlike Protocol 2 where some cards ♣ opened previously may be reused later, such reuse of ♣-cards in the current case violates the independency requirement. Hence we have to remove from the protocol the ♣-cards opened during a Tug-of-War subprotocol without being reused. As a result, each, say ν-th, Tug-of-War subprotocol now requires $3(q_\nu - 1)$ new ♣-cards, and the steps after the loops requires two more new ♣-cards. On the other hand, we do not need to concern about the distributions of the ♡-cards in the protocol and therefore a ♡-card opened at some loop may be reused in Step 5, as at most one ♡-card is opened at each step and the order of turns for ♡-cards in the protocol is determined independently of the input values. These arguments change the number of cards as follows: we need one ♡-card and $3|\boldsymbol{q}| - 3\ell + 2$ ♣-cards in addition to $2|\boldsymbol{q}|$ cards for input commitments, hence $5|\boldsymbol{q}| - 3\ell + 3$ number cards in total. When $\boldsymbol{q} = q^{\times \ell}$, the last value is $(5q-3)\ell + 3$.

In case where each input commitment is made from scratch at the beginning of the protocol by the party knowing the input value, the condition above on the distribution of ♣-cards can be satisfied in the following manner:

1. Before making the input commitments, a CS is applied to all the face-down ♣-cards. Then sufficient numbers of face-down ♣-cards and ♡-cards are separately given to each of Alice and Bob.
2. Alice generates a commitment $\mathsf{qEnc}_{\boldsymbol{q}}(\alpha)$ by permuting her face-down cards privately and appropriately. Bob generates a commitment $\mathsf{qEnc}_{\boldsymbol{q}}(\beta)$ by permuting his face-down cards privately and appropriately.

Although the second step seems to require private permutations, such usage of private permutations might be allowable, as it is reasonable to assume that an input commitment of each party is anyway generated privately. If we adopt this option, the whole protocol uses $2\ell + 2$ PSSs and one CS.

In what follows, we consider another possibility that $\boldsymbol{q}$-ary commitments $\mathsf{qEnc}_{\boldsymbol{q}}(\alpha)$ and $\mathsf{qEnc}_{\boldsymbol{q}}(\beta)$ of input values are given in advance (e.g., as outputs of some other committed-format protocols). In this case, we assume that

> (*) there are disjoint sets $S_{i,\nu}$ ($i \in \{1,2\}$, $\nu \in [0..\ell-1]$) of ♣-cards satisfying that the choice of ♣-cards in the q_ν-vector commitment $\mathsf{vEnc}_{q_\nu}(\alpha_\nu)$ (respectively, $\mathsf{vEnc}_{q_\nu}(\beta_\nu)$) is uniformly random over all sequences of $q_\nu - 1$ distinct cards in the set $S_{1,\nu}$ (respectively, $S_{2,\nu}$).

Now for, say ν-th Tug-of-War subprotocol, the second row at Step 3 consists only of the cards from $\mathsf{vEnc}_{q_\nu}(\alpha_\nu)$. Therefore, the condition (*) implies that the sequence of the q_ν cards opened at Step 3 is a uniformly random sequence of a ♡-card and uniformly random $q_\nu - 1$ distinct ♣-cards from $S_{1,\nu}$, which is independent of the input values. On the other hand, if we naively use $\mathsf{vEnc}_{q_\nu}(\beta_\nu)$ as is, then among the $2q_\nu - 1$ cards opened at Step 8, the cards from $\mathsf{vEnc}_{q_\nu}(\beta_\nu)$

become distinguishable from the others and hence the value of β_ν can be guessed. To avoid the issue, we introduce a pre-processing phase at the beginning of the whole protocol to replace each ♣-card in $\mathsf{qEnc}_{\boldsymbol{q}}(\beta)$ with a random one among the remaining ♣-cards (while keeping the committed value), as follows:

1. A CS is applied to all face-down ♣-cards (not in $\mathsf{qEnc}_{\boldsymbol{q}}(\alpha)$ nor in $\mathsf{qEnc}_{\boldsymbol{q}}(\beta)$).
2. For each $\nu \in [0..\ell - 1]$, we generate a new q_ν-vector commitment $\mathsf{vEnc}_{q_\nu}(\beta_\nu)$ in the following manner:
   (a) Reverse the order of cards of the original $\mathsf{vEnc}_{q_\nu}(\beta_\nu)$.
   (b) Put a face-down ♡-card and $q_\nu - 1$ face-down ♣-cards from left to right at the next row, making a $2 \times q_\nu$ array of cards.
   (c) Apply a column-PSS to the array, open all cards in the first row (i.e., where the original commitment was placed), and rotate each of the two rows synchronously in a way that the face-up ♡-card comes to the right-most. Then use the second row as a new $\mathsf{vEnc}_{q_\nu}(\beta_\nu)$.

This pre-processing itself is secure due to the condition (*). After the pre-processing, the distribution of the ♣-cards opened during the protocol except for Step 3 of each Tug-of-War subprotocol becomes uniformly random. Hence our protocol is secure as well. The pre-processing phase requires $|\boldsymbol{q}|$ more cards, one CS, and ℓ PSSs. In total, our protocol with this option uses $6|\boldsymbol{q}| - 3\ell + 3$ number cards (which is $(6q-3)\ell + 3$ when $\boldsymbol{q} = q^{\times \ell}$), $3\ell + 2$ PSSs, and one CS.

Options for the Protocol. By the same idea as Sect. 3.3, the protocol above can be also modified to have a ternary and/or non-committed output.

- For the case of a ternary and committed output, the steps after the loops now use $|\boldsymbol{q}| - \ell + 1$ new ♣-cards, while it used two new ♣-cards in the original protocol. Hence the total number of cards is increased by $|\boldsymbol{q}| - \ell - 1$, which becomes $(q-1)\ell - 1$ when $\boldsymbol{q} = q^{\times \ell}$.
- For the case of a binary and non-committed output, one of the two new ♣-cards used after the loops becomes not necessary, therefore the total number of cards is decreased by one compared to the original (the ♡-card therein is also not necessary, but it was a reused card and does not affect the total number of cards). We also note that a PSS is removed from the original.
- For the case of a ternary and non-commited output, the total number of cards is decreased further by one compared to the binary and non-committed case.

4.3 Comparison to the Previous Work

We compare the efficiency of our proposed protocol (with binary and committed-format output) with the number-card version of Miyahara et al.'s protocol [3, Section 7], which is (to the authors' best knowledge) the existing protocol with minimal number of shuffles among those based on number cards in the literature. Similarly to the case of binary cards discussed in Sect. 3.4, their protocol consists of $\lceil \log_2 m \rceil$ loops (where m is the size of the input domain), each using an extended version of AND protocol in [4] and, except for the first loop, an XOR protocol in [4]. The total number of cards is $4\lceil \log_2 m \rceil + 4$ and it uses $6\lceil \log_2 m \rceil - 2$ RBCs. See Sect. 7 of [3] for details. On the other hand, our protocol with given $\boldsymbol{q}$-ary commitments for inputs (i.e., not made from scratch), where $\boldsymbol{q} = 2^{\times \ell}$, uses $9\lceil \log_2 m \rceil + 3$ cards, $3\lceil \log_2 m \rceil + 2$ PSSs, and one CS. If we allow the parties to make the input commitments from scratch by using private permutations, the total number of cards is decreased to $7\lceil \log_2 m \rceil + 3$ and the number of shuffles is decreased to $2\lceil \log_2 m \rceil + 2$ PSSs and one CS. In any case, there is a trade-off between the protocol in [3] and ours, the former using less cards but more shuffles, while the latter using more cards but less shuffles. When using larger parameter $q \geq 3$, the number of shuffles in our protocol is decreased further, at the cost of increasing the number of cards further.

Acknowledgements. This work was supported by JSPS KAKENHI Grant Number JP19H01109, Japan.

References

1. Crépeau, C., Kilian, J.: Discreet solitary games. In: Stinson, D.R. (ed.) CRYPTO 1993. LNCS, vol. 773, pp. 319–330. Springer, Heidelberg (1994). https://doi.org/10.1007/3-540-48329-2_27
2. Ishikawa, R., Chida, E., Mizuki, T.: Efficient card-based protocols for generating a hidden random permutation without fixed points. In: Calude, C.S., Dinneen, M.J. (eds.) UCNC 2015. LNCS, vol. 9252, pp. 215–226. Springer, Cham (2015). https://doi.org/10.1007/978-3-319-21819-9_16
3. Miyahara, D., Hayashi, Y., Mizuki, T., Sone, H.: Practical card-based implementations of Yao's millionaire protocol. Theoret. Comput. Sci. **803**, 207–221 (2020)
4. Mizuki, T.: Efficient and secure multiparty computations using a standard deck of playing cards. In: Foresti, S., Persiano, G. (eds.) CANS 2016. LNCS, vol. 10052, pp. 484–499. Springer, Cham (2016). https://doi.org/10.1007/978-3-319-48965-0_29
5. Mizuki, T., Shizuya, H.: A formalization of card-based cryptographic protocols via abstract machine. Int. J. Inf. Secur. **13**, 15–23 (2014)
6. Mizuki, T., Sone, H.: Six-card secure AND and four-card secure XOR. In: Deng, X., Hopcroft, J.E., Xue, J. (eds.) FAW 2009. LNCS, vol. 5598, pp. 358–369. Springer, Heidelberg (2009). https://doi.org/10.1007/978-3-642-02270-8_36
7. Nakai, T., Tokushige, Y., Misawa, Y., Iwamoto, M., Ohta, K.: Efficient card-based cryptographic protocols for millionaires' problem utilizing private permutations. In: Foresti, S., Persiano, G. (eds.) CANS 2016. LNCS, vol. 10052, pp. 500–517. Springer, Cham (2016). https://doi.org/10.1007/978-3-319-48965-0_30
8. Niemi, V., Renvall, A.: Solitaire zero-knowledge. Fund. Inform. **38**(1–2), 181–188 (1999)
9. Ono, T., Shinagawa, K., Nakai, T., Watanabe, Y., Iwamoto, M.: Card-based protocols for any boolean circuit with six cards per gate. In: Proceedings of 2023 Symposium on Cryptography and Information Security (SCIS 2023), article no. 3D2-2 (2023). (in Japanese)

10. Shinagawa, K., et al.: Card-based protocols using regular polygon cards. IEICE Trans. Fundam. Electron. Commun. Comput. Sci. **E100-A**(9), 1900–1909 (2017)
11. Shinagawa, K., Nuida, K.: A single shuffle is enough for secure card-based computation of any boolean circuit. Discret. Appl. Math. **289**, 248–261 (2021)
12. Yao, A.C.-C.: Protocols for secure computations. In: Proceedings of FOCS 1982, pp. 160–164 (1982)

Check Alternating Patterns: A Physical Zero-Knowledge Proof for Moon-or-Sun

Samuel Hand[1], Alexander Koch[2], Pascal Lafourcade[3], Daiki Miyahara[4,5](✉), and Léo Robert[6]

[1] University of Glasgow, Glasgow, UK
[2] Paris Cité University, Paris, France
[3] University Clermont Auvergne, LIMOS, CNRS UMR 6158, Aubière, France
pascal.lafourcade@uca.fr
[4] The University of Electro-Communications, Tokyo, Japan
miyahara@uec.ac.jp
[5] National Institute of Advanced Industrial Science and Technology, Tokyo, Japan
[6] University of Limoges, XLIM, Limoges, France

Abstract. A zero-knowledge proof (ZKP) allows a party to prove to another party that it knows some secret, such as the solution to a difficult puzzle, without revealing any information about it. We propose a physical zero-knowledge proof using only a deck of playing cards for solutions to a pencil puzzle called *Moon-or-Sun*. In this puzzle, one is given a grid of cells on which rooms, marked by thick black lines surrounding a connected set of cells, may contain a number of cells with a moon or a sun symbol. The goal is to find a loop passing through all rooms exactly once, and in each room either passes through all cells with a moon, or all cells with a sun symbol.

Finally, whenever the loop passes from one room to another, it must go through all cells with a moon if in the previous room it passed through all cells with a sun, and visa-versa. This last rule constitutes the main challenge for finding a physical zero-knowledge proof for this puzzle, as this must be verified without giving away through which borders the loop enters or leaves a given room. We design a card-based zero-knowledge proof of knowledge protocol for Moon-or-Sun solutions, together with an analysis of their properties. Our technique of verifying the alternation of a pattern along a non-disclosed path might be of independent interest for similar puzzles.

Keywords: Physical Zero-knowledge Proof · Pencil Puzzle · Card-based Cryptography · Moon-or-Sun · Nikoli Puzzle

1 Introduction

A Zero-Knowledge Proof (ZKP) protocol is a cryptographic tool enabling a party to prove a statement without revealing information about it. Due to their

J. Shikata and H. Kuzuno (Eds.): IWSEC 2023, LNCS 14128, pp. 255–272, 2023.
https://doi.org/10.1007/978-3-031-41326-1_14

versatility, numerous variants of these protocols exist with different possible applications. For instance, a ZKP could help to determine if a database contains information without revealing it. A ZKP protocol is also used for e-voting system to ensure that ballots are correctly shuffled. Lastly, ZKP protocols are also used for cryptocurrencies like Monero or ZCash to allow anonymous transactions.

We focus on a particular ZKP: interactive Zero-Knowledge Proof of Knowledge protocols. In this context, there are two parties involved: a prover P and a verifer V. The prover wishes to convince the verifier that it knows specific information without revealing it. These protocols have three properties:

- Completeness: if P knows a secret s then the protocol ends without failure (meaning that V is convinced P has s);
- (Perfect) Soundness: if P does not have the solution s then the protocol will abort (with probability 1);
- Zero-Knowledge: V learns nothing about s.

We design a ZKP protocol for the Moon-or-Sun puzzle. The goal of our protocol is that if a prover P has the solution for a given instance of the Moon-or-Sun puzzle, then it will be able to convince a verfier V of this fact, and the protocol will end (as stated by the *completeness* property). Further, any information revealed during the protocol should not leak any information about the solution (as stated by the *zero-knowledge* property). Finally, if P does not have the solution, then the protocol should abort (as stated by the *soundness* property).

In a nutshell, the protocol is done in two major steps: (1) the prover P commits its solution, and (2) the verifier V checks that the committed values are respecting the rules.

The Moon-or-Sun rules are given in Fig. 1. We also illustrate an example in Fig. 2 taken from Nikoli's webgpage[1].

In [10], the Moon-or-Sun puzzle is proven to be NP-complete which implies that a ZKP protocol exists, as proved in [2]. While the latter work is a constructive proof which implies the existence of a ZKP protocol, there is always the need to design a specific protocol for a given problem. Indeed, the generic construction is not efficient, nor interesting in itself.

Related Work. The first physical ZKP protocol [8] for a Sudoku grid was constructed using a deck of cards. Since this novel protocol was devised, several papers have proposed physical ZKP protocols using a deck of cards for pencil puzzles, such as Sudoku [29,30], Akari [4], Takuzu [4], Kakuro [4,14], KenKen [4], Makaro [5], Norinori [7], Slitherlink [13], Suguru [21], Nurikabe [18], Ripple Effect [26], Numberlink [24], Bridges [25], Cryptarithmetic [9], and Nonogram [6,23]. More recent puzzles have been considered such as Shikaku [27], Makaro (using a standard deck of cards) [28], Nurimisaki [19], Topswops [11], Pancake Sorting [12], and Usowan [20].

[1] https://www.nikoli.co.jp/en/puzzles/moon_or_sun/.

<u>Moon-or-Sun Rules:</u>

1. Construct a loop.
2. The loop never crosses itself, branches off, or goes through the same cell twice.
3. The loop goes through each *room* (*i.e.*, continuous cells delimited by thick edges) only once.
4. The loop goes through all moon or all sun for each room. This means that the loop cannot pass through moon and sun cells for a given room.
5. After the loop goes through the moons in one room it has to go through all the suns in the next room it enters and visa versa.

Fig. 1. Rules for Moon-or-Sun [1].

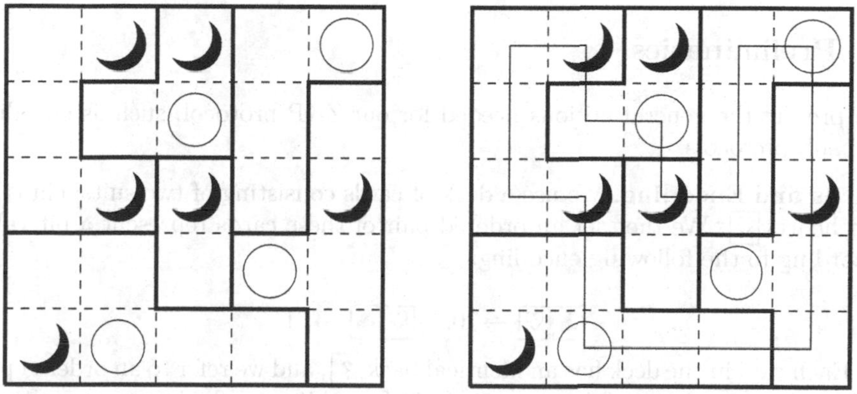

Fig. 2. Example of a Moon-or-Sun instance, with initial values on the left and the solution on the right.

Contributions. We design a card-based, interactive ZKP protocol for the Moon-or-Sun puzzle. We rely on some existing techniques, such as constructing a non-branching loop or computing the sum of multiple commitments, but also propose original and simple sub-protocols, such as showing alternating pattern, to obtain a secure ZKP protocol. Our description is also accompanied of security proofs to show the completeness, perfect soundness and zero-knowledge of our protocol. An overview of our proposed protocol is depicted in Fig. 3.

We also demonstrate that our proposed ZKP protocol is related to a well-known NP-hard problem in graph theory. This may prove the significance of our protocol for a Moon-or-Sun puzzle.

Outline. We begin by introducing notations and existing protocols used in our ZKP protocol in Sect. 2. In Sect. 3, we present our ZKP protocol for a Moon-or-Sun puzzle. In Sect. 4, we prove that our ZKP protocol satisfies the ZKP properties. In Sect. 5, we discuss about our ZKP protocol. We conclude this study in Sect. 6.

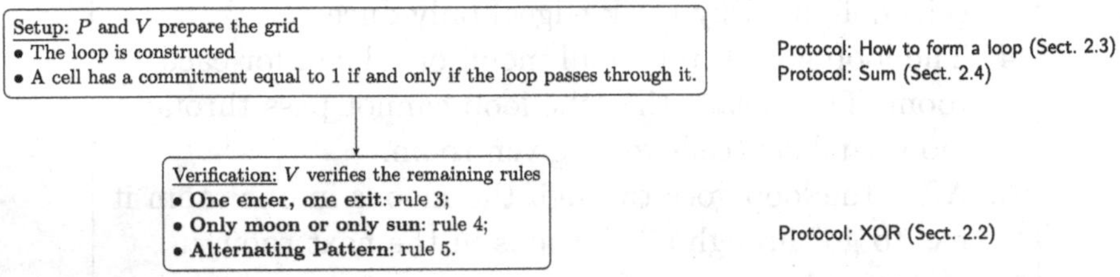

Fig. 3. Overview of our protocol. On the left with rounded corners are the main steps of our construction, and on the right are the main sub-protocols used.

2 Preliminaries

We present the general notions needed for our ZKP protocol, such as encoding and sub-protocols.

Cards and Encoding. We use a deck of cards consisting of two suits: clubs [♣] and hearts [♡]. We then let an ordered pair of these cards represent a bit value according to the following encoding:

$$[\clubsuit][\heartsuit] \rightarrow 0, \quad [\heartsuit][\clubsuit] \rightarrow 1. \tag{1}$$

Each card in the deck has an identical back [?], and we refer to an ordered pair of face-down cards satisfying encoding (1) for a bit $x \in \{0, 1\}$ as a *commitment* to x. Such a commitment to a bit x is then denoted by:

$$\underbrace{[?][?]}_{x}.$$

We also define two converse encodings for integers modulo p [26]:

- ♣-scheme: to encode $x \in \mathbb{Z}/p\mathbb{Z}$ use a row of p cards with one ♣ in position $(x + 1)$ from the left and the remaining $p - 1$ positions occupied by ♡s. As an example, we would represent 2 with [♡][♡][♣][♡] in $\mathbb{Z}/4\mathbb{Z}$.
- ♡-scheme: equivalently as above, but with ♡ and ♣ exchanged. Here 2 is instead represented by [♣][♣][♡][♣] in $\mathbb{Z}/4\mathbb{Z}$.

2.1 Shuffle

We explain two types of shuffles that introduce randomness into the order of a sequence of cards. These shuffles are usually employed in card-based cryptography, particularly within ZKP protocols.

Consider a *pile* consisting of ℓ cards, where $\ell > 0$. Both shuffles are applied to multiple piles of cards, making the order of the piles unknown to everyone, while preserving the order of cards within each pile. Suppose that we have m piles denoted by $(\boldsymbol{p}_1, \boldsymbol{p}_2, \ldots, \boldsymbol{p}_m)$, each containing ℓ cards.

Pile-Scramble Shuffle. This shuffling method, initially introduced in [16], completely randomizes the order of piles. Applying a pile-scramble shuffle to $(\boldsymbol{p}_1, \boldsymbol{p}_2, \ldots, \boldsymbol{p}_m)$ yields $(\boldsymbol{p}_{r^{-1}(1)}, \boldsymbol{p}_{r^{-1}(2)}, \ldots, \boldsymbol{p}_{r^{-1}(m)})$, where r is a random permutation uniformly distributed in a symmetric group of degree m, denoted by S_m. This shuffling is denoted by $[\cdot|\ldots|\cdot]$.

Pile-Shifting Shuffle. This shuffling method, initially introduced in [31], randomly and cyclically shifts the order of piles. Applying a *pile-shifting* shuffle to $(\boldsymbol{p}_1, \boldsymbol{p}_2, \ldots, \boldsymbol{p}_m)$ yields $(\boldsymbol{p}_{s+1}, \boldsymbol{p}_{s+2}, \ldots, \boldsymbol{p}_{s+m})$, where s is chosen randomly and uniformly from $\mathbb{Z}/m\mathbb{Z}$. This shuffling is denoted by $\langle\cdot|\ldots|\cdot\rangle$.

When $m = 2$, this shuffle is called a *random bisection cut* [17], i.e., bisecting a sequence of cards and randomly swapping the two halves. When $\ell = 1$, this shuffle is known as a *random cut* invented by Den Boer [3].

2.2 XOR and Copy Protocols

Our protocol uses the existing card-based protocols for computing a logical function of two-input XOR and duplicating an input commitment [17]. Here, we briefly introduce them, and their full descriptions are in Appendix A.

Given commitments to $a, b \in \{0, 1\}$, the Mizuki–Sone XOR protocol [17] outputs a commitment to $a \oplus b$:

$$\underbrace{\boxed{?}\,\boxed{?}}_{a}\;\underbrace{\boxed{?}\,\boxed{?}}_{b} \rightarrow \cdots \rightarrow \underbrace{\boxed{?}\,\boxed{?}}_{a\oplus b}.$$

Given a commitment to $a \in \{0, 1\}$ along with two commitments to 0, the Mizuki–Sone copy protocol [17] outputs two commitments to a:

$$\underbrace{\boxed{?}\,\boxed{?}}_{a}\;\underbrace{\boxed{?}\,\boxed{?}}_{0}\;\underbrace{\boxed{?}\,\boxed{?}}_{0} \rightarrow \cdots \rightarrow \underbrace{\boxed{?}\,\boxed{?}}_{a}\;\underbrace{\boxed{?}\,\boxed{?}}_{a}.$$

2.3 How to Form a Loop

To verify rule 2, i.e., the loop condition, we use the existing protocol from [13]. Let us introduce an overview of the protocol [13]. This protocol enables a prover P to create any single loop without revealing information about the loop shape, while simultaneously convincing a verifier V that the resulting loop is indeed a single loop. That is, this protocol creates a figure respecting rule 2 rather than verifying it.

Briefly, this protocol starts from the single loop going along the boundary of the board. P and V interactively create the solution P has from the single loop. During this process, V cannot obtain information other than that the process proceeds correctly, and hence, the resulting shape is indeed a single loop.

To represent a loop with a sequence of cards, we place a commitment *between* each cell. The value of such a commitment represents the existence of line, *i.e.*, line passes through them if the value is 1, and no line passes if it is 0 as follows:

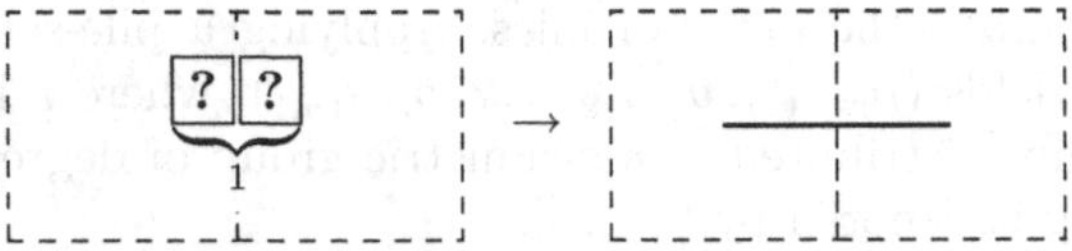

Thus, the protocol [13] begins by placing a commitment to 1 between each cell adjacent to the border of a given board and commitments to 0 on the remaining positions, representing the single loop. Refer to [13] for specific methods on creating the solution P has.

2.4 Sum of Commitments

This protocol is defined in [26]; we give a general description given as an example. Suppose that we have commitments to $a, b \in \{0, 1\}$, and we want to output $a + b \in \mathbb{Z}/3\mathbb{Z}$ (in the $\heartsuit$-scheme, see encoding Eq. (2)):

$$\boxed{?}\boxed{?}\ \boxed{?}\boxed{?}\ \boxed{\clubsuit}\boxed{\heartsuit} \rightarrow \boxed{?}\ \boxed{?}\ \boxed{?}\ .$$
$$\underbrace{\qquad}_{a}\ \underbrace{\qquad}_{b}\qquad\qquad \underbrace{\qquad}_{a+b}$$

1. Swap the two cards of the commitment to a and add a $\boxed{\clubsuit}$ face-down to the right. Those three cards represent a in the $\heartsuit$-scheme in $\mathbb{Z}/3\mathbb{Z}$:

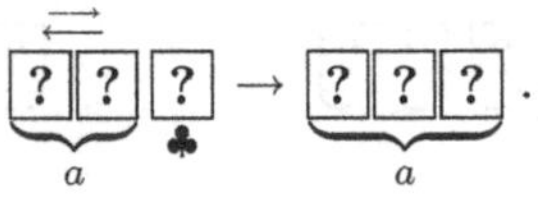

$$\overset{\overleftrightarrow{\ }}{\boxed{?}\boxed{?}}\boxed{?} \rightarrow \boxed{?}\ \boxed{?}\ \boxed{?}\ .$$
$$\underbrace{\qquad}_{a}\ {}_{\clubsuit}\qquad \underbrace{\qquad}_{a}$$

2. Add a $\boxed{\heartsuit}$ on the right of the commitment to b. Those three cards represent b in the $\clubsuit$-scheme in $\mathbb{Z}/3\mathbb{Z}$: $\boxed{?}\boxed{?}\ \boxed{?} \rightarrow \boxed{?}\ \boxed{?}\ \boxed{?}\ .$

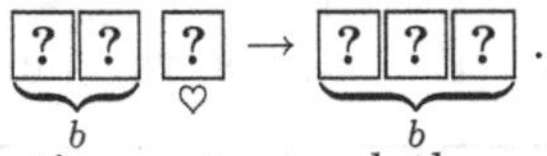

3. Obtain three cards representing $a + r$ and those representing $b - r$ for a uniformly random value $r \in \mathbb{Z}/3\mathbb{Z}$ as follows.
   (a) Place in *reverse* order the three cards obtained in Step 2 below the three cards obtained in Step 1:

$$\underbrace{\boxed{?}\ \boxed{?}\ \boxed{?}}_{a}\ \underbrace{\boxed{?}\ \boxed{?}\ \boxed{?}}_{b} \rightarrow \begin{array}{c} \underbrace{\boxed{?}\ \boxed{?}\ \boxed{?}}_{a} \\[2ex] \underbrace{\boxed{?}\ \boxed{?}\ \boxed{?}}_{2-b} \end{array} .$$

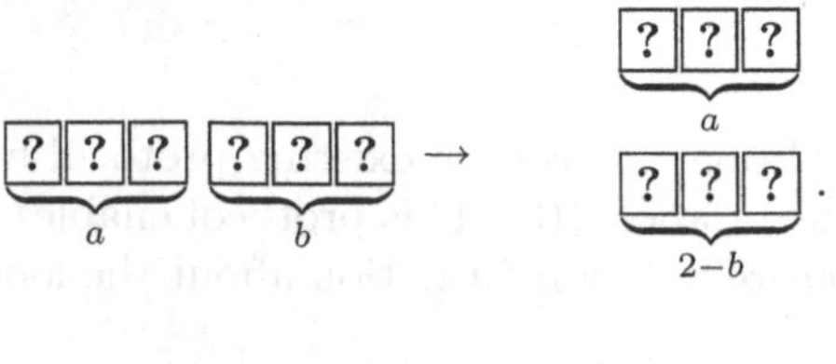

(b) Apply a pile shifting shuffle as follows:

$$\left\langle \begin{array}{c} \boxed{?} \\ \boxed{?} \end{array} \middle\| \begin{array}{c} \boxed{?} \\ \boxed{?} \end{array} \middle\| \begin{array}{c} \boxed{?} \\ \boxed{?} \end{array} \right\rangle \rightarrow \quad \underbrace{\boxed{?}\boxed{?}\boxed{?}}_{a+r} \\ \underbrace{\boxed{?}\boxed{?}\boxed{?}}_{2-b+r} .$$

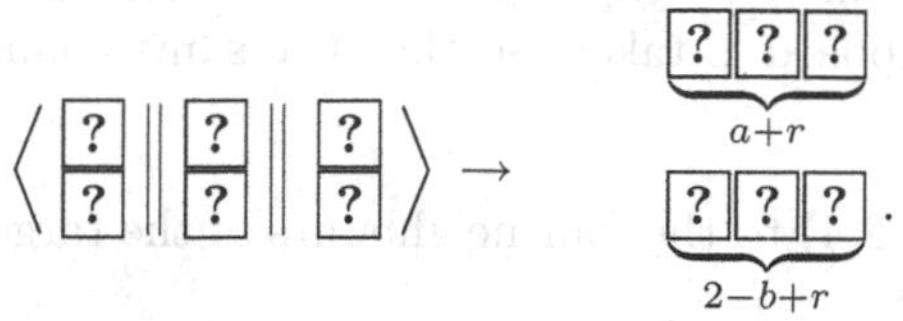

For a uniformly random value $r \in \mathbb{Z}/3\mathbb{Z}$, we obtain three cards representing $a + r$ and $2 - b + r$.

(c) Reverse the order of the three cards representing $2 - b + r$ to obtain $b - r$:

$$\underbrace{\boxed{?}\boxed{?}\boxed{?}}_{a+r} \underbrace{\boxed{?}\boxed{?}\boxed{?}}_{b-r} .$$

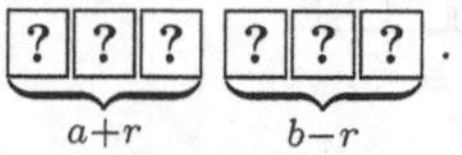

4. Reveal the three cards representing $b - r$, and shift to the right the three cards representing $a + r$ to obtain those representing $a + b$ in the $\heartsuit$-scheme; apply the same routine for the remaining elements to compute the final sum.

Notice that we described the sum protocol for an output of two bit commitments in $\mathbb{Z}/3\mathbb{Z}$. We can generalize by inductively applying the protocol for n bit commitments giving an output in $\mathbb{Z}/(n + 1)\mathbb{Z}$.

3   ZKP Protocol for Moon-or-Sun

We present a card-based ZKP protocol for a Moon-or-Sun puzzle. As shown in Fig. 3, our protocol has two phases: the setup and verification phases. The setup phase constructs a loop with the interaction between a prover P and a verifier V. The verification phase verifies all the rules other than rules 1 and 2.

3.1   Setup

As introduced in Sect. 2.3, a solution is represented with a commitment between each adjacent cells. Moreover, we place a commitment on each cell to represent the loop passing through a symbol (i.e., moon or sun symbol). The setup is done in two steps:

1. Constructing the loop using [13];
2. Placing the commitments inside the cells. Notice that we modify only cells with moon or sun symbol.

Forming the Loop. We directly use the construction of [13] described in Sect. 2.3. At this point, there are commitments between the cells but no commitment inside them.

Filling the Grid. We want to put commitments inside the cells to model the line passing through it (or not). For each cell (corresponding to a moon or sun symbol), if the line passes through it, we observe that the sum of the values of the four *neighbour* commitments on its edge is always equal to two (otherwise, zero).

Based on this observation, we place a commitment inside every cell as follows. We note that we execute the Mizuki–Sone copy protocol introduced in Sect. 2.2 whenever a commitment on the board is taken, so that the same commitment can be used for several times.

1. Apply the sum protocol (Sect. 2.4) to the four neighbours of the targeted cell $\boxed{c_t}$. The result is in $\heartsuit$-scheme:

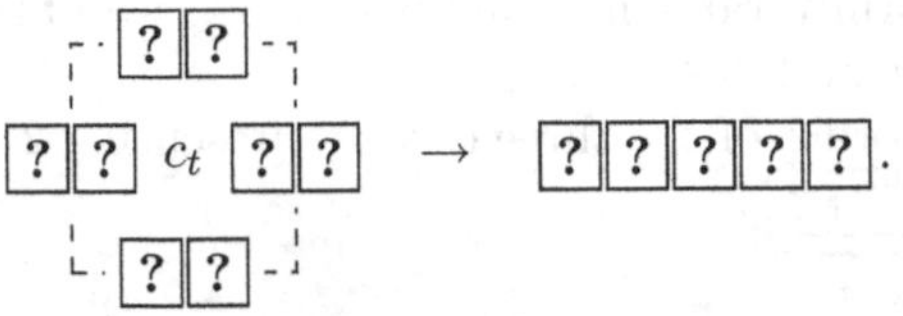

   Remember that if the sum is two, the third card from the left in the resulting sequence is a $\boxed{\heartsuit}$.
2. Make a commitment consisting of the third and first cards in the resulting sequence (in this order) by taking them and place it on $\boxed{c_t}$.

V is convinced that each cell (containing a moon or a sun) is equal to $1 = \boxed{\heartsuit}\boxed{\clubsuit}$ if and only if the line passes through it, *i.e.*, there are two neighbours equal to 1, exactly.

At this point, P has placed commitments according to its solution, and V wants to check that each rule is respected.

3.2 Verification Phases

The loop has been constructed in the previous step, so V wants to check if the other rules are respected.

Only Moon or Only Sun (Rule 4). The loop must pass through only moon or only sun symbols in a given room but exactly one of them. The following verification is done for each room:

1. Consider all the commitments on sun cells, and place them in a sequence (in any order). Apply a random cut introduced in Sect. 2.1 and reveal it. If the result has alternating pattern, then continue; otherwise, abort.
   We show an example when the room has three sun cells as follows:
   $$\langle \boxed{?}\boxed{?}\boxed{?}\boxed{?}\boxed{?}\boxed{?} \rangle \rightarrow \boxed{\clubsuit}\boxed{\heartsuit}\boxed{\clubsuit}\boxed{\heartsuit}\boxed{\clubsuit}\boxed{\heartsuit} \text{ or } \boxed{\heartsuit}\boxed{\clubsuit}\boxed{\heartsuit}\boxed{\clubsuit}\boxed{\heartsuit}\boxed{\clubsuit}.$$
2. Repeat the previous step for moon cells.
3. Execute the Mizuki–Sone XOR protocol [17] with a commitment on any sun cell and a commitment on any moon cell. If the protocol outputs a commitment to 1, then V continues; otherwise, V aborts.

Note that no information is leaked if the rule 4 is respected. Indeed, if the commitments are equal (for a given symbol), the random cut *hides* the initial values of commitments (V does not know if they are 0s or 1s). However, if the rule is not respected, then V knows the number of commitments that are different (*i.e.*, it can deduce the Hamming weight of the sequence).

One Enter, One Exit (Rule 3). The loop must be passing through a room only once. This means that for each room, the loop crosses its edge exactly twice (one for entering and one for exiting the room). The idea is thus to shuffle the commitments located at the edge of a room and reveal them. Formally, we proceed as follows:

1. Consider a room and take all the commitments located at the edge.
2. Apply a pile-scramble shuffle to them.
3. Reveal all the commitments. If exactly two commitments to 1 appears, then continue; otherwise, abort.
4. Repeat the previous step until visiting all rooms.

Alternating Pattern (Rule 5). The loop must pass through a different symbol to the one in the previous room it enters. Let us first present the idea behind our verification for this rule.

Given a solution as in Fig. 2, consider verifying whether a room (referred to as the target) satisfies rule 5 or not. For this, we examine the two rooms connected to the target room (*i.e.*, those through which line passes) and ensure that the loop passes through different symbols within the target room and the connected rooms. That is, we determine whether the two connected rooms are either both "sun rooms" or "moon rooms" and both of them differ to the target room. Our approach follows a similar logic: for every adjacent room, we collect a commitment on any sun cell[2]. Subsequently, from among the commitments, we somehow choose two commitments corresponding to the two connected rooms without leaking any information. The remaining steps are simple; we confirm that the values of the chosen commitments XORed with a commitment on any sun cell within the target room both yields ones.

Now we are ready to describe the verification method. Suppose that we verify the rule 5 for a target room R_0 with $k\ (\geq 2)$ adjacent rooms, $R_1, R_2, \ldots, R_k$. Let n_i, $1 \leq i \leq k$, denote the number of commitments on the border between R_0 and R_i. The verification proceeds as follows.

1. For every adjacent room R_i, let c_j denote each of the n_i commitments on the border between R_0 and R_i, for $1 \leq j \leq n_i$ (in any order). Collect one c_j for every j and add "dummy" commitments to 0 so that the total number of collected commitments (*i.e.*, n_i) becomes $n_{\max} = \max(n_1, \ldots, n_k)$ as follows:

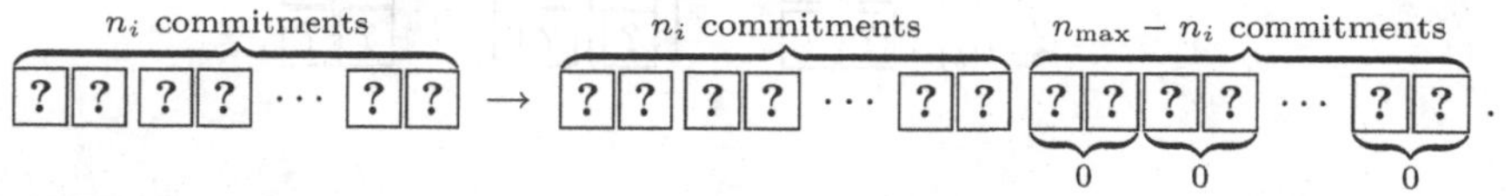

[2] Remember that the value of a commitment on a cell indicates the presence of line passing through the cell.

Let s_i denote the sequence of the $n_{\max}$ commitments. Apply a pile-scramble shuffle to s_i as follows:

$$s_i : \left[\boxed{?}\boxed{?} \,\middle\|\, \boxed{?}\boxed{?} \,\middle\|\, \cdots \,\middle\|\, \boxed{?}\boxed{?}\right] \rightarrow s_i : \boxed{?}\boxed{?}\boxed{?}\boxed{?}\cdots\boxed{?}\boxed{?}.$$

2. For every adjacent room R_i, $1 \leq i \leq k$, let c_i' denote a commitment on any sun cell within R_i. Place one c_i' above s_i. (If R_i has no sun, then let c_i' denote a commitment on any moon cell and swap the two cards constituting c_i' before placing it.)

$$s_i : \boxed{?}\boxed{?}\boxed{?}\boxed{?}\cdots\boxed{?}\boxed{?} \rightarrow \begin{matrix} c_i' : \boxed{?}\boxed{?} \\ s_i : \boxed{?}\boxed{?}\boxed{?}\boxed{?}\cdots\boxed{?}\boxed{?}. \end{matrix}$$

3. Apply a pile-scramble shuffle to the n_k piles consisting of s_i and c_i', $1 \leq i \leq k$, as follows:

$$\left[\begin{matrix} c_1' : \boxed{?}\boxed{?} \\ s_1 : \boxed{?}\boxed{?}\boxed{?}\boxed{?}\cdots\boxed{?}\boxed{?} \end{matrix} \,\middle\|\, \cdots \,\middle\|\, \begin{matrix} c_k' : \boxed{?}\boxed{?} \\ s_k : \boxed{?}\boxed{?}\boxed{?}\boxed{?}\cdots\boxed{?}\boxed{?} \end{matrix}\right].$$

4. Reveal all the commitments constituting s_i for all i, $1 \leq i \leq k$. Then exactly two commitments to 1 should be revealed, each appearing in different s_i (rule 3)[3]. Denote these positions as a and b ($a < b$) as follows:

$$\cdots \begin{matrix} c_{r^{-1}(a)}' : \boxed{?}\boxed{?} \\ s_{r^{-1}(a)} : \boxed{\clubsuit}\boxed{\heartsuit}\cdots\boxed{\heartsuit}\boxed{\clubsuit}\cdots\boxed{\clubsuit}\boxed{\heartsuit} \end{matrix} \cdots \begin{matrix} c_{r^{-1}(b)}' : \boxed{?}\boxed{?} \\ s_{r^{-1}(b)} : \boxed{\clubsuit}\boxed{\heartsuit}\cdots\boxed{\heartsuit}\boxed{\clubsuit}\cdots\boxed{\clubsuit}\boxed{\heartsuit} \end{matrix} \cdots,$$

where $r \in S_k$ is a random permutation generated through the application of a pile-scramble shuffle at step 3.

5. Let c_0' denote a commitment on any sun cell in the target room R_0. (If there is no sun, then denote a commitment on any moon cell by c_0' and swap the two cards constituting c_0'.) Execute an extended version of the Mizuki–Sone XOR protocol [17] with c_0', $c_{r^{-1}(a)}'$, and $c_{r^{-1}(b)}'$ as follows.
   (a) Place c_0', $c_{r^{-1}(a)}'$, and $c_{r^{-1}(b)}'$ and apply a random bisection cut as follows:

$$\begin{matrix} c_0' : \boxed{?}\boxed{?} \\ c_{r^{-1}(a)}' : \boxed{?}\boxed{?} \\ c_{r^{-1}(b)}' : \boxed{?}\boxed{?} \end{matrix} \rightarrow \left[\begin{matrix} \boxed{?} \\ \boxed{?} \\ \boxed{?} \end{matrix} \,\middle\|\, \begin{matrix} \boxed{?} \\ \boxed{?} \\ \boxed{?} \end{matrix}\right] \rightarrow \begin{matrix} \boxed{?}\boxed{?} \\ \boxed{?}\boxed{?} \\ \boxed{?}\boxed{?}. \end{matrix}$$

[3] This means that rule 3 can be simultaneously verified for the target room.

(b) Reveal all the cards. If the values of the middle and bottommost commitments both differ from the value of the topmost commitment, then continue; otherwise, abort.

$$\begin{array}{|c|c|} \hline ? & ? \\ \hline ? & ? \\ \hline ? & ? \\ \hline \end{array} \rightarrow \begin{array}{|c|c|} \hline \clubsuit & \heartsuit \\ \hline \heartsuit & \clubsuit \\ \hline \heartsuit & \clubsuit \\ \hline \end{array} \text{ or } \begin{array}{|c|c|} \hline \heartsuit & \clubsuit \\ \hline \clubsuit & \heartsuit \\ \hline \clubsuit & \heartsuit \\ \hline \end{array} \rightarrow \text{Continue.}$$

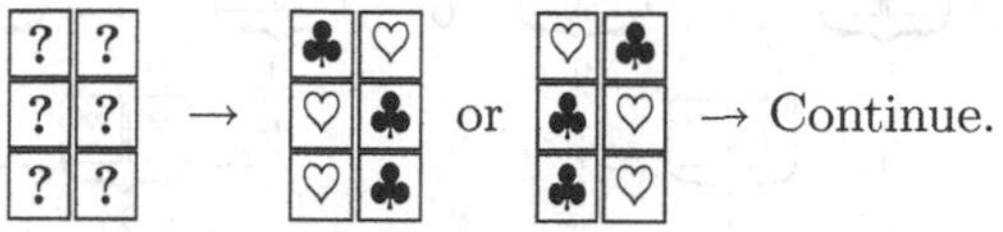

We execute these steps for all the rooms. If V does not abort, then V is convinced that the commitments on the board respect rule 5. We discuss on reducing the number of executions of these steps in Sect. 5.

3.3 Efficiency

Let us evaluate the number of required shuffles for our proposed ZKP protocol for efficiency. Because the verification for rule 5 (alternating pattern) can also verify rule 3 (one enter, one exit) as mentioned, our protocol does not execute the verification for rule 3 in this evaluation. Also, let us omit the evaluation of the part of constructing the single loop [13] because it cannot be included in this paper due to the page length limit.

Let n_r denote the number of rooms in a given Moon-or-Sun puzzle and $p \times q$ denote the size of the puzzle. For verifying rule 4, our protocol uses two random cuts and one random bisection cut (for the XOR protocol [17]) for each room, i.e., $3n_r$. For verifying rule 5 for each room, our protocol uses one pile-scramble shuffle, one random bisection cut, and a number of pile-scramble shuffles corresponding to the number of adjacent rooms. For duplicating commitments, our protocol applies the copy protocol [17], i.e., one random bisection cut, to each commitment between each pair of adjacent rooms and on moon and sun cells. For making a commitment placed on each of moon and sun cells, our protocol applies the sum protocol [26] to the four neighbour commitments, i.e., three pile-shifting shuffles. In total, because the number of commitments between each pair of adjacent rooms (and on moon and sun cells) is less than $p^2 \times q^2$, our protocol uses $\mathcal{O}(p^2 q^2)$ shuffles.

4 Security Proofs

Our protocol needs to verify three security properties given as theorems.

Theorem 1 (Completeness). *If P knows a solution of a Moon-or-Sun grid, then P can always convince V (i.e., V does not abort).*

Proof. In the setup phase described in Sect. 3.1, constructing the loop is directly taken from [13], so we refer readers to this paper for the proof.

For placing a commitment inside a cell, we use the sum protocol [26] so that the value of the commitment represents the presence of line. Because the configuration of the four neighbors is either the following two (up to rotation), the resulting sequence at step 1 is always $\boxed{\clubsuit}\boxed{\clubsuit}\boxed{\heartsuit}\boxed{\clubsuit}\boxed{\clubsuit}$, representing two if line passes through the cell (the loop never branches off):

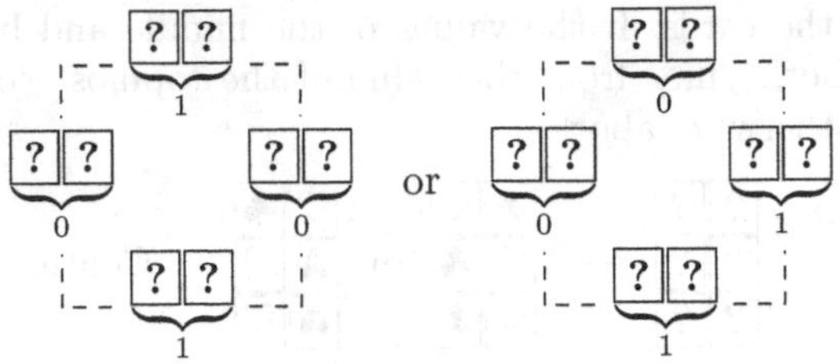

If line does not pass, then the resulting sequence is ♡♣♣♣♣ because all the four neighbors are commitments to 0. Therefore, constructing a commitment with the first and third cards, from the previous sequence, correctly represents the presence of line for a cell.

For the verification phase, described in Sect. 3.2, we divide the proof into three parts, each corresponding to one rule.

Only moon or only sun (rule 4): Because P knows a solution, the values of all the commitments on sun cells considered at step 1 are either 0s or 1s, *i.e.*, ♣♡ ♣♡ ⋯ or ♡♣ ♡♣ ⋯. Thus, applying a random cut to them always yields a sequence having an alternating pattern. This holds true for moon cells at step 2 as well. Finally, because rule 4 implies that the value of a commitment on any sun cell must differ to that on any moon cell within the same room, the XOR protocol [17] always outputs a commitment to 1 at step 3.

One enter, one exit (rule 3): The number of commitments to 1 among all the commitments located at the edge must be two for every room. Therefore, two commitments to 1 always appear when revealing all of them at step 3.

Alternating pattern (rule 5): At step 5, $c'_{r^{-1}(a)}$ and $c'_{r^{-1}(b)}$ come from commitments on any sun cell within different rooms such that lines exist between each of them and R_0. This is because a commitment to 1 is revealed among each of $s_{r^{-1}(a)}$ and $s_{r^{-1}(b)}$, and s_i comes from commitments on the border between R_0 and R_i. Rule 5 implies that the values of $c'_{r^{-1}(a)}$ and $c'_{r^{-1}(b)}$ must be both different to the value of c'_0, *i.e.*, the first configuration at step 5(a) is as follows:

c'_0 : ♡♣ $\qquad$ c'_0 : ♣♡
$c'_{r^{-1}(a)}$: ♣♡ $\quad$ or $\quad$ $c'_{r^{-1}(a)}$: ♡♣
$c'_{r^{-1}(b)}$: ♣♡ $\qquad$ $c'_{r^{-1}(b)}$: ♡♣.

Thus, V never aborts when revealing all the cards at step 5(b). □

Theorem 2 (Soundness). *If P does not know a solution of a Moon-or-Sun grid, then V always rejects (*i.e.*, the protocol aborts).*

Proof. Our protocol is a proof-of-knowledge because commitments placed on the grid after the setup phase represent a solution. Thus, in the remaining part of this proof, we prove that V always aborts if P does not provide a solution, *i.e.*, at least one rule is not respected. Because rule 2 is always respected due to [13], we consider the case that each of the remaining rules is not respected as follows.

Only moon or only sun (rule 4): For a given room, two cases are considered: (1) the loop does not pass through all suns (or moons) but only some of them, and (2) the loop passes through all moons and suns (or nothing). The first case can be detected at either step 1 or step 2 because a sequence of commitments on all sun (moon) cells does not have an alternating pattern, *e.g.*, ♣|♡|♣|♡|♡|♣. The second case can be detected at step 3 because the value of commitment on any sun cell is the same as on any moon cell.

One enter, one exit (rule 3): Because all commitments located at the edge of a given room and the target room are revealed at step 3, the number of times the loop enters the given room is revealed. Thus, V always detect the case in which rule 3 is violated.

Alternating pattern (rule 5): If this rule is violated, it means that for a given room, there is at least one adjacent room such that line exists between them but the loop passes through the same symbol (assuming that rule 4 is respected). As stated in the above proof, because $c'_{r^{-1}(a)}$ and $c'_{r^{-1}(b)}$ come from commitments on any sun cell within such rooms at step 5, V learns whether the values of them are equal to c'_0 using the XOR protocol [17]. Thus, V always aborts.

In any case, the verifier always rejects. □

Theorem 3 (Zero-knowledge). *V learns nothing about P's solution of the given grid G.*

Proof. We use the same proof technique as in [8], namely the description of an efficient *simulator* which simulates the interaction between an honest prover and a cheating verifier. As described in [8], this simulator does not have a correct solution, but has an ability that a sequence of cards can be swapped with the same number of cards during the application of shuffling; this ability is the replaced one with the rewind ability in cryptographic ZKP protocols.

Informally, our protocol is zero-knowledge because it applies an appropriate shuffling to a sequence of cards before revealing them. The simulator can always swap the sequence such that the real and simulated protocols are indistinguishable.

Formally, in the setup phase, the simulator first constructs arbitrary loop executing [13]. Subsequently, it applies the sum protocol [26] introduced in Sect. 2.4. Note that this existing protocol [26] is proved to be zero-knowledge. In the verification phase, for each of the remaining rules, it acts as follows.

Only moon or only sun (rule 4): At steps 1 and 2, during each application of a random cut, the simulator swaps the commitments with commitments to 1. Because a random cut cyclically and randomly shifts a sequence of cards, this swapping results in any of the alternating patterns with a probability of 1/2, which is indistinguishable from a real execution. At step 3, it executes the Mizuki–Sone XOR protocol [17] that is zero-knowledge.

One enter, one exit (rule 3): At step 2, the simulator swaps the commitments with the ones where the number of commitments to 1 is exactly two. Because a pile-scramble shuffle randomly rearranges the order of piles consisting cards, the two commitments to 1 appear in random positions.

Alternating pattern (rule 5): At step 1, the simulator swaps the $n_{\max}$ commitments with the ones having exactly one commitment to 1 if $i = 1, 2$ and with $n_{\max}$ commitments to 0 otherwise. At step 3, it acts nothing, but applying pile-scramble shuffles results in the case where the two commitments to 1 appears in different sequences of random positions. Finally, at step 5, it swaps c'_0, $c'_{r^{-1}(a)}$, and $c'_{r^{-1}(b)}$ with commitments to 1, 0, and 0, respectively. Because applying a random bisection cut to them results in either commitments to 1, 0, and 0 or commitments to 0, 1, and 1 with a probability of 1/2, V learns nothing other than that the value of c'_0 differs to those of $c'_{r^{-1}(a)}$ and $c'_{r^{-1}(b)}$. □

5 Discussion

Here, we discuss whether we can reduce the number of executions of our method for rule 5 described in Sect. 3.2. Suppose that we execute the verification phase described in Sect. 3.2 for all rooms surrounding a given room. Then we prove that such a room does not need to be verified for rule 5 as in the following theorem.

Theorem 4. *A room always satisfies rule 5 if all rooms surrounding the room satisfy all the rules.*

Proof. Suppose, for the sake of contradiction, that there exists a room R that does not satisfy rule 5, while all rooms surrounding R are verified to satisfy all the rules through the execution of our verification phase described in Sect. 3.2. Then, as R does not satisfy rule 5, there should exist a room R' such that the line passes between R and R', passing through the same symbol in both.

However, R' surrounds R, and this contradicts our assumption that all rooms surrounding R satisfy all the rules. Therefore, our initial assumption must be false, and hence, R satisfies rule 5. □

Theorem 4 implies that we do not need to verify all rooms for rule 5. We observe that optimally reducing the number of rooms for which rule 5 is verified in our protocol is related to one of the classical NP-hard problems, namely, the *minimum vertex cover problem.* This connection emerges if we consider a Moon-or-Sun puzzle as an undirected graph, wherein a vertex set comprises rooms, and an edge denotes the adjacency of rooms. A vertex cover of graph is a set of vertices where every edge of the graph has at least one vertex in the set. The minimum vertex cover problem asks the minimum size of such vertex covers if they exist.

Because a vertex cover represents rooms surrounding all the remaining rooms, it suffices to verify whether such rooms satisfy rule 5, as indicated in Theorem 4. However, if we wish to verify rule 5 for a minimum number of rooms we must initially find a minimum vertex cover. As mentioned, finding such a cover is an

NP-hard problem, even on planar graphs, thus we are unable to perform this initial step efficiently. Although techniques for evaluating the execution time of card-based protocols exist [15], doing so in this case is non-trivial, due to this additional computationally intensive step. Additionally, constructing ZKP protocols for a Moon-or-Sun puzzle may prove more challenging than those in existing work because in essence, rule 5 involves not verifying a given room itself but comparing a given room with all of its adjacent rooms.

It is still possible to bound the number of rooms that we must verify rule 5 for, without requiring a computational step of infeasible running time. To begin, we note that any planar graph always has a vertex cover with at most $\frac{3n}{4}$ vertices, and thus we have the following theorem:

Theorem 5. *It is possible to convince the verifier that all rooms satisfy rule 5 by checking this rule for at most $\frac{3}{4}$ of the rooms.*

Proof. It follows from Theorem 4 that it suffices to verify rule 5 only for rooms in a vertex cover. Furthermore every planar graph has a vertex cover containing at most $\frac{3}{4}$ of the vertices. Thus it is only ever necessary to verify rule 5 for only $\frac{3}{4}$ of the rooms. □

Furthermore, we know that we can find a cover of this size in polynomial time. To do so, we find a four coloring of the graph, and then take our cover to be the union of the three smallest color classes, yielding a cover that is of size most $\frac{3n}{4}$. It is possible to compute a four coloring for a planar graph in polynomial (quadratic) time [22].

6 Conclusion

We proposed a ZKP protocol for Moon-or-Sun, which has an interesting rule: the loop must pass through different symbols within two consecutive rooms. Through the construction, we found this rule to be related to a well-known problem in graph theory, which leads some challenging problems.

Acknowledgements. We thank the anonymous referees, whose comments have helped us improve the presentation of the paper. The fourth author was supported in part by Kayamori Foundation of Informational Science Advancement and JSPS KAKENHI Grant Number JP23H00479. The third and fifth authors were partially supported by the French ANR project ANR-18-CE39-0019 (MobiS5). Other programs also fund to write this paper, namely the French government research program "Investissements d´Avenir" through the IDEX-ISITE initiative 16-IDEX-0001 (CAP 20-25) and the IMobS3 Laboratory of Excellence (ANR-10-LABX-16-01). Finally, the French ANR project DECRYPT (ANR-18-CE39-0007) and SEVERITAS (ANR-20-CE39-0009) also subsidize this work.

A Full Description of XOR and Copy Protocols

XOR Protocol. Given commitments to $a, b \in \{0, 1\}$, the Mizuki–Sone XOR protocol [17] outputs a commitment to $a \oplus b$:

$$\underbrace{\boxed{?}\boxed{?}}_{a}\;\underbrace{\boxed{?}\boxed{?}}_{b} \rightarrow \cdots \rightarrow \underbrace{\boxed{?}\boxed{?}}_{a\oplus b}.$$

This protocol proceeds as follows.

1. Rearrange the sequence: $\overset{1}{\boxed{?}}\overset{2}{\boxed{?}}\overset{3}{\boxed{?}}\overset{4}{\boxed{?}} \rightarrow \overset{1}{\boxed{?}}\overset{3}{\boxed{?}}\overset{2}{\boxed{?}}\overset{4}{\boxed{?}}$.
2. Apply a random bisection cut: $[\,\boxed{?}\boxed{?}\,|\,\boxed{?}\boxed{?}\,] \rightarrow \boxed{?}\boxed{?}\boxed{?}\boxed{?}$.
3. Rearrange the sequence: $\overset{1}{\boxed{?}}\overset{2}{\boxed{?}}\overset{3}{\boxed{?}}\overset{4}{\boxed{?}} \rightarrow \overset{1}{\boxed{?}}\overset{3}{\boxed{?}}\overset{2}{\boxed{?}}\overset{4}{\boxed{?}}$.
4. Reveal the first and second cards in the sequence to obtain the output commitment as follows: $\boxed{\clubsuit}\boxed{\heartsuit}\underbrace{\boxed{?}\boxed{?}}_{a\oplus b}$ or $\boxed{\clubsuit}\boxed{\heartsuit}\underbrace{\boxed{?}\boxed{?}}_{\overline{a\oplus b}}$.

Copy Protocol. Given a commitment to $a \in \{0, 1\}$ along with two commitments to 0, the Mizuki–Sone copy protocol [17] outputs two commitments to a:

$$\underbrace{\boxed{?}\boxed{?}}_{a}\;\underbrace{\boxed{?}\boxed{?}}_{0}\;\underbrace{\boxed{?}\boxed{?}}_{0} \rightarrow \cdots \rightarrow \underbrace{\boxed{?}\boxed{?}}_{a}\;\underbrace{\boxed{?}\boxed{?}}_{a}.$$

This protocol proceeds as follows.

1. Rearrange the sequence as follows:
$$\overset{1}{\boxed{?}}\overset{2}{\boxed{?}}\overset{3}{\boxed{?}}\overset{4}{\boxed{?}}\overset{5}{\boxed{?}}\overset{6}{\boxed{?}} \rightarrow \overset{1}{\boxed{?}}\overset{3}{\boxed{?}}\overset{5}{\boxed{?}}\overset{2}{\boxed{?}}\overset{4}{\boxed{?}}\overset{6}{\boxed{?}}.$$
2. Apply a random bisection cut to the sequence as follows:
$$[\,\boxed{?}\boxed{?}\boxed{?}\,|\,\boxed{?}\boxed{?}\boxed{?}\,] \rightarrow \boxed{?}\boxed{?}\boxed{?}\boxed{?}\boxed{?}\boxed{?}.$$
3. Rearrange the sequence as follows:
$$\overset{1}{\boxed{?}}\overset{2}{\boxed{?}}\overset{3}{\boxed{?}}\overset{4}{\boxed{?}}\overset{5}{\boxed{?}}\overset{6}{\boxed{?}} \rightarrow \overset{1}{\boxed{?}}\overset{4}{\boxed{?}}\overset{2}{\boxed{?}}\overset{5}{\boxed{?}}\overset{3}{\boxed{?}}\overset{6}{\boxed{?}}.$$
4. Reveal the first and second cards in the sequence to obtain the output commitments as follows:
$$\boxed{\clubsuit}\boxed{\heartsuit}\underbrace{\boxed{?}\boxed{?}}_{a}\;\underbrace{\boxed{?}\boxed{?}}_{a} \text{ or } \boxed{\heartsuit}\boxed{\clubsuit}\underbrace{\boxed{?}\boxed{?}}_{\overline{a}}\;\underbrace{\boxed{?}\boxed{?}}_{\overline{a}}.$$

References

1. Nikoli, Moon-or-Sun. https://www.nikoli.co.jp/en/puzzles/moon_or_sun/
2. Ben-Or, M., et al.: Everything provable is provable in zero-knowledge. In: Goldwasser, S. (ed.) CRYPTO 1988. LNCS, vol. 403, pp. 37–56. Springer, New York (1990). https://doi.org/10.1007/0-387-34799-2_4
3. Boer, B.: More efficient match-making and satisfiability *the five card trick*. In: Quisquater, J.-J., Vandewalle, J. (eds.) EUROCRYPT 1989. LNCS, vol. 434, pp. 208–217. Springer, Heidelberg (1990). https://doi.org/10.1007/3-540-46885-4_23
4. Bultel, X., Dreier, J., Dumas, J., Lafourcade, P.: Physical zero-knowledge proofs for Akari, Takuzu, Kakuro and KenKen. In: Fun with Algorithms. LIPIcs, vol. 49, pp. 8:1–8:20. Schloss Dagstuhl, Dagstuhl (2016)
5. Bultel, X., et al.: Physical zero-knowledge proof for Makaro. In: Izumi, T., Kuznetsov, P. (eds.) SSS 2018. LNCS, vol. 11201, pp. 111–125. Springer, Cham (2018). https://doi.org/10.1007/978-3-030-03232-6_8
6. Chien, Y.-F., Hon, W.-K.: Cryptographic and physical zero-knowledge proof: from Sudoku to Nonogram. In: Boldi, P., Gargano, L. (eds.) FUN 2010. LNCS, vol. 6099, pp. 102–112. Springer, Heidelberg (2010). https://doi.org/10.1007/978-3-642-13122-6_12
7. Dumas, J.-G., Lafourcade, P., Miyahara, D., Mizuki, T., Sasaki, T., Sone, H.: Interactive physical zero-knowledge proof for Norinori. In: Du, D.-Z., Duan, Z., Tian, C. (eds.) COCOON 2019. LNCS, vol. 11653, pp. 166–177. Springer, Cham (2019). https://doi.org/10.1007/978-3-030-26176-4_14
8. Gradwohl, R., Naor, M., Pinkas, B., Rothblum, G.N.: Cryptographic and physical zero-knowledge proof systems for solutions of Sudoku puzzles. Theory Comput. Syst. **44**(2), 245–268 (2009)
9. Isuzugawa, R., Miyahara, D., Mizuki, T.: Zero-knowledge proof protocol for cryptarithmetic using dihedral cards. In: Kostitsyna, I., Orponen, P. (eds.) UCNC 2021. LNCS, vol. 12984, pp. 51–67. Springer, Cham (2021). https://doi.org/10.1007/978-3-030-87993-8_4
10. Iwamoto, C., Ide, T.: Moon-or-Sun, Nagareru, and Nurimeizu are NP-complete. IEICE Trans. Fundam. **105**(9), 1187–1194 (2022)
11. Komano, Y., Mizuki, T.: Physical zero-knowledge proof protocol for Topswops. In: Su, C., Gritzalis, D., Piuri, V. (eds.) ISPEC 2022. LNCS, vol. 13620, pp. 537–553. Springer, Cham (2022). https://doi.org/10.1007/978-3-031-21280-2_30
12. Komano, Y., Mizuki, T.: Card-based zero-knowledge proof protocol for pancake sorting. In: Bella, G., Doinea, M., Janicke, H. (eds.) SecITC 2022. LNCS, vol. 13809, pp. 222–239. Springer, Cham (2023). https://doi.org/10.1007/978-3-031-32636-3_13
13. Lafourcade, P., Miyahara, D., Mizuki, T., Robert, L., Sasaki, T., Sone, H.: How to construct physical zero-knowledge proofs for puzzles with a "single loop" condition. Theor. Comput. Sci. **888**, 41–55 (2021)
14. Miyahara, D., Sasaki, T., Mizuki, T., Sone, H.: Card-based physical zero-knowledge proof for Kakuro. IEICE Trans. Fundam. **102-A**(9), 1072–1078 (2019)
15. Miyahara, D., Ueda, I., Hayashi, Y., Mizuki, T., Sone, H.: Evaluating card-based protocols in terms of execution time. Int. J. Inf. Secur. **20**, 729–740 (2021)
16. Mizuki, T., Asiedu, I.K., Sone, H.: Voting with a logarithmic number of cards. In: Mauri, G., Dennunzio, A., Manzoni, L., Porreca, A.E. (eds.) UCNC 2013. LNCS, vol. 7956, pp. 162–173. Springer, Heidelberg (2013). https://doi.org/10.1007/978-3-642-39074-6_16

17. Mizuki, T., Sone, H.: Six-card secure AND and four-card secure XOR. In: Deng, X., Hopcroft, J.E., Xue, J. (eds.) FAW 2009. LNCS, vol. 5598, pp. 358–369. Springer, Heidelberg (2009). https://doi.org/10.1007/978-3-642-02270-8_36
18. Robert, L., Miyahara, D., Lafourcade, P., Mizuki, T.: Card-based ZKP for connectivity: applications to Nurikabe, Hitori, and Heyawake. New Gener. Comput. **40**, 149–171 (2022)
19. Robert, L., Miyahara, D., Lafourcade, P., Mizuki, T.: Card-based ZKP protocol for Nurimisaki. In: Devismes, S., Petit, F., Altisen, K., Luna, G.A.D., Anta, A.F. (eds.) SSS 2022. LNCS, vol. 13751, pp. 285–298. Springer, Cham (2022). https://doi.org/10.1007/978-3-031-21017-4_19
20. Robert, L., Miyahara, D., Lafourcade, P., Mizuki, T.: Hide a liar: card-based ZKP protocol for Usowan. In: Du, D., Du, D., Wu, C., Xu, D. (eds.) TAMC 2022. LNCS, vol. 13571, pp. 201–217. Springer, Cham (2022). https://doi.org/10.1007/978-3-031-20350-3_17
21. Robert, L., Miyahara, D., Lafourcade, P., Libralesso, L., Mizuki, T.: Physical zero-knowledge proof and NP-completeness proof of Suguru puzzle. Inf. Comput. **285**, 1–14 (2022)
22. Robertson, N., Sanders, D.P., Seymour, P.D., Thomas, R.: Efficiently four-coloring planar graphs. In: Miller, G.L. (ed.) ACM Symposium on the Theory of Computing, pp. 571–575. ACM (1996)
23. Ruangwises, S.: An improved physical ZKP for Nonogram. In: Du, D.-Z., Du, D., Wu, C., Xu, D. (eds.) COCOA 2021. LNCS, vol. 13135, pp. 262–272. Springer, Cham (2021). https://doi.org/10.1007/978-3-030-92681-6_22
24. Ruangwises, S., Itoh, T.: Physical zero-knowledge proof for Numberlink puzzle and k vertex-disjoint paths problem. New Gener. Comput. **39**(1), 3–17 (2021)
25. Ruangwises, S., Itoh, T.: Physical ZKP for connected spanning subgraph: applications to bridges puzzle and other problems. In: Kostitsyna, I., Orponen, P. (eds.) UCNC 2021. LNCS, vol. 12984, pp. 149–163. Springer, Cham (2021). https://doi.org/10.1007/978-3-030-87993-8_10
26. Ruangwises, S., Itoh, T.: Securely computing the n-variable equality function with 2n cards. Theor. Comput. Sci. **887**, 99–110 (2021)
27. Ruangwises, S., Itoh, T.: How to physically verify a rectangle in a grid: a physical ZKP for Shikaku. In: Fraigniaud, P., Uno, Y. (eds.) Fun with Algorithms. LIPIcs, vol. 226, pp. 24:1–24:12. Schloss Dagstuhl (2022)
28. Ruangwises, S., Itoh, T.: Physical ZKP for Makaro using a standard deck of cards. In: Du, D., Du, D., Wu, C., Xu, D. (eds.) TAMC 2022. LNCS, vol. 13571, pp. 43–54. Springer, Cham (2022). https://doi.org/10.1007/978-3-031-20350-3_5
29. Ruangwises, S., Itoh, T.: Two standard decks of playing cards are sufficient for a ZKP for Sudoku. New Gener. Comput. **40**(1), 49–65 (2022)
30. Sasaki, T., Miyahara, D., Mizuki, T., Sone, H.: Efficient card-based zero-knowledge proof for Sudoku. Theor. Comput. Sci. **839**, 135–142 (2020)
31. Shinagawa, K., et al.: Card-based protocols using regular polygon cards. IEICE Trans. Fundam. **100-A**(9), 1900–1909 (2017)

Author Index

A
Ambrona, Miguel 195

B
Béguinot, Julien 36
Bertani, Alessandro 16
Beunardeau, Marc 195

C
Carminati, Michele 16
Cartor, Max 137
Cartor, Ryann 137
Cheng, Wei 36

D
Danger, Jean-Luc 36

F
Furue, Hiroki 101
Furuya, Isamu 77

G
Giraud, Vincent 3
Guilley, Sylvain 36

H
Hand, Samuel 255
Hu, Lei 59

I
Ikematsu, Yasuhiko 101
Inoue, Akiko 77
Iwata, Tetsu 77

K
Kamada, Shoichi 117
Kasahara, Hayato 77
Koch, Alexander 255
Kudo, Momonari 117

L
Lafourcade, Pascal 255
Lee, Hyeonbum 214
Lewis, Mark 137

M
Marco, Laurane 173
Minematsu, Kazuhiko 77
Miyahara, Daiki 255

N
Naccache, David 3
Nuida, Koji 237

P
Polino, Mario 16

R
Remigio, Riccardo 16
Rioul, Olivier 36
Robert, Léo 255

J. Shikata and H. Kuzuno (Eds.): IWSEC 2023, LNCS 14128, pp. 273–274, 2023.
https://doi.org/10.1007/978-3-031-41326-1

S
Schmitt, Anne-Laure 195
Seo, Jae Hong 214
Smith-Tone, Daniel 137
Song, Ling 59

T
Takagi, Tsuyoshi 117
Talayhan, Abdullah 173
Toledo, Raphaël R. 195
Tran, Bénédikt 152

V
Vaudenay, Serge 152, 173

Y
Yang, Qianqian 59
Yli-Mäyry, Ville 36

Z
Zanero, Stefano 16
Zhang, Nana 59
Zhao, Jiahao 59
Zhu, Haiming 117

Printed in the United States
by Baker & Taylor Publisher Services

Printed in the United States
by Baker & Taylor Publisher Services